AF600179

Motif-Index
of
Folk-Literature

Vol. I

MOTIF-INDEX
OF
FOLK-LITERATURE

A Classification of Narrative Elements in Folktales, Ballads, Myths, Fables, Mediaeval Romances, Exempla, Fabliaux, Jest-Books and Local Legends

REVISED AND ENLARGED EDITION BY

STITH THOMPSON
Indiana University

VOLUME ONE
A-C

INDIANA UNIVERSITY PRESS
BLOOMINGTON & INDIANAPOLIS

Indiana University Press gratefully acknowledges
the support of the L.J. and Mary C. Skaggs Foundation
in the republication of the six volumes of the
Motif-Index of Folk-Literature.

Manufactured in the United States of America

ISBN 0-253-33881-6

6 7 8 9 00 99 98 97

complete set ISBN 0-253-33887-5

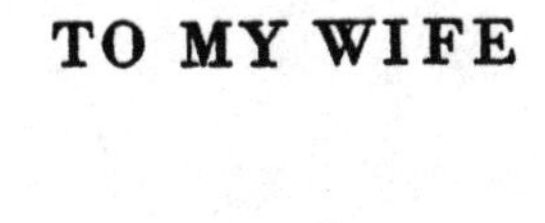

TO MY WIFE

PREFACE TO REVISED EDITION

In the two decades which have now elapsed since the first edition of this work began to appear, the need for a revision and enlargement has become more and more insistent. As the Index has been used for analyzing tales and myths from every quarter of the globe and from almost every narrative literary genre, a large amount of bibliographical material and many new items for the classification have accumulated, so that the revision about doubles the size and scope of the original.

Several very large and important areas have been comprehensively surveyed for motifs during recent years and find place in the present index.

As a result of nearly twenty years of work Professor Tom Peete Cross succeeded in covering the rich field of early Irish literature. Dr. Inger M. Boberg has indexed a large section of the Icelandic sagas and Eddas. There have also been very extensive motif-indexes of the oral tales of India, of the West Indies, of the British and American tale tradition, and of the Talmudic-Midrashic literature — to mention only a few of these important areas. Collections from other parts of the world and from many literary traditions have been examined so as to make the present revision as truly representative as possible of traditional narrative over the entire world.

The introduction to the first edition has been revised to indicate an occasional modification of fact or point of view, to clarify matters about which questions have been raised, and especially to indicate the ways in which the scope of the original index has been widened.

The actual index system has been reconsidered at every point and occasionally changed, but such changes are always minor and are sufficiently indicated. They should facilitate the making of new motif-indexes as well as satisfy the demand of logical arrangement.

The doubling of the scope of material covered, the frequent improvements in the technique of classification, and the amplifying of bibliographic references in the new edition should make the work more useful as a tool for literary and folkloristic research and as a reference work covering a field never before made easily available to the general reader.

Bloomington, Indiana
September, 1955. STITH THOMPSON

INTRODUCTION

PURPOSE OF THE PRESENT WORK

With each passing year the need of a comprehensive classification of the materials in all kinds of traditional narrative becomes more apparent. Our great libraries of folklore, enriched by the ceaseless activity of field workers and scholars, grow daily more difficult to explore. Tales, ballads, myths, and traditions have poured in from all parts of the earth, both civilized and uncivilized, so that no man, however great his industry and skill in languages, can read the thousands of volumes in a lifetime. By a careful division of labor, scholars have, however, examined many parts of this field, with the result that the body of writings about traditional narrative also grows beyond the compass of one man's mastery.

That some kind of systematic indexing of this vast accumulation should be undertaken has been long realized. Though several beginnings of such a work have been made during the past century, no plan has been completed with sufficient thoroughness to warrant general acceptance.

For the special field of the folktale, to be sure, the classification of Antti Aarne [1] has been found useful. In this index some eight hundred complete stories current in Europe have been logically arranged, and by its system the tales of more than a dozen European peoples have now been catalogued. [2] For the European area such an arrangement of tales as Aarne's proves reasonably satisfactory, since popular traditions assume much the same pattern throughout, and the same narrative-complexes are found over much of the continent. [3]

---

[1] **Verzeichnis der Märchentypen,** FFCommunications No. 3, Helsinki, 1910. A revision by the present author appeared as **The Types of the Folk-Tale,** FFCommunications No. 74, Helsinki, 1928.

[2] For a summary of the results of these classifications see R. S. Boggs, **A Comparative Survey of the Folk-tales of Ten Peoples,** FFCommunications No. 93, Helsinki, 1930. In addition to the surveys discussed by Boggs may be mentioned: Andrejev, Ukazatel' Skazochnik sjuzhetov po Sisteme Aarne, and Plenzat, Die ost- und westpreussischen Märchen und Schwänke. For more recent surveys see Thompson, **The Folktale,** pp 420 f.

[3] Every scholar who has constructed a new catalogue of tales has, of course, been obliged to add types of tales not already to be found in the classification, but it has thus far proved practicable as far as European peoples are concerned, to use the Aarne list for the folktale and jest. How far an expansion of the type-index may permit a cataloguing of such partly literary forms as the exemplum and the fabliau, only experiment can tell. As long as the entire tale-complex remains intact in transmission, such an index as **The Types of the Folk-Tale** is useful; when such a condition does not exist, a more analytical list seems necessary.

Outside of Europe, however, Aarne's index is of little use. In the remoter parts of the world, whither any adequate study must lead us, the European tale-types are applicable to very few stories. Yet there is much common matter in the folk-literature of the world. The similarities consist not so often in complete tales as in single motifs. Accordingly, if an attempt is made to reduce the traditional narrative material of the whole earth to order (as, for example, the scientists have done with the worldwide phenomena of biology) it must be by means of a classification of single motifs — those details out of which full-fledged narratives are composed. It is these simple elements which can form a common basis for a systematic arrangement of the whole body of traditional literature. Only after such cataloguing will it be possible to make adequate use of the collections now existing in print and in manuscript.

The work here presented is an attempt at such a classification. In preparing it I have had in mind above all the practical need of using simple principles that will be easily apparent to everyone. According to this plan, motifs dealing with one subject are handled together, irrespective of the literary form in which they may appear. No attempt has been made to determine the psychological basis of various motifs or their structural value in narrative art, for though such considerations have value, they are not, I think, of much practical help toward the orderly arrangement of the stories and myths of a people. [1]

The present problem of classification is analogous to that of the books in a great library. All works on history, of whatever nature and whether good or bad, appear together there, and these in turn are divided into Roman History, French History, and the like. Side by side with Gibbon and Mommsen rests an amateurish dissertation on some minute fact in the life of the Empire. The library cataloguer is not concerned with the merit of the work he includes, nor can he arrange the books according to any principle of literary criticism about which there may be debate. The "literature of knowledge and the literature of power" are illuminating as principles of criticism; they will not serve as a plan for the arrangement of books. The orderly listing of narrative motifs is likewise best accomplished by the simple and usually easy method of placing together all which deal with the same subject.

Acting upon this principle of practical usefulness, I have also made

[1] Division of motifs on philosophical grounds has been made by several scholars. In his **Märchen des Mittelalters** (p. xvii) Albert Wesselski divides the motifs of folktales, novelle, and myths into **Mythenmotive, Gemeinschaftsmotive,** and **Kulturmotive.** By means of this distinction he discusses the difference between the narrative forms. A very elaborate analysis of the concept of motif is found in Arthur Christensen's study, **Motif et Theme** (FFCommunications No. 59). Divisions are made into **"éléments de relation," "motifs," "accessoires épiques," "thème," "motifs sans thème," "motifs à thèmes faibles,"** and the like. The study throws light on the psychological nature of various motifs.

the index very inclusive of various kinds of motifs. Sometimes the interest of a student of traditional narrative may be centered on a certain type of character in a tale, sometimes on an action, sometimes on attendant circumstances of the action. Hence I have endeavored to use all the elements of tales that have in the past been objects of special study and similar elements that are likely to serve as such objects in the future. A glance at the synopsis will indicate the varied nature of the contents of the classification. At some point or other will be found all kinds of motifs or themes which make up the systems of such writers as Wesselski or Christensen, and perhaps many others which a more philosophical approach than mine would rule out. But in spite of the danger of including material that on strictly critical grounds may be unjustified, I have felt that it is in general better to list all elements of a tale that are likely to have interest to the folklorist or the student of literary history. Such an inclusive list may well form the basis for philosophical discussion, but it is in itself quite uncritical of the material involved. The end of this study will have been attained if the multiform materials it treats become thereby easier of investigation and more convenient for reference.

SCOPE OF THE CLASSIFICATION

The purpose of the present study, then, has been to arrange in a single logical classification the elements which make up traditional narrative literature. Stories that have formed part of a tradition, whether oral or literary, find a place here. The folktale, the myth, the ballad, the fable, the mediaeval romance, the fabliau, the jest, the exemplum, and the local tradition have all been included, though some of these divisions have been inadequately recorded. In general, I have used any narrative, whether popular or literary, so long as it has formed a strong enough tradition to cause its frequent repetition.

Certain aspects of folklore have been definitely omitted. I have not treated superstitions, customs, religious beliefs, riddles, or proverbs, except as they happen to form an organic part of a narrative. To have included these would have doubled the size of the index.

Within the chosen field I have made every effort to have the list of motifs as full as possible. Accordingly, in my reading I have been especially desirous of broadening the field of investigation. Certain works introduce the reader to a new world of narrative interest and to a large number of new motifs. Such have been very valuable for my purpose. And the investigations of other folklorists who from their wide reading have brought together lists of versions of tales have also served to increase the scope of the classification.

Some indication of the works from which the largest number of motifs have been gathered may be of interest:

Folktale and Myth.

(a) General

First Edition

Bolte and Polívka's 5 volume notes to Grimm's Household tales — comprehensive for folktales of European, Near Eastern, and Indic tradition.

The Mythology of all Races, 14 volumes.

Feilberg, *Bidrag til en Ordbog over Jyske Almuesmål* — a remarkable general collection of notes on folklore motifs.

MacCulloch, *Childhood of Fiction.*

Cox, *Cinderella,* a pioneer study of the motifs of a single folktale.

Köhler, *Kleinere Schriften* — the erudite folktale annotations of the leading folklorist of the 1870's.

Penzer, *The Pentamerone of Basile* — covering the earliest of all European folktale collections.

FFCommunications. This distinguished series, to which the present work belongs, has surveys of the tales of many different countries and monographs on particular tales.

Dähnhardt's *Natursagen,* especially for its origin legends connected with biblical tradition.

New Edition

Waldemar Liungman's third volume of his collection of Swedish tales, devoted to a study of the provenience of the various European tales. World-wide comparisons.

FFCommunications since 1930.

Numerous monographs on special widely distributed tales and motifs.

(b) European tales and European tradition in other continents

First Edition

Frazer's *Apollodorus,* with learned notes on many Greek mythological themes.

Volumes on Celtic, Eddic, Baltic, Slavic, Finno-Ugric, and Greek mythology in *The Mythology of All Races.*

Surveys of tales of Finland, Estonia, Finnish-Sweden, Norway, Flanders, Czechoslovakia, Livonia, Russia, Spain, Roumania, Hungary, Iceland, Wallonia — mostly in FFCommunications.

The principal reliance for European tales, traditions and myths: Bolte and Polívka.

Notes on Icelandic sagas from Prof. Chester N. Gould.

New Edition

Balys's surveys of Lithuanian tales, legends and songs — covering the very extensive archives in Lithuania.

Dr. Boberg's motif-index of Icelandic Fornaldarsögur and the Eddas

Solheim's index of *Norsk Folkminnelag,* covering scores of volumes published by the Norwegian folklore archives.

Motif-index of McKay's *More West Highland Tales.*

Folktale surveys and monographs in FFCommunications since 1930 — some of prime importance.

Espinosa's new edition of *Cuentos Populares Españoles,* with extensive notes and motif-indexes.

Dawkins's two important new works on modern Greek tales.

T. P. Cross's monumental *Motif-Index of Early Irish Literature,* with extensive folktale material.

A group of important monographs on folktales, particularly Dr. Rooth's study of Cinderella and Dr. Roberts's of the Frau Holle tale.

Baughman's study of the British and American folktale — with bibliography of nearly 1,000 titles.

Flowers's motif-index of the tales of the West Indies (200 titles).

The Frank C. Brown Collection of North Carolina Folklore — tales and legends indexed by motif.

Halpert's analysis of the folktales of the New Jersey Pines country.

Carrière's collection from the French of Missouri and Sister Marie-Ursule from the Quebec French.

Rael's studies of the Spanish tales of New Mexico.

Klipple's exhaustive treatment of the African tales of European and Asiatic tradition (about 500 titles covered).

Frank Goodwyn's unpublished study of the Pedro de Urdemales cycle in Latin America.

Child's *English and Scottish Popular Ballads* (for narrative motifs).

Many additions to Greek mythology from special studies of the Troy story and from Grote's extensive notes in his *History of Greece.*

Anton Nyerges's motif-index of Cheremis folktales in Sebeok's *Studies in Cheremis Folklore.*

(c) The Near East and India

First Edition

Chauvin's *Bibliographie des ouvrages arabes* — a twelve-volume work analyzing the Arabic collections and those from India and Persia which came into Arabic.

Arabian Nights — some notes from Burton's well-known edition, as well as the summaries from Chauvin, mentioned above.

Penzer's ten-volume *Ocean of Story,* with its excellent notes and indexes covering the classical Indic collections.

A sampling of the Jewish field in Moses Gaster's *Exempla of the Rabbis, in Bin Gorion's Der Born Judas,* and in Frazer's *Folklore in the Old Testament.*

For Buddhistic legend, Cowell's Jātaka (6 volumes), and Chavannes' *Cinq cent contes et apologues* (4 volumes) — the latter emanating from China.

Siberian peoples represented in Holmberg's *Siberian Mythology* and in several important monographs.

Persian literary tales like the *Thousand and One Days,* analyzed in Chauvin.

Volumes on Semitic, Armenian, and Indic Mythology from *The Mythology of All Races.*

New Edition

Eberhard and Boratav's types of the Turkish folktales, an exhaustive study of an important field.

Neuman's large motif-index of Talmudic-Midrashic Literature, opening up much biblical and other Jewish material.

Theodor Gaster's *Thespis* and *Oldest Stories in the World,* which explore some Near East material difficult of access.

Thompson-Balys, *Motif and Type-Index of the Oral Tales of India.* Comprehensive — over 200 works indexed.

Bødker's notes on the Panchatantra, from his edition of an old Danish translation.

The Buddhist world explored anew in Malalasekera's *Dictionary of Pali Proper Names.*

(d) The Far East

First Edition

For China, Chavannes' *Cinq cent contes,* mentioned above (Buddhistic), Werner's *Myths and Legends of China* and Ferguson's *Chinese Mythology.*

For Japan, Mitford's rather inadequate collection.

Scott's *Indo-Chinese Mythology.*

New Edition

Eberhard's *Typen chinesischer Märchen,* with its extensive coverage of ancient and modern texts in Chinese.

Graham's new Ch'uan Miao collection, for which I have furnished the type-index.

Hiroko Ikeda's extensive analysis of both published and unpublished Japanese tales.

Zong In-Sob's new *Folk Tales from Korea.*

Hatt's study of Asiatic influences in American Folklore.

(e) Oceania

First Edition

For Indonesia, DeVries's *Volksverhalen uit Oost Indië,* with its extensive comparative notes, as well as special studies such as those by Voorhoeve and Coster-Wijsman.

Fansler's *Filipino Folktales,* with his comparative notes.

The general Pacific area, as covered in Dixon's *Oceanic Mythology.*

New Edition

Cole's Tinguin Folktales — a different Philippine area than covered in Fansler.

Beckwith's *Hawaiian Mythology.*

A comprehensive study, now in progress, of the principal tale and myth collections of Australia, Melanesia, Polynesia, and Micronesia. References are made directly to these works.

Special studies, such as Luomola's *Maui of the Thousand Tricks.*

(f) North and South American Indian

First Edition

Thompson's *Tales of the North American Indians,* with comparative notes.

Alexander's *North American Mythology* and *Latin American Mythology.*

New Edition

Eskimo collections, annotated by Bjorn Winger.

Gayton and Newman's comparative study of the California area.

Mrs. Pessoa's monograph on the flood myths of North and South America.

The Handbook of South American Indians, which in its six volumes gives a good summary of the myths of tribes over the continent.

Various other collections, especially those of Alfred Métraux.

Additional North American Indian references furnished by Dr. Remedios Wycoco Moore in her unpublished Ph. D. thesis *Types of North American Indian Tales.*

(g) Africa

First Edition

Miscellaneous notes from various collections.

New Edition

Native motifs from Klipple's *African Tales with Foreign Analogues.*

Further notes from various collections, chosen so as to be representative of different areas.

Local Legends.

First Edition

Of all fields of traditional literature included in this index, that concerning local legends is least complete. The list is based upon several general books, such as Werhahn's *Die Sage* and the various surveys of *Sagen* in the FFCommunications. In addition, a large number of monographs on special legends have been used.

New Edition

The complete *Handwörterbuch des deutschen Aberglaubens* has been examined for *Sagen.*

Solheim's index to Norsk *Folkminnelag* has added much in this field.

Many newer monographs appearing as special publications and in learned journals have been used.

Kristensen's *Danske Sagn.*

Mediaeval Romances.

First Edition

Wells's *Manual of Writings in Middle English* furnished motifs from romances in English.

Ward's and Herbert's *Catalogue of Romances in the British Museum.*

Special works such as Miss Schoepperle's *Tristan and Isolt,* Dickson's *Valentine and Orson* and Hertz's studies of various romances.

New Edition

Malory's *Morte Darthur* has been indexed by motifs, so as better to represent the Arthurian legend.

Reinhard's study of Geis in the Romance has opened up a special cross section of material.

Exempla and Saints' Legends.

First Edition

Pauli's *Schimp und Ernst,* with Bolte's extensive notes.

Crane's *Exempla of Jacques de Vitry.*

The Catalogue of Romances in the British Museum.

Gaster's *Exempla of the Rabbis.*

Scala Celi.

Alphabetum Narrationum.

New Edition

Keller's *Motif-index of Spanish Exempla.*

Many motifs belonging to this genre are also included in the studies of novelle and jestbooks, mentioned shortly.

Saintyves, *Les Saints Successeurs des Dieux.*

Loomis, *White Magic.*

Jestbooks and Novelle.

First Edition

The jests, of which so many collections were made in the Renaissance, also find a place here. Many have been omitted, particularly those whose only point is obscenity or those depending on some play upon words that cannot be carried over to another language. The foundation of this part of the index has been the very learned works of Wesselski on Hodscha Nasreddin, Bebel, Arlotto, and others, and of Bolte in his editions of Frey's *Gartengesellschaft*, Montanus' *Schwankbücher*, and similar collections. In addition, of course, monographs on particular jests have been used.

New Edition

The Italian novella in prose has been well indexed for motifs by D. P. Rotunda.

A whole series of motifs from the French conteurs of the Renaissance, such as *Les cent nouvelles nouvelles* and the *Heptameron* of Marguerite of Navarre have been furnished by a group of students at the University of South Carolina, whose help is acknowledged in the proper place.

Childers's *Motif Index of the Cuentos of Juan Timoneda* helps fill out this part of the index.

The English jestbooks from *The Hundred Merry Tales* onward have been explored.

Arthur Christensen's two books on noodles, *Molboernes Vise Gerninger* and *Dumme Folk* trace these jests over the world.

Fabliaux.

First Edition

Except for special studies of the various fabliaux, the principal sources for the motifs in that field were Bédier's *Les Fabliaux* and von der Hagen's *Gesammtabenteuer*.

For North Africa and Egypt, Basset's *Mille et un contes arabes* and Müller's *Egyptian Mythology*.

New Edition

A motif-index of the whole corpus of fabliaux has been examined for additional entries. Fabliaux with obscenity as the only point have been excluded, though good jests with risqué elements are retained.

The new *Sources and Analogues of Chaucer's Canterbury Tales* has good studies of certain fabliaux.

Fables.

First Edition

Since the principal purpose in mind was to list the fables, the basis of that part of the work was Wienert's classification of the

Greek and Roman fables (FFCommunications No. 56), supplemented by the oriental fables listed in Chauvin's Arabian *Bibliographie.* The literary history of these tales is well known, so that no attempt was made to supply all of them with bibliographical apparatus, but only to place them definitely in the body of fable literature. In all, some five hundred fables appear in the classification.

New Edition

Certain additions have been suggested by Professor Ben Perry's monumental *Aesopica,* though the expected volume of comparative notes has not been available.

Periodicals Excerpted.

First Edition

Revue des Traditions Populaires.
Mélusine.
Zeitschrift des Vereins fur Volkskunde.
Folk Lore
Journal of American Folklore
Danske Studier
Am Urquell

New Edition

Where continuing, the journals mentioned above have been brought down to date.
Anuario de la Sociedad Folklorica de Mexico
Les Archives de Folklore
Volkskundliche Bibliographie
Annual bibliographies in *Publications of the Modern Language Association of America* and in *Southern Folklore Quarterly.*
Hessische Blätter für Volkskunde
Arv
Folklore (Naples)
A number of local folklore journals from South America, the United States, and France.

Books and periodicals which have been explored with some thoroughness in the search for motif-studies are indicated in the general bibliography by an asterisk. Works which are arranged according to the present index are marked specially (⊙). They need no page reference.

Not all material found in books read has been used, for, of course, much does not belong in this classification. But when I have been in serious doubt, I have always included an item, and only after real consideration has any special treatment of narrative material been rejected.

For the purpose of deciding on inclusion or exclusion, I have had no hard and fast principle. Anything that goes to make up a traditional narrative has been used. When the term *motif* is employed, it is always in a very loose sense, and is made to include any of the elements of narrative structure. In general, any item in tales that other investigators have made notes on has been accepted. Sometimes, as in those treated in Chapter A, the events of creation, or the nature of the creator or of the gods, may be the subject of interest. Again, as in Chapter C, the index may involve incidents based on certain principles of conduct (e. g. tabu); sometimes extraordinary objects or creatures (magic or merely marvelous) may be the focus of attention. Most of the items are found worthy of note because of something out of the ordinary, something of sufficiently striking character to become a part of tradition, oral or literary. Commonplace experiences, such as eating and sleeping, are not traditional in this sense. But they may become so by having attached to them something remarkable or worthy of remembering. Mere eating is usually of no particular interest in a story. Eating on a magic table, food furnished by helpful animals, food that gives magic strength — these become significant and are likely to be handed down by the teller of tales.

Aside from the general principle just given, no rule has been followed in choosing what should go into the classification. I have tried to include all that becomes a part of tradition — all that is found worth retaining when tale, ballad, jest, or myth is transmitted by word of mouth or on the written page from generation to generation or from land to land.

PLAN OF THE WORK

This classification of materials is the result of a gradual evolution, not of any preconceived plan. It has grown out of an attempt to arrange conveniently a large number of notes made from widely divergent fields of narrative. Many groupings have been made and later combined with others which are clearly related; many also have been split up into two or more headings. In the course of time there have emerged from this experimental process twenty-three divisions which have been finally retained.

(a) *The chapters in the classification.*

In a very general fashion the groups may be said to progress from the mythological and the supernatural toward the realistic and sometimes the humorous. But no such progress is to be observed in all parts of the index: the last half is nearly all realistic.

In Chapter A are handled motifs having to do with creation and with the nature of the world: creators, gods, and demigods; the creation and nature of the universe, and especially of the earth; the beginnings of life; the creation and establishment of the animal and vegetable world.

Chapter B is concerned with animals. Not all tales in which animals figure are placed here, for most frequently it is the action and not the particular actor that is significant in such stories. In Chapter B, on the contrary, appear animals that are in some way remarkable as such: mythical animals like the dragon, magic animals like the truth-telling bird, animals with human traits, animal kingdoms, weddings, and the like. Then there are the many helpful or grateful beasts, marriages of animals to human beings, and other fanciful ideas about animals.

Just as the motifs in Chapter B suggest some possible relation to the institution of totemism, those in Chapter C are based upon the primitive idea of tabu. Forbidden things of all kinds are here listed, as well as the opposite of that concept, the unique compulsion.

The most extensive group is that devoted to magic (Chapter D). The divisions are quite simple: transformation and disenchantment, magic objects and their employment, magic powers and other manifestations.

The motifs listed in Chapter E concern ideas about the dead — resuscitation, ghosts, and reincarnation — as well as ideas concerning the nature of the soul.

Aside from magic and the return of the dead, traditional literature records many marvels: journeys to other worlds; extraordinary creatures such as fairies, spirits, and demons; wondrous places, such as castles in the sea; and marvelous persons and events. These form Chapter F.

Because of the prominence of dreadful beings, such as ogres, witches, and the like, these have been given a special division, G. It will be seen that there is naturally much relation between Chapters E, F, and G; for example, between ogres and evil spirits, or between fairies and witches or ghosts. These relationships are noted by means of cross-references.

Beginning with Chapter H, the purely supernatural assumes a minor importance, though it is still occasionally present. Chapter H has been formed gradually from three separate divisions in the original plan. These, however, are all comprehended under the term "Tests". Tales of recognition are really tests of identity; riddles and the like, tests of cleverness; and tasks and quests, tests of prowess. In addition are to be found sundry tests of character and other qualities.

Chapter J was likewise originally three chapters — Wisdom,

Cleverness, Foolishness. Their fundamental unity is apparent: the motivation is always mental. The first part (Wisdom) consists in large part of fable material. The tales of cleverness and of stupidity come in large measure from jest books.

In the motifs in Chapter J the attention is directed primarily to the mental quality of the character. In K, on the contrary, primary importance is given to action. A very large part of narrative literature deals with deceptions. The work of thieves and rascals, deceptive captures and escapes, seductions, adultery, disguises, and illusions constitute one of the most extensive chapters in the classification.

The rest of the work is made up of smaller chapters. In "L" appear such reversals of fortune as the success of the unpromising child or the downfall of the proud. "M" deals with such definite ordaining of the future as irrevocable judgments, bargains, promises, and oaths. In "N" the large part that luck plays in narrative is shown. Tales of gambling, and of the favors and evil gifts of the Goddess Fortuna appear here.

Chapter P concerns the social system. Not all tales about kings and princes belong here, but only such motifs as rest upon some feature of the social order: customs concerning kings, or the relation of the social ranks and the professions, or anything noteworthy in the administration of such activities as law or army. A very great number of cross-references appear in this chapter.

In "Q" are recorded rewards and punishments, in "R" motifs concerning captives and fugitives, and in "S" instances of great cruelty. In "T" are treated together the motifs dealing with sex, though there are, of course, many other parts of the index where such motifs are also of interest. Here particularly come wooing, marriage, married life, and the birth of children, as well as sundry types of sexual relations.

In Chapter U are gathered a small number of motifs, mostly from fable literature, that are of a homiletic tendency. A tale is told with the sole purpose of showing the nature of life. "Thus goes the world" is the text of such tales.

Many incidents depend upon religious differences or upon certain objects of religious worship. These motifs make up Chapter V. In "W" stories designed to illustrate traits of character are classified. The last of the systematic divisions, "X", contains incidents whose purpose is entirely humorous. Many cross-references to merry tales listed elsewhere are, of course, given.

At the end, in Chapter Z, appear several small classifications which hardly deserve a chapter each. In the future should other small classifications seem desirable, they can easily be added as new parts of Chapter Z.

The fact that the classification does with relative completeness really cover the ground chosen was shown during the last six months of work on the first edition of the index. Motifs were excerpted on slips to the number of several thousand, quite without regard to the system. When the time came to throw the slips into the proper place, they nearly always ranged themselves easily and rapidly. This test gave me some confidence in the practical usefulness of the index as a means of cataloguing the materials of traditional narrative. Subsequent experience of those making indexes has confirmed this conviction.

(b). *Organization within the Chapters.*

Within the chapter the items are arranged in grand divisions, to each of which is assigned a hundred numbers, or some multiple of a hundred numbers. Thus B0—B99 concerns mythical animals; B100—B199, magic animals; B200—B299, animals with human qualities; etc.

In a similar manner, within the grand division the arrangement is by tens or groups of tens. The first of these "tens" in a grand division treats the *general idea* of the grand division. Specific ideas are then taken up in the succeeding divisions. The last division in a grand division deals with *miscellaneous* material concerning the grand division. Thus in the grand division B0—B99 (Mythical animals) we have the following divisions: B0—B9. Mythical animals — general. — B10—B19. Mythical beasts. — B20—B29. Beast-men. — B30—B39. Mythical birds. — B40—B49. Bird-beasts. — B50—B59. Bird-men. — B60—B69. Mythical fish. — B70—B79. Fish-beasts. — B80—B89. Fish-men. — B90—B99. Other mythical animals.

Within the division (e. g. B10—B19) the arrangement is according to a similar principle. The first number (ending in "0") refers to the *general* concept for the division. Succeeding numbers are used for specific aspects, and the last number for *miscellaneous* or additional material concerning the division. Thus in the division B10—B19 (Mythical beasts) we have the following sub-divisions: B10. Mythical beasts. — B11. Dragon. — B12. Basilisk. — B13. Unicorn. — B14. Other hybrid animals. — B15. Animals with unusual limbs or members. — B16. Devastating animals. — B19. Other mythical beasts. Usually not all numbers are employed, since room is left for indefinite expansion of the classification. Should more items appear than enough to exhaust the numbers, these can be added indefinitely to the last number (19.1, 19.2, 19.3, etc.).[1]

It is frequently desirable to subdivide a number. This is done by pointing, thus: B11. Dragon. — B11.1. Origin of the dragon. — B11.1.1. Dragon from cock's egg. — B11.1.2. Dragon from transformed horse. — B11.2. Form of dragon. — B11.2.1. Dragon as compound animal. This system of subdivision may be carried on indefinitely. Such an item as E501 with more than two hundred

[1] In case a division is extensive, it may occupy several "tens". When this is true, the numbers ending in "0" and "9" except at beginning and end, are skipped: "0" always refers to the general idea, "9" to miscellaneous or additional examples.

subdivisions will illustrate the manner in which any item may be subdivided, no matter how elaborate the analysis.[1]

A short handling of the classification will undoubtedly make the system clearer than can any explanation, no matter how lucid. Nothing new or strange will be found, but only the well-tested principle of division and subdivision common to all attempts to systematize knowledge.

(c). *Cross-references.*

Many items in this classification are of interest in connection with other parts of the work. Many also could with good reason be assigned to any one of several places. In these instances the use of cross-references becomes necessary. Thus at the beginnings of many grand divisions are listed items from other places that might also be expected at that point, or that for one reason or another are of special interest there. The finding of motifs in the index becomes easier in proportion to the completeness of such cross-references.

(d). *Bibliographical material.*

It has not been my purpose to make a special study of any item listed in this classification. Where I have been able to do so, I have furnished references to books or monographs about a motif, or at least to some reasonably extensive listing of its occurrences. But for many items I know of no such studies. In these cases I have given such references as I happen to have accumulated. At least one instance of the appearance of each motif is listed.[2]

The arrangement of the references has been made according to a relatively uniform plan. First come the names of special treatments and of works listing variants. Here also appears the reference to *The Types of the Folk-Tale.* Special studies are indicated by two asterisks; valuable lists of variants by a single star. Next follow notices of particular versions of the motif, arranged usually by continents or other convenient groupings. Ordinarily these references are additions to those treated in the special studies, though duplication has not been altogether avoided.

It must be said, in defence of the frequently inadequate documen-

---

1 The system is not really decimal, for the subdivisions may go beyond ten. E. g., A2494.5.34, E501.17.5.3. The latter number refers to the third tertiary division of the fifth secondary division of the seventeenth primary division of E501. — A difficult problem in classification has been solved by the use of a "zero" subdivision. In E613, for example, the main idea is "reincarnation as bird." E613.1, E613.2, etc., detail the kind of bird (E613.1. Reincarnation as duck, etc.) Now there are other subdivisions of E613 that refer only to the general idea of bird (not of particular birds). Thus: E613. Reincarnation as bird. — E613.0.1. Reincarnation of murdered child as bird. — E613.0.2. Reincarnation of unbaptized child as bird. — E613.1. Reincarnation as duck. — etc.

2 The appearance of only one or a few references to a motif must not be interpreted to mean that there are not other occurrences.

tation, that the present work is primarily a classified *list* of motifs and that the references appear only to give some preliminary guidance in finding examples of the item concerned. To assume responsibility for bibliographical completeness for so many thousands of motifs has been quite impossible.

SOME SUGGESTIONS AS TO USING THE INDEX

(a). *Finding motifs in the Index.*

A preliminary glance over the general synopsis at the beginning of the first volume will usually serve to indicate the chapter in which a motif is found. The detailed synopsis preceding the appropriate chapter should next be examined for the special division which lists the motif. If the item is not discovered at the point thus indicated, it will probably be listed in the cross-references which are placed there.

Even with careful search a motif may not immediately be found, for often the fundamental nature of an item may not seem to be the same to the searcher as it has seemed to me. To meet such difficulties a detailed alphabetical index appears at the end of the work.

(b). *Using the Index for Cataloguing Tales.*

The principal use of the present index, I hope, will be for cataloguing motifs in various collections of tales and traditions. If gradually all the tales, myths, ballads, and traditions were catalogued according to the same system, great progress would be made in rendering possible completer comparative studies than can now be undertaken.

Each worker must, of course, evolve the details of any plan of work. But by some convenient scheme it will be possible with relative ease to place all motifs in the appropriate chapter (often with cross-references to another chapter). Then the items forming these chapters may in turn be distributed into the proper divisions. It is my hope that the list of motifs in the present index may be so extensive that most items will be found already entered and numbered. Frequently a new motif will be a subdivision of one already in the index. If so, the system of subdivision here used may be continued. If such is not the case, it will ordinarily be found that the new motif will easily fall into a particular "ten". Usually many vacant places are left in each "ten".[1] Should the motif clearly belong to the "hundred" in question, but to none of the "tens" listed, it should go in the last "ten" (usually numbered 90—99, and devoted to "miscellaneous").

The additional motifs suggested by workers during the twenty

[1] If more items must be put in a "ten" than enough to fill the vacant spaces, the additions can be made to the last number in the "ten", e. g. 19.1, 19.2, 19.3, etc.

years since the appearance of the first edition have all been incorporated in the present edition. This has often necessitated slight modifications of the numbers assigned particular motifs. Since such changes are confusing as well as troublesome, it would seem advisable for those who make such indexes in the future not to attempt exact assignment of new motif-numbers but only to indicate the closest approximation possible (e. g. A2685.2+). This will serve for all purposes of reference and will make incorporation into a possible further revision of the index simpler.

In anticipation of the appearance of this index, the numbers have been used in several works. In each of the types given in the Aarne-Thompson *Types of the Folk-Tale*[1] the mention of motifs is immediately followed by the number in brackets. Likewise they are inserted after all additional motifs appearing in Boggs' *Index of Spanish Folktales.* In my *Tales of the North American Indians* the motifs are all listed by the present plan. The numbers are also appearing at appropriate places in the margin of the new *Handwörterbuch des deutschen Märchens.*

The works indexed by this system since its first publication are mentioned on pages 12—18. — Irish and Icelandic myth, Italian, French and Spanish novelle and jestbooks, British and American folktales, African, West Indian, Jewish and Indic tradition, to mention the most important. Such surveys are indicated in the bibliography (p. 37) by a ⊙.

ACKNOWLEDGMENTS

The preparation of this classification has brought with it many pleasant associations, for I have found my fellow-workers in the field extremely kind in their help and encouragement. It is possible here to give but the briefest notice of their help and to express my heartfelt thanks. to them all.

From its very inception I profited by the friendship and advice of Prof. Archer Taylor. Not only did he give the advantage of his deep scholarship, but at the expense of great labor he read the entire manuscript with the critical eye of a foster-father. Prof. Jan de Vries of Leiden explored the entire manuscript, gave me hundreds of references, and during a week in which I was guest in his home made many very valuable suggestions. Large parts of the manuscript were read by Dr. Albert Wesselski of Prague, and by Dr. Reidar Th. Christiansen of Oslo. The main burden of seeing the work through the press rested on the shoulders of Prof. Kaarle Krohn of Helsinki, to whom I am indebted for much help and cordial hospitality.

[1] It is suggested that where references are hereafter made to the present work and to **The Types of the Folk-Tale**, the term **motif** should be used for this Motif-index and **type** for **The Types of the Folk-Tale.** Thus: Motif S31 appears in Type 510.

Without the co-operation of many persons, an undertaking like this cannot be accomplished. It is most pleasant to record my particular appreciation for those who, by furnishing me with the result of their reading in special fields, added to the completeness of the work. Prof. Chester N. Gould of Chicago gave me free access to his rich notes on the Old Norse saga material; Miss Hortense Braden of Indianapolis permitted me to use her classification of incidents in African tales; Miss Thelma James of Detroit turned over to me the manuscript of her classification of the *Alphabetum Narrationum,* as did Dr. Luella Carter of her classification of the tales in the *Scala Celi* and Prof. C. B. Cooper of his notes on Burton's *Arabian Nights* and *the Kathā Sarit Sāgara.* Mr. Bjorn Winger of Indianapolis gave me most valuable help by excerpting motifs from several difficult sources, notably from about half of Feilberg's *Bidrag til en Ordbog over Jyske Almuesmål.* When I excerpted the second half of the work, I realized the magnitude of this kindness so freely given.

Prof. Ernest J. Simmons was good enough to supplement my inadequate knowledge of Russian, so that the motifs in a certain Russian work could be included. Prof. John W. Spargo, of Northwestern University, has in a number of cases enriched the classification from the fields of his special interest. Lastly, must be mentioned a whole group of students of my seminar in the Folk-Tale, who for some years were most generous of their time in excerpting important works.

For the new edition the help for which I am very thankful has continued on all sides through the years. First must be mentioned those who have devoted great labor to the preparation of indexes of special fields and have thus made possible this revision — Jonas Balys, Ernest W. Baughman, Inger Margrethe Boberg, Laurits Bødker, Åke Campbell, Joseph M. Carrière, J. Wesley Childers, Tom Peete Cross, Aurelio M. Espinosa, Paul Delarue, Helen L. Flowers, Theodor H. Gaster, Verrier Elwin, Herbert Halpert, Hiroko Ikeda, William Hugh Jansen, John Esten Keller, May A. Klipple, Waldemar Liungman, Maria de los Angeles Moreno Enriquez, Dov Neuman, Anton Nyerges, Sister Marie-Ursule, Warren E. Roberts, D. P. Rotunda, Archer Taylor, Toni Unger, Maria Alice Moura Pessoa, and Bjorn Winger.

To these may be added a group from the University of South Carolina who have listed motifs from various writers of the French Renaissance — J. Woodrow Hassell, Jr., A. M. Hardee, Cecilia P. Irwin, Sarah C. Pinkney, F. C. Perry, Kenneth Fay and Andrew H. Yarrow.

Aside from those mentioned as having completed motif-indexes, a number of my students have excerpted motifs to the number of many thousand from various fields — Richard Bartel (Greek drama), Kenneth Clarke (Africa), Bacil F. Kirtley (Oceania), Dorothy Thompson Letsinger (Sir Thomas Malory), W. S. Mayer, Jr. (Troy legend), Barbara Harris Mickey (Melanesia), Remedios Wycoco Moore (American Indian, Buddhist, and much else), Henri Stegemeier (German Schwankbücher), and Richard Weir (Modern Greek).

Finally, I have been extremely fortunate in having gifted and willing research assistants whose work has gone far beyond the line of duty — Jonas Balys (1948—52) and Remedios Wycoco Moore (1952—54).

The expense attached to the preparation and publishing of a work such as the present is not trifling. For clerical help the American Council of Learned Societies has twice given me grants. For the second half of the college year 1930—31, this foundation also awarded me funds to permit my taking leave from my university work in order to finish the present classification. Indiana University generously supplemented this grant.

In the years during which the new edition has been prepared generous support of this work has continued. Indiana University has always provided clerical help and for six years a full time research assistant. Preparation of the alphabetical index has been facilitated by a grant from the American Philosophical Society.

The expense of printing the first edition was borne by the Finnish Academy of Sciences and Indiana University. Rosenkilde and Bagger and the Indiana University Press have jointly borne the responsibility for publication of the revised edition. To these and to all who have so generously aided in making this work possible, I wish here to express my thanks.

Bloomington, Indiana
September, 1955 STITH THOMPSON

GENERAL SYNOPSIS OF THE INDEX

A. MYTHOLOGICAL MOTIFS

B. ANIMALS

B0 —B99. Mythical animals
B100 —B199. Magic animals
B200 —B299. Animals with human traits

B300 —B599. *Friendly animals*
- B300 —B349. Helpful animals — general
- B350 —B399. Grateful animals
- B400 —B499. Kinds of helpful animals
- B500 —B599. Services of helpful animals

B600 —B699. Marriage of person to animal
B700 —B799. Fanciful traits of animals
B800 —B899. Miscellaneous animal motifs

C. TABU

C0 —C99. Tabu connected with supernatural beings
C100—C199. Sex tabu
C200—C299. Eating and drinking tabu
C300—C399. Looking tabu
C400—C499. Speaking tabu
C500—C549. Tabu: touching
C550—C599. Class tabu
C600—C699. Unique prohibitions and compulsions.
C700—C899. Miscellaneous tabus
C900—C999. Punishment for breaking tabu

D. MAGIC

D0 —D699. *Transformation*
- D10 —D99. Transformation: man to different man
- D100 —D199. Transformation: man to animal
- D200 —D299. Transformation: man to object
- D300 —D399. Transformation: animal to person
- D400 —D499. Other forms of transformation
- D500 —D599. Means of transformation
- D600 —D699. Miscellaneous transformation incidents

D700 —D799. Disenchantment

D800 —D1699. *Magic objects*
- D800 —D899. Ownership of magic objects
- D900 —D1299. Kinds of magic objects
- D1300—D1599. Function of magic objects
- D1600—D1699. Characteristics of magic objects

D1700—D2199. *Magic powers and manifestations*
- D1710—D1799. Possession and employment of magic powers
- D1800—D2199. Manifestations of magic power

E. THE DEAD

E0 —E199. Resuscitation

E200—E599. *Ghosts and other revenants*
- E200—E299. Malevolent return from the dead
- E300—E399. Friendly return from the dead
- E400—E599. Ghosts and revenants — miscellaneous

E500—E699. Reincarnation
E700—E799. The Soul

F. MARVELS

F0 —F199. Otherworld journeys

F200—F699. *Marvelous creatures*
- F200—F399. Fairies and elves
- F400—F499. Spirits and demons
- F500—F599. Remarkable persons
- F600—F699. Persons with extraordinary powers

F700—F899. Extraordinary places and things
F900—F1099. Extraordinary occurrences

G. OGRES

G10 —G399. *Kinds of ogres*
- G10 —G99. Cannibals and cannibalism
- G100—G199. Giant ogres
- G200—G299. Witches
- G300—G399. Other ogres

G400—G499. Falling into ogre's power
G500—G599. Ogre defeated
G600—G699. Other ogre motifs

H. TESTS

H0 —H199. Identity tests: recognition
H200 —H299. Tests of truth
H300 —H499. Marriage tests

H500 —H899. *Tests of cleverness*
- H500 —H529. Test of cleverness or ability
- H530 —H899. Riddles

H900 —H1199. *Tests of prowess: tasks*
- H900 —H999. Assignment and performance of tasks
- H1000—H1199. Nature of tasks

H1200—H1399. *Tests of prowess: quests*
- H1200—H1249. Attendant circumstances of quests
- H1250—H1399. Nature of quests

H1400—H1599. *Other tests*
- H1400—H1449. Tests of fear
- H1450—H1499. Tests of vigilance
- H1500—H1549. Tests of endurance and power of survival
- H1550—H1569. Tests of character
- H1570—H1599. Miscellaneous tests

J. THE WISE AND THE FOOLISH

J0 —J199. Acquisition and possession of wisdom (knowledge)

J200 —J1099. *Wise and unwise conduct*
- J200 —J499. Choices
- J500 —J599. Prudence and discretion
- J600 —J799. Forethought
- J800 —J849. Adaptability
- J850 —J899. Consolation in misfortune
- J900 —J999. Humility
- J1000—J1099. Other aspects of wisdom

J1100—J1699. *Cleverness*
- J1110—J1129. Clever persons
- J1130—J1199. Cleverness in the law court
- J1200—J1229. Clever man puts another out of countenance
- J1230—J1249. Clever dividing
- J1250—J1499. Clever verbal retorts (repartee)
- J1500—J1649. Clever practical retorts
- J1650—J1699. Miscellaneous clever acts

J1700—J2749. *Fools (and other unwise persons)*
- J1700—J1749. Fools (general)
- J1750—J1849. Absurd misunderstandings
- J1850—J1999. Absurd disregard of facts
- J2000—J2049. Absurd absent-mindedness
- J2050—J2199. Absurd short-sightedness
- J2200—J2259. Absurd lack of logic
- J2260—J2299. Absurd scientific theories
- J2300—J2349. Gullible fools
- J2350—J2369. Talkative fools
- J2370—J2399. Inquisitive fools
- J2400—J2449. Foolish imitation
- J2450—J2499. Literal fools
- J2500—J2549. Foolish extremes
- J2550—J2599. Thankful fools
- J2600—J2649. Cowardly fools
- J2650—J2699. Bungling fools
- J2700—J2749. The easy problem made hard

J2750—J2799. Other aspects of wisdom or foolishness

K. DECEPTIONS

K0 —K99. Contests won by deception
K100 —K299. Deceptive bargains
K300 —K499. Thefts and cheats
K500 —K699. Escape by deception
K700 —K799. Capture by deception
K800 —K999. Fatal deception
K1000—K1199. Deception into self-injury
K1200—K1299. Deception into humiliating position
K1300—K1399. Seduction or deceptive marriage
K1400—K1499. Dupe's property destroyed
K1500—K1599. Deceptions connected with adultery
K1600—K1699. Deceiver falls into own trap

K1700—K2099. *Deception through shams*
- K1700—K1799. Deception through bluffing
- K1800—K1899. Deception by disguise or illusion
- K1900—K1999. Impostures
- K2000—K2099. Hypocrites

K2100—K2199. False accusations
K2200—K2299. Villains and traitors
K2300—K2399. Other deceptions

L. REVERSAL OF FORTUNE

L0 —L99. Victorious youngest child
L100—L199. Unpromising hero (heroine)
L200—L299. Modesty brings reward
L300—L399. Triumph of the weak
L400—L499. Pride brought low

M. ORDAINING THE FUTURE

M0 —M99. Judgments and decrees
M100—M199. Vows and oaths
M200—M299. Bargains and promises
M300—M399. Prophecies
M400—M499. Curses

N. CHANCE AND FATE

N0 —N99. Wagers and gambling
N100—N299. The ways of luck and fate
N300—N399. Unlucky accidents

N400—N699. *Lucky accidents*
- N410—N439. Lucky business ventures
- N440—N499. Valuable secrets learned
- N500—N599. Treasure trove

N600—N699. Other lucky accidents
N700—N799. Accidental encounters
N800—N899. Helpers

P. SOCIETY

P0 —P99. Royalty and nobility
P100—P199. Other social orders
P200—P299. The family
P300—P399. Other social relationships
P400—P499. Trades and professions
P500—P599. Government
P600—P699. Customs
P700—P799. Society — miscellaneous motifs

Q. REWARDS AND PUNISHMENTS

Q10 —Q99. Deeds rewarded
Q100—Q199. Nature of rewards
Q200—Q399. Deeds punished
Q400—Q599. Kinds of punishment

R. CAPTIVES AND FUGITIVES

R0 —R99. Captivity
R100—R199. Rescues
R200—R299. Escapes and pursuits
R300—R399. Refuges and recapture

S. UNNATURAL CRUELTY

S0 —S99. Cruel relatives
S100—S199. Revolting murders or mutilations
S200—S299. Cruel sacrifices
S300—S399. Abandoned or murdered children
S400—S499. Cruel persecutions

T. SEX

T0 —T99. Love
T100—T199. Marriage
T200—T299. Married life
T300—T399. Chastity and celibacy
T400—T499. Illicit sexual relations
T500—T599. Conception and birth
T600—T699. Care of children

U. THE NATURE OF LIFE

U0 —U99. Life's inequalities
U100—U299. Nature of life — miscellaneous

V. RELIGION

V0 —V99. Religious services
V100—V199. Religious edifices and objects
V200—V299. Sacred persons
V300—V399. Religious beliefs
V400—V449. Charity
V450—V499. Religious orders
V500—V599. Religious motifs — miscellaneous

W. TRAITS OF CHARACTER

W0 —W99. Favorable traits of character
W100—W199. Unfavorable traits of character
W200—W299. Traits of character — miscellaneous

X. HUMOR

X0 —X99. Humor of discomfiture
X100—X199. Humor of disability — physical
X200—X599. *Humor of social classes*
    X200—X299. Humor dealing with tradesmen
    X300—X499. Humor dealing with professions
    X500—X599. Humor concerning other social classes
X600—X699. Humor concerning races or nations
X700—X799. Humor concerning sex
X800—X899. Humor based on drunkenness
X900—X1899. Humor of lies and exaggeration

Z. MISCELLANEOUS GROUPS OF MOTIFS

Z0 —Z99. Formulas
Z100—Z199. Symbolism
Z200—Z299. Heroes
Z300—Z399. Unique exceptions
Z400—Z499. Historical, genealogical or biographical motifs
Z500—Z599. Horror stories.

BIBLIOGRAPHY AND ABBREVIATIONS

Works indicated with an asterisk have been examined with some thoroughness for motifs. Those marked with ⊙ have been indexed according to the present work and have references only to motif-numbers. Books infrequently cited are not listed here.

AA n.s. = American Anthropologist, new series. Washington, 1899 ff.

AA o.s. = American Anthropologist, old series. 11 vols. Washington, 1888—1898.

*Aarne, Antti. Vergleichende Märchenforschungen (MSFO XXV). Helsingfors, 1907.

Africa. London, 1928 ff.

Alarcon, J. de Canedo, and Ricardo Pittini. El Chaco Paraguayo y sus tribos. Turin, 1924.

*Alexander *N. Am.* = Alexander, H. B. North American Mythology (The Mythology of all Races X). Boston, 1916.

Lat. Am. = Latin American Mythology (The Mythology of all Races XI). Boston, 1920.

**Alphabet* = Banks, M. M. An Alphabet of Tales, an English 15th century translation of the Alphabetum Narrationum of Etienne de Besançon (EETS Nos. 126, 127). 2 vols. London, 1904—05.

*Ananikian, Mardiros H. Armenian Mythology (The Mythology of all Races VII). Boston, 1925.

*Anderson, W. Nordasiatische Flutsagen (Acta et Commentationes Universitatis Dorpatensis B IV iii [1923]).

Andree, R. Die Flutsagen. Braunschweig, 1891.

Ethnographische Parallelen und Vergleiche. Stuttgart, 1878. Neue Folge, Leipzig, 1889.

*Andrejev, A. N. Ukazatel' Skazočnik Sjuzhetov po Systeme Aarne (Gosud. russ. geogr. obščestvo, otd. etnogr. skazočnaya komissiya). Leningrad, 1929.

Anesaki, Masaharu. Japanese Mythology (The Mythology of all Races VIII). Boston, 1928.

Anssaga Bogsveigis (FAS II 324 ff.).

*Arfert, P. Das Motiv von der unterschobenen Braut. Rostock, 1897.

Argonautica of Apollonius Rhodius (ed. G. W. Mooney). London, 1912.

Arnason, Jón. Íslenzkar þjoðsögur og æfintyri. 2 vols. Leipzig, 1862—64.

Arv. (Tidskrift for Nordisk Folkminnesforskning). Uppsala, 1944 ff.

ASB = Altnordische Saga-Bibliothek (ed. G. Cederschiöld and E. Mogk). 18 vols. Halle a. S., 1892—1929.

Asbjørnson, P. Chr. and Moe, J. Norske Folkeeventyr. 3d edition. Kristiania, 1896.

Asmundarsaga Kappabana (FAS II 460 ff.).

Auning, R. Ueber den lettischen Drachenmythus (Magazin der lettischlitterärischen Gesellschaft XIX 1—128). Mitau, 1891.

Azov, R. F. and D. C. Phillott. "Some Arab Folktales from Hazramut." Journal and Proceedings, Asiatic Society of Bengal (n. s.), II, 399—439; III, 645—680.

Babrius = Babrii Fabulae Aesopeae (ed. O. Crusius). Lipsiae, 1897.

Baldus, Herbert. Ensaios de Etnologia Brasileira. São Paulo, 1937.

Balys, Jonas. *_Ghosts_ and Men, Lithuanian Folk Legends about the Dead (Sub-title: A Treasury of Lithuanian Folklore I). Bloomington, Indiana, 1951.

*Lithuanian _Historical_ Legends. Chicago, 1949.

*Motif-_Index_ of Lithuanian Narrative Folklore. Tautosakos Darbai Vol. II, Publication of the Lithuanian Folklore Archives. Kaunas, 1936.

*Lithuanian Folk _Legends_. Publication of the Lithuanian Folklore Archives I. Kaunas, 1940.

Balzac, Honoré de. Contes drolatiques. Paris (many editions).

BAM = Bulletin of the American Museum of Natural History (New York).

Baring-Gould, S. Curious Myths of the Middle Ages. 2 vols. London, 1868.

*Barker, W. H. and Sinclair, C. West African Folk-tales. London, 1917.

Barrett, W. E. H. A'Kikuyu Fairy Tales (Man XII, XIII).

Barroso, Gustavo. Mythes, Contes et Legendes des Indiens: Folklore Bresilien. Paris, 1930.

Barto, Philip Stephan. Tannhäuser and the Mountain of Venus. New York, 1916.

Basden, G. T. Among the Ibos of Nigeria. London, 1921.

⊙Basile, G. The Pentamerone (trans. and edited by Benedetto Croce and N. M. Penzer). 2 vols. London, 1932.

Baskerville, Rosetta Gage. King of the Snakes and other Folklore: Stories from Uganda. London, 1922.

Basset, René. Contes populaires d'Afrique. Paris, 1903.

*Mille et un contes, récits et légendes arabes. 3 vols. Paris, 1925—27.

*Bateman, G. W. Zanzibar Tales. Chicago, 1901.

⊙Baughman, Ernest Warren. A Comparative Study of the Folktales of England and North America. (Indiana University dissertation.) Ann Arbor, Michigan. Microfilm Service. 1954.

BBAE = Bulletin of the Bureau of American Ethnology.

Beal = Bealoideas: Journal of the Folklore of Ireland Society.

Beauvois, E. L'autre vie dans la mythologie scandinave (Reprint from Muséon). Paris, 1883.

Bebel. See Wesselski.

Beckwith, Martha. Hawaiian Mythology. New Haven, 1940.

*Bédier, Joseph. Les Fabliaux. 2d edition. Paris, 1893.

Bender, C. J. Die Volksdichtung der Wakweli. ZsES Beiheft IV (1922), 38 ff.

Benedict, Ruth. Zuñi Mythology. 2 vols. New York, 1935. (All references are to Volume II.)

Béranger-Feraud, L. J. B. Recueil de Contes Populaires de Sénégambie. Paris, 1879.

Biblioteca Africana (D. A. Drexel ed.) Innsbruck, 1924—31.

*bin Gorion, M. J. Der Born Judas: Legenden, Märchen und Erzählungen. 6 vols. Leipzig, 1918 ff. (Vols. 1—4 cited are second edition, 5 and 6 are first edition).

Bladé, J. F. Contes populaires de Gascogne (Les Littératures Populaires, Nos. 19, 20, 21). 3 vols. Paris, 1886.

*Bleek, W. H. I. Reynard the Fox in South Africa or Hottentot Fables and Tales. London, 1864.

*Bleek, W. H. I., and Lloyd, L. C. Specimens of Bushman Folklore. London, 1911.

Blinkenberg, Chr. The Thunder Weapon in Religion and Folklore. Cambridge, 1911.

Bloomfield, Maurice, Studies in Honor of. New Haven, 1920.

BMB = Bishop Museum Bulletin.

Boas, Franz. Indianische Sagen von der Nord-Pacifischen Küste Amerikas. Berlin, 1895.

⊙Boberg, Inger M. Motif-Index of Early Icelandic Literature (Biblioteca Arnamagnæana). København 1956.

Bødker, Laurits. Christen Nielssen, De Gamle Vijses Exempler oc Hoffsprock. København, 1951, 1953.

Boekenoogen, G. J. Een Schone ende Miraculeuse historie van den Ridder Metter Swane. Leiden, 1931.

Boje, Christian. Über den altfranzösischen roman von Beuve de Hamtone (Beiheft zur Zeitschrift für Romanische Philologie XIX). Halle a. S., 1909.

*Bolte, J. Jakob *Freys* Gartengesellschaft (Bibliothek des Literarischen Vereins in Stuttgart, No. 209). Tübingen, 1896.

*Martin *Montanus* Schwankbücher (Bibliothek des Literarischen Vereins in Stuttgart, No. 217). Tübingen, 1899.

*Valentin *Schumanns* Nachtbüchlein (Bibliothek des Literarischen Vereins in Stuttgart, No. 197). Tübingen, 1893.

*Georg *Wickrams* Werke (Bibliothek des Literarischen Vereins in Stuttgart, Nos. 222, 223, 229, 230, 232, 236, 237, 241). 8 vols. Tübingen, 1901—08.

See BP.
See Fischer.
See Pauli.

Bósasaga (ed. O. L. Jiriczek). Strassburg, 1893.

Bourhill, E. J. and Drake, J. B. Fairy Tales from South Africa. London, 1908.

Bouveignes, Olivier de. Contes d'Afrique. Paris, 1927.

**BP* = Bolte, J. and Polívka, G. Anmerkungen zu den Kinder- und Hausmärchen der Brüder Grimm. 5 vols. Leipzig, 1913—31.

Broderius, John R. The Giant in Germanic Tradition (University of Chicago dissertation). Chicago, 1933.

Brown, A. C. L. Iwain: a Study in the Origins of Arthurian Romance (Harvard Studies and Notes in Philology and Literature VIII). Boston, 1903.

Brown Collection = The Frank C. Brown Collection of North Carolina Folklore. 5 vols. Durham, N. C., 1952—.

Bryan, William F. and Dempster, Germaine. Sources and Analogues of Chaucer's Canterbury Tales. Chicago, 1941.

Bugge, Sophus. Norróne Skrifter af Sagnhistorisk Indhold. Christiania, 1864.

Burton, R. F. Arabian *Nights:* The Book of the Thousand Nights and a Night. London, 1894. (SI, SII, etc. refers to Supplementary Volumes).

Book of the *Sword.* London, 1884.

Büttner, C. G. Lieder und Geschichten der Suaheli. Berlin, 1894.

Caldwell, J. R. Egar and Grime. Cambridge (Mass.), 1933.

*Callaway, H. Nursery Tales, Traditions, and Histories of the Zulus. Vol. I. Natal and London, 1868.

Campbell, J. F. Popular *Tales* of the West Highlands. 4 vols. 2d edition. London, 1890—93.

*Campbell, K. The Seven Sages of Rome. Boston, 1907.

Campbell-McKay = John G. McKay, More West Highland Tales, transcribed and translated from the original Gaelic manuscript of John Francis Campbell. Edinburgh and London, 1940.

Cappelle, H. van. Mythen en Sagen uit West Indië. Zutphen, 1926.

Cardim, Fernão. Tratado da terra e gente do Brasil. Rio de Janeiro, 1925.

*Carnoy, Albert J. Iranian Mythology (The Mythology of all Races VI). Boston, 1917.

Carrière = J. M. Carrière, Tales from the French Folk-Lore of Missouri. Evanston and Chicago, 1937.

Carrington, Hereward and Fodor, Nandor. Haunted People: Story of the Poltergeist down the Centuries. New York, 1951.

Casati, Gaetano. Ten Years in Equatoria and the Return with Emin Pasha (London, New York, 1891).

*Catalogus = Catalogus van Folklore in de Koninklijke Bibliotheek. 3 vols. 'sGravenhage, 1919—22.

CColl = Colorado College Publications, Language Series.

Les Cent Nouvelles Nouvelles. 2 vols. (ed. Pierre Champion). Paris, 1928.

Chantepie de la Saussaye. See Saussaye.

Charpentier, Jarl. Kleine Beiträge zur indoiranischen Mythologie (Uppsala Universitets Årsskrift). Uppsala, 1911.

*Chatelain, Heli. Folk-Tales of Angola (MAFLS I). Boston and New York, 1894.

*Chauvin, Victor. Bibliographie des ouvrages arabes. 12 vols. Liège, 1892—1922.

*Chavannes, Édouard. Cinq cent contes et apologues extraits du Tripitaka chinois. 4 vols. Paris, 1910—34.
*Child, Francis James. The English and Scottish Popular Ballads. 5 vols in 10. Boston, 1882—98.
⊙Childers, J. W. Motif-Index of the Cuentos of Juan Timoneda. Bloomington, Ind., 1947.
Christensen, Arthur, Dumme Folk (DF No. 50). København 1941.
Molboernes vise Gerninger (DF No. 47). København, 1939.
*Christiansen, R. Th. Norske Eventyr (Norske Folkeminder II). Kristiania, 1921.
CI = Publications of the Carnegie Institution of Washington.
*Clark, Mrs. K. M. Maori Tales and Legends. London, 1896.
*Clodd, Edward. Tom-Tit-Tot. London, 1898.
*Clouston, W. A. The Book of *Noodles*. London, 1888.
A Group of Eastern *Romances* and Stories. Glasgow, 1889.
*Popular *Tales* and Fictions. 2 vols. Edinburgh, London, 1887.
CNAE = Contributions to North American Ethnology. Washington, 1877—93.
*Codrington, R. H. The Melanesians: studies in their Anthropology and Folklore. Oxford, 1891.
Cole, Fay Cooper. Traditions of the Tinguian. FM XIV. Chicago, 1915.
*Conzemius, E. Ethnographical survey of the Miskito and Sumu Indians of Honduras and Nicaragua. BBAE CVI, 1932.
Cook, A. B. Zeus: a study in ancient religion. 3 vols. Cambridge, 1914 ff.
Corpus Poeticum Boreale (edited by G. Vigfússon and F. Y. Powell). 2 vols. Oxford, 1883.
*Cosquin, E. Contes populaires de *Lorraine*. 2 vols. Paris, 1887.
**Etudes* folkloriques. Paris, 1922.
*Les contes *indiens* et l'occident. Paris, 1922.
Coster-Wijsman, L. N. Uilespiegel-Verhalen in Indonesië. Santpoort, 1929.
*Cowell, E. B. and others. The Jātaka or Stories of the Buddha's Former Births. 6 vols. and index. Cambridge, 1895—1913.
*Cox, Marian R. Cinderella (PFLS XXXI). London, 1893.
*Coyajee, J. C. Some Shahnameh Legends and their Chinese Parallels. JPASB XXIV (1928).
*Crane, T. F. Liber de *Miraculis* Sanctae Dei Genetricis Mariae. Ithaca (N.Y.) and London, 1926.
*The Exempla of Jacques de *Vitry* (PFLS XXVI). London, 1890.
Crawley, Ernest. The Mystic Rose. London, 1902.
⊙Cross = Tom Peete Cross. Motif-Index of Early Irish Literature. Bloomington, Indiana, 1952.
CU = Columbia University Contributions to Anthropology.
*Curtin, Jeremiah. Seneca Indian Myths. Boston, 1923.
*Cushing, Frank H. Zuñi Folk Tales. New York and London, 1901.

*Dania. 10 vols. København, 1890—1903.
*Danske Studier. København, 1904 ff.
*Davenport, William. Marshallese Folklore Types (JAFL LXVI 219—237).
Dawkins, Richard M. Forty-five Stories from the Dodekanese. Cambridge (England), 1950.
Modern Greek Folktales. Oxford, 1953.
Day, Lal Behary. Folk-Tales of Bengal. London, 1912.
*De Cock, Alfons. *Studien* en Essays over oude Volksvertelsels. Antwerp, 1919.
**Volkssage,* Volksgeloof en Volksgebruik. Antwerp, 1918.
**Volksgeneeskunde* in Vlaanderen. Gent, 1891.
De la Saussaye. See Saussaye.
Dennett, R. E. The Folk-lore of the Fjort (French Congo) (PFLS XLI). London, 1898.
Desparmet, J. Contes populaires sur les ogres, recueillis à Blida. 2 vols. Paris, 1909—10.
Deutschbein, M. Studien zur Sagengeschichte Englands. Göthen, 1906.
De Vries, Jan. "De Sage van het ingemetselde *Kind*". Nederlandsch Tijdschrift voor Volkskunde XXXII (1927) 1—13.
Studiën over *Faerösche* Balladen. Haarlem, 1915.
*Volksverhalen uit Oost Indië. 2 vols. Leiden, 1925, 1928.
*De Vries's list = De Vries, Jan. "Typen-Register der Indonesische Fabels en Sprookjes" (Volksverhalen uit Oost-Indië II 398 ff.)
DF = Danmarks Folkeminder. København, 1908—
**Dh* — Dähnhardt, Oskar. Natursagen. 4 vols. Leipzig, 1909—12.
*Dickson, Arthur. Valentine and Orson, a study in late Medieval Romance. New York, 1929.
Dieterich, Albrecht. Mutter Erde: ein Versuch über Volksreligion. 2d ed. Berlin, 1913.
*Dixon, Roland B. Oceanic Mythology (The Mythology of all Races IX). Boston, 1916.
Dobie, J. Frank. Coronado's Children. Dallas (Texas), 1930.
Dunlop-Liebrecht = Dunlop, J. Geschichte der Prosadichtungen (tr. and revised by F. Liebrecht). Berlin, 1851.
*Dunlop-Wilson = Dunlop, J. History of Prose Fiction. New edition revised by H. Wilson. 2 vols. London, 1888.
Durkheim, Émile. Les formes élémentaires de la vie religieuse. Paris, 1912.
EETS = Early English Text Society Publications. London, 1864 ff.
Ebding, F. "Duala Märchen" (ZsES XVIII, 142—47).
Eberhard, Wolfram. Chinese Fairy Tales and Folk Tales. London, 1937.
*Typen chinesischer Volksmärchen (FFC CCXX, 1937).
*and Boratav, Pertev. Typen türkischen Volksmärchen. Weisbaden, 1953.

Egils saga einhenda ok Ásmundar Berserkjabana (in Lagerholm, Drei Lygisögur, Halle, 1927 pp. 1 ff.).
Ehrenreich, Paul. Die Mythen und Legenden der südamerikanischen Urvölker. Berlin, 1905.
*Einstein, C. Afrikanische Legenden. Berlin, 1925.
Eisler, R. Weltenmantel und Himmelszelt. 2 vols. München, 1910.
*Ellis (Yoruba) = Ellis, A. B. The Yoruba-speaking Peoples of the Slave Coast of West Africa. London, 1894.
*Ellis (Vai) = Ellis, G. W. Negro Culture in West Africa. New York, 1914.
Ellis, T. P. and Lloyd, J. The Mabinogion. 2 vols. Oxford, 1929.
⊙Emeneau, M. B. Kota Texts. 4 vols. Berkeley and Los Angeles, 1944—46.
Encyc. Rel. Ethics = Hastings, J. Encyclopaedia of Religion and Ethics. 12 vols. New York, 1908—22.
Engert, Rolf. Die Sage vom Fliegenden Holländer (Meereskunde, Bd. XV, 7, Heft 173). Berlin, 1927.
Equilbecq, F. V. Contes indigènes de l'Ouest Africain Français. 3 vols. Paris, 1913—16.
Erminy Arismendi, Santos. Huellas Folkloricas. Caracas, 1954.
*Espinosa, Aurelio M. Cuentos populares españoles. 3 vols. 2d edition. Madrid, 1946—47.
Espinosa, Aurelio M., Jr. Cuentos populares de Castilla y Leon. (In press.)
*Eyrbyggja saga (ed. H. Gering). ASB VI. Halle, 1897.
FAS = Rafn, C. C. Fornaldar Sögur Norðrlanda. 3 vols. København, 1829—30.
**Fb* = Feilberg, H. F. Bidrag til en Ordbog over jyske Almuesmål. 4 vols. København, 1886—1914.
*Feilberg, H. F. *Nissens* Historie (DF No. 18). København, 1919.
　Jul. 2 vols. København, 1904.
　Festskrift til (Svenska Landsmål ock svenskt Folkliv). Stockholm, 1911.
*Ferguson, John C. Chinese Mythology (Mythology of all Races VIII). Boston, 1928.
**FFC* = FF Communications, published by the Folklore Fellows. Helsinki, 1907 ff.
*Field, John E. The Myth of the Pent Cuckoo. London, 1913.
Fischer, H. and Bolte, J. Die Reise der Söhne Giaffers (Bibliothek des Litterarischen Vereins in Stuttgart No. 208). Tübingen, 1895.
**FL* = Folklore. London, 1890 ff.
Flateyarbók (ed. Vigfússon and Unger). 3 vols. Christiania, 1860—68.
**FLJ* = Folklore Journal. 8 vols. London, 1883—89.
⊙Flowers, Helen L. A Classification of the Folktales of the West Indies by Types and Motifs. (Indiana University Ph. D. thesis, 1952.) Microfilm Service, Ann Arbor, Michigan, 1953.
**FLR* = Folklore Record. 5 vols. London, 1878—82.
FM = Publications of the Field Columbian Museum, Anthropological Series, Chicago, 1895 ff.

FMS = Fornmannasögur Norðrlanda. 12 vols. København, 1925—37.
FochF = Folkminnen och Folktankar. Lund.
Folklore Studies (The Catholic University of Peking). 6 vols. Peiping, 1942—47.
Fox, William S. Greek and Roman Mythology (Mythology of all Races I). Boston, 1916.
*Frazer, J. G. *Apollodorus:* the Library (Loeb Classical Library). London and New York, 1921.
*The Belief in *Immortality* and the Worship of the Dead. 2 vols. London, 1913.
*The Fasti of *Ovid*. 5 vols. London, 1929.
*Folklore in the *Old Testament*. 3 vols. London, 1918.
*The *Golden Bough*. 3d edition. 12 vols. London, 1907—15.
*Myths of the Origin of *Fire*. London, 1930.
**Pausanias*'s Description of Greece. 6 vols. London, 1898.
Frey. See Bolte.
Frobenius, Leo. *Atlantis:* Volksdichtung und Volksmärchen Afrikas. 12 vols. Jena, 1921—28.
Erlebte *Erdteile*. Frankfurt a. M., 1925 ff.
and Fox, Douglas C. African Genesis. New York, 1937.
FSS = Fornaldarsögur Suðrlanda (ed. G. Cederschiöld). København, 1901.
Gantenbein, B. Sprichwörter und Fabeln der Kamerun-Neger (Mitteilungen der ostschweizerischen Geograph-Commerciellen Gesellschaft II). St. Gallen, 1909.
*Gaster, Moses. *Beiträge* zur vergleichenden Sagen- und Märchenkunde (Gruz' Monatschrift für Geschichte und Wissenschaft des Judentums, XXIX, XXX). Bukarest, 1880, 1881. (Separate reprint, 1882; also included in Studies and Texts in Folklore, cited below).
*The *Exempla* of the Rabbis. London, Leipzig, 1924.
**Studies* and Texts in Folklore, Magic, Medieval Romance, Hebrew Apocrypha and Samaritan Archaeology. 3 vols. London, 1925—28.
⊙Gaster, Theodor H. The *Oldest Stories* in the World. New York, 1952.
⊙*Thespis*. New York, 1950.
Gautreks Saga (ed. W. Ranisch, Palaestra XI). 1900.
Gayton, A. H. and Newman, Stanley S. Yokuts and Western Mono Myths. Berkeley (Calif.), 1940.
*Gerould, Gordon H. The Grateful Dead (PFLS LX). London, 1908.
*Gifford, E. W. Tongan Myths and Tales. BMB VIII. Honolulu 1924.
Giles, Herbert A. Strange Stories from a Chinese Studio. New York, 1927.
Gilgamisch = Ungrad, A. and Gressman, H. Das Gilgamesch-Epos. Göttingen, 1911.
*Golther, Wolfgang. Zur deutschen Sage und Dichtung. Leipzig, 1911.

Göngu Hrólfs saga (FAS III 235 ff.).
Gonzenbach, Laura. Sicilianische Märchen. 2 vols. Leipzig, 1870.
Graf, Arturo. Miti, Leggende e Superstizioni del Medio Evo. 2 vols. Torino, 1892—93.
⊙Graham (Chinese) = Graham, David Crockett. Songs and Stories of the Ch'uan Miao (Smithsonian Miscellaneous Publications CXXIII No. 1). Washington, D. C., 1954.
*Gray, Louis H. Baltic Mythology (Mythology of All Races III). Boston, 1918.
Grenfell = Johnson, Sir Harry. George Grenfell and the Congo, II. London, 1908.
Grettis saga (ed. R. C. Boer). ASB VIII. Halle, 1900.
Grímssaga Loðinkinna (FAS II 143 ff.).
*Grinnell, G. B. Pawnee Hero Stories and Folk-Tales. New York, 1889.
*Grote, George. History of Greece. 3 vols. London, 1888.
Grundtvig, S. Danmarks gamle Folkeviser. 8 vols. København, 1853—.
Grunwald, M. "Spaniolic-Jewish Folktales and Their Motifs", Edoth II (1947), pp. 225—243 (in Hebrew).
GSCan = Publications of the Geological Survey of Canada, Anthropological Series.
Gull-Þóris Saga (ed. Kr. Kaalund). København, 1898.
Gunnlaugs saga Ormstunga (ed. E. Mogk). Altnordische Texte I, 1886.
*Günter, H. Die christliche Legende des Abendlandes. Heidelberg, 1910.
Güntert, H. Der arische *Weltkönig* und Heiland. Halle, 1923.
**Kalypso*. Halle, 1919.
Gutmann, Bruno. Volksbuch der Wadschagga. Leipzig, 1914.
*Hackman, O. Die Polyphemsage in der Volksüberlieferung. Helsingfors, 1904.
Haddon, A. C. Reports of the Cambridge Anthropological Expedition to Torres Straits. 6 vols. Cambridge (Eng.), 1901—35.
*Hagen, Friedrich Heinrich von der. Gesammtabenteuer. 3 vols. Stuttgart and Tübingen, 1850.
Hálfdanar saga Brönufóstra (FAS III 559 ff.).
Hálfdanar saga Eysteinssonar (ed. F. R. Schröder). Halle, 1917.
Hálfs saga ok Hálfsrekka (ed. A. Le Roy Andrews). Halle, 1909.
Halm, K. von. Aisōpeiōn Mythōn Synagōgē. Lipsiae, 1852.
⊙Halpert, Herbert N. Folktales and Legends from the New Jersey Pines. (Indiana University Ph. D. thesis). Typewritten ms. Indiana University Library. Bloomington, Ind., 1947.
*Handbook of South American Indians (ed. Julian H. Steward). BBAE CXLIII. 6 vols. Washington, D. C., 1946—50.
*Handy, E. S. C. Marquesan Legends. BMB LXIX. Honolulu 1930.
Harris, J. R. *Boanerges*. Cambridge (Eng.), 1913.

The Cult of the Heavenly *Twins*. Cambridge, 1906.
Picus who is also Zeus. Cambridge, 1916.

Harris, Joel C. *Uncle *Remus:* his Songs and Sayings. New York, 1880.
*Uncle Remus and his *Friends*. Boston, 1892.
**Nights* with Uncle Remus. Boston, 1883.

*Hartland, E. S. The Legend of *Perseus*. 3 vols. London, 1894 ff.
*Primitive *Paternity*. 2 vols. London, 1909.
*The *Science* of Fairy Tales. London, 1891.

Hatt, Gudmund. *Asiatic Influences in American Folklore. København, 1949.
The Corn Mother in America and Indonesia. (Anthropos XLVI [1951] pp. 853—914.)

**Hdwb. d. Abergl.* = Bächtold-Stäubli, H. and others. Handwörterbuch des deutschen Aberglaubens. 10 vols. Berlin, 1927 ff.

**Hdwb. d. Märch.* = Mackensen, L. and others. Handwörterbuch des deutschen Märchens. Berlin, 1931 ff.

*Heepe, M. Jaunde-Texte. Hamburg, 1919.

Heiðreks saga. See Hervararsaga ok Heiðreks konungs.

*Held, T. v. Märchen und Sagen der africanischen Neger. Jena, 1904.

Heptameron. See Marguerite de Navarre.

*Herbert, J. A. Catalogue of Romances in the Department of Manuscripts in the British Museum. London, 1910. (Vol. 3 only; for vols. 1 and 2 see Ward, H. L. D.)

Herrmann, Paul. Erläuterungen zu den ersten neun Büchern der dänischen Geschichte des *Saxo* Grammaticus. 2 vols. Leipzig, 1901, 1922.
Nordische *Mythologie*. Leipzig, 1903.

Hertel, A. Verzauberte Oertlichkeiten. Hannover, 1908.

*Hertz, Wilhelm. Aus *Dichtung* und Saga (ed. K. Vollmöller). Stuttgart and Berlin, 1907.
*Gesammelte *Abhandlungen* (ed. F. v. d. Leyen). Stuttgart and Berlin 1905.
Parzival. 2d ed. Stuttgart and Berlin, 1914.
Spielmannsbuch. Stuttgart, 1886.
Tristan und Isolde. Stuttgart, 1877.

Hervararsaga ok Heiðreks Konungs (ed. J. Helgason). København, 1924.

Hervieux, L. Les fabulistes latins. 2d ed. 2 vols. Paris, 1893—4.

Hibbard, Laura A. Mediaeval Romance in England. New York, 1924.

HF = Hoosier Folklore. Indianapolis, Ind., 1946 ff.

Hjálmterssaga ok Ölvis (FAS III 453 ff.).

Hock, Stefan. Die Vampyrsagen und ihre Verwertung in der deutschen Literatur. Berlin, 1900.

*Holm, G. Sagn og Fortællinger fra Angmagsalik (Meddelelser om Grønland X 237 ff.).

Holmberg, Uno. *Der *Baum* des Lebens (Annales Academiae Scientiarum Fennicae XVI. B). Helsinki, 1922—3.

*Finno-Ugric Mythology (The Mythology of all Races IV). Boston, 1927.
Gudstrons uppkomst. Uppsala, 1917.
*Siberian Mythology (The Mythology of all Races IV). Boston 1927.
*Holmström, Helge. Studier över svanjungfrumotivet. Malmö, 1919.
*Howey, M. O. The Horse in Magic and Myth. London, 1923.
Hrólfs Saga Kraka (ed. Finnur Jónsson). København, 1904.
*Hromundarsaga Greipssonar (FAS II 363 ff.).
*Huber, P. Michael. Die Wanderlegende von den Siebenschläfern. Leipzig, 1910.
*Huet, G. Les contes populaires. Paris, 1923.
*Hultkrantz, Åke. Conceptions of the Soul Among North American Indians. Stockholm, 1953.
Irwin, Cecilia Pauze. Summaries of the Stories of Béroalde de Verville's La Moyen de Parvenir. Unpublished M. A. thesis, University of South Carolina, 1953.
Ittman, J. *Einiges aus Bankon-Literatur (ZsES XVII).
*Nyang-Märchen (ZsES XVII).
Jacobs, Joseph. Book of Wonder *Voyages*. London, 1896.
*The Fables of *Aesop*. New York, 1894.
Celtic Fairy Tales. London, 1892.
More Celtic Fairy Tales. London, 1894.
English Fairy Tales. London, 1890.
More English Fairy Tales. London, 1895.
*Jacobs' list = Jacobs, Joseph. "List of Folk-Tale Incidents common to European Folk-Tales" in Papers and Transactions of the International Folk-lore Congress, 1891. London, 1892.
*Jacottet, E. The Treasury of Basuto Lore. London, 1908.
**JAFL* = Journal of American Folk-Lore. Boston, etc., 1888 ff.
JAI = Journal of the Royal Anthropological Institute of Great Britain and Ireland. London, 1871 ff.
JAOS = Journal of the American Oriental Society. Boston, etc., 1849 ff.
⊙Jansen, William Hugh. Abraham "Oregon" Smith: pioneer, folk hero, and tale-teller. (Indiana University Ph. D. thesis.) Typewritten MS. Indiana University Library. Bloomington (Ind.), 1949.
JAS = Journal of the African Society. 34 vols. London, 1862—1900.
Jātaka. See Cowell.
JE = Publications of the Jesup North Pacific Expedition. New York, etc., 1898 ff.
*Jegerlehner, Johannes. Sagen und Märchen aus dem Oberwallis. Basel, 1909.
Jenness, Diamond. Notes and Traditions from Northern Alaska (Report of the Canadian Arctic Expedition, Southern Party, 1913—16, XIII). Ottawa, 1924.

Jensen, P. Das Gilgamesch-Epos in der Weltliteratur. Strassburg, 1906.

*Jijena Sanchez, Rafael. El Perro Negro. Buenos Aires, 1952.

Johnson, Sir Harry. George Grenfell and the Congo, Vol. II. London, 1908.

*Jones, Louis C. Spooks of the Valley: ghost stories for boys and girls. Boston, 1948.

JPASB = Journal and Proceedings of the Asiatic Society of Bengal.

JSFO = Journal de la Société Finno-ougrienne. Helsingfors, 1886 ff.

*Junod, H. A. The Life of a South African Tribe, Vol. II. Neuchâtel, 1913.

*Kalevala, the land of heroes (W. F. Kirby, tr.). London, 1907.

Kålund, K. Kirialax Saga. København, 1917.

Keightley, Thomas. Fairy Mythology. London, 1847.

Keith, A. B. Indian Mythology (The Mythology of all Races VI). Boston, 1917.

⊙Keller, John Esten. Motif-Index of Mediaeval Spanish Exempla. Knoxville (Tenn.), 1949.

Kennedy, P. Legendary Fictions of the Irish Celts. London, 1866.

*Ker, Anna. Papuan Fairy Tales. London, 1910.

Ketilssaga Haengs (FAS II 109 ff.).

*Kidd, D. Savage Childhood: a Study of Kaffir Children. London, 1906.

*Kittredge, G. L. *Arthur* and Gorlagon (Harvard Studies and Notes in Philology and Literature VIII). Boston, 1903.

*A Study of *Gawain* and the Green Knight. Cambridge (Mass.), 1916.

**Witchcraft* in Old and New England. Cambridge (Mass.), 1929.

Klapper, Joseph. Erzählungen des Mittelalters. Breslau, 1914.

*Knowles, J. H. Folk-Tales of Kashmir. London, 1893.

*Köhler, Reinhold. *Aufsätze* über Märchen und Volkslieder (ed. J. Bolte and E. Schmidt). Berlin, 1894.

**Köhler-Bolte* = Köhler, R. Kleinere Schriften (ed. J. Bolte). 3 vols. Weimar, 1898—1900.

Kölbing, E. Riddarsögur. København, 1872.

Krappe, A. H. Les Sources du Libro de Exemplos, Bulletin Hispanique, XXXIX, pp. 5—54.

**Balor* with the Evil Eye: Studies in Celtic and French Literature. New York, 1927.

**Études* de mythologie et de folklore germaniques. Paris, 1928.

The *Science* of Folk-Lore. London, 1930.

*Kristensen, Evald Tang. Danske Sagn. 2d ed. 6 vols. København, 1928—36.

Krohn, Kaarle. **Bär* (wolf) und Fuchs (JSFO VI). Helsingfors, 1886.

Der gefangene *Unhold* (Finnische-Ugrische Forschungen VII 129—84). Helsingfors, 1908.

**Mann* und Fuchs. Helsingfors.· 1891.

Krug, Adolph N. Bulu Tales from Kamerun, West Africa (JAFL XXV).
Kruyt, A. C. Het Animisme in den Indischen Archipel. 'sGravenhage, 1906.
*Lagerholm, Å. Drei Lygisǫgur (ASB XVII). København, 1927.
*Laistner, Ludwig. Das Rätsel der Sphinx. 2 vols. Berlin, 1889.
Landau, M. Die Quellen des Dekameron. 2d ed. Stuttgart, 1884.
*Landtman, G. The Folk-Tales of the Kiwai Papuans (Acta Societatis Scientiarum Fennicae XLVII). Helsingfors, 1917.
Lang, Andrew. The Delectable Tale of the Marriage of Cupid and *Psyche,* done into English by William Adlington. London, 1886.
Myth, Ritual and Religion. 2 vols. London, 1887.
*Langdon, S. H. Semitic Mythology (The Mythology of all Races V). Boston, 1931.
Largeau, V. Elements de Grammaire et Dictionnaire Français-Pahouin. Paris, 1901.
Laserstein, Käte. Der Griseldisstoff in der Weltliteratur (Forschungen zur neueren Literaturgeschichte LVIII). Weimar, 1926.
Latchman, Ricardo E. Las creencias religiosas de los antiguos peruanos. Santiago de Chile, 1929.
Lawrence, R. M. The Magic of the Horseshoe. London and Boston, 1898.
Le Braz, A. La Légende de la Mort chez les Bretons armoricains. 2 vols. Paris, 1902.
Lederbogen, Wilhelm. *Kameruner Märchen. Berlin, 1901.
*Duala Märchen (Mittheilungen des Seminars für Orientalische Sprachen, VI, Dritte Abteilung). Berlin, 1903.
Duala Fables. JAS IV (1904—05).
*Lee, A. C. The Decameron, its Sources and Analogues. London, 1909.
*Leland, Charles Godfrey. The Algonquin Legends of New England. Boston, 1884.
Leskien = Leskien, A. and Brugmann, K. Litauische Volkslieder und Märchen. Strassburg, 1882.
*Leyden, F. von der. *Das Märchen,* 3d ed. Leipzig, 1925.
*Das Märchen in den Göttersagen der *Edda.* Berlin, 1899.
Der gefesselte *Unhold* (Prager deutsche Studien, Heft 8, Sonderabzug, 1—29). Prag, 1908.
*Liebrecht, Felix. Zur Volkskunde. Heilbronn, 1879.
*Liljeblad, Sven. Die Tobiasgeschichte und andere Märchen mit toten Helfern. Lund, 1927.
*Liungman, W. En traditionsstudie över sagan om Prinsessan i *Jordkulan.* Göteborg, 1925.
**Två* Folkminnesundersökningar. Göteborg, 1925.
Sveriges Samtliga *Folksagor.* 3 vols. Djursholm (Sweden), 1950—52.
Lloyd, John W. Aw-aw-tam Indian Nights. Westerfield, N. J., 1911.

Loomis, C. Grant. *White Magic:* an Introduction to the Folklore of Christian Legend. Cambridge (Mass.), 1948.
Loomis, R. S. *Celtic Myth* and Arthurian Romance. New York, 1927.
Loorits, Oskar. Grundzüge des estnischen Volksglaubens, Vol. I. Lund, 1949.
Lorentzen, Th. Die Sage vom Rodensteiner. Heidelberg, 1903.
*Löwis, A. von, of Menar. Die Brünhildsage in Russland (Palaestra No. 142). Leipzig, 1923.
*Luomala, Katherine. Maui-of-a-Thousand-Tricks. BMB CXCVIII. Honolulu, 1949.
Luzel, F. M. Contes populaires de Basse-Bretagne. 3 vols. Paris, 1887.
MacCulloch, J. A. **Celtic* Mythology (The Mythology of all Races III). Boston, 1918.
*The *Childhood* of Fiction. London, 1905.
**Eddic* Mythology (The Mythology of all Races II). Boston, 1930.
MacDougall, James, and Calder, George. Folk Tales and Fairy Lore in Gaelic and English. Edinburgh, 1910.
*Máchal, J. Slavic Mythology (The Mythology of all Races III). Boston, 1918.
MacKay, D. E. The Double Invitation in the Legend of Don Juan. Stanford University, 1943.
⊙McKay, J. G. More West Highland Tales. Edinburgh and London, 1940.
MAFLS = Memoirs of the American Folk-Lore Society.
*Malalasekera, George Peiris. Dictionary of Pali Proper Names. 2 vols. London, 1937.
*Malory, Sir Thomas. Morte D'Arthur (many editions).
Mannhart, W. Wald und Feldkulte. 2 vols. 2d ed. Berlin, 1904—05.
*Mansfeld, Alfred. Urwald-Dokumente: Vier Jahre unter den Crossflussnegern Kameruns. Berlin, 1908.
Marie-Ursule, Sœur. Civilisation traditionelle des Lavalois. (Les Archives de Folklore V—VI). Québec, 1951.
*Marguerite de Navarre. Heptameron. 3 vols. (ed. Dillage, Paris, 1879). (Analysis by Sarah C. Pinkney, University of South Carolina).
Meinhof, Carl. Afrikanische Märchen. Jena, 1921.
*Meinhof, Elli. Märchen aus Kamerun. Strassburg, 1889.
*Mélusine. 10 vols. Paris, 1878—1901.
Mensa Philosophica = T. F. Dunn. The Facetiae of the Mensa Philosophica (Washington University Studies, new series, Lang. and Lit. No. 5). St. Louis, 1934.
Métraux, Alfred. *Ethnology* of Easter Island. BMB CLX. Honolulu, 1940.
*Mitos y Cuentos de los Indios Chiriguano. RMLP XXXIII (1932), pp. 119—84.
*Myths of the Toba and Pilaga Indians of the Gran Chaco (MAFLS XL, 1946).

Myths and Tales of the *Matako* Indians. Göteborg, 1939.
Meyer, Elard H. *Germanische* Mythologie. Berlin, 1891.
Mythologie der *Germanen*. Strassburg, 1903.
*Meyer, Johann J. *Hindu* Tales. London, 1909.
*Meyer, Kuno. The Voyage of *Bran,* son of Febal to the Land of the Living (with an essay upon the Irish Vision of the Happy Otherworld and the Celtic doctrine of Rebirth by Alfred Nutt). 2 vols. London, 1895, 1897.
Meyer, Richard M. *Altgermanische* Religiongeschichte. Leipzig, 1910.
Milligan, Robert H. *The *Fetish* Folk of West Africa. Chicago, 1912.
*The *Jungle* Folk of Africa. New York, 1908.
*Mischlich, A. Neue Märchen aus Afrika. Leipzig, 1929.
*Mitford, A. B. F. Tales of Old Japan. 3d edition. London, 1876.
**MLN* = Modern Language Notes. Baltimore, 1886 ff.
Moe, Moltke. Samlede Skrifter. 4 vols. Oslo, 1925 ff.
Mogk Festschrift = Festschrift Eugen Mogk zum 70. Geburtstag. Halle, 1924.
Monteil, C. Contes Soudanais. Paris, 1905.
Moreno Enriquez, Maria de los Angeles. Motivos de narracion tradicionales en los libros de *Esdras*. (Anuario de la Sociedad Folklorica de Mexico VI 7—45.) Mexico, 1947.
MSFO = Mémoires de la Société Finno-ougrienne, Helsingfors.
**MPh* = Modern Philology. Chicago, 1903 ff.
Much, R. Der germanische Himmelsgott (Abhandlungen zur germanischen Philologie: Festgabe für Richard Heinzel, pp. 189 ff.) Halle, 1898.
MWF = Midwest Folklore. Bloomington 1951 ff.
Müller, P. Beitrag zur Kenntnis der Tem-Sprache (Nord-Togo). (Mitteilungen des Seminars für orientalische Sprachen zu Berlin, VIII.)
*Müller, W. Max. Egyptian Mythology (The Mythology of all Races XII). Boston, 1918.
*Nassau, R. H. Where Animals Talk: West African Folklore Tales. London, 1914.
Naumann, Hans. Primitive Gemeinschaftskultur. Jena, 1921.
Neilson, William A. The Origins and Sources of the Court of Love. Cambridge (Mass.), 1899.
*Nekes, Hermann. Lehrbuch der Jaunde-Sprache. Berlin, 1911.
⊙Neuman, Dov. Motif-index to the Talmudic-Midrashic Literature. (Indiana University Ph. D. thesis). Microfilm Service, Ann Arbor, Michigan, 1954.
*Norlind, Tobias. Skattsägner, en studie i jämförande folkminnesforskning. Lund, 1918.
Nornagests þáttr: in Bugge, S. Norroene Skrifter af sagnhistorisk Indhold, pp. 47 ff. Christiania, 1864.
Nouvelles récréations et joyeaux devis (in Oeuvres françoises de Bonaventure des Périers). Vol. II. Paris, 1856.

Nouvelles de Sens (ed. E. Langlois). Paris, 1908.
(Analysis by F. C. Perry, University of South Carolina).
*Nordenskiöld, Erland. Indianerleben, El Gran Chaco (Südamerika). Leipzig, 1912.
Nutt, Alfred. See Meyer, Kuno.
NYFQ = New York Folklore Quarterly.
Nyrop, Kristoffer. Navnets Magt. København, 1887.
*Oberg, Kalervo. Indian Tribes of Northern Mato Grosso, Brazil (Smithsonian Institution, Institute of Social Anthropology, XV). Washington, 1953.
*Oesterley, H. Gesta Romanorum. Berlin, 1872.
Ohrt, F. *Danmarks* Trylleformler (FF Publications, Northern Series III). København, 1917.
Trylleord fremmede og danske (DF XXV). København, 1922.
*Olrik, Axel. Ragnarök: die Sagen vom Weltuntergang (trans. W. Ranisch). Berlin, 1922.
Örvar-Odds Saga (ed. R. C. Boer). Leiden, 1888.
*O'Suilleabhain, S. Scealta Craibhtheacha. Dublin, 1952.
PaAm = Anthropological Papers of the American Museum of Natural History.
PAES = Publications of the American Ethnological Society.
Panchatantra (tr. A. Ryder). Chicago, 1925.
*Panzer, F. *Beowulf* (Studien zur germanischen Sagengeschichte I). München, 1910.
**Hilde-Gudrun*. Halle a. S., 1901.
**Sigfrid*. (Studien zur germanischen Sagengeschichte II). München, 1910.
*Paris, G. Légendes du moyen âge. Paris, 1904.
Parker, Mrs. K. L. Australian Legendary Tales. London, 1896.
*Parkinson, John. Yoruba Folklore. (JAS VIII [1908] p. 165 ff.).
Patch, H. R. *The Goddess *Fortuna* in Mediaeval Literature. Cambridge (Mass.), 1927.
Patch, H. R. *The *Other World* According to Descriptions in Medieval Literature. Cambridge (Mass.), 1950.
Paton, Lucy A. Studies in the Fairy Mythology of Arthurian Romance (Radcliffe College Monographs No. 13). Cambridge (Mass.), 1903.
Pattetta, F. Le Ordalie. Torino, 1890.
**Pauli* = Johannes Pauli. Schimpf und Ernst (ed. Johannes Bolte). 2 vols. Berlin, 1924.
Pauly-Wissowa = Pauly's Real-Encyclopädie der classischen Altertumswissenschaft herausgegeben von G. Wissowa. Stuttgart, 1893 ff.
Pease, Arthur Stanley. M. Tulli Ciceronis De Divinatione. (University of Illinois Studies in Language and Literature, VI Nos. 2, 3; VIII Nos. 3, 4). Urbana (Ill.), 1920—23.
*Pechuël-Loesche, E. Volkskunde von Loango. Stuttgart, 1907.
*Penzer, N. M. The Ocean of Story: being C. H. Tawney's translation

of Somadeva's Kathā Sarit Sāgara. 10 vols. London, 1923 ff. See also Tawney.

Poison-Damsels and other essays in Folklore and Anthropology. London, 1952.

Pétitot, Émile. Traditions indiennes du Canada nord-ouest. Paris, 1886.

PFLS = Publications of the Folklore Society (English).

Phaedrus = Phaedri Fabulae Aesopiae (ed. J. P. Postgate). Oxford, 1920.

Pierre Faifeu = Charles de Bourdigné, Le Légende de Maistre Pierre Faifeu. Paris, 1880.

*Pino Saavedra, Y. Tres Versiones Chilenas de la Princesa Mona o Rana. (Homenaje a Fritz Kruger, Tomo I, pp. 399—407). Mendoza (Argentina), 1952.

*Plenzat, Karl. Die ost- und westpreussischen Märchen und Schwänke nach Typen geordnet (Veröffentlichungen des volkskundlichen Archivs der pädagogischen Akademie Elbing I). Königsberg, 1927.

*Plischke, Hans. Die Sage vom Wilden Heere im deutschen Volke (Leipzig dissertation). Eilenburg, 1914.

*Plummer, Charles. Vitae Sanctorum Hiberniae. 2 vols. Oxford, 1910.

PMLA = Publications of the Modern Language Association of America.

*Potter, Murray Anthony. Sohrab and Rustem. London, 1902.

Radloff, Wilhelm. Die Sprachen der türkischen Stämme Süd-Sibiriens. St. Petersburg, 1866—85.

Ragnarssaga Loðbrókar. See Völsungasaga.

*Rank, Otto. Das *Inzest*-Motiv in Dichtung und Sage. 2d ed. Wien, 1912.

*Der Mythus von der *Geburt* des Helden. Leipzig and Wien, 1912.

Psychoanalytische Beiträge zur Mythenforschung. Leipzig and Wien, 1919.

*Ranke, F. Der Erlöser in der Wiege. München, 1912.

Rasmussen, Knud. *Myter* og Sagn fra Grønland. 3 vols. København, 1921—25.

Rattray (Hausa) = Rattray, R. Sutherland. Hausa Folk-Lore Customs, Proverbs, etc. 2 vols. Oxford, 1913.

Rattray (Ashanti) = Rattray, R. Sutherland. Akan-Ashanti Folk Tales. Oxford, 1930.

RBAE = Annual Report of the Bureau of American Ethnology.

RCHG = Revista Chilena de Historia y Geografia. Santiago de Chile.

Reinhard, John R. The Survival of *Geis* in Mediaeval Romance. Halle a. S., 1933.

Renel, Charles. Contes de Madagascar. Paris, 1910, 1930.

*Rink, Henry. Tales and Traditions of the Eskimo. Edinburgh, 1875.

Rittershaus, Adeline. Die neuisländischen Volksmärchen. Halle, 1902.
RMLP = Revista del Museo de la Plata (Argentina).
*Roberts, Warren E. Aarne-Thompson Type 480 in World Tradition. (Indiana University Ph. D. thesis) Microfilm Service, Ann Arbor, Michigan, 1954.
*Róheim, Géza. *Animism*, Magic, and the Divine King. London, 1930.
Drachen und Drachenkämpfer. Berlin, 1912.
Spiegelzauber. Leipzig and Wien, 1919.
Romanic Review. New York, 1910 ff.
Roscher, W. H. Ausführliches Lexikon der griechischen und römischen Mythologie. Leipzig, 1884 ff.
Rosen, G. Tuti-Nameh, das Papageienbuch. Leipzig, 1858.
Rosén, Helge. Om Själavandringstro i Nordisk Folkföreställning (Folkminnen och Folktankar V p. 89 ff.).
Rosenhuber, P. Simon. Märchen, Fabeln, Rätsel, und Sprichwörter der Kamerun-Neger. Limburg, 1926.
⊙Rotunda, D. P. Motif-Index of the Italian Novella. Bloomington, Indiana, 1942.
RTP = Revue des Traditions Populaires. 32 vols. Paris, 1886—1917.
Rühlemann, Martin. Etymologie des Wortes Harlequin und verwandter Wörter (Halle dissertation). Halle a. S., 1912.
Saga och Sed (Kgl. Gustav Adolfs Akademiens Årsbok). Uppsala, 1932 ff.
Sagan af Illuga Gríðarfóstra (FAS III 648 ff.).
*Saintyves, P. Les Contes de *Perrault* et les recits parallèles. Paris, 1923.
**Essais* de folklore biblique. Paris, 1922.
Les *Saints* Successeurs des dieux. Paris, 1907.
*Saussaye, P. D. Chantepie de la. The Religion of the Teutons (trans. B. J. Vos). Boston, 1902.
**Scala Celi* = Johannes Gobii junior. Scala Celi. Lübeck, 1476.
Schlenker, C. F. A Collection of Temne Traditions, Fables and Proverbs. London, 1861.
Schoolcraft, H. R. *The Myth of *Hiawatha*. Philadelphia and London, 1856.
Algic Researches. New York, 1839.
*Schweda, Valentin. Die Sagen vom Wilden Jäger und vom Schlafenden Heer in der Provinz Posen (Greifswald dissertation). Gnesen, 1915.
*Scott, J. G. *Indo-Chinese* Mythology (The Mythology of all Races XII). Boston, 1918.
*Scott, Robert D. The *Thumb* of Knowledge. New York, 1930.
Sébillot, P. Le Folk-lore de *France*. 4 vols. Paris, 1904—07.
*Les *incidents* des contes populaires de la Haute-Bretagne. Vannes, 1892 (= RTP VII 411 ff, 515 ff.).
*Seligmann, S. Die magischen Heil- und Schutzmittel aus der unbelebten Natur. Stuttgart, 1927.
*Sharp-Karpeles = Sharp, Cecil and Karpeles, Maud. English Folk Songs from the Southern Appalachians. 2 vols. London, 1932.

Showerman, Grant. The Great Mother of the Gods. Madison (Wisconsin), 1901.
Sieber, J. Märchen und Fabeln der Wute (ZsES XII 53 ff., 162 ff.).
Märchen der Kweli in Kamerun (Mitteilungen des Seminars für Orientalische Sprachen zu Berlin, Dritte Abteilung: Afrikanische Studien, XXXV). Berlin, 1932.
Siecke, E. Drachenkämpfe. Leipzig, 1907.
Der Vegetationsgott. 2 vols. Leipzig, 1914.
*Siuts, Hans. Jenseitsmotive im deutschen Volksmärchen (Teutonia XIX). Leipzig, 1911.
Skjöldunga saga. See A. Olrik in Aarbøger for nordisk Oldkyndighed og Historie, II Række, IX (1894), 109.
*Smith, E. W. and Dale, A. The Ila-speaking People of Northern Rhodesia, vol. 2. London, 1920.
*Smith, G. Elliott. The Evolution of the *Dragon*. London, 1919.
Smith, W. Robertson. Lectures on the Religion of the *Semites*. 3d ed. London, 1927.
Snorra Edda (in A. G. Brodeur, The Prose Edda, New York, 1916).
Solheim Register = Solheim, Svale. Register til Norsk Folkeminnelags skrifter Nr. 1—49 (Norsk Folkeminnelag No. 50). Oslo, 1943.
Sörla saga Sterka (FAS III 408 ff.).
Spargo, John Webster. Virgil the Necromancer. Cambridge (Mass.), 1934.
*Sparnaay, H. Verschmelzung legendarischer und weltlicher Motive in der Poesie des Mittelalters. Groningen, 1922.
*Spence, Lewis. Myths and Legends of Babylonia and Assyria. London, 1916.
*Stanley, H. M. My Dark Companions and their Strange Stories. London, 1893.
Stapleton, W. H. Comparative Handbook of Congo Languages. Yakusa, Stanley Falls, 1903.
*Starck, Taylor. Der Alraun, ein Beitrag zur Pflanzensagenkunde. Baltimore, 1917.
*Steere, E. Swahili Tales as told by the Natives of Zanzibar. London, 1922.
*Stigand, C. H. and Mrs. Black Tales for White Children. London and New York, 1914.
*Stimson, J. F. MS. of Tuamotuan Myths. Unpublished. Peabody Museum, Salem, Mass.
*Sturlaugs saga Starfsama (FAS III 592 ff.).
*Swanton, J. R. Myths and Tales of the Southeastern Indians (BBAE LXXXVIII [1929]).
*Sydow, C. W. von. Två *Spinnsagor*. Lund, 1909.
*Sigurds strid med *Fåvne* (Lund Universitets Årsskrift. n. f. Avd. I, Bd. 14, no. 16). Lund, 1918.
*Talbot, P. A. In the Shadow of the Bush. New York and London, 1912.

*Tawney, C. H. Kathā Sarit Sāgara, Ocean of the Streams of Story. 2 vols. Calcutta, 1880—84. See also Penzer.
*Tegethoff, Ernst. Studien zum Märchentypus von Amor und Psyche. Bonn und Leipzig, 1922.
Tessman, Gunter. *Ajongs Erzählungen: Märchen der *Fang*neger. Berlin, 1921.
*Die *Pangwe*. Berlin, 1912.
Thalbitzer, William. A Phonetic Study of the Eskimo Language. Copenhagen, 1904.
*Theal, G. M. *Kaffir* Folk-lore. London, 1886.
*The Yellow and Dark-skinned People of Africa South of the *Zambesi*. London, 1910.
*Thien, J. Uebereinstimmende und verwandte Motive in den deutschen Spielmannsepen im Anschluss an König Rother. Hamburg, 1882.
Thomas, Northcote W. Anthropological Report on the Ibo-Speaking Peoples of Nigeria. 2 vols. London, 1913—14.
⊙Thompson-Balys = Thompson, Stith and Balys, Jonas. Motif and Type Index of the Oral Tales of India. Bloomington (Ind.). (In press).
*Thompson, Stith. European Tales among the North American Indians (CColl II). Colorado Springs, 1919.
**Tales* of the North American Indians. Cambridge (Mass.), 1929.
The *Folktale*. New York, 1946.
*The *Star-Husband* Tale (Studia Septentrionalia IV). Oslo, 1952.
*þiðriks saga (ed. H. Bertelsen). 2 vols. København, 1905—11.
*þorsteinssaga Víkingssonar (FAS II 381 ff.).
*þorsteins þáttr uxafóts (Islendinga þættir).
Thurneysen, Rudolf. Die irische Helden- und Königsage bis zum siebzehnten Jahrhundert. Halle, 1921.
*Tobler, Otto. Die Epiphanie der Seele in deutscher Volkssage. Kiel, 1911.
*Toldo, Peter. Leben und Wunder der Heiligen im Mittelalter (Studien zur vergleichenden Literaturgeschichte I 320, 345; II 87, 304, 329; IV 49; V 337; VI 289; VIII 18; IX 451).
*Torday, E. On the Trail of the *Bushongo*. London, 1925.
Notes ethnographiques sur les .... Bakuba. Bruxelles, 1911.
Travélé, Moussa. Proverbs et contes Bambara. Paris, 1923.
Trilles, R. G. Proverbes, légendes et contes fang (Bulletin de la Société Neuchâteloise de Géographie XVI [1905]).
*Tupper, F. and Ogle, M. B. Master Walter *Map's* Book De Nugis Curialium (Courtiers' Trifles). New York, 1924.
Tuti-Nameh. See Rosen.
**Type* = Aarne, A. and Thompson, Stith. The Types of the Folk-Tale (FFC 74). Helsinki, 1928.
UCal = University of California Publications in American Archaeology and Ethnology.

U Cal Anth Rec. = University of California Anthropological Records.

U Pa = University of Pennsylvania, The University Museum Anthropological Publications.

*Urquell, Am. 6 vols. Lunden, 1890—96.

*Urquell, Der. 2 vols. Leiden and Hamburg, 1898—99.

*Usener, Hermann. Kleine Schriften. 4 vols. Leipzig and Berlin, 1912—14.

U Wash = University of Washington Publications in Anthropology.

Valcarcel, Luis E. El Diluvio (El Aillu, Rev. Peruana de Antr. Etn. Fl. y Linguistica Hist., I. Cusco, Peru).

*Van Wing, J. Folklore Kiyansi: Congo Belge (Bibliotheca Africana, IV [1930—31]).

*Völsunga saga ok Ragnarssaga Loðbrókar (ed. M. Olsen). København, 1906—08.

Von der Hagen. See Hagen.

Von der Leyen. See Leyen.

Von Löwis of Menar. See Löwis.

*Voorhoeve, Petrus. Overzicht van de Volksverhalen der Bataks. Vlissingen, 1927.

Voretzsch, Carl. Einführung in das Studium der altfranzösischen Literatur. 2d ed. Halle a. S., 1913.

Vries, de. See De Vries.

*Wagener, A. J. Afrikanische Parallele zur biblischen Urgeschichte. Bonn, 1927.

*Ward, H. L. D. Catalogue of Romances in the Department of Manuscripts in the British Museum. London, 1883, 1893. (Vols. 1 and 2 only; for vol. 3 see Herbert, J. A.)

Warnke, Karl. Die Quellen des Esope der Marie de France. Halle, 1900.

Weeks, John H. *Among *Congo* Cannibals. London, 1913.
 **Jungle* Life and Jungle Stories. London, 1923.
 Anthropological Notes on the Bangola of the Upper Congo River (JAI XXXIX, 1909).
 Congo *Life* and Folklore. 2 parts. London, 1911.

*Wehrhan, Karl. Die Sage. Leipzig, 1908.

Weicker, G. Der Seelenvogel in der alten Literatur und Kunst. Leipzig, 1902.

*Wells, John Edwin. A Manual of Writings in Middle English. New Haven, 1916.

*Werner, Alice. *African* Mythology (The Mythology of all Races VII). Boston, 1925.

*Werner, E. T. C. *Myths* and Legends of China. London, 1922.

Wesselski, Albert. *Die Schwänke und Schnurren des Pfarrers *Arlotto*. 2 vols. Berlin. 1910.
 *Heinrich *Bebels* Schwänke. 2 vols. München, 1907.
 **Erlesenes* (Gesellschaft deutscher Bücherfreunde in Böhmen VIII). Prag, 1928.

*Die Begebenheiten der beiden *Gonnella*. Weimar, 1920.
*Der Hodscha *Nasreddin*. 2 vols. Weimar, 1911.
*Märchen des Mittelalters. Berlin, 1925.
*Mönchslatein. Leipzig, 1909.
*Die Novellen Girolamo *Morlinis*. München, n. d.
Versuch einer *Theorie* des Märchens. Reichenberg i. B., 1931.
Wessman, V. E. V. Förteckning över Sägentyperna (Finlands Svenska Folkdiktning II). Helsingfors, 1931.
WF = Western Folklore (continuation of California Folklore Quarterly). Berkeley (Cal.), 1942 ff.
*Wheeler, Gerald Camden. Mono-Alu Folklore. London, 1926. Tales referred to by number.
*Wilken, G. A. Verspreide Geschriften. 4 vols. 'sGravenhage, 1912.
*Willans, R. H. K. The Konnoh People (African Society Journal VIII [1908—09]).
*Williams, C. A. Oriental Affinities of the Legend of the Hairy Anchorite. Urbana (Ill.), 1925.
*Wimberly, L. C. Folklore in the English and Scottish Ballads. Chicago, 1928.
*Winger, Bjorn. A Classification of Motifs in Eskimo Folk-Literature. (Unpublished M. A. thesis. Indiana University Library).
*Winter, Leo. Die deutsche Schatzsage. Wattenscheid, 1925.
Wolf, W. Der Mond im deutschen Volksglauben. Bühl (Baden). 1929.
*Woodson, Carter Godwin. African Myths. Washington, D. C., 1928.
Wünsche, A. Die Sagen vom *Lebensbaum* und Lebenswasser, altorientalische Mythen. Leipzig, 1905.
*Der Sagenkreis vom geprellten *Teufel*. Leipzig and Wien, 1905.
*Ynglinga saga (ed. C. Säve). Uppsala, 1854.
*Yngvarssaga vídförla (ed. E. Olson). København, 1912.
*Zachariae, Theodor. Kleine Schriften. Bonn and Leipzig, 1920.
Zingerle, I. V. Sagen aus Tirol. 2d ed. Innsbruck, 1891.
Zong in-Sob. Folk Tales from Korea. London, 1952.
ZsES = Zeitschrift für Eingeborenen-Sprachen.
ZsKS = Zeitschrift für Kolonialsprachen. Berlin, 1913 ff.
**Zs.f.Vksk.* = Zeitschrift des Vereins für Volkskunde. 38 vols. Berlin, 1891—1928. Continued as Zeitschrift für Volkskunde. Berlin, 1929 ff.

Motif-Index of Folk-Literature

A. MYTHOLOGICAL MOTIFS

DETAILED SYNOPSIS

A0 —A99. Creator
- A0. Creator
- A10. Nature of the creator
- A20. Origin of the creator
- A30. Creator's companions
- A40. Creator's advisers
- A50. Conflict of good and evil creators
- A60. Marplot at creation
- A70. Creator — miscellaneous motifs

A100—A499. GODS

A100—A199. The gods in general
- A100. Deity
- A110. Origin of the gods
- A120. Nature and appearance of the gods
- A140. Gods as workmen
- A150. Daily life of the gods
- A160. Mutual relations of the gods
- A170. Deeds of the gods
- A180. Gods in relation to mortals
- A190. Gods — miscellaneous motifs

A200—A299. Gods of the upper world
- A200. God of the upper world
- A210. Sky-god
- A220. Sun-god
- A240. Moon-god
- A250. Star-god
- A260. God of light
- A270. God of dawn
- A280. Weather-god

A300—A399. Gods of the underworld
- A300. God of the underworld
- A310. God of the world of the dead

A400—A499. Gods of the earth
- A400. God of the earth
- A410. Local gods
- A420. God of water
- A430. God of vegetation
- A440. God of animals
- A450. God of trades and professions
- A460. Gods of abstractions
- A490. Miscellaneous gods of the earth

A500—A599. Demigods and culture heroes
- A500. Demigods and culture heroes
- A510. Origin of the culture hero (demigod)
- A520. Nature of the culture hero (demigod)

A530. Culture hero establishes law and order
A560. Culture hero's (demigod's) departure
A570. Culture hero still lives
A580. Culture hero's (divinity's) expected return
A590. Demigods and culture heroes — miscellaneous

A600—A899. COSMOGONY AND COSMOLOGY

A600—A699. The universe
A600—A649. Creation of the universe
A610. Creation of universe by creator
A620. Spontaneous creation of universe
A630. Series of creations
A640. Other means of creating the universe
A650—A699. Nature of the universe
A650. The universe as a whole
A660. Nature of the upper world
A670. Nature of the lower world
A690. Miscellaneous worlds

A700—A799. The heavens
A700. Creation of the heavenly bodies
A710—A739. The sun
A710. Creation of the sun
A720. Nature and condition of the sun
A740—A759. The moon
A740. Creation of the moon
A750. Nature and condition of the moon
A760—A789. The stars
A760. Creation and condition of the stars
A770. Origin of particular stars
A780. The planets (comets, etc.)
A790—A799. The heavenly lights

A800—A899. The earth
A800—A839. Creation of the earth
A810. Primeval water
A820. Other means of creation of earth
A830. Creation of earth by creator
A840. Support of the earth
A850. Changes in the earth
A870. Nature and condition of the earth

A900—A999. Topographical features of the earth
A900. Topography — general considerations
A910—A949. Water features
A910. Origin of water features — general
A920. Origin of the seas
A930. Origin of streams
A940. Origin of other bodies of water
A950—A999. Land features
A950. Origin of the land
A960. Creation of mountains
A970. Origin of rocks and stones
A980. Origin of particular places
A990. Other land features

A1000—A1099. World calamities
A1000. World catastrophe
A1010. Deluge

A1020. Escape from deluge
A1030. World fire
A1040. Continuous winter destroys the race
A1050. Heavens break up at end of world
A1060. Earth-disturbances at end of world
A1070. Fettered monster's escape at end of world
A1080. Battle at end of world
A1090. World calamities — miscellaneous motifs

A1100—A1199. Establishment of natural order
A1110. Establishment of present order: waters
A1120. Establishment of present order: winds.
A1130. Establishment of present order: weather phenomena
A1150. Determination of seasons
A1160. Determination of the months
A1170. Origin of night and day
A1180. Establishment of present order — miscellaneous motifs

A1200—A1699. CREATION AND ORDERING OF HUMAN LIFE

A1200—A1299. Creation of man
A1210. Creation of man by creator
A1220. Creation of man through evolution
A1230. Emergence or descent of first man to earth
A1240. Man made from mineral substance
A1250. Man made from vegetable substance
A1260. Mankind made from miscellaneous materials
A1270. Primeval human pair
A1290. Creation of man — other motifs

A1300—A1399. Ordering of human life
A1310. Arrangement of man's bodily attributes
A1320. Determination of span of life
A1330. Beginnings of trouble for man
A1350. Origin of sex functions
A1360. Man's growth and maturity
A1370. Origin of mental and moral characteristics
A1390. Ordaining of human life — miscellaneous

A1400—A1499. Acquisition of culture
A1400. Acquisition of human culture
A1410. Acquisition of livable environment
A1420. Acquisition of food supply
A1430. Acquisition of other necessities
A1440. Acquisition of crafts
A1460. Acquisition of arts
A1470. Beginning of social relationships
A1480. Acquisition of wisdom and learning
A1490. Acquisition of culture — miscellaneous

A1500—A1599. Origin of customs
A1510. Origin of eating customs
A1520. Origin of hunting and fishing customs
A1530. Origin of social ceremonials
A1540. Origin of religious ceremonials
A1550. Origin of customs of courtship and marriage
A1560. Origin of customs connected with birth
A1570. Origin of regulations within the family
A1580. Origin of laws
A1590. Origin of other customs

A1600—A1699. Distribution and differentiation of peoples
A1610. Origin of various tribes
A1620. Distribution of tribes
A1630. Wandering of tribes
A1640. Origin of tribal subdivisions
A1650. Origin of different classes — social and professional
A1660. Characteristics of various peoples — in personal appearance
A1670. Characteristics of various peoples — in industry and warfare
A1680. Characteristics of various peoples — in habits

A1700—A2199. CREATION OF ANIMAL LIFE

A1700—A1799. Creation of animal life — general
A1710. Creation of animals through transformation
A1730. Creation of animals as punishment
A1750. Animals created through opposition of devil to god
A1770. Creation of animals from unusual primeval mating
A1790. Creation of animals — other motifs

A1800—A1899. Creation of mammals
A1810—A1839. Creation of carnivora
A1810. Creation of *felidae*
A1820. Creation of *mustelidae*
A1830. Creation of *canidae* and other *carnivora*
A1840. Creation of *rodentia*
A1860. Creation of *primata*
A1870. Creation of *ungulata*
A1890. Creation of other mammals

A1900—A1999. Creation of birds
A1910. Creation of *passeriformes*
A1930. Creation of *falconiformes*
A1940. Creation of *charidriiformes*
A1950. Creation of *coraciiformes*
A1960. Creation of *ciconiiformes*
A1970. Creation of miscellaneous birds

A2000—A2099. Creation of insects
A2010. Creation of *hymenoptera*
A2020. Creation of *coleoptera*
A2030. Creation of *diptera*
A2040. Creation of *lepidoptera*
A2050. Creation of *hemiptera*
A2060. Creation of *orthoptera*
A2070. Creation of miscellaneous insects

A2100—A2199. Creation of fish and other animals
A2100—A2139. Creation of fish
A2100. Creation of fish
A2110. Creation of particular fishes
A2140. Creation of reptiles
A2160—A2199. Origin of amphibians and other animal forms
A2160. Origin of *amphibia*
A2170. Origin of miscellaneous animal forms

A2200—A2599. ANIMAL CHARACTERISTICS

A2200—A2299. Various causes of animal characteristics
A2210. Animal characteristics: change in ancient animal
A2220. Animal characteristics as reward
A2230. Animal characteristics as punishment
A2240. Animal characteristics: obtaining another's qualities

A2250. Animal characteristics: result of contest
A2260. Animal characteristics from transformation
A2270. Animal characteristics from miscellaneous causes

A2300—A2399. Causes of animal characteristics: body
A2310. Origin of animal characteristics: body covering
A2320. Origin of animal characteristics: head
A2330. Origin of animal characteristics: face
A2350. Origin of animal characteristics: trunk
A2370. Animal characteristics: extremities
A2380. Animal characteristics: other bodily features

A2400—A2499. Causes of animal characteristics: appearance and habits
A2400. Animal characteristics: general appearance
A2410. Animal characteristics: color and smell
A2420. Animal characteristics: voice and hearing
A2430. Animal characteristics: dwelling and food
A2440. Animal characteristics: carriage
A2450. Animal's daily work
A2460. Animal characteristics: attack and defense
A2470. Animal's habitual bodily movements
A2480. Periodic habits of animals
A2490. Other habits of animals

A2500—A2599. Animal characteristics — miscellaneous
A2510. Utility of animals
A2520. Disposition of animals
A2540. Other animal characteristics

A2600—A2699. Origin of trees and plants
A2600—A2649. Various origins of plants
A2600. Origin of plants
A2610. Creation of plants by transformation
A2620. Plants originate from experience of holy person
A2630. Other types of plant origins
A2650—A2699. Origin of various plants and trees
A2650. Origin of flowers
A2680. Origin of other plant forms

A2700—A2799. Origin of plant characteristics
A2700—A2749. Various origins of plant characteristics
A2710. Plant characteristics as reward
A2720. Plant characteristics as punishment
A2730. Miscellaneous reasons for plant characteristics
A2750—A2799. Origin of various plant characteristics
A2750. Interior and bark of plant
A2760. Leaves of plant
A2770. Other plant characteristics

A2800—A2899. Miscellaneous explanations
A2800—A2849. Miscellaneous explanations: origins
A2850—A2899. Miscellaneous explanations: characteristics

A. MYTHOLOGICAL MOTIFS

A0—A99. Creator.

A0. Creator. — For a general bibliography of creation myths, see Alexander N. Am. 278 n. 15. For bibliographies of North American Indian mythologies arranged by areas, see Thompson Tales 272 n. 1; **Feilberg Skabelses og Syndflodssagn; Jewish: Neuman. — Mexican Indian: (Tarascan) Alexander Lat. Am. 85, (Zapotecan) ibid. 87; Guarayú: Métraux RMLP XXXIII 147; Polynesia: Dixon 21 n. 47; Hawaiian: Beckwith Myth 42; Mono-Alu: Wheeler 28, 66f., 70; Easter Is.: Métraux BMB CLX 313; Marshall Is.: Davenport Folk Tales 221f.; Tahiti: Henry Ancient Tahiti 335ff.; New Hebrides: Codrington II 365. — Armenian: Ananikian 20; African: Werner African 127ff., **Frobenius and Fox, (Loango): Pechuël-Loesche 267; Hindu: Penzer I 10; Buddhist myth: Malalasekera II 338; Icel.: Boberg, MacCulloch Eddic 326; Irish myth: Cross.

A610. Creation of universe by creator. A631. Pre-existing world of gods above. A810.1. God and devil fly together over primeval water. A830. Creation of earth by creator. A923. Ocean from creator's sweat. A1187. Creator appoints chief for each class of created things: Lucifer for demons, Zion for mountains, etc. A1210. Creation of man by creator.

A1. *Identity of creator.*

A1.1. *Sun-god as creator.* — Egyptian: Müller 69; Persian: Carnoy 260.

A220. Sun-god.

A1.2. *Grandfather as creator.* — S. Am. Indian (Paressi): Métraux BBAE CXLIII (3) 359, (Guarayú): Métraux RMLP XXXIII 147.

A1.3. *Stone-woman as creator.* — Paressi: Métraux BBAE CXLIII (3) 359.

A1.4. *Brahma as creator.* — Buddhist myth: Malalasekera II 338.

A2. *Multiple creators.*

A2.1. *Three creators.* — Icel.: Boberg, MacCulloch Eddic 327. — Oceanic: Dixon 24; Hawaii: Beckwith Myth 42.

A2.2. *First human pair as creators.* (Cf. A1270.) Chinese: Eberhard FFC CXX 115 No. 70.

A3. *Creative mother source of everything.* — India: Thompson-Balys.

A5. *Reason for creation.*

A73. Lonely creator.

A5.1. *Gods make earth to have place to rest their feet.* — Hawaiian: Beckwith Myth 43.

A7. *Creator's descendants.* (Cf. A32.)

A7.1. *Creator has two sons.* — Guarayú: Métraux RMLP XXXIII 147.

A10. Nature of the creator. — India: Thompson-Balys.

A11. *Invisible creator.* — Jewish: Neuman. — Ackawoi: Alexander Lat. Am. 269.

A11.1. *Invisibility of creator learned from the impossibility of staring at the sun, his servant.* — Jewish: Neuman.

A12. *Hermaphroditic creator.* The creator is half man and half woman or is thought of as both male and female. — *Lang Myth I 200f., 299; Güntert 324. — Greek: Eisler 396; Egyptian: Maspéro Histoire ancienne des peuples de l'Orient classique 141; Indian (Hindu): Keith 75. — Aztec: Alexander Lat. Am. 88.

A111.3.0.1. God of double sex. F547.2.1. Hermaphroditic pygmies.

A12.1. *Male and female creators.* Japanese: Anesaki 222; Hawaii: Henry Ancient Tahiti 345.

A13. *Animal as creator.*

A13.1. *Beast as creator.*

A13.1.1. *Cow as creator.* *Schröder Altgermanische Kulturprobleme 132; *Güntert Weltkönig 365ff. — Icel.: MacCulloch Eddic 63, 324.

A1245.4. Mankind from salty stone licked by cow. B19.2. Nectar yielding cow.

A13.2. *Bird as creator.* Hawaii: Henry Ancient Tahiti 345.

A13.2.1. *Raven as creator.* Eskimo: Nelson RBAE XVIII 454; Koryak: Jochelson JE VI 218.

A13.2.2. *Eagle as creator of man.* Calif. Indian: Gayton and Newman 94.

A13.2.3. *Black-winged bird as creator.* Greek: Fox 4.

A13.3. *Insect as creator.*

A13.3.1. *Spider as creator.* India: Thompson-Balys.

A13.3.2. *Beetle as creator.* So. Am. Indian (Lengua): Métraux BBAE CXLIII (1) 367.

A13.4. *Reptile as creator.*

A13.4.1. *Snake as creator.* Mono-Alu, Fauru, Buin: Wheeler 67.

A13.4.2. *Worm as creator.* Guarayú: Métraux BBAE CXLIII (3) 437.

A15. *Human creator.*

A15.1. *Female creator.* Chibcha: Kroeber BBAE CXLIII (2) 908.

A15.1.1. *Old woman as creator.* Lepers Is.: Codrington II 372f.

A15.2. *Brothers as creators.* So. Am. Indian (Guaporé River): Levi-Strauss BBAE CXLIII (3) 379.

A15.3. *Old man as creator.*

A15.3.1. *Old man with staff as creator* (cf. A1.2). Inca: Rowe BBAE CXLIII (2) 316.

A15.4. *Artisan as creator.*

A15.4.1. *Potter as creator.* India: Thompson-Balys.

A17. *Angel as creator.* Jewish: Neuman.

A18. *Pictorial representations of creator.*
A137. Pictorial representations of gods.

A18.1. *Creator with dragon's head.* Chinese: Werner 77.

A18.2. *Creator with two horns on head.* Chinese: Werner 76.
A131.6. Horned god. F545.2.2. Horns on forehead.

A18.3. *Dwarfish creator.* Chinese: Werner 76.

A18.4. *Creator clothed in bear-skin* (or in leaves). Chinese: Werner 76.

A18.5. *Creator with hammer and chisel in hands.* Chinese: Werner 76.
A137.1. God with hammer.

A18.6. *Creator with sun and moon in hands.* Chinese: Werner 76.

A19. *Nature of creator — miscellaneous.*

A19.1. *Sun and moon (man and wife) as creators.* So. Am. Indian: (Cashibo) Steward-Métraux BBAE CXLIII (3) 594.

A19.2. *Creator with appearance of Negro.* Africa (Luba): Danohugh V 180.

A20. Origin of the creator.

A21. *Creator from above.*

A21.1. *Woman who fell from the sky.* — Daughter of the sky-chief falls from the sky, is caught by birds, and lowered to the surface of the water. She becomes the creator. — *Iroquois: Thompson Tales n. 27. — Cf. Finnish: Kalevala rune 1.

A21.2. *Old man from sky as creator.* — Old man with his wife comes from the sky. Are the first couple on earth. Have seven sons and seven daughters. Each son marries a daughter. — Ekoi: Talbot 366.

A22. *Creator comes out of chaos.* Chinese: Werner 76, Ferguson 57.

A23. *Creator offspring of dual powers of nature.* (Male and female principles.) — Chinese: Werner 76.

A25. *Creator from below.* God rises from beneath (the center of the spiritual world) and creates the world. — Hottentot: Bleek 74 No. 35.

A25.1. *Creator emerges from lake.* So. Am. Indian (Chibcha): Kroeber BBAE CXLIII (2) 908, (Aymara): Tschopik BBAE CXLIII (2) 570.

A26. *Creator comes from certain direction.*

A26.1. *Creator comes from east.* Africa (Luba): Donahugh V 80.

A27. *Creator born from egg.* Chinese: Eberhard FFC CXX 98f.
A114.2. God born from egg.

A30. Creator's companions. Inca: Rowe BBAE CXLIII (2) 315; Tahiti: Henry 342; Hawaii: Beckwith Myth 45.

A31. *Creator's grandmother.* Casually mentioned in the course of the creation myth. — American Indian: *Thompson Tales 275 n. 13.

A32. *Creator's family.* (Cf. A7.)

A32.1. *Creator's son.* India: Thompson-Balys. — So. Am. Indian: (Chibcha): Kroeber BBAE CXLIII (2) 908.

A32.2. *Creator's daughter.* India: Thompson-Balys.

A32.3. *Creator's wife.* India: Thompson-Balys. — So. Am. Indian (Mundurucu): Horton BBAE CXLIII (3) 281.

A32.3.1. *Creator's wife seduced by his son.* So. Am. Indian (Mundurucu): Horton BBAE CXLIII (3) 281.

A32.3.2. *Creator beats his wife while intoxicated from beverage he invents.* So. Am. Indian (Guarayú): Métraux RMLP XXXIII 147.

A33. *Animal as creator's companion.* India: Thompson-Balys.

A33.1. *Beast as creator's companion.*

A33.1.1. *Creator's dog.* The creator is accompanied by a dog (cf. A63.4). — *Dh I 98—111 passim, especially 108. — Hawaii: Beckwith Myth 347. — Kato: Goddard UCal V 183ff.

A33.2. *Bird as creator's companion.* India: Thompson-Balys; Sumatra: Dixon 160; Samoa, Tonga: ibid. *164 n. 33, 34.

A132.6.2. Goddess in form of bird. B450. Helpful birds.

A33.3. *Insect as creator's companion.*

A33.3.1. *Bee as God's spy.* God, the creator, sends a bee to overhear the devil's secrets. — *Dh I 3, 127ff.

B481.3. Helpful bee. K2375. Secrets learned by deception.

A33.4. *Other animal companions of creator.*

A33.4.1. *Armadillo as creator's companion.* So. Am. Indian (Mundurucu): Horton BBAE CXLIII (3) 281.

A36. *Creator's companions: unicorn, phoenix, tortoise, and dragon.* Chinese: Werner 76.

B11. Dragon. B13. Unicorn. B32. Phoenix.

A37. *Joint creators.*

A37.1. *Falcon and crow as joint creators.* Calif. Indian: Gayton and Newman 54.

A38. *Heavenly bodies as creator's companions.*

A38.1. *Creator's companions: sun and moon.* Jewish: Neuman.

A40. Creator's advisers. Jewish: Neuman.

A41. *Men as God's advisers.* *Dh I 3.

A42. *Angels as God's advisers.* Dh I 3, 31ff., 55, 187; Jewish: Neuman.

A42.1. *Seraphim as creator's advisers.* Jewish: Neuman.

A42.1.1. *God consults two angels on creation.* Jewish: Neuman.

A42.2. *God consults mercy on his right and justice on his left.* Jewish: Neuman.

A43. *Devil as adviser of God.* *Dh I 2f., 6, 12, 28, 31, 42, 44, 127ff., 144, 240, 388. — Siberian: Holmberg Siberian 313ff.

A812.1. Devil as Earth Diver. A810.1. God and Devil fly together over primeval water. A835. Earth from nut in devil's mouth. G303. Devil.

A44. *Tora as God's adviser.* Jewish: Neuman.

A45. *Souls of pious as Creator's advisers.* Jewish: Neuman.

A50. Conflict of good and evil creators. *Dh I 1—89 passim, 172ff. — Jewish: Neuman; India: Thompson-Balys; Persian: Carnoy 261f., 275. — Banks Island: Dixon 106.

A106. Opposition of good and evil gods. A162. Conflict of the gods. A525. Good and bad culture heroes. A716. Dispute at creation of sun. God plans two suns; devil persuades otherwise. A810.1. God and devil fly together over primeval water. A1750. Animals created through opposition of devil to God. G11.0.1.1. As result of fraud, Saturn swallows stone instead of infant Jove. G303. Devil.

A50.1. *Creation of angels and devils.* Jewish: Neuman.

A63. Devil as marplot at creation. G303.1.4. The devil creates other devils.

A51. *Creation of devil(s)* (cf. A63).

A52. *Creation of angels.*

V230. Angels.

A52.0.1. *Angels created to execute God's will.* Jewish: Neuman.

A52.0.2. *Degraded gods become angels.* Jewish: Neuman.

A52.0.3. *Angels existed prior to creation.* Jewish: Neuman.

A52.0.4. *Angels are transformed souls of the pious.* Jewish: Neuman.

A52.0.5. *Angels created from three elements.* Jewish: Neuman.

A52.0.6. *Angels created from words uttered by God.* Jewish: Neuman.

A52.0.7. *God drops water from his finger and the drops become angels.* Lucifer imitated God and created devils. — Lithuanian: Balys Legends No. 2.

A52.0.8. *God created angels by striking one small stone with another.* Lucifer created devils by imitation. Lithuanian: Balys Legends Nos. 1, 3.

G303.1.4.2. Devils are created by striking two stones together.

A52.1. *Creation of individual angels.*

A52.1.1. *Angel of death created by God.* Jewish: Neuman.

A52.1.2. *Angel Michael created from fire.* Jewish: Neuman.

A52.1.3. *Angel Gabriel created from snow.* Jewish: Neuman.

A52.1.4. *Angel Raphael created from water.* Jewish: Neuman.

A52.1.5. *Angel of destruction created from hail and fire.* Jewish: Neuman.

A52.2. *Time of creation of the angels.*

A52.2.1. *Angels created on first day of creation.* Jewish: Neuman.

A52.2.2. *Angels created on second day of creation.* Jewish: Neuman.

A52.2.3. *Angels created on third day of creation.* Jewish: Neuman.

A52.2.4. *Archangels created on first, angels on third day of creation.* Jewish: Neuman.

A52.2.5. *Angels created on fifth day with other winged creatures.* Jewish: Neuman.

A52.3. *Material of which angels are created* (fire, water and snow). Jewish: Neuman.

A54. *Rebel angels.*

A54.1. *Angel of sea rebels at world's creation;* put to death by God. Jewish: Neuman.

A60. Marplot at creation. An evil opponent attempts to undo or mar the work of the creator. — Jewish: Neuman; Siberian: Holmberg Siberian 315f. — Borneo: Dixon 170; Melanesian: *Codrington JAI X 293; Hawaii: Beckwith Myth 45. — So. Am. Indian (Toba, Mataco): Métraux BBAE CXLIII (1) 368f. — India: *Thompson-Balys.

A1217.1. Angels oppose creation of man.

A61. *Coyote as marplot at creation.* *Thompson Tales 285 n. 52.

A63. *Devil as marplot at creation.* *Dh I 6—89 passim, 127—205 passim; *Handwb. d. Abergl. IX (Nachträge) 276f. — Estonian: Loorits Grundzüge I 458f.

A63.1. *Devil works during God's sleep at creation.* *Dh I 2, 42f., 55, 60, 102, 115ff.; India: Thompson-Balys.

A1335.10. Men die because a snake comes to prey on mankind while creator rests.

A63.2. *Devil plans to drown God at time of creation.* *Dh I 184f. — Lithuanian: Balys Index 3005; Balys Legends No. 11.

A63.3. *Devil and God wrestle at time of creation.* *Dh I 184f.

A63.4. *Devil and God create animals.* Wolf created as God's dog. The devil creates goats to destroy things. — BP III 199 (Gr. No. 148); Dh I 127—205 passim.

A33.1.1. Creator's dog. A33.3.1. Bee as God's spy overhears devil's secrets. A106.2. Revolt of Evil Angels against God. A1750. Animals created through opposition of devil to God.

A63.4.1. *God and the devil torment each other with their creations.* Devil pesters God with gnats. God makes a fire and safeguards himself; God plagues the devil with fleas — devil is unable to find means of protecting himself. — Lithuanian: Balys Index 3082; Balys Legends No. 131ff.

A2032. Creation of flea. A2033. Creation of gnat.

A63.5. *Lucifer causes fall of man.* Irish Myth: Cross; Jewish: Neuman.

A63.5.1. *Satan seduces Adam to sin because he is jealous of him.* Jewish: Neuman.

A63.6. *Devil in serpent form tempts first woman* (Satan and Eve). Jewish: Neuman. — India: Thompson-Balys.

A63.7. *Rebel god is author of all poisonous things.* Hawaii: Beckwith Myth 61.

A63.7.1. *Poisonous water created by the devil.* Irish myth: Cross (A63.7).

A63.8. *Satan attempts to create another world.* Jewish: Neuman.

A67. *God makes things and tosses them into the air;* what he catches is good for mankind, what opponent catches is bad. New Hebrides: Beckwith Myth 61.

A70. Creator: miscellaneous motifs.

A71. *Creator tries to devour his son, the culture hero.* Greek: cf. Roscher II 1540. — Tehuelche (Patagonia): Alexander Lat. Am. 335.

A72. *Original creator followed by transformers.* These demigods change the original creation into the present forms. — See A900ff. for work of the transformers, with references. — Aztec: Alexander Lat. Am. 85; So. Am. Indian: *Métraux RMLP XXXIII 122, BBAE CXLIII (3) 437.

A73. *Lonely creator.* The creator is tired of solitude and therefore inaugurates the creation. — Finnish: Kalevala rune 2. — So. Am. Indian (Yuracare): Métraux BBAE CXLIII (3) 503.

A5. Reason for creation.

A74. *Reluctant creator.*

A74.1. *Creation on condition that Israel accept Tora.* Jewish: Neuman.

A74.2. *Creator repents of creating certain things.* Jewish: Neuman.

A75. *Creator as ancestor of heaven and earth.* Chinese: Werner 76.

A76. *Creator's death.* (Cf. A192.) Chinese: Werner 77.

A77. *Creator's works survive him.* Chinese: Werner 77.

A78. *Creator goes to make afterworld.* Calif. Indian: Gayton and Newman 59.

A81. *Creator goes to sky.* Calif. Indian: Gayton and Newman 57.

A84. *Creator of animals.*

A84.1. *Creator of buffaloes.* India: Thompson-Balys.

A85. *Creation match between goddess-wife, god-husband.* India: Thompson-Balys.

A87. *Creator drunk from beverage he invents.* So. Am. Indian (Guarayú): Métraux RMLP XXXIII 147.

A100—A499. GODS

A100—A199. The gods in general.

A100. Deity.

A0. Creator. A2434.2.2. Why foxes do not live on a certain island: driven out by a god. D42. God in guise of mortal. D42.1. God transformed to giant with three heads and six arms. D1380.3. Head of divinity as protection of land. D1981.1. Magic invisibility of gods. E155.2. Annual resuscitation of a god. F63. Person carried to upper world by god. F251.1. Fairies as descendants of early race of gods. V30.1. The eaten god.

A101. *Supreme god.* One god chief of all other gods. (Often not worshipped as other gods are.) — Durkheim 274, 409ff.; Leroy La raison primitive 125ff.; Holmberg Gudstron 61ff.; C. Koch Der römische Juppiter. — Semitic: Smith Semites[3] 529; Jewish: Neuman; Greek: Fox 153, *Grote I 57f.; Assyrian: Spence 206ff.; Babylonian: ibid. 199ff.; Hindu: Keith 21f.; India: Thompson-Balys; Buddhist myth: Malalasekera I 148, 309; Siberian: Karjalainen FFC XLIV 259, 268ff.; Armenian: Ananikian 11, 14, 37; Icel.: MacCulloch Eddic 61; Chinese: Ferguson 50, Eberhard FFC CXX 115 No. 70.— Indonesian: Kruyt Archipel 465ff.; Maori: Clark 32; Tahiti: Henry 121, 128; Hawaii: Beckwith Myth 45. — African: Frobenius Atlantis X 82, Werner African 123ff.; N. A. Indian: Alexander N. Am. 80, 82, 187, 284 n. 28; So. Am. Indian (Guarani): Métraux BBAE CXLIII (3) 93; Africa (Fang): Trilles 130, (Luba): Donohugh V 180.

A101.1. *Supreme god as creator* (cf. A0). Lowie Primitive Religion 85; Goldenweiser Early Civilization 97; Oldenberg Die Religion des Veda 278. — Icel.: MacCulloch Eddic 326; Armenian: Ananikian 20; India: Thompson-Balys; Tarascan: Alexander Lat. Am. 85.

A610. Creation of universe by creator.

A102. *Characteristics of deity.*

A102.1. *Omniscient god.* Icel.: MacCulloch Eddic 47 (Odin); Irish Myth: Cross; Jewish: Neuman. — So. Am. Indian (Chiriguano): Métraux RMLP XXXIII 173, (Guarani): Métraux BBAE CXLIII (3) 93.

D1810.0.1. Omniscience of a god.

A102.2. *All-seeing god.* Jewish: Neuman; Greek: Aeschylus Suppliants line 138.

A102.3. *Immutable god.* Jewish: Neuman.

A102.4. *Omnipotent god.* Jewish: *Neuman.

A102.5. *Omnipresent god.* Jewish: Neuman;India: Thompson-Balys.

A102.6. *Eternal god.* Jewish: Neuman.

A102.7. *Holy god.* Jewish: Neuman.

A102.8. *Sleepless god.* Jewish: Neuman.

A102.9. *Invisible god.* Jewish: Neuman.

A102.10. *Unity of God.* Jewish: Neuman.

A102.11. *Purity of God.* Jewish: Neuman.

A102.12. *Perfect God.* Jewish: Neuman.

A102.13. *Loving kindness of God.* Jewish: Neuman.

A102.14. *Goodness of God.* Jewish: Neuman.

A102.15. *Modesty of God.* Jewish: Neuman.

A102.16. *Justice of God.* Jewish: Neuman.

A102.17. *Anger of God.* Jewish: Neuman.

A102.18. *Imperfect god,* subject to death and rebirth. Buddhist myth: Malalasekera II 959.

A102.19. *Conflict between God's justice and mercy.* Jewish: Neuman.

A103. *Father-god.* Greek: Grote I 3; Hindu: Keith 50ff., 73ff., 82ff.; India: Thompson-Balys.

A1216. Man as offspring of creator. A1271.3. First parents children of god.

A104. *The making of gods.*

A104.1. *Living person becomes god.* Hawaii: *Beckwith Myth 2, ch. I passim.

A104.2. *Dead body becomes god.* Hawaii: Beckwith Myth 2.

A104.3. *Miscellaneous objects become gods.* Hawaii: Beckwith Myth 2.

A104.4. *Spirits become gods.* Hawaii: Beckwith Myth 45.

A106. *Opposition of good and evil gods.* Hindu: Keith 84; *Penzer I 197; India: Thompson-Balys. — Tarahumare (Mexican Indian): Alexander N. Am. 176; S. Am. Indians (Antioquians): Alexander Lat. Am. 197. — Jewish: Neuman.

A50. Conflict of good and evil creators. F531.7.1. Giants and gods in fight.

A106.0.1. *Gods and the demons quarrel over supremacy.* India: Thompson-Balys.

A106.1. *Revolt of bad gods against good.* Babylonian: Spence 75.

A525. Good and bad culture heroes. A1750. Animals created through opposition of devil to God. A1081. Battle of gods at end of world.

A106.1.1. *Goddess rebels against her father* for forbidding her marriage. India: Thompson-Balys.

A106.2. *Revolt of evil angels against God.* Jensen Dania II 180; Olrik ibid. II 67; Irish myth: Cross; India: Thompson-Balys; Lithuanian: Balys Index No. 3002, Legends Nos. 5, 6; Jewish: *Neuman; Irish: Beal. XXI 323.

A106.2.1. *Revolting devil banished to hell.* India: Thompson-Balys; Jewish: Neuman.

A106.2.1.1. *Banished devil appears on earth only on day of dark moon.* India: Thompson-Balys.

A300. God of the underworld.

A106.2.1.2. *Demon (opposed to God) allowed to earth four times a year* (but must let people know who he is and not deceive them). India: Thompson-Balys.

A106.2.2. *Satan's fall from heaven.* Jewish: Neuman.

A106.3. *Created beings rebel against God.* Jewish: Neuman.

A107. *Gods of darkness and light.* Darkness thought of as evil, light as good. — Babylonian: Spence 74; Irish myth: Cross; Jewish: Neuman.

A162.1.0.1. Recurrent battle. A1611.5.4.3. Origin of the Tuatha Dé Danann. A1659.1. Origin of the Fomorians. F200. Fairies. F531. Giant. S262. Periodic sacrifices to monster (giant, Fomorians). Z100.1. Names of giants (Fomorians) with sinister significance.

A108. *God of the living and the dead in the otherworld.* Chinese: Werner 248.

A108.1. *God of the dead.* Irish myth: Cross; Hawaii: Beckwith Myth 60.

A310. God of the world of the dead. A487. God of death. E481.1.1.1. King of the land of the dead. F129.7. Voyage to isle of the dead. V11.6. Sacrifice to the dead.

A109. *Deity: miscellaneous motifs.*

A109.1. *God as a triad.* Hawaii: Beckwith Myth 44; Icel.: Boberg.

A109.2. *Goddess as mother of Pacific Ocean.* Maori: Beckwith Myth 179.

A110. Origin of the gods.

F413. Origin of spirits. T541.4. Birth from person's head.

A111. *Parents of the gods.* Hawaii: Beckwith Myth 171.

A111.1. *Mother of the gods* (cf. A116.2). **Showerman; Smith Dragon viii; *Holmberg Baum 84ff. — Babylonian: Spence 123ff.; Hindu: Penzer I 270ff., 276, VII 231; India: Thompson-Balys; Hittite: Garstang The Hittite Empire 305ff.; Gaster Thespis 179. — Oceanic: Beckwith Myth 294; So. Am. Indian (Apapocuvú-Guarani): Métraux RMLP XXXIII 122.

A485.1. Goddess of war.

A111.2. *Father of the gods.* Icel.: Boberg.

A111.3. *Ancestor of the gods.* Tahiti: Henry 336.

A111.3.0.1. *God of double sex carries within him seed of gods.* Greek: Grote I 16.

A12. Hermaphroditic creator.

A111.3.1. *God dwells with his grandfathers.* Marquesas: Handy 106.

A31. Creator's grandmother.

A111.3.2. *Sea creatures as ancestors of goddess.* Tuamotu: Stimson MS (T-G. 3/600).

A111.3.3. *Great bird as ancestor of gods.* Hawaii: Beckwith Myth 92.

A112. *Birth of gods.* India: Thompson-Balys.

T541.4. Birth from head.

A112.1. *God from incestuous union.* Krappe The Review of Religion (1941); India: Thompson-Balys.

T410. Incest.

A112.1.1. *God from father-daughter incest. Adonis.* Greek: Spence 132. — Icel.: Boberg.

A112.1.1.1. *Goddess of music and dance born of incestuous union* (Brahma and daughter). India: Thompson-Balys.

A112.2. *Male and female creators beget gods.* Japanese: Anesaki 223.

A112.3. *Gods born from various parts of creator's body.* Japanese: Anesaki 224.

A112.4. *God as son of giant.* Icel.: MacCulloch Eddic 139 (Loki), 324 (Odin, Vili, and Ve), Boberg.

A112.4.1. *God as son of giantess.* Icel.: Boberg.

A112.4.2. *Goddess as daughter of giant.* Icel.: Boberg.

A112.5. *God as son of nine giantesses.* Icel.: MacCulloch Eddic 153 (Heimdall).

T541.12. Birth from nine mothers.

A112.6. *Gods as sons of supreme god.* Icel.: MacCulloch Eddic 61. — Tahiti: Henry 147.

A112.7. *God born from peculiar part of parent's body.*

A161.5. Eldest god born in front, younger at back.

A112.7.1. *God born from mother's ear.* Marquesas: Handy 107.

A112.7.2. *God born from mother's armpit.* Marquesas: Handy 107.

A112.7.3. *Goddess born from mother's eyes.* Hawaii: Beckwith Myth 186.

A112.7.4. *God born after prematurely short pregnancy.* Marquesas: Handy 107.

A112.8. *God from adulterous union.* Irish myth: Cross.

A164.2. Adultery among the gods. F252.4.1. Fairies banished for adultery. T481. Adultery.

A112.9. *Gods borne by human woman.* India: Thompson-Balys.

A112.9.1. *Elementary spirits borne by human woman.* India: Thompson-Balys.

A112.10. *Divine child cast out at birth.* Polynesia: Beckwith Myth 257.

A112.11. *Child born from union of God with hen.* Easter Is.: Métraux Ethnology 130.

A113. *Totemistic gods.* Gods which have animal associations; e.g., Athena with the owl, Venus with the sparrow. — Babylonian: Spence 93; India: *Thompson-Balys; Irish myth: Cross.

A131. God with animal features. A132. God in animal form. B2. Animal totems.

A114. *Gods born from object.*

A114.1. *Deity born from sea-foam.* Aphrodite. Greek: Roscher I 402; *Frazer Pausanias III 544.

A1261.1. Man created from sea-foam. T547.1. Birth from sea-foam.

A114.1.1. *Goddess born from sweat of rock washed by sea.* Minahassa (Celebes): Dixon 157.

A1211.2. Man from sweat of creator. A1262. Man created from sweat.

A114.1.1.1. *God born of another god's sweat.* India: Thompson-Balys.

A114.1.1.2. *Origin of lesser gods from spittle of great god.* Hawaii: Beckwith Myth 82.

A114.2. *God born from egg.* Tahiti: Henry 337; Marquesas: Handy 104. — So. Am. Indian (Huamachuco): Métraux RMLP XXXIII 151.

A114.2.1. *Deity born in shape of egg.* Hawaii: Beckwith Myth 169.

A114.3. *Deity born from skull.* Easter Is.: Métraux Ethnology 312.

A114.4. *Deity born from tree.* Hawaii: Beckwith Myth 279, 284. — So. Am. Indian (Tembe): Métraux RMLP XXXIII 122.

A115. *Emergence of deity.*

A115.1. *First deity grows out of primeval chaos.* Japanese: Anesaki 222.

A605. Primeval chaos.

A115.2. *God issues from earth.* Norse: MacCulloch Eddic 328 (Tuisto).

A115.3. *Deity arises from mist.* Hawaii: Beckwith Myth 71.

A115.4. *Deity emerges from darkness of underworld.* Mangia (Cook Is.): Beckwith Myth 224.

A115.5. *Emergence of gods from above and below.* Marquesas: Handy 138.

A115.6. *Deity arises from shell of darkness* where he has been for million ages. Tahiti: Henry.

A115.7. *Gods emerge from hole in tree.* India: Thompson-Balys.

A116. *Twin gods.* *Harris Twins, Boanerges, Picus who is also Zeus; Krappe Études de mythologie 137ff.; Güntert Weltkönig 253ff.; S. Eitrem Die göttlichen Zwillinge bei den Griechen (Christiania 1902); H. Grégoire Saints jumeaux et dieux cavaliers (Paris 1905); J. R. Harris The Dioscuri in the Christian Legends (London 1903); Krappe The Classical Journal XVIII (1923) 502ff.; Zeitschrift für Ethnologie LXVI (1929) 187ff.; "Les dieux jumeaux dans la religion germanique" Acta Philologica Scandinavica (1930); Review of Religion (1944) 123ff.; Revue Celtique XLIX (1932) 96ff; P. Saintyves, "Les Jumeaux, dans l'ethnographie et la mythologie," Revue Anthrop. XXXV (1925) 54—59; T. Gaster Oldest Stories 69. — Germanic: Helm Altgermanische Religionsgeschichte I 321ff.; Irish myth: Cross; Greek: Fox 26; Armenian: Ananikian 40; Hindu: Keith 30f. (Lettish also mentioned). — Zuñi: Alexander N. Am. 188; Mixtec: Alexander Lat. Am. 86; Indians of Central Brazil: Ehrenreich International Cong. of Americanists XIV 661; Chiriguano: Métraux RMLP XXXIII 172.

A515.1.1. Twin culture heroes. T685. Twins.

A116.1. *Twin gods — one mortal, other immortal.* Harris Twins 4ff.

A116.2. *Twin goddesses* (or trinity of goddesses). Irish myth: Cross.

A485.1. Goddess of war.

A116.2.1. *Twin daughters of a god.* India: Thompson-Balys.

A117. *Mortals become gods.*

A117.1. *First men created with eternal life become gods.* India: Thompson-Balys.

A117.2. *Mortal translated to heaven and deified.* India: *Thompson-Balys; Maori: Clark Maori Folk Tales 167.

A117.3. *In extreme old age spirits become gods.* Hawaii: Beckwith Myth 67.

A117.4. *Mortal transfigured to god on mountain top.* Maori: Beckwith Myth 250.

A117.5. *Gods are spirits of deified dead.* Easter Is.: Métraux Ethnology 316.

A118. *Self-created deity.* Tahiti: Henry 336f.

A119. *Origin of gods — miscellaneous.*

A119.1. *God made by magic.* Tahiti: Henry 341. — So. Am. Indian (Apapocuvá-Guarani): Métraux RMLP XXXIII 122.

A119.2. *Goddess produced by heat of earth.* Tahiti: Beckwith Myth 178.

A119.3. *Arrival of the gods in particular country.* Tonga: Gifford 199; Hawaii: Beckwith Myth 2, 3, 11.

A120. Nature and appearance of the gods (cf. A18f.). Jewish: *Neuman.

D1981.1. Magic invisibility of gods. E251.4.4. God with form and characteristics of vampire.

A120.1. *God as shape-shifter.* Irish myth: Cross.

F234.0.2. Fairy as shape-shifter. F237. Fairies in disguise. K1301. Mortal woman seduced by god. K1811. Gods (saints) in disguise visit mortals.

A120.2. *Size-changing god.* Hawaii: Beckwith Myth 127.

A120.3. *Incorporeal god.* Jewish: Neuman.

A120.4. *Formless gods.* Tonga: Beckwith Myth 128.

A121. *Stars as deities.* H. Gressmann Die hellenistische Gestirn-religion (Leipzig 1925); Gaster Thespis 228f. — Zuñi: Alexander N. Am. 187.
A760. Creation of the stars.

A121.1. *Moon as deity* (cf. A240). Jewish: Neuman.

A121.2. *Sun as deity* (cf. A220). Jewish: Neuman; Hawaii: Beckwith Myth 217.

A122. *God half mortal, half immortal.* Hair, skin, flesh, bones and marrow are mortal; mind, voice, breath, eye, and ear are immortal. (Prajāpati). — Hindu: Keith 76; cf. Greek: Grote I 3.

A123. *Monstrous gods.* Jewish: Neuman.
E652. God reincarnated as monster.

A123.1. *God monstrous as to body.*

A123.1.1. *Three-bodied goddess.* Hekate has three bodies standing back to back and looking in three directions. — Greek: Fox 188.
F524.1. Person with three bodies.

A123.1.2. *God with two joined bodies.* Tahiti: Henry 344.

A123.1.3. *God with good looking and ugly bodies.* Marquesas: Handy 124.

A123.1.4. *God with body of earthquake (whirlwind, etc.).* Hawaii: Beckwith Myth 30.

A123.1.5. *God with body of caterpillars.* Hawaii: Beckwith Myth 30.

A123.1.6. *God with body of stream of blood.* Hawaii: Beckwith Myth 30.

A123.1.7. *Goddess with three supernatural bodies: fire, cliff, sea.* Hawaii: Beckwith Myth 496.

A123.2. *God unusual as to face.* Jewish: Neuman.
A282.0.1.1. Facial features of wind-goddess reversed.

A123.2.1. *God with many faces.*

A123.2.1.1. *God with two faces.* *Krappe Balor 7 n. 24; Usener IV 347ff.; *Frazer Ovid II 95ff; India: Thompson-Balys.

A123.2.1.2. *God with three faces.* *Krappe Balor 8 n. 28. — Chinese: Werner 324.

A123.2.1.3. *God with four faces.* Greek: Roscher "Ianus"; Jewish: Neuman; India: Thompson-Balys.

A123.2.1.4. *God with five faces.* Jewish: Neuman.

A123.2.1.5. *God with six faces.* Hindu: Penzer I 73 n. 1, II 102.

A123.2.2. *God's unusual mouth.*

A123.2.2.1. *Maggots squirm from mouth of man-eating god.* Hawaii: Beckwith Myth 506.

A123.2.2.2. *Goddess with eight mouths.* Tonga: Gifford 168.

A123.3. *God unusual as to eyes.*

A123.3.1. *God with many eyes.* *Krappe Balor 19ff. (Argos); Usener IV 223. — Hindu: Penzer II 46 n. 4, VIII 75, 116, IX 19; Keith 110, 134; Chinese: Werner 144.

F512.2.2. Argos.

A123.3.1.1. *Three-eyed god.* *Usener IV 224 n. 1; *Frazer Pausanias III 209; Buddhist myth: Malalasekera II 32; India: Thompson-Balys.

A123.3.1.2. *God with hundred eyes.* Irish myth: Cross; India: Thompson-Balys.

A123.3.1.3. *God with thirteen eyes.* India: Thompson-Balys.

A123.3.1.4. *God with thousand eyes.* India: Thompson-Balys.

A123.3.1.4.1. *Goddess with thousand eyes.* India: Thompson-Balys.

A123.3.2. *God with flashing eyes.* Hawaii: Beckwith Myth 30; Buddhist myth: Malalasekera II 32.

A123.4. *God monstrous as to head.*

A123.4.1. *God with many heads.* Slavic (Elbe): Machal 283f., Boberg. — Chinese: Werner 241, 321.

A123.4.1.1. *God with three heads.* Irish myth: Cross.

D992. Magic head. F511.0.2.2. Three-headed person.

A123.4.1.2. *God with seven heads.* India: Thompson-Balys.

A123.4.1.3. *God with eight heads.* Tahiti: Beckwith Myth 209.

A123.4.2. *God with head of stone.* Hawaii: Beckwith Myth 88.

A123.5. *God unusual as to arms.*

A123.5.1. *God with many arms.* Siva has ten arms. — Hindu: Keith 110; Chinese: Werner 144, 324. — Cf. Greek: Roscher "Briareos"; India: *Thompson-Balys; Irish Myth: Cross.

F516.2. People with many arms.

A123.5.2. *Marvels concerning God's arm and fingers.* Jewish: Neuman.

A123.6. *God unusual at to legs (feet).*

A123.6.1. *God with three legs.* India: Thompson-Balys.

A123.7. *God unusual as to color.*

A123.7.1. *Many-colored god.* Hindu: Keith 81 (Shiva).

A123.7.2. *Black god(dess).* Icel.: *Boberg, MacCulloch Eddic 304; W. Golther Deutsche Myth. (1895) 473f. (Hell); Hindu: Keith 126 (Krsna).

A123.8. *Goddess with one-and-a-half buttocks.* India: Thompson-Balys.

A123.9. *Lotus plants grow from navel of Vishnu.* India: Thompson-Balys.

A123.10. *God (deity) girdled with snakes;* on his forehead shines the moon. India: Thompson-Balys.

A123.11. *God with tail.* Mangaia (Cook Is.): Clark 140; Fiji: Beckwith Myth 76; Tahiti: Beckwith Myth 113.

A124. *Luminous god.* Icel.: MacCulloch Eddic 129 (Balder); India: *Thompson-Balys.

A220. Sun-god. D1162. Magic light. D1645. Self-luminous objects. F541.1. Flashing eyes. F574. Luminous person.

A124.0.1. *God with luminous countenance.* Irish myth: Cross; Jewish: Neuman.

A124.1. *God with blazing eye.* Hindu: Penzer VI 31 n. 1; India: *Thompson-Balys.

A124.2. *White god.* Icel.: MacCulloch Eddic 152 (Heimdall), 129 (Balder).

A124.3. *Goddess with body full of fire.* India: Thompson-Balys.

A124.4. *God's radiance upon Moses' face.* Jewish: Neuman.

A124.5. *God in form of comet.* Hawaii: Beckwith Myth 113.

A125. *Deity in human form.* (The human form is assumed in most mythologies.) — Irish myth: Cross; Jewish: Neuman; Samoa: Henry 346.

D42. God in guise of mortal.

A125.1. *Goddess of war in shape of hag.* Irish myth: Cross.

A485.1. Goddess of war. F234.2.1. Fairy in form of hag.

A125.1.1. *Goddess of war in shape of (red) woman.* Irish myth: Cross.

A485.1. Goddess of war. F233.3. Red fairy. F234.2.5. Fairy (goddess) in form of beautiful young woman.

A125.2. *God with red beard.* Icel.: *Boberg.

A125.3. *God with gold teeth.* Icel.: MacCulloch Eddic 153 (Heimdall).

F544.3.1. Golden teeth.

A125.4. *Beautiful goddess.* So. Am. Indian (Huarochiri): Métraux RMLP XXXIII 169.

A128. *Mutilated god.* Egyptian: Müller 92ff.; Jewish: Neuman; Greek: Argonautica IV line 984 (Chronos); India: Thompson-Balys.

E33. Resuscitation with missing member. S160. Mutilations.

A128.1. *Blind god.* Hödhr. — Icel.: Boberg, De la Saussaye 268. — India: Thompson-Balys; Chinese: Werner 284.

A128.2. *One-eyed god.* Odin. — Harrison (Jane E.) Prolegomena to the Study of Greek Religion 194; Holmberg Finno-Ugric 179. — Irish myth: Cross; Icel.: Boberg, De la Saussaye 226, MacCulloch Eddic 21; Jewish: Neuman.

A1075. End of world heralded by coming of Antichrist, gigantic destructive one-eyed monster. D1273.0.4. Charm chanted standing on one foot, with one eye shut, etc. D2061.2.1. Death-giving glance. D2071. Evil Eye. F512.1. Person with one eye. F531.1.1.1. Giant with one eye in middle of forehead (Cyclops). F541. Remarkable eyes. G121.1. Three giants with one eye. G213.1. One-eyed witch.

A128.2.1. *God with Evil Eye.* Irish myth: Cross.

A955.5. Islands from cow and calf transformed by evil eye of one-eyed god. D2071. Evil Eye.

A128.2.2. *God with single eye, through lid of which passes a polished handle* with which lid is lifted. Irish myth: Cross.

A128.3. *Legless and armless deity supported on animal.* Borneo: Dixon 165.

F516.1. Armless people. F517. Person unusual as to his legs.

A128.3.1. *God with one leg (foot).* Irish myth: Cross.

F517.1.1. Person without feet. S162. Mutilation: cutting off legs (feet).

A128.4. *God with one hand.* Hand cut or bitten off. — *Krappe Études 11ff. — Icel.: Boberg, MacCulloch Eddic 21 (Tyr); Irish myth: Cross.

A172. Gods deposed for a time. A282.1. God of whirlwind. C563.2. Tabu: king having physical blemish. D996. Magic hand. F515. Person unusual as to his hands. F526. Person with compound body. F552. Remarkable hands. P16.2. King must resign if maimed. S161. Mutilation: cutting off hand (arm).

A128.5. *Lame god.* Greek: Fox 205 (Hephaistos).

A128.5.1. *God with thick (iron) shoe.* Icel.: MacCulloch Eddic 159 (Vidarr).

A131. *Gods with animal features.* *De Visser Die nicht menschengestaltigen Götter der Griechen (Leiden 1903). — Egyptian: Müller 15ff. — Mexican: Alexander Lat. Am. 57ff. — Irish myth: Cross.

A113. Totemistic gods. B2. Animal totems. F526.1. Typhon.

A131.1. *God as part man, part fish.* Babylonian: Spence 151 (Dagon); Assyrian: ibid. 216; Jewish: Neuman. — Samoa: Beckwith Myth 76.

A131.2. *God with elephant's face.* Hindu: Penzer II 99ff., 125 n. 1, 147 n. 1, 170, III 155 n. 2, V 196, VII 131, IX 1.

A131.3. *Deity with animal's head.*

A131.3.1. *Deity with cat's head.* Irish myth: Cross.

B29.4.1. Man with cat's head. F511.2.2.1. Person with cat's ears. F514.3. Person with cat's snout.

A131.3.2. *Goddess with pig's head.* Tonga: Beckwith Myth 178.

A131.3.3. *God with ram's head* (cf. A132.14). Egyptian: Müller 135, 405. — Irish myth: Cross.

A131.4. *God in tiger's skin.* Hindu: Keith 81, 111; India: Thompson-Balys.

A131.5. *God with goat-feet.* Greek: Fox 267 (Pan).

A131.6. *Horned god.* Irish myth: Cross; Egyptian: Müller 38 (Hathors).

A131.7. *Winged god.* Jewish: Neuman.

A131.8. *Goddess with pig's teeth.* India: Thompson-Balys.

A132. *God in animal form.* *De Visser Die nicht menschengestaltigen Götter der Griechen (Leiden, 1903). — Egyptian: Müller 15ff.; Chibcha: Alexander Lat. Am. 204 (fox, bear); Irish myth: Cross; India: Thompson-Balys; Chinese: *Krappe "Far Eastern Fox Lore" CFQ III (1944) 124ff.; Jewish: Neuman.

A113. Totemistic gods. A522. Animal as culture hero. D101. Transformation: god to animal. D113.1.2. God assumes form of a wolf. D133.4.1. God assumes form of calf. D142.2. God assumes form of a cat. D197.1. God assumes form of an eel. E611.2.1. Divinity reincarnated as bull. F234.1. Fairy in form of an animal.

A132.0.1. *God in successive animal forms.* India: Thompson-Balys.

A132.0.1.1. *God takes form successively of ants, scorpion, and cobra.* India: Thompson-Balys.

A132.0.1.2. *God in three forms: gecho, shark, or priest.* Tonga: Beckwith Myth 128.

A132.1. *Snake-god.* Smith Dragon 85. — Irish myth: Cross; Jewish: Neuman; Hindu: Penzer X 240 s. v. "Nagas"; India: *Thompson-Balys; Chinese: Eberhard FFC CXX 139. — Fiji: Beckwith Myth 138, 316.

B176. Magic serpent. F234.1.7. Fairy in form of worm (snake, serpent).

A132.1.1. *Deity has snake-children.* India: Thompson-Balys.

A132.2. *Monkey as god.* Chinese: Werner 325ff.; Hindu: Penzer II 73, 197 n. 2, IV 126, VIII 44; India: Thompson-Balys.

A132.3. *Equine god* (goddess).

A132.3.1. *Horse-god.* Irish myth: Cross; Jewish: Neuman; India: Thompson-Balys.

B181. Magic horse. C756.4. Tabu: entering chariot less than three weeks after eating horse flesh. F234.1.8. Fairy in form of horse. Q541.4. Penance for eating horse flesh.

A132.3.1.1. *Mule-god.* Irish myth: Cross; Jewish: Neuman.

A132.3.2. *Horse-goddess.* Irish myth: Cross.

A132.3.3. *Ass-god.* Jewish: Neuman.

A132.4. *Stag-god.* Irish myth: Cross.

A131.6. Horned god. F234.1.4. Fairy in form of stag (deer).

A132.5. *Bear-god* (goddess). Irish myth: Cross.

A132.6. *Bird deity.* Irish myth: Cross.

A132.6.1. *Bird-god.* Irish myth: Cross. — Hawaii: Beckwith Myth 91ff., 370.

D150. Transformation: man (woman) to bird. E732. Soul in form of bird. F234.1.15. Fairy in form of bird. V1.3.10. Bird worship.

A132.6.2. *Goddess in form of bird.* Irish myth: Cross.

A132.6.3. *Cock-god.* Jewish: Neuman; Hawaii: Beckwith Myth 119.

A132.6.4. *Female deities as fly-catchers.* Hawaii: Beckwith Myth 16.

A132.6.5. *Pigeon-god.* Tonga: Gifford 62.

A132.7. *Swine-god.* Irish myth: Cross; India: Thompson-Balys.

A132.8. *Dog (wolf)-god.* Irish myth: Cross; Jewish: Neuman.

A132.9. *Bull-god.* Irish myth: Cross.

D133.2. Transformation: man to bull. D133.4.1. God assumes form of calf. D1812.3.3.6. Prophetic dream by eating meat of bull. E611.2.1. Divinity reincarnated as bull. F234.1.14. Fairy in form of cow (bull).

A132.9.1. *Cow as god.* India: Thompson-Balys.

A132.10. *Tiger-god.* India: *Thompson-Balys.

A132.11. *Seal-god.* Easter Is.: Métraux Ethnology 310.

A132.12. *Eel-god.* Tonga: Gifford 57; Maori: Clark 163.

A132.13. *Fish-god.* Tonga: Beckwith Myth 131, Gifford 79.

A132.14. *Ram-god.* Icel.: Boberg; Jewish: Neuman.

A132.15. *God as tortoise.* Chinese: Eberhard FFC CXX 139.

A133. *Giant god* (cf. A128.2). Irish myth: Cross; India: *Thompson-Balys.

A133.1. *Giant god drinks lakes dry.* (Indra). — Hindu: Keith 33.

A133.2. *Giant goddess bestrides entire land.* One foot is in the north of the country and the other is in the south. — Irish: MacCulloch Celtic 30; Irish myth: Cross.

F531.3.5. Giant steps prodigious distance.

A133.2.1. *Giant god goes with three steps through the world.* Güntert Weltkönig 293ff.; Hopkins JAOS XVI Proc. cxlvii.

A133.2.2. *Heaven as God's throne, earth His footstool.* Jewish: Neuman.

A133.3. *Giant orderly of the gods.* India: Thompson-Balys.

A134. *Dwarf god.* Japanese: Anesaki 229; Hindu: Penzer I 144 n. 2.

E651. God reincarnated as dwarf. F535. Pygmy.

A135. *Man-eating god* (goddess). Hawaii: Beckwith Myth 29f.; Maori: Beckwith Myth 243.

A136. *Gods with unusual transportation.*

A136.1. *God rides unusual animal.*

A155. Animals of the gods. B557. Unusual animal as riding-horse.

A136.1.1. *Deity rides boar.* Icel.: MacCulloch Eddic 22 (Freya), 109 (Frey).

A136.1.2. *God rides unusual horse.*

A136.1.2.1. *Sleipnir: eight-legged horse of Odin.* Icel.: MacCulloch Eddic 43.

A171.1. God rides through air on wind-swift horse. B15.6.3. Animals with many legs.

A136.1.3. *God rides a bull.* Hindu: Keith 111; India: *Thompson-Balys.

A136.1.4. *God rides bird.* Panchatantra (tr. Ryder) 94ff. (Vishnu on Garuda); Penzer Ocean X 159 s. v. Garuda; India: *Thompson-Balys.

A136.1.4.1. *God rides swan.* India: Thompson-Balys.

A136.1.5. *God rides flying elephant.* India: Thompson-Balys.

B45. Air-going elephant.

A136.1.6. *Deity rides a buffalo.* India: Thompson-Balys.

A136.1.7. *Deity rides a lion.* India: *Thompson-Balys.

A136.1.8. *Goddess flies in bird's plumage.* Icel.: MacCulloch Eddic 83, 126, 174.

A136.2. *God's (goddess's) wagon drawn by unusual animals.* Icel.: MacCulloch Eddic 22 (Thor's goats, Freya's cats), 109 (Frey's boars); Greek: *Frazer Pausanias IV 142 (dragons).

B558. Unusual draft animal.

A136.2.1. *Goddess has team of sparrows.* Greek: Sappho Ode to Aphrodite.

A136.2.2. *Goddess's chariot drawn by one-footed horse.* Irish myth: Cross.

A136.3. *God's chariot goes through the air.* India: Thompson-Balys.
A724. Chariot of the sun. F861.2.1. Flying carts.

A136.3.1. *Chariot of fire drawn by four steeds of fire.* Jewish: Neuman.

A137. *Pictorial representations of gods* (cf. A131). Irish myth: Cross.

A137.1. *God with hammer.* Irish myth: Cross; Icel.: Boberg; Gaster Thespis 135, 363.

A137.1.1. *God with axe.* Irish myth: Cross.

A137.2. *God with club.* Irish myth: Cross.

A137.3. *God with wheel.* Irish myth: Cross.

A137.3.1. *Wheel symbol.* Irish myth: Cross.
F531.6.15.6. Giant rolls like wheel.

A137.3.1.1. *Swastika* (hooked cross). Irish myth: Cross.

A137.4. *God (goddess) with basket.* Irish myth: Cross.

A137.4.1. *God carries brothers and sisters on his back in basket.* Hivaoa (Marquesas): Handy 116.

A137.5. *God (goddess) with cornucopia.* Irish myth: Cross.
D1171. Magic vessel.

A137.6. *Squatting god.* Irish myth: Cross.

A137.7. *The bull with three cranes* (cf. A132.6). Irish myth: Cross.
B182. Magic cow (ox, bull).

A137.8. *Small-pox deity rides nude on an ass* with the half of a winnowing fan for an umbrella and with a swing in one hand and a broom in the other. India: Thompson-Balys.

A137.9. *Goddess represented as mounted on a drake,* attended by eight chief snakes attended by snake jewels. India: Thompson-Balys.

A137.10. *God represented as king, world as his kingdom.* Jewish: Neuman.

A137.11. *God represented in cloud.* Jewish: Neuman.

A137.12. *God represented as bridegroom.* Jewish: Neuman.

A137.13. *God represented as priest.* Jewish: Neuman.

A137.14. *God represented with weapon.* Jewish: Neuman.

A137.14.1. *God represented with bow of fire.* Jewish: Neuman.

A137.14.1.1. *God represented with arrow of flames.* Jewish: Neuman.

A137.14.2. *God represented with spears as torches.* Jewish: Neuman.

A137.14.3. *God represented with clouds as shield.* Jewish: Neuman.

A137.14.4. *God represented with lightning flashes as sword.* Jewish: Neuman.

A137.15. *God represented on high throne surrounded by angels.* Jewish: Neuman.

A137.16. *God represented as meteor* (cf. A124). Tahiti: Beckwith Myth 113.

A137.17. *God represented as among seven sheaths of fire.* Jewish: Neuman.

A137.18. *God with long white beard and white moustache.* India: Thompson-Balys.

A138. *God's ineffable name.* Jewish: Neuman.

C431. Tabu: uttering name of god. C432. Tabu: uttering name of supernatural creature.

A139. *Nature and appearance of the gods — miscellaneous.*

A139.1. *Gods (supernatural beings) have many names* (cf. C432). Irish myth: Cross.

A139.2. *Tortoise footstool of God.* India: Thompson-Balys.

A139.3. *Dragon god.* India: Thompson-Balys; Chinese: Eberhard FFC CXX 136.

B11. Dragon.

A139.4. *Vampire goddess.* India: Thompson-Balys.

E251. Vampire.

A139.5. *God's voice.* Jewish: Neuman.

A139.5.1. *God's voice shatters mountain.* Jewish: Neuman.

A139.5.2. *God's voice causes thunder.* Jewish: Neuman.

A1142.1. Origin of thunder.

A139.6. *God's words.* Jewish: Neuman.

A139.7. *Distinctive aroma of gods.* Gaster Thespis 211, 389, 397.

A139.8. *God appears as an object.*

A139.8.1. *God as a tree trunk.* Hawaii: Beckwith Myth 284.

A139.8.2. *Goddess appears as coral reef.* Hawaii: Beckwith Myth 219.

A139.8.3. *Smoldering fire of volcano as head of goddess.* Hawaii: Beckwith Myth 188.

A139.8.4. *God of the wind in shape of kite.* Hawaii: Beckwith Myth 121.

A139.8.5. *Goddess in form of tree.* Hawaii: Beckwith Myth 17.

A139.8.6. *God in shape of an image.* Hawaii: Beckwith Myth 2, Chap. I passim.

A139.9. *Extraordinary physical characteristics of gods.*

A139.9.1. *Goddess with red urine.* Easter Is.: Métraux Ethnology 315.

A139.9.2. *Gods have ichor, not blood: can be wounded but not killed.* Iliad book V line 137.

A139.9.3. *Gods covered with red and yellow feathers.* Tahiti: Henry 338.

A139.10. *God with myriad natures.* Tahiti: Henry 336.

A139.11. *Gods recognized by natural phenomena associated with their worship* — color, scent, etc. Hawaii: Beckwith Myth 4.

A139.12. *Long-suffering God.* Jewish: Neuman.

A139.13. *Tempermental goddess.* Buddhist myth: Malalasekera I 840.

A139.14. *Ugly god.* Chinese: Eberhard FFC CXX 194 No. 135.

A139.15. *Greedy god.* Chinese: Eberhard FFC CXX 215f.

A140. Gods as workmen. Icel.: MacCulloch Eddic 327.

A181. God serves as menial on earth. A1402. The gods build houses, make tongs and tools.

A141. *God as craftsman.* Hephaistos. — Greek: Fox 206. — Tahiti: Henry 342.

A141.1. *God makes automata and vivifies them.* Icel.: Boberg; Greek: Fox 207; Africa (Luba): Donohugh Africa V 180.

D1620. Magic automata.

A141.2. *God builds temple in heaven and brings it later to earth.* Jewish: Neuman.

A141.3. *God bores hole in Hell to cause great heat on earth.* Jewish: Neuman.

A141.4. *God lays foundations of earth.* Jewish: Neuman.

A831.1. Creator of earth.

A142. *Smith of the gods.* Greek: Fox 206; Gaster Thespis 154ff.; *Krappe Archiv f. d. Studium d. neueren Sprachen CLVIII—CLXI passim.; Norse: Herrmann Nordische Mythologie 115ff.; Lithuanian: Gray 330; Irish myth: Cross; India: Thompson-Balys.

A167. Cupbearer of the gods is god of smith-work. A451. Artisan god. A451.1. God of smith-work. F451.3.4.2. Dwarfs as smiths. F531.6.9. Giants as warriors. K1816.12. Disguise as smith. L113.6. Smith as hero. P447. Smith.

A142.0.1. *God as blacksmith.* India: Thompson-Balys.

A142.1. *Brazier of the gods.* Irish myth: Cross.

A143. *Carpenter (wright) of the gods.* Irish myth: Cross; India: Thompson-Balys.

P456. Carpenter.

A144. *Physician of the gods.* Irish myth: Cross.

A454. God of healing. A454.1. Goddess of healing. F274. Fairy physician. P424. Physician.

A145. *Champions of the gods.* Irish myth: Cross.

F610. Remarkably strong man.

A147. *Gods as fishers* (cf. A165.9). Hawaii: Beckwith Myth 24.

A150. Daily life of the gods.

A151. *Home of the gods.* Elysium, Avalon, earthly paradise. — Celtic (general): MacCulloch Celtic 14; Irish: ibid. 37f., 114ff., Cross; Welsh: ibid. 193; Icel.: MacCulloch Eddic 312ff.; Hindu: Penzer I 125 n. 1.; Jewish: Neuman. — Hawaii: Beckwith Myth 67; So. Am. Indian (Apapocuvá-Guarani): Métraux RMLP XXXIII 122; Africa (Fang): Trilles 130.

A102.5. Omnipresent god. A661.1. Valhalla. F130. Location of otherworld. F210. Fairyland.

A151.0.1. *Home of god where he is the only living one.* Jewish: Neuman.

A151.0.2. *God's abode known to none.* Jewish: Neuman.

A151.1. *Home of gods on high mountain.* Mt. Olympus. Patch PMLA XXXIII 618; Gaster Thespis 138, 170ff.; Greek: Fox 8, Grote I 10; Icel.: MacCulloch Eddic 23; Hindu: Penzer X 195 s. v. "Kailasa", Keith 149 (Mount Meru); India: *Thompson-Balys; Jewish: Neuman. — Hawaii: Beckwith Myth 19.

A665.3. Mountain supports sky. F132. Otherworld on lofty mountain. F750. Extraordinary mountains and valleys.

A151.1.1. *Home of gods inside of hill.* Irish myth: Cross. — Cheyenne: Alexander N. Am. 123, 127; Hawaii: Beckwith Myth 39.

F211. Fairyland under a hollow knoll (mound, hill, sid). F721.2. Habitable hill.

A151.1.2. *Home of gods in cave.* Hivaoa (Marquesas): Handy 104; Tonga: Gifford 81.

A151.1.3. *Home of gods in volcano crater.* Hawaii: Beckwith Myth 167, 173.

A151.1.4. *Gods live in cloudland.* Hawaii: Beckwith Myth 64, 67; Tahiti: Beckwith Myth 31.

A151.2. *Garden of the gods.* Hindu: Penzer I 66 n. 1, 68, 96, II 34, III 5, 24, 138, VI 82, VII 129, 148, VIII 73, 165, 170, IX 21, 87 n. 4; Irish myth: Cross; Babylonian: Ungnad Das Gilgamesch Epos IX 163, cf. 148, 163ff.; Jewish: Neuman; Gaster Thespis 171, Oldest Stories 48.

F162.1. Garden in otherworld.

A151.3. *Home of the gods under the sea.* India: Thompson-Balys.

A151.3.1. *Gods live in spring.* Tonga: Beckwith Myth 74.

A151.3.2. *Home of gods on island.* Hawaii: Beckwith Myth 67f., 85; Tahiti: Beckwith Myth 178.

A151.4. *Palaces of the gods.* Icel.: MacCulloch Eddic 327, 329.

A151.4.1. *God's temple of jewels.* Jewish: Neuman.

A151.4.2. *Palace of gods with door at each end for sun's journey.* Virgil Aeneid X line 3.

A151.4.3. *Golden mansions of gods.* Buddhist myth: Malalasekera II 421.

A151.4.4. *House of god with pillars made of dead chief's bones.* Samoa: Beckwith Myth 76.

A151.5. *City of gods (God).* Icel.: MacCulloch Eddic 329; Buddhist myth: Malalasekera I 290, II 961, 1195.

A151.6. *God's home on heavenly bodies.*

A151.6.1. *God (Indra) has palace on Milky Way.* India: Thompson-Balys.

A151.6.2. *Sun and moon as habitations of gods.* Hawaii: Beckwith Myth 85.

A151.7. *Deity lives in forest.* Buddhist myth: Malalasekera II 1059. — Hawaii: Beckwith Myth 36f.

A151.7.1. *Deity resides in tree.* Buddhist myth: Malalasekera II 1319. — India: *Thompson-Balys; Chinese: Eberhard FFC CXX 136.
F441.2.1. Wood-nymph.

A151.7.1.1. *God's home under tree of life* (cf. F441.2.1.). Jewish: Neuman.
E90. Tree of life.

A151.8. *God in sea of milk.* India: *Thompson-Balys.

A151.9. *God originally resident among men.* Jewish: Neuman.

A151.10. *God dwells at particular point on earth.* Jewish: Neuman.

A151.10.1. *Home of God the ark and the temple.* Jewish: Neuman.

A151.11. *God's spirit dwells among mortals.* Jewish: Neuman.

A151.12. *God's landing place (on island).* Hawaii: Beckwith Myth 11.

A151.13. *God dwells alone in darkness.* Hawaii: Beckwith Myth 42.

A151.14. *Various other dwelling places of gods.* Hawaii: Beckwith Myth 3, 11, 43, 67.

A152. *God's throne.* Jewish: Neuman.

A152.1. *God's two thrones* (of mercy and of justice). Jewish: Neuman.

A152.2. *Flames surround God's throne.* Jewish: Neuman.

A152.3. *God's throne on wheels.* Jewish: Neuman.

A152.4. *Attendants around God's throne.* Jewish: Neuman.

A152.5. *Heavenly curtain surrounds God's throne.* Jewish: Neuman.

A152.6. *Footstool before divine throne.* Jewish: Neuman.

A152.7. *Bearers of God's throne.* Jewish: Neuman.

A152.8. *Heavenly throne has Jacob's face engraved on it.* Jewish: Neuman.

A152.9. *God's throne becomes hot because of activities on earth.* Buddhist myth: Malalasekera II 425, 492, 572, 897.

A153. *Food of the gods.* Ambrosia. — Smith Dragon 188; Hindu: Keith 106, Tawney I 425, 478; India: Thompson-Balys; Greek: Roscher I 280. — Hawaii: Beckwith Myth 67; Icel.: MacCulloch Eddic 313; Irish myth: Cross.
C241. Tabu: eating food of gods. D1030. Magic food. F243. Fairies' food.

A153.1. *Theft of ambrosia.* Food of the gods stolen. — Hindu: Keith 139; Persian: Carnoy 283.
A1415. Theft of fire. K 300. Thefts and cheats.

A153.2. *Magic food gives immortality to gods.* Irish: MacCulloch Celtic 54; India: Thompson-Balys.
D1346.3. Food of immortality.

A153.2.1. *Gods' food gives supernatural growth.* Irish Myth: Cross; India: Thompson-Balys; Greek: Grote I 43.
T615. Supernatural growth.

A153.3. *Banquets of the gods.* Icel.: MacCulloch Eddic 23; India: Thompson-Balys; Chinese: Werner 137. — So. Am. Indian (Chiriguano): Métraux RMLP XXXIII 178.

A153.3.1. *Moon steals food from banquet of the gods* (cf. A153.1.). India: Thompson-Balys.

A153.3.2. *Sun, moon and wind dine with their uncle and aunt,* thunder and lightning. India: Thompson-Balys.

A153.4. *Magic food rejuvenates the gods.* Icel.: MacCulloch Eddic 178.
A191. Goddess rejuvenates self when old. A474.1. Goddess of youth.

A153.5. *Food of gods: meat of "cow of plenty".* India: Thompson-Balys.

A153.6. *Why gods only accept blood.* India: Thompson-Balys.

A153.7. *God's preference for cooked food.* India: Thompson-Balys.

A153.8. *Cannibal gods* (cf. G11.). India: Thompson-Balys.

A153.9. *Gods nourished by air.* Hivaoa (Marquesas): Handy 105.

A154. *Drink of the gods.* Greek: Grote I 43; Icel.: MacCulloch Eddic 54, 86, 172, 313; Hindu: Penzer X 243 s. v. "nectar"; Keith 46 and passim; India: *Thompson-Balys; Persian: Carnoy 265; Chinese: Ferguson 130.
D1346.1.2. Nectar of immortality.

A154.1. *Magic drink gives immortality to gods* (cf. D1040). Irish: Mac Culloch Celtic 31, 54; Hindu: Keith 46.
A191.1. Great age of the gods. D1338.1. Magic drink rejuvenates. D1880. Magic rejuvenation. F167.9. Otherworld people ever young, ever beautiful. F172. No time, no birth, no death in otherworld. F251.5. Fairies as sprites who have been given immortality. F259.1. Mortality (immortality) of fairies.

A154.2. *Theft of magic mead by Odin.* *Olrik Edda XXIV 236ff. — Icel.: MacCulloch Eddic 54.
M234.1. Life spared in return for poetic mead.

A154.3. *Gods discover liquor.* India: Thompson-Balys.

A154.4. *Milk of the gods.* India: Thompson-Balys.

A155. *Animals of the gods* (cf. A136). Icel.: MacCulloch Eddic 109, 216.

A155.1. *Cattle of the sun.* Greek: Fox 137.

A155.2. *Horses of the gods* (cf. A171.1). Icel.: MacCulloch Eddic 216; Snorra Edda Gylf. XV.

A155.3. *Birds of the gods* (cf. A165.1.1.). Hawaii: Beckwith Myth 36f., 115, 177.

A155.4. *Gods keep mosquitoes as pets.* India: Thompson-Balys.

A155.5. *God's elephant.* India: Thompson-Balys.

A155.5.1. *God has enormous elephant.* Buddhist myth: Malalasekera I 457.

A155.6. *Goddess sleeps on bed of snakes.* India: Thompson-Balys.

A155.7. *God has his dairies and buffaloes.* India: Thompson-Balys.

A156. *Precious properties of the gods.* Icel.: MacCulloch Eddic 266; Jewish: Neuman.

A156.1. *Jewels of the gods.* Icel.: MacCulloch Eddic 120ff., 140ff.; Jewish: Neuman.

A156.2. *God's crown.* Jewish: Neuman.

A156.3. *God's scepters.* Jewish: Neuman.

A156.4. *God's seal.* Jewish: Neuman.

A156.5. *Chariot of the gods.* Virgil Aeneid X line 635; India: *Thompson-Balys; Buddhist myth: Malalasekera II 77, 916.

A157. *Weapons of the gods.* Buddhist myth: Malalasekera II 32, 965.

A157.1. *Thunderweapon.* Stone weapons (axes) brought down by thunderbolt (from Thunder God). — Blinkenberg The Thunder Weapon 1911; Hdwb. d. d. Aberglaubens II 325; Saintyves Corpus du Folklore Prehistorique en France et dans les Colonies Françaises (1934—36) I—III; J. Balys Tautosakos Darbai III 1937 223ff.; Jewish: *Neuman.

A284. God of thunder. A284.2. Thunderbird. A285. God of lightning. A992.2. Sacred place where thunderbolt fell down. Q552.1. Death by thunderbolt as punishment.

A157.1.1. *Thunderbolt as gods' weapon.* Greek: Fox 159; Buddhist myth: Malalasekera I 214, 309, II 1060.

A284. God of thunder. A284.2. Thunderbird.

A157.2. *God's arrows.* Jewish: Neuman.

A157.3. *God's spear.* Jewish: Neuman.

A157.4. *God's shield.* Jewish: Neuman.

A157.5. *God's sword.* Jewish: Neuman.

A157.6. *God's bow.* Jewish: Neuman.

A157.7. *Hammer of thunder god.* Gaster Thespis 135, 363.

A158. *Clothing of gods.* Eskimo: Holm 73; Jewish: Neuman.

A159. *Daily life of the gods — miscellaneous.*

A159.1. *Deity's special drum.* Buddhist myth: Malalasekera II 965.

C916.2. Animals produced when forbidden drum is beaten.

A160. Mutual relations of the gods.

D45.2. Gods exchange forms.

A161. *Hierarchy of gods.* Persian: Carnoy 260; Irish myth: Cross; Hindu: Müller 142f.; India: Thompson-Balys; Greek: Grote I 3, 9; Buddhist myth: Malalasekera I 729.

A101. Supreme god. A107. Gods of darkness and of light.

A161.1. *Division of control of universe among gods.* Greek: Grote I 3, 9.

A161.2. *King of the gods.* See all references to A101 (Supreme god).

A161.3. *Queen of the gods.* Greek: Grote I 10; Hawaii: Beckwith Myth 13, chap. II passim.

A161.4. *God presides over all male spirits.* Hawaii: Beckwith Myth 13.

A161.5. *Eldest god born in front, younger at back.* (Cf. A112.7.) Hivaoa (Marquesas): Handy 138.

A162. *Conflicts of the gods.* Irish myth: Cross; Greek: Grote I 1, 3, 8; Icel.: MacCulloch Eddic 26ff., 172; Siberian: Holmberg Siberian 356, 411; Hindu: Penzer I 197ff.; India: *Thompson-Balys; Japanese: Anesaki 225; Buddhist myth: Malalasekera I 318, 1104. — Gaster Thespis 115ff., 125.

A1750. Animals created through opposition of devil to God. F277. Battle of the fairies and the gods.

A162.1. *Fight of the gods and giants.* Jünger (F. G.) Die Titanen (Frankfurt a. M. 1944); Mayer Die Giganten und Titanen in der antiken Sage (Berlin 1887). — Greek: Frazer Apollodorus I 11, *42 n. 1, *43 n. 2; Icel.: MacCulloch Eddic 82, Herrmann Saxo II 97ff; Irish myth: Cross; Siberian: Holmberg Siberian 356; Chinese: Werner 159; Hindu: Penzer X 77 s.v. "Asuras", X 118 s.v. "Daityas", X 119 s.v. "Dānavas"; India: *Thompson-Balys; Samoa: Beckwith Myth 254.

A107. Gods of darkness and of light. A255. Star deity and drought demon fight. E155.1.1. Constant replacement of fighters. In contest between gods and demons, latter are constantly slain and replaced Q433.2. Defeated giants imprisoned in lower world.

A162.1.0.1. *Recurrent battle* (everlasting fight) (cf. A165.7.). Irish myth: Cross.

E155.1. Slain warriors revive nightly.

A162.2. *Combat between god of light and dragon of ocean.* Jewish: Neuman; Babylonian and Egyptian: Müller 104; cf. Chinese: Werner 215.

A162.3. *Combat between thundergod and devil* (cf. A157.1, A189.1.1, A284, A285). *Balys "Donner und Teufel in den Volkserzählungen der baltischen und skandinavischen Völker" Tautosakos Darbai VI (1939) 1—220.

G303.3.1.18. Devil as shoemaker is struck by lightning. G303.6.2.12. Devil hides in the folds of clothes of people running from storm. G303.6.3.1.1. Devil appears during thunder storm, seeking shelter among people. K1177. Dupe deceived concerning thunder. Q45.2.1. Man saves the unrecognized devil from thunder. Q552.1. Death by thunderbolt as punishment. Q552.1.0.2. Thunder slays people for disregard for him.

A162.3.1. *Devil (ogre) steals thunder's instruments.* Icel.: Thrymskvida; Lappish, Finnish, Estonian, Latvian, and Lithuanian: *Balys Tautosakos Darbai VI (1939) 33—43.

A162.3.2. *Thunder and lightning slay devils.* Norwegian, Danish, Swedish, Finnish, Estonian, Latvian, and Lithuanian: *Balys Tautosakos Darbai VI (1939) 111—128.

A162.4. *Brahma cursed by other gods: now has no temples.* India: Thompson-Balys.

A162.5. *God reborn of human woman to avenge self on giant* (cf. A179.5.). India: Thompson-Balys.

A162.6. *Battle between God's orderly (giant) and plague.* India: Thompson-Balys.

A162.7. *Single combat between gods.* Hawaii: Beckwith Myth 17, 206; Marquesas: Handy 109; Icel.: Boberg.

A162.8. *Rebellion of lesser gods against chief.* Hawaii: Beckwith Myth 60, 118, 155.

A106.2. Revolt of evil angels against God.

A163. *Contests among the gods.*
H1589.1. Judgment of Paris.

A163.1. *Game between gods.* (Cf. A164.3.1.).

A163.1.1. *Gods play chess.* Chinese: Eberhard FFC CXX 216 No. 165.

A164. *Marriage or liaison of gods.* Irish myth: Cross; Buddhist myth: Malalasekera II 964; India: Thompson-Balys.

A164.1. *Brother-sister marriage of the gods.* Irish myth: Cross; Icel.: MacCulloch Eddic 102; Greek: Grote I 58; Marquesas: Handy 122.
A511.3.2. Culture hero son of king's unmarried sister by her brother. T410. Incest.

A164.1.1. *Mother-son marriage of the gods.* Irish myth: Cross; So. Am. Indian (Mundurucu): Horton BBAE CXLIII (3) 281.
T412. Mother-son incest.

A164.2. *Adultery among the gods.* Irish myth: Cross.
K1563. Husband (god) traps wife and paramour with magic armor.

A164.3. *Polygamy among the gods.* Irish myth: Cross; Buddhist myth: Malalasekera I 186.
T145. Polygamous marriage.

A164.3.1. *Krishna plays cards with his three wives.* (Cf. A163.1.). India: Thompson-Balys.

A164.4. *Matriarchy among the gods.* Irish myth: Cross.
T148. Matriarchy.

A164.5. *Polyandry among the gods.* Irish myth: Cross.
T146. Polyandry.

A164.6. *God as lover of giantess.* Icel.: *Boberg.
F531. Giant.

A164.7. *Jealous wife of god.* India. Thompson-Balys.

A165. *Attendants and servants of the gods.* Greek: Grote I 10, 67; Icel.: *Boberg (A165.3); Jewish: *Neuman; Buddhist myth: Malalasekera II 964f.; Hindu: *Penzer I 200, X 158 s. v. "Ganas", "Gandharvas".
A141. God as craftsman. A155. Animals of the gods.

A165.1. *Animals as attendants of god.*

A165.1.1. *Ravens as attendants of god.* Grimm Deutsche Mythologie I 122. — Icel.: MacCulloch Eddic 65, Boberg.
B122.2. Birds as reporters of sights and sounds. Sit on Odin's shoulder and report what they see and hear. C92.1. Tabu: killing raven (Odin's bird). E501.4.4. Two ravens follow wild huntsman.

A165.1.2. *Eagle as god's bird.* Icel.: Boberg.

A165.1.3. *Red sea-bird god's pet.* Tahiti: Henry 180.

A165.2. *Messenger of the gods.* *Güntert Weltkönig 280; Gaster Thespis 139. — Greek: Fox 191 (Hermes, Iris), Grote I 43; Irish: Beal XXI 319, 336; India: *Thompson-Balys; Jewish: *Neuman; Huichol: Alexander Lat. Am. 122. — Tahiti: Beckwith Myth 31, Henry 164.

A165.2.0.1. *Deity's messenger can assume any guise he wishes.* Buddhist myth: Malalasekera II 906.
D630. Transformation and disenchantment at will.

A165.2.1 *Animals as messengers of the gods.*

A165.2.1.1. *Wild beasts as messengers of the gods.* Jewish: Neuman.

A165.2.1.1.1. *Wolves as god's dogs.* *Fb "ulv" III 971, BP III 199. — Icel.: MacCulloch Eddic 65.

B575.1. Wild animals kept as dogs.

A165.2.1.1.2. *Tiger as god's messenger.* India: Thompson-Balys.

A165.2.1.1.3. *Elephant as god's messenger.* India: Thompson-Balys.

A165.2.1.1.4. *Bears as God's messengers.* Jewish: Neuman.

A165.2.1.1.5. *Leopards as God's messengers.* Jewish: Neuman.

A165.2.1.1.6. *Lions as God's messengers.* Jewish: Neuman.

A165.2.2. *Birds as messengers of the gods.* Irish myth: Cross; India: Thompson-Balys; Pawnee: Alexander N. Am. 81; Hawaii: Beckwith Myth 177.

A132.6.2. Goddess in form of bird. B450. Helpful birds. F234.1.15. Fairy in form of bird.

A165.2.2.1. *Cock as ambassador of god.* Fjort: Dennett 105 No. 29.

A165.2.3. *Angels as God's messengers.* Jewish: Neuman.

A165.2.4. *Powers of nature (sun, moon, etc.) as God's messengers.* Jewish: Neuman.

A165.3. *Cupbearer of the gods.* Greek: Frazer Apollodorus II 37 n. 4.

A165.3.1. *Cupbearer of the gods is god of smith-work.* *MacCulloch Celtic 31.

A142. Smith of the gods.

A165.3.2. *Cupbearer of the gods controls waters.* Irish myth: Cross.

D2151. Magic control of waters.

A165.4. *Watchman of the gods.* Icel.: MacCulloch Eddic 152 (Heimdall), 276, 303, 313, 331 (Cock), 328 (Thor), 329 (Heimdall). — Tahiti: Beckwith Myth 221.

A165.4.1. *Demons as watchmen of the gods upon earth.* Greek: *Grote I 63.

A165.5. *Doorkeeper of the gods.* Icel.: MacCulloch Eddic 186 (Syn).

A165.6. *Scribe of the gods.* Siberian, Babylonian, Egyptian: Holmberg Siberian 410; Armenian: Ananikian 30ff.

A465.3.1. God of eloquence and learning.

A165.7. *Army of the gods* (cf. A162). Icel.: Herrmann Nordische Mythologie 279 (Einherjar), Neckel Walhall 68ff; India: Thompson-Balys.

E155.1. Slain warriors revive nightly.

A165.8. *Magician of the gods.* India: Thompson-Balys.

A165.9. *Fisherman of the gods.* Gaster Thespis 154. — Maori: Clark 56.

A166. *Dancers of the gods.* Hindu: Keith 143; Buddhist myth: Malalasekera I 186.

A167. *Assembly of gods.* Buddhist myth: Malalasekera I 310, II 958, 1098.

A167.1. *Council of the gods.* India: *Thompson-Balys.

A168. *Family of gods* (cf. A111, A164). Greek: Fox 151ff. passim. — Tahiti: Henry 231; Easter Is.: Métraux Ethnology 311; Buddhist myth: Malalasekera II 964.

A169. *Mutual relations of the gods — miscellaneous.*

A169.1. *Judge and tribunal of the gods.* Icel.: *Boberg.

A170. Deeds of the gods.

A171. *Gods ride through air.* India: *Thompson-Balys.

A136.6. God rides flying elephant. F32. God visits earth. K1811. Gods in disguise visit mortals.

A171.0.1. *God drives chariot over waves.* Irish myth: Cross.

A421. Sea-god. B71. Sea-horse. B181.4. Magic horse travels on sea or land. D1114. Magic chariot. D1533.1.2. Magic land and water chariot.

A171.0.2. *God ascends to heaven.* Hawaii: Beckwith Myth 109; Maori: Beckwith Myth 83; So. Am. Indian (Huamachuco): Métraux RMLP XXXIII 151.

A171.0.3. *God descends from heaven.*

F32. God visits earth. K1811. Gods in disguise visit mortals.

A171.0.3.1. *God descends on rainbow.* Tahiti: Henry 232; Hawaii: Beckwith Myth 37.

F152.1.1. Rainbow bridge to otherworld.

A171.0.3.2. *God descends in form of shooting star.* New Zealand: Beckwith Myth 113.

A171.1. *God rides through air on wind-swift horse.* Icel.: MacCulloch Eddic 43.

A136.1.2.1. Sleipnir: eight-legged horse of Odin. B41.2. Flying horse.

A171.1.1. *God rides through air in chariot.* Jewish: Neuman.

A136.2. God's chariot.

A171.1.2. *Valkyries ride through air and water.* Icel.: Boberg.

A171.2. *God flies in bird plumage.* Icel.: MacCulloch Eddic 83, Boberg; Greek: Iliad and Odyssey passim.

A171.3. *God flies in pillar of floating clouds, thunder, and lightning.* Hawaii: Beckwith Myth 29.

A172. *Gods intervene in battle.* Irish myth: Cross; Greek: Iliad passim; Norse: Herrmann Nordische Mythologie 291ff, Boberg; Gaster Thespis 349; Hindu: Tawney I 412, II 473—477; Jewish: *Neuman.

A185. Gods and goddesses help the men, heroes, whom they like. A185.1. God aids half-mortal son in battle. A536. Demigods fight as allies of mortals. D2163.2. Magic reinforcements. F349.2. Fairy aids mortal in battle. F394.2. Mortals aid fairies in war. K1845. Substitute in battle. N817.0.1. God as helper.

A173. *Gods deposed for a time.* Irish myth: Cross; Icel.: De Vries FFC XCIV 38ff., Herrmann Saxo II 109ff.; Hindu: Tawney II 581. — Hawaii: Beckwith Myth 11, 17, 177.

A128.4. God with one hand. P16.2. King must resign if maimed (disfigured).

A173.1. *In god's absence his function ceases.* Death, reproduction, etc., suspended until the god's return. — *Wesselski Archiv Orientální I 300ff.

A431.1. Goddess of fertility.

A173.2. *Gods imprisoned.* Irish myth: Cross.

A175. *God reduces the elements to order.* Greek: Fox 9; Irish myth: Cross; Jewish: *Neuman. — Hawaii: Beckwith Myth 20ff.

A530. Culture hero establishes law and order.

A175.1. *God supplies reproductive energy to all things.* Hawaii: Beckwith Myth 20, 32.

A176. *God ordains ceremonies and regulations.* Jewish: *Neuman; India: Thompson-Balys; Hawaii: Beckwith Myth 40.

A1500. Origin of customs.

A177. *God as thief.* Greek: *Frazer Apollodorus II 6 n. 1 (Hermes).

F365. Fairies steal.

A177.1. *God as dupe or trickster.* Irish myth: Cross.

A521. Culture hero as dupe or trickster. K232.2.1. Fairy loses stronghold by consenting to lend it for "a day and a night".

A178. *God as prophet.* Irish myth: Cross; Jewish: *Neuman.

M301. Prophets.

A179. *Deeds of the gods — miscellaneous.*

A179.1. *God as rath-builder.* Irish myth: Cross.

D1136.1. Fort produced by magic. F531.6.6. Giants as builders of great structures.

A179.2. *God given dominion over floating island. Hawaii:* Beckwith Myth 71.

F737. Wandering island.

A179.3. *God deliberately has enemies kill him.* Hivaoa (Marquesas): Handy 105.

A179.4. *Head of god bitten off by shark.* Hivaoa (Marquesas): Handy 108.

A179.5. *Deity reincarnated.* Hawaii: Beckwith Myth 279.

A162.5. God reborn of human woman.

A179.6. *God has power to create men.* Marquesas: Handy 122.

A179.7. *God divests self of earthly raiment and clothes self with lightning.* Maori: Beckwith Myth 83.

A179.8. *God hides from sun in shadow of a cloud.* Tuamotu: Stimson MS (T-G 3/191).

A179.9. *God plays with leviathan.* Jewish: Neuman.

A844.7. God rests on leviathan. B61. Leviathan.

A180. Gods in relation to mortals. Irish myth: Cross; Norse: Olrik Kilderne til Sakses Oldhistorie I (1892) 30ff., 32ff.

B641.3. Marriage to god in bull form. C50. Tabu: offending the gods. C191. Tabu: mortal lusting after goddess. C312.1.1. Tabu: man looking at nude goddess. C313.1.1. Tabu: goddess seeing mortal husband naked. D42. God in guise of mortal. D42.1. God transformed to giant with three heads and six arms. D101. Transformation: god to animal. D1814.3. Advice from god (or gods). D1983.1. Invisibility conferred by a god. D2161.5.3. Cure by deity. E121.1. Resuscitation by a god. E605.2. Reincarnation: god reborn as man. E605.3. Reincarnation: man becomes god. F32. God visits earth. K1811. Gods (saints) in disguise visit mortals. M226. Immortal exchanges immortality with mortal. M414.1. Goddess cursed. N817. Deity as helper. P535.2.1. Ireland given to mortals by gods in payment of eric for death of their leader. Q1. Hospitality rewarded — opposite punished. Q221. Personal offences against gods.

punished. Q255. Punishment of woman who prefers mortal lover to gods. S260. Sacrifices. T91.8. Mortal and supernatural being in love. T111.1. Marriage of a mortal and a god. T611.1.1. Child nourished by sucking thumb of a god. V227. Saints have divine visitors.

A181. *God serves as menial on earth.* Greek: *Frazer Apollodorus II 20 n. 1, Grote I 36, 53, 108; Irish: MacCulloch Celtic 142; Buddhist myth: Malalasekera II 962; India: *Thompson-Balys.

F346.2. Fairy serves mortal. K1816.0.1. God disguised as menial. L113.1. Menial hero. Q482. Punishment: noble person must do menial service. V233.1. Angel of death spares mother who is suckling children. As punishment angel must serve as sexton.

A181.1. *God clears plains.* Irish myth: Cross.

A537. Culture hero clears plains. A901. Topographical features caused by experiences of primitive hero. F271.5. Fairies clear land. F614.9. Strong man clears plain.

A181.2. *God as cultivator.* India: Thompson-Balys; Hawaii: Beckwith Myth 17.

A182. *God reveals himself to mortals.* Jewish: *Neuman.

A182.0.1. *God does not reveal himself; men unable to endure his glory.* Jewish: Neuman.

A182.0.2. *Human intellect unable to conceive God's essence.* Jewish: Neuman.

A182.1. *God reveals secrets (mysteries) to mortals.* Jewish: Neuman.

A182.1.1. *Household gods speak to explain events.* Virgil Aeneid III line 155.

A182.2. *God gives name to child.* Jewish: Neuman.

A182.3. *God (angel) speaks to mortal.* Jewish: Neuman.

V227. Saints have divine visitors. V235. Mortal visited by angel.

A182.3.0.1. *God speaks to Moses from bush.* Jewish: Neuman; Moreno Esdras.

D1610.2.2. Speaking bush.

A182.3.0.1.1. *Angel speaks to Patrick from bush* that merely seems to burn. Irish myth: Cross.

A182.3.0.2. *God speaks to saint in prison.* Rüttgers Der Heiligen Leben (Leipzig, 1921) 103.

A182.3.0.3. *Saint speaks with God each Thursday.* Irish myth: Cross.

A182.3.0.3.1. *Saint goes to heaven every Thursday (each day) and talks with angels.* Irish myth: Cross.

Q172.8.1. Saint goes to heaven every Thursday.

A182.3.0.4. *God does not directly address women; uses interpreter.* Jewish: Neuman.

A182.3.0.5. *God speaks from mountain.* Jewish: Neuman.

A182.3.1. *God consoles mortal.* Jewish: Neuman.

A182.3.2. *God rebukes mortal.* Jewish: Neuman.

A182.3.3. *God blesses mortal.* Jewish: Neuman.

A182.3.4. *God makes promises to mortal.* Jewish: Neuman.

A182.3.4.1. *God in form of fakir visits king and gives him advice.* India: Thompson-Balys.

A182.3.4.2. *God promises mortal prosperity for man and offspring.* India: Thompson-Balys.

A182.3.5. *God advises mortal.* Jewish: Neuman.

A182.3.6. *Moon-god, overcome in contest with mortal, threatens to withold rain and game.* Eskimo: Holm 75, Rink 442.
A1421.1. Hoarded game.

A183. *Deity invoked.* Greek: Odyssey IX line 528, Iliad I 218, et passim; Hawaii: Beckwith Myth 2, chap. 1 passim.

A183.1. *Male god invoked in east; female in west.* Hawaii: Beckwith Myth 12.

A184. *God as founder and protector of certain peoples.*

A184.1. *God as protector of Israel.* Jewish: *Neuman.

A185. *Deity cares for favorite individuals.* Greek: Fox 33, 170f., 197; Icelandic: Volsunga Saga chap. 13, Boberg; Jewish: Neuman; Chinese: Eberhard FFC CXX 187f.

A185.1. *God helps mortal in battle.* Jewish: Neuman; Irish myth: Cross.
A172. Gods intervene in battle. A528. Culture hero has supernatural helpers. A536. Demigods act as allies of mortals. F349.2. Fairy aids mortal in battle. N800. Helpers.

A185.2. *Deity protects mortal.* Jewish: Neuman; Greek myth passim.

A185.2.1. *God rescues sleeping man from attack.* Jewish: Neuman.

A185.2.2. *God makes man's hand rigid so he can no longer torment captive.* Jewish: Neuman.
D2072. Magic paralysis.

A185.2.3. *God makes sword drop from assailant's hands.* Jewish: Neuman.

A185.3. *Deity teaches mortal.* Jewish: Neuman.

A185.4. *Deity buries dead mortal.* Jewish: Neuman.

A185.5. *Deity assists at man's wedding.* Jewish: Neuman.
T150. Happenings at weddings.

A185.6. *Deity particular friend to one mortal.*

A185.6.1. *God kisses mortal.* Jewish: Neuman.

A185.6.1.1. *Kiss of God causes painless death.* Jewish: Neuman.

A185.7. *God prepares food for mortal.* Jewish: Neuman.

A185.8. *Deity promises to restore city.* Jewish: Neuman.

A185.9. *Covenant between God and mortal.* Jewish: Neuman.
M200. Bargains and promises.

A185.10. *Deity accompanies mortal on journey as guide.* Jewish: Neuman; Oahu (Hawaii): Beckwith Myth 328; Tahiti: ibid. 221; Africa (Fang): Einstein 94.

A185.11. *God rewards mortal for pious act.* Jewish: Neuman.
Q20. Piety rewarded.

A185.12. *Deity provides man with soul.* Jewish: Neuman.

A1217. Devil's unsuccessful attempt to vivify his creations as God has done. E700. The soul.

A185.12.1. *God resuscitates man.* Jewish: Neuman; Chinese: Eberhard FFC CXX 188 No. 128.

E0. Resuscitation.

A185.12.2. *God removes mortal's soul.* Jewish: Neuman.

E700. The soul.

A185.13. *God puts mortal to test.* Jewish: Neuman.

H. Tests.

A185.14. *God controls mortals' sinning.*

A185.14.1. *God causes mortals' sin.* Jewish: Neuman.

A185.14.2. *God witholds mortal from sinning.* Jewish: Neuman.

A185.15. *God establishes peace between mortals.* Jewish: Neuman.

A185.16. *God pities mortal.* Jewish: Neuman.

A185.17. *God visits sick mortal.* Buddhist myth: Malalasekera II 1116.

A187. *Gods and men judge each other.*

A187.1. *God as judge of men.* Greek: Fox 227, Wienert FFC LVI 36; Icel.: MacCulloch Eddic 162 (Forseti); Jewish: *Neuman; India: Thompson-Balys, Penzer I 198ff., II 249, IV 238, 275f., VIII 64, 108 n. 1, 163 n. 1, 184, 215.

A187.2. *Mortal as umpire of quarrel between gods.* Icel.: Boberg; Celtic-Norse: FFC LXXXIII, xxxviii-xli. — India: *Thompson-Balys.

D832. Magic object acquired by acting as umpire for fighting heirs. F451.5.23. Dwarfs seek human help in their fights and troubles.

A188. *Gods and goddesses in love with men.* Babylonian: Gilgamesch Epos VI (Ishtar). — Irish myth: Cross; Norse: Herrmann Saxo Gr. II 238ff., *Boberg; Greek: Fox 29, 157, 199, 211. — Tahiti: Henry 231, Beckwith Myth 37, Porapora (Society Is.): *Beckwith Myth 38; Maori: Clark 148; So. Am. Indian (Chiriguano): Métraux RMLP XXXIII 154, 165.

T91.8. Love of goddess for mortal. T111. Marriage of mortal and supernatural being.

A188.1. *Philandering god.* Greek: Grote I 58; India: *Thompson-Balys.

D658.1. Transformation to husband's (lover's) form to seduce woman. K1301. Mortal woman seduced by god. K1315.1. Seduction by posing as a god.

A188.2. *Gods as ancestors of mankind.* Irish myth: Cross (A188.1); Hawaii: Beckwith myth 2, 70, 294, 300; Tahiti: Beckwith Myth 37; Tuamotu: Stimson MS (T-G. 3/1010); Easter Is.: Métraux 310; So. Am. Indian (Chiriguano): Métraux RMLP XXXIII 171; Inca: Rowe BBAE CXLIII (2) 315.

A189. *Gods in relation to mortals — miscellaneous.*

A189.0.1. *"Gods and not-gods".* Irish myth: Cross (A189).

A189.1. *Mortal as ally of gods.*

A189.1.1. *Man as helper of thundergod.* Lithuanian, Latvian, Livonian, Estonian, Ukrainian, Polish, and Rumanian: *Balys Tautosakos Darbai VI 53—83, 107f.; Lithuanian: Balys Index No. *1147A; Prussian: Plenzat 60.

A162.3. Thundergod pursues and slays the devil. G303.10. Allies and possessions of the devil. G303.25.7. Man shoots the devil with a silver gun.

A189.2. *God summoned by weeping.* India: Thompson-Balys.

E361. Return from the dead to stop weeping. E381. Ghost summoned by weeping.

A189.3. *Man cheats a god in throwing dice.* India: Thompson-Balys.

A189.4. *God jealous of a mortal.* India: Thompson-Balys.

A189.5. *Goddess' throne shakes when some mischance befalls her faithful worshipper.* India: Thompson-Balys.

A189.6. *Deity appears before human being after prayers.* India: Thompson-Balys.

A189.7. *Deity ascertains destiny of newborn babe and inscribes it upon* his forehead. India: Thompson-Balys.

N121. Fate decided before birth.

A189.8. *Accountants of god keep lists of good and bad acts* of human beings. India: Thompson-Balys.

A189.9. *Early period when gods and men lived together,* gods ruling men, ordaining how they should live and originating various customs. — India: Thompson-Balys.

A189.10. *Goddesses come down to earth by a silken thread,* are offended by raja and produce drought. India: Thompson-Balys.

F37. God visits earth. K1811. Gods (saints) in disguise visit mortals.

A189.11. *Mortal adopted son by god.* India: Thompson-Balys.

A189.12. *Goddess protects animals from hunters.* India: Thompson-Balys.

A189.13. *Gods forced by mortals to take refuge underground.* Irish myth: Cross (A183.1.).

A151.1.1. Home of gods inside of hill.

A189.14. *God's enemies.* Jewish: Neuman.

A189.15. *God as fructifier of mankind and the earth.* Jewish: Neuman.

A189.16. *Gods give divinity to mortal.* Tahiti: Henry 231.

A189.17. *Night the period of gods,* day the period of mankind. Hawaii: Beckwith Myth 14.

A190. Gods: miscellaneous motifs.

A191. *Goddess rejuvenates self when old.* Navaho: Alexander N. Am. 164.

A153.4. Magic food rejuvenates the gods. A474.1. Goddess of youth. D1881. Magic self-rejuvenation.

A191.1. *Great age of the gods.* Irish myth: Cross.

A154.1. Magic drink gives immortality to gods. A564. Remarkable longevity of culture heroes. D1345. Magic object gives longevity. D1857. Magic longevity. F172. No time, no birth, no death in otherworld. F251.5. Fairies as sprites who have been given immortality. F531.6.4. Age of giants. F571. Extremely old person. V229.2.12. Extraordinary longevity of saints.

A192. *Death or departure of the gods.*

A192.1. *Death of the gods.* Icel.: MacCulloch Eddic 340ff. (at the Doom); Irish myth: Cross; India: Thompson-Balys; Hawaii: Beckwith Myth 110; Tahiti: Henry 231; Chinese: Werner 99, Eberhard FFC CXX 141; Africa: Bouveignes 12.

F259.1. Mortality of fairies.

A192.1.1. *Old god slain by young god.* Irish myth: Cross.

A525.2. Culture hero (god) slays his grandfather.

A192.1.2. *God killed and eaten.* Easter Is.: Métraux Ethnology 311.

A192.2. *Departure of gods.* Tonga: Gifford 102, Nukuhiva (Marquesas): Handy 123.

A560. Culture hero's (demi-god's) departure.

A192.2.1. *Deity departs for heaven (skies).* Polynesia: Moriori (Chatham Is.), Pora Pora (Society Is.), Samoa: Beckwith Myth 38, 43, *241ff., 254; So. Am. Indian (Apapocuvá-Guarani): Métraux RMLP XXXIII 122.

A192.2.1.1. *Deity departs for moon.* Polynesia: Hawaii, Beckwith Myth 220, *241; Tuamotu: Stimson MS (T-G. 3/931).

A192.2.2. *Divinity departs in boat over sea.* Hawaii: Beckwith Myth 29, *37.

A192.2.3. *Divinity departs to submarine home.* Hawaii: Beckwith Myth 206.

A192.2.4. *Divinity departs in column of flame.* Pora Pora (Society Is.): Beckwith Myth 38.

A192.3. *Expected return of deity.* Banks Is. (Fiji): Beckwith Myth 316.

A192.4. *Divinity becomes mortal.* Tonga: Beckwith Myth 75.

A193. *Resurrection of gods.* Chinese: Werner 99.

A194. *Divinity's emotions.*

A194.1. *Divinity weeps.* Jewish: Neuman.

A194.2. *God's vengeance.* Jewish: Neuman.

A194.3. *God's jealousy.* Jewish: Neuman.

A194.4. *God's joy.* Jewish: Neuman.

A195. *Divinity's companions.*

A195.1. *God dealing with his angels.* Jewish: Neuman.

A195.2. *Wisdom as God's companion.* Jewish: Neuman.

A195.3. *Bird as the shadow of a god.* Tahiti: Henry 121.

A196. *Deity's limitations.*

A196.1. *Fate controls gods.* Greek: Fox 162; Icel.: MacCulloch Eddic 74; Semitic: Langdon 102, 307.

A196.2. *Decree of gods irrevocable.* India: Thompson-Balys.

M10. Irrevocable judgments.

A196.2.1. *Deity changes decision.* Jewish: Neuman.

A197. *Deity controls elements.* Jewish: *Neuman; Greek: "Zeus the cloud gatherer"; Icel.: MacCulloch Eddic 10, 15ff., 32ff., 68—96, et passim. — Tahiti: Henry 337.

D2140. Magic control of the elements.

A199. *Gods — additional motifs.*

A199.1. *Spirit of deity animates earthen jar* when it is placed beneath banyan tree. India: Thompson-Balys.

A199.2. *God has magic vision only from his throne.* Icel.: MacCulloch Eddic 22.

D1820. Magic sight.

A199.3. *Deity's child becomes fire as soon as he is born.* India: Thompson-Balys.

A199.4. *Wind drives buffaloes for god.* India: Thompson-Balys.

A199.5. *God's day is one thousand years.* Jewish: Neuman.

A199.6. *Deity authenticates sacred writings in heaven.* Jewish: Neuman.

A199.7. *Drums and flutes off-shore announce approach of gods.* Hawaii: Beckwith Myth 16 n. 3.

A200—A299. Gods of the upper world.

A200. God of the upper world.

A101. Supreme god.

A205. *Witch-woman of upper world.* Tuamotu: Stimson MS (Z-G. 13/249).

A210. Sky-god. *Cook Zeus; *Cook Classical Review XVII 270, XVIII 365, FL XV 301, XVI 260; *Hommel "Der allgegenwärtige Himmelsgott" Archiv f. Religionsgeschichte XXIII 193; *Koch Der römische Juppiter (Frankfurt a. M. 1937). — Greek: Fox 152 (Zeus); Babylonian: Spence 76, 121ff.; Hindu: Keith 21, 24 (Dyaus, Varuna); India: Thompson-Balys; Icel.: De la Saussaye 243 (Tiu); Much Der germanische Himmelsgott; Finno-Ugric: *Holmberg Finno-Ugric 217ff.; Irish myth: Cross. — Estonian: Loorits Grundzüge I 583ff.; Hawaii: Beckwith Myth 114, 294; Africa (Luba): Donohugh V 180.

A101. Supreme god. A220. Sun-god. F499.1. Sky-spirit.

A210.1. *Sky-goddess.* Egyptian: Müller 37 (Hathor and others), 41 (Nut). — Tonga: Gifford 16.

A211. *God of heaven* (cf. A210). Icel.: De la Saussaye 233 (Odin); Jewish: Neuman; Gaster Thespis 122f. — Siberian: Holmberg Siberian 390; Armenian: Ananikian 11, 14, 37; Chinese: Werner 331, Graham; Hindu: Penzer III 257, IV 177 n. 1. — African: Werner African 127. — Pawnee: Alexander N. Am. 80 ("Father Heaven"); Hivaoa (Marquesas): Handy 133.

A216. *God of the air.* *Encyc. Religion and Ethics s. v. "Air and gods of the air"; Greek: Grote I 3; India: Thompson-Balys.

A220. Sun-god. **Frobenius Das Zeitalter des Sonnengottes (Berlin 1904); Smith Dragon viii; Montelius FL XXI (1909) 60; Krappe "The Anatolian Lion God" JAOS LXV (1945) 144—154; Krappe "Apollon" Studi i Materiali di Storia delle Religioni XIX—XX (1943—1946); *Koch Gestirnverehrung im alten Italien (Frankfurt a. M. 1933). —

Greek: Gaster Thespis 127, 205, 339f., Fox 241 (Helios); Egyptian: Müller 24ff., 129 (Amon); Babylonian: Spence 109ff., 187, 189; Irish myth: Cross; Persian, Hindu: Keith 24—29, 232; Armenian: Ananikian, 11, 33, 37, 43; Finno-Ugric: Holmberg Finno-Ugric 223; Siberian: Holmberg Siberian 422; Chinese: Ferguson 90; Russian: Machal 273, 297, 299; India: *Thompson-Balys; Buddhist myth: Malalasekera II 735. — Navaho: Alexander N. Am. 165; Pima: ibid. 176; (Pawnee and Plains in general): ibid. 81, 87; Huichol: Alexander Lat. Am. 121.

A450.1., God "of many arts". A720. Nature and condition of the sun.

A220.0.1. *Sun-god commits adultery.* India: Thompson-Balys.

A220.0.2. *Sun-god couples with the moon.* India: Thompson-Balys.

A220.1. *Sun-goddess.* Gaster Thespis 30f., 127, 205, 339; Japanese: Anesaki 225ff., *Ikeda, Beckwith Myth 102; Irish myth: Cross.

A270.1. Goddess of dawn.

A220.2. *The sun-god and his family.* India: Thompson-Balys.

A221. *Sun-father.* *Fb "sol" III 457b. — Pawnee: Alexander N. Am. 81, 87; Zuñi: ibid. 187; S. Am. Indian (Guarani): Métraux BBAE CXLIII (3) 93.

A222. *Sun-god bitten by snake, leaves earth for heaven.* Egyptian: Müller 80ff.

A225. *Son of the sun.* Irish myth: Cross. — Central Brazil: Ehrenreich International Congress of Americanists XIV 661; Navaho: Matthews MAFLS V 104ff.

A116. Twin gods (or trinity of gods).

A226. *Sun father-in-law.* American Indian: *Thompson Tales 312 n. 123.

A227. *Two sun-gods.*

A227.1. *Male sun-god while ascending; female while setting.* Hawaii: Beckwith Myth 12, chap. 2 passim.

A227.2. *One sun-god for night; another for day* (Osiris, Horus). Egyptian: Müller 113.

A240. Moon-god. D. Nielson Die altarabische Mondreligion und die mosaische Ueberlieferung (Strassburg 1904); **Siecke Hermes der Mondgott; Gaster Thespis 291. — Irish myth: Cross; Greek: Fox 186; Egyptian: Müller 32, 33; Maspéro Histoire ancienne des peuples de l'Orient classique 145; Hindu: Keith 90f., Oldenberg Religion des Veda 193, Penzer III 161 n. 1, India: Thompson-Balys, Buddhist myth: Malalasekera I 854, II 735, 962; Japan: Beckwith Myth 102; Finno-Ugric: Holmberg Finno-Ugric 223; Armenian: Ananikian 11.

A240.1. *Moon-goddess.* Usener IV 1; Irish myth: Cross; Greek: Fox 186f. (Artemis, Hekate); India: Thompson-Balys; Tonga: Gifford 181.

A250. Star-god. Gressmann Die hellenistische Gestirnreligion (Leipzig 1925). — Chinese: Werner 106; India: Thompson-Balys.

A116. Twin gods. A121. Stars as deities.

A251. *God of morning star.* *Handwb. d. Abergl. IX Nachträge 17f.; Greek: Fox 247 (Phosphoros).

A252. *God of evening star.* Greek: Fox 247 (Hesperos).

A253. *God of north star.*

A253.1. *Goddess of north star.* Chinese: Werner 144.

A255. *Star-deity and drought-demon fight.* Persian: Carnoy 268.
D2144.2. Contest of heat and cold.

A260. **God of light.** Greek: Fox 179 (Apollo); Icel.: De la Saussaye 253ff. (Balder); Maori: Clark 14, 171n.
A162.2. Combat between god of light and dragon of ocean.

A260.1. *Goddess of light.* India: Thompson-Balys.

A270. **God of dawn.** Gaster Thespis 228.

A270.1. *Goddess of dawn.* Hindu: Keith 32; Greek: Roscher I 1252 s. v. "Eos"; Irish myth: Cross.

A280. **Weather-god.** Irish myth: Cross, Beal XXI 326, 334.
A210. Sky-god. D900. Magic weather phenomena. D2140. Magic control of the elements. F430. Weather-spirits.

A281. *Storm-god.* See also A282. — Babylonian: Spence 95ff., 188; Assyrian: ibid. 218ff.; Persian: Carnoy 264; Japanese: Anesaki 225; Irish myth: Cross.

A281.1. *Storm-goddess.* Hindu: Penzer I 272. — Eskimo: Boas RBAE VI 600.

A282. *Wind-god.* Greek: Grote I 287; Icel.: MacCulloch Eddic 40ff. (Odin), 102 (Njord), De la Saussaye 225; Hindu: Keith 37, 40; India: *Thompson-Balys. — Penzer IV 110 n. 4, VIII 163 n.; Siberian: Holmberg Siberian 457; Finno-Ugric: Holmberg Finno-Ugric 232; Chinese: Ferguson 73. — Maori: Dixon 32; Marshall Is.: Davenport 222; Hawaii: Beckwith Myth 86, 121. — Eskimo: Rasmussen Myter I 99—102; S. Am. Indian (Arua): Lévi-Strauss BBAE CXLIII (3) 379; Bushman: Bleek and Lloyd 101.
F432. Wind-spirit.

A282.0.1. *Wind-goddess.* Eskimo: Rasmussen Myter I 100, Holm 95.

A282.0.1.1. *Facial features of wind-goddess reversed.* Eskimo: Rasmussen Myter I 102.
A123. Monstrous gods.

A282.0.2. *Wind-angel.* Jewish: Neuman.

A282.1. *God of whirlwind.* Typhon. He is represented as having serpents' heads on his shoulders, as having a voice like the sound of many beasts and eyes which flash fire. — Greek: Fox 9.
F526.1. Typhon.

A283. *Cloud-god.* Finno-Ugric: Holmberg Finno-Ugric 234; India: *Thompson-Balys.

A283.1. *Cloud-angel.* Jewish: Neuman.

A284. *God of thunder.* *Harris Boanerges 13ff., 20; Montelius FL XXI (1909) 60. — Icel.: De la Saussaye 236 (Thor); Lithuanian: Gray 319, Balys "Der Donner im lithauischen Volksglauben" Tautosakos Darbai III (1937) 149—238; Finno-Ugric: Holmberg Finno-Ugric 227; Estonian: Eisen Estnische Mythologie 156ff.; Siberian: Holmberg Siberian 443; Armenian: Ananikian 11; Chinese: Werner 198, 201; Greek: Fox 159 (Zeus); Egyptian: Müller 103 (Seth); Hindu: Keith 37 (Parjanya). —

Maori: Beckwith Myth 250; S. Am. Indian (Chiriguano): Métraux RMLP XXXIII 172; American Indian: Alexander N. Am. 287 n. 32.
A791.1. Rainbow as bow of thunder god.

A284.0.1. *Angel of thunder.* Jewish: Neuman.

A284.1. *Goddess of thunder.* Maori: Dixon 57.

A284.2. *Thunderbird.* A mythical giant bird usually thought of as a thunder-god. — *Harris Boanerges 13—30 passim, Harris Picus who is also Zeus vii; *Encyc. Religion and Ethics I 529a; Hatt Asiatic Influences 36ff.; Gaster Thespis 135, 363. — Babylonian: Spence 193; Siberian: Holmberg Siberian 439; India: Thompson-Balys. — African: Werner African 237. — N. A. Indian: Alexander N. Am. 387 n. 32, *Thompson Tales 318 n. 151c.; S. Am. Indian (Chiriguano): Lowie BBAE CXLIII (3) 55, (Toba): Métraux Myths 110. — Cf. Persian: Carnoy 289 (Saēna).
B31. Giant birds.

A284.3. *Appearance of thunder-spirit.* Eskimo: Rasmussen Myter III 61.
F434. Thunder spirits.

A284.3.1. *Thunder god or spirit has very long mouth.* India: Thompson-Balys.

A284.3.2. *Thunder spirit lives in world below earth.* India: Thompson-Balys.

A285. *God of lightning.* Gaster Thespis 213; Irish myth: Cross; Hindu: Keith 36; Chinese: Dawsel Magie und Geheimwissenschaft 150. — Maori: Beckwith Myth 250.

A285.0.1. *Angel of lightning.* Jewish: Neuman.

A285.1. *Lightning weapon of the gods.* Irish myth: Cross.
D1080. Magic weapons. F832.1.1. Gaí bulga. V1.8. Worship of weapons.

A287. *Rain-god.* Gaster Thespis 122f.; *Smith Dragon vii ff., 77f., 86. — Greek: Fox 159 (Zeus); Hindu: Keith 39, 135, 233; India: *Thompson-Balys; Buddhist myth: Malalasekera II 98, 412; Chinese: Werner 206; Maya: Alexander Lat. Am. 134; Antilles: ibid 25; Aztec: ibid. 71; Hawaii: Beckwith Myth 97; Samoa ibid. 19; Easter Is.: Métraux Ethnology 310.
B11.7. Dragon as rain-spirit. D2143.1. Rain produced by magic.

A287.0.1. *Rain-god and wind-god brought back* in order to make liveable weather. Have been banished by sun-god. — India: Thompson-Balys.
A282. Wind-god. L351. Contest of wind and sun.

A287.1. *Rain-goddess.* India: Thompson-Balys.

A287.2. *St. Peter as ruler for the air and rain.* Often misunderstands the orders of God. — Lithuanian: Balys Legends No. 31.
D2140. Magic control of the elements.

A288. *Rainbow-goddess.* Greek: Fox 241 (Iris). — Chibcha: Alexander Lat. Am. 204.

A289. *Other weather-gods.*

A289.1. *Frost-god.* Gaster Thespis 345; Type 480 (*Roberts 120). — Finno-Ugric: Holmberg Finno-Ugric 233; Icel.: Boberg.

A300—A399. Gods of the underworld.

A300. God of the underworld. Gaster Thespis 136; Greek: Grote I 3; Irish myth: Cross; Babylonian: Spence 105, 150; Buddhist myth: Malalasekera II 695; Korean: Zong in-Sob 92 No. 50; Chinese: Eberhard FFC CXX 200f.; Hawaii: Beckwith Myth 114; Fiji: Beckwith Myth 138; Nukuhiva (Marquesas): Handy 122. — Aztec: Alexander Lat. Am. 57.

F80. Journey to lower world.

A300.1. *Goddess of underworld* (cf. A310.1). Oceania: Beckwith Myth 294; Polynesia: Beckwith Myth 114; Tuamotu: Stimson MS (z-G. 3/1241); Nukuhiva (Marquesas): Handy 121; Tonga: Beckwith Myth 178.

A302. *Angel of hell.* Jewish: Neuman.

A305. *Demigod of underworld.* Tuamotu: Stimson MS (z-G 13/221, 249, 317); Hawaii: Beckwith Myth 155 n. 33.

A307. *Deity ruler of lowest heaven.* Buddhist myth: Malalasekera II 938.

A651. Hierarchy of worlds.

A3[illegible] *Warrior chieftain of underworld.* Tuamotu: Stimson MS (z-G. [illegible]

A3[illegible] of the world of the dead. *Meyer "Der irische Totengott und die Toteninsel" Stzb. d. preussischen Akad. d. Wissenschaften XXXII 537. — Greek: Fox 233 (Hades); Icel.: De la Saussaye 227 (Odin), Boberg; Irish myth: Cross; Siberian: Holmberg Siberian 486; Egyptian: Müller 97 (Osiris); Hindu: Keith 159; India: *Thompson-Balys; Chinese: Eberhard FFC CXX 201f. — Jicarilla Apache: Alexander N. Am. 175, Goddard PaAM VIII 194 n. 1; Aztec: Alexander Lat. Am. 77, 80; Huichol: ibid. 122; Maya: ibid. 139.

A108.1. God of the dead. A487. God of death. A671. Hell. E481. Land of the dead. E481.9. King of the land of the dead. F81. Descent to lower world of dead.

A310.1. *Goddess of world of the dead.* Greek: Fox 230 (Persephone); Icel.: De la Saussaye 280 (Hel), 276 (Freyja), *Boberg, MacCulloch Eddic 303ff.; Armenian: Ananikian 35; Babylonian: Spence 129. — New Zealand (Maori): Dixon 74; Eskimo: Thompson Tales 272 n. 2.

A485.1. Goddess of war.

A310.2. *God of the slain.* Icel.: MacCulloch Eddic 44 (Odin).

A310.3. *God of the hanged.* Icel.: MacCulloch Eddic 43ff. (Odin).

A310.4. *God of suicide.* Hawaii: Beckwith Myth 177.

A311. *Conductor of the dead.* Greek: Farnell Cults of the Greek States V 15ff.; Egyptian: Müller 111. Hawaii: Beckwith Myth 72, 110.

A316. *Goddess divides time between upper and lower worlds.* Persephone spends six months on earth and six in Hades. — *Frazer Apollodorus I 41 n. 2.

A317. *Demon god lies in wait for spirits descending to underworld.* Tuamotu: Stimson MS (T-G 3/18).

A318. *Rank of the gods in Hades.* Chinese: Werner 98.

A400—A499. Gods of the earth.

A400. God of earth. Greek: *Grote I 3; Irish myth: Cross; Egyptian: Müller 42; Persian: Carnoy 260; India: Thompson-Balys; Chinese: Graham, Eberhard FFC CXX 42, 120.

A400.0.1. *Gods of earth.* Irish myth: Cross.

A1611.10. Origin of the Tuatha Dé Danann. A1659.1. Origin of the Fomorians. F251.1. Fairies as descendants of early race of gods. F251.1.2. Fairies as gods. V1.16.1. Fairies seek to induce mortal to worship them.

A400.1. *Goddess of earth.* Gaster Thespis 128 n., 51; Finnish: Holmberg Finno-Ugric 243ff., 413ff.; Livonian: Loortis Liivi rahva usund I 256; Lithuanian, Chuvashan: Wolter "Die Erdgöttin der Tschuwaschen und Litauer" Archiv f. Religionswiss. II 358ff.; Icel.: MacCulloch Eddic 194; Hindu: Penzer II 241, IV 177 n. 1; India: Thompson-Balys. — Haitian: Alexander Lat. Am. 34; Aztec: ibid. 74f.; Chibcha: ibid. 204.

A111. Mother of the gods.

A400.2. *Angel of earth.* Jewish: Neuman.

A401. *Mother Earth.* The earth is conceived of as the mother of all things (cf. A431.1). — **Dieterich Mutter Erde; A. Mayer Erdmutter und Hexe (München 1936); *Lang Myth. 299ff.; Fb. "jord" II 44b IV 247a; Nöldeke "Mutter-Erde bei den Semiten" Archiv f. Religionswiss. VIII 161. — Icel.: MacCulloch Eddic 194, 328; Finnish: Holmberg Finno-Ugric 239; Siberian: Holmberg Siberian 459; Hindu: Keith 230; India: *Thompson-Balys. — African: Werner African 125. — N. Am. Indian: *Thompson Tales 280 n. 37a, Alexander N. Am. 91f., 289 n. 34.

A111. Mother of the gods. A625. World parents: sky-father and earth-mother. A1234.1. Earth as virgin mother of Adam.

A401.1. *Mother Earth pregnant with Adam.* Jewish: Neuman.

A405. *Nature gods.* Hawaii: Beckwith Myth 2, chap. I passim.

A410. Local gods. Chinese: Graham; Irish myth: Cross.

A411. *Household gods.* Irish myth: Cross; Istrian: Machal 229; Slavic (general): ibid. 240ff.; Germanic: Meyer Germanen 213ff.; Roman: (Lares and Penates) *Frazer Ovid II 470 n. 1, IV 12ff., Roscher II 1868 s. v. "Lares"; Siberian: Holmberg Siberian 454; Finno-Ugric: Holmberg Finno-Ugric 113ff.; Estonian: Loorits Grundzüge I 543—570; Chinese: Ferguson 75.

B593. Animal as house spirit. F480. House-spirits.

A411.1. *Door-gods.* Chinese: Werner 172.

A411.2. *Kitchen-gods.* Chinese: Werner 166; India: Thompson-Balys.

A411.3. *Dairy-god.* India: Thompson-Balys.

A411.4. *Hearth-god.* Greek: Grote I 55 (Hestia, Vesta).

A412. *City-gods.* Chinese: Werner 403, Eberhard FFC CXX 42, 67.

D1380.0.1. Magic object protects a city.

A413. *God of roads (streets).* *Frazer Pausanias II 417. — Irish myth: Cross.

A413.1. *God of cross-roads.* Frazer Ovid II 453ff. — Irish myth: Cross.

A414. *God of boundaries.* *Frazer Ovid I 95ff., II 481ff. — India: Thompson-Balys.

A415. *God of clans or nations.* Jewish: Neuman. — Hopi: Alexander N. Am. 189.

M119.2. Swearing by clan gods.

A417. *Gods of the Quarters.* A god or spirit for each of the world-quarters, north, south, east, and west. — Japanese: Anesaki 243; Chinese: Werner 240. — Marshall Is.: Davenport 222; American Indian: *Alexander N. Am. 286 n. 31; Maya: Alexander Lat. Am. 137.

A871. Earth square with four quarters. A1127. Winds of the four quarters established. A1182. Determination of world quarters.

A417.1. *Beast guardians of the four quarters.* Hindu: Penzer VIII 75f., 108 n. 1 (elephants). — Sia: Alexander N. Am. 203.

Z71.2.1. Formula: north, south, east, west (the cardinal directions).

A418. *Deity of particular mountain* (cf. A495). Buddhist myth: Malalasekera II 529; Korean: Zong in-Sob 170 no. 73; Chinese: Eberhard FFC CXX 185ff.

A418.1. *Angel of mountains.* Jewish: Neuman.

A419. *Local gods — miscellaneous.*

A419.1. *Deity of particular forest.* Hawaii: Beckwith Myth 17.

A419.1.1. *Angel of the bush.* Jewish: Neuman.

A419.2. *Deity of the deserts.*

A419.2.1. *Angel of the deserts.* Jewish: Neuman.

A419.3. *Gods of seat-braces on canoe.* Hawaii: Beckwith Myth 16.

A420. God of water. Irish myth: Cross; Icel.: MacCulloch Eddic 167; Babylonian: Spence 76, 111ff.; Persian: Carnoy 260; India: Thompson-Balys; Chinese: Werner 217, 222; Finno-Ugric: Holmberg Die Wassergottheiten der finno-ugrischen Völker (MSFO XXXII); Gaster Thespis 123. — S. Am. Indian (Toba): Métraux MAFLS XL 52; Hawaii: Beckwith Myth 541.

A1110. Establishment of present order: waters. F420. Water-spirits.

A420.1. *Water-goddess.* India: Thompson-Balys.

A421. *Sea-god.* Gaster Thespis 123; Icel.: MacCulloch Eddic 102 (Njord), 171 (Aegir); Irish myth: Cross; Greek: Fox 210, *Grote I 3, 10, 173. — Society Is., Cook Group: Dixon 39; Hawaii: Beckwith Myth 19, 61, 97; Tahiti: Beckwith Myth 360, Henry 122; Tuamotu: Stimson MS (z-G. 13/441); Tonga: Gifford 87; Easter Is.: Métraux Ethnology 311.

A121.0.1. God as shape-shifter. A171.0.1. God drives chariot over waves. F531.6.15.6. Giant rolls like wheel. V11.2. Sacrifice to sea. Z118.1. Sea personified as tresses of sea-god's wife.

A421.0.1. *Angel of the deep.* Jewish: *Neuman.

A421.1. *Sea-goddess.* Greek: *Grote I 173 (Thetis); Icel.: MacCulloch Eddic 190 (Ran); Babylonian: Gilgamesch X line 1ff., cf. p. 136ff. (Jensen's edition); India: Thompson-Balys; Japanese: Anesaki 269; Chinese: Ferguson 72; Buddhist myth: Malalasekera II 492. — Tuamotu: Stimson MS (z-G 13/441).

A421.1.1. *Sea-queen and hand maidens entice lovers.* Tuamotu: Stimson MS (z-G. 13/441).

B53. Siren.

A423. *Waves as girls, daughters or widows of the sea-god.* Icel.: Boberg, MacCulloch Eddic 190.

A425. *River-god.* Greek: Fox 256, *Frazer Pausanias II 527; Egyptian: Müller 45ff.; Russian: Rambaud La Russie épique 216f.; India: *Thompson-Balys; Jewish: Neuman; Chinese: Werner 336, Eberhard FFC CXX 135—141.

D1432. Waters magically pursue man.

A425.0.1. *Angel of rivers.* Jewish: Neuman.

A425.1. *River goddess.* Irish myth: Cross; Hindu: Penzer II 189 n. 1; India: *Thompson-Balys.

F424. Water-nymph. N815.0.2.1. Gift of gold bracelet from river goddess.

A425.1.1. *Stream is wife of deity.* India: Thompson-Balys.

A427. *God of springs.*

A427.1. *Goddess of springs and wells.* In Greek myth, the nymphs were regarded as deities of springs. In Babylonian, Ishtar, the goddess of fertility had this function. — Greek: Fox 257; Persian and Babylonian: Carnoy 278.

V134. Sacred (holy) wells.

A430. God of vegetation. **Siecke Der Vegetationsgott. — Irish myth: Cross; Persian: Carnoy 260; Chinese: Graham. — Aztec: Alexander Lat. Am. 76.

F440. Vegetation spirits.

A430.0.1. *Angel in charge of vegetation.* Jewish: Neuman.

A430.1. *Goddess of vegetation.* Irish myth: Cross.

A111. Mother of the gods.

A430.1.1. *Goddess of splendor of spring.* Hindu: Penzer I 112; Japanese: Anesaki 233.

A430.1.2. *Goddess of autumn leaves.* Japanese: Anesaki 234.

A431. *God of fertility.* Irish myth: Cross; Greek: Fox 160; Roman: Frazer Ovid II 172; Icel.: De la Saussaye 252; Krappe "Ingvi-Frey and Aengus Mac Oc" Scandinavian Studies (1943) 174—178. — Hawaii: Beckwith Myth 13, 93, chap. II passim; Marshall Is.: Davenport 222.

A431.1. *Goddess of fertility* (cf. A401). Irish myth: Cross; Greek-Roman: Fox 292; Babylonian: Carnoy 278 (Ishtar), Spence 124; Lappish: Reuterskiöld De Nordiska Lapparnas Religion 102ff. — Hawaii: Beckwith Myth 185; Icel.: Boberg.

A111. Mother of the gods. A427.1. Goddess of springs and wells. As goddess of fertility. A475.1. Goddess of love.

A431.1.1. *In absence of goddess of fertility, no reproduction of life.* Wesselski Archiv Orientální I 304.

A431.1.2. *Goddess of fertility of wild forest plants.* Hawaii: Beckwith Myth 289.

A431.1.3. *Goddess causes famine.* Hawaii: Beckwith Myth 289.

A431.1.4. *Goddess of dryness and sterility.* Chinese: Eberhard FFC CXX 203f.

A432. *God of agriculture.* Irish myth: Cross; Roman: Frazer Ovid III 2 n. 1; Finno-Ugric: Holmberg Finno-Ugric 244; India: Thompson-Balys; Japanese: Anesaki 232; Chinese: Werner 239. — Maori: Dixon 32; Hawaii: Beckwith Myth 15, 20, 61, and chap. II passim.

A431. God of fertility. A1440. Acquisition of crafts. V1.7. Plough worship.

A432.0.1. *God plants fields.* *Dh I 192ff. India: Thompson-Balys.

A432.0.2. *Plowman god.* Irish myth: Cross.
A1441.2. Origin of yoking oxen.

A432.1. *Goddess of agriculture.* Irish myth: Cross (A432.0.2); Greek: Fox 230.

A433. *Gods or goddesses of special crops.* Mangaia (Cook Is.): Clark 140.

A433.1. *Corn-god (goddess).* *Frazer Golden Bough VII passim; Gaster Thespis 373. — Finno-Ugric: Holmberg Finno-Ugric 241; Greek: Fox 226; Jewish: Neuman; India: Thompson-Balys; Chinese: Eberhard FFC CXX 231 No. 177. — Aztec: Alexander Lat. Am. 75; Zuñi: Alexander N. Am. 188; Pawnee: ibid. 81, 92; Arikara: ibid. 107.

A433.1.1. *God of rice-fields.* India: *Thompson-Balys.
D1432.1. Water gradually envelops girl filling pitcher. Work of malevolent rice spirit.

A433.2. *The seven grain sisters.* India: Thompson-Balys.

A433.3. *God of the vine.* Greek: Grote I 239 (Dionysus).

A433.4. *God (goddess) of fruit.* Roman: Fox 290 (Pomona); Jewish: Neuman.

A433.5. *God (angel) of grass.* Jewish: Neuman.

A434. *Goddess (god) of flowers.* Roman: *Frazer Ovid III 417; India: Thompson-Balys. — Aztec: Alexander Lat. Am. 77f.

A435. *God of trees and forests.* Greek: Fox 267 (Pan); Buddhist myth: Malalasekera I 283, II 253; Jewish: Neuman. — Maori: Dixon 32.
F440. Vegetation spirit. F441.2. Tree spirit. V1.1. Worship of trees. V114. Sacred groves (forests).

A435.1. *Bamboo goddess.* India: Thompson-Balys.

A435.2. *Fig tree as god.* India: Thompson-Balys.

A440. God of animals. Jewish: Neuman; Irish myth: Cross.
A113. Totemistic gods. A131. Gods with animal features. A132. God in animal form.

A440.1. *Goddess of animals.* Penzer I 272 (Ishtar).

A441. *God (goddess) of domestic animals.* Persian: Carnoy 260; Irish myth: Cross.

A441.1. *God of domestic beasts.*

A441.1.1. *Goddess of buffaloes.* India: Thompson-Balys.

A441.1.2. *God of flocks.* Russian: Machal 300.
F241.5. Fairies have herds of deer.

A441.2. *God of domestic fowls.* Hawaii: Beckwith Myth 120.

A443. *God (goddess) of wild animals.* Irish myth: Cross.

A443.1. *God of wild beasts.*

A443.2. *God of wild fowls.*

A443.2.1. *God of owls.* Hawaii: Beckwith Myth 123.

A445. *God of fish.* Hawaii: Beckwith Myth 11, 60, 90.

A445.0.1. *Angel of fishes.* Jewish: Neuman.

A445.1. *God of the squid.* Hawaii: Beckwith Myth 60.

A445.2. *God of eels.* Maori: Clark 163; Samoa: Clark 70.

A446. *God of reptiles.*

A446.1. *God of lizards.* Maori: Clark 91.

A446.1.1. *God whose shadow on earth is a lizard.* Tahiti: Beckwith Myth 360.

A446.2. *God of the cutworm.* Hawaii: Beckwith Myth.

A450. God of trades and professions.

A450.1. *God "of many arts".* Irish myth: Cross.

A451. *Artisan-god.* Irish myth: Cross; Hindu: Keith 50 (Tvastr).
A141. God as craftsman.

A451.1. *God of smith-work.* Gaster Thespis 136, 154f.; Irish: MacCulloch Celtic 28; Greek: Fox 206 (Hephaistos); Norse: Herrmann Nordische Mythologie 115ff. (Weland).
A142. Smith of the gods.

A451.1.1. *Goddess of smith-work.* Irish myth: Cross.

A451.2. *God of carpenters.* Tonga: Beckwith Myth 317.

A451.2.1. *God as canoe builder.* Hawaii: Beckwith Myth 15.

A451.3. *God of handicrafts.*

A451.3.1. *Goddess of weaving and spinning.* Greek: Grote I 51.

A451.4. *Goddess of pottery.* Greek: Grote I 51.

A452. *God of hunting.* Icel.: MacCulloch Eddic 156 (Ullr); Assyrian: Spence 216. — Cherokee: Alexander N. Am. 69.

A452.1. *Goddess of hunting.* Greek: Fox 183; Icel.: MacCulloch Eddic 103ff., Boberg.
A440. God of animals.

A453. *Shepherd-god.* Greek: Grote I 57; Babylonian: Spence 126ff. (Tammuz); India: Thompson-Balys.

A454. *God of healing.* *Jayne The Healing Gods of Ancient Civilizations (New Haven 1925); *Hopf Die Heilgötter und Heilstätten des Altertums (Tübingen 1904). — Irish myth: Cross; Greek: Fox 179, *Grote I 166f.; Hindu: Penzer III 258; India: Thompson-Balys; Chinese: Werner 247. — Hawaii: Beckwith Myth 115.
A220. Sun-god. D1240. Magic waters and medicines. D2161. Magic healing power. F344. Fairies heal mortals. P424. Physician.

A454.0.1. *Angel of healing* (Raphael). Jewish: Neuman.

A454.1. *Goddess of healing.* Icel.: MacCulloch Eddic 186 (Eir); Irish myth: Cross; Greek: Fox 184 (Artemis); India: Thompson-Balys.

A455. *God of fishing.* Hawaii: Beckwith Myth 15.

A456. *God of sailors.*

A456.1. *Goddess of sailors.* India: Thompson-Balys.

A457. *God of thieves.* Tahiti, Mangaia, Rarotonga, Maori: Beckwith Myth 447; Easter Is.: Métraux Ethnology 310.

A459. *God of trades and professions — miscellaneous.*

A459.1. *God or goddess of skiing (or snow-shoes).* Icel.: MacCulloch Eddic 105 (Skadi), 156 (Ullr), Boberg.

A460. Gods of abstractions. Greek: Fox 299.

Z110. Abstractions personified.

A461. *God of wisdom.* Irish myth: Cross; Norse: Herrmann Nordische Mythologie 320 (Odin); Greek: Grote I 10 (Apollo); Babylonian: Spence 184ff.

A461.1. *Goddess of wisdom.* Greek: Grote I 10 (Athene). — Tahiti: Henry 85.

A111. Mother of the gods. A454.1. Goddess of healing. A465.1.1. Goddess of poetry.

A462. *God of beauty.* Tahiti: Henry 128.

A462.1. *Goddess of beauty.* Hindu: Penzer VII 129 n. 4, 137; India: Thompson-Balys; Buddhist myth: Malalasekera II 767.

A463. *God of fate.* Irish myth: Cross; Greek: Grote I 10; Egyptian: Müller 52; Slavic (general): Machal Slavic 249ff.; Siberian: Holmberg Siberian 392.

A178. God (goddess) as prophet. M300. Prophecies. N110. Luck and fate personified.

A463.0.1. *God of fate in shape of golden frog.* India: Thompson-Balys.

D195. Transformation: man to frog.

A463.1. *The Fates.* Goddesses who preside over the fates of men. — Wehrhan Die Sage 81; Gaster Thespis 348. — Norse: De la Saussaye 312, Corpus Poeticum Boreale I 32, 36, 47, 131, MacCulloch Eddic 238ff., *Boberg; Greek: Grote I 7; Irish myth: Cross, Beal. 21, 318, 336; Lappish: Holmberg Finno-Ugric 256ff.; Estonian: Loorits Grundzüge I 527f. — India: Thompson-Balys.

F315. Fairy predicts birth of child. F317. Fairy predicts future greatness of (new-born) child. F343.11. Fairy offers man change of form and feature for aid in battle. F347. Fairy adviser. F 361. Fairy's revenge. F362. Fairies cause disease. F363. Fairies cause death. G201. Three witch sisters. N110. Luck and fate personified.

A463.1.1. *The Fates weave.* Icel.: Boberg.

A463.1.2. *Three fates in house in woods allot destiny to people.* Lithuanian: Balys Index No. *936.

A464. *God of justice.* Icel.: MacCulloch Eddic 162 (Forseti); Jewish: Neuman; Assyrian: *Spence 222; Persian: Carnoy 260f.; Hindu: Penzer I 4, 84 n. 1; India: Thompson-Balys.

A464.1. *Goddess of justice.* Greek: Fox 6 (Themis).

A465. *God of the arts.* Greek: Grote I 43 (Apollo).

A450.1. God "of many arts."

A465.0.1. *The Nine Muses, patronesses of the arts.* Greek: Fox 239, Grote I 10.

A465.1. *God of poetry.* Greek: Fox 181; Irish myth: Cross; Icel.: Mac Culloch Eddic 55 (Odin), 160 (Bragi).

A527.4. Culture hero as poet (musician). A1464.1. Acquisition of poetry. Z117. Poetry personified.

A465.1.1. *Goddess of poetry.* Irish: MacCulloch Celtic 40, Cross.

A465.2. *God of music.* Greek: Fox 181.

A465.2.0.1. *God as harper.* Irish myth: Cross.

A465.2.1. *Goddess of music.* Hindu: Penzer I 243; India: Thompson-Balys; Japanese: Anesaki 268.

A112.1.1.1. Goddess of music and dance born of incestuous union.

A465.3. *God of eloquence and learning.* Irish myth: Cross.

A465.3.0.1. *God of eloquence and learning as inventor of ogam alphabet.* Irish myth: Cross.

A541.1. Culture hero invents and teaches the Irish language. A1469.2. Origin of ogam inscriptions. D1266.1.1. Magic ogam writing.

A465.3.1. *Goddess of eloquence and learning.* Hindu: Penzer I 1 n. 4, 18 n. 1, 31 n. 3.

A465.4. *God of the dance.* Hawaii: Beckwith Myth 16.

A465.4.1. *Goddess of the dance.* India: Thompson-Balys.

A465.5. *God of pictorial art.*

A465.5.1. *God of tattooing.* Tahiti: Henry 234.

A466. *Goddess of fame.* Hindu: Penzer II 90, 116.

A467. *God of happiness.* Chinese: Werner 169.

A467.1. *Angel of peace.* Jewish: Neuman.

A468. *The three Graces.* Greek: Fox 236, Grote I 10.

A471. *God of prophecy.* Greek: Fox 178; Norse: Herrmann Nordische Mythologie 306ff. (Odin); India: *Thompson-Balys.

A178. God (goddess) as prophet. M300. Prophecies.

A471.1. *Goddess of prophecy.* Irish myth: Cross; Icel.: Boberg.

A461. God (goddess) of wisdom.

A472. *God of sleep.*

A472.0.1. *Angel of insomnia.* Jewish: Neuman.

A472.1. *Goddess of sleep.* Hindu: Penzer V 197.

A473. *God of wealth.* Irish myth: Cross; Greek: Roscher III 2572 s. v. "Plutos"; Icel.: Herrmann Nordische Mythologie 204; Hindu: Penzer X 163 s. v. "God of Wealth", X 205 s. v. "Kuvera"; Chinese: Werner 170, Eberhard FFC CXX 176, 196.

A473.0.1. *Angel of poverty.* Jewish: Neuman; India: Thompson-Balys (A489.3).

A473.1. *Goddess of wealth.* Irish myth: Cross. — Hindu: Penzer X 206 s. v. "Lakshmi"; India: *Thompson-Balys; Japanese: Anesaki 268.

A111. Mother of the gods. N111. Fortuna.

A473.1.1. *Goddess of prosperity.* India: Thompson-Balys.

A474. *Gods of youth and age.*

A474.1. *God of youth.* Irish myth: Cross.

A474.1.1. *Goddess of youth.* Icel.: MacCulloch Eddic 178 (Idunn); Greek: Fox 240.

A153.4. Magic food rejuvenates the gods. A191. Goddess rejuvenates self when old.

A474.2. *God (goddess) of longevity.* Chinese: Werner 171, 214, Ferguson 81; Japanese: Anesaki 280.

A191.1. Great age of the gods.

A475. *God of love.* Krappe "Diarmuid and Grainne" FL XLVII (1936) 347—361. — Irish myth: Cross; Hindu: Keith 141; Penzer X 163 s. v. "God of Love"; Greek: Roscher I 1339 s. v. "Eros".

T0. Love. T56.2. Image of God of Love sent to fetch bride.

A475.0.1. *Cupid with arrows of lead and gold.* *Reinhard PMLA XXXVIII 438 n. 42.

A475.0.2. *Marriage-god.* India: *Thompson-Balys.

A475.1. *Goddess of love.* Krappe "The Bearded Venus" FL LVI (1945) 325—335. — Irish myth: Cross; Greek: Fox 198, Grote I 5; Norse: MacCulloch Eddic 120 (Freya); Armenian: Ananikian 24f., 38f.; Babylonia: Spence 124. — Hawaii: Beckwith Myth 185, 186; Aztec: Alexander Lat. Am. 78; S. Am. Indian (Chibcha): Kroeber BBAE CXLIII (2) 908.

A111. Mother of the gods. A431.1. Goddess of fertility.

A475.1.1. *Goddess of love with thousand faces.* India: Thompson-Balys.

A475.1.1.1. *Goddess of thousand eyes discovered by lousing.* India: Thompson-Balys.

A123.3. God with many eyes. G253. Witch's horns discovered by lousing her.

A476. *Goddess of chastity.* Greek: Fox 185; Icel.: Boberg.

T300. Chastity and celibacy.

A477. *Goddess of childbirth.* *Ploss Das Kind I 18ff.; Penzer I 272. — Greek: Fox 164, 167, 185.; Finno-Ugric: *Holmberg Finno-Ugric 252ff.; Armenian: Ananikian 25; Siberian: Holmberg Siberian 414. — India: Thompson-Balys. — Hawaii: Beckwith Myth 285.

T500. Conception and birth. T584. Parturition.

A477.1. *Goddess of cradle.* India: Thompson-Balys.

A478. *God of disease.*

A478.1. *Goddess of pestilence.* *Krappe "Artemis Mysia" Classical Philology XXXIX (1944) 178—183. — Hindu: Penzer I 147.

F493. Spirit of plague.

A478.2. *God (goddess) of smallpox.* India: *Thompson-Balys; Korean: Zong in-Sob 57 No. 32.

A478.3. *God (goddess) of cholera.* India: *Thompson-Balys.

A478.4. *God of fevers.* India: Thompson-Balys.

A478.5. *Devil of leprosy.* India: Thompson-Balys.

A478.6. *Angel (demon) of blindness.* Jewish: Neuman.

A481. *God of intoxication* (or of wine). W. F. Otto, Dionysos: Mythos und Kultus (Frankfurt a. M. 1933). — Greek: Fox 219; Hindu: Keith 46; India: Thompson-Balys. — S. Am. Indian (Chibcha): Kroeber BBAE CXLIII (2) 908.

A482. *God of gambling* (luck). Hindu: Penzer IV 240 n. 1.
N0. Wągers and gambling. N111. Fortuna.

A482.1. *Goddess of ill-luck.* Hindu: Penzer VI 106; India: *Thompson-Balys.

A482.1.1. *Spirit of ill-luck a son of a god.* India: Thompson-Balys.

A482.2. *Goddess of good luck* (Lakshmi). India: Thompson-Balys.

A483. *God of mercy.* Jewish: Neuman.

A483.0.1. *Angel of mercy.* Jewish: Neuman.

A483.1. *Goddess of mercy.* Chinese: Werner 251.

A484. *God of oaths.*

A484.1. *Goddess of oaths.* Icel.: MacCulloch Eddic 186 (Vár).

A485. *God of war.* *H. Lommel Der arische Kriegsgott (Frankfurt a. M. 1939). — Irish myth: Cross; Greek: Fox 189; Norse: MacCulloch Eddic 40, 55 (Odin), 98 (Tyr); Armenian: Ananikian 42; Hindu: Penzer VII 137, VIII 180; Chinese: Ferguson 95; Babylonian: Spence 106ff.; Jewish: Neuman. — Aztec: Alexander Lat. Am. 58; Maya: ibid. 139. — Tahiti: Henry 120; Maori: Clark 14; Marquesas: Handy 110; Hawaii: Beckwith Myth 15.

A485.1. *Goddess of war.* Gaster Thespis 136; Irish myth: Cross; Roman: Frazer Ovid IV 151ff.; Assyrian: Spence 213; India: Thompson-Balys.
A125.1. Goddess of war in shape of hag. A172. Gods intervene in battle. F418. Spirits hover in air shrieking over battle. Z129.2. War personified.

A485.2. *Valkyries* (shield-maidens). Demigoddesses who attend battle. — *Handwb. d. Abergl. IX Nachträge 240ff; **Golther "Der Valkyrenmythus" Abhandl. d. Akad. d. Wiss. (München), 1. Kl., XVIII, Abt. 2, 401ff.; *Krappe Modern Language Review XXI 55 ff.; *Hertz Aus Dichtung und Sage 31ff. — Irish myth: Cross; Norse: De la Saussaye 304ff., MacCulloch Eddic 248ff., 259, 283—84, 314, Penzer X 345 s. v. "Valkyries".

A485.3. *God of single-combats.* Norse: MacCulloch Eddic 156 (Ullr).

A486. *The Furies.* Goddesses of vengeance. — Greek: Fox 275, Frazer Apollodorus I 5 n. 4; India: Thompson-Balys. — Hawaii: Beckwith Myth 115.

A487. *God of death.* *Wesselski Archiv Orientální I 300ff. — Hindu: Penzer X 365 s. v. "Yama"; Buddhist myth: Malalasekera II 680; India: *Thompson-Balys; Maori: Clark 8, 135; Marshall Is.: Davenport 222; S. Am. Indian (Toba): Métraux Myths 19; Icel.: Boberg.
A107. Gods of darkness and of light. A108.1. God of the dead. A310. God of the world of the dead. A1335.11. God of world of the dead demands that men die so he will have subjects. D651.1.3. Queen transforms herself to defeat god of death. F160.0.2. Fairy otherworld confused with land of the dead. Z111. Death personified.

A487.0.1. *Death kills only those whose time it is to die.* India: Thompson-Balys.

M341.1. Prophecy: death at certain time.

A487.1. *Goddess of death.* Hindu: Penzer IV 110 n. 3.

A488. *God of destruction.* India: Thompson-Balys

A489. *Gods of abstractions — miscellaneous.*

A489.1. *Goddess of protection.* India: Thompson-Balys.

A489.2. *God of strength.* India: Thompson-Balys.

A489.3. *God of fear.*

A489.3.1. *Angel of fear.* Jewish: Neuman.

A489.4. *God of laughter.* Greek: Hesiod (Momus).

A490. Miscellaneous gods of the earth. *Hartmann Die germanische Gottheit des Jahres und des Lebens (Halle 1935).

A491. *God of travelers.* Greek: Fox 195; Chinese: Ferguson 82; Tahiti: Beckwith Myth 221.

A413. God of roads (streets). A413.1. God of cross-roads.

A492. *God of metals.* Irish myth: Cross; Persian: Carnoy 260.

V1.8. Worship of weapons.

A493. *God of fire.* Greek: Fox 205; Russian: Machal 298; Persian: Carnoy 260, 284; Jewish: Neuman; Hindu: Keith 43, Penzer X 163 s. v. "God of Fire" (Agni); India: *Thompson-Balys; Buddhist myth: Malalasekera I 952, II 8; Armenian: Ananikian 33; Finno-Ugric: Holmberg Finno-Ugric 235; Siberian: Holmberg Siberian 454; Chinese: Ferguson 76, Werner 237, 283. — Huichol: Alexander Lat. Am. 121; Maori: Clark 41; Hawaii: Beckwith Myth 170; Tahiti: Henry 130, 241; Icel.: Boberg.

A220. Sun-god. D1271. Magic fire.

A493.0.1. *Angel of fire.* Jewish: Neuman.

A493.1. *Goddess of fire.* India: Thompson-Balys; Oceanic: Beckwith Myth 167ff.

A493.2. *God of the furnace.* India: Thompson-Balys.

A494. *Food-goddess.* India: Thompson-Balys; Japanese: Anesaki 232.

A495. *Mountain-god.* Chinese: Ferguson 91.

A496. *God of the seasons.* India: *Thompson-Balys.

A496.1. *God of spring.* Buddhist myth: Malalasekera I 992.

A497. *Echo.*

D2065.6. Person abducted by Echo crazed and dumb.

A497.1. *Echo invisible.* India: Thompson-Balys.

A498. *Deity of stone.* India: *Thompson-Balys.

A499. *Other deities.*

A499.1. *Python-goddess.* India: Thompson-Balys.

A499.2. *Goddess of the hair.* India: Thompson-Balys.

A499.3. *God of stones.* Hawaii: Beckwith Myth 88.

A499.4. *God of sorcery.* Hawaii: Beckwith Myth 15, 29f., 108.

A499.4.1. *Goddess of sorcery.* Hawaii: Beckwith Myth 114.

A499.5. *God of dreams.* Greek: Grote II 115.

A499.6. *God of poison.* Hawaii: Beckwith Myth 112.

A499.7. *Goddess of the parasol.* Buddhist myth: Malalasekera I 421.

A500—A599. Demigods and culture heroes.

A500. Demigods and culture heroes. Irish myth: Cross; Hawaii: *Beckwith Myth 60.

C566. Tabus of heroes. Z200. Heroes.

A501. *Groups of demigods.*

A501.1. *Seven demigods.* Siberian and Indo-Iranian: Holmberg Siberian 402ff.

A502. *Heroes or demigods as fourth race of men.* Greek: Grote I 62.

A504. *Male virgin demigod.* Tuamotu: Stimson MS (z-G. 3/1301).

A506. *Half-spirit, half-man.* Samoa: Beckwith Myth 368.

A510. Origin of the culture hero (demigod).

A510.1. *Culture hero as god.* Irish myth: Cross.

A510.2. *Culture hero reborn.* Irish myth: Cross.

E600. Reincarnation.

A511. *Birth and rearing of culture hero* (demigod). Irish myth: Cross.

T510. Miraculous conception. T540. Miraculous birth.

A511.1. *Birth of culture hero.* Hawaii: Beckwith Myth 227.

A511.1.1. *Culture hero snatched from mother's side.* *Dh I 11. — Finnish: Kalevala rune 1. — S. Am. Indian (Tehuelche): Alexander Lat. Am. 335, (Jivaro): Métraux RMLP XXXIII 148f., (Warrau): Métraux ibid. 146, (Kaiguà): Métraux ibid. 139, (Chiriguano): Métraux ibid. 156, (North Peru): Métraux ibid. 133, (Eastern Brazil): Lowie BBAE CXLIII (1) 434.

T584.1. Birth through the mother's side.

A511.1.1.1. *River flows from corpse of mythical mother of culture hero.* S. Am. Indian (Amuesha): Métraux RMLP XXXIII 131.

A511.1.2. *Culture hero speaks before birth.* Krappe Zeitschrift für deutsches Altertum LXXII (1935) 161—171. — African: Werner African 213.

T575. Child speaks before birth.

A511.1.2.1. *Twin culture heroes quarrel before birth.* (Cf. A515.1.1.) — Dh I 11; Jewish: Neuman.

A525. Good and bad culture heroes. T575.1.3. Twins quarrel before birth in mother's womb.

A511.1.2.2. *Culture hero in mother's womb indicates direction* to be taken by her. S. Am. Indian (Tupinamba): Métraux BBAE CXLIII (3) 132, (Apapacuvo-Guarani): Métraux RMLP XXXIII 139.

A511.1.3. *Culture hero incarnated through birth from virgin.* Siberian: Holmberg Siberian 387.

A1411.2. Theft of light by being swallowed and reborn. E600. Reincarnation.

A511.1.3.1. *Demigod son of king's unmarried sister (daughter) by god.* Irish myth: Cross.

A188. Gods (goddesses) unite with mortals. Z255. Hero born out of wedlock.

A511.1.3.2. *Demigod son of king's unmarried sister by her brother.* Irish myth: Cross.

A164.1. Brother-sister marriage of the gods. T415. Brother-sister incest.

A511.1.3.3. *Immaculate conception of culture hero.* Hawaii: Beckwith Myth 227; S. Am. Indian (Chiriguano): Métraux BBAE CXLIII (3) 484, (Manasi): Metraux ibid. 393.

A511.1.4. *Magic origin of culture hero.*

A511.1.4.1. *Origin of culture hero from bursting stone.* Oceanic (Banks Group, Tonga, Celebes, Union Group, Gilbert Group): Dixon 111.

A511.1.4.2. *Hero formed by god out of mother's apron.* Maori: Beckwith Myth 231.

A511.1.4.3. *Birth of culture heroes from human bones* swallowed by jaguar's human wife. S. Am. Indian (Bacairi): Levi-Strauss BBAE CXLIII (3) 347.

A511.1.4.4. *Culture hero creates a companion from a toenail.* S. Am. Indian (Yurakare): Métraux RMLP XXXIII 144.

A511.1.5. *Culture hero son of mortal (half-mortal) father.* Irish myth: Cross.

L100. Unpromising hero.

A511.1.6. *Culture hero posthumous child.* Irish myth: Cross.

A516. Expulsion and return of culture hero.

A511.1.7. *Culture hero born three times.* Irish myth: Cross.

E600. Reincarnation.

A511.1.8. *Culture hero son of animal.*

B630. Offspring of marriage to animal.

A511.1.8.1. *Culture hero son of deer mother.* Irish myth: Cross.

B635.3.1. Culture hero licked by deer mother. D114.1. Transformation: man to deer.

A511.1.8.2. *Culture hero offspring of woman and jaguar.* S. Am. Indian (Eastern Brazil): Lowie BBAE CXLIII (1) 434, (Bakairi): Métraux RMLP XXXIII 145.

A511.1.8.3. *Mythical lizards parents of culture hero.* S. Am. Indian (Amuesa): Métraux RMLP XXXIII 149.

A511.1.9. *Culture hero born from egg.* S. Am. Indian (Jivaro): Métraux RMLP XXXIII 148, (Huamachuco): ibid. 151, (North Peru): Métraux ibid. 133.

A511.2. *Care of culture hero.*

A511.2.1. *Abandonment of culture hero at birth.* S. Am. Indian (Tupinamba): Métraux RMLP XXXIII 135, (Chiriguano): Métraux ibid. 142; Maori: Clark 29.

A511.2.1.1. *Abandoned culture hero captured by use of net.* S. Am. Indian (Amuesa): Métraux RMLP XXXIII 132.

L111.2.1. Future hero found in boat (basket, bushes). T572.2.3. Hero an abortion thrown into the bushes. T612. Child born of slain mother cares for itself during infancy. Z210.1. Lodge-boy.

A511.2.2. *Nursing of culture hero.*

B535. Animal nurse. T611. Suckling of children.

A511.2.2.1. *Culture hero suckled by wolf.* Irish myth: Cross.

A511.2.2.2. *Culture hero cared for by tiger.* S. Am. Indian (Yurakari): Métraux RMLP XXXIII 144.

A511.2.3. *Culture hero is hidden in order to escape enemies.* S. Am. Indian (Bakairi): Métraux RMLP XXXIII 145, (Tembe, Kaigua): Métraux ibid. 139.

A511.3. *Education of culture hero.*

A511.3.1. *Culture hero reared in seclusion.* Irish myth: Cross.

A511.3.2. *Culture hero reared (educated) by extraordinary (supernatural) personages.* Irish myth: Cross.

F311.1. Fairy godmother. F311.3. Fairy foster-mother. F340. Gifts from fairies. F345. Fairies instruct mortals.

A511.4. *Growth of culture hero.*

A511.4.1. *Miraculous growth of culture hero.* Philippine (Tinguian): Cole 38, 87, 102; S. Am. Indian (Tupinamba): Métraux RMLP XXXIII 135.

T615. Supernatural growth.

A512. *Parentage of culture hero.* (Cf. also A511.1.8.).

A512.1. *Culture hero's grandmother.* Eskimo (Kodiak): Golder JAFL XVI 16.

A31. Creator's grandmother.

A512.2. *Culture hero creator's son.* Norse: MacCulloch Eddic 328. — S. Am. Indian (Ackawoi) (Orinoco): Alexander Lat. Am. 269, (Guaporé River): Levi-Strauss BBAE CXLIII (3) 378, (Guarani): Métraux BBAE CXLIII (3) 92f.

A0. Creator.

A512.3. *Culture hero as son of god.* Irish myth: Cross; Greek: Grote I 94. — Hawaii: Beckwith Myth 13.

A512.4. *Sun as father of culture hero.* S. Am. Indian (Warrau, Carib): Métraux RMLP XXXIII 123, 145.

A220. Sun-god. A225. Son of the sun.

A513. *Coming of culture hero (demigod).*

A513.1. *Demigods descend from heaven.* Irish myth: Cross. — S. Am. Indian (Tapirapé): Wagley-Galvão BBAE CXLIII (3) 178; Maori: Clark 30.

A1611.10. Origin of the Tuath Dé Danann regarded as an early tribe.

A513.2. *Culture hero arrives (and departs) in boat.* Norse: Boberg, Mac Culloch Eddic 262f.; Old English: Beowulf.

A563. Divinity's departure in boat.

A515. *Pair of culture heroes.* Amazon tribes: Alexander Lat. Am. 311.

A515.1. *Culture heroes brothers.* Araucanian: Alexander Lat. Am. 330; N. Am. Indian: *Thompson Tales 280 n. 35.

A515.1.1. *Twin culture heroes.* (Cf. A511.1.2.1.). P. Saintyves "Les Jumeaux dans l'ethnographie et la mythologie" Revue Anthrop. XXV (1925) 54ff. — Jewish: Neuman; N. Am. Indian (Plains Tribes): Alexander N. Am. 104, 106, (Pima): ibid. 176, (Sia): ibid 204; S. Am. Indian (Jíbaros, Eastern Ecuador): Karsten Myths of the Jíbaros (cf. Boas JAFL XXXII 446), Amazon tribes: Alexander Lat. Am. 311, (Warrau, Carib, Tupinamba, Kaigua, Tembe, Apapocuvá-Guarani, Bakairi, Kaingang, Amuesha, Huamachucho, Chiriguano): Métraux RMLP XXXIII 123, 135f., 138, 145ff., 158—165, (Tenetchara): Wagley-Galvão BBAE CXLIII (3) 147, (Cashinawa, Guarani, Guarayú): Métraux BBAE CXLIII (3) 92f., 438, 685, (Toba): Métraux BBAE CXLIII (1) 368, (Bakairi): Lévi-Strauss BBAE CXLIII (3) 347, (Paressi): Métraux BBAE CXLIII (3) 359. — Tonga: Gifford 20.

A116. Twin gods.

A515.1.1.1. *Twin culture heroes sired by two fathers.* S. Am. Indian (Guarani): Métraux BBAE CXLIII (3) 92f., RMLP XXXIII 136.

T587.1. Birth of twins an indication of unfaithfulness in a wife.

A515.1.1.2. *Twin culture heroes — one foolish, one clever.* (Cf.A525.) S. Am. Indian (Bacairi): Lévi-Strauss BBAE CXLIII (3) 347, (Tupinamba): Métraux RMLP XXXIII 135, (Chiriguano): ibid 163.

A515.1.1.3. *Twin culture heroes conceived of as sun and moon.* S. Am. Indian (Amuesha): Métraux RMLP XXXIII 150, (Chiriguano): ibid. 158ff.

A515.1.2. *Sworn brothers as culture heroes.* India: Thompson-Balys.

P311. Sworn brethren.

A515.2. *Father and son as culture heroes.* Irish myth: Cross. — Amazon tribes: Alexander Lat. Am. 311.

A515.3. *Culture hero has blood brother.* Irish myth: Cross.

P312. Blood-brotherhood.

A515.4. *Culture hero has faithful attendant.* Irish myth: Cross.

A515.5. *Culture hero fights with (encounters) son without recognizing him.*

N731.2. Father-son combat.

A516. *Expulsion and return of culture hero.*

L111.1. Exile returns and succeeds. S140. Cruel abandonments and exposures. S300. Abandoned or murdered children. S350.2. Child driven out (exposed) brought up in secret.

A520. Nature of the culture hero (demigod).

A520.1. *Gods as culture heroes.* Hawaii: Beckwith Myth 16, chap. 2 passim.

A521. *Culture hero as dupe or trickster.* Celtic: MacCulloch Celtic 30; Irish myth: Cross. — S. Am. Indian (Yunca, Peru): Alexander Lat.

Am. 229, (Chiriguano): Métraux BBAE CXLIII (3) 484; N. Am. Indian: *Thompson Tales 294 n. 78; Hawaii: Beckwith Myth 20; New Hebrides: Codrington 152—166; African: Werner African 213.

A177.1. God as dupe or trickster. J1700. Fools.

A522. *Animal as culture hero.*

A132. God in animal form. D100. Transformation: man to animal.

A522.1. *Beast as culture hero.*

A522.1.1. *Dog as culture hero.* Aztec: Alexander Lat. Am. 82f.

A522.1.1.1. *Culture hero acts as watch-dog;* named "Hound". Irish myth: Cross.

B421. Helpful dog.

A522.1.2. *Rabbit as culture hero.* Central Algonquian tribes: Thompson PMLA XXXVII 130ff.

A522.1.3. *Coyote as culture hero.* N. Am. Indian: Alexander N. Am. 141ff., 298 n. 48.

A522.1.4. *Fox as culture hero.* S. Am. Indian (Chaco): Métraux BBAE CXLIII (1) 369, (Chiriguano): Métraux BBAE CXLIII (3) 484.

A522.1.5. *Mink as culture hero.* N. Am. Indian: Boas RBAE XXXI 585.

A522.2. *Bird as culture hero.*

A132.6.1. Bird-god. B122. Bird with magic wisdom. B450. Helpful birds.

A522.2.1. *Blue Jay as culture hero.* N. A. Indian: Boas RBAE XXXI 646 and passim.

A522.2.2. *Raven as culture hero.* Krappe "Arturus Cosmocrator" Speculum 1945, 405ff. — Irish myth: Cross; N. A. Indian: *Boas RBAE XXXI 567ff.

D151.5. Transformation: man to raven.

A522.2.3. *Hawk as culture hero.* S. Am. Indian (Toba): Métraux MAFLS XL 3, BBAE CXLIII (1) 368.

A522.2.4. *Aquatic bird as culture hero.* S. Am. Indian (Toba): Métraux MAFLS XL 3.

A522.3. *Other animals as culture hero.*

A522.3.1. *Spider as culture hero.* Dakota: Dorsey JAFL II 134. — African: Werner African 213.

A523. *Giant as culture hero.* Irish myth: Cross; Persian: Carnoy 294; Chinese: Werner 305.

A133. Giant god.

A523.1. *Giant sword of culture hero.* Fb. "sværd" III 691a.; Irish myth: Cross.

D1081. Magic sword.

A524. *Extraordinary possessions of culture hero.*

A524.1. *Culture hero's extraordinary animals.*

A524.1.1. *Culture hero has marvelous dogs.* Irish myth: Cross.

B187. Magic dog.

A524.1.2. *Culture hero has marvelous horses.* Irish myth: Cross.

A132.3. Horse-deity.

A524.2. *Extraordinary weapons of culture hero.* Irish myth: Cross.
D1080. Magic weapons.

A525. *Good and bad culture heroes.* Walapai: Alexander N. Am. 180; S. Am. Indian (Guarani): Métraux BBAE CXLIII (3) 93; Melanesia: Dixon 122ff.; Polynesia, Micronesia: ibid. 122 n. 1.
A50. Conflict of good and evil creators. A71. Creator tries to devour his son, the culture hero. A106. Opposition of good and evil gods. A107. Gods of darkness and of light. A511.1.2.1. Twin culture heroes quarrel before birth. A1750. Animals created through opposition of devil to God.

A525.1. *Culture hero fights with his elder brother.* Ojibwa: Jones-Michelson PAES VII (1) 19.

A525.2. *Culture hero (god) slays his grandfather.* Irish myth: Cross.
A192.1. Old god slain by young god. E765.4.3. Father will die when daughter bears son. M311.1. Prophecy: king's grandson will dethrone him. M343.2. Prophecy: murder by grandson.

A526. *Physical characteristics of culture hero (demigod).*

A526.1. *Culture hero can be wounded.* Irish myth: Cross.
F254.4. Fairies can be wounded.

A526.2. *Culture hero as mighty hunter.* Irish myth: Cross.
F679.5. Skillful hunter.

A526.3. *Culture hero has irresistible beauty spot* (ball seirc). Irish myth: Cross.
D1355.13. Love-spot.

A526.4. *Culture hero has three heads of hair of different colors.* Irish myth: Cross.
D991. Magic hair. F555.5.1. Person with three heads of hair.

A526.5. *Culture hero has seven pupils in each eye,* seven toes on each foot, seven fingers on each hand. Irish myth: Cross.
F541.3.3. Eye with seven pupils. F551. Remarkable feet.

A526.5.1. *Culture hero with different colored eyes,* one brown, one green. Maori: Clark 30.

A526.6. *Culture hero, when angry, subject to contortions.* Irish myth: Cross.
D50. Magic changes in man himself. F873.0.1. Battle rage. F969.3.2. Hero's light (luau láith). F1041.2. Horripilation. F1041.16. Extraordinary physical reactions to anger.

A526.7. *Culture hero performs remarkable feats of strength and skill.* Irish myth: Cross.
F610. Remarkably strong man. F684. Marvelous jumps. F697.1. Culture hero as marvelous ball player. F698. Skill in juggling with swords, balls, etc. H1563. Test of skill.

A526.8. *Culture hero can turn feet and knees backwards.* Irish myth: Cross.
F517.1.5. Person with knees backward. F531.1.3.2. Giant with heels in front. F531.1.6.8. Giant with knees backwards. G303.4.5.6. Devil's knees are backwards.

A526.9. *Lightning flashes from armpits of hero.* Maori: Beckwith Myth 250.

A527. *Special powers of culture hero.*

A527.1. *Culture hero precocious.* Irish myth: Cross.
A511.4. Growth of culture hero. T615. Supernatural growth.

A527.1.1. *Divine twins make selves a bow and arrow.* S. Am. Indian (Chiriguano): Métraux RMLP XXXIII 143, 156, (Carib): ibid. 147.

A527.2. *Culture hero has knowledge-giving member* (thumb, tooth). Irish myth: Cross.

D1009.2. Magic tooth. D1810.3. Magic knowledge from touching "knowledge tooth" with thumb. D1811.1.1. Thumb of knowledge.

A527.3. *Culture hero as magician* (drai). Irish myth: Cross.

D1711. Magician. M364.7.2. Coming of saint (Christianity) prophesied by heathen. P427 Druid (magus).

A527.3.1. *Culture hero can transform self.* S. Am. Indian (Caingang): Métraux BBAE CXLIII (1) 473.

D630. Transformation and disenchantment at will.

A527.3.1.1. *Culture hero assumes ugly and deformed guise.* S. Am. Indian (Tupinamba): Métraux RMLP XXXIII 168.

K1815. Humble disguise.

A527.4. *Culture hero as poet (musician).* Irish myth: Cross.

A465.1. Goddess of poetry. A465.2. God of music.

A528. *Culture hero has supernatural helpers.* Irish myth: Cross.

N810. Supernatural helpers.

A530. Culture hero establishes law and order. Norse: Boberg; Greek: Fox 103; Jewish: Neuman.

A175. God reduces elements to order. A1175. Purchase of night by culture hero.

A530.1. *Culture hero completes work of creator.* S. Am. Indian (Guarani): Métraux BBAE CXLIII (3) 93, (Tucuna): Nimuendajú BBAE CXLIII (3) 724.

A531. *Culture hero (demigod) overcomes monsters.* Norse: Boberg; Greek: Grote I 189; Irish myth: Cross, Beal XXI 327; Babylonian: Spence 158; Hindu: Keith 34, 172; India: *Thompson-Balys; Chinese: Coyajee JPASB XXIV 189; Japanese: Anesaki 303; Persian: Carnoy 287, 293, 300. — American Indian: *Thompson Tales 272 n. 1; *Farrand-Frachtenberg JAFL XXVIII 216 (N. Pac. Coast, Chinook, Kathlamet, Shoshone, Maidu, Coos, Alsea, Molala, Kalapuya); and add (Maidu) Dixon PAES IV 59 No. 2, (Joshua) Farrand-Frachtenberg JAFL XXVIII 235 No. 18, (Navaho) Alexander N. Am. 165, (Arikara) ibid. 108; Jicarilla Apache: Mooney AA old ser. XI (1898) 204; S. Am. Indian (Toba): Métraux MAFLS XXXX 4, 8, 62, 66f., 73, 77, (Tucuan): Nimuendajú BBAE CXLIII (3) 724, (Huamachuco): Métraux RMLP XXXIII 151, (Apapocuvá-Guarani): Métraux RMLP XXXIII 138.

A162.1. Fight of the gods and giants. A1071. Fettering of underground monster. A1111. Impounded water. A1125. Wind caused by flapping wings. Culture hero tames the monster bird. B11.11. Fight with dragon. Q433.2. Defeated giants imprisoned in lower world.

A531.1. *Culture hero spares certain evil spirits.* Old Age, Cold, Poverty, and Hunger beg the culture hero not to destroy them because of their real usefulness to man. — Navaho: Matthews MAFLS V 130ff.

A531.1.1. *Culture hero banishes demons.* Irish myth: Cross. — Easter Is.: Métraux Ethnology 370.

V229.5. Saint banishes demons.

A531.2. *Culture hero banishes snakes.* *Krappe "St. Patrick and the Snakes" Traditio V (1947) 323—330; Irish: Cross, Giraldus Cambrensis

Topography of Ireland I 23, Bede Historia Ecclesiastica I 18 (St. Patrick); Swiss: Jegerlehner Oberwallis 300 No. 9, 303 No. 22.

A531. Culture hero overcomes monsters. A2434.2.2. Why foxes do not live on certain island: driven out by a god. D2176.1. Snakes banned by magic. V229.3. Saint banishes snakes.

A531.3. *Culture hero exterminates race of tigers.* S. Am. Indian (Caingang): Métraux RMLP XXXIII 148, (Amuesha): ibid. 150, (Apapocuvu-Guarani): ibid. 138.

A531.4. *Culture hero conquers sea monster.* Chinese-Persian: Coyajee JPASB XXIV 190.

A531.4.1. *Demigod conquers great octopus.* Hawaii: Beckwith Myth 22.

A532. *Culture hero tames winds in caves.* Western Mono: Gifford JAFL XXXVI 326ff. Nos. 9, 10.

A1122. Cave of winds. D2142. Wind produced by magic.

A533. *Culture hero regulates rivers.*

A533.1. *Culture hero stays current of river.* India: Thompson-Balys.

A535. *Culture hero swallowed and recovered from animal.* Irish myth: Cross; Persian: Carnoy 302.

F913. Victims rescued from swallower's belly.

A536. *Demigods fight as allies of mortals.* Irish myth: Cross; Jewish: Neuman.

A172. Gods intervene in battle. A185.1. God aids his half-mortal son in battle. A581.2. Culture hero returns and aids followers in battle. F343.10. Fairy gives mortal equipment for soldiers. F349.2. Fairy aids mortal in battle. F394.2. Mortal aids fairies in war. N810. Supernatural helpers.

A536.1. *Culture hero (saint) defends Ireland against foreign invasions.* Irish myth: Cross.

A537. *Culture heroes clear plains.* Irish myth: Cross.

A901. Topographical features caused by experiences of primitive hero. F271.5. Fairies clear land. F614.9. Strong man clears land.

A538. *Culture hero builds raths.* Irish myth: Cross.

A179. God as rath-builder. A1435.2. Origin of raths. D1136.1. Fort produced by magic. F531.6.6. Giants as builders of great structures. P427.6.3. Druids as rath-builders. P447.2. Smith as rath-builder.

A541. *Culture hero teaches arts and crafts.* Jewish: Neuman; India: *Thompson-Balys. — American Indian: in practically all the mythologies — see Thompson Tales 272 n. 1; Eskimo (Bering Strait): Nelson RBAE XVIII 456; S. Am. Indian (Maya): Alexander Lat. Am. 131ff., (Bakairi): Alexander Lat. Am. 313, (Toba): Métraux MAFLS XXXX 78, 84, 86, 112ff., Métraux BBAE CXLIII (1) 368, (Guaporé River): Lévi-Strauss BBAE CXLIII (3) 379, (Chiriguano): Métraux BBAE CXLIII (3) 484, (Guarayú): Métraux BBAE (3) 437, (Cubeo): Goldman BBAE CXLIII (3) 789, (Cashinawa): Métraux BBAE CXLIII (3) 685. — Hawaii: Beckwith Myth 115; New Hebrides (Banks Is.): Codrington 152—166.

A432.0.1. God plants fields. A450. God of trades and professions. A1400. Acquisition of human culture.

A541.1. *Culture hero invents and teaches the Irish language.* Irish myth: Cross.

A465.3.1.1. God of eloquence and learning as inventor of ogam alphabet.

A541.2. *Culture hero as god of agriculture.* Irish myth: Cross.

A432. God of agriculture.

A545. *Culture hero establishes customs.* India: Thompson-Balys. — Mixtec: Alexander Lat. Am. 86; S. A. Indian (Bakairi): Lévi-Strauss BBAE CXLIII (3) 347, (Tupinamba): Métraux BBAE CXLIII (3) 93, (Toba): Métraux MAFLS XL 79, 367, (Mataco): Métraux ibid. 105, 367, (Cubeo): Goldman BBAE CXLIII (3) 798, (Tucuna): Nimuendaju BBAE CXLIII (3) 724.

A1313.3. Misplaced genitalia. Originally genitals are misplaced; conception and childbirth are not understood. All is arranged by culture hero. A1500. Origin of customs. P600. Customs.

A546. *Culture hero establishes social system.* Persian: Carnoy 317; India Thompson-Balys.

A1500. Origin of customs. P. Society.

A547. *Culture hero dispenses food and hospitality.* Irish myth: Cross.

P320. Hospitality.

A560. **Culture hero's (demigod's) departure.** Irish myth: Cross; Finnish: Kalevala rune 50; India: Thompson-Balys.

A513.2. Culture hero arrives (and departs) in boat. A692. Islands of the blessed. F0. Journey to the otherworld. F111. Journey to earthly paradise. F134. Otherworld on an island.

A561. *Divinity's departure for west.* American Indian: *Thompson Tales 274 n. 11; S. A. Indian (Inca): Alexander Lat. Am. 240, (Yuracare, W. Brazil): ibid. 315, (Guarayú): Métraux BBAE CXLIII (3) 437, Métraux RMLP XXXIII 147.

A692. Islands of the blest. Elysium situated in the west.

A562. *Divinity's departure for east.* S. A. Indian (Tehuelche, Patagonia): Alexander Lat. Am. 336.

A564. *Remarkable longevity of culture heroes.* Irish myth: Cross; Jewish: Neuman.

A191.1. Great age of the gods. A570. Culture hero still lives.

A565. *Dying culture hero.* The culture hero teaches people how to die by dying himself. — Irish myth: Cross; California Indians: *Thompson Tales 285 n. 52a.

A978. Origin of minerals from body of dead culture hero. F323. Fairy women take body of dead hero to fairyland. F399.1. Fairies bear dead warrior to fairyland.

A566. *Culture hero returns to upper world.* S. Am. Indian (Apapocuvá-Guaraní): Métraux RMLP XXXIII 136ff., (Chiriguano): Métraux RMLP XXXIII 148f., 157.

A566.1. *Return of mortal reincarnation of celestial being* to the country of the gods after his mission has been accomplished on earth. India: Thompson-Balys.

A511.3. Culture hero incarnated through birth from virgin.

A566.2. *Culture hero ascends to heaven* guided by blind ancestress. Maori: Beckwith Myth 249.

A567. *Divinity retires to the end of the world.* S. Am. Indian (Yuracare): Métraux BBAE CXLIII (3) 503.

A570. **Culture hero still lives.** Köhler-Bolte I 411; Irish myth: Cross.

A564. Remarkable longevity of culture heroes.

A571. *Culture hero asleep in mountain.* Köhler-Bolte I 411. — Irish myth: Cross; Welsh: MacCulloch Celtic 194 (Arthur); Norse: Mac Culloch Eddic 316; Eng., Scot.: Baughman.

A580. Culture hero's expected return. D1960.2. King asleep in mountain. F721.2. Habitable hill.

A571.1. *Culture hero still alive in hollow hill.* Irish myth: Cross.

A151.1.1. Home of gods inside of hill. F211. Fairyland under a hollow knoll. F759.2. Hollow mountain.

A571.2. *Culture hero still alive on mysterious island.* Irish myth: Cross.

A692. Islands of the blest. E481.4.1. Avalon. F134. Otherworld on island.

A572. *Culture hero still keeps watch over earth.* S. Am. Indian (Apapocuvá-Guaraní): Métraux RMLP XXXIII 138.

A572.1. *Culture hero still resides in the zenith.* S. Am. Indian (Guaraní): Métraux BBAE CXLIII (3) 93.

A575. *Departed deity grants requests to visitors.* N. A. Indian: *Thompson Tales 276 n. 17.

D1720. Acquisition of magic powers. D1761. Magic results produced by wishing. F12. Journey to see deity. L220. Modest request best. Q338.1. Request for immortality punished by transformation into tree.

A580. Culture hero's (divinity's) expected return. Divinity or hero is expected to return at the proper time and rescue his people from their misfortunes. Often joined with A571. — *Norlind "Skattsägner". — Danish: Bolte Zs. f. Vksk. XXIX 74; Fb. "Holger Danske"; Norse: Olrik Ragnarök 108ff., 478 (Balder); Irish myth: Cross; Welsh: Mac Culloch Celtic 194 (Arthur); Eng., Scot.: Baughman; Finnish: Kalevala rune 50. — Jewish: Neuman; Persian: Carnoy 339. — N. A. Indian: *Thompson Tales 274 n. 11a.; Aztec: Alexander Lat. Am. 66.

A571. Culture hero asleep in mountain. B19.3. Horse born of egg. Mythical hero will come riding on such a horse. D1960.2. King asleep in mountain.

A581. *Culture hero (divinity) returns.* Irish myth: Cross.

E300. Friendly return from the dead. F116.1. Voyage to the land of youth. F379.1. Return from fairyland.

A581.1. *Culture hero returns and assists mortals.* Irish myth: Cross.

F393. Fairy visits among mortals.

A581.2. *Culture hero returns and aids followers in battle.* Irish myth: Cross.

A172. Gods intervene in battle. A536. Demigods act as allies of mortals. F349.2. Fairy aids mortal in battle.

A581.3. *Culture hero returns to prove power of saint.* Irish myth: Cross.

E367.4. Return from dead to convert to Christianity. V220. Saints.

A590. Demigods and culture heroes—miscellaneous.

A591. *Semi-divine hero granted free access to men's wives.* India: Thompson-Balys.

T281. Sex hospitality.

A592. *Culture heroes and descendants.*

A592.1. *Demigod and witch woman of upper world have son.* Tuamotu: Stimson MS (z-G. 13/249).

A592.2. *Virgin daughter of culture hero.* S. Am. Indian (Tupinamba): Métraux RMLP XXXIII 168.

A592.2.1. *Daughter of culture hero gives birth to boy.* S. Am. Indian (Tupinamba): Métraux RMLP XXXIII 169.

A600—A899. COSMOGONY AND COSMOLOGY

A600—A699. The universe.

A600—A649. CREATION OF THE UNIVERSE

A600. Creation of the universe. In addition to other references in this section A600—A649, see: *Encyc. Rel. Ethics s. v. "Creation"; *Lang Myth. 163ff.; Henne am-Rhyn Das Jenseits: Kulturgeschichtliche Darstellung über Schöpfung, etc. (1881); Schlieper Die kosmogonischen Mythen der Urvölker (Bonn 1932, diss.); *Hdwb. d. Abergl. IX Nachträge 274—284; Feilberg Skabelses og Syndflodssagn (1915). — Norse: Boberg, MacCulloch Eddic 327ff.; Irish myth: Cross; Persian: Carnoy 275; Jewish: Neuman; India: Thompson-Balys; Chinese: Werner 406. — Cherokee: Mooney Am. Urquell II 85ff.; Quiché: Alexander Lat. Am. 160f.; Maya: ibid. 152ff.; Hawaii: Beckwith Myth 43ff.; Tahiti: Henry 336ff.

A0. Creator.

A601. *Universe created in specified time and order.* Jewish: Neuman; Hawaii: Beckwith Myth 45.

A601.1. *Universe created in five periods of time.* Hawaii: Beckwith Myth 44.

A601.2. *Universe created in six days.* Hawaii: Beckwith Myth 45.

A605. *Primeval chaos.* *Sayce Encyc. Religion and Ethics III 363 s. v. "Chaos". — Greek: Roscher I 871 s. v. "Chaos"; Icel.: De la Saussaye 340f.; Jewish: Neuman; Egyptian: Müller 47; Babylonian: Spence 71; Japanese: Anesaki 222. — Pima: Alexander N. Am. 177; Mixtec: Alexander Lat. Am. 86; Marquesas Is.: Dixon 10 n. 13; Maori: ibid. 6ff.; Nias Is.: ibid. 167; Hawaii: Beckwith Myth 42; Tahiti: Henry 336, 340.

A115. First deity grows out of primeval chaos. A620. Spontaneous creation of universe. A810. Primeval water.

A605.1. *Primeval darkness.* S. Am. Indian (Guaraní): Métraux BBAE CXLIII (3) 93; Hawaii: Beckwith Myth 312; Africa (Luba): Donohugh Africa V 180.

A605.2. *Primeval cold.* Icel.: Boberg.

A610. Creation of universe by creator. The creator is existing before all things. — Irish myth: Cross; Jewish: Neuman; Hindu: Oldenberg Religion des Veda 278; Chinese: Werner 76, 90. — Mexican: Alexander Lat. Am. 85; Guiana: ibid. 256ff.. — Society Is.: Dixon 11 n. 18, 12 n. 19; Marquesas Is.: ibid. 11 n. 14; Maori: ibid. 11 n. 16, 17, 13 n. 20; Hawaii: Beckwith Myth 42; Australian: Goldenweiser Early Civilization 105. — Uganda: ibid. 97.

A0. Creator. A101.1. Supreme god as creator. A830. Creation of earth by creator. A901. Topographical features caused by experiences of primitive hero (demigod, deity).

A610.1. *All things created in pairs* (heaven and earth, etc.). Jewish: Neuman.

A610.2. *Creation of heaven, earth, and hell.* Jewish: Neuman; Hawaii: Beckwith Myth 42.

A661. Heaven. A671. Hell.

A611. *Fiat creation.* Universe is created at command of creator. — Irish myth: Cross; Hebrew: Genesis ch. 1; Jewish: Neuman. — Pelew Group, Western Caroline Is., Central Caroline Is., Gilbert Group: Dixon 248; Mono-Alu (Fauru): Wheeler 66; Tahiti: Henry 338.

D1765. Magic results produced by command. M0. Judgments and decrees.

A611.0.1. *Creator uses particular formula (letters) to create universe.* Jewish: Neuman.

A611.1. *Druids as creators.* Irish myth: Cross.

P427. Druid (magus).

A612. *Creation: materialization of creator's thinking.* Creator "thinks outward in space" and thus produces the universe. — *Dh I 10f., 15, 17ff., 58, 113; Jewish: Neuman. — Zuñi: Cushing RBAE XIII 379ff.; Thompson Tales 280 n. 36.

A612.1. *World-soul.* The universe a manifestation of the creator. — Society Is.: Dixon 12 n. 19.

A613. *Creation from creator's tears.* Dh I 31f.

A614. *Universe from parts of creator's body.* Ymir makes the world from his members — mountains from bones, cliffs from teeth, heavens from skull, etc. — Norse: Dh I 111 n. 1; Lang Myth I 234 ff. — Mexican: Danzel Kultur und Religion des primitiven Menschen 60; Kalmuck, Chinese, Hindu: Holmberg Finno-Ugric 372; Chinese: Eberhard FFC CXX 96 No. 55.

A1211. Man made from creator's body.

A614.1. *Universe from parts of man's body.* (Cf. A831.2) — Kabyle: Frobenius Atlantis I 101; Madagascar: Dandonau Contes pop. de Sakalava No. 58; Papuan: Landtmann The Kiwai Papuans 551; Sumatra: Pleyte Bataksche Vertellingen 68.

A615. *Universe as offspring of creator.* The Sky Father begets various parts of the universe by his various wives. — Maori: Dixon 8 n. 9.

A645. Creation of universe: genealogical type. A begets B, who begets C, etc.

A615.1. *Universe from creator's masturbation* with water, with stone, and with earth. (Cf. A1216.1). Easter Is.: Métraux Ethnology 314.

A615.2. *Universe from copulation of various objects to produce others.* Easter Is.: Métraux Ethnology 320f.

A617. *Creation of universe from clam-shell on primeval water by creator.* — Nauru (Pleasant Island): Dixon 249; Tahiti: Henry 337.

A617.1. *Creation of universe from clay pot set afloat on primeval waters.* India: Thompson-Balys.

A810. Primeval water.

A617.2. *Creation of universe from calabash.* Hawaii: Beckwith Myth 304f.

A618. *Universe created by various activities of creator.*

A618.1. *Universe coughed into being.* Mono-Alu: Wheeler 67.

A636. New creation shouted away.

A618.2. *Universe created by spitting.* Melanesia: Wheeler 66.

A620. Spontaneous creation of universe. Greek: *Grote I 4. — Maori: Dixon 6ff.; Marquesas Is.: ibid. 10 n. 13; Tahiti: Henry 343.

A605. Primeval chaos.

A620.1. *Spontaneous creation — evolutionary type.* From primeval chaos gradually arise worlds and life. — Norse: MacCulloch Eddic 327ff.; Greek: Fox 3f.; Hawaiian: Dixon 15 n. 25, 26, Beckwith Myth 3; Maori: ibid. 6, 7, nn. 2, 3, 4, 5; Marquesas Is.: ibid. 11 n. 14.

A645. Creation of universe: genealogical type. A begets B, who begets C, etc. A1220. Creation of man through evolution.

A620.2. *Spontaneous encroachment of heavens and earth checked by creator.* Jewish: Neuman.

A621. *Universe from congealed vapor.* Kachin (North Burma): Scott Indo-Chinese 263; Chinese: Werner 136.

A621.1. *Creation from vapor-produced primeval giant.* Vapors from half-frozen primeval river origin of giant Ymir, from whom universe is created. — Icel.: MacCulloch Eddic 327ff.

A642. Universe from body of slain giant.

A622. *Universe created out of fire world.* Icel.: MacCulloch Eddic 279, 324, 326.

F702. Land of fire.

A623. *Universe created out of ice and mist.* Icel.: MacCulloch Eddic 324—26, 304, 329, Herrmann Saxo II 584.

A625. *World parents: sky-father and earth-mother* as parents of the universe. The sky-father descends upon the earth-mother and begets the world. — Greek: *Frazer Apollodorus I 2 n. 1, Fox 5, 272; Icel.: MacCulloch Eddic 194, 328; Hindu: Keith 16; India: Thompson-Balys. — Eastern Indonesia: Dixon 166; Chatham Is.: ibid. 10 n. 12; Cook and Hervey Is.: ibid. 14 n. 21; Maori: ibid. 7 n. 3, 8 n. 7, 9 n. 10, 31; Tahiti: Henry 337f.; N. A. Indian: *Thompson Tales 280 n. 37; S. Am. Indian (Cora): Alexander Lat. Am. 121, (Antilles): ibid. 24; African: Werner African 124.

A401. Mother earth.

A625.1. *Heaven-mother — earth-father.* Kachin (North Burma): Scott Indo-Chinese 263.

A625.2. *Raising of the sky.* Originally the sky is near the earth (usually because of the conjunction of the sky-father and earth-mother). It is raised to its present place. — Gaster Oldest Stories 133; Egyptian: Müller 30; Babylonian: Spence 81, 114; Mongolian: Holmberg Siberian 330; India: *Thompson-Balys; Chinese: Eberhard FFC CXX 97. — Indonesian: Dixon 36, 178 nn. 124—133, (Rotti) Jonker Rottineesche Texten No. 58; Pleasant Island (Micronesia): Dixon 250; Central and Western Polynesia, Hawaii, Samoa: ibid. 50f.; Maori: ibid. 31; Chatham Is., Cook Group, Society Is., Samoa, Union Group, Hawaii: ibid. 35; Maori: Clark 13, 15, 171; Philippine: Gifford 23; Tonga: Gifford 18, 23. — N. A. Indian (Mohave): Alexander N. Am. 179; S. Am. Indian (Aztec): Alexander Lat. Am. 93, (Bakairi): ibid. 313, Lévi-Strauss BBAE CXLIII (3) 348, (Botocudo): Métraux BBAE CXLIII (1) 540, (Cashinawa): Métraux BBAE CXLIII (3) 684, (Yuracare): Métraux ibid. 504. — African: Frobenius Atlantis VII 304.

A727. Raising the sun.

A625.2.1. *Heaven and earth originally connected by navel string.* Navel string cut. — India: Thompson-Balys.

F51. Sky-rope.

A625.2.2. *Why the sky receded upward:* it was struck by a woman's pestle. India: Thompson-Balys.

A625.2.3. *Raising the sky:* striking with broom. Old woman's hump strikes clouds as she sweeps. She strikes at sky with broom and thus raises it. — India: Thompson-Balys.

A625.2.4. *Deity clothes his father the sky* after he has separated him from earth. Maori: Clark 16.

A625.2.5. *After sky is lifted, plants and shrubs begin to grow.* Maori: Clark 15.

A630. Series of creations.. The present universe is the last of a succession of creations. — Etruscan: Fox 289. — Navaho: Alexander N. Am. 159ff.; Aztec: Alexander Lat. Am. 91.

A651. Hierarchy of worlds. A1101. The four ages of the world. A1220.1. Man created after series of unsuccessful experiments.

A631. *Pre-existing world of gods above.* Such a world is assumed before the real creation of the universe. Though this belief is not explicitly set forth in many mythologies, it seems to be implied in most of the North American Indian systems. See, for example, motif A31, Creator's grandmother. — Jewish: *Neuman. — Samoa: Dixon 18f.; Hawaii: Beckwith Myth 45.

A632. *Succession of creations and cataclysms.* From the ruins of each earlier creation a new one is raised. — Jewish: Neuman. — Inca: Alexander Lat. Am. 240; Hawaiian: Dixon 15 n. 24.

A633. *Earlier universe opposite of present.* Everything in the earlier world was the reverse of the present world. Cf. A855. — California tribes (Capistrano, Luiseño, Diegueño, Mohave): Waterman AA n. s. XI 52.

A636. *New creation shouted away.* It is unstable and therefore unsatisfactory. — American Indian: Kroeber JAFL XXI 224, (California): Gayton and Newman 56.

A640. Other means of creating the universe.

A641. *Cosmic egg.* The universe brought forth from an egg. — Lang Myth. I 252; Dh I 19. — Finnish: Kalevala rune 1; Esthonian: Eisen Estnische Mythologie 170, Loorits Grundzüge I 447f.; Hindu: Keith 74; Society Is., Hawaiian, Maori: Dixon 20; Hawaii: Henry 345. — African: Frobenius Atlantis X 119.

A655. World as egg. A701.1. Origin of sky from egg brought from primeval water. A1222. Mankind originates from eggs.

A641.1. *Heaven and earth from egg.* They are the two halves of an egg shell. Eros escapes as they are separated. — Greek: Fox 5. — Indonesian: L. d. Backer L'Archipel indien 232.

A641.2. *Creation from duck's eggs.* Upper vault from half shell, lower vault from half shell, moonbeams from whites, sunshine from yellows, starlight from motley parts, clouds from dark parts. — Finnish: Kalevala rune 1.

A642. *Universe from body of slain giant.* Ymir. See A621.1. — Icel.: *De la Saussaye 341.

A642.1. *Primeval woman cut in pieces:* houses, etc., made from her body. India: Thompson-Balys.

A644. *Universe from pre-existing rocks.* Originally rocks are assumed and everything is made from them. — Samoa: Dixon 17.

A645. *Creation of universe: genealogical type.* A begets B, who begets C, etc. Finally the universe is brought forth in its present form. — Nias Is. (Indonesia): Dixon 166.

A615. Universe as offspring of creator. A715. Sun born of first couple.

A647. *Universe from cosmic fowl.* Hawaii: Beckwith Myth 217ff.

A650—A699. NATURE OF THE UNIVERSE

A650. The universe as a whole.

A651. *Hierarchy of worlds.* A series of worlds, one above the other. — Irish myth: Cross; Egyptian: Müller 366 n. 7; Siberian: Holmberg Siberian 307, 309f., 410; Hindu: Keith 15, 134, 228; India: *Thompson-Balys. — N. A. Indian: *Thompson Tales 287 n. 58, Alexander N. Am. 7, 60, 105, 136, 263, *275 n. 11 (Eskimo, Cherokee, Mandan, Kiowa, Thompson River, Bella Coola); Aztec: Alexander Lat. Am. 52f.; Maya: ibid. 140; Amazon: ibid. 307; Bororo: ibid. 296; S. Am. Indian (Chaco): Métraux MAFLS XL 24, Métraux BBAE CXLIII (1) 366, (Witoto): Métraux MAFLS XL 25; Chuckchee: Bogoras AA n. s. IV 590; Maori: Dixon 59. — Cf. Icel.: De la Saussaye 346 n. 4.

A630. Series of creations. E755.1.1. Heavenly hierarchy.

A651.0.1. *Nine worlds.* India: Thompson-Balys; Buddhist myth: Malalasekera II 974.

A651.0.2. *Four world systems.* Buddhist myth: Malalasekera I 117, 1033.

A651.1. *Series of upper worlds.* Japanese: Holmberg Siberian 344.

F10. Journeys to the upper world.

A651.1.0.1. *Highest of celestial worlds consists of twenty heavens.* Buddhist myth: Malalasekera II 336.

A651.1.1. *Three heavens.* Icel.: Snorra Edda Gylf XVII, Boberg. — Hawaii: Thrum 15, Beckwith Myth 42, 74; Maori: Clark 163ff.; S. Am. Indian (Chamacoco): Métraux MAFLS XL 25.

A651.1.1.1. *Third sky above prevents earth being burned by sun.* S. Am. Indian (Witoto): Métraux MAFLS XL 25.

A651.1.1.2. *Region above the three worlds.* Hindu: Penzer II 242.

A651.1.2. *Four heavens.* Irish myth: Cross (A651.1.6.). — S. Am. Indian (Chamacoco): Métraux MAFLS XL 25.

A651.1.3. *Five heavens.* S. Am. Indian (Chamacoco): Métraux MAFLS XL 25, BBAE CXLIII (1) 366.

A651.1.4. *Seven heavens.* A series of seven upper worlds. — Irish myth: Cross; Jewish: *Neuman; Hindu: Penzer VII 246; Mohammedan: Hartland Science 224; Siberian: Holmberg Siberian 400f. —Sumatra: Dixon 160.

D1273.1.3. Seven as magic number.

A651.1.5. *Eight heavens.* Samoa: Beckwith Myth 210.

A651.1.6. *Nine heavens.* Siberian: Holmberg Siberian 400f. — Fiji: Beckwith Myth 150; Aztec: Alexander Lat. Am. 77.

A651.1.6.1. *The nine ranks (orders) of heaven.* Irish myth: Cross (A651.1.2.1.).

D1273.1.3.1. Nine as magic number.

A651.1.7. *Ten heavens.* Jewish: Neuman; Maori: Clark 186; Tonga: Gifford 18; Tahiti: Henry 164, 343.

A651.1.8. *Series of upper worlds — miscellaneous.* Jewish: *Neuman.

A651.1.8.1. *Seventeen-storied heaven.* Siberian: Holmberg Siberian 405.

A651.2. *Series of lower worlds.* Irish myth: Cross.

E755.2.9. Series of hells. F80. Journey to the lower world.

A651.2.0.1. *Creator lives in lowest sky beneath us.* S. Am. Indian (Witoto): Métraux MAFLS XL 25.

A307. Deity ruler of lowest heaven.

A651.2.1. *Two lower worlds.* S. Am. Indian (Chamacoco): Métraux MAFLS XL 25, BBAE CXLIII (1) 366.

A651.2.2. *Three lower worlds.* Finno-Ugric: Holmberg Finno-Ugric 77. — S. Am. Indian (Witoto): Métraux MAFLS XL 25.

A651.2.3. *Seven lower worlds.* Hindu: Penzer IV 21 n. 1, VIII 162 n. 1.

A651.3. *Worlds above and below.*

A651.3.1. *Seven worlds above and below.* An angel upholds the seven worlds on his shoulders. Under him in turn are: rock, bull, fish, vast sea, air, fire, and serpent. — *Chauvin VII 58 No. 77 n. 1.

A651.3.2. *Worlds above and below — miscellaneous.* Hawaii: Beckwith Myth 42; S. Am. Indian (Chamacoco): Métraux MAFLS XL 25.

A652. *World-tree.* Tree extending from lowest to highest world. (Cf. A878.) — **Holmberg Baum des Lebens. — Irish myth: Cross; Norse: MacCulloch Eddic 331ff., De la Saussaye 346ff.; Hagen MPh I (1903—4) 57; **Olrik Danske Studier, 1917, 49ff.; Babylonian: Spence 138; N. A. Indian: *Thompson Tales 286 n. 56a.

A714.2. Sun and moon placed in top of tree. A878. Earth-tree. D950. Magic tree. E90. Tree of life. F162.3.1. Tree of Life in otherworld.

A652.1. *Tree to heaven.* Lithuanian and Lettish: Gray 325; Finnish: Kalevala rune 2; India: Thompson-Balys. — N. A. Indian: *Alexander N. Am. 294f. n. 42; Maya: Alexander Lat. Am. 140; S. Am. Indian (Chaco): Métraux MAFLS XL 24f.

A665.4. Tree supports sky. F54. Tree to upper world.

A652.1.1. *Tree to heaven from goddess' necklace* which she hangs on branch. India: Thompson-Balys.

A652.2. *Tree hanging from sky.* A tree hangs upside down in the sky. By its branches men pass back and forth to the upper world. — Indonesian and Micronesian: Dixon 38 (n. 113, 114), 249.

A652.3. *Tree in upper world.* Iroquois: Alexander N. Am. 35.

A652.4. *Sky as overshadowing tree.* Shadowing the earth. — Egyptian: Müller 35.

A653. *Earth under umbrella.* Hindu: Penzer II 125 n. 3.

A654. *Primary elements of universe.* (Earth, air, fire, water, etc.). — Jewish: *Neuman; Chinese: Werner 84. Cf. the early Greek philosophers.

A655. *World as egg.* The two halves are heaven and earth. — Hindu: Penzer I 10 n. 3; Greek: Fox 5.

A641. Cosmic egg. A701.1. Origin of sky from egg brought from primeval water.

A657. *River connecting earth and upper and lower worlds.* Norse: Mac Culloch Eddic 304, 313; Siberian: Holmberg Siberian.

A657.1. *Bridge connecting earth and heaven.* Icel.: Boberg.

F152. Bridge to otherworld.

A657.2. *Heaven and earth touch each other at east, west, and south.* Jewish: Neuman.

A658. *Size and distances of the universe.*

A658.1. *Nine days' fall from heaven to earth;* the same from earth to hell. — Frazer Apollodorus I 4 n. 2.

A658.1.1. *Nine nights' riding from heaven (or earth) to hell.* Icel.: MacCulloch Eddic 304.

A658.2. *Five hundred years travel across universe.* Jewish: Neuman.

A659. *The universe as a whole — miscellaneous.* Jewish: Neuman.

A659.1. *Music of the spheres.* Jewish: Neuman. (The general philosophical theory of the music of the spheres is not treated here).

D1615.9. Singing heavens and earth.

A659.2. *Big lake under the earth.* S. Am. Indian (Chamacoco): Métraux MAFLS XL 25.

A659.3. *River's source where sky and earth meet.* S. Am. Indian (Toba): Métraux MAFLS XL 24.

A659.4. *Each world corresponds to different color.* S. Am. Indian (Chamacoco): Métraux BBAE CXLIII (1) 366.

A660. Nature of the upper world.

A1131.3. Rain from sea in upper world. F10. Journey to upper world. F56. Sky window. H1260. Quest to the upper world.

A661. *Heaven.* A blissful upper world. — Kohler Heaven and Hell in Comparative Religion (New York 1923); Jeremias Hölle und Paradies bei den Babyloniern (Leipzig 1903); Gaster Thespis 286; Irish myth: Cross, Beal XXI 330; Norse: MacCulloch Eddic 312; German: Grimm Nos. 3, 35, 81, 82, 112, 167, 175, 178; Egyptian: Müller 176; Persian: Carnoy 345; Hindu: Keith 99, 131, 201. — Japanese: Anesaki 237, 241. —Haida: Alexander N. Am. 263; Eskimo: ibid. 7; Aztec: Alexander Lat. Am. 81; Maya: ibid. 138, 140; Isthmian tribes (Panama): ibid. 193.

A211. God of heaven. E481.4. Beautiful land of dead. E754.2. Saved soul goes to heaven. E755.1. Souls in heaven. F11. Journey to heaven (upper-world paradise). Q172. Reward: admission to heaven. Q565. Man admitted to neither heaven nor hell. V511.1. Visions of heaven. V520. Salvation.

A661.0.1. *Gate of heaven.*

F59.1. Gate to upper world. F91. Door entrance to lower world. F156. Door to otherworld.

A661.0.1.1. *Gate of heaven guarded by clap of thunder and mysterious sword.* Chinese: Werner.

A661.0.1.1.1. *Doors of heaven guarded by rivers of fire.* Irish myth: Cross.

A671.2.4. The fires of hell. E755.1.2. River in heaven burns wicked and gives joy to righteous.

A661.0.1.1.2. *Veils of fire and ice before chief door of heaven.* Irish myth: Cross.

A671.3.3. Alternate heat and cold in hell.

A661.0.1.2. *Saint Peter as porter of heaven.* *Types 800, 801, 804; *Köhler Aufsätze 48; *Fb. "Sankt Peder". — Irish: Beal XXI 329; Breton: Sébillot Incidents s. v. "Antoine" (St. Anthony); French Canadian: Barbeau JAFL XXIX 25; U.S.A.: *Baughman.

K2371.1. Heaven entered by a trick. V220. Saints.

A661.0.1.3. *Archangels Michael and Ariel as porters of two of the doors of heaven.* Irish myth: Cross.

A661.0.1.4. *Abersetus as guardian of river of fire* at one of the doors of heaven. Irish myth: Cross.

A661.0.1.5. *Virgins with iron rods as guardians of two of the doors in heaven.* Irish myth: Cross.

A661.0.2. *Music in heaven.* India: Thompson-Balys; Jewish: Neuman.

A661.0.2.1. *Heavenly music caused by four columns under Lord's chair.* Irish myth: Cross. (Cf. A661.0.3.).

B251.3. Birds in otherworld sing religious songs. F774.3. Musical pillar (stone).

A661.0.2.2. *Music produced by precious stones in heaven.* Irish myth: Cross.

A661.0.3. *Chairs in heaven.* Irish myth: Cross.

V515.1.1. Allegorical vision of chairs in heaven. Z71.1.2. Three chairs in heaven for three saints.

A661.0.4. *Cleansing fountain in heaven.* Irish myth: Cross.

A661.0.5. *Bridge of heaven.* Irish myth: Cross.

F152. Bridge to otherworld.

A661.0.5.1. *Soul-bridge:* easy for righteous to cross, more difficult for others. Irish myth: Cross.

H1573.4.1. Ability to cross bridge as test of righteousness.

A661.0.6. *Windows in heaven:* sixty-six (seventy-two) windows in the firmament. Irish myth: Cross.

A1171.1. Windows in firmament shed light. F165.3.5. Windows in otherworld.

A661.0.7. *Self-illuminating precious stones in heaven.* Irish myth: Cross.

F162.0.1.2. (Luminous) precious stones in otherworld (dwelling).

A661.0.8. *Sweet odor in heaven.* Irish myth: Cross.

A661.0.9. *Heaven surrounded by seven walls.* Irish myth: Cross.

F169.5. Fence of metal or crystal in otherworld.

A661.0.10. *Land of the saints surrounded by fiery circle.* Irish myth: Cross.

V511.4. Visions of land of the saints.

A661.1. *Valhalla.* The hall of warriors who go to Odin. They die and are resurrected daily. — **Neckel Walhall (Dortmund, 1913); M. Olsen Acta Philol. Scand. VI 151f.; MacCulloch Eddic 312; Irish myth: Cross.

A151. Home of the gods. E155.1. Slain warriors revive nightly.

A661.1.0.1. *Valhalla has five hundred and forty doors.* Icel.: Boberg.

A661.1.0.2. *Goat (Heidrún) in Valhalla gives mead.* Icel.: Boberg.

A661.1.0.3. *Hog (Sæhrímnir) in Valhalla gives meat.* Icel.: Boberg.

A661.1.0.4. *Deer (Eikþyrnir) in Valhalla fills the fountain Hvergelmir.* Icel.: Boberg.

A661.1.0.5. *Cock in Valhalla awakens the gods.* Icel: Boberg.

A661.1.1. *Inhabitants of heaven divided into companies.* Irish myth: Cross.

A661.1.2. *Saint sees vision of three cities in heaven:* a city of gold, a city of silver, a city of glass. Irish myth: Cross.

F761. City of precious metals and stones. V511.1. Visions of heaven.

A661.2. *The eight paradises.* Hindu: Penzer VII 246.

A661.3. *Five trees of paradise.* Hindu: Penzer VIII 248 n.

A661.4. *Girls dancing in heaven.* India: Thompson-Balys.

A662. *Upper world (heaven) as a mountain.* The sky is the hollowed under side of the mountain. — Siberian: Holmberg Siberian 341ff.

A663. *The plains of heaven.* Irish myth: Cross.

F160.1. Otherworld as plain. F756.2. Plain that is earthly paradise.

A665. *Support of the sky.*

A702.3. Sky supported by north star.

A665.0.1. *God stabilizes the sky.* Tahiti: Henry 180.

A665.1. *God of space upholds sky.* Egyptian: Müller 44.

J2273.1. Bird thinks that the sky will fall if he does not support it.

A665.2. *Pillar supporting sky.* *Holmberg Baum des Lebens 12ff. — Siberian: Holmberg Siberian 333ff.; Norse: MacCulloch Eddic 334ff.

A841. World columns: two (four). F58. Tower (column) to upper world.

A665.2.0.1. *Pillars supporting sky.* Tahiti: Henry 342; Eskimo (Ungava): Turner RBAE XII (266), (Cape York): Rasmussen III 169, (Greenland): Rink 440.

A665.2.1. *Four sky-columns.* Four columns support the sky. — Cook Zeus II 140ff.; Frobenius Erdteile VI 165ff. — Egyptian: Müller 35.

A841. Four world-columns.

A665.2.1.1. *Four gods at world-quarters support the sky.* India: Thompson-Balys. — Aztec: Krickeberg Märchen der Azteken 208, 316.

A842. Atlas.

A665.2.1.2. *Four dwarfs support the sky.* Icel.: MacCulloch Eddic 264—65.

A665.2.1.3. *Sky extended by means of pillars.* Tahiti: Henry 342.

A665.3. *Mountain supports sky.* India: Thompson-Balys; Siberian: Holmberg Siberian 341ff.

A151.1. Home of gods on high mountain. F132. Otherworld on lofty mountain.

A665.3.1. *Four mountains support sky.* Patch PMLA XXXIII 618 n. 61.

A665.4. *Tree supports sky.* (Cf. A652.1.).

A665.5. *Sky held against earth by great octopus.* Tahiti: Henry 338.

A665.6. *Serpent supports sky.* S. Am. Indian (Yuracare): Métraux BBAE CXLIII (3) 503.

A666. *Ladder to heaven* (applied to saint). Irish myth: Cross.

A666.1. *Eight (symbolical) steps of the ladder of heaven.* Irish myth: Cross.

A666.2. *Rodent gnaws away ladder to other world* and thus ghosts remain on earth. S. Am. Indian (Brazil): Oberg Mato Grosso 109.

A667. *Language of heaven.* Irish myth: Cross.

A1482.1. Hebrew the language of the inhabitants of heaven.

A669. *Nature of the upper world — miscellaneous.*

A669.1. *Judges in the upper world.* Gaster Thespis 186; Icel.: Boberg.

A669.2. *Sky of solid substance.* S. Am. Indian (Chiriguano): Métraux RMLP XXXIII 164.

A670. Nature of the lower world.

F80. Journey to lower world. H1270. Quest to lower world.

A671. *Hell.* Lower world of torment. — Jeremias Hölle und Paradies bei den Babyloniern (Leipzig 1903); Kohler Heaven and Hell in Comparative Religion (New York 1923); *Landau Hölle und Fegfeuer in Volksglaube, Dichtung, und Kirchenlehre (Heidelberg, 1909); *Jātaka Index s. v. "hell". — Norse: De la Saussaye 256, 291, Mac Culloch Eddic 303, Herrmann Saxo Gr. II 588, *Boberg; Greek: Fox 143; Egyptian: Müller 179; Babylonian: Spence 128; Persian: Carnoy 345; Hindu: Penzer X 169 s. v. "Hades", Keith 100, 160; India: Thompson-Balys. — Japanese: Anesaki 237. — Aztec: Alexander Lat. Am. 80; Maya: ibid. 138; Chaco: ibid. 324; Chibcha: ibid. 198; Eskimo: Alexander N. Am. 7.

A310. God of the world of the dead. B11.3.6. Dragons in hell. D191.1. Lucifer as serpent. D1738. Magic arts learned in hell. E480. Abode of the dead. E481.1. Land of dead in lower world. E755. Destination of the soul. F81. Descent to lower world of dead. Q560. Punishments in hell. Q565. Man admitted to neither heaven nor hell. V511.2. Visions of hell. V520. Salvation.

A671.0.1. *Hell located to the north.* Irish myth: Cross; Icel.: MacCulloch Eddic 319.

E481.6.1. Land of death in north. E755.2.5. Punishment by cold in hell. G633. North as abode of evil spirits.

A671.0.1.1. *Other locations for hell.* Jewish: Neuman.

A671.0.2. *Creation of hell.* Lithuanian: Balys Legends Nos. 2, 5, 7; Jewish: Neuman.

A671.0.2.1. *Fire in hell.* Christ created fire in hell from his blood; formerly hell was cold. Lithuanian: Balys Legends No. 26.

A671.0.3. *Entrance to cave as gate to hell.* Irish myth: Cross; Jewish: Neuman. (Cf. A671.5.).

F156. Door to otherworld. F158. Pit entrance to otherworld. F211.1. Entrance to fairyland through door in knoll. V511.2.2. Vision of gate to hell.

A671.0.4. *Hell confused with fairy land.* Irish myth: Cross.

F160.0.2. Fairy otherworld confused with land of the dead. F165.6.1. Otherworld (fairy land) as place of sorrowful captivity. F251.7. Fairies as demons. F360. Malevolent or destructive fairies.

A671.0.5. *Size and arrangements of hell.* Jewish: Neuman; Buddhist myth: Malalasekera II 786.

A671.1. *Doorkeeper of hell.* Breton: Sébillot Incidents s. v. "Chabert".

E755.2.3. Lost soul to serve as porter in hell for seven years.

A671.2. *Horrible sights in hell.* Irish myth: Cross; Gaster Thespis 187f.

E755.2. Souls in hell. Q560. Punishments in hell.

A671.2.1. *Serpents in hell.* Wimberly Folklore in Ballads 424; Icel.: MacCulloch Eddic 319, 321, 332, Boberg; Irish myth: Cross.

A671.2.1.1. *Adders in hell.* Irish myth: Cross.

Q566.1. Fiery chains in the form of adders about waists of souls tormented in hell.

A671.2.2. *Rivers of blood in hell.* Wimberly Folklore in Ballads 128.

A671.2.2.1. *Rivers of poison in hell.* Irish myth: Cross; Icel.: MacCulloch Eddic 319f.; Jewish: Neuman.

A671.2.2.2. *River in hell filled with weapons.* Icel.: MacCulloch Eddic 320, 321.

A671.2.2.3. *Rivers of fire in hell.* Irish myth: Cross.

F142. River of fire as barrier to otherworld.

A671.2.2.4. *Rivers of black water in hell.* Irish myth: Cross.

D1293.4. Black as magic color. E481.2. Land of dead across water.

A671.2.2.5. *Four (three) rivers in hell.* Irish myth: Cross.

F162.2.1. The four (three) rivers of paradise.

A671.2.2.6. *Other rivers in hell.* Irish myth: Cross; Jewish: Neuman (A671.2.29).

F162.2. Rivers in other world.

A671.2.3. *Tree in hell made of living heads of the dead.* Quiché: Alexander Lat. Am. 171.

A671.2.4. *The fires of hell.* Irish myth: Cross.

E750. Perils of the soul. Q566. Punishments by heat in hell. V511.2.1. Vision of fires of hell.

A671.2.4.1. *Sea of fire in hell.* Irish myth: Cross.

A671.2.4.2. *Islands in sea of fire in hell.* Irish myth: Cross.

D911. Magic sea.

A671.2.4.3. *Fiery showers in hell.* Irish myth: Cross.

Q566.9. Showers of fire fall on sinners in hell. Q566.10. Demons shoot fiery arrows at souls in hell.

A671.2.4.4. *Burning plains in hell.* Irish myth: Cross.

A671.2.4.5. *Fiery glens in hell.* Irish myth: Cross.

E750.2.2. Perious valley in (on way to) land of dead. F151.1.2. Perilous glen on way to otherworld. F756.4. Glen of witchcraft.

A671.2.4.6. *Fiery wheels in hell.* Irish myth: Cross.

Q566.2. Fiery wheels about necks of souls tormented in hell.

A671.2.4.7. *Fiery chains in hell.* Irish myth: Cross.

Q566.1. Fiery chains in the form of adders about waists of souls tormented in hell. Q566.6 Fiery red overgarments worn by sinners in hell.

A671.2.4.8. *Fiery sticks in hell.* Irish myth: Cross.

A671.2.4.9. *Fiery stones in hell.* Irish myth: Cross.

A671.2.4.10. *Fiery nails in hell.* Irish myth: Cross.

Q566.3. Fiery nails through tongues of souls tormented in hell.

A671.2.4.11. *Fiery columns in hell.* Irish myth: Cross.

F169.1. Pillars of silver and glass in otherworld. Q566.4. Tormented souls bound to fiery columns in hell.

A671.2.4.12. *Swift, flaming winds in hell.* Irish myth: Cross.

A671.2.4.13. *Four fires in hell.* Irish myth: Cross.

D1273.1.2. Four as magic number. F162.2.1. The four rivers of paradise.

A671.2.5. *Dragons in hell.* Irish myth: Cross; Icel.: MacCulloch Eddic 319, 332 (Nidhogg).

A671.2.6. *Wolf in hell.* Icel.: MacCulloch Eddic 319.

A671.2.7. *Gnats in hell.* Irish myth: Cross.

A671.2.8. *Toads in hell.* Irish myth: Cross.

B776.5.1. Blood of toad venemous.

A671.2.9. *Scorpions in hell.* Irish myth: Cross; Jewish: Neuman.

A671.2.10. *Griffins in hell.* Irish myth: Cross.

B42. Griffin.

A671.2.11. *Birds made of iron in hell.* Irish myth: Cross.

A671.2.12. *Lions in hell.* Irish myth: Cross.

A671.2.13. *Scratching cats in hell.* Irish myth: Cross.

A671.2.14. *Tigers in hell.* Irish myth: Cross.

A671.3. *Frigidity of hell.* Irish myth: Cross; Buddhist myth: Malalasekera II 786.

D2144. Magic control of cold and heat. E481.7. Icy inferno. E755.2.5. Icy hell. Q567. Punishments by cold in hell.

A671.3.1. *Coldness in hell.* Irish myth: Cross.

A671.3.2. *Rugged, icy mountains in hell.* Irish myth: Cross.

F750. Extraordinary mountains and other land features.

A671.3.3. *Alternate heat and cold in hell.* Irish myth: Cross.

Q562. Pain of souls tormented in hell alternately ebbs and flows.

A671.4. *Well in hell* (Hvergelmir). Icel.: MacCulloch Eddic 319, 324, 332.

A671.5. *Gate around hell.* Icel.: MacCulloch Eddic 130, Boberg.

A671.6. *Beings born in hell have long bodies* and cling with long nails to walls. Buddhist myth: Malalasekera II 786.

A672. *Stygian river.* River in lower world. In Greek myth five such rivers in Hades, Styx (hate), Acheron (mourning), Kokytus (lamentation), Lethe (forgetfulness) and Pyrephlegethon (flame). — Gaster Oldest Stories 50; Greek: Fox 143; Norse: De la Saussaye 350, Mac Culloch Eddic 330, Boberg. — Chibcha: Alexander Lat. Am. 198; India: Thompson-Balys.

E481.2. Land of dead across water. F162.2.1. The four rivers of paradise.

A672.1. *Ferryman on river in lower world (Charon).* Irish myth: Cross; Greek: Fox 142; Egyptian: Müller 176; Icel.: MacCulloch Eddic 45; Babylonian: Jensen Gilgamesch-Epos X, XI, 46ff., cf. 136ff.

F90. Access to lower world.

A672.1.1. *Charon exacts fee to ferry souls across Styx.* Greek: Fox 142; Italian Novella: Rotunda.

E431.11. Coin placed in mouth of dead to prevent return. E489.3. Forgetting Charon's fee.

A672.2. *Maiden at the bridge to hell.* Icel.: MacCulloch Eddic 130, 304.

A673. *Hound of hell.* Cerberus (monstrous dog) guards the bridge to the lower world. — *Encyc. Rel. Ethics I 493a; *Fb "hund" III 678b. — Gaster Thespis 214; Greek: Fox 88; Frazer Apollodorus I 232 n. 1; Norse: Herrmann Nordische Mythologie 599ff., MacCulloch Eddic 303f.; Persian and Hindu: Keith 69. — Eskimo (Greenland): Rink 326, (Cumberland Sound): Boas BAM XV 165.

B15.7.1. Cerberus. B187. Magic dog. B325.1. Animal bribed with food. B576.1. Animal as guard of person or house. E481.2.1. Bridge to land of dead. E572.5. Hell-hounds accompany soul to lower world. F150.2. Entrance to otherworld guarded by monsters. F152.0.1. Bridge to otherworld guarded by animals. H1271. Quest for Cerberus in hell.

A673.1. *Dogs in hell.* Irish myth: Cross.

B187. Magic dog.

A673.2. *Cock of hell.* Icel.: Boberg.

A675. *Judges in the lower world.* Greek: Fox 143. — Chinese: Eberhard FFC CXX 206 No. 155; Japanese: Anesaki 238.

A676. *Ship of hell.* Icel.: MacCulloch Eddic 340, 343.

A677. *Workmen and tradesmen of hell.*

A677.1. *Smith of hell.* Irish myth: Cross.

A677.2. *Miller of hell.* Irish myth: Cross.

P443. Miller.

A678. *In other world one room contains the dead,* another contains souls of the unborn waiting to enter the wombs of women, and a third contains all the evil spirits. India: Thompson-Balys.

A681. *Sun in the underworld.* S. Am. Indian (Viracocha): Steward-Métraux BBAE CXLIII (3) 550.

A682. *Hole to lower world up which people come.* S. Am. Indian (Terino): Métraux BBAE CXLIII (1) 367.

A1232. Mankind ascends from under the earth.

A689. *Nature of the lower world — miscellaneous.*

A689.1. *Dark puddles in hell.* Irish myth: Cross.

Q568.1. Sinners in hell forced to sit in dark puddles up to their middles.

A689.2. *Foul odor in hell.* Irish myth: Cross.

A689.3. *Hunger in hell.* Irish myth: Cross. (A679.4.).

A689.3.1. *Dogs incited to devour souls in hell.* Irish myth: Cross (A679.4.1).

A690. Miscellaneous worlds. Irish myth: Cross.

F110. Journey to terrestrial otherworlds.

A692. *Islands of the blest.* Irish myth: Cross. — Greek: Fox 147, Grote I 62, Güntert Kalypso 81; Gaster Oldest Stories 50. — Oceanic: Kruyt Het Animisme 368ff.; Landman Kiwai Papuans 12; Lévy-Bruhl L'âme primitive 382ff.

A561. Divinity's departure for west. D936. Magic island. D981.1.1. Magic apple from Garden of the Hesperides. E480. Abode of the dead. E481.2. Land of dead across water. F111. Journey to earthly paradise. Land of happiness. F112. Journey to land of women. F116. Journey to land of the immortals. F129.7. Voyage to island of the dead. F134. Otherworld on island. F213. Fairyland on island. F730. Extraordinary islands.

A692.1. *Overseas otherworld in the west.* Irish myth: Cross; S. Am. Indian (Guarayú): Métraux RMLP XXXIII 147.

A693. *Intermediate future world.* Residence for those whose good and evil deeds exactly counterbalance. — Irish myth: Cross; Persian: Carnoy 344.

D1856.1.1. The two sorrows of the kingdom of heaven. Q0. Rewards and punishments. V511.3. Visions of purgatory. V520. Salvation.

A694. *Christian paradise.* Irish myth: Cross.

F11. Journey to heaven (upper-world paradise). F111. Journey to earthly paradise.

A694.1. *Christian paradise (Terra Repromissionis) corresponding to pagan Celtic otherworld* (Ireland). Irish myth: Cross.

F110. Journey to terrestrial otherworlds. F160.0.3. Pagan otherworld identified with Christian paradise. F756.2. Plain that is earthly paradise.

A695. *Moon as next world.* (Cf. A750.) Hindu: Keith 101.

A696. *World of serpents.* Hindu: Keith 154.

A697. *Various Buddhist otherworlds.*

A697.1. *Brahma world.* Buddhist myth: Malalasekera II 796.

A697.2. *Tusita world.* Buddhist myth: Malalasekera I 1034.

A697.2.1. *Years are days in Tusita world.* Buddhist myth: Malalasekera I 1033.

D2011. Years thought days.

A697.3. *Deva world.* Buddhist myth: Malalasekera I 861, II 892, 909.

A700—A799. The heavens.

A700. Creation of the heavenly bodies. Irish myth: Cross; Pawnee: Alexander N. Am. 108; Navaho: ibid. 163; Persian: Carnoy 276; Babylonian: Spence 115.

D1546. Magic object controls heavenly bodies. F961. Extraordinary behavior of heavenly bodies.

A700.1. *Heavenly bodies from objects thrown into sky.* The Christ Child throws mud pies into the sky and creates sun, moon, and stars. — *Dh II 78ff.; Icel.: MacCulloch Eddic 325—26.

A714. Sun from object thrown into sky. A741. Origin of moon from object (person) thrown into sky. A763. Stars from objects thrown into sky.

A700.2. *Heavenly bodies vomited up by creator.* Bushongo: Werner African 144.

A700.3. *A woman has four children: sun, moon, fire, and water.* India: Thompson-Balys.

A700.4. *Heavenly bodies created after the plant world.* Jewish: Neuman.

A700.5. *Sun, moon, and stars forged by smith.* African (Togo): Einstein 14f.

A700.6. *Sun and moon purchased.* African (Togo): Einstein 9f.

A700.7. *Sun, moon, and stars nourished on fire.* African (Fang): Einstein 33.

A700.8. *Sun, moon, and darkness as god's three children.* African (Kamerun): Mansfield 234.

A701. *Creation of the sky.* Babylonian: Spence 79; Hebrew: Genesis, ch. 1; Jewish: Neuman; Estonian: Loorits Grundzüge I 384; India: Thompson-Balys; Chinese: Graham.

A701.0.1. *Creation of firmament.* Jewish: Neuman.

A701.1. *Origin of sky from egg brought from primeval water.* — Borneo: Dixon 165; Tahiti: Henry 339.

A641. Cosmic egg. A655. World as egg. A812.2. Earth from egg from bottom of sea.

A701.2. *Origin of sky from Ymir's skull.* Icel.: MacCulloch Eddic 325—26.

A702. *Nature of the sky.* Chinese: Graham.

F51. Sky rope. F55. Mountain reaches to sky. F56. Sky window. F791. Rising and falling sky.

A702.1. *Sky of water.* The sky consists of water. — *Eisler Weltenmantel und Himmelszelt 204ff. — Egyptian: Müller 34f.

A702.2. *Sky as solid vault (tent).* Siberian: Holmberg Siberian 336; Hatt Asiatic Influences 63; Eskimo (Labrador): Hawkes GSCan XIV 153. — African: Werner African 130. — Cf. Isaiah, ch 40.

A702.3. *Sky supported by north star* ("nail of the north") around which it revolves. (Cf. A665, A774.) — Gaster Thespis 170; Icel.: MacCulloch Eddic 335; Estonian: Loorits Grundzüge I 386. — Finno-Ugric: Holmberg Finno-Ugric 221. — Siberian: Holmberg Siberian 337.

A702.3.1. *Celestial bodies attached to a wheel* in heaven around which they move. Jewish: Neuman.

A702.4. *Why the sky is blue.* India: Thompson-Balys.

A702.5. *Marriage of earth and sky.* India: Thompson-Balys.

A702.6. *Sky measured by bird.* Chinese: Graham.

A702.7. *Clouds as props of the sky.* Maori: Clark 18.

A702.8. *Sky is black because once raised by means of dirty stick.* Tonga: Gifford 23.

A625.2. Raising the sky.

A702.9. *Sky immortal, changing skin like a snake.* S. Am. Indian (Bacairi): Lévi-Strauss BBAE CXLIII (3) 348.

A703. *Angels arrange course of heavenly bodies.* Jewish: Neuman.

A705. *Origin and nature of clouds.*

A705.1. *Origin of clouds.* India: Thompson-Balys; Icel.: Boberg.

A705.1.1. *Creator makes clouds from own vitals.* Tahiti: Henry 339.

A705.1.2. *Clouds as tapa beaten out by woman in moon.* Samoa: Clark 120.

A705.2. *Nature of clouds (covered with skin).* (Cf. A702.9.) — India: Thompson-Balys.

A710—A739. THE SUN

A710. **Creation of the sun.** *Rühle Sonne und Mond im primitiven Mythus (Tübingen, 1925). — Irish myth: Cross; India: Thompson-Balys. — Indonesian: Dixon 177; Australian: ibid. 275; Navaho: Alexander N. Am. 166ff.; Hopi: ibid. 205; Quileute: Farrand JAFL XXXII 254f.; Sinkyone: Kroeber JAFL XXXII 346f.; Tahltan: Teit JAFL XXXII 205. — Inca: Alexander Lat. Am. 240; Africa (Luba): Donohugh Africa V 180.

F961.1. Extraordinary behavior of sun.

A711. *Sun as man who left earth.* Man, usually of supernatural birth, ascends to the sky and becomes the sun. — India: Thompson-Balys; Bushman: Bleek and Lloyd 45; Gold Coast: Barker and Sinclair 97 No. 18; Ekoi: Talbot 357, 359; British New Guinea: Dixon 113; Tuamotu: Stimson MS (T-g 3/191); S. Am. Indian (Eastern Brazil): Lowie BBAE CXLIII (1) 434, (Guarayú): Métraux RMLP XXXIII 147, (Kaigua): Métraux RMLP XXXIII 138ff., (Manasi): Métraux BBAE CXLIII (3) 393, (Chiriguano): Métraux RMLP XXXIII 122, 158—165, (Guaporé River): Lévi-Strauss BBAE CXLIII (3) 379.

A711.1. *Sun and moon as uncle and nephew who ascended to the sky.* Tunja (Colombia): Alexander Lat. Am. 200.

A711.2. *Sun as a cannibal.* India: Thompson-Balys; Crow: Lowie PaAM XV 157.

A736.4.1. Sun-moon quarrel when sun eats up all their children but two.
G11. Kinds of cannibals.

A711.3. *Originally a moon but no sun.* Africa (Luba): Donohugh Africa V 180.

A711.4. *Originally no sun.* Africa (Bushongo): Torday 247.

A712. *Sun as fire* rekindled every morning. Australian: Dixon 274f.

A712.1. *Moon from light, sun from fire.* Jewish: Neuman.

A713. *Sun and moon from cave.* Haiti: Alexander Lat. Am. 28.

A713.1. *Sun and moon from belly of a fish.* India: Thompson-Balys.

A714. *Sun from object thrown into sky.* Bushman: Bleek and Lloyd 54; Pelew Is. (Micronesia): Dixon 253; Cook Group: ibid. 37; Admiralty Is., Woodlark Is.: ibid 112; Australian: ibid 275.

A700.1. Heavenly bodies from objects thrown into sky.

A714.1. *Sun and moon placed for eyes in the sky.* Maori, Society Is., Samoa, Cook Group: Dixon 37.

A714.2. *Sun and moon placed in top of tree.* Hero makes the sun and moon and fastens them to the top of the "World Tree" (cf. A652), but they give no light at first. — Finnish: Kalevala rune 49, cf. FFC LXXII 108.

D1576.1. Magic song causes tree to rise to sky. Has moon and Great Bear in its branches.

A714.3. *Sun from fire flung into sky.* Siberian: Holmberg Siberian 421.

A714.4. *Sun and moon metal mirrors in sky.* Siberian: Holmberg Siberian 419; India: *Thompson-Balys.

A714.5. *Sun as grindstone full of fire.* India: Thompson-Balys.

A714.6. *Sun and moon as spangle* which falls from creator's forehead into his own urine. India: Thompson-Balys.

A714.7. *Sun and moon as eyes of Rama* which he tore out after his brother's death. India: Thompson-Balys.

A714.8. *Wooden circles that were the sun and moon animated* after human sacrifice of blood. India: Thompson-Balys.

A740. Creation of the moon.

A715. *Sun born of first couple.* Gilbert Is.: Dixon 254; Samoa: Beckwith Myth 254; S. Am. Indian (Tupinamba, Tembé, Apapocuva): Métraux RMLP XXXIII 123, (Jivaro): Stewart-Métraux BBAE CXLIII (3) 627, (Guarani): Métraux BBAE CXLIII (3) 93, (Paressi): Métraux ibid. 359, (Viracocha): Stewart-Métraux ibid. 550.

A715.1. *Sun and moon born from a woman.* *Fb "sol" III 457b.

A645. Creation of universe: genealogical type.

A715.2. *Sun and moon born from a goddess impregnated by the wind.* India: Thompson-Balys.

T524. Conception from wind.

A715.3. *Sun and moon born from an ogre.* India: Thompson-Balys.

A715.4. *Sun and moon from breasts of mother earth.* (Cf. A401.) India: Thompson-Balys.

A715.5. *Sun as offspring of moon.* Babylonia: Spence 145.

A715.6. *Sun and moon born of lizard.* S. Am. Indian (Amuesha): Métraux RMLP XXXIII 149.

A716. *Dispute at creation of sun.* God and devil discuss creation. God plans two suns; devil persuades him to create only one. — Dh I 128ff.; cf. Pauli (ed. Bolte) No. 498.

A716.1. *Four suns at first: culture hero shoots three down.* — Siberian: Holmberg Siberian 420.

A717. *Hero makes sun and moon from tree* and sends them alternately into sky. India: Thompson-Balys.

A717.1. *Hero makes sun and moon from tree and vivifies them with blood of creator's son.* India: Thompson-Balys.

A718. *Sun from transformation.*

A718.1. *Sun from head of youth offered in sacrifice.* India: Thompson-Balys.

A718.2. *Sun and moon as divine bodies of gods.* Hawaii: Beckwith Myth 85.

A718.3. *Sun from fruit kernels thrown into water of flood.* S. Am. Indian (Cashinawa): Métraux BBAE CXLIII (3) 683.

A718.4. *Sun from transformed maggots.* Maori: Beckwith Myth 101.

A719. *Creation of sun — miscellaneous.*

A719.1. *Sun emerges from lake.* S. Am. Indian (Amyra): Tschopik BBAE CXLIII (2) 571.

A719.2. *After world catastrophe, new sun reappears* and starts new epoch. S. Am. Indian (Chiriguano): Métraux RMLP XXXIII 154ff.

A1000. World catastrophe.

A719.3. *Sun created on fourth day of creation.* Jewish: Neuman.

A720. Nature and condition of the sun. Chinese: Graham.

A220. Sun-god. D1546.1. Hat which turns the sun. F17. Visit to land of the sun.

A720.1. *Formerly seven suns.* India: Thompson-Balys.

A720.2. *Formerly great heat of sun causes distress to mankind.* India: Thompson-Balys.

A721. *Sun kept in box.* Siberian: Holmberg Siberian 421.

A754. Moon kept in box. A1411.1. Light kept in box (basket).

A721.0.1. *Sun and moon kept in pots* when they do not shine. S. Am. Indian (Bakairi, Amazon): Alexander Lat. Am. 313, (Cashinawa): Métraux BBAE CXLIII (3) 683. Cf. N. A. Indian: Thompson Tales 282 n. 45 (light kept in box or basket).

A721.0.2. *Sun shut up in pit.* India: Thompson-Balys; Chinese: Graham.

A721.0.3. *Sun kept in a case.* Jewish: Neuman.

A721.1. *Theft of sun.* The sun, which is kept by a monster, is stolen and brought to earth. — BP III 288; Dh I 136ff., III 113ff. — Cf. Kaffir: Kidd 238 No. 7; Finnish: Kalevala runes 47, 49. — Eskimo (Bering Strait): Nelson RBAE XVIII 483; Calif. Indian: Gayton and Newman 60; S. Am. Indian (Cashinawa): Métraux BBAE CXLIII (3) 683.

A758. Theft of the moon. A1411. Theft of light. A1415. Theft of fire.

A721.2. *Sun swallowed and spit out.* In theft of sun, the raven (or devil) thus succeeds. — Dh III 113ff.

A721.2.1. *Great darkness due to awk swallowing the sun.* India: Thompson-Balys.

A721.3. *Stolen sun restored to sky.* Calif. Indian: Gayton and Newman 83; India: Thompson-Balys.

A721.4. *Pale sun made right again by using egg, yellow grass,* etc. India: Thompson-Balys.

A721.5. *Sun falls but is lifted back to sky and tied to it.* S. Am. Indian: (Mocovi): Métraux MAFLS XXXX 34.

A722. *Sun's night journey. Around or under the earth.* — Armenian: Ananikian 50; S. Am. Indian (Mundurucu): Horton BBAE CXLIII (3) 281.

J2272.3. Fools believe sun sleeps at certain woman's house.

A722.1. *Sun's night journey in golden goblet.* Helios' chariot is conveyed eastward at night in a golden goblet (or bed). — Greek: Fox 243. Cf. A724.

A722.2. *Sun's night journey with reversed face.* It returns from west to east by the same way that it came, but it turns its light side to the sky and leaves the earth in darkness. — Hindu: Keith 16.

A722.3. *Sun's night journey: in land of dead.* Gaster Thespis 195; Egyptian: Müller 27, 84; Armenian: Ananikian 50; India: Thompson-Balys.

A722.4. *Sun at night closes doors. In evening goes home and shuts doors and windows.* — Africa (Ekoi): Talbot 357.

A722.5. *Sun at night lowers arm.* The sun, a man, lies with arm uplifted. The shining comes from his armpits. When his arm is lowered the shining ceases. — Bushman: Bleek and Lloyd 45.

A722.5.1. *Sun bathes in stream of fire at night.* Jewish: Neuman.

A722.5.2. *Sun led through stream to cool off heat at night;* otherwise might consume earth. Jewish: Neuman.

A722.6. *Sun hidden at night because afraid to wander.* India: Thompson-Balys.

A722.7. *Mountain where sun goes through.* Babylonian: Jensen Gilgamesch Epos IX 37.

A722.7.1. *Sun at night enters fissure between sky and earth.* S. Am. Indian (Toba): Métraux MAFLS XL 19.

A722.8. *Sun sits on back of a male buffalo.* India: Thompson-Balys.

A722.9. *At dawn sun comes to play with the moon.* India: Thompson-Balys.

A722.10. *Sun and moon to remain half their time in underworld.* India: Thompson-Balys.

A722.11. *Sun worships God by night.* Jewish: Neuman.

A722.12. *Visible sun is the "pet" of real sun.* S. Am. Indian (Bacairi): Lévi-Strauss BBAE CXLIII (3) 348.

A722.13. *Sun is man during day.* Philippine (Tinguian): Cole 33.

A723. *Boat of the sun.* Egyptian: Müller 26; Icel.: cf. Du Chaillu The Viking Age 100ff., 107; Almgren Hällristningar och Kultbruk (Stockholm, 1926—27) passim.

A724. *Chariot of the sun.* *Helm Altgermanische Religionsgeschichte I 178, 256; Cook Zeus I 205ff. — Greek: Fox 243, cf. A722.1., Grote I

313; Icel.: MacCulloch Eddic 198; Babylonian: Spence 236; Jewish: Neuman; India: Thompson-Balys.

A136.2.1. God's chariot.

A724.1. *Charioteer of the sun.* Sun drives his horses and chariot across sky. — Howey Horse in Magic and Myth 114ff. — Icel.: MacCulloch Eddic 196; Greek: Fox 243; Hindu: Penzer I 143 n. 2, II 150ff.

B41.2. Flying horse. F1021.2.1. Flight so high that sun melts glue of artificial wings. L421. Attempt to fly to heaven punished.

A724.1.0.1. *Coyote rides with sun.* Calif. Indian: Gayton and Newman 85.

A724.1.1. *Phaëton.* Sun entrusts his chariot to another (his son) and the horses run away. The world is almost burnt up. — Krappe "Phaëthon", The Review of Religion (1944) 115—129. — Greek: *Roscher s.v. "Phaëthon", *Frazer Pausanias II 59. — N. A. Indian: *Thompson Tales 291 n. 66.

A724.1.2. *Chariot of sun accompanied by angels.* Jewish: Neuman.

A724.2. *The sun a golden bowl* on the rim of which sits a peacock; both bowl and peacock are in a crystal box, which rests on a flying chariot. — India: Thompson-Balys.

A721. Sun kept in box.

A725. *Man controls rising and setting of sun.* Irish myth: Cross; Jewish: *Neuman.

D1546.2. Magic spell controls sun.

A725.1. *Sun does not set for a year through power of saint.* Irish myth: Cross.

V222. Miraculous manifestation acclaims saint.

A726. *Daily course of sun across sky.*

A726.1. *Sun and moon make daily tour under direct orders of God.* Jewish: Neuman.

A726.2. *Wings of sun.* Jewish: Neuman.

A727. *Raising the sun.* Originally low, it is raised little by little by conjurors. — Cherokee: Alexander N. Am. 60; Navaho: ibid. 167ff.

A625.2. Raising the sky.

A727.1. *Sun originally so hot that it threatens all life.* India: Thompson-Balys.

A728. *Sun caught in snare.* Luomala Oceanic, American Indian, and African Myths of Snaring the Sun (BMB No. 168 [Honolulu, 1940]); *Dh III 120ff. — India: Thompson-Balys; African: Frobenius Atlantis V 38, 70f., XII 160, 185f.

H1023.23. Task: to tie the sun with a gold chain.

A728.1. *Sun-snarer: burnt mantle.* A boy is angered because the sun burned his mantle. He makes a snare and catches the sun and delays him so that everything is burning up. A mouse finally gnaws the snare in two. — American Indian: *Thompson Tales 290 n. 65. Cf. Luomala.

A728.2. *Sun-snarer: fast sun.* The sun goes too fast to dry clothing. The hero snares the sun's legs with a rope as he is climbing up from the underworld. He releases the sun upon the promise to go more slowly. — Polynesian: *Dixon 44ff. n. 26; Society Is., Samoan: ibid. 46; Hawaii: Beckwith Myth 10, 227, 230; Marquesas: Handy 103. Cf. Luomala.

A728.3. *Sun visits earth in form of black bull,* caught by man, thus causing night. India: Thompson-Balys.

A728.4. *Sun and moon carried through sky by animals.* Speed depends upon hour and season. — S. Am. Indian (Bacairi): Lévi-Strauss BBAE CXLIII (3) 348.

A731. *Sun as king of sky and earth.* India: Thompson-Balys; Jewish: Neuman; Africa: Bouveignes 14.

A731.1. *Sun sits on throne.* Jewish: Neuman.

A731.2. *Crown of the sun.* Jewish: Neuman.

A732. *The sun's animals.*

A732.1. *Cattle and sheep of the sun.* 350 of each (= days and nights of the lunar year). — Greek: Fox 242.

H721. Riddle of the year.

A732.2. *Horse of the sun.*

A732.2.1. *Slave shoots arrow into leg of sun's horse.* India: Thompson-Balys.

A733. *Heat and light of the sun.*

A733.1. *Why sunlight is so much stronger than moonlight.* Jewish: Neuman.

A733.2. *Mortal cannot look at sun* since God's name is engraved on it. Jewish: Neuman.

A733.3. *Two faces of the sun:* fire, directed toward earth; hail, directed toward heaven. Jewish: Neuman.

A733.4. *Beams of light are snares* with which sun is tied to earth. Cf. A728. — Maori: Clark 46.

A733.5. *Sun dries out earth with its heat.* Jewish: Neuman.

A734. *Sun hides.*

A734.1. *Sun hides in cave.* India: Thompson-Balys.

A735. *Pursuit of sun by moon.* Aztec: Alexander Lat. Am. 89; N. A. Indian: *Thompson Tales 274 n. 9. — Philippine (Tinguian): Cole 189; African: Frobenius Atlantis XII 181, (Fang): Einstein 34, Trilles 173, (Dahomé): Einstein 30.

A735.1. *Moon tied to sun* so that when sun sinks moon is dragged up to light earth. Maori: Clark 46.

A735.2. *Sun and moon pursued by dark planet* in black chariot. India: Thompson-Balys.

A736. *Sun as human being.*

A736.1. *Sun and moon as man and woman.* India: Thompson-Balys; Macobi: Alexander Lat. Am 319; Africa: Meinhof 200.

A736.1.1. *Sun sister and moon brother.* Brother visits sister at night. She marks him to identify him. He flees and she follows with flaming brand. She is sun and he the moon. — *Rank Das Inzestmotiv 446ff.; Frazer Ovid III 31. — Icel.: MacCulloch Eddic 196;

Lappish: Friis Lappisk Mythologi 79; German: Hdwb. d. deutschen Aberglaubens I 642, II 1511; India: Thompson-Balys; Korean: Zong in-Sob 10 No. 3. — Eskimo: *Thompson Tales 273 note 6; S. Am. Indian (Chaco): Métraux BBAE CXLIII (1) 366, (Manasi): Métraux BBAE CXLIII (3) 393, (Witoto, Shipaya, Canelo, Warrau, Arawak): Lowie BBAE CXLIII (3) 54; African (Baluga): Einstein 176.

A751.7.1. Moon wants to marry his sister the sun. She is angered and throws hot ashes on his face. H58. Tell-tale hand-mark. Clandestine lover is identified by paint marks left on his skin by his mistress. R321.1. Sister escapes to the stars to avoid marrying brother. T415. Brother-sister incest.

A736.1.2. *Sun-brother and moon-sister.* Icel.: De la Saussaye 344; India: *Thompson-Balys. — N. A. Indian (Montagnais and Menominee): Alexander N. Am. 25.

T415. Brother-sister incest.

A736.1.3. *Sun and moon as lovers.* (Cf. A736.1.1.). — India: Thompson-Balys. — S. Am. Indian (Amazon): Alexander Lat. Am. 306, (Caviña, Tumupasa): Métraux BBAE CXLIII (3) 448; African (Ekoi): Talbot 359.

A753. Moon as wooer.

A736.1.4. *Sun and moon married.* *Fb. "sol" III 457b. — Lettish: Gray 321; Jewish: Neuman; India: *Thompson-Balys; Chinese: Werner 133, Eberhard FFC CXX 113. — African: Werner African 232, (Fang): Trilles 171f.; Hatt Asiatic Influences 74f. — Tlingit: Alexander N. Am. 257; S. Am. Indian (Fuegian): Alexander Lat. Am. 342, (Jivaro): Stewart-Métraux BBAE CXLIII (3) 627, Métraux RMLP XXXIII 129, (Aymara): Tschopik BBAE CXLIII (2) 571, (Chibcha): Kroeber ibid. 908.

A736.1.4.1. *Sun and moon quarrel when sun eats up all their children but two.* India: Thompson-Balys. Cf. Africa: Meinhof 200.

A711.2. Sun as cannibal.

A736.1.4.1.1. *Moon kills sun's children.* Africa (Fang): Milligan Jungle 248.

A736.1.4.2. *Moon, sun are sister and brother, wife and husband.* India: Thompson-Balys. Cf. A736.1.2.

A736.1.4.3. *Creator separates sun and moon* to prevent birth of more stars. India: Thompson-Balys.

A736.2. *Sun as woman.* S. Am. Indian (Mocoví): Métraux MAFLS XXXX 20.

A736.3. *Sun and moon as brothers.* N. Am. Indian (Klikitat): Jacobs Northwest Sahaptin Texts 16; S. Am. Indian (Guarani): Métraux BBAE CXLIII (3) 93, (Chiriguano): Métraux ibid. 484; (Guaporé River): Lévi-Strauss ibid. 379.

A736.3.1. *Sun and moon as twin brothers.* S. Am. Indian (Mataco, Chamacoco): Métraux BBAE CXLIII (1) 366, (Amuesa): *Métraux RMLP XXXIII 131.

A515.1.1. Twin culture heroes.

A736.3.2. *Sun and moon brothers: sun clever, moon stupid.* S. Am. Indian (Mataco, Chamacoco): Métraux BBAE CXLIII (1) 366, (Timbira, Sherente, Caingang, Mashachali): Lowie BBAE CXLIII (1) 397, 515.

A736.3.3. *Sun and his brother rise and set alternately.* India: Thompson-Balys.

A736.4. *Sun and moon as sisters, daughters of sky-god.* India: Thompson-Balys.

A736.5. *Children of the sun.* Tonga: Gifford 115.

A736.5.1. *Son of sun so hot no one can hold it.* S. Am. Indian (Cavina, Tumupasa): Métraux BBAE CXLIII (3) 448.

A736.5.2. *Children from union with the sun turn into bit of blood* in daytime as soon as they are exposed to sun; take human form (shape) again at sunset. — India: Thompson-Balys.

T521. Conception from sunlight.

A736.6. *Sun and moon as friends.* India: Thompson-Balys.

A736.7. *Sun's affection for human girl rouses moon's jealousy.* India: Thompson-Balys.

A736.7.1. *Sun marries woman.* Philippine (Tinguian): Cole 35.

A736.8. *Original moon changed into sun and sun into moon.* India: Thompson-Balys.

A736.9. *Sun cursed by moon.* India: Thompson-Balys.

A736.10. *Human son of sun.* Tonga: Gifford 114.

A736.11. *Contest between sun and moon.* Chinese: Eberhard 219.

A737. *Causes of eclipses (sun or moon).* *Hdwb. d. deutschen Aberglaubens II 1511; Penzer II 81f. — Estonian: Loortis Grundzüge I 153, 410ff.; Icel.: De la Saussaye 344; Jewish: Neuman; Korean: Zong in-Sob 11 No. 4; Hindu: Keith 137, 151, 192, 232f.; India: *Thompson-Balys. — Montagnais: Alexander N. Am. 25; Mataguaya (Pampean): Alexander Lat. Am. 319.

A1046. Continuous world eclipse.

A737.0.1. *Origin of eclipse of moon.* India: *Thompson-Balys.

A737.1. *Eclipse caused by monster devouring sun or moon.* *Fb "solulv"; *Encyc. Religion and Ethics I 492a.; Gaster Oldest Stories 234; Gaster Thespis 206. — Icel.: MacCulloch Eddic 279; Finnish: Kalevala rune 47; Jewish: Neuman; Siberian: Holmberg Siberian 424; Jugo-Slav: Machal Slavic Myth 229; Armenian: Ananikian 48. — Buddhist myth: Malalasekera II 736; India: Thompson-Balys; Indonesian: Wilken Indische Gids (1885) I 240; Tahiti: Henry 227; S. Am. Indian (Chiriguano): Métraux RMLP XXXIII 123, 158, 165, (Mocoví): Métraux MAFLS XL 20, (Manao): Métraux BBAE CXLIII (3) 712, (Guarani, Manasí, Guarayú, Chiriguano): Métraux BBAE CXLIII (3) 93, 393, 483, (Guayaki): Métraux-Baldus BBAE CXLIII (1) 444, (Toba, Abipón, Mocovi, Mataco, Vilela): Métraux BBAE CXLIII (1) 366, (Eastern Brazil): Lowie ibid. 434 (Tucuna): Nimuendajú BBAE CXLIII (3) 724.

A737.2. *Cause of eclipses: mother's curse laid upon her third son.* India: Thompson-Balys.

A737.3. *Toad causes eclipses of the sun.* India: Thompson-Balys.

A737.4. *Ghosts of the sun's children return to cause eclipse.* India: Thompson-Balys.

E225. Ghost of murdered child.

A737.5. *Moon's eclipse caused by moon's interfering* between attacker and person attacked. India: Thompson-Balys.

A737.6. *Eclipses caused by animal hiding sun behind his body.* S. Am. Indian (Bacairi): Lévi-Strauss BBAE CXLIII (3) 348, (Lule): Métraux BBAE CXLIII (1) 366.

A737.7. *Eclipses from quarrels between moon and sun.* S. Am. Indian (Botocudo): Métraux BBAE CXLIII (1) 540.

A737.8. *Eclipses when sun smears his face on account of mourning.* S. Am. Indian (Caviña, Tumupasa): Métraux BBAE CXLIII (3) 448.

A737.8.1. *Sun hides face in shame: eclipse.* Africa: Meinhof 207.

A737.9. *Eclipse as punishment by deity.* Jewish: Neuman.

A737.10. *Eclipses because sun cannot endure tragic happenings of history.* Jewish: Neuman.

A737.11. *Partial eclipses because of ailments of sun or moon.* S. Am. Indian (Mojo): Métraux BBAE CXLIII (3) 424.

A738. *Attributes of sun.*

A738.1. *Physical attributes.*

A738.1.1. *Sun and moon are balls of feathers.* S. Am. Indian (Bacairi): Lévi-Strauss BBAE CXLIII (3) 347f., (Paressi): Métraux ibid. 360.

A738.1.2. *Sun a fat woman walking across sky.* S. Am. Indian (Toba): Métraux MAFLS XL 19.

A738.2. *Mental powers and disposition of sun.*

A738.2.1. *Religious sun and moon.* Jewish: Neuman.

A738.2.2. *Sun endowed with wisdom and passion.* Jewish: Neuman.

A738.3. *Sun's healing powers.* Jewish: Neuman.

A738.4. *Sun's power over plants.* Jewish: Neuman.

A739. *Nature and condition of the sun — miscellaneous.*

A739.1. *Sun at the edge of the sky.* Chinese: Graham.

A739.2. *War with the sun.* India: Thompson-Balys.

A739.3. *Each of sun brothers works for a month* and plays for the other eleven; were they to work all together, the world would be burned up by the heat. — India: Thompson-Balys.

A739.4. *Reason for variations in seasonal heat of sun.* India: Thompson-Balys.

A739.5. *Why the sun is red.* India: Thompson-Balys; Africa (Kamerun): Mansfield 235.

A739.6. *Sun sets and refuses to rise:* must be coaxed back from underworld. India: Thompson-Balys.

A739.7. *Sun's all-seeing eye.* Greek: Grote I 313.

A739.8. *Sun as caretaker of the poor.* S. Am. Indian (Chiriguano): Métraux RMLP XXXIII 165.

A739.9. *Sun has weapons of iron to repel enemies.* S. Am. Indian (Toba): Métraux MAFLS XL 19.

A740—A759. THE MOON

A740. Creation of the moon. (Cf. A710 to A719, where many of the motifs refer to the moon). — *Rühle Sonne und Mond im primitiven Mythus (Tübingen, 1925); *Roheim Mondmythologie und Mondreligion (Leipzig, 1927); Nielsen Die altarabische Mondreligion (Strassburg, 1904); Harley Moon Lore (London, 1885); Wolf Der Mond im deutschen Volksglauben (Bühl, Baden, 1929). — Irish myth: Cross; India: Thompson-Balys; Babylonian: Spence 79. — Indonesian: Dixon 177; Australian: ibid. 276ff.; Gold Coast: Barker and Sinclair 97 No. 18; Hopi: Alexander N. Am. 205; Quileute: Farrand JAFL XXXII 254ff.; Tahltan: Teit JAFL XXXII 205; Inca: Alexander Lat. Am. 240.

A711.1. Sun and moon as uncle and nephew who ascended to the sky. A713. Sun and moon from cave. A714.1. Sun and moon placed for eyes in the sky. A714.8. Wooden circles that were sun and moon animated after human sacrifices of blood.

A741. *Moon from object (person) thrown into sky.* Admiralty Is.: Dixon 112; Cook Group: ibid. 37; Hawaii: Beckwith Myth 215.

A700.1. Heavenly bodies from objects thrown into sky. A714.2. Sun and moon placed in top of tree.

A741.1. *Moon is water slung into sky.* Siberian: Holmberg Siberian 421.

A741.2. *Chest of sacrificed youth becomes the moon.* India: Thompson-Balys.

A741.3. *Moon as grinder which brings fire out of the sun.* India: Thompson-Balys.

A742. *Moon made from shining fragments.* A cap is opened and shining things fall out. Children pick them up and put them into a box. At the end of the month the box is full. The full moon shines when all the fragments are gathered together. — Africa (Ekoi): Talbot 349.

A743. *Moon from transformed object.*

A743.1. *Origin of moon from shell.* Nauru (Pleasant Is.), Micronesia: Dixon 250.

A744. *Heavenly smith is hammering on the moon.* Africa (Sudanese): Frobenius Atlantis VII 18f.

A745. *Family of the moon.*

A745.1. *Moon born from first couple.* Gilbert Is. (Micronesia): Dixon 254.

A745.2. *Mother of the moon: the most distant star in the sky.* India: Thompson-Balys.

A745.3. *Moon younger brother of the sun.* India: Thompson-Balys; S. Am. Indian (Chiriguano): Métraux RMLP XXXIII 158, 165.

A736.3. Sun and moon as brothers.

A747. *Person transformed to moon.* India: *Thompson-Balys; S. Am. Indian (Chiriguano): Métraux RMLP XXXIII 165, (Cashinawa): Métraux BBAE CXLIII (3) 684, (Warrau): Kirchoff ibid. 879, (Chibcha): Kroeber BBAE CXLIII (2) 908; Norse: Boberg.

D200. Transformation: man to object.

A750. Nature and condition of the moon. Many motifs in A720 to A739 refer to the moon and are not here repeated.

A695. Moon as next world. F16. Visit to land of moon.

A751. *Man in the moon.* A man is said to be seen in the moon. Various explanations are given as to how he came to be there. — *Dh I 134; *Volksmann Am Urquell V 285, VI 75, 126, 199; *Cornelissen Ons Volksleven VI 168ff., 189ff.; *Köhler-Bolte III 597; *Robinson Complete Works of Geoffrey Chaucer (Boston 1933) 929; *Brown English Lyrics of the Thirteenth Century (Oxford 1932) 234ff.; *Hench JAFL XLVIII 384; *G. de Raille RTP III 129ff.; Basset RTP XXIII 220 and references to earlier volumes. — Breton: *Sébillot Incidents s. v. "homme"; Estonian: *Aarne FFC XXV 140 No. 7, Loorits Grundzüge I 427f.; Livonian: *Loorits FFC LXVI 81 No. 8; Siberian: Holmberg Siberian 423; Armenian: Ananikian 52; Flemish: *De Meyer FFC XXXVII 82 No. 8; Chinese: Eberhard FFC CXX 37, 214 No. 163, 221, 250. — Maori: Dixon 88; N. A. Indian (general): *Thompson Tales 291 n. 69, (Haida, Tlingit, Kwakiutl): Alexander N. Am. 257, (Loucheux): Barbeau JAFL XXVIII 255; Hottentot: Bleek 72 No. 33; Am. Negro (Georgia): Harris Friends 130 No. 17.

A751.1. *Man in moon is person thrown or sent there as punishment.* *Dh I 254ff.; *ibid. II 242 (Judas); Köhler-Bolte I 114 (Judas), III 597; *Fb "måne" II 659b.; Kristensen Danske Sagn II (1893) 275ff., (1928) 171; Lithuanian: Balys Index No. 3907; Rumanian: Schullerus FFC LXXVIII 84 No. 4; Chinese: Eberhard FFC CXX 37f. No. 25; Madison County Virginia (U.S.A.): Hench JAFL XLVIII 384. — Isthmian tribes (Panama): Alexander Lat. Am. 192 (punishment for incest); Yuracare (West Brazil): Alexander ibid. 314.

A751.1.1. *Man in moon has punishment for burning brush on Sunday.* **Hench The Man in the Moon and his Sticks (SFQ XIV 169). — North Carolina: Brown Collection I 631.

C631. Tabu: breaking the sabbath. C950. Person carried to other world for breaking tabu. E501.3.6. Wild huntsman wanders for hunting on Sunday.

A751.1.2. *Man in moon is put there as punishment for cursing God.* U.S.: Baughman.

A751.1.3. *Man in moon as punishment for disdainful sacrifice* (Cain). Emerson "Medieval Legends of Cain" PMLA XXI 840ff.

V10. Religious sacrifices.

A751.1.4. *Man in moon banished there for stealing bundle of thorns.* Emerson PMLA XXI 840ff.

A751.2. *Man in the moon a rabbit* (hare, other animal). *Werhan Die Sage 65; Fb "måne" II 659b. — Hindu: Keith 137, Penzer I 109 n. 1, II 82, V 101 n. 2, IX 143, Jātaka Index s. v. "moon", Buddhist myth: Malalasekera II 675, 1079; India: *Thompson-Balys; Japanese: Anesaki 339. — Aztec: Alexander Lat. Am. 57, 89; S. Am. Indian (Yuracare): Métraux BBAE CXLIII (3) 503 (jaguar).

A751.3. *Frog in moon.* S. Am. Indian (Warrau): Métraux RMLP XXXIII 123.

A751.3.1. *Man in moon a frog which has jumped into person's face* and remains there. *Köhler-Bolte I 473ff. — N. A. Indian: *Thompson Tales 291 n. 69.

Q551.1. Undutiful son punished by toad clinging to face.

A751.4. *Man in the moon: tarring of the moon.* Man sets out to tar the moon and remains with his tar-bucket in the moon. — Finnish: *Aarne FFC VIII 4 No. 8; XXXIII 51 No. 8; Livonian: *Loorits FFC LXVI 81 No. 7; Estonian: *Aarne FFC XXV 140 No. 6.

A751.5. *Man in the moon from scratches or paint.* S. Am. Indian (Caviña, Tumupasa): Métraux BBAE CXLIII (3) 448, (Chamacoco): Métraux BBAE CXLIII (1) 366, (Guarani): Métraux BBAE CXLIII (3) 93, (Tembe): Métraux RMLP XXXIII 140, (Toba): Métraux MAFLS XL 142f., (Peru): Métraux RMLP XXXIII 123.

A751.5.1. *Man in the moon: moon's face scratched by hare* in retaliation for injury to hare. (Cf. A2216.3.) — Hottentot: Bleek 72 No. 33.

A751.5.2. *Man in the moon: dung (ashes) on moon's face smeared there by sun.* India: Thompson-Balys.

A751.5.2.1. *Moon wants to marry his sister the sun.* She is angered and throws hot ashes on his face. — India: Thompson-Balys.

A736.1. Sun sister and moon brother. A763.3. Sun and moon as lovers. A753. Moon as wooer.

A751.5.3. *Mark of her mother's hand to be seen on moon's shoulder.* India: Thompson-Balys.

A751.5.4. *Mark of tiger's paw on moon.* India. Thompson-Balys.

A751.5.5. *Moon spots are tattoo marks.* India: Thompson-Balys.

A751.6. *Cotton tree and nettles on moon.* India: Thompson-Balys.

A751.6.1. *Spots on moon a banyan tree* planted there by creator to diminish its light. India: Thompson-Balys; Chinese: Graham.

A751.7. *Two children in moon with yoke and bucket.* Icel.: MacCulloch Eddic 184, Boberg.

A751.8. *Woman in the moon.* Hawaii: Beckwith Myth 242, Tuamotu: Stimson MS (T-G. 3/1010).

A751.8.1. *Man in the moon is an old woman busy with her spindle.* India: Thompson-Balys.

A751.8.2. *Man in moon is a woman threshing corn with a dog by her side.* India: Thompson-Balys; Chinese: Graham.

A751.8.3. *Goddess in moon with calabash at her side.* Hawaii: Beckwith Myth 221.

A751.8.4. *Woman in moon's oven seen on clear nights.* Samoa: Clark 120.

A751.8.5. *Girl with tree carried to moon and is seen there.* Samoa: Clark 119.

A751.8.6. *Goddess in moon beating tapa beneath tree.* Tonga: Gifford 181.

A751.9. *Miscellaneous images on moon.*

A751.9.1. *Rows of palm trees (black spots) on the moon.* India: Thompson-Balys.

A751.9.2. *Bag in the moon.* Samoa: Clark 89.

A751.9.3. *Giant in moon.* Buddhist myth: Malalasekera II 736.

A751.10. *Particular individual is man in the moon.*

A751.10.1. *Joshua as man in the moon:* Jewish: Neuman.

A751.10.2. *Jacob as man in the moon.* Jewish: Neuman.

A751.11. *Other marks on the moon.* India: Thompson-Balys; Philippine (Tinguian): Cole 192.

A753. *Moon as a person.*

A753.1. *Moon as wooer.* The moon is enamored of a mortal. — Greek: *Frazer Apollodorus I 61 n. 2 (Endymion); Estonian: Loorits Grundzüge I 427. — N. A. Indian: *Thompson Tales 273 n. 6a.

A736.3. Sun and moon as lovers. T111.1. Marriage of a mortal and a god.

A753.1.1. *Moon abducts woman.* Eskimo (Kodiak): Golder JAFL XVI 29, (Cape York): Rasmussen III 50.

A753.1.2. *Moon (man) cohabits with woman.* Maori: Beckwith Myth 74; Eskimo (Greenland): Holm 47; S. Am. Indian (Cubeo): Goldman BBAE CXLIII (3) 798.

A753.1.3. *Moon (goddess, woman) cohabits with mortal man.* Maori: Beckwith Myth 244.

A753.1.4. *Moon married to mortal woman.* India: Thompson-Balys (A753.2); Eskimo (Kodiak): Golder JAFL XVI 29ff., (Cumberland Sound): Boas BAM XV 198, (Greenland): Rasmussen III 50, 52, Rink 441, Holm 47.

A753.1.4.1. *Moon married to son of sky-god.* India: Thompson-Balys.

A753.1.4.2. *Moon is wife to all twelve brothers of the sun* and they have her a month at a time because she ate up her sisters. India: Thompson-Balys.

A753.1.5. *Moon and mortal have child.* Eskimo (Cumberland Sound): Boas BAM XV 199, (Greenland): Holm 47.

A753.2. *Moon has house.* Eskimo (Kodiak): Golder JAFL XVI 30, (Central Eskimo): Boas RBAE VI 598, (Greenland): Rasmussen I 81, 83, II 25, 33, III 51, 170, Rink 442, Holm 73, 75, 80.

A753.3. *Moon as person — miscellaneous.*

A753.3.1. *Moon deceives sun.* India: Thompson-Balys.

A753.3.2. *Moon steals from a garden.* India: Thompson-Balys.

A753.3.3. *During day moon stays with his mother under the earth.* S. Am. Indian (Ipurina): Métraux MAFLS XL 19.

A753.3.4. *Moon endowed with wisdom and passion.* Jewish: Neuman.

A754. *Moon kept in box.* (Cf. A755.1). — French Canadian: Barbeau JAFL XXIX 11. — N. A. Indian: Thompson Tales 282 n. 45; German New Guinea: Dixon 112. — Siberian: Holmberg Siberian 421; Chinese: Graham.

A754.1. *Moon buried in pit.* India: Thompson-Balys.

A754.1.1. *Moon falls into pit but is rescued by man.* S. Am. Indian (Guayaki): Métraux-Baldus BBAE CXLIII (1) 444.

A755. *Causes of moon's phases.* Irish: Beal XXI 323; Icel.: MacCulloch Eddic 183; Baltic: (Lithuanian and Lettish): Gray 320; Estonian:

Loorits Grundzüge I 422f.; Lappish: Qvigstad FFC LX 34 No 4; Hindu: Oldenberg Religion des Veda 171; Yakuts: Holmberg Siberian 424; India: *Thompson-Balys. — Maori: Dixon 88. — African: Werner African 227f. (Ekoi): Talbot 349, (Fang): Trilles 172.

A755.1. *Moon's phases caused by its being put in box.* (Cf.A754). When it is closed up in the box, it is dark; when taken out of the box, light. — Ekoi: Talbot 344.

A755.2. *Moon's phases caused by watcher's death.* Moon is hung in tree and is tended by four men. As one dies it loses a quarter. Later it is united in the lower world. — BP III 288ff. (Gr. No. 175). — Cf. Ekoi: Talbot 344.

A755.3. *Moon's waning caused by her sickness.* Belden MLN XX 205; Penzer VI 119 n. 1. — Maori: Clark 182; S. Am. Indian (Toba): Métraux MAFLS XL 19.

A755.3.1. *Sacrifice made to free moon from sickness and allow waxing.* India: Thompson-Balys.

A755.4. *Moon cut in two by sun: hence waxes and wanes.* India: Thompson-Balys.

A755.4.1. *Moon cut in half.* India: Thompson-Balys.

A755.4.2. *Moon stolen and divided into quarters.* German: Grimm No. 175.

A755.4.3. *Moon's phases caused by animals gnawing at edge.* S. Am. Indian (Paressi): Métraux BBAE CXLIII (3) 360.

A755.5. *Moon's phases caused by feeding or starving.* S. Am. Indian (Toba): Métraux MAFLS XL 19, (Ipurina): Métraux ibid. 20.

A755.6. *Moon's phases as punishment for moon's misdoing.* Jewish: Neuman.

A755.7. *Moon's waning caused by menstrual period.* India: Thompson-Balys.

A756. *Moon as sun's representative at night.* Egyptian: Müller 84.

A757. *Moon-boat.* Lappish: Friis Lappisk Mythologi 79.

A757.1. *Moon-chariot.* Icel.: Boberg.

A758. *Theft of moon.* Moon is kept by a monster. It is stolen and brought to earth. — *BP III 288f. Cf. Thompson Tales 281 n. 42; Eskimo (Bering Strait): Nelson RBAE XVIII 483. — Finnish: Kalevala runes 47, 49.

A721.1. Theft of the sun. A1411. Theft of light. A1415. Theft of fire.

A759. *Condition and nature of the moon — miscellaneous.* For eclipse of the moon see A737, where both eclipses of the sun and moon are handled.

A759.1. *Moon has wooden weapons, therefore vulnerable.* S. Am. Indian (Toba): Métraux MAFLS XL 19.

A759.2. *Sun and moon as divine hero's wedding presents.* India: Thompson-Balys.

A759.3 *Why the moon is pale.* India: Thompson-Balys.

A759.4. *Moon is hare covered with silver,* which lives in crystal house with fifteen windows. It rests on a chariot and travels around Mount Meru. — India: Thompson-Balys.

A759.5. *Formerly seven moons.* India: Thompson-Balys.

A759.6. *Moon under direct control of deity.* Buddhist myth: Malalasekera I 854.

A759.7. *Planet Mars lies on moon* to impart warmth to her lest she freeze the earth. (Cf. A780). Jewish: Neuman.

A760—A789. THE STARS

Note: the question of implicit meanings assumed by the proponents of "astralmythology" is not discussed here; only explicit statements in original sources are considered.

A760. Creation and condition of the stars. *Normann Mythen der Sterne (Gotha 1925) 75ff. — Icel.: MacCulloch Eddic 325—26; Irish myth: Cross; Babylonian: Spence 79; India: Thompson-Balys; Chinese: Graham. — Tahltan: Teit JAFL XXXII 205; Eskimo (Ungava): Turner RBAE XI 266; Maori: Clark 16; S. Am. Indian (Jivaro): Métraux RMLP XXXIII 148.

A121. Stars as deities. E741.1. Soul in form of star. F961.2. Extraordinary behavior of stars.

A760.1. *Stars created by creator.* Jewish: Neuman.

A760.2. *Star from union of girl with peacock.* India: Thompson-Balys.

A761. *Ascent to stars.* People or animals ascend to the sky and become stars. — *Dh I 289. — Estonian: Loorits Grundzüge I 534f.; India: *Thompson-Balys; Korean: Zong in-Sob 14 No. 6; Japanese: Ikeda. — Hawaii: Henry 345; Tonga: Gifford 20; Maori: Clark 50; Australian: Dixon 299; Eskimo (Cumberland Sound): Boas BAM XV 174; S. Am. Indian (Jivaro): Métraux RMLP XXXIII 129, 140f., Steward-Métraux BBAE CXLIII (3) 627, (Toba): Métraux MAFLS XL 34, (Yuracari): Métraux RMLP XXXIII 144, (Eastern Brazil): Lowie BBAE CXLIII (1) 434, (Tapirape): Wagley-Galvão BBAE CXLIII (3) 178, (Amyara): Tschopik BBAE CXLIII (2) 571; Ekoi: Talbot 355.

F15. Visit to star-world. R321. Escape to the stars. Fugitives rise in air and become stars.

A761.1. *River taken to sky becomes star.* Eridanos. — Fox 244.

A761.2. *Chariot from heaven takes couple to live with sages in the Great Bear.* India: Thompson-Balys.

A761.3. *Stars as transformed lovers.* India: Thompson-Balys.

A761.4. *Stars as fires in the hearths of ghosts.* India: Thompson-Balys.

A761.5. *Stars are men peering through holes in sky.* Eskimo (Kodiak): Golder JAFL XVI 30.

A761.6. *Stars thought of as living beings.* S. Am. Indian (Warrau): Kirchoff BBAE CXLIII (3) 879.

A762. *Star descends as human being.* Persian: Carnoy 269; India: Thompson-Balys; Chinese: Eberhard FFC CXX 56.

A788.2. Shooting star a star that has come down to graze. A788.3. Shooting stars spirits coming down to earth to make a woman pregnant.

A762.1. *Star-husband.* Star takes mortal maiden as wife. — **Thompson "The Star-husband Tale," Studia Septenrionalia IV (Oslo 1953) 93—163; N. A. Indian: Thompson Tales 330 n. 193, Alexander N. Am. 94, Hatt Asiatic Influences. Cf. Estonian: Loorits Grundzüge I 538f.

A762.2. *Mortal marries star-girl.* Chinese: Graham; African (Lamba): Doke Lamba Folk-Lore 14 No. 11; S. Am. Indian (Camacan): Métraux-Nimuendajú BBAE CXLIII (1) 552, (Chaco): Métraux ibid. 369, (Sherente): Louis ibid. 516, (Mataco): Métraux MAFLS XL 48, (Caraja): Métraux ibid. 49, (Chamacoco): ibid. 48, (Apinaye, Canella): ibid. 48.

A763. *Stars from objects thrown into sky.* Germanic: Herrmann Nordische Mythologie 365, 440; Icel.: MacCulloch Eddic 328; India: Thompson-Balys; Siberian: Holmberg Siberian 431. — African: Frobenius Atlantis I 85. — Fox: Jones PAES I 73.

A700.1. Heavenly bodies from objects thrown into sky.

A763.1. *Stars from arrows shot at sky.* India: Thompson-Balys.

A763.2. *Stars hung by god in heavens to decorate it.* India: Thompson-Balys.

A764. *Stars as pieces of the moon.* *BP I 232; Köhler-Bolte I 484, 505; Jewish: Neuman.

J2271.2.2. Stars made from the old moon.

A764.1. *Stars as children of the moon.* Cook Zeus I 523 n. 6. — Jewish: Neuman; India: Thompson-Balys; Indonesian: Kruyt Bijdragen tot de Taal-, Land-, en Volkenkunde van Nederlandsch-Indië LXXIX 470; Philippines: Beckwith Myth 537; S. Am. Indian (Amyara): Tschopik BBAE CXLIII (2) 571.

A764.1.1. *Stars as children of sun eaten by their father.* Hence no stars in the day. — Frazer Ovid III 205; Hatt Asiatic Influences 74f. — India: Thompson-Balys; Africa (Fang): Trilles 172.

A764.1.2. *Sun eats all his own children except morning star,* while moon keeps all her children in hiding. India: Thompson-Balys.

A764.1.3. *Stars as children of sun and moon.* Africa (Fang): Trilles 171, 174.

A764.2. *Stars as drops of the moon's blood.* India: Thompson-Balys.

A764.3. *Most brilliant stars children of the sun;* others are children of the moon. India: Thompson-Balys.

A764.4. *Stars are transformed spittle of the moon.* India: Thompson-Balys.

A765. *Naming the stars.* The "Great Star" names the stars. — Bushman: Bleek and Lloyd 79.

A766. *Origin of constellations.* India: Thompson-Balys; Chinese: Werner 176. — Quileute: Farrand JAFL XXXII 266; Ojibwa: Carson JAFL XXX 493; S. Am. Indian (Amazon): Alexander Lat. Am. 288, (Mojo): Métraux BBAE CXLIII (3) 424, (Bacairi): Lévi-Strauss ibid. 348. — African: Werner African 229. — For the origin of particular constellations see A770—A779.

R321. Escape to the stars. Fugitives rise in the air and become stars.

A767. *Stars sing together.* Hebrew: Job 38:7; Jewish: Neuman; Pawnee: Alexander N. Am. 110.

A659.1. Music of the spheres.

A769. *Creation of the stars — miscellaneous.*

A769.1. *Stars are trees growing on the clouds.* India: Thompson-Balys.

A769.2. *Stars rebel against God.* Jewish: Neuman.

A769.3. *Stars supervised by angels.* Jewish: Neuman.

A769.4. *Speaking stars.* Jewish: Neuman.

A769.5. *Sun gives light to stars.* S. Am. Indian (Viracocha): Steward-Métraux BBAE CXLIII (3) 550.

A770. Origin of particular stars. **Normann Mythen der Sterne (Gotha 1925); *Frazer Ovid V 7 s.v. "constellations". — Chinese: Werner 189.

A771. *Origin of the Great Bear* (Ursa Major). *Andree Ethnographische Parallelen (1878) 104; *Handwb. d. Aberglaubens IX Nachträge 681f.; *Basset RTP XXVIII 112 with references to earlier volumes. — Danish: Kristensen Danske Sagn II (1893) 276; Greek: Fox 21 (Kallisto), 251; Jewish: Neuman; Lappish: Qvigstad FFC LX 34 No. 5; Livonian: Loorits FFC LXVI 81 Nos. 10, 11; Egyptian: Müller 59; Siberian: Holmberg Siberian 426; Hindu: Keith 102; Chinese: Graham; Korean: Zong in-Sob 12 No. 5. — N. A. Indian (Eskimo, Iroquois, Assiniboine, Blackfoot, Mandan, Sioux): Alexander N. Am. 9, 26, 96, *278 n. 14; Aztec: Alexander Lat. Am. 93.

D1576.1. Magic song causes tree to rise to sky. Has moon and Great Bear in its branches.

A771.1. *Origin of the Southern Cross.* Analogous legends in the southern hemisphere with those of Ursa Major in the northern. — Andree Ethnographische Parallelen (1878) 113. — Macobi (Pampean): Alexander Lat. Am. 319.

A772. *Origin of Orion.* Andree Ethnographische Parallelen (1878) 108; *RTP XXI 102 and references to earlier volumes; *Handwb. d. Abergl. IX Nachträge 684f. — Icel.: MacCulloch Eddic 177; Greek: Fox 249f.; Egyptian: Müller 57; India: *Thompson-Balys. — Siberian: Holmberg Siberian 429; Livonian: Loorits FFC LXVI 81 No. 12. — S. A. Indian (Tarahumare and Tepehuane): Alexander N. Am. 176; (Amazon) Alexander Lat. Am. 307; N. American Indian (California): Gayton and Newman 67; Africa (Tonga): Gifford 100.

A773. *Origin of the Pleiades.* *Andree Ethnographische Parallelen (1878) 106; Frazer Ovid III 197 n. 4; *Basset RTP XXIII 396 and references to earlier volumes; *Dh II 83; Frazer Golden Bough VII 307ff.; *Fb "syvstjærne"; *Handwb. d. Abergl. IX N. 687f. — Lithuanian: Balys Legends No. 29; Siberian: Holmberg Siberian 336, 417, 427, 430. — India: Thompson-Balys; Chinese: Eberhard FFC CXX 56. — N. A. Indian: *Thompson Tales 291 n. 71; (Blackfoot) Alexander N. Am. 96; (California) Gayton and Newman 65; — S. A. Indian (Tarahumare and Tepehuane): Alexander N. Am. 176; (Chaco, Pampean): Alexander Lat. Am. 323; (Amazon) ibid. 306. — Maori: Clark 106, 178. — Eskimo (Smith Sound): Kroeber JAFL XII 173. — Africa: Werner African 229.

A773.1. *Pleiades a princess and six suitors* among whom she could not choose. *Köhler-Bolte I 439f.

T92. Rivals in love.

A773.2. *Pleiades six repudiated wives.* They have been cast out for apparent infidelity. — Hindu: Keith 140.

S410. Persecuted wife.

A773.3. *Pleiades girls who died of grief.* Greek: Fox 248.

A773.4. *Pleiades seven illegitimate children.* *Fb "pige" II 816b.

A773.5. *Pleiades from hunters marooned in sky* after felling world-tree. S. Am. Indian (Mataco): Métraux MAFLS XL 25, BBAE CXLIII (1) 366.

A652. World-tree.

A773.6. *Pleiades as swarm of bees.* S. Am. Indian (Chiriguano): Métraux BBAE CXLIII (3) 483.

A773.7. *Two stars from Great Bear constellation transferred to Pleiades.* Jewish: Neuman.

A774. *Origin of the North Star.* (Cf. A702.3.) — *Basset RTP XXII 355 and references to earlier volumes. — Hindu: Keith 165.

A775. *Origin of Hyades.* Greek: Fox 46, 248ff., Frazer Apollodorus I 321 n. 5; African: Werner African 229; S. Am. Indian (Toba): Métraux BBAE CXLIII (1) 365, MAFLS XL 21.

A776. *Origin of constellation Lyra.* Greek (Orpheus's lyre).

A776.1. *Origin of Vega* (Alpha Lyrae). Maori: Beckwith Myth 101; Korean: Zong in-Sob No. 6.

A777. *Origin of constellation Scorpio.* Maori: Clark 56; Cook Is.: Clark 81, 83; S. Am. Indian (Chiriguano): Métraux BBAE CXLIII (3) 483, (Toba, Vilela): Métraux MAFLS XL 21f.

A778. *Origin of the Milky Way.* *Andree Ethnographische Parallelen (1878) 109; *Basset RTP XXII 167 and references to earlier volumes; *Fb "mælkevej" II 642. — Welsh: MacCulloch Celtic 100; Armenian: Ananikian 37; Bulgarian: ibid. 49. — Ekoi: Talbot 366; Hawaii: Beckwith Myth 74; S. Am. Indian (Yuracari): Métraux BBAE CXLIII (3) 503f.

A778.0.1. *Origin of Magellanic Clouds.* Tonga: Gifford 105, 109; S. Am. Indian (Toba): Métraux MAFLS XL 21f., 47, (Chiriguano): Métraux BBAE CXLIII (3) 483.

A778.1. *Milky Way a hunting party.* Siberian: Holmberg Siberian 436. — Tehuelche (Pategonia): Alexander Lat. Am. 336.

A778.1.1. *Milky Way is the Wild Hunt.* German: Brunk Zs. f. Vksk. XIII 184; Russian: Ralston Songs of the Russian People 109; Hungarian: Spolyi Zs. f. deutsche Myth. II 161; Finno-Ugric: Holmberg Finno-Ugric 82; Greek-Latin: Cook Zeus II 37.

E501. The Wild Hunt.

A778.2. *Milky Way as a road.* S. Am. Indian (Toba): Métraux MAFLS XL 20, Métraux BBAE CXLIII (1) 365.

A778.2.1. *Milky Way as path of souls* (demons). Finno-Ugric: Holmberg Finno-Ugric 82. — Mandan, Pawnee: Alexander N. Am. 96, 117; S. Am. Indian (Amazon): Alexander Lat. Am. 307, (Chaco, Pampean): ibid. 323.

E481.2.1. Bridge to land of dead. E700. The Soul. F152.1.1. Rainbow bridge to otherworld.

A778.3. *Milky Way as a river.* Siberian: Holmberg Siberian 435; Japanese: Ikeda. — Blackfoot: De Josselyn de Jong Blackfoot Texts 29ff.

A778.4. *Milky Way as a stitched seam in the sky.* Siberian: Holmberg Siberian 336, 434.

A778.5. *Milky Way as milk from breast of a woman.* Siberian: Holmberg Siberian 414.

A778.6. *Milky Way as the sperma of the gods.* Eisler Weltenmantel und Himmelszelt 482.

A778.7. *Milky Way as path of a bird of passage.* Siberian: Holmberg Siberian 434; S. Am. Indian (Pañ'): Métraux BBAE CXLIII (3) 93, (Chiriguano): Métraux ibid. 483.

A778.8. *Milky Way is smoke (ashes).* African: Werner African 231; S. Am. Indian (Toba): Métraux MAFLS XL 21, (Mocoví): Métraux BBAE CXLIII (1) 365.

A778.9. *Milky Way as race track.* Calif. Indian: Gayton and Newman 66.

A778.10. *Abyss at end of Milky Way.* S. Am. Indian (Toba): Métraux MAFLS XL 20f.

A779. *Origin of stars — miscellaneous.* Jewish: Neuman; Buddhist myth: Malalasekera I 22; S. Am. Indian (Toba): Métraux MAFLS XL 21f.

A779.1. *Origin of Coal Sack.* S. Am. Indian (Toba): Métraux MAFLS XL 22, 47.

A779.2. *Origin of constellation Aquila.* Gaster Thespis 293.

A779.3. *Origin of constellation Argo.* Greek: Grote I 221.

A780. The planets (comets, etc.). — *Normann Mythen der Sterne (Gotha 1925). — Chinese: Graham.

A759.7. Planet Mars lies on moon to impart warmth to her lest she freeze the earth.

A780.1. *Planets supervised by angels.* Jewish: Neuman.

A781. *Origin of Venus (planet).* *RTP XVII 227 and references to earlier volumes. — Estonian: Loorits Grundzüge I 434f., 535—540; India: Thompson-Balys; Siberian: Holmberg Siberian 432. — Eskimo: Alexander N. Am. 9; S. Am. Indian (Toba): Métraux BBAE CXLIII (1) 365, (Viracocha): Steward-Métraux BBAE CXLIII (3) 550; Africa (Fang): Trilles 136.

A781.1. *Origin of Morning Star.* Buddhist myth: Malalasekera I 466; Chinese: Graham. — Maori: Clark 50; S. Am. Indian (Toba): Métraux MAFLS XL 23, (Warrau): Kirchoff BBAE CXLIII (3) 880.

A781.2. *Origin of Evening Star.* Greek: Fox 247; Maori: Clark 50; Tonga: Gifford 110.

A782. *Origin of Jupiter (planet).* Africa: Werner African 229; S. Am. Indian (Toba): Métraux MAFLS XL 19.

A786. *Origin of comets.* Frazer Ovid III 198 n. 4. — Tahiti: Henry 227; S. Am. Indian (Viracocha): Steward-Métraux BBAE CXLIII (3) 551.

A787. *Relation of the planets to human life.* Irish myth: Cross.

A788. *Origin of meteors.* S. Am. Indian (Toba): Métraux MAFLS XL 24, (Viracocha): Steward-Métraux BBAE CXLIII (3) 551.

A788.1. *Falling stars as pieces of the moon.* S. Am. Indian (Guayaki): Métraux-Baldus BBAE CXLIII (1) 444.

A788.2. *Shooting star one that has come down to graze.* India: Thompson-Balys.

A762. Star descends as human being.

A788.3. *Shooting stars spirits coming down to earth to make woman pregnant.* India: Thompson-Balys.

A788.4. *Shooting stars are star-dung.* India: Thompson-Balys; S. Am. Indian (Toba): Métraux MAFLS XL 624.

A788.5. *Shooting stars are unfaithful wives.* Africa (Fang): Trilles 174.

A790. The heavenly lights.

A790.1. *Heavenly lights originate from firmament.* Jewish: Neuman.

A791. *Origin of the Rainbow.* *Wünsche "Der Regenbogen in den Mythen und Sagen der Völker" Nord und Süd LXXXII (1898) 70—82; *RTP XXIII 221 and references to earlier volumes. — Irish myth: Cross; Lithuanian: Balys Legends No. 30; India: Thompson-Balys. — Hawaii: Beckwith Myth 234; S. Am. Indian (Amuesha): Métraux RMLP XXXIII 149, (Botocudo): Métraux BBAE CXLIII (1) 540, (Toba): Métraux MAFLS XL 38; Zulu: Callaway 293, 295.

N516. Treasure at end of rainbow.

A791.1. *Rainbow as bow of deity.* Gaster Thespis 261 n. 21; Siberian: Holmberg Siberian 443f.

A791.2. *Rainbow as snake.* African: Werner African 234; S. Am. Indian (Moré): Métraux BBAE CXLIII (3) 406, (Ashluslay): Métraux BBAE CXLIII (1) 366, (Toba): Métraux MAFLS XL 38, (Vilela): ibid. 40.

A791.3. *Rainbow made as bridge by the gods.* Icel.: MacCulloch Eddic 329.

F152.1.1. Rainbow bridge to otherworld.

A791.4. *Rainbow has three colors.* Icel.: MacCulloch Eddic 329.

A791.5. *Rainbow is a transformed king;* the lesser rainbow is the king's wife. India: Thompson-Balys.

A791.6. *Rainbow from gods' emptying their drinking cups.* India: Thompson-Balys.

A791.7. *Rainbow is horse of rain-god.* India: Thompson-Balys.

A791.8. *Rainbow comes out of an anthill.* India: Thompson-Balys.

A791.8.1. *Rainbow lives in a hole.* S. Am. Indian (Toba): Métraux MAFLS XL 38.

A791.9. *Origin of rainbow: transformed butterflies* (souls of lovers). Chinese: Eberhard FFC CXX 266.

A791.10. *Rainbow as covenant between creator and men.* Jewish: Neuman.

A795. *Origin of the Northern Lights* (Aurora Borealis). Estonian: Aarne FFC XXV 140 No. 8; Finnish: Aarne VIII 4 No. 9; Finno-Ugric: Holmberg Finno-Ugric 81, 287. — Eskimo (Labrador): Hawkes GSCan XIV 153, (Ungava): Turner RBAE XI 266.

A796. *Origin of the signs of the zodiac.* Jewish: Neuman.

A797. *Origin of colors at sunrise and sunset.* Tuamotu: Stimson MS (T-G. 3/191).

A800.—A899. The earth.

A800. Creation of the earth. *H. F. Feilberg Skabelses og Syndflodssagn (1915); A. Kühn Berichte über den Weltanfang bei den Indochinesen und ihren Nachbarvölker (1935); Irish myth: Cross; Persian: Carnoy 280; India: *Thompson-Balys; Chinese: Graham. — N. A. Indian (general): Thompson Tales 272 n. 1, (Ojibwa) Skinner JAFL XXXII 287, (Kaska) Teit JAFL XXX 441ff. — See also all references in this section (A800-839).

A401. Mother Earth. A625. World parents: sky-father and earth-mother.

A801. *Earth born of Chaos.* Greek: Grote I 4ff.

A605. Primeval chaos.

A802. *China first land to appear in our world.* India: Thompson-Balys.

A810. Primeval water: In the beginning everything is covered with water. — **Dh I 1—89 passim; Gaster Oldest Stories 69. — Irish myth: Cross; Icel.: MacCulloch Eddic 325—26; Finnish: Kalevala rune 1; Egyptian: Müller 48; Babylonian: Spence 71; Jewish: Neuman; Siberian: Holmberg Siberian 313ff.; Buddhist myth: Malalasekera II 786; India: *Thompson-Balys. — Batak: Voorhoeve Oversicht 63ff.; Marquesas: Handy 122; Marshall Is.: Davenport 221; Oceanic: Dixon 8 n. 7 (Maori), 18f. (Samoa), 20 (Society Is., Tonga), 105 (Admiralty Is., Polynesia, Indonesia, Micronesia), 157 (Minahassa), 158f. (Borneo), 248f. (Marshall Is., Yap), 270 (Arunta); Bushongo: Werner African 144, African: Stanley 5; S. Am. Indian (Guarayu): Métraux BBAE CXLIII (3) 437. — N. A. Indian: *Thompson Tales 279 n. 29, Alexander N. Am 260 (Haida), (Calif.): Gayton and Newman 53; Mixtec: Alexander Lat. Am. 86; Quiché: ibid. 160.

A810.1. *God and Devil fly together over primeval water.* Dh I 6.

A50. Conflict of good and evil creators.

A810.2. *Primeval water to subside in a specified time.* Calif. Indian: Gayton and Newman 55.

A810.2.1. *Waters of heaven would engulf earth were it not for firmament.* Jewish: Neuman.

A811. *Earth brought up from bottom of primeval water.* (Cf. A812.) — India: Thompson-Balys. — New Britain, New Hebrides: Dixon 105.

A811.1. *Earth originates from fish brought from bottom of sea.* The fish is hacked with knives; hence, mountains. — Oceanic (Maori, Hawaiian, Central Polynesian, Tonga, Samoan, New Hebrides, Union Group, Gilbert Is., New Britain): Dixon 43f.

A962. Mountains from hacked-up fish drawn from primeval water.

A811.2. *Earth brought up by three gods.* Icel.: MacCulloch Eddic 326.

A812. *Earth Diver.* From a raft in the primeval sea, the creator sends down animals to try to bring up earth. After a number of animals have failed, one (often the muskrat) succeeds. The earth is made from the bit brought up. — **E. W. Count The Earth Diver and the Rival Twins (Proceedings 29th International Congress of Americanists [Chicago, 1952] 55—62); Walk "Die Verbreitung des Tauchmotivs in den Urmeerschöpfungs- (und Sintflut-) Sagen" Mitteil. d. anthrop. Gesellschaft Wien LXIII (1933) 60—76. — Siberian: Holmberg Siberian 318, *322ff.; Hatt Asiatic Influences 12—36; India: *Thompson-Balys. — N. A. Indian: *Thompson Tales 279 n. 30, (Calif. Indian): Gayton and Newman 53.

A812.1. *Devil as Earth Diver.* Satan dives for earth at instance of God. Succeeds only third time (by use of right formula). He hides the earth under his tongue. It swells, and he must be rescued by God. — *Dh I 2—89 passim; *Handwb. d. Abergl. IX Nachträge 277ff. — Finnish: Aarne FFC VIII 3 No. 1; Estonian: Loorits Grundzüge I 455f., Aarne FFC XXV 139 No. 1; Livonian: Loorits FFC LXVI 80 No. 1; Lithuanian: Balys Index No. 3005; Legends Nos. 7—10, 12f.; Siberian: Holmberg Siberian 313ff.

A43. Devil as adviser of God.

A812.2. *Earth from egg from bottom of sea recovered by bird.* — Borneo: Dixon 165.

A701.1. Origin of sky from egg brought from primeval water.

A812.3. *Creator sends crow, after creating her, to scout for earth-nucleus.* — India: Thompson-Balys.

A813. *Raft in primeval sea.* Creator is on the raft and there creates the earth. (Cf. A812.) — India: Thompson-Balys; Sumatra: Dixon 162.

A813.1. *Earth in form of raft supported by spirits.* S. Am. Indian (Yuracare): Métraux BBAE CXLIII (3) 503.

A813.2. *Lotus-leaf raft in primeval sea.* India: Thompson-Balys.

A813.3. *Creator rests on tree or stake.* Calif. Indian: Gayton and Newman 55.

A814. *Earth from object thrown on primeval water.* India: Thompson-Balys.

A814.1. *Earth from stone thrown on primeval water.* Oceanic: Dixon 18 (Samoa), 158 (Borneo), 163 n. 29—32. (Philippines, Samoa, Tonga, Micronesia).

A814.2. *Earth from sand strewn on primeval water.* India: Thompson-Balys; Yap: Dixon 249.

A814.3. *Earth from decayed matter on primeval water.* Mongolian, Japanese, Tungus: Holmberg Siberian 328f.; Japanese: Anesaki 223. — Hawaii: Dixon 15.

A814.4. *Earth from tree grown in primeval water.* Tungus: Holmberg Siberian 329.

A814.5. *Earth from steam made by fire thrown into primeval water.* Tungus: Holmberg Siberian 330.

A814.6. *Earth scattered in a circuit in four directions on primeval water.* India: Thompson-Balys; Calif. Indian: Gayton and Newman 55.

A814.7. *Earth from primeval water mixed with seeds of tobacco.* Calif. Indian: Gayton and Newman 55.

A814.8. *Earth from lotus seed placed on water.* India: Thompson-Balys.

A814.9. *Earth from egg breaking on primeval water.* (Cf. A1222). — India: Thompson-Balys.

A814.10. *Earth from creator's spittle falling on primeval water.* — India: Thompson-Balys.

A814.10.1. *Earth from spittle of primeval potter* spreading on surface of water. India: Thompson-Balys.

A815. *Earth from turtle's back.* Earth erected on back of a turtle floating in primeval water. (Cf. A844.1.). — N. A. Indian: *Thompson Tales 279 n. 31.

A815.1. *Earth from serpent's head.* Earth reared on head of serpent floating in primeval water. — Borneo, Sumatra: Dixon 159f.

A842.1. Serpent supports the earth. A876. Midgard serpent.

A816. *Earth rises from sea.* *Handwb. d. Abergl. IX Nachträge 279. — Icel: *Olrik Ragnarök 23, MacCulloch Eddic 325. — Mixtec: Alexander Lat. Am. 86.

A816.1. *Stone emerges from primeval water.* Devil sits on the stone, which becomes a mountain. — *Dh I 6.

A816.2. *Ocean under this world.* India: Thompson-Balys.

A816.3. *God causes primeval sea to roll back* and leave bare all the hills. India: Thompson-Balys.

A817. *Earth let down from sky on to primeval ocean.* Siberian: Holmberg Siberian 330.

A820. Other means of creation of earth.

A821. *Earth made of lac.* India: Thompson-Balys.

A822. *Earth made by mud shaken from back of primeval boar.* India: Thompson-Balys.

A822.1. *World is transformed mud parrot in golden cage.* India: Thompson-Balys.

A823. *Earth made by cups of earth placed on spider's web.* India: Thompson-Balys.

A824. *Earth made by transformation of broken ground.* India: Thompson-Balys.

A825. *Earth made by first couple dancing on bit of cloth laid on water.* India: Thompson-Balys.

A826. *Earth sets like curds.* India: Thompson-Balys.

A827. *Earth made by drying up of primeval water.* India: Thompson-Balys.

A828. *Earth from worm scratched by creator's nails.* India: Thompson-Balys.

A828.1. *Earth excreted by worm.* India: Thompson-Balys.

A830. Creation of earth by creator. Genesis ch. I. — Irish myth: Cross; India: Thompson-Balys; Tahiti: Henry 341; Marquesas: Handy 122; Pawnee: Alexander N. Am. 109.

A0. Creator. A610. Creation of universe by creator.

A831. *Earth from body of person* (animal).

A831.1. *Earth from body of son of deity.* India: Thompson-Balys; Kamchadale: Holmberg Siberian 330.

A831.2. *Earth from giant's body* (Ymir). (Cf. A614.1.). *Handwb. d. Abergl. IX Nachträge 282. — Icel: MacCulloch Eddic 325; India: Thompson-Balys.

A831.3. *Earth by sacrifice of son and daughter of first couple.* India: Thompson-Balys.

A831.4. *Earth by murder of first brother and sister.* India: Thompson-Balys.

A831.5. *Earth from the body of murdered child.* India: Thompson-Balys.

A831.6. *Earth from body of slain animal.* India: Thompson-Balys.

A831.7. *Earth from body of divine suicide.* India: Thompson-Balys.

A831.8. *Gods create the earth from their dead victim's blood and bones* India: Thompson-Balys.

A831.9. *Earth created from Adam's body.* Jewish: Neuman.

A832. *Creation because of creator's lonesomeness.* Dissatisfied at being alone in center of primeval water, God creates the earth. — *Dh I 35; India: Thompson-Balys.

A833. *Earth from creator's cuticle.* (Cf. A1211 5.). India: Thompson-Balys; San Carlos Apache: Goddard PaAM XXIV 7.

A835. *Earth from nut in devil's mouth.* God throws a nut over his left shoulder. The devil catches it in his mouth. The nut grows rapidly and the devil spits it out. — Livonian: Loorits FFC LXVI 80 No. 1.

A43. Devil as adviser of God.

A835.1. *Earth created from snow under divine throne.* Jewish: Neuman

A836. *Creator prepared earth's nucleus as one would a rice cake.* India: Thompson-Balys.

A837. *Creator creates earth piecemeal.* Jewish: Neuman.

A840. Support of the earth. India: Thompson-Balys.

A841. *World-columns.* Four (two, etc.) columns or supports sustain the earth. — Irish myth: Cross; Estonian: Loorits Grundzüge I 385, 400; Jewish: Neuman; Greek: *Grote I 70; India: Thompson-Balys; Chinese: Eberhard FFC CXX III No. 66. — Sumatra: Dixon 163; N. A. Indian: *Thompson Tales 286 n. 56; Maya: Alexander Lat. Am. 154. — See also references to A665.2.1.

A665.2.1. Four sky-columns. F58. Column to upper world. F736.1. Island supported on four feet. F736.2. Otherworld island supported on pedestal.

A841.0.1. *The four world-columns fastened immovably by two gods with their mother's hairs.* India: Thompson-Balys.

A841.1. *Four world-cords.* Earth is suspended from the sky by cords at four corners. India: Thompson-Balys; Cherokee: Alexander N.Am. 60.

A841.2. *Four maidens as earth-supports.* One is at each of the cardinal points. (Cf. A842.). — Hindu: Keith 134.

A841.3. *Twelve iron pillars steady the earth.* India: Thompson-Balys.

A841.4. *Four earth-nails.* India: Thompson-Balys.

A842. *Atlas.* A man supports the earth on his shoulders. — Greek: Fox 88, *Grote I 70; Gaster Oldest Stories 129. — N. A. Indian: *Thompson Tales 286 n. 56b; Chibcha: Alexander Lat. Am. 203.

A665.2.1.1. Four gods at world-quarters support the sky. F623. Strong man holds up mountain.

A842.1. *Goddess standing on her head supports earth.* India: Thompson-Balys.

A842.2. *Old woman supports earth on her head.* India: Thompson-Balys.

A843. *Earth supported on post.* The post has an old woman as guardian. When she is hungry the post shakes, causing earthquakes. — Finno-Ugric: Holmberg Finno-Ugric 222. — N. A. Indian (Tlingit, Hare): Boas RBAE XXXI 732.

A843.1. *Earth supported on cross of wood.* S. Am. Indian (Guarani): Métraux BBAE CXLIII (3) 93, (Apapocuvá): Métraux RMLP XXXIII 136.

A844. *Earth rests on animal's back.* *Encyc. Religion and Ethics I 491b.

A1145. Earthquakes from movements of monster.

A844.1. *Earth rests on turtle's back.* (Cf. A815.). — Siberian: *Holmberg Siberian 327; India: *Thompson-Balys. — N. A. Indian: *Thompson Tales 279 n. 31.

A844.2. *Earth supported by bull.* Siberian: Holmberg Siberian 311; Armenian: Ananikian 93.

A844.3. *Earth supported by fish.* *Handwb. d. Abergl. IX Nachträge 281. — Siberian: Holmberg Siberian.

A844.4. *Earth supported by frog.* Siberian: Holmberg Siberian 311.

A844.5. *Earth rests on the horns of a bull who rests upon a fish.* India: Thompson-Balys.

A844.6. *Earth rests on tortoise, serpent, elephant.* (Cf. A1145.1.). — India: Thompson-Balys.

A844.7. *Earth rests on elephant's back.* India: Thompson-Balys.

A844.8. *Earth rests on cobra's head.* India: Thompson-Balys.

A844.9. *Earth supported on great boar's tusk.* India: Thompson-Balys.

A844.10. *Earth supported on vast number of birds' legs.* India: Thompson-Balys.

A844.11. *Earth rests on leviathan.* Jewish: Neuman.

A844.12. *Serpent supports the earth.* (Cf. A844.6.). Hindu: Keith 120, 155, Penzer VI 71 n. 1 (thousand-headed serpent); India: *Thompson-Balys.

A815.1. Earth from serpent's head. A876. Midgard serpent. *B15.1.6.1. Thousand-headed serpent.

A849. *Support of the earth — miscellaneous.*

A849.1. *Earth founded on stone.* Jewish: Neuman.

A849.2. *Earth rests on God's arm.* Jewish: Neuman.

A849.3. *Earth supported by prop.* S. Am. Indian (Apapocuvá-Guaraní): Métraux MAFLS XL 36.

A850. Changes in the earth.

A625.2. Raising of the sky. Originally sky is low and is raised to its present place.

A851. *How the earth became oblong.* God the Father situated on one side of the earth, the Son on the other. — Finnish: Aarne FFC VIII 3 No. 2; Estonian: Aarne FFC XXV 139 No. 3.

A852. *Making the earth smaller.* Earth made too large. God learns from devil by trickery how to make it smaller. — *Dh I 3—89 passim, 127ff.

A853. *Making the earth larger.* Gradually extended during creation. See references to A812 in which this idea is always involved. — Siberian: Holmberg Siberian 317. — Oceanic: Dixon 29; India: Thompson-Balys. — N. A. Indian: *Thompson Tales 279 n. 30.

A853.1. *Doubling size of the earth.* Increase of population necessitates change. — Persian: Carnoy 307.

A855. *Opposite of present.* Everything on the earth — courses of rivers, height of mountains, human reproduction, etc. — are at first the reverse of the present condition. — N. A. Indian: Kroeber JAFL XXI 225.

A633. Earlier universe opposite of present.

A856. *Hardening of the earth.* At first it is soft, but is hardened by sun's rays. — India: Thompson-Balys. — Carib: Alexander Lat. Am. 39.

A856.1. *Primeval earth hardened by wind.* India: Thompson-Balys.

A856.2. *Ground, previously all wet, dries up* when first woman cuts her little finger and blood drips on ground. India: Thompson-Balys.

A857. *Steadying the earth.* India: Thompson-Balys; Jewish: Neuman.

A857.1. *Why earth becomes warm and wet:* two huge copper vessels steaming over fire are underneath earth. — India: Thompson-Balys.

A857.2. *Creator's giant servant puts a valley where earth's crust is heavy* and a mountain where it is light so as to stabilize it. — India: Thompson-Balys.

A857.3. *Creator's giant servant puts trees to hold earth together* where it slipped. India: Thompson-Balys.

A857.3.1. *Roots created to hold land firm.* Tahiti: Henry 342.

A870. Nature and condition of the earth. Icel.: MacCulloch Eddic 325.

A871. *Earth square with four quarters.* Irish myth: Cross; Siberian: Holmberg Siberian 308.

A417. Gods of the quarters. A651.1.6. Heavens (world) divided into four quarters. A1127. Winds of the four quarters established. A1182. Determination of world-quarters. D1273.1.2. Four as magic number.

A871.0.1. *Taprobane at eastern end of the world.* Irish myth: Cross.

A871.0.2. *Unextinguishable fire at end of earth.* S. A. Indian (Mbayá, Mataco): Métraux BBAE CXLIII (1) 367.

A871.1. *Four streams from four corners of earth.* Patch PMLA XXXIII 623 n. 77.

A871.2. *Four rivers, rising in paradise, water primitive world.* Irish myth: Cross.

A671.2.2.5. Four rivers in hell. D1273.1.2. Four as magic number. F162.2.1. The four rivers of paradise.

A872. *River that flows around the world.* Greek: *Grote I 220, 232, 310 (River Ocean); Jewish: Neuman; India: Thompson-Balys.

A872.1. *Seven seas encircle the world.* India: Thompson-Balys.

A873. *Above and below the earth are great clouds.* India: Thompson-Balys.

A875. *Earth wheel-shaped (flat and round).* Greek: Grote I 4, 310; Hindu: Keith 16; Siberian: Holmberg Siberian 308.

A875.1. *Navel of the earth.* Omphalos, the central point on the earth disc. — *Holmberg Baum des Lebens 150 s.v. "Mittelpunkt"; *Frazer Pausanias V 314f.; *Pease Cicero De Divinatione 353 (Bk. II 115); *Roscher Abh. kgl. Sächs. Ges. d. Wiss. (Phil. hist. Kl.) XXIX (1913) 9, XXXI (1915) 1, Berichte d. kgl Sächs. Ges. d. Wiss. (Phil. hist. Kl.) LXX (1918) 2; Warren Paradise Found (1885) 225ff.; Gaster Thespis 170f.; Jewish: Neuman; Norse: Boberg.

A1181. Determination of world center. H681.3. Riddle: what is the center of the earth?

A875.1.1. *Mountain at center of earth.* Buddhist myth: Malalasekera II 1136.

A875.2. *Well in the midst of earth from which eleven rivers originate.* (Cf. A871.1.) Icel.: Boberg.

A876. *Midgard Serpent.* A serpent surrounds the earth. — Icel.: De la Saussaye 346, MacCulloch Eddic 279, 328, Boberg; Siberian: Holmberg Siberian 345; Western Asia (general): Frobenius Erdteile VI 196; India: Thompson-Balys. — Arapaho: cf. Dorsey FM IV 13; Aztec: Alexander Lat. Am. 57.

A815.1. Earth from serpent's head. A842.1. Serpent supports the earth. A1082.3. Thor battles Midgard serpent at end of world. B91. Mythical serpents. B873.1. Giant serpent. H1149.2. Task: lifting a certain cat (Midgard serpent).

A876.1. *The leviathan that surrounds the globe.* Irish myth: Cross; Jewish: Neuman.

A1145.2. Earthquakes from movements of sea-monster. B61. Leviathan. B91. Mythical serpent.

A878. *Earth-tree.* Tree of life or fate. — *Wünsche "Das Wasser des Lebens in den Märchen der Völker" Zs. f. vgl. Litteraturgeschichte XIII 166ff.; **Holmberg Baum; Dh I 6 (five eastern branches given to man, others forbidden); *Albright Am. Jour. Semitic Langs. XXXIX 161. — *Handwb. d. Abergl. IX Nachträge 150ff., 200. — Icel.: Mac Culloch Eddic 331ff. (Yggdrasil); Irish Myth: Cross; Egyptian: Müller 36.

A652. World tree. C621.1. Tree of knowledge forbidden. D950. Magic tree. E90. Tree of life. F162.3.1. Tree of life in otherworld.

A878.1. *Stream of paradise from roots of world-tree.* Holmberg Baum 70ff.; Icel.: MacCulloch Eddic 320f., 334.

F162.2.1. The four rivers of paradise.

A878.1.1. *Other streams from roots of earth-tree.* Icel.: Boberg.

A878.1.2. *Three wells under the three roots of earth-tree.* Icel.: Boberg.

A878.2. *Lake of milk by tree of life.* Siberian: Holmberg Siberian 414.

A878.3. *Animals at earth-tree.*

A878.3.1. *Snake at roots of earth-tree.* Icel.: MacCulloch Eddic 319, 332; Boberg; Siberian: Holmberg Siberian 357.

A878.3.2. *Hart(s) eating of the earth-tree.* Holmberg Baum 67ff. — Icel.: MacCulloch Eddic 332ff., Boberg.

A878.3.3. *Chattering squirrel in the earth-tree.* Holmberg Baum 67ff. Icel.: MacCulloch Eddic 332ff., Boberg.

A878.3.4. *Wise eagle in the earth-tree.* Holmberg Baum 67ff. — Icel.: MacCulloch Eddic 332ff., Boberg.

A878.3.5. *Hawk in the earth-tree.* Holmberg Baum 67ff. — Icel.: Mac Culloch Eddic 332ff., Boberg.

A878.3.6. *Golden çock in earth-tree.* Icel.: Boberg.

A878.4. *Earth-tree furnishes health-giving and hunger-satisfying sap.* Siberian: Holmberg Siberian 350, 353.

D1472. Food and drink from magic objects.

A881. *Zones of earth corresponding to Zodiac.* Jewish: Neuman.

A900—A999. Topographical features of the earth.

A900 Topography — general considerations.

A72. Original creator followed by transformers. D683.1. Transformers.

A901. *Topographical features caused by experiences of primitive hero* (demigod, deity). Footprints of the gods, thoroughfares of heroes, etc. — *Dh II 8, 68, 199; *Hdwb. d. deutschen Aberglaubens III 240 s.v. "Fussspur"; *Wehrhan Die Sage 65; *Basset and others RTP XXIV 299 and references to earlier volumes. — Irish myth: Cross; Breton: MacCulloch Celtic 135; Icel.: De la Saussaye 280; Swiss: Jegerlehner Oberwallis 303 Nos. 22, 23; Finnish: Kalevala rune 1; Lithuanian: Balys Index No. 3008, Legends Nos. 12ff.; Greek: Fox 250. — Siberian: Holmberg Siberian 331; Japanese: Anesaki 248f.; Indo-Chinese: Scott Indo-Chinese 291; Buddhist myth: Malalasekera II 31, 768, 957, 1211. — Hawaii: Beckwith Myth 18; Aztec: Alexander Lat. Am. 70; Africa (Fang): Trilles 153. — Cf. A911, A920.1.2, A920.1.5, A924, A931, A932, A933, A941.1, A941.2, A951, A955, A964, A972, A982.1, A984.

A2271.5. Trees bear first buds to commemorate reign of primitive hero. F960.1. Extraordinary nature phenomena at birth (death) of hero (holy person). F979.11. Trees spring up to commemorate birth of primitive hero (demigod, deity).

A901.1. *Topographical changes or landmarks due to battle between gods.* India: Thompson-Balys.

A901.2. *Natural features because of combat of huge rock columns* with each other. Marquesas: Handy 133.

A902. *Topographical features of the earth arranged by creator.* (Cf. A0.) — Jewish: Neuman; India: Thompson-Balys. — African: Werner African 143. — N. A. Indian: Thompson Tales 30.

A902.1. *Two creators go by different route to establish features of the earth.* Calif. Indian: Gayton and Newman 59.

A903. *Topographical features caused by animals.* Cheremis: Sebeok-Nyerges.

A910—A949. WATER FEATURES

A910. Origin of water features — general.

A910.1. *Waters created on first day of creation.* Jewish: Neuman.

A910.2. *Waters created as punishment.* Jewish: Neuman.

A910.3. *Bodies of water in primitive abyss sink.* Jewish: Neuman.

A910.4. *Bodies of water remnant of flood.* S. A. Indian (Tupinamba): Métraux BBAE CXLIII (3) 133.

A1010. Deluge.

A910.5. *Waters created by divine twins.* S. A. Indian (Chiriguano): Métraux RMLP XXXIII 167.

A116. Twin gods.

A911. *Bodies of water from tears.* (Cf. A901, A920.1.5, A941.2, A1012.) — Irish: MacCulloch Celtic 135; Nebraska: Pound WF VI 305—316; Finnish: Kalevala rune 4; African (Upoto): Einstein 127.

A913. *Origin of tides.* *Hdwb. d. deutschen Aberglaubens II 513 s. v. "Ebbe und Flut". — Persian: Carnoy 278. — Shetland Is.: Teit JAFL XXXI 198. — N. A. Indian: *Thompson Tales 293 n. 76a, and add (Malecite) Speck JAFL XXVIII 60, (Tahltan) Teit JAFL XXXII 201.

A913.1. *Tidal wave or surge marks place of death of person.* (Cf. A920.1.4, A936.) — Irish myth: Cross.

D911.1. Magic wave. F931.4. Extraordinary behavior of waves.

A913.2. *Tide caused by breathing of sea-monster.* Maori: Clark 180.

A913.3. *Ebb-tide goes to great whirlpool.* Tonga: Gifford 144.

A913.4. *Tub that drips at high tide but holds water at low tide.* Irish myth: Cross.

D1171.14. Magic tub.

A914. *Mountains push water westward.* Calif. Indian: Gayton and Newman 54.

A915. *Why waters do not engulf the earth.* Jewish: Neuman.

A917. *Quarrel between earth and waters.* Jewish: Neuman.

A918. *Male and female waters.* Jewish: Neuman.

A920. Origin of the seas. Jewish: Neuman; Persian: Carnoy 270, 277f. — Gold Coast: Barker and Sinclair 87; Buin: Wheeler 28. — Hatt: Asiatic Influences 17.

D2151.1.1. Sea produced by magic. F930. Extraordinary occurences concerning seas or waters.

A920.1. *Origin of lakes.* Fb "sø" III 731a. — Irish: MacCulloch Celtic 135 (cf. A911), Cross; Indo-Chinese: Scott Indo-Chinese 291 (cf. A901). — Tahltan: *Teit JAFL XXXII, 219f.; Malecite: Speck JAFL XXX 481.

D1486.1. Magic stone makes rivers and lakes. F934.2. Lake rises from bramble bush.

A920.1.0.1. *Origin of particular lake.* India: Thompson-Balys.

A920.1.1. *Inexhaustible buckets as source of lakes.* Chinese: Werner 221.

D1652.5. Inexhaustible vessel.

A920.1.2. *Lakes from digging of primeval ox.* (Cf. A901.) — Kirghis: Holmberg Siberian 331.

X958. Lie: hero responsible for topographical features.

A920.1.3. *Lake bursts forth to drown thief.* Irish myth: Cross.

A939.1. River bursts from well in pursuit. F934. Extraordinary occurrences connected with lakes. Q212. Theft punished. Q552.19. Miraculous drowning as punishment.

A920.1.4. *Lakes burst forth to commemorate birth, death, battle, etc., of primitive hero.* Irish myth: Cross.

A901. Topographical features caused by experiences of primitive hero (demigod, deity). A936. Rivers burst forth to commemorate birth, death, battle, etc., of primitive hero. F960.1. Extraordinary nature phenomena at birth of holy person.

A920.1.5. *Lakes originate from tears.* (Cf. A901, A911.) Irish myth: Cross.

A920.1.5.1. *Lakes originate from belches.* Irish myth: Cross.

D921.2. Lake produced by belches after magic draught.

A920.1.6. *Lake from urine of horse.* (Cf. A933.) Irish myth: Cross.

A920.1.7. *Lake created by fairies.* Irish myth: Cross.

F212. Fairyland under water.

A920.1.7.1. *Lake bursts forth to quell fairy war.* Irish myth: Cross.

F277.0.1. War between fairy settlements.

A920.1.8. *Lake bursts forth to drown impious people.* Kristensen Danske Sagn III (1895) 241ff., (1931) 162ff.; Fb "sø" III 731a; G. Schütte in Danske Studier (1925) 117ff.

F944. City sinks in the sea. Q220. Impiety punished.

A920.1.8.1. *Lake from violating tabu.* Irish myth: Cross; Africa: Bouveignes 21—29.

C900. Punishment for breaking tabu. F933.6. Spring miraculously breaks forth against wrongdoer. F934.2. Lake rises from bramble bush.

A920.1.9. *Lake bursts forth where island is plowed out.* (See A951.) — Olrik Danske Studier (1910) 1ff.

A920.1.10. *Lakes made by giant or devil.* Lithuanian: Balys Historical.

A920.1.11. *Woman transformed to pool of water.* Irish myth: Cross.

D283. Transformation: woman to pool of water.

A920.1.12. *Lake bursts forth where blind king plucks rushes.* Irish myth: Cross.

D1505.5. Magic water restores sight. F934.2. Lake rises from bramble bush.

A920.1.13. *Lake of milk formed through virtue of saint.* Irish myth: Cross.

D921.3.1. Lake of milk created through merit of saint.

A920.1.14. *Lakes are daughters of the gods.* India: Thompson-Balys.

A920.1.15. *Origin of the Dead Sea.* Jewish: Neuman.

A920.1.16. *Lake originally filled with palm wine.* Africa (Bushonga): Torday 235.

A920.2. *Origin of sea channels.* Tonga: Gifford 87, 94.

A921. *Ocean the son of Earth and Heaven.* Greek: Fox.

A922. *Ocean made from blood.* Icel.: MacCulloch Eddic 325f.; Finnish: Aarne FFC XXXIII 51 No. 7**; Livonian: Loorits FFC LXVI 86 No. 45. — Oceanic: Dixon 37 n. 107, 108 (Polynesia, Samoa, Marquesas).

A923. *Ocean from creator's sweat.* Corpus Poeticum Boreale I 64. — Polynesian: Dixon 37 n. 106.

A610. Creation by creator.

A923.1. *Ocean from urine.* (Cf. A933.) — Buin: Wheeler Mono-Alu 28, Aurora (New Hebrides): Codrington II 372.

A924. *Miscellaneous origins of the ocean.*

A924.1. *Origin of sea from overturned calabash.* Haitian: Alexander Lat. Am. 29.

A924.2. *Origin of sea from rotting snakes.* Buin: Wheeler Mono-Alu 28.

A924.3. *Sea released from tree-top.* Papua: Kerr 25.

A924.4. *Sea from earth excavation.* Buddhist myth: Malalasekera II 973.

A925. *Origin of various qualities of the sea.*

A925.1. *Origin of high sea waves.* Tuamotu: Stimson MS (z-G. 13/441).

A925.2. *Origin of sea's color.* Jewish: Neuman.

A925.3. *Origin of foul odor of sea.* Jewish: Neuman; Tuamotu: Stimson MS (z-G. 3/1110).

A925.4. *Origin of fresh water welling up in sea.* Hawaii: Beckwith Myth 96.

A925.5. *Origin of mournful sound of sea.* Hawaii: Beckwith Myth 21.

A925.6. *Origin of surf.* Hawaii: Beckwith Myth 436.

A925.7. *Origin of shining patches beneath sea.* Tonga: Gifford 200.

A928. *Giant drinks up ocean.* Hindu: Keith 146. — Cf. Icel.: Meyer Mythologie der Germanen (1903) 244 (Thor lowers level of ocean).

F531.3.18.1. Hero's demon guide drinks streams dry on their journey. H1142.2. Task: drinking the sea dry.

A930. Origin of streams. Irish myth: Cross; India: Thompson-Balys.

D915. Magic river. D1486.1. Magic stone makes rivers and lakes. D1549.3. Magic object controls river. D2151. Magic control of waters. D2151.2. Magic control of rivers. F932. Extraordinary occurences connected with rivers.

A930.1. *Creator of rivers.* Jewish: Neuman.

A930.1.1. *Snake as creator of rivers and lakes.* Papua: Kerr 57; Mono-Alu: Wheeler 67.

A931. *Meander-pursuit.* (Cf. A901.) — A fugitive's doublings cause a river's windings. — N. A. Indian: Kroeber JAFL XXI 224, (Micmac): Speck JAFL XXVIII 60, (Calif.): Gayton and Newman 62.

A933. *River from urine of goddess* (giantess). — Irish myth: Cross; Icel.: Herrmann Nordische Mythologie 368, Boberg; French: Sébillot France II 327ff.; Sudanese: Frobenius Atlantis VI 219; India: Thompson-Balys; Korean: Zong in-Sob 15 No. 7.

A933.1. *River from the slaver of the Fenris-wolf.* Icel.: MacCulloch Eddic 328; cf. India: Thompson-Balys.

A933.2. *River from vagina of first woman.* S. A. Indian (Paressi): Métraux BBAE CXLIII (3) 359.

A934. *Various origins of rivers.*

A934.1. *Rivers from digging of primeval ox.* (Cf. A920.1.2.) — Kirghis: Holmberg Siberian 331.

A934.2. *Rivers formed where certain stones are placed.* Each of seven children are to go in a different direction, to walk a mile and put down a stone, then another mile and a stone, etc. Thus rivers are formed. — Ekoi: Talbot 366.

A934.3. *Rivers burst forth to commemorate birth, death, battle, etc., of primitive hero.'* (Cf. A901, A920.1.4.) — Irish myth: Cross.

A934.4. *Rivers where god drags his staff.* India: Thompson-Balys.

A934.5. *Rivers originate through saint's prayer during drought.* Irish myth: Cross.

D1713. Magic power of hermit (saint). D1766.1. Magic results produced by prayer.

A934.6. *Hail-storm leaves twelve chief rivers in Ireland.* Irish myth: Cross.

F962. Extraordinary precipitation (rain, snow, etc.).

A934.7. *River bursts from well in pursuit.* Irish myth: Cross.

A920.1.3. Lake bursts forth to drown thief. A920.1.8.1. Lake from violating tabu. F932. Extraordinary occurences connected with rivers.

A934.8. *Rivers from mythical well.* Icel.: MacCulloch Eddic 330, 333.

A934.9. *Stream unexpectedly bursts from side of mountain.* Irish myth: Cross.

F715.3.2. Marvelous stream containing little black fish bursts forth from mountain.

A934.10. *Origin of river: from a girl drowned in a well.* India: Thompson-Balys.

A934.11. *River from transformation.*

A934.11.1. *Girl reincarnated as river* so god Vishnu can lie in its bed in the form of a stone. India: Thompson-Balys.

A934.11.2. *Person transforms self to river.* India: Thompson-Balys.

A934.11.3. *Goddess in anger breaks herself into five parts: hence, five branches of a river.* India: Thompson-Balys.

A934.11.4. *Origin of river: transformed flowing honey.* India: Thompson-Balys.

A934.12. *Peacock shows rivers the way to the big valley* so they will not go round and round. India: Thompson-Balys.

A935. *Origin of falls (cataracts).* Irish myth: Cross. — Malecite: Speck JAFL XXX 480; S. A. Indian (Chibcha): Kroeber BBAE CXLIII (2) 908; African (Upoto): Einstein 135.

A937. *Why there is no mist on a certain river: fanned away with a pair of eagle's wings.* India: Thompson-Balys.

A938. *Rivers and streams offspring of marriage of Ocean and his sister.* Greek: Grote I 6.

A940. Origin of other bodies of water.

A941. *Origin of springs.* Irish myth: Cross; Jewish: Neuman. — Japanese: Ikeda; Chinese: Eberhard FFC CXX 114 No. 69; S. A. Indian (Amuesa): Métraux RMLP XXXIII 131.

D927.1. Magic spring. D2151. Magic control of waters. F933. Extraordinary occurrences connected with springs.

A941.0.1. *Origin of a particular spring.* India: Thompson-Balys.

A941.1. *Springs originate from horse's hoof-prints.* (Cf. A901.) — Malten Jahrb. d. kaiserlichen deutschen archäologischen Inst. XXIX 185. — Icel.: MacCulloch Eddic 134, 328, Herrmann Saxo II 216; Greek: Fox 40, 213; Hungarian: Ipolyi Zs. f. deutsche Mythologie u. Sittenkunde II 273; German: Hdwb. d. deutschen Aberglaubens s.v. "Brunnen"; India: Thompson-Balys.

A941.1.1. *Spring from urine of horse.* (Cf. A920.1.6., A933.) — Irish myth: Cross.

A941.1.2. *Spring breaks forth where fairy horse lies down.* Irish myth: Cross.

A1012.3. Flood caused by loosing fairy horse and allowing it to stale. B181. Magic horse. F241.1. Fairies' horses.

A941.2. *Springs originate from tears.* (Cf. A901, A911.) — Greek: Fox 41; Jewish: Neuman.

A941.3. *Spring from striking earth with sword.* Sébillot France II 181ff.; Chinese: Eberhard FFC CXX 114 No. 69.

D927.1. Spring made by magic. D1567.6. Stroke of staff brings water from rock.

A941.3.1. *Spring breaks forth where magic spear strikes ground.* (Cf. A941.5.1.). Irish myth: Cross.

D1084. Magic spear.

A941.3.2. *Spring where god throws his staff or spear.* Oceanic: Beckwith Myth 64ff.

A941.4. *Spring breaks forth to commemorate experiences of hero (deity).* (Cf. A901, A913.1, A920.1.4.)

A941.4.1. *Spring breaks forth to commemorate place of death or burial.* Irish myth: Cross; Hawaii: Beckwith Myth 188.

A941.4.2. *Spring breaks forth at primitive hero's need.* Irish myth: Cross.

A172. Gods intervene in battle. A536. Demigods act as allies of mortals. N815. Fairy as helper. N817.0.1. God as helper.

A941.4.2.1. *Spring breaks forth at need of demigod's warriors.* Icel.: Herrmann Saxo II 216, MacCulloch Eddic 134, Boberg.

A941.5. *Spring breaks forth through power of saint.* Irish myth: Cross; India: Thompson-Balys.

D1567. Magic object produces fountain. D1713. Magic power of hermit (saint). F933.1. Miraculous spring (lake) bursts forth for holy person.

A941.5.0.1. *Fountain breaks forth through power of Virgin Mary.* Irish myth: Cross.

A941.5.0.2. *Wells break forth at birth of Christ.* Irish myth: Cross.

V211.1. Nativity of Christ.

A941.5.1. *Spring breaks forth where saint smites rock.* (Cf. A941.3.1.) Irish myth: Cross.

D927. Magic spring. D1567.6. Stroke of staff brings water from rock.

A941.5.2. *Many-colored fountain breaks forth where saint strikes earth with his foot.*

F718.2. (Perfectly round) well contains vari-colored water.

A941.5.3. *Spring breaks forth through power of saint at place where leper pulls out clump of rushes.* Irish myth: Cross.

D2161.1.1. Magic cure for leprosy. F933.5. Rushes uprooted revealing spring. F934.2. Lake rises from bramble-bush. F955. Miraculous cure for leprosy.

A941.5.4. *Spring breaks forth where animal delivers* book left behind by saint. Irish myth: Cross.

B548. Animal retrieves lost object.

A941.5.5. *Spring breaks forth where saint's stolen cow is found.* Irish myth: Cross.

A941.5.6. *Cloth from goddess, when spread by holy man over a spot, causes water to spring from earth.* India: Thompson-Balys.

A941.5.7. *Origin of springs where deity dug.* Hawaii: Beckwith Myth 212.

A941.5.8. *Spring from innocent king's blood.* Icel.: Boberg.

A941.6. *Breaking forth of springs partial cause of Flood.* Irish myth: Cross; Jewish: Neuman.

A1010. Deluge. A1011.1. Flood partially caused by breaking forth of springs.

A941.7. *Springs from beneath magic (holy) object.*

A941.7.1. *Spring from beneath world-tree.* Icel.: MacCulloch Eddic 330—333; Jewish: Neuman.

A652. World-tree.

A941.7.2. *Spring from roots of sacred tree when arrow is shot into it.* Fiji: Beckwith Myth 317.

A941.7.3. *Stream from under holy of holies in temple.* Jewish: Neuman.

A942. *Origin of hot springs* (geysers). Jewish: Neuman.

A942.1. *Hot springs rise where Christ bathed his feet.* (Cf. A901.) — Dh II 68.

A942.2. *Origin of salt springs.* Icel.: MacCulloch Eddic 326.

A950—A999. LAND FEATURES

A950. Origin of the land. Chinese: Graham; Eskimo (Cape York): Rasmussen III 47.

A951. *Contours of land caused by plowing of goddess.* (Cf. A901.) — *Olrik in Danske Studier (1910) 1ff.; Icel.: MacCulloch Eddic 181; Danish: De la Saussaye 280.

A951.1. *River valley licked out by giant beast.* Irish myth: Cross.

A951.2. *Contours of land caused by rooting of swine.* Irish myth: Cross.

A951.3. *Contours of land caused by occult hero driving harrow.* India: Thompson-Balys.

A952. *Land rises out of sea.* Tuamotu: Beckwith Myth 75.

A953. *Land thrown down from heaven.* Tonga: Gifford 15.

A954. *Land born from goddess.* Hawaii: Beckwith Myth 302.

A955. *Origin of islands.*

A955.0.1. *Islands created by order of deity.* Marquesas: Handy 122f.; Marshall Is.: Davenport 221.

A955.1. *Islands as deity's stepping-stones.* (Cf. A901.) — Greek: Fox 250.

A955.2. *Island created by shooting arrow.* (Cf. D936, D1092.) — Greek: Pauly-Wissowa s.v. "Anaphe" 2060, Apollonius Rhodius IV 1709ff.

A955.3. *Origin of island's shape and position.*

A955.3.1. *Origin of an island's shape.* India: Thompson-Balys.

A955.3.2. *Origin of island's position.* Mono-Alu, Farau: Wheeler 70.

A955.3.2.1. *Primeval hero moves islands into their present position.* *Frazer Pausanias II 48. — Japanese: Anesaki 248ff., Ikeda; Marshall Is.: Davenport 222.

A955.4. *Island plowed out by goddess.* (See A951.).

A955.5. *Islands from cow and calf transformed by evil eye of one-eyed god.* Irish myth: Cross.

A128.2.1. God with Evil Eye.

A955.6. *Islands from stones cast by giantess.* (Cf. A901, A963.5.) — Irish myth: Cross.

A955.7. *Islands from webs woven by primeval spiders.* India: Thompson-Balys.

A955.8. *Island fished-up by demigod (hero).* Hawaii: Beckwith Myth 61, 227, 308; Tonga: Beckwith Myth 369, Gifford 15, 20; Maori: Clark 48ff.; Marquesas: Handy 103; Tuamotu: Stimson MS (x-G. 13/52).

A955.9. *Goddess gives birth to islands.* Tonga: Gifford 102.

A955.10. *Islands from transformed object or person.* Hawaii: Beckwith Myth 347; Tahiti: Henry 129, 346; Marshall Is.: Davenport 222; Tonga: Gifford 24, 68, 179; Marquesas: Handy 44.

A955.11. *Islands originally form continent, later separated.* Tahiti: Beckwith Myth 468; Hawaii: Beckwith Myth 216f., 230, 328; Marquesas: Handy 112; Tonga: Gifford 81; Easter Is.: Métraux Ethnology 389.

A955.12. *Old woman as guardian of floating islands of the gods.* Hawaii: Beckwith Myth 68.

F737. Wandering island.

A956. *Origin of peninsulas.* Greek: Aeschylus Suppliants line 542. — Tonga: Gifford 68.

A957. *Origin of desert.* Jewish: Neuman.

A960. Creation of mountains (hills). Norwegian: Solheim Register 22; Persian: Carnoy; Chinese: Graham; Eskimo (Cape York): Rasmussen III 47.

D932.1. Mountains created by magic. D1593.1. Magic flower thrown down creates mountain. D2152. Magic control of mountains.

A961. *Mountains from primeval animal.*

A961.1. *Hills from flapping of primeval bird.* Hills and valleys are formed from the flapping of a giant turkey-buzzard when the earth is still plastic. — Yuchi: Alexander N. Am. 62.

A961.2. *Mountains from hacked-up fish* drawn from bottom of primeval water. Earth originates from a fish drawn from the water. It is hacked up and thus made to form mountains. — Maori: Dixon 43.

A811.1. Earth originates from fish brought from bottom of sea.

A961.3. *Mountain from accident to primeval lizard.* Lizard passing through a mountain is broken; his fore and hinder parts become mountains. — Bushman: Bleek and Lloyd 215.

A961.4. *Mountains spring from scattered parts of slain giant serpent's body.* India: Thompson-Balys.

A961.5. *Mountains (cliffs) from bones of killed giant.* Icel.: Boberg.

A962. *Mountains (hills) from ancient activities of god (hero).*

A962.1. *Mountain from part of deity's (hero's) body.* Hawaii: Beckwith Myth 170 (bones), 188f.; Maori: Beckwith Myth 379 (navel); Tahiti: Henry 339 (ribs, spine).

A962.2. *Mountains made with God's hand.* Jewish: Neuman.

A962.3. *Mountains from primeval journeys of a god.* (Cf. A901.) — Siberian: Holmberg Siberian 332.

A962.4. *Mountains pressed together by God.* Finnish: Aarne FFC VIII 4 No. 4, XXXIII 51 No. 4.

A962.5. *Mountains made with the hand.* Jewish: Moreno Esdras.

A962.6. *Mountains originated from primeval journeys of the first man.* Lithuanian: Balys Legends No. 14.

A962.7. *Hills from hero's striking (earth) with sword.* Irish myth: Cross.

F626.1. Strong man flattens hill.

A962.8. *Origin of hills and ridges: pieces of shattered god's head.* India: Thompson-Balys.

A962.9. *Mountains and hills are former sons, daughters of gods.* India: Thompson-Balys.

A962.10. *Hills represent loads from culture-hero's shoulders.* India: Thompson-Balys.

A963. *Mountains from stones (soil, sand) dropped or thrown.*

A963.1. *Mountains from stones dropped from giant's clothes.* He carries the stones in his clothes but loses them as he walks. — German: Grimm Deutsche Mythologie I 443; Hdwb. d. Abergl. I 1043; French: Sébillot France IV 7ff.; Swedish: Wessman 68 Nos. 581—3. — Indonesian: L. de Backer L'archipel indien 232ff.

A963.2. *Mountains from breaking of God's sieve.* He is sifting stones and the bottom of the sieve breaks, letting huge stones and mountains fall through. (Cf. A971.) — Finnish: Aarne FFC VIII 4 No. 5; Lappish: Qvigstad FFC LX 34 No. 1.

A963.3. *Soil dropped to form mountains.* Calif. Indian: Gayton and Newman 59.

A963.4. *Mountains and hills from stones thrown by giant at church.* Germanic: Hdwb. d. deutschen Aberglaubens s. v. "Findlingssteine"; Celtic: Thurneysen Irische Helden- und Königssage 431; Danish: Schmidt Danmarks Kæmpesten (1932) (DF XXXIX) 66ff.; Kristensen Danske Sagn III (1895) 19ff., (1931) 11ff.; Lithuanian: Balys Legends Nos. 493—96; Finnish-Swedish: Wessman 68 Nos. 586—591.

A963.5. *Hills from stones cast by giants.* Irish myth: Cross.

A955.6. Islands from stones cast by giantess. F531.6.6. Giants as builders of great structures.

A963.6. *Hill from anvil (cast by supernatural smith).* Irish myth: Cross.

A142. Smith of the gods. D1202. Magic anvil. F624. Mighty lifter.

A963.7. *Hill from sand left by passersby.* — Lithuanian: Balys Historical.

A963.8. *Hill as unfinished tower built in the likeness of Nimrod's tower.* Irish myth: Cross.

A963.9. *Clay soil dropped from sky to form hill.* Tonga: Gifford 39.

A964. *Mountains (hills) from ancient contest (fight).*

A964.1. *Holes in hills result of fight between gods.* India: Thompson-Balys.

A964.2. *Mountains fight each other: cause of their present shape.* India: Thompson-Balys.

A1185. Wings cut from flying mountains.

A964.2.1. *Mountains fight each other for honor of being the spot for the revelation.* Jewish: Neuman.

A964.3. *Battle of demons: hills torn up.* India: Thompson-Balys.

A965. *Origin of mountain chain.*

A965.1. *One mountain in love with another stretches leg out to meet her:* origin of a mountain chain. India: Thompson-Balys.

A966. *Origin of volcanoes.* Maori: Clark 43.

A967. *Origin of mounds.* Tonga: Gifford 121.

A967.1. *Mounds from horns cast by cattle.* Irish myth: Cross.

B182. Magic cow (ox, bull). B301.6. Faithful cattle fight at master's grave until they cast their horns.

A968. *Origin of cliffs.*

A968.1. *Cliffs become hard.* Were formerly soft but become hard by God's order. (Cf. A975.) — Finnish: Aarne FFC VIII 3 No. 3; Estonian: Aarne FFC XXV 139 No. 2.

A968.2. *Cliff from lovers' leap.* Lovers in despair throw themselves from a high place. This becomes a cliff. — *Crane Vitry 220f. No. 214; Ward Cat. Romances III 17; U.S.: Baughman. — Common among the North American Indians.

T80. Tragic love. T211.3. Husband and wife kill themselves so as not to be separated.

A969. *Creation of mountains and hills — miscellaneous.*

A969.1. *Mountain from buried giant.* India: Thompson-Balys.

F531.Exceptionally large or small men. G100. Giant ogre.

A969.2. *Cloud on lofty male mountain induced by a beautiful female mountain to bow to her feet:* hence their present shape. India: Thompson-Balys.

A969.3. *Mountains and valleys formed from great fire.* India: Thompson-Balys.

A969.4. *Hills because sky asked earth to wrinkle up its feet.* India: Thompson-Balys.

A969.5. *Water freezes and forms mountains.* Eskimo (Bering Strait): Nelson RBAE XVIII 482.

A969.6. *Hill brought to country as adopted child.* Hawaii: Beckwith Myth 379.

A969.7. *Origin of mountains as punishment.* Jewish: Neuman.

A969.8. *Origin of crevasse.* Africa (Bushongo): Torday 251.

A969.9. *Mountain or hills from actions of the devil.* England: *Baughman.

A970. Origin of rocks and stones. Icel.: MacCulloch Eddic 325f.; Jewish: Neuman. — Eskimo (Cape York): Rasmussen III 47.

A1599.1 Origin of warning beacon. D231. Transformation: man to stone. D931. Magic rock (stone). D2153. Rock in sea created by magic. F531.3.2. Giant throws a great rock. F636. Remarkable thrower. F800. Extraordinary rocks and stones.

A971. *Origin of rocks from breaking of God's sieve.* See references in A963.2.

A972. *Indentions on rocks from prints left by man (beast).* (Cf. A901.) — *Fb "sten" III 552b; *Andree Ethnographische Parallelen (1878) 96; Dh II 8. — Irish: Thurneysen Irische Helden-u. Königssagen 189, Cross; Icel.: Boberg; Danish: Schmidt DF XXXIX 13ff.; French: Sébillot France I 369ff.; India: Thompson-Balys. — N. A. Indian: Krickeberg Indianermärchen aus Nordamerika 245, Calif. Indian: Gayton and Newman 59; Aztec: Krickeberg Märchen der Azteken 60, 204, and passim; S. Am. Indian (Tupinamba): Métraux BBAE CXLIII (3) 132.

A972.1. *Indentions on rocks from imprint of gods and saints.* *Toldo Studien zur vgl. Literaturgeschichte V 337ff.; Andree Ethnographische Parallelen (1878) 95. — Irish myth: *Cross; Eng., Scot., Ire., Wales, U.S.: *Baughman; Jewish: Neuman; India: Thompson-Balys; Buddhist myth: Malalasekera II 977; Greek: *Grote I 180. — Hawaii: Beckwith Myth 65, 142, 212f.; S. Am. Indian (Mundurucu): Horton BBAE CXLIII (3) 281.

A972.1.1. *Indentions on rocks from footprints of Christ.* Dh II 199. — Irish myth: Cross; Icel.: Kirialaxsaga 66.

V211.2. Christ on earth.

A972.1.2. *Priest stamps on stone to prove truth of pope; print is still visible.* England: Baughman.

A972.1.3. *Footprints of holy man are still seen in stone where he stood to preach.* England: Baughman.

A972.2. *Indentions on rocks from footprints of fairies* (angels, devils). Jegerlehner Oberwallis 303 Nos. 22, 23. — Lithuanian: Balys Legends No. 500ff.

A972.2.1. *Indention on rock from footprint of angel.* Irish myth: Cross; Jewish: Neuman.

A972.2.2. *The devil's footprint.* Eng., Wales, U.S.: *Baughman.

A972.3. *Holes in stones caused by piercing by saint's finger.* Irish: Plummer Vitae Sanctorum Hiberniae clvi.

A972.3.1. *Holes in stone caused by saint (warrior).* Irish myth: Cross.

A972.3.1.1. *Indentions on rock from weapons (limbs) of robbers* through power of saint. Irish myth: Cross.

A972.3.1.2. *Indentions on rocks from footprints of saint's cow.* Irish myth: Cross.

A972.4. *Imprint of horse in rocks.* — French: Sébillot France I 383ff.; Danish: Thiele Danmarks Folkesagn I 209, II 47, Schmidt DF XXXIX 22—23; German: þidriks saga I 157, 220. — India: Thompson-Balys; Japanese: Ikeda.

A972.5. *Indentions on rocks from marks of various persons.*

A972.5.1. *Indentions on rocks from head of infant hero* (saint). Irish myth: Cross.

A972.5.2. *Chasms between rocks mark "leaps" of giants, heroes,* etc. Irish myth: Cross.

F1071. Prodigious jump.

A972.5.3. *Indentions on rock from paws of King Arthur's dog.* Irish myth: Cross.

A524.1. Culture hero has marvelous dogs. A526.2. Culture hero as mighty hunter.

A972.5.4. *Indentions on rocks from weapons, knees, and elbows* (of persons slain by hero). Irish myth: Cross.

A972.5.5. *Rocks or hill-tops flat because persons (gods) slept or cooked on them.* Irish myth: Cross.

A988. Cairn marks burial place.

A972.5.6. *Hole in stone caused by weapon of warrior.* Irish myth: Cross.

A972.6. *Indentions on rocks caused by giants.* Irish myth: Cross.

F531.6.6. Giants as builders of great structures.

A972.7. *Great fish killed by hero and cut into sixteen pieces: the great stones may still be seen.* India: Thompson-Balys.

A973. *Origin of stones: punishment for discourtesy.* Jesus asks a man what he is sowing. He answers, "Stones." Jesus turns the crop to stones. This is how stones originate. — *Dh II 95. — Estonian: Aarne FFC XXV 140 No. 4; Livonian: Loorits FFC LXVI 80 No. 2; England: Baughman.

A974. *Rocks from transformation of people to stone.* Greek: Fox 175; Icel.: Boberg. — Hawaii: Beckwith Myth 175; Marshall Is.: Davenport 229; Tonga: Gifford 99, 130; Marquesas: Handy 106; India: Thompson-Balys; Eskimo: Boas RBAE VI 639; Calif. Indian: Gayton and Newman 97.

A974.1. *Certain stones are druids transformed by power of saint.* Irish myth: Cross.

D231. Transformation: man to stone. D661. Transformation as punishment. P427. Druid (magus). Q551.5. Scoffers turned to stone by saint. V229.6. Saint in conflict with druid.

A974.2. *Certain stones are transformed giants.* Irish myth: Cross.
F531.6.13. Graves of giants.

A975. *Why stones became hard.* By God's order. (Cf. A968.1.) — Schmidt DF XXXIX 36; von Sydow Folkeminder och Folktankar VI 73; Fb "Adam" IV 3a. — Finnish: Aarne FFC VIII 3 No. 3; Estonian: Aarne FFC XXV 139 Nr. 2; Livonian: Loorits FFC LXVI 80 Nos. 3, 4. — Oceanic: Beckwith Myth 88.

A975.1. *Why stones no longer grow.* Devil sows stones; God sends cold to prevent their growing. Lithuanian: Balys Index No. 3015, Legends Nos. 16f.

A975.1.1. *Why stones no longer grow: punishment for injuring foot of holy person.* Lithuanian: Balys Index No. 3015. Legends Nos. 19, 25.
F802. Growing rocks. J1889. Objects supposed to be born, grow, and die. J2212.7. Boat taken to graze in order to grow.

A975.2. *Why certain rock produces fire when struck with steel.*

A975.2.1. *Fire producing rock result of contest between god of fire and god of rain.* India: Thompson-Balys.

A976. *Why rocks at river are covered with moss.* Jamaica Negro: Beckwith MAFLS XVII 259 No. 49.

A977. *Origin of particular stones or groups of stones.*

A977.1. *Giant responsible for certain stones.* (Cf. A963.1.) — Canada, England, U.S., Wales: *Baughman; Icel.: Boberg.

A977.2. *Devil throws stones.* England, U.S.: *Baughman.

A977.2.1. *Devil and man throw stones in contest.* England, Wales: *Baughman.

A977.2.2. *The devil throws stones at church or churchmen.* (Cf. A963.4.) — England: *Baughman.

A977.2.3. *Devil throws down quoits when he is told that it is wrong to play on Sunday.* They remain as stones to this day. — England: *Baughman.*

A977.3. *Devil drops stones.* England: *Baughman.

A977.3.1. *The devil drops stones from apron.* (Cf. A963.1.) — England, Ireland: *Baughman.

A977.4. *The devil turns object or animal to stone which is still seen.* England, U.S.: *Baughman.

A977.5. *Origin of particular rock.* India: Thompson-Balys.

A977.5.1. *Certain stones are cheeses transformed by saint.* (Cf. A974.) — Irish myth: Cross.
Q552.16.1.2. Women carrying cheeses concealed pretend that they are carrying webs or balls of thread. Saint changes cheeses to stones.

A977.5.2. *Pile of stones in certain chapel formed of fragments of salmon transformed by saint.* Irish myth: Cross.
D176. Transformation: man to salmon. Q552.16.1.1. Fishermen cut fish into pieces and claim that they have none.

A977.5.3. *Stone column is membrum virile of ancient hero.* Irish myth: Cross.
F547. Remarkable sexual organs.

A977.5.4. *Two rocks from split and transformed lapdog.* Irish myth: Cross.

B187.0.1. Toy (lap) dogs.

A978. *Origin of minerals.*

A1432. Acquisition of metals.

A978.1. *Origin of minerals from body of dead culture hero.* Persian: Carnoy 294.

E630. Reincarnation in object.

A978.2. *Iron created to punish cedar's pride.* Jewish: Neuman.

A978.3. *Origin of emeralds from marvelous vase broken into pieces.* India: Thompson-Balys.

A979. *Other stories about stone origins.* Tahiti: Henry 341; Marquesas: Handy 132; Hawaii: Beckwith Myth 18, 22.

A979.1. *Stone rent at time of crucifixion.* England: Baughman.

A980. Origin of particular places.

A983. *Origin of valleys or hollows.* Jewish: Neuman; Tonga: Gifford 89.

A984. *Pillars of Hercules at Gibraltar set up by Hercules.* (Cf. A901.) — Greek: Fox 86.

A986. *Bridge of the Gods.* A conflict of the gods breaks a primeval bridge and thus causes a rapid in a river (the Columbia River at The Dalles, Oregon). — Salishan: Alexander N. Am. 134.

A988. *Cairn marks burial place.* Irish myth: Cross.

A989. *Origin of particular places — miscellaneous.*

A989.1. *Dark brown patches on soil mark place where marvelous cow (Glas) and her calf lay.* Irish myth: Cross.

B182. Magic cow (ox, bull).

A989.2. *Roads marked out by supernatural cows.* Irish myth: Cross.

B72.1. Three sea-cows, one red, one white, one black.

A989.3. *Certain stones are druids' (saints') seats (chairs).* Irish myth: Cross.

A989.4. *Pile of stones (cairn) marks site of battle.* Irish myth: Cross.

P554. Battle-cairn.

A990. Other land features.

A991. *Origin of villages.* Jegerlehner Oberwallis 308 No. 36; India: Thompson-Balys.

A992. *Origin of sacred places.* Lithuanian: Balys Index No. 3725; India: Thompson-Balys.

A992.1. *Origin of sacred post* (placed there by ancestral culture hero). India: Thompson-Balys.

A992.2. *Sacred place where thunderbolt fell down.* Blinkenberg The Thunderweapon (Cambridge 1911); Handwb. d. Abergl. II 325 "Donnerkeil".

A992.3. *Ground bursts open and a temple rises from it.* India: Thompson-Balys.

A994. *Five great roads of Ireland "discovered" on night of king's birth.* Irish myth: Cross.

F1099.2.1. Roads miraculously appear on day of hero's birth.

A995. *Origin of cities.* Jewish: Neuman.

A996. *Origin of settlements* (places later to be settled). Jewish: Neuman.

A997. *Origin of boundaries.* Jewish: Neuman.

A998. *Origin of clay.* India: Thompson-Balys.

A1000—A1099. World calamities and renewals.

A1000. World catastrophe. The world is destroyed. The incidents are usually the same whether a final destruction is thought of or a destruction which may be overcome by a renewal of the earth. — **Olrik Ragnarök; Fb "verden" III 1039ab; *G. Neckel Studien zu den germanischen Dichtungen vom Weltuntergang (Stzb. d. Heidelberger Akad. d. Wissenschaften 1918); **H. Fischer Weltwenden (1928); **Henne-am Rhyn Das Jenseits: kulturgeschichtliche Darstellung der Ansichten über .... Weltuntergang (1881); **Reitzenstein Weltuntergangsvorstellungen (Kyrkohistoriska Årsskrift [Uppsala 1924]). — Icel.: MacCulloch Eddic 336ff.; Irish myth: *Cross; Jewish: *Neuman; Egyptian: Smith Dragon 111; Hindu: Keith 105. — S. Am. Indian (Guaraní): *Métraux RMLP XXXIII 124.

M357. Prophecy: world catastrophe.

A1001. *Series of world catastrophes.* **Olrik Ragnarök; Icel.: MacCulloch Eddic 336ff.; Lithuanian: Balys Index No. 3012, Legends No. 15. — Aztec: Alexander Lat. Am. 95.

A1002. *Doomsday.* Catastrophes precede the Day of Judgment. *Olrik Ragnarök. — Icel.: MacCulloch Eddic 336ff.; Irish myth: Cross; Estonian: Loorits Grundzüge I 461ff.; Jewish: Moreno Esdras (M307), *Neuman; Hindu: Keith 105; India: Thompson-Balys; Buddhist myth: Malalasekera I 279. — Pawnee: Alexander N. Am. 116ff. — Cf. Revelations passim.

A1075. End of world heralded by coming of Antichrist. B259.8. Birds' wings drip blood when birds hear of Day of Judgment. E751. Souls on Judgment Day. M341.2.20. Prophecy: wholesale slaughter to be inflicted by colossal wheel rolling over Europe. Q155.1. Condemned souls released from hell on Doomsday at request of saint.

A1002.1. *Widespread calamity when feast of John the Baptist shall fall on certain day.* Irish myth: Cross.

V70.3.1. Feast of Saint John the Baptist.

A1002.2. *Signs before the Day of Judgment.* **Heist Fifteen Signs Before Doomsday (East Lansing, Michigan, 1952). — Irish myth: Cross.

A1075. End of world heralded by coming of Antichrist. M363.0.1. Coming of Antichrist prophesied. Z71.16.14.3. Fifteen signs before doomsday.

A1002.2.1. *No rainbow for fifteen years before the Day of Judgment.* Irish myth: Cross.

A1002.2.2. *Bleeding wood as sign of Doomsday.* Jewish: Moreno Esdras (M307.3.).

A1002.2.3. *Talking stone as sign of Doomsday.* Jewish: Moreno Esdras (M307.4).

A1002.2.4. *Unusual migration of birds as sign of Doomsday.* Jewish: Moreno Esdras (M307.5.).

A1003. *Calamity as punishment for sin.* Jewish: *Neuman; India: Thompson-Balys; Maori: Beckwith Myth 317; S. Am. Indian (Chiriguano): Métraux RMLP XXXIII 158.

A1005. *Preservation of life during world calamity.* (Cf. A1020, A1038, A1045.) — Persian: Carnoy 308; S. Am. Indian (Chiriguano): Métraux BBAE CXLIII (3) 484.

A1005.1. *Preservation of life of certain persons in Ireland during Flood.* (Cf. A1006.5.) — Irish myth: Cross.

A1005.2. *Inclosure made during world calamity and only best types of animals and men preserved.* Persian: Carnoy 308; India: Thompson-Balys.

A1005.3. *Holy Land not ravaged by deluge.* Jewish: Neuman.

A1006. *Renewal of world after world calamity.* Icel.: De la Saussaye 352, Boberg; Jewish: *Neuman. — S. Am. Indian (Bakairi): Lévi-Strauss BBAE CXLIII (3) 347, (Namicuara): Lévi-Strauss ibid. 369.

A719.2. After world catastrophe, new sun appears and starts new epoch.

A1006.1. *New race from single pair (or several) after world calamity.* (Cf. A1038, A1045.) — *Olrik Ragnarök 479 s.v. "Erneuerung". — Greek: *Grote I 93; Jewish: Neuman; India: Thompson-Balys. — Marquesas: Handy 110; Ellice Is.: Beckwith Myth 270; Hawaii: ibid. 315; Calif. Indian: Gayton and Newman 91; S. Am. Indian (Yuracare): Métraux RMLP XXXIII 144, (Chiriguano): ibid. 157, 163, 170f., (Guaporé River): Lévi-Strauss BBAE CXLIII (3) 379; African (Lamomi): Bouveignes 29.

A1245.1. New race from stones thrown over head after deluge. A1254.1. New race from seeds thrown over head after deluge.

A1006.2. *New race from incest* after world calamity. Hindu: Keith 92; India: Thompson-Balys; Chinese: Graham.

T410. Incest.

A1006.3. *New race made of red earth* after world calamity. Smith Dragon 121.

A1241. Man made from clay (earth).

A1006.4. *New race from union of girl and rat.* India: Thompson-Balys.

A1006.5. *Ireland repopulated by persons who escape flood.* Irish myth: Cross.

A1021.0.1. Persons excluded from Noah's ark build another ark and sail to Ireland.

A1006.6. *Ireland, waste for centuries after flood, is repopulated by immigrants.* Irish myth: Cross.

A1006.7. *Whole tribe descended from lone woman-survivor* of doomed city. India: Thompson-Balys.

A1006.8. *One bear-child escapes death, is ancestor of all bears.* India: Thompson-Balys.

A1006.9. *After world-fire life recreated from tree.* Africa (Fang): Trilles 132f.

A1007. *World calamity will begin in Palestine.* Jewish: Neuman.

A1009. *World catastrophes — miscellaneous.*

A1009.1. *First race of men perishes when sun first rises.* S. Am. Indian (Aymara): Tschopik BBAE CXLIII (2) 571, (Chibaya): La Barre ibid. 585.

A1009.2. *Animate and inanimate objects attempt to destroy humanity.* S. Am. Indian (Chiriguano): Métraux RMLP XXXIII 158.

A1009.3. *Large stone falls from sky killing all but one couple.* S. Am. Indian (Moré): Métraux BBAE CXLIII (3) 406.

A1010. Deluge. Inundation of whole world or section. — **Anderson Nordasiatische Flutsagen; **Andree Die Flutsagen (Braunschweig, 1891); **Diestel Die Sintflut und die Flutsagen des Altertums[2] (Berlin 1876); *Woods Encyc. Religion and Ethics s.v. "Deluge"; **Winternitz Die Flutsagen des Altertums (Wien 1901); **Fischer Weltwenden: Die grossen Fluten in Sage und Wirklichkeit (Leipzig 1925); **Gerland Der Mythus von der Sintflut (Bonn 1912); **Usener Die Sintflutsagen untersucht (Bonn 1899); Ley Eiszeit (Anhang: Eiszeit u. Sintflut) (Erfurt 1928); *Riem Die Sintflut in Sage und Wissenschaft (Hamburg 1925); *F. von Schwarz Sintflut und Völkerwanderung (Stuttgart 1894); **Feilberg Skabelses og Syndflodssagn (1915); *Maria Alice Moura Pessoa A Bibliographic Study of the Deluge Myth in the Americas (MA Thesis, Columbia University 1948). —Irish myth: Cross; Greek: Fox 19, *Frazer Apollodorus I 55 n. 1, II 88 n. 2; Egyptian: Müller 75f.; Persian: Carnoy 270; Hindu: Keith 105, Charpentier Kleine Beiträge 34 n. 1; India: Thompson-Balys; Indo-Chinese: Scott 267, 278ff.; Chinese: Graham; Korean: Zong in-Sob 16 No. 8; Siberian: Holmberg Siberian 361ff. — Indonesian: Dixon 178ff., 256f.; Philippine (Tinguian): Cole 189; Melanesian: ibid. 119f.; Polynesian: ibid. 38; Samoan: ibid. 17; Australian: ibid 280; Hawaii: Beckwith Myth 307, 314. — N. A. Indian (general): *Thompson Tales 286 n. 57, Alexander N. Am. 299 f. n. 49, also 177, 180, 203, 205 (Pima, Walapai, Sia, Hopi); Sinkyone: Kroeber JAFL XXXII 347; Calif. Indian: Gayton and Newman 55; Eskimo (Central): Boas RBAE VI 637, (Bering Strait): Nelson RBAE XVIII 452, (Cape York): Rasmussen III 48, (Northwest Canada): Pétitot Traditions 2; Maya: Alexander Lat. Am. 152f.; Mixtec: ibid. 87; S. Am. Indian (Carib): Alexander Lat. Am. 39, (Chibcha): ibid. 203, (Amazon tribes): ibid. 311, (Jivaro, Yugua): Steward-Métraux BBAE CXLIII (3) 627, 736, (Cubeo): Goldman ibid. (3) 798, (Aymara): Tschopik ibid. (2) 571, (Zaparoans, Pebans): Steward ibid. (3) 532, (Bacairi): Lévi-Strauss ibid. (3) 347, (Nambicuara): Lévi-Strauss ibid. (3) 369, (Guaporé): Lévi-Strauss ibid. (3) 379, (Caingang): Métraux ibid. (1) 473, (Eastern Brazil): Lowie ibid. (1) 397. — African: *Wagener 13ff.

A925. Origin of ocean from flood. A2211.7. Birds cling to sky in flood: cause of tail colors. A2231.9. Fish in deluge deride God: are flattened with blow. A2291. Animal characteristics obtained during deluge. Q150.1 Rescue from deluge as reward.

A1010.1. *Sun and moon do not shine during deluge.* Jewish: Neuman.

A1010.2. *Great flood lasts eight months.* Maori: Beckwith Myth 316.

A1011. *Local deluges.* **Schmarsel Die Sage von der untergegangenen Stadt; *RTP XXVIII 27 and references to earlier volumes. — Irish myth: Cross; Greek: Frazer Apollodorus II 81 n. 2; Jewish: Neuman.

B91.6. Serpent causes flood.

A1011.1. *Flood partially caused by breaking forth of springs.* Irish myth: Cross; India: Thompson-Balys.

A941.6. Breaking forth of springs partial cause of flood.

A1011.2. *Flood caused by rising of river.* S. A. Indian (Chiriguano): Métraux RMLP XXXIII 170.

A1011.3. *God's promise never to destroy world by water does not apply to local floods.* Jewish: Neuman.

A1012. *Flood from fluids of the body.*

A1012.1. *Flood from tears.* N. A. Indian: *Thompson Tales 287 n. 57b; Polynesian: Dixon 38 n. 117.

A1131.1. Rain from tears. D1567.2. Saint's tears produce fountain.

A1012.1.1. *Flood from Adam's tears of repentance.* Dh I 223.

A1012.1.2. *Flood from tears of grieving lover.* N. Am. Indian (N'tlaka'-panaq): British Association for the Advancement of Science LXIX 574f.; S. Am. Indian (Chaco): Nordenskiöld Indianerleben 253f.

A1012.2. *Flood from urine.* *Jochelson JE VI 367 (Koryak, Eskimo, Athapascan Indians).

A933. River from urine of goddess (giantess).

A1012.2.1. *Flood caused by loosing fairy horse and allowing it to stale.* Irish myth: Cross.

A1012.3. *Flood from blood.* American Indian (Mono): Gifford JAFL XXVI 306.

A1012.3.1. *Flood from slain giant's blood.* Icel.: Boberg.

A1013. *Flood from belly.* It flows from pierced belly of monster.—Indonesian: Dixon 196 n. 33; N. A. Indian: *Thompson Tales 287 n. 57c.; S. Am. Indian (Toba): Métraux MAFLS XL 127.

A1013.1. *Vomiting of a whale causes flood.* N. Am. Indian (Déné): Petitot Traditions (Paris 1886) 318f.

A1015. *Flood caused by gods or other superior beings.* (Cf. A1018.) — Babylonian: Jensen Gilgamesch Epos XI 53ff., 69ff.; Marquesas: Handy 109f.; S. Am. Indian (Tupinamba): Métraux BBAE CXLIII (3) 133, (Yuracare): ibid. 503.

A1015.1. *Flood from conflict of gods.* Sea god and rain god. — Cook Group: Dixon 39 n. 121, 122; S. Am. Indian (Chiriguano): Campana Archivio per l'Antropologia et la Etnologia XXXII 22.

A1015.1.1. *Flood from conflict of monsters (giant animals).* S. Am. Indian (Araucanian): Cooper BBAE CXLIII (2) 753, (Aymara): Tschopik ibid. (2) 571, (Chiriguano): Métraux ibid. (3) 484.

A1015.2. *Spirit causes deluge.* Jegerlehner Oberwallis 299 No. 10. — S. Am. Indian (Eastern Brazil): Lowie BBAE CXLIII (1) 434, (Guaporé River): Lévi-Strauss ibid. (3) 379.

A1015.3. *Flood caused by deity stamping on floor of heavens.* Maori: Beckwith Myth 250, Clark 162.

A1016. *Pseudo-scientific explanations of the flood.* S. Am. Indian (Cashinawa): Métraux BBAE CXLIII (3) 684; Tuamotu: Beckwith Myth 267.

A1016.1. *Flood from animals' boring into ground* (turtles, crawfishes, etc.). American Negro (Georgia): Harris Remus No. 5.

A1016.2. *Deluge produced by hot liquid which burns as it floods.* American Indian (Salinan): Mason JAFL XXVII 163f., (Krawak): Ehrenreich Mythen und Legenden 49.

A1016.3. *Flood caused by melting of ice after great spell of cold.* N. Am. Indian (Déné): Petitot Traditions 373—378; S. Am. Indian (Gusinde): Métraux MAFLS XL 37.

A1016.4. *Flood from broken calabashes of water.* American Indian (Puerto Rico): Fewkes RBAE XXV 73f., (Carajá): Baldus Ensaios de Etnologia Brasileira 174, Lowie Encyc. Rel. Ethics s.v. "flood".

A1016.5. *Making mountains out of flat earth causes flood.* N. Am. Indian (Apache): Goddard PaAM XXIV 28f.

A1016.6. *Moon falls into sea and causes flood by overflowing.* S. Am. Indian (Fueginos): Coazzi Rev. Chil. Hist. Geogr. X 31.

A1016.7. *Flood whenever shard at earth's core moves.* Jewish: Neuman.

A1017. *Flood caused to satisfy emotional need.*

A1017.1. *Desire of man for sun causes flood.* S. Am. Indian (Chaco): Métraux BBAE CXXXIV 26.

A1017.2. *Flood caused by prayer.* Maori: Beckwith Myth 316.

D1766.1. Magic results produced by prayer.

A1017.3. *Flood caused by curse.* S. Am. Indian (Chiriguano): Métraux BBAE CXLIII (3) 484.

D1792. Magic results from curse.

A1018. *Flood as punishment.* *Frazer Old Testament I 144—360; Spanish Exempla: Keller. — Jewish: Neuman; Greek: Fox 158; Babylonian: Spence 45f.; India: Thompson-Balys; Buddhist myth: Malalasekera II 1056. — Society Is.: Dixon 39 n. 120; Hawaiian, Maori, Marquesas: ibid. 40; N. Am. Indian (Calif.): Gayton and Newman 59, (Pomo): Angelo JAFL XLVI 241, (Wishosk): Kroeber JAFL XVIII 96, (Apache): Goddard PaAM XXIV 8, (Hopi): Voth FM VIII 53, (Zuñi): Benedict Zuñi Mythology I 10ff.; Caribbean (Cuan): Stout CU IV 267; S. Am. Indian (Chaco): Métraux BBAE CXLIII (1) 369, (Cubeo): Goldman JAFL LIII 244, (Toba): Métraux MAFLS XL 29, (Inca): Rowe BBAE CXLIII (2) 315. — See also references to "Sintflut" in A1010 and A1015, where in nearly all cases the gods produce the flood as punishment.

Q200. Deeds punished. Q595.5. Flood as punishment for murder.

A1018.1. *Flood as punishment for breaking tabu.* Fiji, Tahiti, Maori, Andaman: Beckwith Myth 316—319; S. Am. Indian (Toba, Mataco, Lengua): Métraux BBAE CXLIII (1) 367.

A1018.2. *Flood as punishment for incest.* American Indian (Namba): Muller Anthropos XXIX 186.

Q242. Incest punished. T410. Incest.

A1018.3. *Flood brought as revenge for injury.* Tuamotu: Beckwith Myth 318; N. Am. Indian (Carrier): Jennes JAFL XLVII 141ff., (Ts'etsaut): Boas JAFL IX 262, (North Pacific Tribes): Boas Indianische Sagen 79, (Haida): Swanton BBAE XXIX 142, (Kwakiutl): Boas and Hunt JE III 100, (Mono): Gifford JAFL XXVI 326, (Shasta): Dixon JAFL XXIII 36, (Pima): Lloyd Aw-Aw-Tam 36ff., (Ojibwa): Jones-Michelson PAES VII 151, 271, (Menomini): Skinner and Satterlee PaAM XIII

255—260, Hoffman RBAE XIV 133; Central and S. Am. Indian (Cahita): Beals BBAE CXLII 216f., (Bororo): Baldus Ensaios de Etnologia Brasileira 176ff., (Tupinamba): Métraux BBAE CXLIII (3) 133.

A1019. *Deluge — miscellaneous.*

A1019.1. *Subsidence of earth beneath flood.* India: Thompson-Balys.

A1019.2. *Serpent king causes flood by damming rivers.* India: Thompson-Balys.

A1019.3. *Flood because earth has become too thickly populated.* India: Thompson-Balys.

A1019.4. *Flood puts out world-fire.* (Cf. A1030.) — S. Am. Indian (Tupinamba): Métraux BBAE CXLIII (3) 133, (Tucuna): Nimuendajú ibid. 724, (Cubeo): Goldman JAFL LIII 244.

A1020. Escape from deluge.

A1021. *Deluge: escape in boat (ark).* *Dh I 258ff. — Irish myth: Cross; Icel.: MacCulloch Eddic 324, Boberg; Spanish Exempla: Keller; Greek: Fox 19, Grote I 93; Hebrew: Genesis, ch. 6, 7, 8; Jewish: Moreno Esdras; Babylonian: Spence 173f.; Hindu: Keith 99; India: Thompson-Balys; Buddhist myth: Malalasekera II 1056; Chinese: Graham, Eberhard FFC CXX 84; Siberian: Holmberg Siberian 364. — Pelew Is. (Micronesia): Dixon 257; Maori: Beckwith Myth 316. — American Indian: *Thompson CColl II 452, (Eskimo): Boas RBAE VI 637f., (Carrier): Jenness JAFL XLVII 141ff., (Chipewyan): Lowie PaAM X 195, (Coos): Frachtenberg CU I 45—49, (Kathlamet): Boas BBAE XXVI 23, (Nootka): Sapir JAFL XXXII 353ff., (Chimariko): Dixon UCal. V 304, (Salishan): Teit MAFLS XI 13, 132; (Crow): Lowie PaAM XXV 16, (Cochiti): Benedict BBAE XCVIII 2ff., (White Mountain Apache): Goodwin MAFLS XXXIII 50ff., (Objibwa): Radin JAFL XLI 70ff., (Chochtaw): Bushnell AA n. s. XII 528f., (Shawnee): Spencer JAFL XXII 319, (Natchez): Swanton BBAE LXXXVIII 121, 214, (Aztec): Alexander Lat. Am. 85f., (Arawak): ibid 273, (Carib): ibid. 39, (Mbaya): Muller Anthropos XXIX, (Mura): Nimuendajú BBAE CXLIII (3) 265, (Taulipang): Camara Cascudo Antologia de Folclore Brasileira 124ff. (These are only a selection of the American Indian references).

C12.5.1. Noah's curse admits devil to ark. Z356. Unique survivor.

A1021.0.1. *Persons excluded from Noah's ark build another ark and sail to Ireland.* Irish myth: Cross.

A1006.5. Ireland repopulated by persons who escape flood.

A1021.0.2. *Escape from deluge in wooden cask (drum).* Chinese: Graham; S. A. Indian (Guaporé): Lévi-Strauss BBAE CXLIII (3) 379.

A1021.0.3. *Deluge: escape in gourd.* India: Thompson-Balys.

A1021.0.4. *Deluge: escape on floating tree.* Korean: Zong in-Sob 16 No. 8.

A1021.0.5. *Deluge: escape in hollow tree trunk.* American Indian (Seneca): Curtin-Hewitt RBAE XXXII 636ff., (Mexican): Bancroft Native Races of the Pacific States of America (New York 1874—76) III 66ff.

A1021.0.6. *Deluge: escape on floating building.* American Indian (Tlingit): Bancroft Native Races V 14, (Cahita): Beals BBAE CXLII 216f.

A1021.1. *Pairs of animals in ark.* Seed of all beings put into ark to escape destruction. — See references to "Sintflutsage" in A1010; also Dh I 267ff. — Irish myth: Cross; Hebrew: Genesis 6:19; Babylonian: Spence 175; Hindu: Keith 147. — Aztec: Alexander Lat. Am. 85f.

A1853.2. Mice engendered after flood from rottenness: no mice on ark. A2145.2. Snake preserved in ark: to stop hole with tail. A2214.3. Unicorn thrown from ark and drowned: hence extinct. A2232.4. Griffin disdains to go on ark: drowned: hence extinct. B754.4. Male rabbit bears young: female rabbit escaped Noah on ark and drowned. F681.8. Marvelous runner captures two of every wild animal. F989.6. One bull, one cow survive plague. H1154.9. Task: capturing pair of every wild animal in the land.

A1021.2. *Bird scouts sent out from ark.* *Dh I 283. — Irish myth: Cross; Hebrew: Genesis 8:7ff., Neuman; Babylonian: Spence 176.

A2221.7. Dove returns to ark in obedience to Noah: rewarded. A2234.1.1. Raven does not return to ark in obedience to Noah: punished. B291.1. Bird as messenger. B450. Helpful bird.

A1022. *Escape from deluge on mountain.* Greek: Grote I 93; Hebrew: Genesis 8:4, Neuman; Hindu: Keith 99; India: Thompson-Balys. — Philippine: Dixon 179; Borneo: ibid. 180; West Caroline Is.: ibid. 257; Australian: ibid. 280; Polynesian: ibid 38 n. 118; Cook Group: ibid. 39 n. 121; Hawaii: Beckwith Myth 215. — N. Am. Indian (Bella-Bella): Boas MAFLS XXV 1f., (Tahltan): Teit JAFL XXXII 232ff., (Luiseño): Du Bois UCal VIII 157, (Shasta): Dixon JAFL XXIII 36, (Blackfoot): Wissler PaAM II 19, (Chiricahua Apache): Opler MAFLS XXXVII 1f., (Zuñi): Benedict CU XXI 10ff.; S. Am. Indian (Araucanian): Alexander Lat. Am. 330, (Inca): ibid. 230, (Yunca, Peru): ibid. 230, (Caingang, Amazon): ibid. 312. (Only a selection of references for North and South America.).

A1023. *Escape from deluge on tree.* India: Thompson-Balys. — American Indian (Paiute): Steward UCal XXXIV 372, (Plains Cree): Skinner JAFL XXIX 350, (Fox): Jones JAFL XIV 233ff., (Catawba): Speck CU XXIV 23, (Ackawoi): Alexander Lat. Am. 270, (Caingang): ibid. 312, (Guayaki): Métraux-Baldus BBAE CXLIII (1) 444, (Maina): Steward-Métraux BBAE CXLIII (3) 649.

R311. Tree refuge.

A1024. *Escape from deluge in cave.* Andaman Is.: Beckwith Myth 319; American Indian (Cheyenne): Dorsey FM IX 36, (Arawak, Antis, Yuracare): Spence The Problem of Atlantis 95.

A1025. *Escape from deluge on island.* Society Is.: Dixon 39.

A1005.1.Preservation of life of certain persons in Ireland during flood. A1006.5. Ireland repopulated by persons who escape flood.

A1026. *Escape from deluge on foot.* Chinese: Eberhard FFC CXX 84.

A1027. *Rescue from deluge by fish.* Hindu: Keith 75, 99.

B551. Fish carries man across water.

A1028. *Bringing deluge to end.*

A1028.1. *Trickster sticks spear in ground and leads water to sea,* ending deluge. S. Am. Indian (Chaco): Métraux BBAE CXLIII (1) 369.

A1028.2. *Birds fill sea with dirt and overcome flood.* S. Am. Indian (Caingang): Métraux BBAE CXLIII (1) 473.

A1029. *Escape from deluge — miscellaneous.*

A1029.1. *Marvelous tree survives deluge.* Irish myth: Cross.

F811.2.1. Marvelous tree (trees) of extraordinary age.

A1029.2. *(Four) persons who, in four quarters of the world, survived the flood* and thus preserved ancient tradition. Irish myth: Cross.

A1029.3. *Escape from deluge in pot or jar.* S. Am. Indian (Chiriguano): Métraux RMLP XXXIII 170, (Guarayu): Métraux BBAE CXLIII (3) 438.

A1029.4. *Flood: refuge in huge gourds* with seven rooms in each. India: Thompson-Balys.

A1029.5. *Escape from deluge in box or basket.* American Indian (Thompson River): Teit JE VIII 230, (Apache): Gould JAFL XXXIV 319, Russell JAFL XI 253ff., (Guarayu): Métraux BBAE CXLIII (3) 438, (Cubeo): Goldman ibid. (3) 798, (Chaco): Nordenskiöld Indianerleben 253f.

A1029.6. *Survivors of flood establish homes.* S. Am. Indian (Chiriguano): Métraux RMLP XXXIII 170f.

A1030. World-fire. A conflagration destroys the earth. Sometimes (as with the flood legends) the tradition is somewhat local and does not refer to an actual destruction of the whole earth; sometimes the fire marks the end of the world. — **Olrik Ragnarök 483 s. v. "Weltbrand", *Danske Studier (1913) 204ff.; *Eisler Weltenmantel und Himmelszelt 452. — Icel.: MacCulloch Eddic 336ff., Boberg; Greek: Grote I 94; Lithuanian: Balys Tautosakos Darbai VI 133f.; Jewish: Neuman; Babylonian: Meissner Babylonien und Assyrien II 118; Siberian: Holmberg Siberian 368ff.; Hindu: Keith 105; India: Thompson-Balys; Chinese: Eberhard FFC CXX 84. — Maori: Dixon 47 n. 33; N. Am. Indian: *Thompson Tales 287 n. 57d.; S. Am. Indian (Yuracare, W. Brazil): Alexander Lat. Am. 313, (Araucanian): ibid. 330, (Chaco, Tupinamba, Apapocuva-Guarani, Tembè, Shipaya, Carajá, Mura, Cashinawa, Witoto, Arawak, Yuracare): Métraux MAFLS XL 36 (Mataco): ibid. 35, (Toba): ibid. 33, (Tucuna): Nimuendaju BBAE CXLIII (3) 724, (Bacairi): Lévi-Strauss ibid. (3) 347.

A1031. *Causes of world-fire.*

C984.6. General conflagration from violation of tabu.

A1031.1. *A "flame of fire swifter than a blast of wind" as punishment for the sin of the Irish.* Irish myth: Cross.

A1031.2. *World-fire after theft of fire.* India: Thompson-Balys.

F962.2. Fire from heaven. Q552.13. Death by fire from heaven as punishment.

A1031.3. *Evil demons set world on fire.* S. Am. Indian (Yuracare, Tupinamba, Arawak): Métraux MAFLS XL 36.

A1031.4. *Fall of sun causes world-fire.* S. Am. Indian (Toba, Mataco, Lengua): Métraux BBAE CXLIII (1) 367, (Mocovi): Métraux MAFLS XL 34.

A1031.4.1. *All countries burned while the wife of sun god pours fire from a small bowl.* India: Thompson-Balys.

A1031.5. *World-fire because of man's arrogance.* African (Fang): Trilles 131.

A1031.6. *Miscellaneous reasons for world-fire.* S. Am. Indian (Witoto, Apapocuva-Guarani): Métraux MAFLS XL 36, (Toba): ibid. 19, (Inca): Rowe BBAE CXLIII (2) 316.

A1035. *Quenching the world-fire.*

A1035.1. *Rain invoked to destroy world-fire.* Maori, Melanesian: Dixon 49.

A1035.2. *Creator puts out world-fire with his staff.* S. A. Indian (Inca): Rowe BBAE CXLIII (2) 316.

A1036. *Earth recreated after world-fire.* S. Am. Indian (Mundurucu): Horton BBAE CXLIII (3) 282.

A1038. *Men hide from world-fire and renew race.* (Cf. A1006.1., A1045.) — Swiss: Jegerlehner Oberwallis 311 No. 47; India: Thompson-Balys. — S. Am. Indian (Toba, Arawak, Mura, Yuracare, Tupinamba): Métraux MAFLS XL 34—36, (Chiriguano): Métraux RMLP XXXIII 158; African (Fang): Trilles 133f.

A1039. *World-fire — miscellaneous.*

A1039.1. *Vulture sent out as scout to see whether earth has cooled from world-fire.* (Cf. A1021.2.).

A1040. Continuous winter destroys the race. Spoken of as "Fimbulwinter". It ushers in the end of the world. — *Olrik Ragnarök 479; Icel.: MacCulloch Eddic 336ff.; Persian: Carnoy 309. — S. Am. Indian (Toba, Pilagá, Tierra del Fuego): Métraux MAFLS XL 30, 37, (Chaco): Métraux BBAE CLXIII (1) 367.

A1045. *One pair escapes continuous winter and renews race.* (Cf. A1006.1, A1038.) — *Olrik Ragnarök 479 s. v. "Fimbulwinter".

A1046. *Continuous world-eclipse.* India: Thompson-Balys. — S. Am. Indian (Toba, Mocovi, Mataco, Choroti): Métraux BBAE CXLIII (1) 367, (Tupinamba): Métraux ibid. (3) 131, (Guarani): Métraux MAFLS XL 33.

A1046.1. *World-eclipse ended by bat making sun smile.* India: Thompson-Balys.

A1050. Heavens break up at end of world. *Olrik Ragnarök 480 s. v. "Himmel".

A1051. *Behavior of stars at end of world.*

A1051.1. *Stars fall down at end of world.* *Olrik Ragnarök 482 s. v. "Sterne"; Irish myth: Cross.

A1051.2. *End of world when stars* in one constellation overtake those in another. Siberian: Holmberg Siberian 425.

A1052. *Behavior of sun at end of world.*

A1052.1. *Sun devoured by monster at end of world.* *Olrik Ragnarök 482 s.v. "Sonne".

A1052.2. *Sun shining at night as sign of Doomsday.* Jewish: Moreno Esdras (M307.1).

A1052.3. *End of world when four (seven) suns appear in sky.* Buddhist myth: Malalasekera I 157, II 566.

A1053. *Behavior of moon at end of world.*

A1053.1. *Moon shining by day as sign of Doomsday.* (Cf. A1002.) Jewish: Moreno Esdras (M307.2).

A1057. *Seven days silence in whole universe at the end of the world.* Jewish: Moreno Esdras (M307.10).

A1058. *End of world when culture hero removes one of the world-props.* S. Am. Indian (Guaraní): Métraux BBAE CXLIII (3) 93.

A1060. Earth-disturbances at end of world. Irish myth: Cross; Jewish: Neuman.

A1002. Doomsday.

A1061. *Earth sinks into sea at end of world.* *Olrik Ragnarök 479 s.v. "Erde".

A1061.1. *Earthquakes at the end of the world.* Jewish: Moreno Esdras (M307.12). — S. Am. Indian (Chiriguano): Métraux RMLP XXXIII 158.

A1062. *Mountains fall together at end of world.* *Olrik Ragnarök 484 s. v. "Zusammenstürzen".

A1063. *Water-disturbances at end of world.*

A1063.1. *Sea makes extraordinary noise and throws out fishes at end of world.* Jewish: Moreno Esdras (M307.6).

A1063.2. *Sea water mixes with fresh water at end of the world.* Jewish: Moreno Esdras (M307.8).

A1065. *Continuous drought at end of world.* Buddhist myth: Malalasekera II 736; S. Am. Indian (Chiriguano): Métraux RMLP XXXIII 171.

A1066. *Sun will lock moon in deep ditch in earth's bottom and will eat up stars* at end of world. Africa (Fang): Einstein 36.

A1067. *Extraordinary wind at end of the world.* Jewish: Moreno Esdras (M307.15).

A1068. *Sun thrown on fire: period of darkness, rain.* Calif. Indian: Gayton and Newman 83.

A1069. *Flow of molten metal at end of world.* Persian: Carnoy 262.

A1070. Fettered monster's escape at end of world. Giant, or monster, is fettered in depths of the earth. His movement causes earthquakes. When he succeeds in freeing himself from the fetters and escapes, the world will end. — *Olrik Ragnarök 278, 478ff. s.v. "Erdbebenriese", "Schlange", "Raubtier", "Ungeheuer", Danske Studier (1913) 3ff.; Anholm Danske Studier (1904) 141; *Krohn Der gefangene Unhold; *Von der Leyen Der gefesselte Unhold. — Irish myth: Cross; Icel.: De la Saussaye 246; Lettish and Lithuanian: Gray 322; Persian: Carnoy 324; Babylonian: Spence 78.

A1145.1. Earthquakes from movements of subterranean monster. R210. Escapes.

A1070.1. *Birth of monsters as sign at end of world.* Jewish: Moreno Esdras (M307.7).

A1071. *Fettering of underground monster.* Gaster Thespis 160, 329.

F864.1. Fetter for Fenris wolf. Q433.2. Defeated giants imprisoned in lower world. Q434. Punishment: fettering.

A1071.1. *Underground monster fettered by trick.* Is persuaded to try on fetters. (Sometimes told of fettering Satan, who plays same role.) —

*Type 803; *Olrik Ragnarök 204ff., 248ff.; Lithuanian: Balys Lithuanian Legends of the Devil in Chains (Tautosakos Darbai III [1937] 321—331.)

A1071.2. *Forging of chain for fettered monster.* Smiths hit once in three or four times on the bare anvil. All of these blows go to forging chains for the monster (devil). — Olrik Ragnarök 204ff., 248ff., 253 (Prometheus), 269 (Loki).

A1072. *Form of fettered monster.*

A1072.1. *Fettered monster in human form.* *Olrik Ragnarök 83f.

A1072.2. *Fettered monster as ferocious animal.* *Olrik Ragnarök 85, 481 s.v. "Erdbebenriese". — S. Am. Indian (Guarani): Métraux BBAE CXLIII (3) 93.

A1072.3. *Fettered monster as snake.* *Olrik Ragnarök 84, 482 s. v. "Schlange".

A1072.4. *Fettered monster as dragon.* Irish myth: Cross; Gaster Thespis 160, 329.

B11. Dragon.

A1074. *Fettered monster's captivity.*

A1074.1. *Monster fettered with sword just out of reach.* If he reaches it he will free himself. — *Olrik Ragnarök 136ff., 184ff., 225.

A1074.2. *Fettered monster's vain attempt to reach sword with man's help.* Could he reach it he would escape. — *Olrik Ragnarök 139ff., 185, 223ff.

A1074.3. *Fettered monster questions visitor.* He asks "Are lambs still being produced?" or the like; i.e. is nature still normal? He must remain fettered till he hears that nature's laws no longer hold. — *Olrik Ragnarök 149ff., 180ff.

A1074.4. *Fettered monster preyed upon by vulture.* Cf. Prometheus. — *Olrik Ragnarök 151ff., 183f., 288.

Q501.4. Punishment of Prometheus.

A1074.5. *Fettered monster kept just out of reach of water.* The water is always drunk by vulture as he is ready to take it. — *Olrik Ragnarök 151ff., 183f., 288.

Q501.2. Punishment of Tantalus. Stands in pool that ever recedes from his lips.

A1074.6. *Fettered monster vainly loosens his stake.* Each time he loosens it, it is driven in the ground. — *Olrik Ragnarök 186f., 289.

A1074.7. *Fettered monster's weakened chains renewed by supernatural power.* Are almost licked in two by dog but then renewed. — *Olrik Ragnarök 152, 189ff., 217f., 289.

A1074.8. *Fettered monster's weakened chains renewed by stroke of a smith.* (Cf. A1071.2.) — *Olrik Ragnarök 152, 189ff., 217f., 289; Fb "smed" III 402a.

A1075. *End of world heralded by coming of Antichrist,* a gigantic destructive one-eyed monster. Irish myth: Cross.

M363.0.1. Coming of Antichrist prophecied.

A1075.1. *Signs before the birth of Antichrist.* Irish myth: Cross.

A1002.2. Signs before the day of judgment.

A1080. Battle at end of world. Armageddon. — Revelations 16:16; Fb "krig" II 296b.; Irish myth: Cross; Jewish: Neuman, Moreno Esdras (N307.13).

A1080.1. *Horse shall wade in blood at Armageddon.* *Fb "hest" I 600a.

A1081. *Battle of the gods at end of world.* *Olrik Ragnarök 480 s.v. "Götterschlacht".

A1082. *Battle of gods and monster at end of world.* Jewish: Neuman.

A1082.1. *Battle of gods and giants at end of world.* *Olrik Ragnarök 480 s.v. "Götterschlacht".

A1082.2. *Odin battles Fenris Wolf at end of world.* (Cf. A1070.) — *Olrik Ragnarök 479 s.v. "Fenris-wolf".

A1082.2.1. *Other gods battle Fenris wolf at end of world.* Icel.: Boberg.

A1082.2.2. *God battles hound of hell at end of world.* Icel.: Boberg.

A1082.3. *Thor battles Midgard serpent at end of world.* *Olrik Ragnarök 481 s.v. "Midgardschlange".

A876. Midgard serpent.

A1082.3.1. *End of world to come at disease and death of snake encircling the world. India:* Thomson-Balys.

A1082.4. *God battles Leviathan at end of world.* Jewish: Neuman.

A1082.5. *God conquers Satan at end of world.* Jewish: Neuman.

A1082.6. *Battle of saints with Lucifer at end of world.* *Hdwb. d. Abergl. II 781ff.; Lithuanian: Balys Tautosakos Darbai VI 133f.

A1082.7. *Battle of angels with Leviathan and Behemoth at end of world.* Jewish: Neuman.

A1084. *Prophecy of defeat in battle as sign of end of the world.* Jewish: Moreno Esdras (M324.1).

A1085. *End of the gods.* *Olrik Ragnarök 51f.; Irish myth: Cross.

A192. Death of the gods.

A1087. *Monsters kill each other off at end of world.* Jewish: Neuman.

A1090. World calamities and renewals: miscellaneous motifs.

A1091. *Natural laws inoperative at end of world.* *Olrik Ragnarök 46ff.; Irish myth: Cross; Chinese: Graham.

A1091.1. *Three horses from dove's egg on last day.* *Fb "hest" I 600a.

A1093. *End of world announced by trumpet.* *Olrik Ragnarök 116ff.

A1095. *The Messianic Age.* Jewish: **Neuman.

A1097. *Extraordinary man at end of the world.* Jewish: Moreno Esdras (M307.16).

A1099. *World calamities — additional motifs.*

A1099.1. *World destroyed by rain of stones.* India: Thompson-Balys.

A1099.2. *World devoured by ogre.* India: Thompson-Balys; Chinese: Graham.

A1099.3. *World turned topsy-turvy and eaten by an earthworm.* India: Thompson-Balys.

A1100—A1199. Establishment of natural order.

A1100. Establishment of natural order.

A530. Culture hero establishes law and order. A1300. Ordering of human life. M0. Judgments and decrees.

A1101. *The four ages of the world.* A development of the present order through four stages or periods, the golden, silver, bronze, and iron ages, or the like. — **Encyc. Religion and Ethics s.v. "Ages of the World". — Irish myth: Cross; Greek: Fox 17, Grote I 62; Hindu: Keith 105, Penzer IV 240 n. 1, VII 1 n. 5; Chinese: Ferguson 33.

A630. Series of creations.

A1101.1. *Golden age.* A former age of perfection. — Hdwb. d. Abergl. III 927ff. — Irish myth: Cross; Icel.: De la Saussaye 165, MacCulloch Eddic 327, 378 n. 49, Boberg; Lappish: Qvigstad FFC LX 35 No. 8; Greek: Fox 105, Grote I 62; Jewish: Neuman; Persian: Carnoy 300, 305; Hindu: Keith 103; India: Thompson-Balys. — Tuamotu: Stimson MS (z-G 13/50); Aztec: Alexander Lat. Am. 66; Carib: ibid 262; Ackawoi: ibid. 269.

A1346.2. Man must labor for a living: at first everything too easy. M324. Prophecy: future golden age.

A1101.1.1. *Reign of peace and justice (under certain king).* Icel.: Herrmann Saxo II 377; Irish myth: Cross; Persian: Carnoy 300, 305; Jewish: Neuman; Chinese: Ferguson 33.

P12.5. Good king never retreats in battle. Q153. Nature benign and fruitful during reign of good king. Q552.3. Failure of crops during reign of wicked king.

A1101.1.2. *Even trees could speak in golden age.* India: Thompson-Balys.

A1101.1.3. *Former age: spirits and ogres lived with men, and gods appeared in human guise.* India: Thompson-Balys.

A1101.2. *Reversal of nature in former age.*

A1101.2.1. *Formerly men plowed and cattle were their masters.* India: Thompson-Balys.

A1101.2.2. *Formerly men ate grass: cattle ate rice and pulse.* India: Thompson-Balys.

A1101.2.3. *Formerly men dumb: birds and animals talked.* India: Thompson-Balys.

A1101.2.4. *Formerly men could go safely beneath the sea.* Tuamotu: Stimson MS (z-G. 13/50).

A1102. *Why powers of nature work on Sabbath.* Jewish: Neuman.

A1103. *Nature transformed by God once in seven years.* Jewish: Neuman.

A1110. Establishment of present order: waters.

A1111. *Impounded water.* Water is kept by monster so that mankind cannot use it. A hero defeats the monster and releases the water. (The monster is sometimes a giant frog.) — *Chauvin VI 3 No. 181, VII 132 No. 399. — Hindu: Keith 33 (guarded by dragon); India:

Thompson-Balys; Chinese: Ferguson 155; Japanese: Anesaki 276. — Australian: Dixon 279, 297; Papua: Ker 25; Baining of New Britain: ibid. III; Samoan, Melanesian: ibid 38 n. 109, 110. — N. A. Indian: *Thompson Tales 293 n. 76, (Tahltan): Teit JAFL XXXII 201, 203; S. Am. Indian (Bacairi, Amazon): Alexander Lat. Am. 313, (Botocudo): Métraux BBAE CXLIII (1) 540, (Caingang): Lowie ibid. (1) 397, (Bolivia, Peru): Jijena Sanchez Perro Negro 134. — Africa: Stanley 8, (Basuto): Jacottet 148 No. 21, 154 No. 22 cf. 8 No. 1, (Hottentot): Bleek 27 No. 14, (Ekoi): Talbot 144, 197, (Ababua): Einstein 101.

A263.3. Person sacrificed to water-spirit to secure water supply. A420. God of water. A531. Culture hero overcomes monsters. A1421. Hoarded game released. B11.7.1. Dragon controls water-supply. D2151.2.3.1. Evil spirit holds back water. F914.1. Princess stands in middle of dried up tank so serpent will release the water which he had swallowed up completely. G346.3. Evil spirit drinks water supply dry.

A1113. *God promises never again to destroy world by water.* Jewish: Neuman.

A1020. Escape from deluge.

A1115. *Why the sea is salt.* New Guinea: Ker 25; Hawaii: Beckwith Myth 43.

A1115.1. *Why the sea is salt: because of wrecked salt ship.* — Fb "hav" I 565b, IV 203a. — Dutch: Volkskunde XVII 23.

K420. Thief loses his goods or is detected. Q212 Theft punished.

A1115.2. *Why the sea is salt: magic salt mill.* Stolen by sea-captain, who takes it aboard and orders it to grind. It will stop only for its master; ship sinks and mill keeps grinding salt. — *Type 565; *BP II 438ff. — Icel.: MacCulloch Eddic 283; cf. Chinese: Eberhard FFC CXX 108.

C916. Continuous action started by breaking tabu. D1263. Magic mill. D1601.21.1. Self-grinding salt-mill. D1651. Magic object obeys master alone.

A1115.3. *Why the sea is salt: heavy rain showers on ashes of wood burnt by primeval fire.* S. Am. Indian (Tupi): Ehrenreich 16, (Tupinamba): Métraux BBAE CXLIII (3) 133.

A1116. *Origin of sea-waves.*

A1116.1. *Sea-waves are (manes of) sea-god's horses.* Irish myth: Cross.

A421. Sea-god.

A1117. *Origin of foam on waters.* West Indian: Parsons JAFL XXXII 443.

A1118. *Origin of swirling motion of water.* Animals and birds scratch in it. — Icel.: MacCulloch Eddic 283f.; Finnish: Aarne FFC VIII 4 No. 7, XXXIII 51 No. 7; Estonian: Aarne FFC XXV 140 No. 5; Livonian: Loorits FFC LXVI 81 No. 6.

A1119. *Establishment of present order: waters — miscellaneous.*

A1119.1. *Why sea is blue.* New Guinea: Ker 25.

A1119.2. *Why sea waters are warm:* kept so by Leviathan. Jewish: Neuman.

A1119.3. *Origin of sea's unpleasant odor.* Jewish: Neuman.

A1120. Establishment of present order: winds. Jewish: Neuman; India: Thompson-Balys. — Tonga: Gifford 16; Quileute: Farrand JAFL XXXII 269ff.; Tahltan: Teit JAFL XXXII 224.

C322.1. Bag of winds. D906. Magic wind. D1543. Magic object controls wind. D2142. Wind produced by magic.

A1121. *Breathing of deity (spirit) causes winds.* Chinese: Werner 77; Maori: Clark 19; Eskimo (Bering Strait): Nelson RBAE XVIII 175, (Labrador): Hawkes GSCan XIV 153, (Ungava): Turner RBAE XI 267; S. Am. Indian (Toba): Métraux MAFLS XL 28.

A1122. *Cave of winds.* Winds originally confined in caves. — Roman: Virgil Aeneid I lines 52 ff.; Siberian: Holmberg Siberian 457. — Maori: Dixon 55; Western Mono: Gifford JAFL XXXVI 328 No. 9.

A532. Culture hero tames winds in caves. F757.2. Wind continually blows from cave.

A1122.1. *Hole of winds: stopper destroyed.* The hole is stopped with a wooden stopper, which is destroyed. The country dries up. — Chauvin II 110 No. 75.

A1122.2. *Wind a bird dwelling in mountain-hole.* Bushman: Bleek and Lloyd 107.

A1122.3. *Lost wind found in hollow tree: has been banished and is needed by men.* India: Thompson-Balys.

A1122.4. *Wind comes through holes in sky when gut covering is cut.* Eskimo (Bering Strait): Nelson RBAE XVIII 498.

A1123. *Winds as children of titans (giants).* Greek: Grote I 6.

A1125. *Winds caused by flapping wings.* A giant bird causes the wind with his wings. The wings are cut by the culture hero so that the bird cannot flap so hard. — Gaster Thespis 158; Icel.: MacCulloch Eddic 276; Babylonian: Spence 117; India: Thompson-Balys. — N. A. Indian: *Thompson Tales 292 n. 74; American Negro (Georgia): Harris Friends 39ff. No. 5.

B31. Giant birds.

A1125.1. *Wind caused by flapping of ears of giant.* Peigan: Uhlenbeck Verhandelingen der Koninklijke Akademie van Wetenshappen XIII (1) 64.

A1126. *Wind caused by wind-god's movements.* When the son of the wind lies down, the wind blows. — Bushman: Bleek and Lloyd 101ff.

A1127. *Winds of the four quarters established.* Winnebago, Omaha: Alexander N. Am. 99; Quileute: Farrand-Meyer JAFL XXXII 271 No. 13.

A417. Gods of the Quarters. A651.1.6. Heavens (world) divided into four quarters. A871. Earth square with four quarters. A1182. Determination of world quarters.

A1127.1. *Effect of the four winds on weather.* Jewish: Neuman. — Tahltan: Teit JAFL XXXII 224; Ojibwa: Jones JAFL XXIX 372.

A1127.1.1. *North wind tempers fury of south wind.* Jewish: Neuman.

A1127.1.2. *South wind causes heat and hurricanes.* Jewish: Neuman.

A1127.2. *Gentle west wind said to be exhausted from fleeing deity.* Maori: Clark 46.

A1128. *Regulation of winds.* India: Thompson-Balys.

A1128.1. *Angels' wings protect earth from winds.* Jewish: Neuman.

A1128.2. *When wind-spirit is awake it storms; asleep, it is calm.* Tonga: Gifford 53.

A1129. *Establishment of present order: winds — miscellaneous.*

A1129.1. *Colors of winds.* Irish myth: Cross.

A1129.1.1. *Creator establishes twelve winds, each a different color.* Irish myth: Cross.

A1129.2. *Origin of monsoon: from chewed skin and spit* of pair of divine friends eating guavas. India: Thompson-Balys.

A1129.3. *Wind is blind.* India: Thompson-Balys.

A1130. Establishment of present order: weather phenomena.

A1127.1. Effect of the four winds on weather. D900. Magic weather phenomena. D1540. Magic object controls elements. D2140. Magic control of the elements.

A1130.1. *Angels set over clouds, winds, and rains.* Jewish: Neuman.

A1130.2. *Origin of storms in sixth heaven.* Jewish: Neuman.

A651.1. Series of upper worlds.

A1131. *Origin of rain.* India: Thompson-Balys; Bushman: Bleek and Lloyd 113.

A1131.0.1. *Regulation of rains.* India: Thompson-Balys; Chinese: Graham.

A1131.0.2. *Why it rains most in the hills.* India: Thompson-Balys.

A1131.1. *Rain from tears.* Jewish: Neuman; Ekoi: Talbot 344; Kaska: Teit JAFL XXX 448; Maori: Clark 19.

A1012. Flood from tears.

A1131.1.1. *Rain from urine.* Eskimo (Cape York): Rasmussen III 61, (Central Eskimo): Boas RBAE VI 600, (East Greenland): Rasmussen I 100; Koryak: Jochelson JE VI 142.

A1131.2. *Rainy weather sent by saint as punishment.* *Dh II 176ff.

A1131.3. *Rain from sea in upper world.* Fb "hav" IV 203a. — Jewish: Neuman; Eskimo (East Greenland): Rasmussen I 81; S. Am. Indian (Toba): Métraux MAFLS XL 26, (Cashinawa): Métraux BBAE CXLIII (3) 684.

A1131.4. *Rain from container in sky.* Gaster Thespis 192; Eskimo (Ungava): Turner RBAE XI 266, (Labrador): Hawkes GSCan XIV 153, (Central Eskimo): Boas RBAE VI 600, (East Greenland): Holm 95; S. Am. Indian (Chamacoco, Ashluslay): Métraux BBAE CXLIII (1) 366.

A1131.4.1. *Rain kept in waterskin dragged along sky floor.* India: Thompson-Balys.

A1131.5. *Rain from rain-god (rain spirit).* See all references to A287. — Greek: Fox 159 (Zeus); S. Am. Indian (Toba, Chamacoco, Mataco): Métraux BBAE CXLIII (1) 366, MAFLS XL 26f.

A1131.6. *Rain shed by stars.* Gaster Thespis 212.

A1132. *Origin of dew.* Knoop Zs. f. Vksk. XXII 89; Icel.: MacCulloch Eddic 331ff.; Jewish: Neuman.

A1133. *Origin of clouds.* Jewish: Neuman; Maori: Clark 19; Hawaii: Beckwith Myth 97; Eskimo (Labrador): Hawkes GSCan XIV 79; S. Am. Indian (Chamacoco): Métraux BBAE CXLIII (1) 366.

A1133.1. *Origin of clouds from Ymir's brain.* Icel.: MacCulloch Eddic 325f., Boberg.

A1133.2. *Origin of clouds: creator ornaments the sky* with clouds so that the mountains are sometimes shaded. India: Thompson-Balys.

A1133.3. *Clouds as smoke rising to sky.* S. Am. Indian (Toba): Métraux MAFLS XL 26f.

A1133.4. *Clouds as God's shield.* Jewish: Neuman.

A1134. *Origin of mist (fog).* India: Thompson-Balys; Eskimo (Cumberland Sound): Boas BAM XV 176.

A1135. *Origin of wintry weather.*

A1135.1. *Origin of cold in winter.*

A1135.1.1. *Origin of cold: sun turns fiery face upward.* Jewish: Neuman.

A1135.2. *Origin of snow.* Irish myth: Cross; Flemish: De Meyer FFC XXXVII 83 No. 9b; Jewish: Neuman. — Eskimo (West Greenland): Rasmussen II 33, Rink 44.

A1135.2.1. *Snow from feathers or clothes of a witch* (Frau Holle). — *Hoffmann-Krayer Zs. f. Vksk. XXV 119 n. 5; *Fb "sne" III 427b.

G283. Witches have control over weather. G303.11.4.2. Devil's grandmother is bleaching when it snows.

A1135.3. *Origin of frost.* S. Am. Indian (Toba): Métraux MAFLS XL 22; India: Thompson-Balys.

A1135.4. *Origin of hail.* S. Am. Indian (Aymara): Tschopik BBAE CXLIII (2) 571.

A1137. *Causes of hot weather:* God bores hole in hell. Jewish: Neuman.

A1141. *Origin of lightning.* Jewish: Neuman. — Bushman: Bleek and Lloyd 113; Liberia: Bundy JAFL XXXII 422f.; Nootka: Sapir JAFL XXXII 354; Eskimo (Cape York): Rasmussen III 61, (Cumberland Sound): Boas BAM XV 175, (Central Eskimo): Boas RBAE VI 600.

A1141.1. *Lightning as fiery snake.* Siberian, Finnish: Holmberg Siberian 445.

J2271.2.1. Lightning made from the old moon.

A1141.2. *Lightning from flashing sword.* India: Thompson-Balys.

A1141.3. *Lightning from heavenly horses striking hoofs against stars.* India: Thompson-Balys.

A1141.4. *Lightning as god's whip.* Gaster Thespis 157; Jewish: Neuman.

A1141.5. *Lightning as God's messenger.* Jewish: Neuman.

A1141.6. *Lightning produced by deity.* Greek: Grote I 8; Jewish: Neuman; Maori: Clark 168.

A1141.7. *Lightning from fire.* S. Am. Indian (Chorotí, Lengua, Ashluslay): Métraux BBAE CXLIII (1) 366, (Tupinamba): Métraux ibid. (3) 132.

A1141.7.1. *Lightning as torches of invisible dancers.* Africa (Fang): Trilles 174.

A1141.8. *Origin of lightning — other motifs.* S. Am. Indian (Toba, Mataco, Chamacoco): Métraux MAFLS XL 27f., (Huamachuco): Métraux RMLP XXXIII 151.

A1142. *Origin of thunder.* *Blinkenberg The Thunderweapon in Religion and Folklore (Cambridge 1911); *Saintyves Pierres magiques (Paris 1936); Flemish: DeMeyer FFC XXXVII 82 No. 9a.; India: Thompson-Balys; Jewish: Neuman. — Cook Group: Dixon 88; Eskimo (Cumberland Sound): Boas BAM XV 175, (Labrador): Hawkes GSCan XIV 153, (Cape York): Rasmussen III 62; Nootka: Sapir JAFL XXXII 354; S. Am. Indian (Cashinawa): Métraux BBAE CXLIII (3) 683f.; Africa (Angola): Chatelain 97, (Bushman): Bleek and Lloyd 113, Liberian: Bundy JAFL XXXII 422f.

A284. God of thunder. F434. Thunder-spirits.

A1142.0.1. *Origin of thunderbolt.* India: Thompson-Balys.

A1142.1. *Creator's (deity's) voice makes thunder.* Jewish: Neuman; Chinese: Werner 77.

A1142.2. *Thunder from flying dragon.* Siberian: Holmberg Siberian 440.

B11. Dragon.

A1142.3. *Persons escape to sky and become thunder.* Calif. Indian: Gayton and Newman 96; S. Am. Indian (Chiriguano): Métraux RMLP XXXIII 177.

A761. Ascent to stars.

A1142.4. *Origin of thunder clouds: from wings of mountains.* India: Thompson-Balys.

A1142.5. *Thunder is sound of God's gun.* India: Thompson-Balys.

A1142.5.1. *Thunder caused by God beating his weapon.* India: Thompson-Balys.

A1142.5.1.1. *Thunder from crashing of stones in moon* as goddess beats tapa. Samoa: Clark 121.

A1142.5.1.2. *Thunder from thunder-spirit beating his children.* S. Am. Indian (Cashinawa): Métraux BBAE CXLIII (3) 684.

A1142.6. *Cause of thunder: sounds of the horses' hoofs* as gods play ball. India: Thompson-Balys.

A1142.6.1. *Thunder from clashing weapons of warring spirits in sky.* S. Am. Indian (Chamacoco): Métraux MAFLS XL 26.

A1142.7. *Thunder from deity separating the winds which try to unite.* India: Thompson-Balys.

A1142.8. *Thunder is noise of waterskin which rain-god drags along sky floor.* India: Thompson-Balys.

A1142.9. *Thunder made by giants in sky.* Greek: Grote I 5, 8, 12 (Cyclops).

A1142.9.1. *Thunder the drums of dead.* Africa (Fang): Trilles 174.

A1145. *Cause of earthquakes.* India: Thompson-Balys.

A1145.1. *Earthquakes from movements of subterranean monster.* (Cf. A844). — *Encyc. Religion and Ethics I 491b; *Olrik Ragnarök 278; Icel.: De la Saussaye 264. — Greek: Fox 211 (Poseidon); Jewish: Neuman; Egyptian: Müller 104; Siberian: Holmberg Siberian 311f.; Armenian: Ananikian 93; India: Thompson-Balys. — S. Am. Indian (Chibcha): Kroeber BBAE CXLIII (2) 908.

A843. Earth supported on post. Cause of earthquakes. A1070. Fettered monster. In depths of earth: movement causes earthquakes.

A1145.2. *Earthquakes from movements of sea-monster.* Irish myth: Cross.

A876.1. The Leviathan that surrounds the globe. B16.8.1. Leviathan causes cataclysm by striking earth with tail.

A1147. *Origin of stormy sky.*

A1147.1. *Origin of red sky* (blood). Kaska: Teit JAFL XXX 448; Tahiti: Henry 339.

A1148. *Origin of tornado sunsets;* i. e., peculiar sunsets foreboding tornadoes. — Ekoi: Talbot 364.

A1150. Determination of seasons. Greek: Frazer Apollodorus II 87 n. 3; India: Thompson-Balys. — N. A. Indian: *Thompson Tales 288 n. 60, (Ojibwa): Jones JAFL XXIX 372, Carson JAFL XXX 493, (Tahltan): Teit JAFL XXXII 226, 246, (Naskapi): Speck JAFL XXVIII 76.

D2145. Magic control of seasons.

A1150.1. *Establishment of times for sowing and reaping.* India: Thompson-Balys.

A1151. *Theft of the seasons.* Certain seasons are lacking. A culture hero steals the season from a monster and brings it to his people. — N. A. Indian: *Thompson Tales 288 n. 60a.

A1152. *Boneless man turned over to produce seasons.* N. A. Indian: Thompson Tales 276 n. 16.

C100.1. Sex tabu broken: child born without bones. F529.7. Person with gristle instead of bones.

A1153. *Seasons produced by marriage of North and South.* N. A. Indian: *Thompson Tales 288 n. 61.

A1154. *Genealogy of summer and winter.* Icel.: Boberg.

A1155. *Why days lengthen in spring.* Flemish: DeMeyer FFC XXXVII 83 No. 9d.

A1156. *Why days shorten in autumn:* the real sun sets very early because the red cockscomb plant, used to kill his brother sun with, grows to its full height during this time. — India: Thompson-Balys.

A1157. *Causes of seasons — deities push sun back and forth at solstices.* Hawaii: Beckwith Myth 119.

A1160. Determination of the months. Jewish: Neuman. — Ojibwa: Carson JAFL XXX 493.

A1161. *February's shortage of days.* Days stolen by January and March. — *Köhler-Bolte I 380f.; Destriche RTP II 53; Gaidoz Mélusine VII No. 11 (with references to earlier numbers); Shaineanu Romania XVIII 107.

A1170. Origin of night and day. India: Thompson-Balys.

A1411. Theft of light. B755. Animal calls the dawn. The sun rises as result of the animal's call. D2146. Magic control of day and night. J2272.1. Chanticleer believes that his crowing makes the sun rise.

A1171. *Origin of day.*

A1171.1. *Opening of creator's eyes creates day.* (Cf. A0.) — Chinese: Werner 78.

A1171.2. *Windows in firmament shed light.* Irish myth: Cross.

A661.0.6. Windows in heaven. D1162. Magic light.

A1171.3. *Angels of the day:* Jewish: Neuman.

A1171.4. *Origin of day: son of the night and the dawn.* Icel.: Boberg.

A1172. *Determination of night and day.* After much discussion, the relative length of these divisions is determined. — Jewish: Neuman; India: Thompson-Balys; Maori: Clark 43, 46; N. A. Indian: *Thompson Tales 289 n. 62; S. Am. Indian (Cashinawa): Métraux BBAE CXLIII (3) 683; African (Fang): Einstein 169.

A1172.1. *Regulation of sunshine.* India: Thompson-Balys.

A1172.2. *Wallet containing night and day.* Sébillot Incidents s.v. "bissac".

J2327. Man who asks for good weather given a box full of hornets. He thinks it is filled with the weather.

A1172.3. *Night and day have steeds and chase each other.* Icel.: Mac Culloch Eddic 200.

A1174. *Origin of night.* India: Thompson-Balys; Tahltan: Teit JAFL XXXII 205.

A1174.1. *Night (darkness) in package.* Released. — Mundurucu: Alexander Lat. Am. 310; Arawak, Carib, Surinam: ibid. 274.

C322.1. Bag of winds.

A1174.2. *Why some nights are dark and some light.* India: Thompson-Balys.

A1174.3. *Purchase of night.* Originally no night. Culture hero goes to distant land and buys it. He introduces sleep, etc. Cock to crow for day. (Cf. B755, J2272.1.). — Banks Is.: Dixon 113.

A721.0.1. Sun and moon kept in pots. A721.1. Theft of sun.

A1174.3.1. *Night stolen and kept in jar.* S. Am. Indian (Cashinawa): Métraux BBAE CXLIII (3) 683.

A1174.4. *Night caused by deity wrapping himself in dark mantle.* Maori: Clark 17, 21.

A1177. *Why sun shines on Saturday (Friday).* *Dh II 30. — Flemish: DeMeyer FFC XXXVII 83 No. 9c; Jewish: Neuman.

A1178. *Origin of "yesterday" and "today."* India: Thompson-Balys.

A1179. *Origin of night and day — miscellaneous.*

A1179.1. *Origin of twilight.*

A1179.1.1. *Twilight reflection of fires of hell.* Jewish: Neuman.

A1179.2. *Origin of dawn.*

A1179.2.1. *Dawn reflection of roses of paradise.* Jewish: Neuman.

A1180. *Establishment of present order — miscellaneous motifs.*

A1181. *Determination of world center.* By reaching to its ends. — N. A. Indian: Kroeber JAFL XXI 223.

A875.1 Navel of the earth. H681.3. Riddle: what is the center of the earth.

A1182. *Determination of world quarters.* The four cardinal points. — Yuma: N. Curtis Craftsman XVI 560.

A417. Gods of the Quarters. A651.1.6. Heavens (world) divided into four quarters. A871. Earth square with four quarters. A1127. Winds of the four quarters established.

A1185. *Wings cut from flying mountains.* In beginning mountains have wings. They are cut off by thunderbolt. — Hindu: Penzer VI 3 n. 1; India: Thompson-Balys.

A969.1. Mountains fight each other: cause of their present shape. F750. Extraordinary mountains and valleys.

A1186. *Measuring the world.* India: Thompson-Balys.

A1187. *Creator appoints a chief for each class of created things:* Lucifer for demons, Sion for mountains, etc. — Irish myth: Cross; Jewish: Neuman.

A1191. *All things receive names.* Chinese: Graham; Jewish: Neuman.

A1195. *Origin of echo.* Eskimo (Cumberland Sound): Boas BAM XV 172.

A1196. *Why salt disappeared from forests.* S. Am. Indian (Yuracare): Métraux BBAE CXLIII (3) 503.

A1200—A1699. CREATION AND ORDERING OF HUMAN LIFE

A1200—A1299. Creation of man.

A1200. Creation of man. *Hdwb. d. Abergl. I 460 s.v. "Anthropogonie"; *DeCock Volkssage, 146ff.; *Basset RTP XVIII 542 and references to earlier volumes. — Lappish: Qvigstad FFC LX 34 No. 6; Jewish: *Neuman; Siberian: Holmberg Siberian 371ff. — N. A. Indian: *Thompson Tales 283 n. 49, (Calif.): Gayton and Newman 94; Eskimo (Bering Strait): Nelson RBAE XI 338, (N. Alaska and Mackenzie River): Jenness 80, (Labrador): Hawkes GSCan XIV 152, (Cumberland Sound): Boas BAM XV 167; Quiché: Alexander Lat. Am. 163.

A1614.3 Dark and light-skinned peoples made from dark and light coconuts. D2178.6. People created by magic.

A1201. *Man created to rule the earth.* Africa (Fang): Trilles 131.

A1205. *Unacceptable gods as first inhabitants of earth.* Hawaii: Beckwith Myth 60.

A1210. Creation of man by creator. *Dh I 89. — Irish myth: Cross; Greek: *Grote I 71; Spanish Exempla: Keller; Lithuanian: Balys Index No. 3030; India: Thompson-Balys; Chinese: Werner 81. — Maori: Dixon 23, 26; Easter Is.: Métraux Ethnology 312; Hawaiian, Tahitan: Dixon 26; Aztec: Alexander Lat. Am. 92; S. Am. Indian (Cashinawa): Métraux BBAE CXLIII (3) 684, (Tucuna): Nimuendajú ibid. 724; Africa (Fjort): Dennett 105, (Ibo of Nigeria): Basden 282, (Ekoi): Talbot 373.

A0. Creator. A141.1. God makes automata and vivifies them. A1614.5. Negroes made from left-over scraps at creation. G312.5. Fierce flesh-eating creatures made by creator in fit of anger.

A1211. *Man made from creator's body.* India: Thompson-Balys.

A614. Universe from parts of creator's body.

A1211.0.1. *Man springs into existence from deity's body by his mere thinking.* India: Thompson-Balys.

A1211.1. *Man from dirt mixed with creator's blood.* Eitrem Opferritus und Voropfer der Griechen und Römer (Skrifter Akad. Oslo 1914 No. 1 426). — Gaster Oldest Stories 69; Babylonian: Spence 81. — New Britain: Dixon 107 (figures drawn on ground and sprinkled with creator's blood).

A1211.2. *Man from sweat of creator.* Dh I 113; Lithuanian: Balys Legends No. 33. — Persian: Carnoy 293.

A114.1. Goddess born from sweat of rock washed by sea. A1262. Man created from sweat.

A1211.3. *Man from spittle of creator.* Lithuanian: Balys Legends No. 32; Oceanic: Dixon 24.

D1001 Magic spittle.

A1211.3.1. *Being made from spittle of the gods.* Icel.: De la Saussaye 233.

M201.3. Spitting of all parties into vessel to seal bargain.

A1211.4. *Man made from creator's eye.* Egyptian: Müller 70ff.

A1211.5. *Man made from dirt rubbed from creator's (hero's) body.* (Cf. A833). India: Thompson-Balys.

A1211.5.1. *Man made from broken off toenail of creator.* S. Am. Indian (Yuracare): Métraux BBAE CXLIII (3) 503.

A1211.6. *Primeval human pair spring from two drops of urine of creator* (woman from half-drop). India: Thompson-Balys.

A1211.7. *First man the result of maid having licked semen-stained loin cloth* of creator's teacher. India: Thompson-Balys.

A1211.8. *Primeval crab pulls first five living creatures out of his side.* India: Thompson-Balys.

A1212. *Man created in creator's image.* Jewish: *Neuman; Hawaii: Beckwith Myth 43.

A1215. *Man originates from god who comes to earth.* West Caroline Is.: Dixon 250.

A1216. *Man as offspring of creator.* Greek: Fox 11. — India: Thompson-Balys; Indonesian: Dixon 156, 167, Voorhoeve Overzicht 64.

A1271.3. First parents children of god. A1275.4. Creator makes woman and then begets man by her.

A1216.1. *Mankind from masturbation of creator with earth.* (Cf. A615.1.) Easter Is.: Métraux Ethnology 314.

A401. Mother Earth.

A1217. *Devil's unsuccessful attempt to vivify his creations as God has done.* Succeeds only in making animal. — Dh I 90ff., 156ff.; *Fb "menneske" II 578a. — Lithuanian: Balys Legends Nos. 4, 39, 41, 149; Jewish: *Neuman; Hawaii: Beckwith Myth 61; Maidu: Dixon BAM XVII 39ff. No. 1.

A63. Devil as maplot at creation. A185.12. Deity provides man with soul. A1335.2. Origin of death from unsuccessful imitation of bad creator.

A1217.1. *Rebel angels oppose creation of man. Jewish: *Neuman.*

A1218. *Man created by co-operation of the gods.* *BP III 54. — Icel.: De la Saussaye 263, MacCulloch Eddic 327; Lithuanian: Balys Legends No. 39; Jewish: Neuman; Greek: Fox 15.

A1220. Creation of man through evolution. Hawaiian: Dixon 15f.; Samoan: ibid. 18, 28; Maori: ibid. 27.

A620.1. Spontaneous creation: evolutionary type.

A1220.1. *Progressive degeneration to present race of men.* Greek: *Grote I 64.

A1221. *Mankind from unusual primeval mating.* India: Thompson-Balys.

A1221.1. *Mankind begotten by giant's two feet.* He touches one foot with the other and begets progeny. — Icel.: De la Saussaye 342 (Ymir).

A1221.2. *Mankind from "Peace and Quiet fructified by Light."* Hawaiian: Dixon 16.

A1221.3. *Mankind from mating of pairs of reeds.* Igorot (Luzon): Dixon 176.

A1221.4. *Mankind from mating of tree and vine.* Borneo: Dixon 159; Samoan: ibid. 164 n. 37.

A1221.5. *Mankind from mating of frog and "daughter of fire."* Africa: Bouvergnes 33, 40.

A1221.6. *Mankind from human-animal mating.* Chinese: Eberhard FFC CXX 88.

B600. Marriage of person to animal.

A1222. *Mankind originates from eggs.* Chinese: Eberhard FFC CXX 89 No. 49; India: Thompson-Balys; Oceanic: Dixon 109 (Fiji, Torres Straits, Admiralty Is.), 109 n. 17 (Polynesia, Indonesia, Micronesia), 160 (Sumatra), 169f. (Indonesia), Handy 125 (Marquesas); S. Am. Indian (Jivaro): Métraux RMLP XXXIII 148, (Mbaya): Métraux BBAE CXLIII (1) 367.

A641. Cosmic egg. A1261.2. Man created from egg formed from sea-foam.

A1224. *Descent of man from animals.* *Lang Myth I 179, 184; *Hdwb. d. Abergl. I 465; *Frazer Old Testament I 33ff. — Australian: Van Gennep Mythes et légendes d'Australie 2f., 8f.; Koryak: Jochelson JE VI 374; Eskimo (Smith Sound): Kroeber JAFL XII 168, (Ungava): Turner RBAE XI 261, (Greenland): Rink 471, (Cape York): Rasmussen III 85, (W. Hudson Bay): Boas BAM XV 359, (Labrador): Hawkes GSCan XIV 152, (Bering Strait): Nelson RBAE XVIII 482, (Mackenzie River): Jenness RCanAE XIII 81; S. Am. Indian (Toba): Métraux MAFLS XL 104.

A511.10. Culture heroes born from an animal. B2. Animal totems.

A1224.0.1. *Mankind is descended from marriage of human being and animal.* Eskimo (Bering Strait): Nelson RBAE XVIII 482, cf. Thompson Tales n. 2; S. Am. Indian (Yuracare): Métraux BBAE CXLIII (3) 503.

A1224.1. *Mankind descended from tadpoles.* Wa (Indo-Chinese): Scott Indo-Chinese 293.

A1224.2. *Mankind descended from worms or larvae.* Eastern Indonesian: Dixon 169; Tonga: Gifford 15f.; S. Am. Indian (Cashinawa): Métraux BBAE CXLIII (3) 684.

A1224.3. *Woman created from dog's tail.* Eve. — *Dh I 114ff.; *Bolte Zs f. Vksk. XI 255 n. 3; Polívka ibid. XVI 212. — Finnish: Aarne FFC VII 5 No. 11, XXXIII 52 No. 11; Estonian: Aarne FFC XXV 140 No. 10; Livonian: Loorits FFC LXVI 82 No. 17; Flemish: DeMeyer XXXVII 83 No. 11; Lithuanian: Balys Legends Nos. 36ff., 52, 65.

A1224.4. *Mankind born from a cow.* India: Thompson-Balys.

A1224.5. *Descent of men from monkeys.* Chinese: Graham.

A1224.5.1. *Men are monkeys who have lost their tails.* Chinese: Graham.

A1224.6. *Mankind descended from fish.* S. Am. Indian (Tucuna): Nimuendajú BBAE CXLIII 93, 294.

A1224.7. *Creation of man by creator from ants.* He commands them to become men. — Greek: Fox 11.

A1225. *First men undeveloped.* Rudimentary and amorphous, gradually assume present shape. — Arunta: Dixon 272; Borneo: ibid. 159; Society Is.: ibid. 29, 164; Nias Is., Samoan: ibid. 164 n. 35, 36.

A1225.1. *First couple organically united.* Like Siamese twins. (Cf. A1275.2.) — Jewish: Neuman. — S. Am. Indian (Chaco): Alexander Lat. Am. 322, (Lengua): Métraux BBAE CXLIII (1) 267.

A1225.2. *Man originally without hands and feet.* Boy steals them from Python, and afterward men have them. — Africa (Ekoi): Talbot 376.

A1225.2.1. *Man given hands, feet, mouth and nose by monkey.* S. Am. Indian (Cashinawa): Métraux BBAE CXLIII (3) 68.

A1226. *Man created after series of unsuccessful experiments.* Greek: *Grote I 62; Quiché: Alexander Lat. Am. 163ff.; Cakchiquel: ibid. 180; Banks Is.: Beckwith Myth 61.

A630. Series of creations. A1401. Culture originated by previous race of man.

A1226.1. *Creator makes man out of butter first;* it would not stand up and melted. India: Thompson-Balys.

A1227. *Different types of men produced from one original type.* Jewish: Neuman.

A1230. Emergence or descent of first man to earth.

A1231. *First man descends from sky.* *Lang Myth I 75; India: *Thompson-Balys; German New Guinea: Dixon 111; Northern Australia: ibid. 274; Kei Is. (Indonesia): ibid. 156; Eastern Indonesian: ibid. 167. — N. A. Indian: Krickeberg Indianermärchen aus Nordamerika 10; Eskimo (Bering Strait): Nelson RBAE XVIII 517; Carib: Alexander Lat. Am. 38; S. Am. Indian (Inca): Rowe BBAE CXLIII (2) 315, (Yagua): Steward-Métraux ibid. (3) 736, (Warrau): Kirchoff ibid. (3) 880, (Bacairi): Lévi-Strauss ibid. (3) 347, (Tiatinagua): Métraux ibid. (3) 448, (Toba, Mataco): Métraux ibid. (1) 367, Métraux MAFLS XL 21f., 101. — African: Werner African 152.

F30. Inhabitant of upper world visits earth.

A1231.1. *Mankind from featherless bird sent from sky.* Sumatra: Dixon 169.

A1232. *Mankind ascends from under the earth.* (Cf. A1631.) Jewish: Neuman; India: Thompson-Balys. — S. Am. Indian (Chaco, Pampean): Alexander Lat. Am. 322, (Tereno, Caduveo, Mbaya): Métraux BBAE CXLIII (1) 367, (Inca): Rowe ibid. (2) 315, (Mundurucu): Horton ibid. (3) 281, (Viracocha): Steward-Métraux ibid. (3) 550, (Chamacoco): Métraux MAFLS XL 25; N. Am. Indian (Zuñi): *Benedict 337.

A682. Hole to lower world up which people come.

A1232.1. *Mankind from bones of dead brought from underworld.* Aztec: Alexander Lat. Am. 90.

A1232.2. *Mankind emerges from lake.* A woman and boy. They marry and populate earth. — Chibcha (with reference to other South American tribes): Alexander Lat. Am. 199.

A1232.2.1. *Mankind emerges from water.* India: Thompson-Balys.

A1232.3. *Mankind emerges from caves.* India: Thompson-Balys; Haitian: Alexander Lat. Am. 30; S. Am. Indian (Inca): Rowe BBAE CXLIII (2) 317, (Aymara): Tschopik ibid. (2) 571, (Araucanian): Cooper ibid. (2) 753, (Yuracare): Métraux ibid. (3) 503, (Mbaya): Métraux ibid. (1) 367, (Tiatinagua): Métraux ibid. (3) 449, (Caduveo): Métraux MAFLS XL 106; African: Werner African 147.

A1232.3.1. *Mankind emerges from a pit.* India: Thompson-Balys.

A1234. *Mankind emerges from ground.* Greek: *Grote I 177; Australian: Dixon Oc. Myth. 271; Papuan (British New Guinea): ibid. 110; Indonesian: ibid. 169 n. 79—81; Easter Is.: Métraux Ethnology 312; Eskimo (Cape York): Rasmussen III 47; African: Werner African 147.

A1234.1. *Earth as virgin mother of Adam.* *Denk Zs. f. Vksk. XII 352.
A401. Mother Earth.

A1234.1.1. *Primeval human pair spring from womb of Mother Earth.* (Cf. A1270.) — India: Thompson-Balys.

A1234.2. *Mankind emerges from mountain.* Pijaos (Colombia): Alexander Lat. Am. 200.

A1234.3. *Spontaneous generation.* Scientists find child on deserted island. They suggest that he has emerged from the ground. Italian Novella: Rotunda.

A1234.4. *Earth gives birth to woman.* Chinese: Graham.

A1236. *Mankind emerges from tree.* (Cf. A1251.) — Indonesian: Dixon 168f.; Papuan (British New Guinea): ibid. 110; Sumatra: ibid 160. — S. Am. Indian (Warrau): Kirchoff BBAE CXLIII (3) 880, (Chamacoco): Métraux ibid. (1) 367; African: Werner African 145f.

A1236.1. *Mankind emerges from buds on trees.* Nias Is.: Dixon 167; Sumatran: ibid. 160.

A1236.2. *Tribes emerge from melon.* Lao, Wa (Indo-China): Scott Indo-Chin. 286, 289.

A1240. Man made from mineral substance.

A1241. *Man made from clay (earth).* *Dh I 89-III passim; Barton JAOS XXXIX 287; *Frazer Old Testament I 3—29. — Irish myth: Cross; Greek: *Frazer Apollodorus I 51 n. 5, Fox 10f., 13, 208; Jewish: *Neuman; Hindu: Penzer III 59; Babylonian: Spence 86; Siberian: Holmberg Siberian 373; Chinese: Eberhard FFC CXX 114ff. — Polynesian (Maori, Hawaii, Tahiti, Society Is., Marquesas): Dixon 24—26; Indonesian: ibid. 172ff. n. 96—100, 104—106; Australian: ibid. 273; Marquesas: Handy 122f.; Hawaii: Beckwith Myth 44ff.; Easter Is.: Métraux Ethnology 315. — Eskimo (Bering Strait): Nelson RBAE XVIII 454; N. A. Indian: Krickeberg Indianermärchen 267, 307, 321f., (Calif.): Gayton and Newman 56; S. Am. Indian (Lengua): Métraux BBAE CXLIII (1) 367, (Apapocuva-Guarani): Métraux RMLP XXXIII 136; Aztec: Alexander Lat. Am. 85; Quiché: ibid. 163.
A401. Mother Earth. A1006.3. New race made of red earth after world calamity.

A1241.1. *Man made from piece of clay thrown on ground.* Babylonian: Spence 162.

A1241.2. *Man made from sand sprinkled with water.* Muzo (Colombia): Alexander Lat. Am. 200.

A1241.3. *Man made from clay image and vivified.* (Cf. A1241.2, A1252.1.) — Lithuanian: Balys Legends Nos. 4, 34f.; Jewish: *Neuman, Moreno Esdras; Indonesian: Dixon 172ff.; Banks Is., New Hebrides: ibid. 107; Hawaii: *Beckwith Myth 43—46; S. Am. Indian (Inca): Rowe BBAE CXLIII (2) 315, (Yuracare): Métraux ibid. (3) 504; Calif. Indian: Gayton and Newman 94.

A1241.4. *Man made from earth reddened with blood of human sacrifice.* India: Thompson-Balys.

A1241.4.1. *Man from clay and animal's blood.* Africa (Loango): Pechuël-Loesche 267.

A1241.5. *Man made of earth brought from four different places.* Irish myth: Cross; Jewish: Neuman.

A1291. Adam's body made of eight (four) things.

A1245. *Man created from stones.* Hdwb. d. Abergl. I 463. — Greek: *Frazer Apollodorus I 55 n. 2; Fox 11. — Nauru (Pleasant Is.): Dixon 252; Tongan, Samoan, Melanesian: ibid. 158; Indonesian: Kruyt Het Animisme 469. — Central American: Van Cappelle Mythen en Sagen uit West Indië 19; S. Am. Indian (Inca): Rowe BBAE CXLIII (2) 315, (Paressi): Métraux ibid. (3) 359.

A1245.1. *New race from stones thrown over head after deluge.* (Cf. A1254.1.). — Greek: Frazer Apollodorus I 55 n. 2, Fox 19.

A1006. Renewal of world after world calamity.

A1245.2. *Mankind from vivified stone image.* (Cf. A1241.3, A1252.1.). — Indonesian: Dixon 174.

A1245.3. *Mankind from cleft rock.* Formosa: Dixon 170; Gilbert Is.: ibid. 251.

A1245.4. *Mankind from salty stone (ice block) licked by cow.* (Audhumla). — Icel.: MacCulloch Eddic 63, 324, Boberg.

A14. Cow as creator.

A1245.5. *Man born from mountains.* India: Thompson-Balys.

A1246. *Mankind originates from shell.* New Hebrides: Dixon 110.

A1247. *Mankind originates from metals.* Aztec: Alexander Lat. Am. 85.

A1250. Man made from vegetable substance.

A1251. *Creation of man from tree.* (Cf. A1236, A1275.6.) — Hdwb. d. Abergl. I 461, 955; Holmberg Baum 69; BP III 54. — Icel.: Herrmann Nordische Mythologie 579, MacCulloch Eddic 327f., Boberg; Greek: Fox 11; Hindu: Berguigne La religion védique I 100. — Australian: Dixon 274; Island of Nieue: ibid. 30; Melanesian: ibid. 106; Solomon Is.: ibid. 110; Ceram, Amboina, Formosa, Borneo, Nias: ibid. 168; Indonesian: Voorhoeve Overzicht 65, Kruyt Het Animisme 465. — Central American: Van Cappelle 18; S. Am. Indian (Tembe): Métraux RMLP XXXIII 140.

A1252. *Creation of man from wood.* Borneo: Dixon 174f.; S. Am. Indian (Paressi): Métraux BBAE CXLIII (3) 360.

A1252.1. *Mankind from vivified wooden image.* (Cf. A1241.3, A1245.2) — Indonesian: Dixon 172ff.; Admiralty Is., Banks Is.: ibid. 106; India:

Thompson-Balys; S. Am. Indian (Bacairi, Amazon): Alexander Lat. Am. 312.

D435.1.1. Transformation: statue comes to life.

A1253. *Creation of man from fruit (nut).*

A1253.1. *Creation of man from fruit.*

A1253.1.1. *Creation of man from fig.* S. Am. Indian (Brazil): Oberg 108.

A1253.1.2. *First man born from apple.* Chinese: Eberhard FFC CXX 90 No. 49.

A1253.2. *Creation of man from nut.*

A1253.2.1. *Creation of woman from coconut.* The first man throws a coconut on the ground and thus creates the first woman. — New Britain: Dixon 107f.

A1253.2.2. *Men from long nuts, women from short ones.* S. Am. Indian (Brazil): Oberg 108.

A1254. *Man created from seeds.* Burmese: Scott Indo-Chin. 281; Eskimo (Bering Strait): Nelson RBAE XVIII 450; Isthmian tribes (Panama): Alexander Lat. Am. 193; S. Am. Indian (Cashinawa): Métraux BBAE CXLIII (3) 684.

A1254.1. *New race from seeds thrown over head after deluge.* (Cf. A1245.1., A1006.) — Tamanac (Carib): Alexander Lat. Am. 271.

A1255. *Man made from plant.* Sulka (New Britain): Dixon 130, 132 n. 2.

A1255.1. *Man from sugar-cane stalks.* Solomon Is., New Britain: Dixon 110.

A1255.2. *Man from ears of corn.* Navaho: Alexander N. Am. 158.

A1256. *Man made from herb.* Tunja (Colombia): Alexander Lat. Am. 200.

A1256.1. *Man made from grass.* Hindu: Penzer IV 128. — Ata (Mindanao): Dixon 176.

A1260. Mankind made from miscellaneous materials. Indonesian: Dixon 176.

A1260.1. *Man made from combination of different objects.* Grimm Deutsche Mythologie I 468ff. — Siberian: Holmberg Siberian 371.

A1260.1.1. *Man made of four elements.* Irish myth: Cross; Jewish: Neuman.

A1260.1.2. *Man made of substances from eight different sources.* Irish myth: Cross.

A1260.1.3. *Adam's body made of eight (four) things.* Body, earth; bones, stones; veins, roots; blood, water; hair, grass; thoughts, wind; spirit, clouds — or warmth, fire; cold, air; dryness, earth; instability, water. — *Dh I 111ff.; Köhler-Bolte II 1ff. — Icel.: MacCulloch Eddic 326f.; Siberian: *Holmberg Siberian 376.

A614. Universe from parts of creator's body. A1241.5. Man made of earth brought from (four) different places. D1273.1.2. Four as magic number. V211.4.1. Cross of Christ made of four kinds of wood.

A1260.1.4. *Seven substances employed in composition of human body.* Jewish: Neuman.

A1260.1.5. *Man made of clay with bones of stone, with blood of water and with vines for veins.* India: Thompson-Balys.

A1261. *Man made from water.* Greek: Fox 10; Jewish: Neuman.

A1261.1. *Man created from sea-foam.* *Dh I 18f., cf. 23.

A114. Goddess born from sea-foam. T547.1. Birth from sea-foam.

A1261.2. *Man created from egg formed from sea-foam.* Minahassa (Celebes): Dixon 157.

A1222. Mankind originate from eggs.

A1262. *Man created from sweat.* Icel.: De la Saussaye 342.

A114.1. Goddess born from sweat of rock washed by sea. A1211.2. Man from sweat of creator.

A1262.1. *Man created from sweat, heat, and breath.* Irish myth: Cross.

A1263. *Man created from part of body.*

A1211. Man made from creator's body.

A1263.1. *Man created from blood.* Jewish: Neuman.

A1263.1.1. *Man created from blood-clot.* Chatham Is., Samoan, Melanesian: Dixon 30; Admiralty Is., Polynesian, Indonesian, Melanesian, New Britain: *ibid. 109 n. 17.

T541.1.1. Birth from blood-clot. T541.1.1.1. Boy created by saint from blood-clot.

A1263.1.2. *Man from blood of game animal.* S. Am. Indian (Cashinawa): Métraux BBAE CXLIII (3) 684.

A1263.2. *Man created from fingernail.* Yuracare (West Brazil): Alexander Lat. Am. 314.

A1263.3. *Man created from rubbings of skin.* India: Thompson-Balys; Zuñi: Parsons JAFL XXIX 394 n. 1.

A1263.4. *Man created from spittle of holy person.* *Fb "spytte" III 515b.

A1263.5. *Man created from animal horns that bloomed and bore him as fruit.* Chinese: Graham.

A1263.6. *Man created from culture hero's genitals.* Koryak: Jochelson JE VI 139, 165, 168, 178, 218.

A1263.7. *Man created from animal bone.* Jewish: Neuman; Eskimo (Cape York): Rasmussen III 51.

A1265. *Men created from sown dragon's teeth.* Cadmus, Jason. — Grierson FL XXXIII (1922) 380. — Greek: Fox 10, 45, 112; Frazer Apollodorus I 315 n. 2.

B11. Dragon.

A1266. *Man created from food.*

A1266.1. *Man made from meat-ball.* Chinese: Eberhard FFC CXX 89 No. 49.

A1268. *Man created from ashes (cinders).* India: Thompson-Balys; Gilbert Is. (Micronesia): Dixon 252; Aztec: Alexander Lat. Am. 85.

A1268.1. *Tribe born from fire.* India: Thompson-Balys.

A1270. Primeval human pair. India: *Thompson-Balys; S. Am. Indian (Apapocuva-Guarani): Métraux RMLP XXXIII 138, (Yuracare): Métraux ibid. 144, (Paressi): Métraux BBAE CXLIII (3) 359.

A1270.1. *Primeval human pair live in innocence.* Tonga: Gifford 15.

A1271. *Origin of first parents.*

A1271.1. *Sun, moon, and stars bring forth first parents.* Sun and moon beget son; morning and evening star beget daughter; these, the first parents, are at first without understanding, but it is awakened later by demigods. — Pawnee: Alexander N. Am. 110.

A1271.2. *Sun and moon beget stones and birds: these transformed to first parents.* Baining of New Britain: Dixon 110.

D350. Transformation: bird to person. D430. Transformation: object to person.

A1271.3. *First parents children of god.* Persian: Carnoy 294; Chinese: Eberhard FFC CXX 88.

A1216. Man as offspring of creator.

A1271.4. *First parents originate from gold* which is from body of first man. Born fifteen years old. — Persian: Carnoy 294.

A1273. *Twin first parents.* Persian: Carnoy 294f.

A1273.1. *Incestuous first parents.* India: *Thompson-Balys; Philippine: Dixon 171f.

Brother-sister marriage of children of first parents. T410. Incest.

A1275. *Creation of first man's (woman's) mate.* Irish myth: Cross; India: Thompson-Balys.

A1275.1. *Creation of first woman from man's rib.* *Dh I 115ff.; *Frazer Old Testament I 9f.; India: Thompson-Balys; Jewish: Neuman. — Spanish Exempla: Keller; Lithuanian: Balys Legends Nos. 34, 36ff., 52, 65; Siberian: Holmberg Siberian 379; Hawaiian: Dixon 24; cf. Central Caroline Is.: ibid. 251, Beckwith Myth 43, 46.

A1275.1.1. *Deity creates princess from prince's body and gives her to him.* India: Thompson-Balys.

A1275.2. *First man split in two to form mate.* (Cf. A1225.1.) — Jewish: Neuman; Hindu: Carnoy 316.

A1275.3. *Of ten original men one magically changes sex.* New Hebrides: Dixon 107; Eskimo (Cape York): Rasmussen III 49.

D658.3. Transformation to female to seduce.

A1275.4. *Creator makes woman and then begets man by her.* New Zealand: Dixon 24f.; Society Is.: ibid. 25; Marquesas: ibid. 26.

A1275.5. *Man creates a woman from melted butter,* sour milk, sour cream and curds offered on the waters. India: Thompson-Balys.

A1275.6. *First woman's mate made from transformed tree.* S. Am. Indian (Yuracare): Métraux RMLP XXXIII 144.

A1275.7. *First man created from nothing wanders until he finds mate.* Eskimo (Ungava): Turner RBAE XI 261.

A1275.8. *Why Eve was not made at first along with Adam.* Irish myth: Cross.

A1275.9. *First man descends on earth, falls in love with and marries a fairy.* India: Thompson-Balys.

A1275.10. *First created man catches woman in his snare.* India: Thompson-Balys.

A1276. *Man chosen as best gift by primeval women.* In beginning only women on earth. Deity kills one by accident and promises anything as reparation. They choose man. — Ekoi: Talbot 98.

J1545.4. The exiled wife's dearest possession.

A1277. *Offspring of first parents.*

A1277.1. *First parents devour offspring.* Persian: Carnoy 297.

A1277.2. *Primeval human pair allowed to bear all children they wish.* Lithuanian: Balys Legends No. 67.

A1277.3. *Son of first human couple murdered by tiger sent by god; his head becomes the sun, his chest the moon, and his blood gives the red earth its color.* India: Thompson-Balys.

A1277.4. *First man and woman bring in children and clothe them.* Eskimo (Cape York): Rasmussen III 47.

A1279. *Primeval human pair — miscellaneous.*

A1279.1. *Of first parents husband so hideous he is kept hidden.* India: Thompson-Balys.

A1280. First man (woman). Hawaii: Beckwith Myth 276, 280f.; Tahiti: Beckwith Myth 120; Easter Is.: Métraux Ethnology 315.

A1281. *Condition of first man (woman).*

A1281.1. *First man covered with horny substance.* (Cf. A1310.1.) — *Dh I 225; Jewish: Neuman. — Lithuanian: Balys Legends No. 34; Siberian: Holmberg Siberian 376.

F558. Man covered with horn.

A1281.2. *Man at first covered with hair.* Lithuanian: Balys Legends No. 34; Siberian: Holmberg Siberian 383.

A1281.2.1. *Change of animal and human skin in ancient times.* India: Thompson-Balys.

A1281.3. *Man at first naked.* Irish myth: Cross; India: Thompson-Balys.

A1383.1. Shame for nakedness appears to first woman (leaves for clothes). F568.1. Naked man (body). H812. Riddle: what were the clothes of Adam and Eve.

A1281.4. *Men originally self-luminous.* Jewish: Neuman; Siberian: Holmberg Siberian 385.

A1281.5. *First man created circumcised.* Jewish: Neuman.

A1281.6. *Adam at first nameless.* Irish myth: Cross; Jewish: Neuman.

Z252. Hero at first nameless.

A1281.6.1. *Adam's name composed of initial letters of four stars from the four quarters of the heavens.* Irish myth: Cross.

A651.1.6. Heavens (world) divided into four quarters.

A1282. *The mother of men.* Calif. Indian: Gayton and Newman 93.

A1282.1. *Mother of the world gives birth to three sons.* India: Thompson-Balys.

A1285. *Activities of first man.*

A1285.1. *First man made chief over whole world.* Hawaii: Beckwith Myth 44.

A1285.1.1. *In response to Adam's prayer, God sends him to earth* to be father of mankind. India: Thompson-Balys.

A1290. Creation of man—other motifs.

A1291. *Man created by supernatural creature, not deity.*

A1291.1. *Man created by angels.* Jewish: Neuman.

A1293. *Devil in God's absence puts sickness in Adam's body.* Dh I 98ff.

A63. Devil as marplot at creation.

A1295. *Creation in covered vessel.* Men (or animals) created in a basket or from a bundle, or from under a blanket. — N. A. Ind.: Kroeber JAFL XXI 223; S. Am. Indian (Cashinawa): Métraux BBAE CXLIII (3) 684.

A1296. *Multiplication of man by fragmentation.* S. Am. Indian (Inca): Rowe BBAE CXLIII (2) 406.

A1297. *First human being killed by jealous brothers* (reptiles and insects). India: Thompson-Balys.

A1300—A1399. Ordering of human life.

A1300. Ordering of human life. India: Thompson-Balys.

A530. Culture hero establishes law and order. A541. Culture hero teaches arts and crafts. M0. Judgments and decrees.

A1301. *Men at first as large as giants.* Dh I 242ff.; Irish myth: Cross; Greek: *Grote I 5; Jewish: Neuman.

A523. Giant as culture hero. F232.6. Fairies as giants. F531. Giant.

A1310. Arrangement of man's bodily attributes.

A1310.1. *Change in bodily form at fall of man.* Adam's body was formerly horn-like. (Cf. A1281.1.) — Dh I 225. — Lithuanian: Balys Index No. 3035, Balys Legends Nos. 34, 45—49.

A1310.2. *Assembling the body.* India: Thompson-Balys.

A1310.3. *Why men are clothed in skin.* India: Thompson-Balys.

A1310.4. *Why women have marks on the belly.* India: Thompson-Balys.

A1311. *Origin of hands and feet.* India: Thompson-Balys.

A1311.1. *The lizard hand.* Man's hand is modeled on that of the lizard. — N. A. Indian: *Thompson Tales 288 n. 59; Calif. Indian: Gayton and Newman 56.

A2375.2.6. Why mole has hand like man.

A1311.2. *Why God changed right hand into left.* Man loses hand with which he gives devil a box on ears. — Finnish: Aarne FFC VIII 6 No. 19.

A1311.3. *Origin of fingernails.* India: Thompson-Balys.

A1312. *Origin of human skeleton.*

A1312.1. *Origin of knee-caps.* A stone that magically joins self to woman's body. — Ekoi: Talbot 394.

A1312.2. *Why an uneven number of ribs.* Livonian: Loorits FFC LXVI 83 Nos. 21, 22. — Tahltan: Teit JAFL XXXII 226 (floating ribs).

A1313. *Origin of sex-organs.*

A1313.0.1. *Origin of eunuchs.* India: Thompson-Balys.

A1313.0.2. *Origin of sex differentiations.* Africa (Loango): Pechuël-Loesche 267.

A1313.1. *Origin of male sex-organs.* Finnish: Aarne FFC VIII 6 No. 21, XXXIII 52 No. 21; India: Thompson-Balys; Jewish: Neuman. — Estonian: Aarne FFC XXV 141 No. 14; Lithuanian: Balys Index No. 3040, Balys Legends Nos. 50—57; Livonian: Loorits FFC LXVI 83f. Nos. 28—30; Flemish: DeMeyer FFC XXXVII 84 No. 21. — Plains Ojibwa: Skinner JAFL XXXII 283; Plains Cree: Skinner JAFL XXIX 351.

A1313.2. *Origin of female sex-organs.* Finnish: Aarne FFC VIII 6 No. 22, XXXIII 52 No. 22; India: *Thompson-Balys; Estonian: Aarne FFC XXV 141 No. 14; Lithuanian: Balys Index No. 3040, Balys Legends Nos. 50—57; Livonian: Loorits FFC LXVI 83f. Nos. 27, 29, 30; Flemish: DeMeyer FFC XXXVII 84 No. 22.

A1313.2.1. *Origin of clitoris.* India: Thompson-Balys.

A1313.3. *Misplaced genitalia.* Originally genitals are misplaced. They are properly arranged by the culture hero. — Lithuanian: Balys Legends Nos. 56f.; India: Thompson-Balys; Chinese: Graham. — N. A. Indian: *Thompson Tales 288 n. 59a.; Hatt Asiatic Influences 84f.

A1351. Origin of childbirth. A2229.8. Bird has red spot on its tail as reward for having moved woman's organ to its present position. F529.2. People without anuses.

A1313.3.1. *Vaginal teeth broken.* Women originally had toothed vaginas. Culture hero breaks teeth so that women will be harmless to men. (See practically all references to F547.1.1, *Vagina Dentata.*) — S. Am. Indian (Toba, Mataco): Métraux MAFLS XL 99, 105, Métraux BBAE CXLIII (1) 367.

A1313.4. *Origin of women's breasts.* Finnish: Aarne FFC VIII 6 No. 20; Livonian: Loorits FFC LXVI 83 No. 27; Lithuanian: Balys Legends Nos. 53ff.; India: Thompson-Balys. — S. Am. Indian (Apapocuva-Guarani): Métraux RMLP XXXIII 137.

A1313.4.1. *Women at first with breasts on their foreheads.* S. Am. Indian (Yuracare): Métraux BBAE CXLIII (3) 503.

A1313.5. *Origin of placenta.* India: Thompson-Balys.

A1315. *Origin of hair and beard.* India: Thompson-Balys.

A1315.1. *Why men become gray-headed.* Dh I 314. — Finnish: Aarne FFC VIII 6 No. 18.

A1315.2. *Origin of bald heads.* Christensen Molboerne 212 No. 70; Finnish: Aarne FFC VIII 6 No. 17, XXXIII 52 No. 17; Livonian: Loorits FFC LXVI 82 No. 20; Flemish: DeMeyer FFC XXXVII 84 No. 17; India: Thompson-Balys.

A1315.3. *Origin of beard.* *Dh I 228ff. — Finnish: Aarne FFC VIII 5 Nos. 13, 14, XXXIII 52 No. 13; Livonian: Loorits FFC LXVI 83 Nos. 23, 24; Estonian: Aarne FFC XXV 141 No. 11; Lithuanian: Balys Legends Nos. 58—62, 70.

A1315.4. *Origin of hair around mouth and eyes.* Original dispute between Hair and Stomach. Stomach compelled to stay on inside of man. Hair stands on guard at mouth and eyes to see that Stomach does not escape. — Ekoi: Talbot 394.

A1315.5. *Origin of pubic hairs.* India: Thompson-Balys.

A1315.6. *Origin of eyelashes.* India: Thompson-Balys.

A1316. *Origin of facial features.* India: Thompson-Balys.

A1316.0.1. *Man at first with two faces, separated at birth of first woman.* Jewish: Neuman.

A1316.1. *Distribution of noses.* The earlier comers receive big noses, the later small. — Finnish: Aarne FFC VIII 5 No. 15.

A1316.1.1. *Forming of the nose.* Nose was made from clay taken from the posterior of the already created man. — Lithuanian: Balys Legends No. 35.

A1316.2. *Why men blink.* India: Thompson-Balys.

A1316.3. *Origin of eyes.* India: Thompson-Balys.

A1316.3.1. *Distribution of eyes.* Jewish: Neuman.

A1316.3.2. *Why there are one-eyed women.* S. Am. Indian (Toba): Métraux MAFLS XL 104.

A1316.3.3. *Men originally blind: eyes opened by accident.* Africa (Dahomey): Einstein 18f.

A1316.4. *Origin of ears.* India: Thompson-Balys.

A1316.5. *Origin of tongue.* India: Thompson-Balys.

A1316.6. *Origin of teeth.* India: Thompson-Balys.

A1317. *Origin of urine and excreta.* India: Thompson-Balys.

A1319. *Origin of other bodily attributes.*

A1319.1. *Origin of Adam's apple.* Forbidden fruit sticks in Adam's throat. — *Dh I 208ff.; *Fb "Adamsæble" IV 4. — Finnish: Aarne FFC VIII 5 No. 16, XXXIII 52 No. 16; Lappish: Qvigstad FFC LX 35 No. 10; Lithuanian: Balys Legends No. 34; U.S.: Baughman; Jewish: Neuman.

A1319.2. *Why men lack tails.* Chinese: Eberhard FFC CXX 117 No. 72; Piegan: Michelson JAFL XXIX 409.

A1319.3. *Why ear-wax is inside the ear.* Cameroons: Gantenbein 69ff., Lederbogen Mitt. d. Sem. f. orient. Spr. IV 175f. No. 11.

A1319.4. *Why the posterior of man is large.* Lithuanian: Balys Legends No. 35.

A1319.5. *Origin of the liver.* India: Thompson-Balys.

A1319.6. *Origin of blood.* Jewish: Neuman; India: Thompson-Balys.

A1319.7. *Why the center of man's eye is black:* blackened by spirits to make themselves invisible. India: Thompson-Balys.

A1319.8. *Origin of sweat.* Jewish: Neuman; India: Thompson-Balys.

A1319.9. *Origin of sneezing.* India: Thompson-Balys.

A1319.10. *Origin of itching.* India: Thompson-Balys.

A1319.11. *Origin of the sensation of tickling.* India: Thompson-Balys.

A1319.12. *Originally man rejuvenated himself by snake-like change of skin.* Chinese: Eberhard FFC CXX 411.

A1319.12.1. *Why man does not change his skin:* ancient contest lost by toad, representing man, won by lizard. India: Thompson-Balys.

A1319.13. *Why man's neck is its present size.* Marshall Is.: Davenport 231.

A1319.14. *Origin of man's skin.* Jewish: Neuman.

A1320. Determination of span of life. *Köhler-Bolte I 42. — N. A. Indian: *Thompson Tales 288 n. 60b.

A1321. *Men and animals readjust span of life.* At first, thirty years are given to all animals and to man. For the animals it is too long, for man too short. Man is given a portion of animals' lives. Years 1—30 vigorous (man's own); 30—48 burdens and blows (ass's); 48—60 no teeth (dog's); 60—70 foolish (monkey's). — *BP III 290 (Gr. No. 176); *Fb "menneske" II 577b; Halm Aesop No. 173; Wesselski Bebel II 135 No. 103. — Lithuanian: Balys Index No. 3060, Balys Legends Nos. 113f.; India: *Thompson-Balys.

B592. Animals bequeath characteristics to man.

A1321.1. *Why children learn to walk later than animals.* African (Cameroon): Mansfield 231, 237.

A1322. *Determination of relation between birth-rate and death-rate.* Japanese: Anesaki 224.

A1323. *Long span of life for first man.* Jewish: Neuman; India: Thompson-Balys; Buddhist myth: Malalasekera I 108.

A1325. *Short span of life for first men.* Chinese: Eberhard FFC CXX 116, 411 s.v. "Alter."

A1326. *Why babies die so easily.* S. Am. Indian (Toba): Métraux MAFLS XL 103.

A1330. Beginnings of trouble for man. Shasta and Athapascan: Frachtenberg JAFL XXVIII 225; Africa (Congo): Weeks 205.

A1331. *Paradise lost.* Original happy state forfeited because of one sin. — *H. Schmidt Die Erzählungen von Paradies und Sündenfall (Tübingen 1931); J. Feidmann Paradies und Sündenfall (1913); *Frazer Old Testament I 45—76; Irish myth: Cross; Jewish: Neuman; Persian: Carnoy 296, 309; Burmese: Scott Indo-Chin. 265, 269f.; Hawaii: Beckwith Myth 43ff., 61.

A2236.2. Animal characteristics from carrying devil into paradise. A2612.1 Tears of Adam and Eve leaving paradise become trees. C600. Unique prohibition. G303.3.3.15.1. The devil in form of snake. Tempts Eve. C937. God's favor lost for breaking tabu. M400. Curses. Q541.1.1. Standing in (Jordan and Tigris) rivers as penance (by Adam and Eve).

A1331.1. *Paradise lost because of forbidden fruit (drink).* (Cf. A1346). — *Dh I 208ff.; *Frazer Old Testament I 45ff.; Irish myth: Cross; Spanish Exempla: Keller; Lithuanian: Balys Legends No. 34. — Persian: Carnoy 297; India: Thompson-Balys; Burmese, Indo-Chinese: Scott 265, 289. — Hawaii: Beckwith Myth 45; Quiché: Alexander

Lat. Am. 171; Yuracare: ibid. 315; Biloxi: Dorsey and Swanton BBAE XLVII 32; African (Baluba): Einstein 199.

B176.1. Serpent as deceiver in paradise. C621. Forbidden fruit.

A1331.1.1. *Paradise lost because of forbidden food.* India: *Thompson-Balys.

A1331.2. *Paradise lost because of brother-sister incest.* Persian: Carnoy 310.

A1331.2.1. *Paradise lost because first woman is seduced.* Hawaii: Beckwith Myth 43, 61.

A1333. *Confusion of tongues.* Originally all men speak same language. Because of a sin they come to speak different languages. — *Frazer Old Testament I 384ff.; Jewish: Neuman; Irish myth: Cross. — India: Thompson-Balys; Chin (Indo-China): Scott 266f.; Siberian: Holmberg Siberian 365. — N. A. Indian: *Thompson Tales 285 n. 53; Maya: Alexander Lat. Am. 132.

A1616. Origin of particular languages. C771.1. Tabu: building too high a tower. (Tower of Babel). C966. Change of language for breaking tabu.

A1333.1. *Confusion of tongues partly due to lack of understanding* of difference between the word for "stick" and the word for "stone." Irish myth: Cross.

A1335. *Origin of death.* S. S. Cohon The Origin of Death (Journal of Jewish Lore and Philosophy [1919]); Irish myth: Cross; Jewish: Neuman; India: *Thompson-Balys; Chinese: Graham; Siberian: Holmberg Siberian 377; Japanese: Anesaki 224, 233; Burmese: Scott Indo-Chinese 264. — Africa (Angola): Wagener Afrikanische Parallelen 9ff., Chatelain 249, (Bushman): Bleek and Lloyd 60, (Congo): Weeks 217 No. 12, (Ekoi): Talbot 177, (Liberian): Bundy JAFL XXXII 407f., (Fang): Trilles 131. — Philippine (Tinguian): Cole 178; Maori: Dixon 54; Australian: ibid. 285; Melanesian: ibid. 117f. *n. 53; Micronesian: ibid. 252f.; Indonesian: ibid. 170 (Borneo), 174, *182; Hawaii: Beckwith Myth 43; Raratonga: ibid. 158; Banks Is.: ibid. 61. — N. A. Indian: R. Dangel Mythen vom Ursprung dies Todes bei den Indianern Nordamerikas (Mitt. der Anthrop. Gesellschaft in Wien LVIII [1928] 341—374); *Krappe Nieuw Theologisch Tijdschrift (1928) 242ff.; *Thompson Tales 284 n. 51; Chitimacha: Swanton JAFL XXX 476; Sinkyone: Kroeber JAFL XXXII 346; Tahltan: Teit *JAFL XXXII 206f.; Calif. Indian: Gayton and Newman 64; Eskimo (Kodiak): Golder JAFL XX 486, (Cape York): Rasmussen III 48, (Cumberland Sound): Boas BAM XV 173; S. Am. Indian (Chiriguano): Métraux RMLP XXXIII 171, (Cubeo): Goldman BBAE CXLIII (3) 798, (Yuracare): Métraux ibid. (3) 503, (Warrau): Kirchoff ibid. (3) 880.

C937.1. Immortality lost because of broken tabu. F1041.1.3.2.2. First woman in Ireland to die of grief for the death of her husband. K1581. Originator of death first sufferer.

A1335.1. *Origin of death from falsified message.* *Dh III 22; *Wesselski Theorie 43; Gaster Oldest Stories 91. — African: Werner African 160ff., 167, (Hottentot): Bleek 69 No. 31, 71 No. 32, 72 No. 33, 74 No. 35, (Basuto): Jacottet 46 No. 6, (Gold Coast): Barker and Sinclair 129 No. 23, (Togo): Einstein 5, (Sandeh): Casati I 222; S. Am. Indian (Cashinawa): Métraux BBAE CXLIII (3) 684, (Tropical Forests): Lowie ibid. (3) 55.

A2276. Animal characteristics from falsified message. K511. Uriah letter changed. K1851. Substituted letter.

A1335.1.1. *Origin of death: wrong messenger goes to God.* Wesselski Theorie 44.

A1335.2. *Origin of death from bad creator's unsuccessful imitation.* The bad creator attempts in vain to endow his creations with life like the good creator. Fails and thus introduces death. — Banks Is.: Dixon 106; Hawaii: Beckwith Myth 61.

A63. Devil as marplot at creation. A1217. Devil's unsuccessful attempt to vivify his creations. J2400. Foolish imitation.

A1335.3. *Origin of death from unwise choice.* Choice between two bundles, one containing tempting articles, the other everlasting life. People choose the large bundle and lose everlasting life. — Congo: Weeks 218 No. 13.

L211. Modest choice: three caskets type.

A1335.4. *Origin of death when early people put on new skins.* Child fails to recognize mother, who puts old skin back on. — Wesselski Theorie 45.

A1335.5. *Origin of death: serpent given immortality instead of man.* Renews his skin. — **Delarue Nouvelle Revue des Traditions Populaires (1950) 262—275; Wesselski Theorie 45; Gaster: Oldest Stories 81.

A1335.6. *Origin of death: punishment for scorning deity.* Wesselski Theorie 45; India: Thompson-Balys.

A1335.6.1. *Origin of death: disrespectful answer to God.* India: Thompson-Balys.

A1335.7. *First son who died before his father after the Flood.* Irish myth Cross; Jewish: Neuman.

A1335.8. *Origin of death because world is overpopulated.* India: *Thompson-Balys; Eskimo (Cumberland Sound): Boas BAM XV 173; S. Am. Indian (Chiriguano): Métraux RMLP XXXIII 171.

A1335.9. *Origin of death because people weary of living.* India: Thompson-Balys.

A1335.9.1. *Death sent into the world by culture hero (God) when he got tired of man.* India: Thompson-Balys.

A1335.10. *Men die because a snake comes to prey on mankind while creator rests.* India: Thompson-Balys.

A63.1. Devil works during God's sleep at creation.

A1335.11. *God of world of the dead demands that men die* so he will have subjects. (Cf. A487) India: Thompson-Balys.

A1335.12. *Death origin: God sends a woman to sell poisoned curds to man.* India: Thompson-Balys.

A1335.13. *God sends centipede down to introduce death* into the world through its poisoned sting. India: Thompson-Balys.

A1335.14. *Death comes into the world by treachery of the gods:* stick used by man for scratching his back is changed into cobra. — India: Thompson-Balys.

A1335.15. *God punishes man by killing his child:* origin of death. Chinese: Eberhard FFC CXX 187.

A1336. *Origin of murder.* Hebrew: Genesis 4:8ff.; Jewish: Neuman; Greek: Grote I 7. — Congo: Weeks 207 No. 4; Ila of Rhodesia: Smith and Dale 350 No. 5.

F839.3. Cain slays Abel with bone of camel.

A1337. *Origin of disease.* *Dh I 98ff. — Finnish Kalevala rune 45; Greek: Grote I 72 (Pandora's Box); Buddhist myth: Malalasekera I 461; India: *Thompson-Balys; Chinese: Eberhard FFC CXX 187. — Africa (Ekoi): Talbot 278, 282; Hawaii: Beckwith Myth 113, 502; Shasta: Frachtenberg JAFL XXVIII 227; S. Am. Indian (Cubeo): Goldman BBAE CXLIII (3) 798.

A1337.0.1. *Disease caused by the gods.* India: Thompson-Balys.

A1337.0.1.1. *Pestilence brought to man in box* by messenger from creator. S. Am. Indian (Inca): Rowe BBAE CXLIII (2) 318.

A1337.0.2. *Disease caused by ghosts.* India: Thompson-Balys.

A1337.0.3. *Disease caused by witchcraft.* India: Thompson-Balys.

A1337.0.4. *Disease caused by menstrual blood.* (Cf. D1003.) — India: Thompson-Balys.

A1337.0.5. *Disease as punishment.* India: Thompson-Balys.

A1337.0.6. *Disease to prevent man enjoying himself too much.* India: Thompson-Balys.

L482.5. Men enjoy themselves too much.

A1337.0.7. *Origin of sickness and misfortune: monstrous births from brother-sister incestuous union.* India: Thompson-Balys.

C114. Tabu: incest.

A1337.1. *Origin of ulcers.* Estonian: Aarne FFC XXV 142 No. 21; Lithuanian: Balys Legends No. 42.

A1337.2. *Origin of cholera.* India: Thompson-Balys.

A1337.3. *Origin of epilepsy.* India: Thompson-Balys.

A1337.4. *Origin of fever.* India: Thompson-Balys.

A1337.5. *Origin of itch.* India: Thompson-Balys.

A1337.6. *Origin of leprosy.* India: Thompson-Balys.

A1337.7. *Origin of smallpox.* India: Thompson-Balys.

A1337.8. *Origin of illness from fire and cold.* Africa (Togo): Einstein 5f.

A1338. *Origin of physical defects.* Wicked people entering heaven on rope fall to earth and are injured. St. Peter misunderstands what God says and lets them fall. — Spanish: Boggs FFC XC No. 758A.

A1338.1. *Origin of cripples.* Chinese: Eberhard FFC CXX 114f.

A1339.1. *Origin of blindness.* Jewish: Neuman; S. Am. Indian (Toba): Métraux MAFLS XL 145.

A1341. *Origin of war among men.* Irish myth: Cross; Kaska: Teit JAFL XXX 469; Africa (Konnoh): Willans 136.

A1341.1. *Origin of battle-shouting.* Irish myth: Cross.

A1341.2. *Origin of duelling.* Irish myth: Cross.

A1341.3. *Origin of thefts and quarrels.* India: Thompson-Balys.

A1342. *Origin of quarrelling.* Greek: Grote I 7; S. Am. Indian (Yuracare): Métraux BBAE CXLIII (3) 503.

A1343. *Origin of lying.* Greek: Grote I 7; Buddhist myth: Malalasekera I 113, 911; Jewish: Neuman.

A1344. *Origin of tears and sighs.* Wienert FFC LVI 37; Halm Aesop Nos. 138, 355; Greek: Grote I 7, 72; Jewish: Neuman; India: Thompson-Balys.

A1344.1. *The "three first cries that made their way to God":* the cry of the blood of Abel, etc. Irish myth: Cross.

A1345. *Origin of hunger.* Greek: Grote I 7; Jewish: Neuman; India: Thompson-Balys; Liberian: Bundy JAFL XXXII 421f.; Tahltan: Teit JAFL XXXII 216, 221.

A1345.1. *Origin of thirst.* India: Thompson-Balys.

A1346. *Man to earn bread by sweat of his brow.* (Cf. A1331.1.) — Irish myth: Cross; Greek: Fox 158; Jewish: Neuman; India: *Thompson-Balys.

A1346.1. *Man must work as punishment for theft of fire.* Greek: Fox 14.

A1415. Theft of fire.

A1346.2. *Man must labor for a living: at first everything too easy.* Full crops produce themselves, trees drop sugar etc. — Greek: Grote I 61; Jewish: Neuman; India: *Thompson-Balys; Seneca: Curtin-Hewitt RBAE XXXII 462; S. Am. Indian (Mataco): Métraux MAFLS XL 59f.

L482. Men too prosperous (happy), so that things are made more difficult.

A1346.2.1. *Cotton at first already spun into threads.* India: Thompson-Balys.

A1346.2.2. *First people have everything they wish (life without work).* India: Thompson-Balys; Africa (Fang): Trilles 144.

A1346.2.3. *Men are too happy: pain and sickness created.* India: Thompson-Balys.

A1346.2.4. *Canoes at one time self-propelling.* Marshall Is.: Davenport 222.

A1348. *Mankind's escape from trouble.*

A1348.1. *Wren helps mankind restore prosperity to the world.* India: Thompson-Balys.

A1350. Origin of sex functions. (Cf. A1556.)

A1351. *Origin of childbirth.* Irish myth: Cross; Jewish: Neuman; India: *Thompson-Balys. — Maori: Dixon 78; Polynesian, Melanesian, Micronesian: ibid. 79 n. 79—82; Maori, Hawaii, Cook Is., Fijis: Beckwith Myth 502—504; Hawaii: ibid. 284; Marquesas: Handy 58, 122, 128; N. A. Indian: *Thompson Tales 288 n. 59a, (Tahltan): *Teit JAFL XXXII 207 n. 2.

A1313.3. Misplaced genitalia. T500. Conception and birth.

A1351.1. *Origin of childbirth pains.* Jewish: Neuman; Africa (Togo): Einstein 8f.

A1351.2. *Origin of abortions.* Jewish: Neuman.

A1352. *Origin of sexual intercourse.* Lithuanian: Balys Legends Nos. 63—66; India: *Thompson-Balys; Japanese: Ikeda; Tonga: Gifford 18;

S. Am. Indian (Cashinawa): Métraux BBAE CXLIII (3) 684; Africa (Mkulwe): Einstein 18f., (Loango): Pechuël-Loesche 267.

A1550. Origin of customs of courtship and marriage. A2236.6 Why dogs get stuck in sexual intercourse. A2496. Sexual intercourse of animals.

A1352.1. *Origin of unrestricted sexual intercourse between husband and wife.* Cheremis: Sebeok-Nyerges.

A1352.2. *Means of persuading persons to intercourse.* India: Thompson-Balys; Chinese: Graham.

A1352.3. *Former intercourse by navel.* India: Thompson-Balys.

A1355. *Origin of menstruation.* Finnish: Aarne FFC VIII 6 No. 25, XXXIII 53 No. 25; Jewish: Neuman; India: *Thompson-Balys.

A1355.1. *Origin of menstruation — Eve and the serpent.* It is a punishment because Eve had intercourse with the serpent. — Dh I 211; Jewish: Neuman.

Q243. Incontinence punished.

A1355.1.1. *Origin of menstruation:* punishment because Eve ate forbidden fruit. Irish myth: Cross; Jewish: Neuman.

A1331.1. Paradise lost because of forbidden fruit.

A1355.2. *Origin of menstruation — Virgin Mary's garment.* She hides her garment and a maiden finds it. — Finnish: Aarne FFC VIII 6 No. 24; Jewish: Neuman.

V250. The Virgin Mary.

A1355.3. *Previously men menstruated.* India: *Thompson-Balys.

F569.2. Men menstruate.

A1357. *Culture hero teaches women how to rear their children.* S. Am. Indian (Toba): Métraux MAFLS XL 112f.

A1358. *Origin of sterility among women.* India: Thompson-Balys.

A1360. Man's growth and maturity.

A1361. *Why children are helpless for so long.* Livonian: Loorits FFC LXVI 84 No. 36; Lithuanian: Balys Legends Nos. 43f.; Flemish: DeMeyer FFC XXXVII 83 No. 11c.

A1365. *Why a lad at puberty is energetic and later lazy.* Tahltan: Teit JAFL XXXII 239.

A1370. Origin of mental and moral characteristics.

A1371. *Why women are bad.* Irish myth: Cross; Jewish: Neuman.

A1371.1. *Bad women because of head exchanged with devil.* Devil (serpent) and woman fight. St. Peter cuts off their heads and exchanges them. — Flemish: DeMeyer FFC XXXVII 83 No. 11b.; Lithuanian: Balys Index No. 3047, Balys Legends Nos. 82—93.

A1371.2. *Bad women combination of nine different animals.* Stiefel Zs. f. Vksk. VIII 163.

A2733. Poppy characteristics from series of reincarnations.

A1371.3. *Bad women from transformed hog and goose.* Peter, having only one daughter, foolishly promises her to three men. He asks the Lord to create two others. This request is granted. The first creature he meets on two successive mornings he is to greet, and they will be transformed. He meets a hog and a goose. His two new daughters have these characteristics. — *Dh II 191ff.; Fb "so" III 449b.; Lithuanian: Balys Index No. 411.

D336. Transformation: swine to person. D364. Transformation: goose to person. D526. Transformation through greeting. E601.1. Man by magic sees his wives in their former incarnations as dog and sow.

A1372. *Origin of other special characteristics of women.*

A1372.1. *Why women are prattlers.* Flemish: DeMeyer FFC XXXVII 83 No. 11a.

A1372.2. *Why women laugh much.* When Eve sees her first child she laughs over its smallness. — Estonian: Aarne FFC XXV 141 No. 16.

A1372.3. *Why women are roving.* Lithuanian: Balys Legends No. 73; Africa (Ekoi): Talbot 114.

A1372.4. *Why women have a treble voice.* Estonian: Aarne FFC XXV 141 No. 13; Livonian: Loorits FFC LXVI 84 No. 34.

A1372.5. *Why women are deceitful.* Kaska: Teit JAFL XXX 462.

A1372.6. *Why some women are good-looking.* Tahltan: Teit JAFL XXXII 220.

A1372.7. *Origin of pleasant and unpleasant women.* Contest arranged by Virgin Mary — laughter forbidden for some time. — Lithuanian: Balys Legends No. 79.

A1372.8. *Why women never have leisure.* Because they refused to show God the way, saying they had no time. — Lithuanian: Balys Index No. 3046, Balys Legends Nos 74—78.

A2231.1. Animal characteristics: punishment for discourteous answer to God (saint).

A1372.9. *Why women are subservient to men.* Lithuanian: Balys Legends No. 70ff.; India: Thompson-Balys; S. Am. Indian (Mundurucu): Horton BBAE CXLIII (3) 282.

A1557. Why woman is master of her husband.

A1372.10. *Why women keep washing themselves.* St. Andrew, sent to get salt to keep people clean, gets drunk and forgets. There is only enough for men. — Venezuela: Dominguez Collection II No. 33 (Archive of Venezuelan Institute of Folklore).

A1373. *Why women attract men.*

A1373.1. *Why good-looking but soft, useless women attract men.* Tahltan: Teit JAFL XXXII 220; cf. Kaska: Teit JAFL XXX 456.

A1375. *Origin of jealousy and selfishness.* Irish myth: Cross; Gold Coast: Barker and Sinclair 112 No. 19.

W151. Greed. W152. Stinginess. W181. Jealousy.

A1375.1. *Why some married people quarrel* and accuse each other of infidelity. Kaska: Teit JAFL XXX 456.

A1376. *Why man excels woman.* Africa (Cameroon): Mansfield 236.

A1377. *Origin of laziness.* Tahltan: Teit JAFL XXXII 238f.

A1381. *Origin of bravery.*

A1381.1. *Why people do not fear earthquakes.* Tahltan: Teit JAFL XXXII 227.

A1382. *Origin of fear.*

A1382.1. *Why man is fearful in the jungle.* Africa: Stanley 78.

A1383. *Origin of shame for nakedness.*

C312.1. Tabu: man looking at nude woman.

A1383.1. *Shame for nakedness appears to first woman.* (Leaves for clothes). — Jewish: Neuman; India: Thompson-Balys; Africa (Baluba): Einstein 19.

A1282. First people go naked.

A1384. *Origin of evil inclinations.*

A1384.1. *Origin of evil inclinations: punishment for fall of man.* Jewish: Neuman.

A1384.2. *Evil inclination enters body at time of conception.* Jewish: Neuman.

A1386. *Origin of drunkenness.* Jewish: Neuman.

A1388. *Origin of hatred.* Jewish: Neuman.

A1388.1. *Hate released among mankind.* Greek: Fox 78.

A1390. Ordaining of human life—miscellaneous.

A1391. *Why other members must serve belly.* Result of a debate between members of the body. — India: Thompson-Balys; Africa (Ekoi): Talbot 393.

J461.1. The belly and the members. Debate.

A1391.1. *Why all limbs are dependent on body.* Africa (Cameroon): Mansfield 234.

A1392. *First walk by Adam.* Irish myth: Cross.

A1394. *Men live by the breath of the gods.* (Cf. A1241.3.) — India: Thompson-Balys.

A1399. *Ordaining of human life — additional motifs.*

A1399.1. *Origin of laughter.* India: Thompson-Balys.

A1399.2. *Origin of dreams.* India: Thompson-Balys.

A1399.2.1. *Origin of sleep.* India: Thompson-Balys; S. Am. Indian (Tucuna): Nimuendajú BBAE CXLIII (3) 724.

A1399.3. *Origin of spitting.* India: Thompson-Balys.

A1399.4. *Origin of coughing.* India: Thompson-Balys.

A1400—A1499. Acquisition of culture.

A1400. Acquisition of human culture.

A541. Culture hero teaches arts and crafts.

A1401. *Culture originated by previous race of men.* N. A. Indian: Kroeber JAFL XXI 226 s.v. "Departed race."

A630. Series of creations. A1220.1. Man created after series of unsuccessful experiments.

A1402. *The gods build houses, and fashion tools.* Icel.: MacCulloch Eddic 327.

A140. Gods as workmen.

A1403. *God teaches people to work.* Lithuanian: Balys Index No. 3057, Balys Legends Nos. 110f.

A1404. *Gods teach people all they know.* Marquesas: Handy 123; S. Am. Indian (Cariri): Lowie BBAE CXLIII (1) 559.

A1405. *Culture originated by ancestor of tribes.* Jewish: Neuman; S. Am. Indian (Tucuna): Nimuendajú BBAE CXLIII (3) 724.

A1410. Acquisition of livable environment.

A1411. *Theft of light.* Light originally absent is stolen by culture hero. — Jewish: Neuman; Hindu: Keith 34. — N. A. Indian: *Thompson Tales 281 n. 42; Eskimo (Smith Sound): Kroeber JAFL XII 205; S. Am. Indian (Tapirape): Wagley-Galvão BBAE CXLIII (3) 178. Cf. Finnish: Kalevala rune 47.

A721.1. Theft of sun. A758. Theft of moon. A1151. Theft of the seasons.

A1411.1. *Light kept in box (basket).* Stolen. — N. A. Indian: *Thompson Tales 282 n. 45.

A721. Sun kept in box. A754. Moon kept in box.

A1411.2. *Theft of light by being swallowed and reborn.* The hero transforms himself to a particle. The daughter of the guardian of light swallows him as she is drinking water. He is reborn. As a child in the house he steals light. — India: Thompson-Balys; N. A. Indian: *Thompson Tales 282 n. 44.

A511.3. Culture hero incarnated through birth from virgin. D646.2. Transformation to child to be adopted. D861.10. Magic object carried away; child allowed to play with it. E607.2. Person transforms self, is swallowed and reborn in new form. F392. Fairy transforms self to fly, allows self to be swallowed by woman and reborn as fairy. T511. Conception from eating.

A1412. *Origin of light — miscellaneous.* Jewish: Neuman.

A1412.1. *Light originated from shield of old cobra supporting the earth.* India: Thompson-Balys.

A1412.2. *Origin of light: souls of dead in heaven.* Eskimo (Cape York): Rasmussen III 48.

E741.1.3. Soul as light.

A1412.3. *Acquisition of daylight by culture hero.* S. Am. Indian (Tucuna): Nimuendajú BBAE CXLIII (3) 724.

A1414. *Origin of fire.* **Frazer Fire. — Irish myth: Cross; Persian: Carnoy 284. — Micronesian: Dixon 254f.; N. A. Indian (Kaska): *Teit JAFL XXX 443, (Tahltan): Teit JAFL XXXII 219, (Sinkyone): Kroeber JAFL XXXII 347, (Shasta): Frachtenberg JAFL XXVIII 210, (Calif. Indian): Gayton and Newman 63; Aztec: Alexander Lat. Am. 93; S. Am. Indian (Jibaro, Peru): Karsten (rev. JAFL XXXII 446), (Tropical Forest): Lowie BBAE CXLIII (3) 55, (Chiriguano): Métraux RMLP XXXIII 158, 171.

A1414.1. *Origin of fire — rubbing sticks.* Greek: Fox 192 (Hermes); Jewish: Neuman. — Kaffir: Kidd 253 No. 13; Marquesas: Handy 13.

A1414.1.1. *Fire drill invented.* India: Thompson-Balys; Calif. Indian: Gayton and Newman 61; Africa (Bushongo): Torday 237; S. Am. Indian (Kaskiha): Métraux BBAE CXLIII (1) 367, (Toba): Métraux MAFLS XL 3.

A1414.2. *Origin of fire — found in person's own body.* Australian, New Guinea, Torres Str., Massim (British New Guinea): Dixon 115 n. 47; Marquesas: Handy 13; S. Am. Indian (Warrau): Métraux RMLP XXXIII 146.

A1414.3. *Origin of fire — children strike rocks together,* accidentally produce fire. Calif. Indian: Gayton and Newman 60.

A1414.4. *Origin of fire — gift from god* (supernatural person). India: Thompson-Balys. — Maori: Clark 42; Isabel Is.: Beckwith Myth 504; Hawaii: ibid. 499; S. Am. Indian (Sherente): Lowie BBAE CXLIII (1) 515, (Cashiba): Steward-Métraux ibid. (3) 595, (Chamacoco): Métraux ibid. (1) 368, (Warrau): Kirchoff ibid. (3) 880, (Caviña, Tumupasa): Métraux ibid. 448, (Chiriguano): *Métraux RMLP XXXIII 171, (Toba): Métraux MAFLS XL 54; Africa: Bouvergnes 14f., (Bushongo): Torday 237, (Congo): Weeks 205f.

A1414.5. *Origin of flint and tinder.* India: Thompson-Balys.

A1414.6. *Bird as guardian of primordial fire.* S. Am. Indian (Apapocuvú-Guarani): Métraux RMLP XXXIII 171.

A1414.7. *Repository of fire.*

A1414.7.1. *Tree as repository of fire.* Calif. Indian: Gayton and Newman 61; S. Am. Indian (Chiriguano): Métraux RMLP XXXIII 158.

A1414.7.2. *Rock as repository of fire.* Calif. Indian: Gayton and Newman 61.

A1414.7.3. *Cave as repository of fire.* Marquesas: Handy 103.

A1415. *Theft of fire.* Mankind is without fire. A culture hero steals it from the owner. — **Frazer Fire; *Dh I 142ff.; *Hdwb. d. März. II 109b n. 14—15. — Greek: Fox 13, *Frazer Apollodorus I 51 n. 6; Hindu: Keith 36; Finnish: Holmberg Finno-Ugric 238. — Oceanic: Dixon 47 n. 31 (Maori), 47 n. 34 (Polynesia — general), 48 n. 35, 36 (Melanesia), 49 (Maori, Chatham Is., Marquesas, Melanesia, Hawaii, Micronesia), 112 (Woodlark Is.), 114 (Motu and Massim of British New Guinea), 182ff. (Indonesia), 281 (Australia); Indonesian: Voorhoeve Overzicht 65; Marquesas: Handy 104; Hawaii: Beckwith Myth 227; Tonga: Gifford 22; Eskimo (Ungava): Turner RBAE XI 340; N. A. Indian: *Thompson Tales 289 n. 63, Alexander N. Am. 256, 301f. n. 51; S. Am. Indian (Baikairi, Amazon): Alexander Lat. Am. 313; (Caingang): Métraux BBAE CXLIII (1) 473, (Botocudo): Métraux ibid. (1) 550, (Tucuna): Nimuendajú ibid. (3) 724, (Tenethara): Wagley-Galvão ibid. (3) 147, (Guarani): Métraux ibid. (3) 93, (Guarporé): Lévi-Strauss ibid. (3) 379, (Tapirape): Wagley-Galvão ibid. (3) 178, (Chamacoco): Métraux MAFLS XL 111, (Choco, Western Colombia): Métraux ibid. 112, (Apapocuvú-Guarani): Métraux RMLP XXXIII 138. —African: Frobenius Atlantis XII 80, (Bushongo): Torday 237, cf. Congo: Weeks 206. Cf. Finnish: Kalevala rune 47.

A153.1. Theft of ambrosia. A1031. World-fire after theft of fire. A1346.1. Man must work as punishment for theft of fire. A2229.4. Fly steals fire from spider: may eat everywhere. H1264. Quest to upper world for fire. Q501.4. Punishment of Prometheus.

A1415.0.1. *Fire witheld from men as punishment.* Greek: *Grote I 71.

A1415.0.2. *Original fire property of one person (animal).* Marquesas: Handy 12, 103; Hawaii: Beckwith Myth 115, 121, 216; S. Am. Indian (Ashlushlay): Métraux BBAE CXLIII (1) 367, (Tapirape): Wagley-Galvão ibid. (3) 178, (Mundurucu): Horton ibid. (3) 294, (Warrau, Chiriguano): *Métraux RMLP XXXIII 129.

A1415.1. *Fire stolen in hollow reed.* Greek: Fox 13, *Frazer Apollodorus I 51 n. 6; *Hdwb. d. März. II 109b nn. 9—13. —N. A. Indian: Thompson Tales 290 n. 64; S. Am. Indian (Jivaro, Eastern Ecuador): Karsten Myths of the Jibaros (reviewed JAFL XXXII 446) (fire preserved in bark of tree), (Tenetehara): Wagley-Galvão BBAE CXLIII (3) 147.

S352.1. Animal preserves fire for abandoned children in a clam shell.

A1415.1.1. *Fire carried from heaven in fingernails.* Jewish: Neuman.

A1415.2. *Theft of fire by animals.* *Dh III 92ff.; Lithuanian: Balys Index No. 3020, Balys Legends Nos. 27f.; Eng.: Baughman; North Carolina: Brown Collection I 632. — Massim of British New Guinea: Dixon 115; Africa (Ekoi): Talbot 370, (Ila, Rhodesia): Smith and Dale 345, (Fang): Nassau No. 3; N. A. Indian: *Thompson Tales 289 n. 63 (practically every reference); S. Am. Indian (Guarani): Métraux BBAE CXLIII (3) 93, (Mataco, Toba): Métraux ibid. (1) 367, (Eastern Brazil): Lowie ibid. (1) 434, (Chiriguano): Métraux ibid. (3) 484, RMLP XXXIII 172, (Toba): Métraux MAFLS XL 107—109.

A2436. Why animals lack fire. B500. Services of helpful animals.

A1415.2.1. *Theft of fire by bird.* Persian: Carnoy 264 (storm god in form of bird); India: Thompson-Balys; S. Am. Indian (Cashinawa): Métraux BBAE CXLIII (3) 685, (Jivaro): Steward-Métraux ibid. (3) 627, (Toba): Métraux MAFLS XL 6.

A1415.3. *Theft of fire — trick exchange.* Child of fire-owner is stolen and then given back in exchange for fire. — *Dh III 110ff.

D831. Magic object acquired by trick exchange. K300. Thefts and cheats.

A1415.4. *Vain attempts to circumvent theft of fire.* *Dh III 109ff. — Polynesian: Dixon 47; Massim (British New Guinea): ibid. 115 n. 48.

A1416. *Country ridded of ogres and made peaceful.* India: Thompson-Balys.

A531. Culture hero (demigod) overcomes monsters.

A1417. *Theft of tablets of fate.* From heaven by bird Zu. — Babylonian: Carnoy 264.

A1420. Acquisition of food supply for human race. India: Thompson-Balys.

A2813. Origin of honey. A2814. Origin of spices.

A1420.1. *Origin of food from body of slain food-goddess.* (Cf. A2611.1). Japanese: Anesaki 232, Ikeda.

A1420.2. *Gods teach how to seek and prepare food.* Marquesas: Handy 114; Africa (Luba): Donohugh Africa V 180.

A1420.3. *Creator of food items.* Mono-Alu-Fauru: Wheeler 66.

A1420.4. *Food originally obtained without effort.* Jewish: Neuman; Calif. Indian: Gayton and Newman 59.

A1346.2. Man must labor for a living: at first everything too easy.

A1420.5. *After Fall first parents fed and clothed from one palm-tree.* Irish myth: Cross; Jewish: Neuman.

A1420.6. *At beginning people start to eat the earth.* Calif. Indian: Gayton and Newman 56.

A1421. *Hoarded game released.* Animals are kept imprisoned by malevolent creature. Released by culture hero. Hindu: Keith 33f.; India: Thompson-Balys; Kodiak: Jochelson JE VI 143, 164, 187, 367; Tonga:

Gifford 91; Hawaii: Beckwith Myth 434f.; S. Am. Indian (Yunca, Peru): Alexander Lat. Am. 229 (fish); Eskimo (Bering Strait): Nelson RBAE XVIII 515, (Greenland): Rink 442, Holm 75, (Cape York): Rasmussen III 51.

A1111. Impounded water.

A1421.0.1. *Hoarded rice made available once more to men by culture hero.* India: Thompson-Balys.

A1421.1. *Man given dominion over beasts.* Jewish: Neuman; India: *Thompson-Balys.

A1421.1.1. *Man rules all animals.* God gives greatest strength to lion, but because of man's wisdom lion is in his power. Lithuanian: Balys Index No. 3110, Legends No. 215.

A1422. *Assignment of edible animals.* Certain animals may be eaten by man. — Hebrew: Leviticus ch 11; Jewish: Neuman; India: *Thompson-Balys; Africa (Ekoi): Talbot 78, 149, (Hottentot): Bleek 73 No. 34.

A1681.2. Why Jews do not eat pork.

A1422.0.1. *Animals sources of food because they were once unfaithful, disobedient wives* of a visitor from god-country. India: Thompson-Balys.

A1422.0.2. *What animals are to be eaten by man.* India: Thompson-Balys.

A1422.1. *Why men may eat hares.* India: *Thompson-Balys.

A1422.1.1. *Why Santals eat entrails of hare.* India: *Thompson-Balys.

A1422.2. *Why Birhors eat flesh of monkeys and baboons.* India: Thompson-Balys.

A1422.3. *Why the wild boar is hunted by man for food:* once a faithless wife killed by her husband. India: Thompson-Balys.

A1423. *Acquisition of vegetables and cereals.* Jewish: Neuman; India: Thompson-Balys; Samoa: Beckwith Myth 439; Isabel Island: ibid. 504; Hawaii: ibid. 61, 63; Tonga: Gifford 194; Easter Island: Métraux Ethnology 364; African (Angola): Chatelain 249, (Gold Coast): Barker and Sinclair 179 No. 35, (Ekoi): Talbot 240, (Ila, Rhodesia): Smith and Dale 348 No. 3; S. Am. Indian (Guarayu): Métraux RMLP XXXIII 147.

A1423.0.1. *Hoarded plants released.* Rarotonga, Cook Island: Beckwith Myth 236; Hawaii: ibid. 290, 432; S. Am. Indian (Cashinawa): Métraux BBAE CXLIII (3) 685.

A1423.1. *Origin of yams* (sweet potatoes, taro). Samoa, Maori, Tonga: Beckwith Myth 101; Kai of New Guinea: ibid. 104; Tonga: Gifford 163, 169; Easter Island: Métraux Ethnology 317.

A1423.2. *Acquisition of rice.* (Cf. A2685.) — India: *Thompson-Balys; Chinese: Eberhard FFC CXX 130f. No. 86.

A1423.3. *Origin of coconut.* Maniliki, Cook Island: Beckwith Myth 256; Tonga: Gifford 182.

A1423.4. *Acquisition of manioc.* Africa (Bushongo): Tardau 249.

A1425. *Origin of seed.* India: Thompson-Balys; S. Am. Indian (Chiriguano): Métraux BBAE CXLIII (3) 484.

A1425.0.1. *Hoarded seeds.* S. Am. Indian (More): Métraux BBAE CXLIII (3) 424.

A1425.1. *All the kinds of seed in a bamboo* that culture hero cuts down. India: Thompson-Balys.

A1426. *Acquisition of food supply — miscellaneous.*

A1426.1. *Discovery of oil.* India: Thompson-Balys; Africa (Bushongo): Torday 249.

A1426.2. *Acquisition of ale.* Irish myth: Cross.

A1426.2.1. *Introduction of brewing.* Irish myth: Cross.

A1426.2.2. *Origin of rice-beer.* India: Thompson-Balys.

A1427. *Acquisition of spiritous liquors.* India: Thompson-Balys; Buddhist myth: Malalasekera I 636: S. Am. Indian (Guarayu): Métraux RMLP XXXIII 147.

A1456. Origin of distilling.

A1427.0.1. *Liquor discovered when birds get drunk.* India: Thompson-Balys.

A1427.0.2. *Liquor discovered by rain-god.* India: Thompson-Balys.

A1427.0.3. *Intoxicating drink first used at the wedding feast of the first couple.* India: Thompson-Balys.

A1427.0.4. *Creator gives liquor to his servant giant to drink.* India: Thompson-Balys.

A1427.1. *Acquisition of brandy.* Devil teaches how to burn brandy. (Cf. A1456.) — Finnish: Aarne FFC VIII 7 No. 31, XXXIII 52 No. 31; Livonian: Loorits FFC LXVI 87 No. 54; Lithuanian: Balys Index No. 3291; India: Thompson-Balys.

A1427.2. *Origin of whiskey.* Lithuanian: Balys Legends No. 340ff.

A1428. *Acquisition of wine.* Greek: Fox 47, 222; India: Thompson-Balys; Chinese: Graham. — Africa (Tshi): Ellis 337, (Fang): Einstein 44, Trilles 162.

A1429. *Acquisition of food supply — miscellaneous.*

A1429.1. *Discovery of oil (edible).* India: Thompson-Balys; Africa (Bushongo): Torday 249.

A1429.2. *Origin of yeast:* wasp stole it from the old woman underneath the earth. India: *Thompson-Balys.

A1429.3. *Acquisition of water.* (Cf. A1111.) — Irish Myth: Cross.

A1429.3.1. *First wells dug.* Irish myth: Cross.

A1429.3.2. *Gods provide drinkable water.* (Cf. A941.) — Hawaii: Beckwith Myth 63f.

A1429.4. *Acquisition of salt.* India: Thompson-Balys; S. Am. Indian (Jivaro): Steward-Métraux BBAE CXLIII (3) 627.

A1430. Acquisition of other necessities.

A2823. Origin of churning stick. A2824. Origin of drum. A2825. Origin of canoes.

A1431. *Origin of coal.* Flemish: DeMeyer FFC XXXVII 84 No. 29; Africa (Fang): Trilles 132.

A1432. *Acquisition of metals.*
A978. Origin of minerals.

A1432.1. *Origin of iron.* Finnish: Kalevale rune 9; India: Thompson-Balys; Jewish: Neuman; Africa (Bushongo): Torday 235.

A1432.1.1. *Iron at first was made for food,* not for weapons. India: Thompson-Balys.

A1432.2. *Acquisition of gold.* Irish myth: Cross; India: Thompson-Balys.

A1432.2.1. *Gold comes from gourd received from fishes.* India: Thompson-Balys.

A1432.3. *Acquisition of brass.* India: Thompson-Balys.

A1432.4. *Acquisition of copper.* India: Thompson-Balys.

A1433. *Acquisition of money.* Jewish: Neuman; India: Thompson-Balys.

A1433.0.1. *First money received from kettle* which two dead men try in vain to carry from hell to heaven. Finnish: Aarne FFC VIII 7 No. 32.

A1433.1. *Origin of gold coins.* Surinam: Penard JAFL XXX 248.

A1433.2. *Origin of silver coins.* India: Thompson-Balys.

A1433.2.1. *Silver coins from pumpkin* received from fishes. India: *Thompson-Balys.

A1433.3. *Origin of shell money.* Mono-Alu: Wheeler 12, 57.

A1435. *Acquisition of habitations.* Irish myth: Cross; India: *Thompson-Balys.

A1435.0.1. *Origin of cave-digging.* Irish myth: Cross.

A1435.1. *Acquisition of guest-houses.* Irish myth: Cross.

A1435.2. *Origin of raths* (duns, stone forts). Irish myth: Cross.

A1435.2.1. *Raths marked out with brooch.* Irish myth: Cross.

A1435.3. *Origin of grass huts to replace caves as dwellings.* Papua: Ker 135.

A1436. *Acquisition of vehicles.* Irish myth: Cross.

A1437. *Acquisition of clothing.* India: *Thompson-Balys; Eskimo (Bering Strait): Nelson RBAE XVIII 456.

A1438. *Origin of medicine (healing).* Greek: Fox 279ff.; Irish: MacCulloch Celtic 70f.; Icel.: MacCulloch Eddic 202, 205f.; Jewish: Neuman; Chinese: Ferguson 14; Hawaii: Beckwith Myth 116f., 119; N. A. Indian (Joshua): Frachtenberg JAFL XXVIII 230; S. Am. Indian (Toba): Métraux MAFLS XL 3, 69; (Manasi): Métraux BBAE CXLIII (3) 393.
A454. God of healing. D1342. Magic object gives health. D1500. Magic object controls disease. D2161. Magic healing power. F950. Marvelous cures.

A1438.1. *Origin of medicine: shaman sent down by the Creator equipped with it.* India: Thompson-Balys.

A1439. *Acquisition of other necessities.*

A1439.1. *Acquisition of marble.* India: Thompson-Balys.

A1439.2. *Origin of dyes.* India: Thompson-Balys; Easter Is.: Métraux Ethnology 317.

A1439.3. *Origin of rubber* S. Am. Indian (Chiriguano): Métraux BBAE CXLIII (3) 484.

A1439.4. *Origin of cauldrons.* Irish myth: Cross.

D1171.2. Magic cauldron (kettle).

A1440. Acquisition of crafts. Irish: MacCulloch Celtic 137; Icel.: Boberg; Jewish: Neuman; India: Thompson-Balys.

A141. God as craftsman. A450.1. God "of many arts". A541. Culture hero teaches arts and crafts.

A1440.1. *Assignment of crafts and professions:* creator opens shop and from it distributes plough, pen, bottle, pair of scales, fishing-net and loom to various groups. India: Thompson-Balys..

A1440.2. *Origin of distribution of work.* India: Thompson-Balys.

A1440.3. Patriarchs because of long life made inventions. Tupper and Ogle Map 4.

A1323. Long span of life for first men.

A1441. *Acquisition of agriculture.* India: *Thompson-Balys; Chinese: Graham; Greek: *Grote I 163; Jewish: Neuman; Marquesas: Handy 128; Kai of New Guinea: Beckwith Myth 104; Philippine (Tinguian): Cole 177. — S. Am. Indian (Guarayu): Métraux BBAE CXLIII (3) 437, (Guaporé R.): Lévi-Strauss ibid. (3) 379, (Tupinamba): Métraux ibid. (3) 132, (Cubeo): ibid. (3) 798, (Tapirape): Wagley-Galvão ibid. (3) 178, (Cashinawa): Métraux ibid. (3) 685.

A432.0.1. God plants field. A541.2. Culture hero as god of agriculture.

A1441.1. *Origin of plowing.* Greek: Fox 171, Alphabet of Tales No. 654; Jewish: Neuman; India: Thompson-Balys; Hawaii: Beckwith Myth 69; S. Am. Indian (Caingang): Métraux BBAE CXLIII (1) 473.

A1441.2. *Origin of custom of yoking oxen.* Irish myth: Cross.

A1441.3. *Origin of water wheel and rice growing.* Chinese: Graham.

A1441.4. *Origin of sowing and planting.* Greek myth: Grote I 41; Kauai: Beckwith Myth 367; S. Am. Indian (Toba): Métraux MAFLS XL 115.

A1441.4.1. *Origin of periodic sowing.* India: Thompson-Balys.

A1441.5. *Origin of onion-growing.* Korean: Zong in-Sob 21 No. 10.

A1442. *Origin of milling.* (Cf. A1446.5.3.) Irish myth: Cross; Jewish: Neuman.

A1443. *Origin of domestication of animals.* Lithuanian: Balys Index No. 3108; Greek: Aeschylus Prometheus Bound, lines 462—465; Jewish: Neuman; India: Thompson-Balys; Africa: Stanley 43, 196, (Bushongo): Torday 242f., (Fang): Tessman 18f.

A1421.1. Man given dominion over beasts. A1422. Assignment of edible animals.

A1443.1. *First shepherder.* Irish myth: Cross; Jewish: Neuman; India: Thompson-Balys.

A1445. *Acquisition of building crafts.*
A1435. Acquisition of habitations.

A1445.1. *Origin of boat-building.* Greek: Aeschylus Prometheus Bound, line 468; Jewish: Neuman; Africa (Benga): Nassau No. 3, (Fang): Trilles 159; Marquesas: Handy 128; Hawaii: Beckwith Myth 15; Samoa: ibid. 271.

A1445.2. *Origin of carpentry.* Irish myth: Cross; Greek: Aeschylus Prometheus Bound line 447; Hawaii: Beckwith Myth 70.
A143. Carpenter (wright) of the gods. P456. Carpenter.

A1445.2.1. *Why carpenters are found everywhere:* flood scatters them on raft over world. Tonga: Gifford 201, Beckwith Myth 317.

A1445.2.2. *Man learns housebuilding from wasp.* S. Am. Indian (Cashinawa): Métraux BBAE CXLIII (3) 685.

A1446. *Acquisition of tools.* India: *Thompson-Balys.

A1446.0.1. *Culture hero steals tools for men.* S. Am. Indian (Tapirape): Wagley-Galvão BBAE CXLIII (3) 178.

A1446.1. *Origin of the saw.* Invented by devil. — Flemish: DeMeyer FFC XXXVII 85 No. 30b.

A1446.2. *Origin of the axe.* Irish myth: Cross; Jewish: Neuman; India: Thompson-Balys; Carib: Penard JAFL XXX 258.

A1446.3. *Origin of the ox-goad.* India: Thompson-Balys.

A1446.4. *Origin of the adze.* India: Thompson-Balys.

A1446.5. *Acquisition of household implements.* Irish myth: Cross; India: Thompson-Balys.

A1446.5.1. *Origin of the broom.* India: Thompson-Balys.

A1446.5.2. *Origin of the pestle.* India: Thompson-Balys.

A1446.5.3. *Origin of the grindstone.* India: Thompson-Balys.

A1446.5.4. *Origin of the winnowing-fan.* India: Thompson-Balys.

A1446.5.5. *Origin of baskets.* India: Thompson-Balys.

A1446.5.6. *Origin of the oil-press.* India: Thompson-Balys.

A1447. *Origin of metal-working.* Hebrew: Genesis 4:22; Greek: Fox 171; Jewish: Neuman; India: *Thompson-Balys.
A142. Smith of the gods. A1465.3.2. Origin of metal ornaments. P447. Smith.

A1447.1. *Origin of the bellows.* India: Thompson-Balys.

A1447.2. *Origin of blacksmith work.* Irish myth: Cross.

A1447.3. *Origin of goldsmith work.* Irish myth: Cross.

A1447.4. *Origin of smelting.* Africa: Bouvergnes 16, (Babuka): Einstein 166, (Bushongo): Torday 235, 248.

A1448. *Origin of mining.* Irish myth: Cross.

A1451. *Origin of pottery.* Jewish: Neuman; India: *Thompson-Balys; African (Basuto): Jacottet 50 No. 7; S. Am. Indian (Paressi): Métraux BBAE CXLIII (3) 359, (Yagua): Steward-Métraux ibid. (3) 736, (Jivaro): ibid. (3) 627, (Toba): Métraux MAFLS XL 86.

A1452. *Origin of charcoal making.* India: Thompson-Balys.

A1453. *Origin of cloth-making.* India: Thompson-Balys.

A1453.1. *Origin of spinning.* Greek: Fox 171, *Grote I 163; S. Am. Indian (Chibcha): Kroeber BBAE CXLIII (2) 909.

A2091.1. Arachne transformed to spider. Vies with goddess in spinning.

A1453.2. *Origin of weaving.* Irish myth: Cross; Greek: Fox 171; Finnish: Aarne FFC VIII 7 No. 27; India: *Thompson-Balys; S. Am. Indian (Toba): Métraux MAFLS XL 113, (Cashinawa): Métraux BBAE CXLIII (3) 685.

A1453.3. *Origin of dyeing.* Irish myth: Cross.

A1453.4. *Origin of leaf-dress.* Jewish: Neuman; India: Thompson-Balys.

A1453.5. *Origin of bark-cloth.* India: Thompson-Balys.

A1453.6. *Creator paints on clay models of men clothes that they are to wear.* S. Am. Indian (Inca): Rowe BBAE CXLIII (2) 315.

A1453.7. *Origin of raffia cloth.* Africa (Bushongo): Torday 249.

A1454. *Origin of shoemaking.* Finnish: Aarne FFC VIII 7 No. 28; Jewish: Neuman.

A1455. *Origin of cooking.* Greek: Grote I 163; India: *Thompson-Balys; Marquesas: Handy 104, 128; S. Am. Indian (Toba): Métraux MAFLS XL 108f.; Africa (Ekoi): Talbot 373 (water for cooking.)

A1455.1. *Origin of the domestic hearth.* India: Thompson-Balys.

A1456. *Origin of distilling.* Learned from devil. (Cf. A1427.2.) — Flemish: DeMeyer FFC XXXVII 85 No. 31; cf. Livonian: Loorits FFC LXVI 86, 87 No. 52, 53; India: Thompson-Balys; S. Am. Indian (Toba): Métraux MAFLS XL 54.

A1457. *Origin of fishing.* Jewish: Neuman; India: Thompson-Balys; S. Am. Indian (Cubao): BBAE CXLIII (3) 798.

A1457.1. *Origin of the fish hook.* Easter Island: Métraux Ethnology 317, 363; Tahltan: Teit JAFL XXXII 210.

A1457.2. *Origin of custom of catching fish by day as well as by night.* Irish myth: Cross.

A1457.3. *Origin of the net for fishing.* Icel.: MacCulloch Eddic 146; Maori: Clark 27f.; Tonga: Gifford 16.

A1457.4. *Origin of fishing stations.* Hawaii: Beckwith Myth 19, 22f.

A1457.5. *Origin of fish-traps.* Hawaii: Beckwith Myth 194f.

A1457.6. *Origin of fish ponds.* Hawaii: Beckwith Myth 19.

A1458. *Origin of hunting.* India: Thompson-Balys; New Hebrides: Codrington 368; S. Am. Indian (Yagua): Steward-Métraux BBAE CXLIII (3) 736, (Toba): Métraux ibid. (1) 368, MAFLS XL 3, 84.

A1458.1. *Origin of pitfall.* Irish myth: Cross.

A1459. *Acquisition of crafts — miscellaneous.*

A1459.1. *Acquisition of weapons.* Irish myth: Cross; Jewish: Neuman.

A1459.1.1. *Origin of bows and arrows.* India: *Thompson-Balys; Chinese: Graham.

A1459.1.2. *Introduction of broad-headed spears into Leinster.* Irish myth: Cross.

A1459.1.2.1. *Origin of obsidian-tipped spears.* Easter Is.: Métraux Ethnology 376.

A1459.1.3. *Origin of sling-stones.* Irish myth: Cross.

A1459.1.4. *Invention of gai bulga.* Irish myth: Cross.
F832.1.1. Gai bulga.

A1459.1.5. *Origin of horse-whips.* Irish myth: Cross.
A1535.6. Origin of horse-racing.

A1459.2. *Acquisition of seamanship* (sailing, etc.). Hawaii: Beckwith Myth 86.

A1459.3. *Acquisition of sorcery.* Hawaii: Beckwith Myth 115.
D1710. Possession of magic powers.

A1460. Acquisition of arts.

A1460.1. *Arts taught man by angel.* Jewish: Neuman.
A465. God of the arts.

A1461. *Acquisition of music.* Wallaschek Sagen und Märchen über den Ursprung der Musik (Leipzig 1903). — Irish myth: Cross; Jewish: Neuman; India: Thompson-Balys.

A1461.1. *Origin of violin.* Flemish: DeMeyer FFC XXXVII 84 No. 30a; India: Thompson-Balys.

A1461.2. *Origin of lyre.* Hermes makes it from a tortoise. — Greek: Fox 192, Frazer Apollodorus II 9 n. 2. — Finnish: Kalevala rune 40 (from bones of a pike); cf. rune 44.

A1461.2.1. *Origin of harp.* Irish myth: Cross; Jewish: Neuman.
A465.2.0.1. God as harper. F262.3.1. Fairy as harper. P427.10. Harper.

A1461.3. *Origin of organ.* Finnish: Aarne FFC VIII 7 No. 30; Irish myth: Cross.

A1461.4. *Origin of the use of the rattle.* Ojibwa: Skinner JAFL XXXII 290.

A1461.5. *Origin of whistle.* Irish myth: Cross.

A1461.6. *Origin of shepherd's pipe.* Greek: Fox 267f.

A1461.7. *Origin of nose-flute.* Hawaii: Beckwith Myth 538.

A1462. *Origin of dancing.* India: Thompson-Balys.

A1464. *Origin of literary arts.* Irish myth: Cross.

A1464.1. *Acquisition of poetry.* Irish myth: Cross; Icel.: Boberg.
A465.1. God of poetry. P427.7. Poet.

A1464.1.1. *First poetry composed in imitation of tones of hammer on anvil.* Irish myth: Cross.

A1464.2. *Origin of hymn.* Irish myth: Cross.
D1275.3. Magic hymn.

A1464.2.1. *Origin of particular song.* India: Thompson-Balys.

A1464.3. *Origin of satire.* Irish myth: Cross.
D1273. Magic formula (charm). D1275. Magic song. M400.1. Satire.

A1465. *Origin of decorative art.*

A1465.1. *Origin of tatooing.* India: Thompson-Balys; Maori: Dixon 73, Clark 139.

A1465.2. *Origin of embroidery.* Irish myth: Cross.

A1465.3. *Origin of ornaments.* India: Thompson-Balys; Jewish: Neuman.

A1465.3.1. *Origin of gadaba ornaments.* India: Thompson-Balys.

A1465.3.2. *Origin of designs on cloth.* Hawaii: Beckwith Myth 100.

A1465.3.3. *Origin of metal ornaments.* India: Thompson-Balys.
A142. Smith of the gods. A1447. Origin of metal working.

A1465.4. *Origin of polishing stone.* Maori: Clark 103.

A1465.5. *Origin of wood carving.* Maori: Clark 114.

A1465.6. *Origin of masks.* Africa (Bushongo): Torday 250; (Bakuba): Einstein 163f.

A1466. *Origin of church bells.*
V115. Church bells.

A1466.1. *First church bell built on model of bluebell.* Finnish-Swedish: Wessman 72 No. 606.

A1468. *Origin of games of skill (indoor).*

A1468.1. *Invention of chess game.* Irish myth: Cross.
Z21.1. Origin of chess.

A1470. Beginning of social relationships.
A1500. Origin of customs. P. Society.

A1471. *Origin of commerce.* Irish myth: Cross; Jewish: Neuman; India: Thompson-Balys; Africa (Benga): Nassau No. 3.

A1471.1. *Origin of trade between two places.* India: Thompson-Balys.

A1471.2. *Origin of weights and measures.* Jewish: Neuman.

A1472. *Beginning of division of labor.*

A1472.1. *Division of labor: religious and lay activities.* Jewish: Neuman; India: *Thompson-Balys.

A1473. *Origin of slavery.* Jewish: Neuman.

A1480. Acquisition of wisdom and learning.

A1481. *Origin of human wisdom.* It is kept hidden by monster and is later stolen. It escapes and spreads through the world. (Cf. A1111, A1421.) — Africa (Gold Coast): Barker and Sinclair 33 No. 2.
A461. God (goddess) of wisdom.

A1482. *Origin of language.* Irish myth: Cross; Jewish: Neuman.
A1333. Confusion of tongues. A1616.2. Origin of Irish language. D1815. Magic knowledge of strange tongues.

A1482.1. *Hebrew the language of the inhabitants of heaven.* Irish myth: Cross; Jewish: Neuman.

B212.0.1. All kinds of animals understand language of heaven. V249.2.2. Hebrew, the language of the angels.

A1484. *Origin of reading and writing.* Jewish: Neuman; India: Thompson-Balys.

A1484.1. *Origin of ogam inscriptions.* Irish myth: Cross.

A465.3.1.1. God of eloquence and learning as inventor of ogam alphabet. A541.1. Culture hero invents and teaches the Irish language. D1266.1.1. Magic ogam writing.

A1484.2. *Origin of alphabet.* Jewish: Neuman.

A1485. *How people learned about calculating time and the seasons.* Chinese: Graham.

A1487. *Origin of sciences.* Jewish: Neuman.

A1487.1. *Origin of astronomy.* Jewish: Neuman.

A1487.1.1. *Origin of astrology.* Jewish: Neuman.

A1487.2. *Origin of medical books.* Jewish: *Neuman.

A1438. Origin of medicine.

A1490. Acquisition of culture — miscellaneous.

A1491. *Origin of art of walking on stilts.* Marquesas: Handy 114.

A1495. *Origin of outdoor games.*

A1495.1. *Origin of ball game.* Mangaia (Cook Island): Beckwith myth: 336.

A1500—A1599. Origin of customs.

A1500. Origin of customs — general. Irish: Beal XXI 324—326; Jewish: Neuman.

A545. Culture hero establishes customs. P600. Customs.

A1501. *Tribal customs established by diviner.* (Man who sees future.) — India: *Thompson-Balys.

D1712. Soothsayer.

A1502. *All customs for the year established.* India: Thompson-Balys.

A1503. *Creator gives men customs and songs before their emergence.* S. Am. Indian (Inca): Rowe BBAE CXLIII (3) 315.

A1234. Mankind emerges from ground.

A1510. Origin of eating customs. India: Thompson-Balys.

A1422. Assignment of edible animals. A1539.1. Origin of seating arrangements in royal hall.

A1511. *Origin of time for meals.* Esthonian: Aarne FFC XXV 141 No. 17; Jewish: Neuman.

A1511.1. *Mealtimes from confused message from God.* India: Thompson-Balys; Chinese: Eberhard FFC CXX 120 No. 77.

A1512. *Origin of custom of not eating in the dark:* devil eats from plates. India: *Thompson-Balys.

A1514. *Origin of compulsory drinking at feast.* Jewish: Neuman.

A1514.1. *Origin of drinking ceremonies.* Tonga: Gifford 35, 47, 72, 74.

A1515. *Origin of custom of eating certain animals.*

A1515.1. *Origin of custom of eating flesh of buffalo.* India: Thompson-Balys.

A1516. *Origin of cannibalism.* Maori: Clark 15; Easter Is.: Métraux Ethnology 377.

G10. Cannibalism.

A1517. *Origin of eating tabus.* Tonga: Gifford 80; New Guinea: Ker 13, 52; Africa: Bouveignes 15.

C220. Tabu: eating certain things.

A1518. *Why food is cooked.* New Guinea: Ker 97.

A1520. Origin of hunting and fishing customs. Irish myth: Cross.

A1525. *Origin of customs: game-division.* Africa (Ekoi): Talbot 243f.

A1526. *Why Indians cache their meat.* Chitimacha: Swanton JAFL XXX 467.

A1527. *Custom of catching fish with nets.* S. Am. Indian (Toba): Metraux MAFLS XL 53.

A1528. *Why one presents stranger with first fish caught.* Hawaii: Beckwith Myth 22.

A1530. Origin of social ceremonials.

A1533. *Origin of peace ceremonies.* Tahltan: Teit JAFL XXXII 213.

A1534. *Origin of "guesting."* Irish myth: Cross.

A1435.1. Acquisition of guest-houses.

A1535. *Origin of secular feasts.* Jewish: Neuman.

V70. Religious feasts and fasts.

A1535.1. *Origin of the potlatch.* A feast of the Indians of the Northwest Coast of America in which large amounts of property are given away to the guests. These feasts must be returned. Quileute: Farrand JAFL XXXII 258.

A1535.2. *Origin of games and fairs.* Irish myth: Cross.

A1535.3. *Origin of games (fair) at Telltown (Tailtiu).* Irish myth: Cross.

V70.3. Festival of Lugnasad (Telltown, Tailtiu).

A1535.4. *Origin of feast of Tara.* Irish myth: Cross.

A1541.3. Origin of Hallowe'en. V70.5. Festival of Samhain (Hallowe'en).

A1535.5. *Festival of Beltane.* Irish myth: Cross.

A1535.6. *Origin of horse-racing.* Irish myth: Cross.

A1537. *Origin of social etiquette.* Jewish: Neuman.

A1537.1. *Origin of wishing long life to person who sneezes.* Buddhist myth: Malalasekera I 731.

A1539. *Origin of social ceremonials — miscellaneous.*

A1539.1. *Origin of seating arrangements in royal hall.* Irish myth: Cross.
A1510. Origin of seating customs. P632. Customs concerning recognition of rank.

A1540. **Origin of religious ceremonials.** Flemish: DeMeyer FFC XXXVII 85 Nos. 36a, 43d. — India: *Thompson-Balys; Philippine (Tinguian): Cole 171f.

A1541. *Origin of religious feasts and fasts.* Irish myth: Cross; Jewish: Neuman; India: Thompson-Balys.
V70. Religious feasts and fasts.

A1541.1. *Origin of feast for the dead.* (Cf. A1543.1.) — Tahltan: Teit JAFL XXXII 238.

A1541.1.1. *Origin of grave-digging.* Irish myth: Cross.

A1541.1.2. *Communion feast to placate dead.* India: Thompson-Balys.

A1541.2. *Origin of feasts in honor of certain god (goddess).* Irish myth: Cross; India: Thompson-Balys.
A1535.3. Origin of games (fair) at Telltown (Tailtiu).

A1541.2.1. *Origin of feast for Zise.* India: Thompson-Balys.

A1541.3. *Origin of Hallowe'en.* Irish myth: Cross.
V70.5. Festival of Samhain (Hallowe'en, Tara [Temau]).

A1541.3.1. *Origin of Hallowe'en as a mystic night.* Irish myth: Cross.

A1541.4. *Origin of Sabbath.* Jewish: Neuman.

A1541.4.0.1. *Holy day established on seventh day.* Hawaii: Beckwith Myth 45.

A1541.4.1. *Origin of Sabbath from a feast to Venus.* Spanish Exempla: Keller.

A1541.4.2. *Origin of dragon festival.* Chinese: Eberhard FFC CXX 238 No. 185.

A1541.5. *Origin of passover.* Jewish: Neuman.

A1541.6. *Origin of Pentecost.* Jewish: Neuman.

A1541.7. *Origin of religious fasts.* Jewish: Neuman.

A1542. *Origin of religious dances.* Jewish: Neuman; India: Thompson-Balys; Hawaii: Beckwith Myth 359.

A1542.1. *Origin of particular manner of dancing.* India: Thompson-Balys.

A1542.2. *Origin of particular dance.*

A1542.2.1. *Origin of crocodile dance.* Africa (Fang): Einstein 48.

A1543. *Origin of religious songs (chants)*

A1543.1. *Origin of the death chant.* (Cf. A1541.1.) — Tahltan: Teit JAFL XXXII 239; Irish myth: Cross.
V69.2. Funeral song sung over dead.

A1544. *Origin of religious images (idols).* Jewish: Neuman; India: *Thompson-Balys; Hawaii: Beckwith Myth 516; Easter Is.: Métraux Ethnology 261.

A1544.0.1. *Why Jews do not worship idols.* Jewish: Neuman.

A1545. *Origin of sacrifices.* Greek: *Grote I 25f., 28; Irish myth: Cross; Icel.: Boberg; Jewish: Neuman; India: Thompson-Balys; Africa (Ekoi): Talbot 36, 59, 199.
S260. Sacrifices. V10. Religious sacrifices.

A1545.1. *Regulations for sacrifices.* Hebrew: Leviticus ch. 1—7; Greek: *Grote I 25f., 28; Jewish: Neuman; Africa (Ekoi): Talbot 64, 70, 198, 397; Tahltan: Teit JAFL XXXII 238.

A1545.2. *Animal substituted for human sacrifice.* Jewish: Neuman; India: Thompson-Balys.

A1545.3. *Origin of animal sacrifices.* India: *Thompson-Balys.

A1545.3.1. *Origin of dog sacrifices.* India: Thompson-Balys.

A1545.3.2. *Origin of calf sacrifices.* India: Thompson-Balys.

A1545.3.3. *Origin of cock sacrifice.* Chinese: Eberhard FFC CXX 120 No. 78.

A1545.4. *Custom of sacrifice begun at harvest and sowing times.* India: Thompson-Balys.

A1545.5. *Origin of human sacrifice.* India: *Thompson-Balys; Hawaii: Beckwith Myth 370.

A1545.5.1. *Origin of the custom of wife self-sacrifice (suttee).* India: *Thompson-Balys.
P16.4.1. Suttee.

A1545.6. *Why animal bones only are used in sacrifice.* Greek: Grote I 59.

A1546. *Origin of worship.* (Cf. V0—V99.) — Irish myth: Cross; Jewish: *Neuman.

A1546.0.1. *Origin of symbols of worship.* India: Thompson-Balys.

A1546.0.2. *Origin of prayers.* Jewish: *Neuman; Hawaii: Beckwith Myth 19ff., 69; Easter Is.: Métraux Ethnology 313.

A1546.0.3. *Origin of calf-statues in temples.* Chinese: Eberhard FFC CXX 136.

A1546.1. *Origin of worship of rivers.* India: *Thompson-Balys.

A1546.2. *Origin of worship of particular god(s).* India: Thompson-Balys.

A1546.3. *Origin of Christian worship.*

A1546.3.1. *First convert to Christianity in Ireland.* Irish myth: Cross.
V331.0.2. Three (two) Irishmen who believed in Christianity before the coming of St. Patrick.

A1546.3.2. *First monk, first pilgrim.* Irish myth: Cross.

A1546.4. *Origin of Jewish worship.* Jewish: Neuman.

A1546.5. *Origin of worship from holy books.* India: Thompson-Balys.

A1546.6. *Origin of fire worship.* Jewish: Neuman.

A1546.7. *Origin of animal worship.*

A1546.7.1. *Origin of crocodile worship.* Africa (Fang): Einstein 50.

A1547. *Origin of funeral customs.* Jewish: Neuman; India: *Thompson-Balys.

A1541.1.1. Origin of grave-digging. A1543.1. Origin of death chant. V60. Funeral rites.

A1547.1. *Origin of funeral sacrifices.* (Cf. A1545.) — India: Thompson-Balys.

A1547.2. *Origin of lute-playing at funerals.* India: Thompson-Balys.

A1547.3. *Origin of lamentations for the dead.* India: Thompson-Balys.

A1548. *Origin of tithing.* Jewish: Neuman.

A1549. *Origin of religious ceremonials — miscellaneous.*

A1549.1. *Origin of commemorative religious meal* (to memorialize death or actions of ancestor or holy person). India: Thompson-Balys.

G13.1. Ritual cannibalism: the corpse of a hero (demi-god) eaten to acquire his strength.

A1549.2. *Origin of sundry religious ceremonials* — Jewish: Neuman.

A1549.3. *Origin of religious games.* Hawaii: Beckwith Myth 40.

A1549.4. *Origin of penance for sin.* Jewish: Neuman.

A1550. Origin of customs of courtship and marriage. India: *Thompson-Balys.

T130. Marriage customs.

A1551. *Why women do not woo.* Esthonian: FFC XXV 142 No. 18; Jewish: Neuman; S. Am. Indian (Toba): Métraux MAFLS XL 54.

A1552. *Marriage between close relatives.*

A1552.1. *Why brothers and sisters do not marry.* India: *Thompson-Balys.

F1075. Blood of brother and sister (and smoke from their funeral pyres) refuses to mingle. T100. Marriage T415. Brother-sister incest.

A1552.2. *Origin of royal marriages with close relatives.* Tonga: Gifford 187.

A1552.3. *Brother-sister marriage of children of first parents.* Lithuanian: Balys Legends No. 68.

A1270. Primeval human pair. T415.5. Brother-sister marriage.

A1553. *Origin of exogamy and endogamy.*

A1553.1. *Origin of exogamy.* India: Thompson-Balys.

A1554. *Origin of love-songs.* China: Eberhard FFC CXX 118.

A1555. *Origin of marriage.* Finnish: Aarne FFC VIII 7 No. 26, XXXIII 52 No. 26; Flemish: DeMeyer FFC XXXVII 84 No. 26; Irish myth: Cross; India: Thompson-Balys; Chinese: Graham.

T100. Marriage. H317. Long term of service imposed on suitor.

A1555.1. *Origin of wedding ceremony.* Jewish: Neuman; India: Thompson-Balys.

A1555.1.1. *Origin of custom of throwing fruits on bridal couple.* Jewish: Neuman.

A1555.2. *Origin of custom of purchasing wives.* Irish Myth: Cross.

P532.5. Women as tribute. T141.2. Wives exchanged.

A1555.3. *Why umbrellas are used to welcome bride to new home.* Chinese: Graham.

A1556. *Origin of sexual restrictions.* India: Thompson-Balys.
A1350. Origin of sex functions. C100. Sex tabu. T130. Marriage customs.

A1556.1. *Beginning of law against rape.* India: Thompson-Balys.

A1556.2. *Origin of celibacy.* Lithuanian: Balys Legends No. 109.
T300. Chastity and celibacy.

A1556.3. *Origin of adultery.* It occurs in the primeval human family. Lithuanian: Balys Legends No. 69.
K1500. Deception connected with adultery. T481. Adultery.

A1556.3.1. *Origin of decrying female sinners.* Irish myth: Cross.

A1556.4. *Origin of jus primae noctis.* Jewish: Neuman.
T161. Jus primae noctis.

A1557. *Why woman is master of her husband.* (Cf. A1372.9.) Africa (Ekoi): Talbot 98.

A1558. *Origin of divorce.* Africa (Akan-Ashanti): Rattray 242 No. 62.

A1559. *Origin of customs of courtship and marriage — miscellaneous.*

A1559.1. *Origin of the village dormitory.* India: Thompson-Balys; Chinese: Graham.

A1560. Origin of customs connected with birth. India: Thompson-Balys.
T500. Conception and birth.

A1562. *Origin of medical treatment during pregnancy.*

A1562.1. *Origin of charms for pregnant women.* Africa (Ekoi): Talbot 181.

A1565. *Origin of diet during confinement.* Africa (Basuto): Jacottet 54.

A1566. *Parents learn how to wean their children.* S. A. Indian (Toba): Métraux MAFLS XL 120.

A1567. *Origin of circumcision.* Jewish: Neuman.

A1567.1. *Why dust is strewn on wound at circumcision.* Jewish: Neuman.

A1570. Origin of regulations within the family.
P200. The family.

A1571. *Origin of code of conduct between husband and wife.*

A1571.1. *Why husband and wife shall not exchange hats.* Africa (Ekoi): Talbot 117.

A1575. *Origin of relation of mother and children.*
P230. Parents and children.

A1575.1. *Why a mother has prior claim on her children.* Africa (Ekoi): Talbot 101.

A1576. *Origin of code of conduct for parents toward children of polygamous marriage.* India: Thompson-Balys.

A1577. *Origin of personal names.* Irish myth: Cross; Jewish: Neuman; Liberian: Bundy JAFL XXXII 422.
A1296. Adam at first nameless.

A1577.1. *Adam named from first letters of four stars.* Irish myth: Cross.

A1578. *Origin of family insignia.*

A1578.1. *Origin of family crests.* Tahltan: Teit JAFL XXXII *235—238.

A1579. *Origin of regulation within the family — miscellaneous.*

A1579.1. *Why children are not left alone in the house to sleep.* Marquesas: Handy 51.

A1580. Origin of laws. Irish myth: Cross; India: Thompson-Balys.
A530. Culture hero establishes law and order. A1471. Origin of commerce.

A1580.1. *Origin of justice.* Irish myth: Cross.

A1580.1.1. *First judgment in Ireland.* Irish myth: Cross.

A1580.2. *Laws given directly by deity.* Jewish: Neuman.

A1581. *Origin of special penalties.*

A1581.1. *Origin of penalty for murder.* Africa (Ekoi): Talbot 401.
A1336. Origin of murder. Q211. Murder punished.

A1581.2. *Origin of penalty for theft.* India: Thompson-Balys.

A1582. *Origin of government.* India: Thompson-Balys.
P500. Government.

A1583. *Origin of kingdom.* Irish myth: Cross.

A1585. *Origin of laws:* division of property in a family. India: Thompson-Balys.

A1586. *First surety.* Irish myth: Cross.

A1587. *Origin of tabus.* Mono-Alu: Wheeler 67; Papua: Kerr 90.
C. Tabu.

A1587.1. *Tabus instituted by God or creator.* India: Thompson-Balys.

A1587.2. *Tabus instituted by culture hero.* S. A. Indian (Tupinamba): Métraux BBAE CXLIII (3) 132.

A1589. *Origin of laws — miscellaneous.*

A1589.1. *Why women are disqualified as witness in court.* Jewish: Neuman.

A1590. Origin of other customs.
H41. Recognition of royalty by personal characteristics or traits. H71. Marks of royalty.

A1591. *Origin of burial.* Irish myth: Cross; Icel.: Boberg; Finnish: Aarne FFC VII 9 No. 41, XXXIII 53 No. 41. — India: Thompson-Balys; Africa (Ekoi): Talbot 226; Maidu: Dixon BAM XVII 44 No. 1.
A1547. Origin of funeral rites. V60. Funeral rites.

A1591.1. *Burial learned from watching raven bury its dead.* Dh I 249.

A1592. *Origin of cremation.* Icel.: Boberg; India: Thompson-Balys; Tahltan: Teit JAFL XXXII 239ff.

A1593. *Why men no longer know time of death.* Custom changed when men began to repair fences with stalks when they knew they were to die the next day. — Irish myth: Cross; *Babler Sudetendeutsche Zs. f. Vksk. VII (1934) 171ff.; Lithuanian: Balys Index No. 3062, Legends Nos. 115—120. — Esthonian: Aarne FFC XXV 142 No. 19; Livonian: Loorits FFC LXVI 84 No. 37.

A1594. *Origin of physicians.* India: Thompson-Balys.

A1594.1. *Establishment of doctor's fees.* Africa (Ekoi): Talbot 279.

A1595. *Origin of tatooing.* Easter Island: Métraux Ethnology 316f., 367.

A1596. *Origin of army.* Irish myth: Cross.
A1459.1. Acquisition of weapons. P551. Army.

A1596.1. *Origin of custom of paying soldiers.* Irish myth: Cross.

A1597. *Origin of custom of wearing a beard.* Irish myth: Cross.
C565. Tabus of bearded men.

A1597.1. *First men without beards:* Cain, Abel. Irish myth: Cross; Jewish: Neuman.
F545.4. Beardless men. K1821.4. Youths wear false beards. Q566.2.1. Mark of Cain. Z212. Beardless hero.

A1597.2. *Origin of custom of shaving.* Irish myth: Cross.

A1598. *Origin of customs of hospitality.* Jewish: Neuman.
P320. Hospitality.

A1599. *Origin of additional customs.*

A1599.1. *Origin of warning beacon.* Irish myth: Cross.

A1599.2. *Origin of erection of monuments to mark boundaries.* Irish myth: Cross; Jewish: Neuman.

A1599.3. *Why women wear veils in India.* India: Thompson-Balys.

A1599.4. *Why the face must be wiped dry after washing.* Lithuanian: Balys Index No. 3070; Legends No. 122.

A1599.5. *Why in addressing anyone the second plural should be used.* Lithuanian: Balys Index No. 3072.

A1599.6. *Why earthworms are killed whenever earth is dug.* India: Thompson-Balys.

A1599.7. *Why dagger must be always cleaned on the inside of the robe.* India: Thompson-Balys.

A1599.8. *Inequalities of fortune among men, otherwise the work of the world will not go on.* India: Thompson-Balys.
U0—U99. Lifes inequalities.

A1599.9. *Origin of custom of committing suicide by strangling.* India: Thompson-Balys.

A1599.10. *Origin of witchcraft.* India: Thompson-Balys.

A1599.11. *Origin of quarrels.* India: Thompson-Balys.
A2575. Quarrels introduced among animals.

A1599.11.1. *Origin of war.* Africa (Togo): Einstein 8.

A1599.12. *Origin of covenanted friendships.* India: Thompson-Balys.
P311. Sworn brethren.

A1599.13. *Why certain caste is kind to animals.* India: *Thompson-Balys.

A1599.14. *Why a lamp must be lighted in a house at least every fortnight.* — India: Thompson-Balys.

A1599.15. *Origin of begging.* India: Thompson-Balys.

A1599.16. *Origin of allusive expression for the story of gods' incest and trickery.* Marquesas: Handy 123.

A1600—A1699. Distribution and differentiation of peoples.

A1600. Distribution and differentiation of peoples — general. Irish myth: Cross; India: Thompson-Balys.

A1601. *Number of nations of the world* (70, 72, 140). Jewish: Neuman.

A1610. Origin of various tribes. Icel.: MacCulloch Eddic 328; Persian: Carnoy 298. — Finnish: Aarne FFC XXXIII 52 No. 12**; Livonian: Loorits FFC LXVI 85 No. 39; Lappish: Qvigstad FFC LX 34 No. 7, 35 No. 9; Flemish: DeMeyer FFC XXXVII 85 No. 43a; India: Thompson Balys

A1610.1. *Unworthy origin ascribed to hostile tribes.* *Dh II 184; Jewish: Neuman; S. Am. Indian (Paressi): Métraux BBAE CXLIII (3) 359.

A1610.1.1. *Foreigners heads exchanged with those of devils in fight.* Lithuanian: Balys Legends Nos. 94ff.

A1610.2. *Couples placed to establish tribes.* Calif. Indian: Gayton and Newman 54, 92, 94, 98.

A1610.3. *Origin of races from mixed offspring of animal marriage.* Eskimo (Cape York): Rasmussen III 85, 125, 200, (East Greenland): Rasmussen I 363, Holm 57.
B601.2. Marriage to dog.

A1610.4. *Tribes from fruits of various trees.* S. Am. Indian (Brazil): Oberg 108.

A1610.5. *Different tribes result from choice of things Sun offers people.* S. Am. Indian (Bacairi): Lévi-Strauss BBAE CXLIII (3) 348.

A1610.6. *Tribes from clay models made by creator.* S. Am. Indian (Inca): Rowe BBAE CXLIII (2) 315.

A1611. *Origin of particular tribes.* India: Thompson-Balys.

A1611.1. *Origin of American Indian tribes.*

A1611.1.1. *Origin of the Ojibwa.* Ojibwa: Jones JAFL XXIX 388, *Skinner JAFL XXXII 290.

A1611.1.2. *Origin of Eskimo.* Eskimo (East Greenland): Holm 57.

A1611.2. *Origin of Gypsies.* Finnish: Aarne FFC VIII 5 No. 12; Irish: Beal XXI 304, 325f.

A1611.3. *Origin of various African tribes.* Jewish: Neuman.

A1611.3.1. *Origin of Bushmen.* Hottentot: Bleek 83 No. 40.

A1611.4. *Origin of various tribes of India.* India: Thompson-Balys.

A1611.5. *Origin of various European peoples.*

A1611.5.1. *Origin of Greeks.* Jewish: Neuman.

A1611.5.2. *Origin of Italians.* Jewish: Neuman.

A1611.5.3. *Origin of Germans.* Jewish: Neuman.

A1611.5.4 *Origin of Celts.* Irish myth: Cross (A1611.8).

A1611.5.4.1. *Origin of women in Ireland.* Irish myth: Cross.

F1041.1.3.2.2. First woman in Ireland to die of grief for the death of her husband.

A1611.5.4.2. *Origin of the Maic Milid (Milesians, Gaels).* Irish myth: Cross.

A1611.5.4.3. *Origin of the Tuatha Dé Danann regarded as an early tribe.* Irish myth: Cross.

A107. Gods of darkness and of light. A400.0.1. Gods of earth. F211.0.2.1. Tuatha Dé Danann, conquerors of Ireland, are overcome by invaders.

A1611.6. *Origin of various Near Eastern peoples.* Jewish: Neuman.

A1614. *Origin of white and colored races.* Africa (Fjort): Dennett 101 No. 27, (Ekoi): Talbot 387, (Loango): Pechuël-Loesche 268, (Fang): Trilles 143, 152, 155, Einstein 178, (Cameroon): Rosenhuber 20 No. 3; American Negro (Georgia): Harris Remus 163 No. 33.

A1614.1. *Negroes as curse on Ham for laughing at Noah's nakedness.* Dh I 290; *BP III 311; Jewish: Neuman.

M400. Curses.

A1614.1.1. *Origin of luchrupain (leprechauns, dwarfs, pygmies) from curses of Ham.* Irish myth: Cross.

F451. Dwarf. F451.0.1. Luchrupain (leprechauns) (as fairies).

A1614.1.2. *Origin of "goat-heads" from curse of Ham.* Irish myth: Cross.

B29.5. Man-goat.

A1614.2. *Races dark-skinned from bathing after white men.* All peoples bathe in the river, the white man first, then in turn, the Spaniard, the Indian, and the negro — each becoming darker because of the condition of the water. — N. A. Indian (Biloxi): Swanton BBAE XLVII 32; Carib: Alexander Lat. Am. 271; American Negro: Harris Remus 163; Africa (Loango): Pechuël-Loesche 268, (Cameroon): Rosenhuber 57. Cf. Dh. I 247 (Danish).

A1614.3. *Light and dark-skinned peoples made from light and dark coconuts.* New Britain: Dixon 108.

A1614.4. *Origin of tribes from choices made.*

A1616.4.1. *Origin of tribes from kinds of meat they choose.* India: Thompson-Balys.

A1614.4.1.1. *Origin of race colors from eating of ox.* Those who eat livers are black; those who eat lungs and blood are red. — Herero: Werner African 150.

A1614.4.2. *Origin of different peoples according to choice of chairs.* India: Thompson-Balys.

A1614.4.3. *Origin of different peoples according to choice of bows and arrows* or else guns, horses and cattle. Indians choose the former, whites the latter. — S. Am. Indian (Paressi): Métraux BBAE CXLIII (3) 360.

A1614.5. *Negroes made from left-over scraps at creation.* North Carolina: Brown Collection I 632.

A1614.6. *Origin of light and dark skin color.* India: Thompson-Balys.

A1614.7. *Indians and whites from different legs of first man.* S. Am. Indian (Brazil): Oberg 108.

A1614.8. *Black tribe because woman is put on fire.* S. Am. Indian (Chiriguano): Métraux RMLP XXXIII 175.

A1614.9. *Origin of white man.* Eskimo (Ungava): Turner RBAE XI 261, (Smith Sound): Kroeber JAFL XII 168.

A1616. *Origin of particular languages.* Estonian: Aarne FFC XXV 142 No. 25; Finnish: Aarne FFC VIII 9 Nos. 45—47; Livonian: Loorits FFC LXVI 85 Nos. 38, 40; Lappish: Qvigstad FFC LX 35 No. 11; Icel.: Snorra Edda Prologue V; Lithuanian: Balys Legends No. 123; Jewish: Neuman.

A1616.1. *Cold before theft of fire impedes speech: explanation of difficulty of certain languages.* Calif. Indian: Gayton and Newman 63.

A1616.2. *Origin of Irish language.* Irish myth: Cross.
A541.1. Culture hero invents and teaches the Irish language.

A1617. *Origin of place-name.* India: Thompson-Balys. (No attempt is given here to collect references to place-name origins. Stories of this kind are world wide.)

A1618. *Origin of inequalities among men.* India: Thompson-Balys.
U0—U99. Lifes inequalities.

A1620. Distribution of tribes. Hebrew: Genesis ch. 10; Indo-Chinese: Scott 292. — Africa (Ekoi): Talbot 149, (Fjort): Dennett 108 No. 31; India: Thompson-Balys. — N. A. Indian: (general) *Thompson Tales 285 n. 54, (Hopi): Alexander N. Am. 205, (Tahltan): Teit JAFL XXXII 213; Cakchiquel: Alexander Lat. Am. 181; S. Am. Indian (Yuracare): ibid. 315.

A1621. *Reasons for difference in population sizes in different areas.* New Guinea: Ker.138.

A1630. Wandering of tribes. Icel.: Snorra Edda Prologue IV-V, Hermann Saxo II 85ff.; Hebrew: Exodus, Leviticus, Numbers, Deuteronomy; Jewish: Neuman; Armenian: Ananikian 65. — N. A. Indian (Thompson, Gros Ventre, Sarcee, Blackfoot, Cheyenne): *Teit MAFLS XI 48ff., (Creek): Alexander N. Am. 63, (Sia): ibid. 203f.; S. Am. Indian (Yuracare): Métraux BBAE CXLIII (3) 503, (Mundurucú): Horton ibid. (3) 281, (Brazil): Oberg. 108.

A1631. *Emergence of tribe from lower world.* Creek: Alexander N. Am. 62; Choctaw: ibid. 63; Mandan, Kiowa: ibid. 105; Arikara: ibid. 107; Navaho: ibid. 159; Pima: ibid. 177; Sia: ibid. 203; Hopi: ibid. 205; Warrau (Carib): Alexander Lat. Am. 273; Amazon tribes: ibid. 309.
A1232. Mankind ascends from under earth.

A1631.1. *Emergence of tribe from lower world stopped by fat woman* or pregnant woman who becomes lodged in the hole of egress. — Warrau (Carib tribe): Alexander Lat. Am. 272 (references to Kiowa, Mandan, and Pueblo).

A1631.2. *Tribe climbs down from sky to earth.* S. Am. Indian (Tropical Forest): Lowie BBAE CLXIII (3) 55.

A1231. First man descends from sky.

A1640. Origin of tribal subdivisions. India: Thompson-Balys; Siberian: Holmberg Siberian 502. — Tahltan: Teit JAFL XXXII 207; S. Am. Indian (Tropical Forest): Lowie BBAE CXLIII (3) 53.

A1611. Origin of particular tribes.

A1641. *Characteristics of tribal subdivisions.* Tahltan: Teit JAFL XXXII 216; Laguna and Zuñi: Parsons JAFL XXXI 263.

A1650. Origin of different classes — social and professional. Icel.: MacCulloch Eddic 153.

P0—P99. Royalty and nobility. P100—P199. Other social orders.

A1650.1. *The various children of Eve.* Eve has so many children that she is ashamed when God pays her a visit. She hides some of them and they fail to receive the blessing that God gives those in sight. Thus arises the differences in classes and peoples. — *BP III 308ff. (Gr. No. 180); *Dh I 247, II 98f. — Livonian: Loorits FFC LXVI 85 No. 41; Spanish: Boggs FFC XC 87 No. 758.

A1861.1. Monkeys from children hidden by Eve when God visited her. F251.4. Underworld people from children which Eve hid from God. Q220. Impiety punished.

A1650.2. *Custom of differentiating social classes by color of dress introduced.* Irish myth: Cross.

A1650.3. *Origin of different trades.* Cheremis: Sebeok-Nyerges.

A1650.3.1. *Why some men are good basket-makers.* India: Thompson-Balys.

A1650.3.2. *How God distributed professions:* according to the bodily appearance of men. Lithuanian: Balys Index No. 3056, Balys Legends No. 107.

A1641. *Origin of castes.* India: Thompson-Balys.

A1651.0.1. *Attitude to untouchables.* India: Thompson-Balys.

A1651.1. *Origin of castes from instructions received in dream.* India: Thompson-Balys.

J157. Wisdom (knowledge) from dream.

A1651.2. *Caste determined by what kind of tree one catches while crossing a river.* India: Thompson-Balys.

A1653. *Origin of royalty.*

A1653.1. *Origin of kings* (from god(s)). Icel.: Corpus Poeticum Boreale I 241 (Rigsthula), Snorra Edda Prologue.

P10. Kings.

A1653.2. *Origin of a king's family* from a fairy prince. India: Thompson-Balys.

A1654. *Origin of priesthood* (shamanism, etc.)

A1654.1. *Origin of priests.* India: Thompson-Balys.

A1654.2. *Origin of diviners.* India: Thompson-Balys.
D1712. Soothsayer.

A1655. *Origin of peasantry.* Icel.: Corpus Poeticum Boreale I 237 (Rigsthula); African (Senegambia): Bérenger-Feraud II 185ff. No. 2.

A1655.1. *Why peasant is always busy:* he is eager to produce food for all living beings. Lithuanian: Balys Legends No. 108.

A1656. *Origin of noblemen.* Icel.: Corpus Poeticum Boreale I 239 (Rigsthula).

A1656.1. *Origin of Polish noblemen:* from wheat dough that a bitch devours. Lithuanian: Balys Index No. 3050, Balys Legends Nos 97, 104ff.
X561. Jokes about the gentry.

A1657. *Origin of slaves.* Icel.: Corpus Poeticum Boreale I 235 (Rigsthula); Irish myth: Cross; Jewish: Neuman.
P170. Slaves.

A1657.1. Origin of subject tribes (aithech-thuatha). Irish myth: Cross.

A1657.2. *Origin of the Fir Bolg ("Men of the Sacks");* so-called because as slaves they were forced to carry earth in sacks (builg). Irish myth: Cross.
H1129.11. Task: carrying soil to cover stony ground.

A1658. *Origin of professional warriors.* Irish myth: Cross.
P551.0.1. Band of professional warriors.

A1658.1. *Origin of fiana* (bands of professional warriors). Irish myth: Cross.

A1659. *Origin of different classes — miscellaneous.*

A1659.1. *Origin of the Fomorians (giants).* Irish myth: Cross.
A107. Gods of darkness and of light. A123. Monstrous gods. F531. Giant. G100.1. Giant ogre (Fomorian). G301. Monsters. R111.1.4. Rescue of maiden from Fomorian. S262. Periodic sacrifices to a monster (giant, Fomorian). Z100.1. Names of giants (Fomorians) with sinister significance.

A1659.1.1. *Fomorians descended from Ham* (or Cain). Irish myth: Cross.

A1660. Characteristics of various peoples — in personal appearance. Icel.: MacCulloch Eddic 153, Corpus Poeticum Boreale I 234 ff. Irish myth: Cross.

A1661. *Hair and beard of various peoples.* Irish myth: Cross.

A1661.1. *How the white man got his beard.* Cheyenne: Campbell JAFL XXIX 407.
A1597. Origin of custom of wearing a beard.

A1661.2. *Why the white man has short hair.* Cheyenne: Campbell JAFL XXIX 408.

A1661.3. *Why Canaanites have curly hair.* Jewish: Neuman.

A1662. *Peculiar smell of body.*

A1662.1. *Why Jews smell bad.* They rubbed Christ's body with garlic. Lithuanian: Balys Index No. *1867A.
G303.16.19.3.3. Task: washing a Jew to rid him of his evil smell.

A1663. *Heads of various people.*

A1663.1. *Why Babylonians are round headed.* Jewish: Neuman.

A1664. *Beauty of various peoples.* Jewish: Neuman.

A1665. *Feet of various peoples.*

A1665.1. *Why Africans have bad feet.* Jewish: Neuman.

A1666. *Eyes of various peoples.*

A1666.1. *Why Canaanites have red eyes.* Jewish: Neuman.

A1666.2. *Why Palmyrenes have narrow eyes.* Jewish: Neuman.

A1667. *Intelligence of various people.*

A1667.1. *Why Europeans know more than natives.* Marquesas: Handy 138.

A1670. Characteristics of various peoples — in industry and warfare.

A1671. *Tribal characteristics — labor.*

A1671.1. *Why the negro works.* S. Carolina Negro: Davis JAFL XXVII 244; N. Carolina Negro: Brown Collection I 633; Africa (Cameroon): Mansfield 225.

A1673. *Tribal characteristics — industry.*

A1673.1. *Why the Haidas surpass in certain industries.* Tahltan: Teit JAFL XXXII 213.

A1674. *Tribal characteristics—stealing.*

A1674.1. *Why it is not a sin for a Gypsy to steal:* helpful at crucifixion. Lithuanian: Balys Index No. *1638, Balys Legends No. 102.

A1674.2. *Why Russians like thefts and robberies.* Lithuanian: Balys Legends No. 100.

A1675. *Tribal characteristics — warfare.* Irish myth: Cross.

A1459.1.2. Introduction of broad-headed spears into Leinster.

A1676. *Tribal characteristics — bravery or cowardice.*

A1676.1. *Why the Chittagongs are not as brave as they used to be.* India: Thompson-Balys.

A1680. Characteristics of various peoples — in habits. Irish myth: Cross.

X682. Humorous habits of persons of certain cities.

A1681. *Tribal characteristics — eating.*

A1681.1. *Why Indians chew spruce gum.* Loucheux: Barbeau JAFL XXVIII 256.

A1681.2. *Why Jews do not eat pork.* Jaworskij Der Urquell II 196; Fb "svin" III 676b. — Estonian: Aarne FFC XXV 142 No. 23; Lithuanian: Balys Index No. 1867A; Livonian: Loorits FFC LXVI 85 No. 42; Flemish: DeMeyer FFC XXXVII 85 No. 43c.

A1422. Assignment of edible animals. C221.1. Tabu: eating flesh of certain animal., P715.1. Jews. V360. Christian traditions concerning Jews.

A1681.3. *Why the Muria eat snakes.* India: Thompson-Balys.

A1681.4. *Why the Agaria eat rats.* India: Thompson-Balys.

A1683. *Tribal characteristics — dress.*

A1683.1. *Why Russians wear their shirts outside their breeches.* Estonian: Aarne FFC XXV 142 No. 24.

A1683.1.1. *Why Russians wear red shirts.* Lithuanian: Balys Legends No. 99.

A1683.2. *Why a certain tribe wear clothes like dogs* (supposed descendants of a bitch mother). India: Thompson-Balys.

A1683.3. *Origin of custom of wearing mantles.* Irish myth: Cross.

A1683.4. *Why certain peoples go nude.*

A1683.4.1. *Why Canaanites go nude.* Jewish: Neuman.

A1683.5. *Why certain peoples wear only loincloths.* S. Am. Indian (Toba): Métraux MAFLS XL 94.

A1687. *Tribal characteristics — decoration.*

A1687.1. *Why Zuñi girls rub flour on their faces as they grind.* Zuñi: Parsons JAFL XXIX 394.

A1689. *Other origins and originators.* Irish myth: Cross.

A1689.1. *Why Bhuiya yoke the cow and the bullock together to the plough.* India: Thompson-Balys.

A1689.2. *Why Agaria are not afraid of fire.* India: Thompson-Balys.

A1689.3. *Why the Gond and Baiga are omnivorous.* India: Thompson-Balys.

A1689.4. *Why Saora wave axes and swords and shout while dancing.* India: Thompson-Balys.

A1689.5. *Why the Kamar offer liquor to gods and spirits.* India: Thompson-Balys.

A1689.6. *Why Jews read and write from right to left:* because of the ugly name of the king of the Jews. Lithuanian: Balys Index No. *1867C.

A1689.7. *Origin of the Russian calendar.* Lithuanian: Balys Legends No. 101.

A1689.8. *Why Chapperbands coin false money for a living.* India: Thompson-Balys.

A1689.9. *Why Chenchu women are ugly.* India: Thompson-Balys.

A1689.10. *Why the Agaria are cultivators.* India: Thompson-Balys.

A1689.11. *Why one people is superior in power to another.*

A1689.11.1. *English more powerful than Hindus* since latter were late at distribution of qualities. (Both defecating, but Hindu must wash, while Englishman uses paper.) — India: Thompson-Balys.

A2235. Animal characteristics caused by animal's lateness at distribution of qualities.

A1689.12. *Why Egyptians are fond of asses.* Jewish: Neuman.

A1689.13. *Why Jews keep aloof from other peoples.* Jewish: Neuman.

A1690. Distribution and differentiation of people — miscellaneous.

A1691. *Differentiation between "free" (saer) and "unfree" (daer).* Irish myth: Cross.

A1611.9. Origin of the Maic Milid (Milesians, Gaels).

A1700—A2199. CREATION OF ANIMAL LIFE

A1700—A1799. Creation of animal life — general.

A1700. Creation of animals. (Cf. Chapter B, Animals.) Quiché: Alexander Lat. Am. 162; Ekoi: Talbot 149.

D2178.4. Animals created by magic.

A1701. *Creation of animals by God.* India: Thompson-Balys.

A1702. *Creation of animals by creator.* (Cf. A0.) — Jewish: Neuman.

A1703. *Culture hero creates useful animals.* S. Am. Indian (Caingang): Métraux BBAE CXLIII (1) 473.

A1704. *All animals created in couples.* Jewish: Neuman.

A1705. *Animals created to serve man.* Jewish: Neuman.

A1710. Creation of animals through transformation. (Cf. A1811.1, A1833.2, A1861.1, A1861.2, A1863, A1887). — India: Thompson-Balys; Chinese: Graham, Eberhard FFC CXX 79, 96, 122f. No. 82; Calif. Indian: Gayton and Newman 98.

D100. Transformation: man to animal.

A1711. *Animals from transformations after deluge or world calamity.* S. Am. Indian (Amazon Tribes): Alexander Lat. Am. 311f., Métraux BBAE CXLIII (1) 367.

A1713. *Creator sent for water: Meantime animals assume present forms.* Calif. Indian: Gayton and Newman 59.

A60. Marplot at creation. A2286.1.1. Creation of hog incomplete since God has to go to a fire: cause of hog's round snout.

A1714. *Animals from various transformed objects.* India: Thompson-Balys; Hawaii: Beckwith Myth 22, 465; Eskimo (Kodiak): Golder JAFL 20 171, (Cumberland Sound): Boas BAM XV 167, 169, (Central Eskimo): Boas RBAE VI, 588, (East Greenland): Rasmussen I, 82, 96, (Ungava): Turner RBAE XI 261, (Labrador): Hawks GSCan XIV 155, (Cape York): Rasmussen III 79; S. Am. Indian (Caingang): Métraux BBAE CXLIII (1) 473, (Araucanian): Cooper ibid. (2) 753, (Inca): Rowe ibid. 315, (Cashinawa): Métraux ibid. (3) 684.

A1714.1. *Animals from transformed cloth.* India: Thompson-Balys.

A1714.2. *Animals from bark thrown on ground.* Borneo: Dixon 176.

A1252. Creation of man from wood.

A1714.3. *Animals created from earth.* India: Thompson-Balys.

A1241. Man made from clay (earth).

A1714.3.1. *Buffaloes emerge from earth, the first man holding the tail of last one.* India: Thompson-Balys.

A1715. *Animals from transformed man.* (Cf. A2005, A2011.2.) Lithuanian: Balys Index No. 3115, Balys Legends Nos. 216—219, 261f.; India: Thompson-Balys; Maori: Clark 15; Hawaii: Beckwith Myth 422; Rarotanga (Cook Island): ibid. 101; Tuomatu: Stimson MS (z-G 3/1100); S. Am. Indian (Tiatinagua): Métraux BBAE CXLIII (3) 449, (Mundurucu): Horton ibid. 281, (Cashinawa): Métraux ibid. 685, (Toba): Métraux MAFLS XL 31, 79, (Mataco): Métraux ibid. 64.

A1715.1. *Animals from Pharaoh's drowned army.* From the army crossing the Red Sea came the various animals. — Dh I 318.

A1715.2. *Animals from men transformed for discourtesy to God* (Jesus). (Cf. A1831, A1862, A1871.) — *Dh. II 99ff. India: Thompson-Balys.

A1730. Creation of animals as punishment. C841.1. Tabu: killing stork. Bird was once maiden. Q221.1. Discourtesy to god punished.

A1715.3. *Seven whistlers are the souls of the Jews who crucified Christ.* (Cf. F456.1.1.1.) — England, U.S.: *Baughman.

A1715.4. *Animals from transformed men according to favorite food.* One man asks for flesh, one for blood, etc. They are changed to mice, cats, and bugs. (Cf. A1811, A1853.) — Finnish: Aarne FFC XXV 150 No. 71.

A1715.5. *Animals from transformed survivors of shipwreck.* India: Thompson-Balys.

A1895. Creation of bat.

A1716. *Animals from transformed ogre or giant.* Maori: Clark 101.

A1716.1. *Animals from different parts of body of slain giant.* Giant person, cow, ox, etc. — Persian: Carnoy 288. — Borneo, Philippines: Dixon 177.

A2001. Insects from body of slain monster. A2611.3. Coconut tree from head of slain monster. E610. Reincarnation as animal. E613.0.5. Severed heads of monster become birds. G100. Giant ogre.

A1724. *Animals from transformed parts of the body (animal or human).* India: Thompson-Balys.

A1724.1. *Animals from body of slain person.* India: Thompson-Balys.

A1724.1.1. *Animals from severed fingers of woman.* (Cf. A2102.) — N. A. Indian: Thompson Tales 272; India: Thompson-Balys.

A1724.2. *Animals from transformed hair.* India: Thompson-Balys.

A1724.3. *All living things from Jesus' spattered blood.* Laguna, Zuñi: Parsons JAFL XXXI 257.

A1725. *Animals from parts of body of deity or saint.*

A1725.1. *Animals from spittle of deity (saint).* (Cf. A2181, A2182.) — *DhII 107ff.

D1001. Magic spittle.

A1725.2. *Animals from body dirt of deity* (hero). India: Thompson-Balys.

A1727. *Primordial animal mutilated to produce present form.* Maori: Clark 50; Hawaii: Beckwith Myth 135, 436, 500.

A1730. Creation of animals as punishment. India: Thompson-Balys.

A1715. Animals from men transformed for discourtesy to God (Jesus). A2011.2. Creation of ant: avaricious man transformed.

A1731. *Creation of animals as punishment for beating forbidden drum.* Gold Coast: Barker and Sinclair 89 No. 16.

A2231.10. Crab beats deity's forbidden drum: eyes lift out of body. C916.2. Animals produced when forbidden drum is beaten.

A1732. *Creation of animals to take revenge.* India: Thompson-Balys.

A1733. *Creation of animals as punishment for incest.* India: Thompson-Balys.

A1734. *Animals from frogs sent as one of Egypt's plagues.* Jewish: Neuman.

A1750. Animals created through opposition of devil to god.

A50. Conflict of good and evil creators. A63.4. Devil and God create animals.

A1751. *The devil's animals and God's.* In the contest between God and the devil, certain animals are made by each. Dh. I 164 (with lists of the animals). Lithuanian: Balys Index No. 3081, Legends Nos. 124—130; German: Grimm No. 148.

A2286.2. Animal characteristics result of contest between God and devil. A2286.2.1. Devil's animals devour God's. God makes white fish, devil a pike to eat it up, etc. K483. Color of devil's cows changed while he sleeps so that he does not know them. Only those not changed (all black, all red, etc.) belong to the devil.

A1751.1. *Mouse created by Lucifer; cat by Michael to destroy mouse.* (Cf. A1811. A1853.) — Irish myth: Cross.

A1755. *Devil's unsuccessful creation produces certain animals.* (Cf. A1811, A1833.1, A1862, A1893.) — Dh I 156.

A1756. *Devil produces animals only in God's name.* He tries unsuccessfully without using God's name. Dh I 146ff. Lithuanian: Balys Index No. 3086; Legends Nos. 139—146, 152.

A1757. *Dualism of animal creation.* Persian: Carnoy 291.

A1758. *Animals created while god Mahadeo quarrels with his wife.* India: Thompson-Balys.

A1770. Creation of animals from unusual primeval mating. S. Am. Indian (Paressí): Métraux BBAE CXLIII (3) 359.

A1771. *Animals from mating of sun and moon.* S. Am. Indian (Jivaró): Steward-Métraux BBAE CXLIII (3) 627.

A1772. *Animals born from primeval mating of snake and person.* S. Am. Indian (Tapirapé): Wagley-Galvão BBAE CXLIII (3) 253.

A1790. Creation of animals — other motifs.

A1791. *Giant ox ancestor of all animals.* Persian: Carnoy 289.

B871.1.1. Giant ox.

A1792. *Animals vomited up by creator.* Bushongo: Werner African 144.

A1793. *Animals emerge from tree.* Hawaii: Beckwith Myth 287; S. Am. Indian (Warrau): Kirchhoff BBAE CXLIII (3) 880.

A1795. *Animals drop from clouds.* India: Thompson-Balys.

A1800—A1899. Creation of mammals.

Note: A1800—A1899 is based upon the following classification of mammals:

A1810—A1819. Felidae.
A1811. Cat. A1812. Puma. A1813. Leopard. A1814. Lion. A1815. Tiger. A1816. Lynx. A1817. Jaguar.

A1820—A1829. Mustelidae.
A1821. Otter. A1822. Mink. A1823. Weasel. A1824. Marten. A1825. Wolverine. A1826. Skunk. A1827. Badger.

A1830—A1839. Canidae and other carnivora.
A1831. Dog. A1832. Fox. A1833. Wolf. A1834. Coyote and other canidae. A1835. Raccoon. A1836. Bear. A1837. Seal. A1838. Walrus.

A1840—A1859. Rodentia.
A1841. Woodchuck. A1842. Prairie-dog. A1843. Chipmunk. A1844. Squirrel. A1847. Beaver. A1848. Gopher. A1851. Muskrat. A1852. Lemming. A1853. Mouse. A1854. Rat. A1856. Hare (rabbit). A1857. Mongoose. A1858. Porcupine.

A1860—A1869. Primata.
A1861. Monkey. A1862. Ape. A1863. Baboon. A1864. Gorilla. A1865. Orangutan.

A1870—1889. Ungulata.
A1871. Hog. A1872. Hippopotamus. A1873. Camel. A1874. Giraffe. A1875. Deer. A1876. Moose (elk). A1877. Cow. A1878. Bison (buffalo). A1881. Horse. A1882. Ass. A1883. Zebra. A1884. Sheep. A1885. Goat. A1886. Rhinoceros. A1887. Elephant.

A1890—1899. Other mammals.
A1891. Opossum. A1892. Kangaroo. A1893. Mole. A1894. Hedgehog. A1895. Bat. A1896. Anteater. A1897. Armadillo.
Since whales are thought of as fish in folk-literature they have been catalogued under that heading rather than under mammals, where they strictly belong.

A1800. Creation of mammals. Irish myth: Cross; Jewish: Neuman; India: Thompson-Balys.

A1810—A1839. CREATION OF CARNIVORA

A1810. Creation of felidae.

A1811. *Creation of cat.* Esthonian: Aarne FFC XXV 150 No. 71 (cf. A1715.4); Finnish: Aarne FFC VIII 11 No. 55, XXXIII 53 No. 55, Dh I 166, 273 (cf. A1751.); ibid. I 157 (cf. A1755.) — Lithuanian: Balys Index No. 3120, Legends No. 133, 195, 220f.; Jewish: Neuman; India: Thompson-Balys.

A1751.1. Mouse created by Lucifer: cat by Michael to destroy mouse.

A1811.1. *Cat from transformed eagle.* Eagle mistakes stick of wood for fish and gets feet caught. Wind blows off feathers and makes hair. (Cf. A1710.) — Finnish: Aarne FFC VIII 11 No. 54.

A1811.2. *Creation of cat: sneezed from lion's nostrils.* Devil as mouse gnaws hole in bottom of ark. Noah asks lion's help. Lion sneezes and cat comes from lion's nostril and eats mouse. *Dh I 271ff.

A1811.3. *Cat of divine origin; is really praying when he purrs.* India: Thompson-Balys.

A1815. *Creation of tiger.* India: *Thompson-Balys; S. Am. Indian (Apapocuvu-Guaraní): Métraux RMLP XXXIII 138.

A1817. *Creation of jaguar.* S. Am. Indian (Mojo): Métraux BBAE CXLIII (3) 424.

A1820. Creation of mustelidae.

A1821. *Creation of otter.*

A1821.1. *Creation of sea otter.* Eskimo (Kodiak): Golder JAFL XX 139.

A1824. *Creation of marten.* Kaska: Teit JAFL XXX 432.

A1830. Creation of canidae and other carnivora.

A1831. *Creation of dog.* Dh I 164 (Cf. A1751); ibid. II 101 (Cf. A1715.2). — Irish: Beal XXI 330; Jewish: Neuman; India: *Thompson-Balys; Chinese: Eberhard FFC CXX 72; Hawaii: Beckwith Myth 436, 500; Maori: Clark 50; Eskimo (Cape York): Rasmussen III 47; Ojibwa: Jones JAFL XXIX 376.

A1831.1. *Dog created as watch-dog for Jesus.* Jesus, left to watch the herd, creates the dog to drive off the wolf. *Dh II 118.

A1831.2. *First lapdog in Ireland.* Irish myth: Cross.

B1870.1. Toy (lap) dogs.

A1832. *Creation of fox.* India: Thompson-Balys; Cheremis: Sebeok-Nyerges.

A1833. *Creation of wolf.* (Cf. A1751.) Dh I 147ff., I 164. — Quileute: Farrand JAFL XXXII 259.

A1833.1. *Devil makes wolf; God gives him life.* (Cf. A1755.) — Esthonian: Aarne FFC XXV 145 No. 39. Lithuanian: Balys Index No. 3086; Legends Nos. 139—146.

G303.25.1. Wolf is the devil's craftiest enemy.

A1833.2. *Wolf from man transformed by magician.* (Cf. A1710.) — Finnish: Aarne FFC VIII 14 No. 76.

A1833.3. *Wolf as God's dog.* German: Grimm No. 148.

A1834. *Creation of coyote and other canidae.*

A1834.1. *Creation of coyote.*

A1834.2. *Creation of jackal.* India: Thompson-Balys.

A1834.3. *Creation of hyena.* India: Thompson-Balys.

A1836. *Creation of bear.* Dh II 99 (Cf. A1715.2.) — Esthonian: Aarne FFC XXV 146 No. 41; Lithuanian: Balys Index No. 3112; Legends Nos. 175, 216ff.; India: Thompson-Balys; Ojibwa: Jones JAFL XXIX 370, Eskimo (Cumberland Sound): Boas BAM XV 171, (West Hudson Bay): Boas ibid. 307, (Smith Sound): Kroeber JAFL XII 172.

A1837. *Origin of seal.* Eskimo (Central): Boas RBAE VI 637, 639.

A1838. *Origin of walrus.* Eskimo (Central): Boas RBAE VI 587.

A1840. Creation of rodentia.

A1853. *Creation of mouse.* Esthonian: Aarne FFC XXV 150 No. 71 (Cf. A1715.4); Lithuanian: Balys Index No. 3120. Legends No. 220f.

A1751.1. Mouse created by Lucifer; cat by Michael to destroy mouse.

A1853.1. *Creation of mouse by devil in ark.* (Cf. A1811.2.) — *Dh I 166, 273; *Fb "mus" II 632a.; Finnish: Aarne FFC VIII 11 No. 55, XXXIII 53 No. 55.

A1853.1.1. *Mice engendered after flood from rottenness:* no mice on ark. Nouvelles Récreations No. 66.

A1854. *Creation of rat.* India: Thompson-Balys.

A1854.1. *Why we have rats: one escapes from slaughter of rats.* India: Thompson-Balys.

A1856. *Creation of hare (rabbit).* Dh I 164; India: Thompson-Balys; Eskimo (Central): Boas RBAE VI 639, (Ungava): Turner RBAE XI 263.

A1857. *Creation of mongoose.* India: Thompson-Balys.

A1858. *Creation of porcupine.* India: Thompson-Balys.

A1860. Creation of primata. India: Thompson-Balys.

A1861. *Creation of monkey.* India: *Thompson-Balys; Chinese: Graham; Philippine (Tinguian): Cole 189f.; S. Am. Indian (Macovi): Métraux MAFLS XL 35.

A1861.1. *Monkeys from children hidden by Eve when God visited her.* (Cf. A1650.1, A1710.) — BP III 320f.; Dh I 247.

Q220. Impiety punished.

A1861.2. *Creation of monkeys: old woman thrown into fire.* In unsuccessful imitation of Christ, the smith throws an old woman into the fire. She becomes a monkey. (Cf. A1710.) — Dh II 168. — Finnish: Aarne FFC VIII 13 No. 68; Esthonian: Aarne FFC XXV 146 No. 46; Flemish: DeMeyer FFC XXXVII 86 No. 68; German: Grimm No. 147. — Cf. Type 753.

E15. Resuscitation by burning. J2400. Foolish imitation.

A1861.3. *Creation of monkey: lazy man.* *Fb "abe" IV 2a.

A1862. *Creation of ape.* Dh I 156ff. (Cf. A1755); ibid. I 164 (Cf. A1751); ibid. II 100 (Cf. A1715.2.) — Indonesian: De Vries's list No. 74; Palestine: Schmidt-Kahle Volkserzählungen aus Palestina I No. 59; Jewish: Neuman; Chinese: Eberhard FFC CXX 121f. 411 s.v. "Affen entstehen"; Africa (Cameroon): Rosenhuber 38.

A1863. *Creation of baboon.* Ila (Rhodesia): Smith and Dale 349 No. 4; Zulu: Callaway 178 (transformed men, cf. A1710).

A1870. Creation of ungulata.

A1871. *Creation of hog (pig).* Dh II 102 — Esthonian: Aarne FFC XXV 144 No. 34; Livonian: Loorits FFC LXVI 88 No. 68; India: Thompson-Balys; Rarotonga (Cook Island): Beckwith Myth 101.

A1871.0.1. *God's urine used to make pig.* India: Thompson-Balys.

A100. Deity. D1006. Magic urine.

A1871.1. *Origin of wild boar.* Jewish: Neuman.

A1871.2. *Origin of peccary.* S. Am. Indian (Cashinawa): Métraux BBAE CXLIII (3) 685.

A1872. *Creation of hippopotamus.* Africa (Ekoi): Talbot 386.

A1873. *Creation of camel.* India: Thompson-Balys.

A1875. *Origin of deer.* India: Thompson-Balys (A1888).

A1875.0.1. *First deer in Ireland — introduced by Tuatha Dé Danann.* Irish myth: Cross (A1888.1).

A1875.1. *Origin of reindeer.* Kodiak: Jochelson JE VI 224; Eskimo (Central): Boas RBAE VI 215 588, (Bering Strait): Nelson RBAE XVIII 454; N. Am. Indian (Kathlamet): Boas RBAE XXVI 109.

A1876. *Creation of moose (elk).* Quileute: Farrand JAFL XXXII 258.

A1876.1. *Creation of caribou.* Eskimo (Cumberland Sound): Boas BAM XV 167, 306, (Mackenzie Area): Jenness 80.

A1877. *Creation of cow.* Dh I 164 (Cf. A1751). — India: *Thompson-Balys; Chinese: Eberhard FFC CXX 120 No. 77; Masai: Werner African 149.

A1877.1. *First cattle in Ireland.* Irish myth: Cross.
B182. Magic cox (ox, bull).

A1878. *Creation of bison (buffalo).* Cheyenne: Alexander N. Am. 127; India: *Thompson-Balys.

A1878.1. *Origin of wild and domestic buffalo.* India: *Thompson-Balys.

A1881. *Creation of horse.* Dh. I 155, 164 (Cf. A1751); *Fb "hest" I 599; Howey Horse in Magic and Myth 213 ff. — Finnish: Aarne FFC VIII 11 No. 58; Lithuanian: Balys Index No. 3092, Legends No. 135f., 153—160; Jewish: Neuman; India: *Thompson-Balys; Philippine (Tinguian): Cole 189.
B181. Magic horse.

A1881.0.1. *Horse lives from time of Adam on.* Irish myth: Cross.
B841. Long-lived animals.

A1881.1. *Creation of white horse.* Man takes skin of horse and substitutes a white bedspread. Dh. III 86. — Finnish: Aarne FFC VIII 12 No. 60.

A1882. *Creation of ass.* (Cf. A1751.) Dh I 164. — Jewish: Neuman.

A1882.1. *Creation of ass: proud horse.* (Cf. A1730.) Flemish: DeMeyer FFC XXXVII 86. No. 58a.

A1884. *Creation of sheep.* Dh I 154f., 164 (Cf. A1751). — India: Thompson-Balys; S. Am. Indian (Toba): Métraux MAFLS XL 115.
B189.1. Magic sheep.

A1884.0.1. *First sheep in Ireland.* Irish myth: Cross.

A1884.1. *Creation of mountain sheep.* Eskimo (Bering Strait): Nelson RBAE XVIII 454.

A1885. *Creation of goat.* Dh I 153f., 164 (Cf. A1751); Fb "gjed" IV 178a.; Lithuanian: Balys Index No. 3090, Legends Nos. 149—152; German: Grimm No. 148; India: Thompson-Balys.

A1887. *Creation of elephant.* Benga: Nassau No. 3 (Cf. A1710); Ila (Rhodesia): Smith and Dale 363 No. 15; India: Thompson-Balys.

A1889. *Creation of ungulata — miscellaneous.*

A1889.1. *Creation of tapir.* S. Am. Indian (Mundurucu): Horton BBAE CXLIII (3) 281.

A1890. Creation of other mammals.

A1893. *Creation of mole.* Dh I 156ff. (Cf. A1755). — England, U.S.: *Baughman.

A1895. *Creation of bat.* Dh I 155f. (Cf. A1755), ibid. III 268 (Cf. A1710.) — Finnish. Aarne FFC VIII 16 No. 84 (Cf. A1751), ibid. 15 No. 81; Esthonian: Aarne FFC XXV 146 No. 45; Flemish: DeMeyer XXXVII 86 No. 81; India: *Thompson-Balys.

A1896. *Creation of anteater.* S. Am. Indian (Cashinawa): Métraux BBAE CXLIII (3) 685.

A1897. *Creation of armadillo.* S. Am. Indian (Cashinawa): Métraux BBAE CXLIII (3) 685.

A1900—A1999. Creation of birds.

Note: A1900—A1999 is based on the following classification of birds.

A1910—A1929. Passeriformes.
A1911. Lark. A1912. Thrush (nightingale, robin). A1913. Bluebird. A1914. Thrasher. A1915. Mocking-bird. A1916. Wren. A1917. Swallow. A1918. Titmouse. A1919. Crow (raven). A1921. Jay. A1922. Magpie. A1923. Tanager. A1924. Blackbird. A1925. Oriole. A1926. Finch. A1927. Sparrow. A1928. Starling (myna).

A1930—A1939. Falconiformes.
A1931. Vulture. A1932. Turkey-buzzard. A1934. Falcon. A1935. Buzzard. A1936. Eagle. A1937. Hawk. A1938. Kite.

A1940—A1949. Charidriiformes.
A1941. Plover. A1942. Snipe. A1943. Curlew. A1944. Sandpiper. A1945. Gull (tern). A1946. Quail. A1947. Pigeon. A1948. Dove.

A1950—A1959. Coraciiformes.
A1951. Kingfisher. A1952. Hoopoe. A1953. Humming-bird. A1954. Whippoorwill. A1955. Nighthawk. A1956. Swift. A1957. Woodpecker (flicker). A1958. Owl.

A1960—A1969. Ciconiiformes.
A1961. Cormorant. A1962. Pelican. A1963. Gannet. A1964. Heron. A1965. Bittern. A1966. Stork. A1967. Flamingo.

A1970—A1999. Miscellaneous birds.
A1971. Ostrich. A1974. Penguin. A1975. Loon (diver). A1976. Grebe. A1977. Albatross. A1978. Fulmar. A1979. Petrel. A1981. Swan. A1982. Goose. A1983. Duck. A1985. Quail. A1986. Partridge. A1987. Grouse. A1988. Chicken. A1991. Coot. A1992. Crane. A1993. Cuckoo. A1994. Parrot (cuckatoo). A1995. Turkey. A1996. Peacock.

A1900. Creation of birds. Lappish: Qvigstad FFC LX 38 No. 46; Jewish: Neuman; India: Thompson-Balys; Chinese: Eberhard FFC CXX 123 No. 83, 127; Maori: Clark 15; S. Am. Indian (Toba): Métraux MAFLS XL 29, (Cashinawa): Métraux BBAE CXLIII (3) 685.

A1901. *Various birds from Pharaoh's drowned army.* (Cf. A1715.1). — Finnish: Aarne FFC VIII 15 No. 82; Esthonian: Aarne FFC XXV 146 No. 48; Lappish: Qvigstad FFC LX 38 No. 45.

A1903. *God makes birds, devil reptiles.* (Cf. A1751). — Finnish: Aarne FFC VIII 19 No. 105, XXXIII 54 No. 105; Estonian: Aarne FFC XXV 148 No. 58; Lithuanian: Balys Legends No. 124—129.

A1904. The oldest bird. Irish Myth: Cross.
B841. Long-lived animals.

A1910. Creation of passeriformes.

A1911. *Creation of lark.* Dh I 164 (Cf. A1751). — Lithuanian: Balys Index No. 3148; Legends Nos. 124ff., 258f.

A1912. *Creation of thrush (nightingale).*

A1912.1. *Creation of thrush.* Dh I 164 (Cf. A1751).

A1912.2. *Creation of nightingale.* Estonian: Aarne FFC XXV 147 No. 52; Livonian: Loorits FFC LXVI 90 No. 78; Lithuanian: Balys Index No. 3150; Greek: Grote I 182 (Philomela).

A1912.3. *Creation of robin.* Naskapi: Speck JAFL XXVIII 74.

A1917. *Creation of swallow.* Dh III 414ff. (cf. A1710); ibid. I 164 (cf. A1751). — Greek: Grote I 182 (Procne); Finnish: Aarne FFC VIII 15 No. 83, 16 No. 85 (cf. A1751); Estonian: Aarne FFC XXV 147 No. 50; Livonian: Loorits FFC LXVI 90 No. 79 (cf. A1710); Lithuanian: Balys Legends No. 127; Spanish: Boggs FFC XC 37 No. *243.
D511.1. Man calls wife "my swallow"; she becomes swallow.

A1918. *Creation of titmouse.* (Cf. A1710.) — Livonian: Loorits FFC LXVI 90 No. 80.
D151.6. Transformation: man to titmouse.

A1919. *Creation of crow (raven).* Dh I 164 (Cf. A1751). — India: Thompson-Balys.

A1921. *Creation of jay.* Dh I 164 (cf. A1751). — Finnish: Aarne FFC XXXIII 54 No. 96** (cf. 1715.2), No. 95**.

A1922. *Creation of magpie.* Dh I 164 (cf. A1751). — Finnish: Aarne FFC VIII 16 No. 88.

A1924. *Creation of blackbird.* Irish myth: Cross.
A1904. The oldest bird.

A1926. *Creation of finch.* Dh I 164 (cf. A1751).

A1927. *Creation of sparrow.* Dh I 165 (cf. A1751). — Lithuanian: Balys Legends No. 130; India: Thompson-Balys.

A1928. *Creation of myna* (bird). India: *Thompson-Balys.

A1930. Creation of falconiformes.

A1931. *Creation of vulture.* India: *Thompson-Balys.

A1937. *Creation of hawk.* Finnish: Aarne FFC VIII 17 No. 95 (cf. A1710); India: Thompson-Balys.

A1938. *Creation of kite.* India: Thompson-Balys.

A1940. Creation of charidriiformes. Finnish: Aarne FFC VIII 18 No. 101 (waterbird).

A1941. *Creation of plover* (known as seven whistlers). (Cf. A1715.1.) — England, U.S.: Baughman.

A1942. *Origin of snipe.*

A1942.1. *Snipe from man admitted neither to heaven nor to hell.* Finnish: Aarne FFC VIII 18 No. 99. Cf. Type 330A and 330B.
Q565. Man admitted to neither heaven nor hell.

A1944. *Creation of sandpiper.*

A1944.1. *Creation of sandpiper: Pharaoh's cook calls drowned army to dinner.* Finnish: Aarne FFC XXXIII 53 No. 82**.

A1945. *Creation of gull.*

A1945.1. *Gull from transformed cat.* A cat catches a strong fish with her claws. The fish carries the cat on its back to the sea, where the gull originates from the cat. (Cf. A1710.) — Finnish: Aarne FFC VIII 18 No. 102.

A1945.2. *Gull a transformed ravished maiden.* While he is sleeping, the maiden the hero has stolen is ravished by another man. The hero thereupon turns her into a gull. (Cf. A1710.) — Finnish: Kalevala Rune 38.

A1946. *Creation of quail.* India: Thompson-Balys.

A1947. *Creation of pigeon.* India: Thompson-Balys.

A1947.1. *Creation of sea pigeon.* Eskimo (Ungava): Turner RBAE XI 263, (Labrador): Hawks GSCan XIV 161.

A1948. *Creation of dove.* Dh I 164 (cf. A1751). — S. Am. Indian (Chiriguano): Métraux RMLP XXXIII 178.

A1950. Creation of coraciiformes.

A1951. *Creation of the kingfisher.* India: Thompson-Balys; Chinese: Graham.

A1952. *Creation of hoopoe.* Transformed shepherd. (Cf. A1710, A2261.1.) — *BP III 286 (Gr. No. 173); Dh III 394; Greek: Grote 182 (Tereus).

A1957. *Creation of woodpecker.*

A1957.1. *Woodpecker from devil's herdsman transformed.* The devil strikes his herdsman so that he turns into a bird who continually calls after his beloved cow. (Cf. A1710.) — Livonian: Loorits FFC LXVI 90 No. 80.
D153.1. Transformation: man to woodpecker.

A1958. *Creation of owl.* (Cf. A1710.) — Fb "ugle" III 964b. — Lappish: Qvigstad FFC LX 38 No. 47; India: Thompson-Balys.
E613.2. Reincarnation as owl.

A1958.0.1. *The owl is a baker's daughter* who objected to the size of the dough put into the oven for Jesus when he appeared in her house as a beggar. Type 751A (woodpecker). (Cf. A1710.) England, U.S.: Baughman.*

A1960. Creation of ciconiiformes.

A1965. *Creation of bittern.* Maori: Clark 101.

A1965.1. *Bittern from Pilate transformed.* (Cf. A1710.) — Estonian: Aarne FFC XXV 148 No. 56.

A1965.2. *Bittern from transformed shepherd.* (Cf. A1710, A2261.1.) — *BP III 286 (Gr. No. 173); Dh III 394.

A1966. *Creation of stork* (Cf. A1715.) — Dh II 102; India: Thompson-Balys.

C841.1. Tabu: killing stork. Bird was once maiden.

A1970. Creation of miscellaneous birds.

A1975. *Creation of diver* (bird). Greek: Frazer Apollodorus II 45 n. 2 (cf. A1710).

A1981. *Origin of swan.*

A1981.0.1. *Origin of swans from two fowls fed in Urd's well.* Icel.: Snorra Edda Gylf. XVI, Boberg.

A1983. *Creation of duck.* India: Thompson-Balys.

A1988. *Creation of chicken.* India: Thompson-Balys.

A1992. *Creation of crane.* Irish myth: Cross; India: Thompson-Balys.

D162. Transformation: man (woman) to crane.

A1993. *Creation of cuckoo.* Dh II 99, 101 (Cf. A1715.2.) — Livonian: Loorits FFC LXVI 90 No. 78; Flemish: DeMeyer FFC XXXVII 88 No. 94a; Lithuanian: Balys Index No. 3134ff., Legends Nos. 248—252; India: Thompson-Balys.

A1993.1. *Cuckoo a transformed baker.* *Fb "bager" IV 20b.

A1994. *Creation of parrot.* India: Thompson-Balys; S. Am. Indian (Yuracare): Métraux BBAE CXLIII (3) 503, (Paressi): Métraux ibid. 359.

A1996. *Creation of peacock.* India: Thompson-Balys.

A1997. *Creation of papiha.* India: Thompson-Balys.

A2000—A2099. Creation of insects.

A2000. Creation of insects. Knortz Die Inzekten in Sage, Sitte und Literatur (Annaberg 1910). Jewish: Neuman; India: Thompson-Balys.

A2001. *Insects from body of slain monster.* Usually the monster is burnt; sometimes the insects come from his head, sometimes from his body as it burns. (Cf. A1716.1.) — *Dh I 279, III 152ff., 164ff., 170ff. (dragon); *Fb "myre", "myg"; Persian: Carnoy 288; Siberian: Holmberg Siberian 386; Chinese: Eberhard FFC CXX 23, 128; Japanese: Ikeda; N. Am. Indian: *Thompson Tales 354 n. 275.

A2034.2. Mosquitoes from bones of slain demon flung into the air. B713. Bees born from carcass of ox. E616. Reincarnation as insect. G100. Giant ogre. G655. Ogre's ashes cast on stream cause rapids to stop.

A2001.1. *Insects from brains, blood, and bones of slain helpful animal.* India: Thompson-Balys.

A2002. *Origin of insects from various experiences of saint.* Dh I 192f.

A901. Topographical features caused by experiences of primitive hero (demigod, deity). B259.5. Fly, wren, fox live with cleric.

A2002.1. *The god Mahadeo turns wood chips into insects.* India: Thompson-Balys.

A2003. *Origin of insects: released from sack.* God places them in a sack and gives it to hare to carry to stream. He must not look in the sack. When he does so the insects escape. The hare laughs and this is the cause of his split lip. — Livonian: Loorits FFC LXVI 93 No. 104; Lithuanian: Balys Index No. 3131, Legends Nos. 232—244.

A2342.1. Why hare's lip is split. C322. Tabu: looking into bag.

A2004. *Insects from devil's post-hole.* Devil is given enough land to dig a post-hole. From this come all kinds of insects. To stop them a burning log is put in the hole. Insects therefore hate smoke. Dh I 173 — Finnish: Aarne FFC VIII 21 No. 120, XXXIII 55 No. 120.

A2005. *Origin of insects: God throws sand on lazy shepherds.* (Cf. A1716.1). — Esthonian: Aarne FFC XXV 150 No. 70.

A2006. *Origin of insects: monstrous births* from brother-sister incest. India: Thompson-Balys.

A2010. Creation of hymenoptera.

A2011. *Creation of ant.* *Fb "myre" (cf. A2001); India: Thompson-Balys.

A2011.1. *Creation of ant by devil.* *Fb "myre". India: Thompson-Balys; Chinese: Eberhard FFC CXX 23 (cf. A2001).

A2011.2. *Creation of ant: avaricious man transformed.* (Cf. A1715, A1730.) — Dh IV 272f. — Wienert FFC LVI 79 (ET 450), 134 (ST 395); Halm Aesop 294.

Q272. Avarice punished.

A2012. *Creation of bee.* Jewish: Neuman; India: Thompson-Balys.

A2012.0.1. *Creation of honey-bees: transformed man.* India: Thompson-Balys.

A1710. Creation of animals through transformation. D180. Transformation: man to insect.

A2012.1. *Creation of bee to provide wax* for candles in church. (Cf. B259.4.) — *Dh II 129ff.

V133. Holy candles.

A2012.2. *First bees in Ireland.* Irish myth: Cross.

A2012.3. *God sends stinging bees to punish men.* Chinese: Eberhard FFC CXX 187.

A2013. *Creation of hornet.* India: Thompson-Balys.

A2020. Creation of coleoptera.

A2021. *Creation of beetle.* Lappish: Qvigstad FFC LX 39 No. 63.

A2021.1. *Beetle's special sacredness.* India: Thompson-Balys.

A2030. Creation of diptera.

A2031. *Creation of fly.* India: Thompson-Balys.

B259.5. Fly, wren, fox live with cleric.

A2031.1. *Creation of fly: punishment for laziness.* (Cf. A1730.) — Dh II 111ff.

Q321. Laziness punished.

A2031.2. *Flies on the ark.* Noah tries to keep them out. Devil says that either the flies go in or he does. Noah chooses the lesser of two evils. Later the devil slips in nevertheless. Dh I 268.

A2032. *Creation of flea.* Cf. Type 276**. — Japanese: Ikeda.

A2032.1. *Creation of flea: punishment for laziness.* (Cf. A1730.) — Dh II 111ff.

A2032.2. *Creation of flea: to give women work.* (Cf. A2051.1.) — Flemish: DeMeyer FFC XXXVII 89 No. 125a; cf. Livonian: Loorits FFC LXVI 93 No. 103.

A2032.3. *Origin of flea: from squirrel.* (Cf. A1710.). — Livonian: Loorits FFC LXVI 93 No. 105.

A2032.4. *Creation of flea: God plagues the devil with fleas.* Lithuanian: Balys Legends No. 131ff.

A2033. *Creation of gnat.* Livonian: Loorits FFC LXVI 93 No. 102.
A671.2.7. Gnats in hell.

A2033.0.1. *Gnats created by devil to worry God.* Lithuanian: Balys Legends No. 131f.
A63.4.1. God and devil torment each other with their creations.

A2033.1. *Origin of gnats in Lapland.* Lappish: Qvigstad FFC LX 39 No. 60.

A2034. *Origin of mosquitoes.* India: Thompson-Balys; Japanese: Ikeda; Hatt Asiatic Influences 89f.; Eskimo (Ungava): Turner RBAE XI 264; S. Am. Indian (Tucuna): Nimuendajú BBAE CXLIII (3) 294; N. Am. Indian (Kaska): Teit JAFL XXX 445.

A2034.1. *Deity's wife creates mosquitoes to drive her husband out of jungle.* India: Thompson-Balys.

A2034.1.1. *Mosquitoes created by goddess to make sleeping outside impossible to men.* Chinese: Eberhard FFC CXX 128.

A2034.1.2. *Deity creates mosquitoes to irritate other gods.* Chinese: Eberhard FFC CXX 128.

A2034.2. *Mosquitoes from bones of slain demon flung into the air.* (Cf. A2001.) — India: Thompson-Balys.

A2034.3. *Mosquitoes from ashes of bad woman.* (Cf. A2001.) — Chinese: Eberhard FFC CXX 128.

A2040. Creation of lepidoptera.

A2041. *Creation of butterfly.* India: Thompson-Balys.

A2050. Creation of hemiptera.

A2051. *Creation of louse.* Lappish: Qvigstad FFC LX 39 No. 61; Eskimo (Ungava): Turner RBAE XI 263.

A2051.1. *Louse created to give women work.* (Cf. A2032.2.) — *Fb "lus".

A2052. *Creation of bugs.* Esthonian: Aarne FFC XXV No. 71.

A2053. *Creation of maggots.* India: Thompson-Balys.

A2060. Creation of orthoptera.

A2061. *Creation of cockroach.* India: Thompson-Balys.

A2061.1. *Origin of cockroach in Finland.* Finnish: Aarne FFC VIII 22 No. 125.

A2062. *Origin of locust.* Flemish: DeMeyer FFC XXXVII 90 No. 125b. — Bushman: Bleek and Lloyd 76.

A2063. *Creation of cricket.* India: Thompson-Balys.

A2064. *Creation of grasshopper.* India: Thompson-Balys.

A2070. Creation of miscellaneous insects.

A2091. *Origin of spider.* [1] (Cf. A1751.) — Finnish: Aarne FFC VIII 22 No. 122; India: Thompson-Balys.

A2091.1. *Arachne transformed to spider: vies with goddess in spinning.* Greek: Roscher Lexikon s.v. "Arachne".

A2231.5. Spider vies with Virgin Mary in spinning: cursed. D181 Transformation: man to spider.

A2092. *Origin of scorpion.* India: Thompson-Balys.

A2092.1. *Origin of leaf-scorpion.* India: Thompson-Balys.

A2093. *Origin of mantis.* India: Thompson-Balys.

A2094. *Creation of fireflies.* India: Thompson-Balys.

A2095. *Creation of lac insects.* India: Thompson-Balys.

A2100—A2199. Creation of fish and other animals.

A2100—A2139. CREATION OF FISH

A2100. Creation of fish. India: Thompson-Balys; Jewish: Neuman; Hawaii: Beckwith Myth; 287, 422; Tuamotu: Stimson MS (z—G 3/1100); S. Am. Indian: (Toba): Métraux MAFLS XL 84.

A2110. Creation of particular fishes.

A2111. *Creation of pike.* Lappish: Qvigstad FFC LX 39 No. 56.

A2112. *Creation of mullet.* Hawaii: Beckwith Myth 63.

A2115. *Origin of olachen.* Tahltan: Teit JAFL XXXII 203f.

A2121. *Creation of mackerel.* Dh I 156.

A2122. *Origin of bonito.* Tonga: Buford 57.

A2125. *Origin of salmon.* Tahltan: Teit JAFL XXXII 206.

A2126. *Origin of flounder.*

A2126.0.1. *Origin of flounder from Virgin Mary's half-eaten fish.* (See A2305.1.2.) — *Dh II 1ff. — Finnish: Aarne FFC VIII 21 No. 116, XXXIII 55 No. 116; Livonian: Loorits FFC LXVI 91 No. 91; Esthonian: Aarne FFC XXV 149 No. 64; Lithuanian: Balys Index No. 3180, Legends No. 282.

A2126.1. *Origin of sole.* New Hebrides: Codrington 372.

A2127. *Origin of catfish.* India: Thompson-Balys.

D177. Transformation: man (woman) to catfish.

[1] In folk thought the spider is classed as an insect and not with the other arachnida.

A2131. *Creation of eel.* Finnish: Aarne FFC XXV 149 No. 62; Lithuanian: Balys Legends No. 287.

A2132. *Creation of prawns.* India: Thompson-Balys.

A2135. *Origin of whale.* [1] Eskimo (Central): Boas RBAE VI 637; Kaska: Teit JAFL XXX 452.

A2135.1. *Origin of narwhal.* Eskimo (Cumberland Sound): Boas BAM XV 169, (Cape York): Rasmussen III 79.

A2135.2. *Creation of leviathan.* Jewish: Neuman.
B61. Leviathan.

A2137. *Creation of sharks: from a savage tribe.* India: Thompson-Balys.
A1710. Creation of animals through transformation.

A2140. Creation of reptiles. India: *Thompson-Balys.

A2145. *Creation of snake (serpent).* Finnish: Aarne FFC VIII 19 No. 106; Lappish: Qvigstad FFC LX 38 No. 54; Estonian: Aarne FFC XXV 149 No. 62; Jewish: Neuman; India: *Thompson-Balys; Buin: Wheeler Mono-Alu 28; Chinese: Eberhard FFC CXX 96; S. Am. Indian (Tembe): Métraux RMLP XXXIII 140; Africa (Congo): Weeks 213.
D551.6.3. Transformation by eating snake eggs.

A2145.0.1. *Origin of horned serpent.* N. Am. Indian (Creek): Swanton BBAE LXXXVIII 32f.
B91.3. Horned snake.

A2145.1. *Snake from blood of slain monster.* Medusa. (Cf. A1724, A2001.) — Greek: Fox 34.

A2145.2. *Snake preserved in ark: to stop hole with tail.* Dh I 277. — Finnish: Aarne FFC VIII 19 No. 107, XXXIII 54 No. 107; Esthonian: Aarne FFC XXV 149. No. 61; Lithuanian: Balys Legends Nos. 192ff.
A1021.1. Pairs of animals in ark. B527.2. Helpful animal stops leak in Noah's ark.

A2145.3. *Snake created to suck poison from earth.* Esthonian: Aarne FFC XXV 149 No. 60; India: *Thompson-Balys.
D2161.4.10.2.2. Snake sucks poison from snake bite.

A2145.4. *Snake from devil's slaver.* Estonian: Aarne FFC XXV 148 No. 59.

A2145.5. *Adder harmful to holy person transformed to blindworm.* (Cf. A1710, A1730, A2231.7.) — Dh II 7.

A2146. *Creation of crocodile.* India: Thompson-Balys.

A2147. *Creation of tortoise (turtle).* India: Thompson-Balys; Chinese: Eberhard FFC CXX 96; Hawaii: Beckwith Myth 22, 465; S. Am. Indian (Cashinawa): Métraux BBAE CXLIII (3) 685.

A2148. *Creation of lizard.* Jewish: Neuman; India: Thompson-Balys.

A2148.1. *Creation of chameleon.* India: Thompson-Balys.

A2148.2. *Origin of salamander.* Jewish: Neuman.

---

[1] In folk thought, a fish.

A2160—A2199. ORIGIN OF AMPHIBIANS AND OTHER ANIMAL FORMS

A2160. Origin of amphibia.

A2161. *Origin of toad.* *Fb "lærke" II 499b (Cf. A1755). — Lithuanian: Balys Legends Nos. 124ff., 128f.; Jewish: Neuman.

A2162. *Origin of frog.* Finnish: Aarne FFC XXXIII 55 No. 11; Lappish: Qvigstad FFC LX 38 No. 55 (Cf. A1710). — Lithuanian: Balys Legends Nos. 127fl, 202; Jewish: Neuman; India: Thompson-Balys; Naskapi: Speck JAFL XXVIII 74.

A2170. Origin of miscellaneous animal forms. India: Thompson-Balys.

A2171. *Origin of crustaceans.*

A2171.1. *Origin of crayfish.*

A2171.1.1. *Crayfish from devil's fleas shaken off in water.* (Cf. A1710.) — Estonian: Aarne FFC XXV 151 No. 73.

A2171.2. *Creation of crab.* India: Thompson-Balys.

A2171.3. *Origin of lobster.* Tahiti: Henry 339.

A2171.4. *Origin of shrimp.* Tahiti: Henry 339.

A2181. *Origin of snail.*

A2182. *Origin of worm.*

A2182.1. *Origin of silkworm.* *Dh II 107ff. (cf. A1725.1). — Chinese: Eberhard FFC CXX 79.

A2182.2. *Origin of leech.* India: Thompson-Balys.

A2182.3. *Origin of earth-worm.* India: Thompson-Balys.

A2182.4. *Origin of cutworm.* Hawaii: Beckwith Myth 135.

A2182.5. *Origin of multipede.* Jewish: Neuman.

A2200—A2599. ANIMAL CHARACTERISTICS

A2200—A2299. Various causes of animal characteristics.

A2200. Cause of animal characteristics. See "Register" to Dähnhardt (III 537ff.); also articles scattered through RTP , e. g., V 244, VI, 314, 473, VII 479, VIII 557, IX 165, 491, 646, X 26, 176, 301, 363, XII 667, XIII 344, XIV 379, XV 425, XVI 445, XVII 150, 344, 578. — Jewish: Neuman; Australian: Dixon 290; Miwok: Powers CNAE III 359; Karok: ibid. 36; Alsea: Frachtenberg BBAE LXVII 47ff.; Southern Ute: Lowie JAFL XXXVII 14 No. 6.

A2201. *All qualities of animals appear with their creation.* Jewish: Neuman.

A2210. Animal characteristics: change in ancient animal. (Cf. A2311.) — Dh III 7ff.

B1. Animal elders. Mythical ancestors of tne present animals.

A2211. *Animal characteristics: accidental action of ancient animal.*

A2211.1. *Lynx views country from mountainside: cause of his squint.* (Cf. A2330.2.) — Ojibwa: Jones-Michelson PAES VII (II) 131 No. 10.

A2211.2. *Rabbit laughs: cause of hare-lip.* (Cf. A2216.3, A2234.4, A2342.1.) — *Type 47A; *BP III 75 n. 1. — Finnish: Aarne FFC XXV 144 No. 35; Livonian: Loorits FFC LXVI 89 No. 71; India: Thompson-Balys.

A2211.3. *Wolf falls out of nest: cause of straight back.* (Cf. A2356.2.2.) — Finnish: Aarne FFC XXXIII 53 No. 76**.

A2211.4. *Why some whales die on land: first whale did so.* Tuamotu· Stimson MS (z—G 13/320).

A2211.5. *Shrew blows nose into snout.* Sent after fire, he finds but a little which he tries to revive by hard blowing. — Fang: Nassau 234 No. 3.

A2211.6. *Spider carries large stone on head and drops it: hence spiders under stones.* (Cf. A2433.5.3.) — Gold coast: Barker and Sinclair 84 No. 13.

A2211.7. *Birds cling to sky in flood: cause of tail colors.* (Cf. A2412.2.) — N. Am. Indian: *Thompson Tales 287 n. 57a.

A1020. Escape from deluge. A2291. Animal characteristics obtained during deluge.

A2211.8. *Lizard dips head in palm-oil: cause of red head.* (Cf. 2320.3.) — Ibo (Nigeria): Basden 278.

A2211.9. *Lizard swallows fish bone: hence head bobs up and down.* (Cf. A2474.1.) — Ibo (Nigeria): Basden 278.

A2211.10. *Tortoise left out in rain: hard shell develops.* (Cf. A2312.1.) — — Gold Coast: Barker and Sinclair 115 No. 20.

A2211.11. *How rattlesnake became harmful: earthworm feeds him chili pepper.* S. Am. Indian (Toba): Métraux MAFLS XL 68.

A2211.12. *Buffalo helps tiger quench fire: white mark left* on buffalo's neck where tiger held on while being ducked in water. India: Thompson-Balys.

A2412.1. Markings of mammals.

A2211.13. *Stag defeated by snail vomits his gall-bladder.* India: Thompson-Balys.

A2211.14. *Rat defecates on octopus's head: origin of tubercles on head.* Tonga: Gifford 206.

A2211.15. *Goddess scatters pubic hairs on fish: why he has so many bones.* Tuamotu: Stimson MS (t—G 2/44).

A2212. *Animal characteristics from great fear.* *Dh III 243ff.

A2212.1. *Frightened rabbit puts head in charred tree: hence black ears.* (Cf. A2325.2.) — Finnish: Aarne FFC VII 13 No. 71.

A2212.2. *Frightened animals scatter: cause of present habitat of each.* (Cf. A2433.1.) — Kaffir: Theal 172, 176.

A2213. *Animal characteristics from squeezing or stretching* ancient animal (See A2231.9).

A2213.1. *Ancient animal squeezed: hence small size.* (Cf. A2302.) — Dh III 2—7 (hazel-grouse, squirrel, eagle, wolf, snake's head.)

A2213.2. *Animal pressed: hence facial or bodily marks.* (Cf. A2412.4.) — Dh III 54, (cf. I 201f., 248, II 195); India: Thompson-Balys.

A2213.2.1. *Wildcat's (Lynx's) face mashed in.* (Cf. A2230.1.) — Dh III 5, 6. — N. Am. Indian: *Thompson Tales 300 n. 99; Australian: Dixon 290 (wombat).

A2213.2.2. *Tortoise pressed into earth: hence humpy back.* (Cf. A2356.2.9.) Africa (Ekoi): Talbot 380.

A2213.2.3. *Baboon pressed on hot, flat rock: hence bald place on his back.* (Cf. A2317.10.) — Africa (Hottentot): Bleek 39 No. 19; Indonesian: De Vries's list No. 74.

A2213.2.4. *Why lobster is shallow: insulted cattle step on it.* Chinese: Eberhard FFC CXX 13, No. 2.

A2213.3. *Animals' size increased by stretching.* (Cf. A2312.1, A2301.) — Dh III 2—5 (fish, bat, flying squirrel, monkey).

A2213.4. *Animal characteristics changed by stretching.*

A2213.4.1. *Coyote's muzzle pulled out long.* (Cf. A2335.4.4.) — Dh III 3

A2213.4.2. *Fox's tail pulled out long.* (Cf. A2378.3.4.) —Dh III 3.

A2213.4.3. *Mouse's nose pulled out long.* Salinan: Mason U. Cal. XIV 64

A2213.5. *Animal characteristics from being struck.*

A2213.5.1. *Mole struck on head in attempt to steal fire: hence his flat head.* S. Am. Indian (Toba): Métraux MAFLS XL 109.

A2213.5.2. *Fish struck by coconut: hence flat tail.* Tuamotu: Stimson MS (t—G 3/600).

A2214. *Animal characteristics from dropping ancient animal from air.*

A2214.1. *Swallow thrown on his tail: cause of split tail.* (Cf. A2378.5.1.) — Dh II 126, III 419. — Aarne FFC VII 16 No. 85; Flemish: DeMeyer FFC XXXVII 87 No. 85.

A2214.2. *Ant thrown from heaven: hence narrow waist.* God decides dispute between ant and spider in spider's favor. (Cf. A2355.1.2.) — Finnish: Aarne FFC VII 22 No. 124, XXXIII 55 No. 124; Esthonian: Aarne FFC XXV 149 No. 66; Flemish: DeMeyer FFC XXXVII 89 No. 124; Lithuanian: Balys Index No. 3200, Legends Nos 291—94; India: Thompson-Balys.

A2214.3. *Unicorn thrown from ark and drowned: hence no longer exists.* Dh I 287f.

A2291. Animal characteristics obtained during deluge. B13. Unicorn.

A2214.4. *Crab thrown to ground: breaks into small pieces.* Hence crabs are small. India: Thompson-Balys.

A2214.5. *Tortoise hurled on rock: half falls on land, half in water. Therefore amphibious.* African (Nigeria): Herskovits JAFL XLIV 448ff.

A2433.6. Haunts of reptiles, etc.

A2214.5.1. *Tortoise dropped by eagle: hence cracks in his shell.* (Cf. A2312.1.1.) — Ila (Rhodesia): Smith and Dale 373 No. 23.

J657.2. Tortoise lets self be carried by eagle. Dropped and eaten. K1041. Borrowed feathers. Dupe lets himself be carried aloft by bird and dropped.

A2214.6. *Bat falls from high perch due to extreme heat of sun's rays, breaks bones,* etc. Hence peculiar feet and nose. India: Thompson-Balys.

A2215. *Animal characteristics from throwing members at ancient animal.*

A2215.1. *Stick (leaf) thrown at animal's rump: hence tails.* (Cf. A2378.3.3.) — Finnish: Aarne FFC VIII 14 No. 77 (wolf). — Banks Is.: Dixon 144 (rat).

A2215.2. *Hare runs away at creation; almost loses tail.* When, as the most timid of all beasts, he runs away, God throws a tail at him from a pile of tails. (Cf. A2378.4.1.) — Dh III 185. — Finnish: Aarne FFC VIII 13 No. 72; Flemish: DeMeyer FFC XXXVII 86 No. 72.

A2215.3. *Bowl placed on turtle's back: hence his shell.* (Cf. A2312.1.) — British New Guinea: Dixon 145.

A2215.4. *Red fruit thrown at rail's (bird's) head: hence red lump on head.* (Cf. A2321.8.) — Banks Is: Dixon 144.

A2215.5. *Fox struck with churn-dash: hence white tail.* (Cf. A2378.8.1.) — Cf. Type 3. — Finnish: Aarne FFC VIII 15 No. 79; Estonian: Aarne FFC XXV 146 No. 43.

A2215.6. *God throws diver's feet after him; hence his feet reach backward.* (Cf. A2371.2.9.) Dh III 46. — Finnish: Aarne FFC VIII 18 No. 103.

A2216. Animal characteristics: members bitten or cut off. Tuamotu: Stimson MS (z—G 13/441).

A2216.1. *Bear fishes through ice with tail: hence lacks tail.* (Cf. A2378.2.4.) — *Type 2; Dh III 49. — Finnish: Aarne FFC VIII 14 No. 78; Esthonian: Aarne FFC XXV 146 No. 42; Flemish: DeMeyer FFC XXXVII 86 No. 78; Japanese: Ikeda.

K1021. The tail fisher.

A2216.2. *Devil pulls off goats' tails: hence lack tails.* (Cf. A2378.2.2.) — *BP III 200 (Gr. No. 148).

A2216.3. *Moon splits hare's lip with hatchet: hence hare-lip.* (Cf. A2211.2, A751.5.1, A2342.1.) — Hottentot: Bleek 72 No. 33.

A2216.4. *Bush-rat bites off tortoise's tail: hence tortoise's short tail.* (Cf. A2378.4.4.) — Ibo (Nigeria): Thomas 70.

A2216.5. *Hawk's tail cut in two by sword* as he is being transformed. Cause of his forked tail. (Cf. A2378.5.2.) — Dh III 54.

A2216.6. *God as falcon has tail cut off: hence falcon's short tail.* Icel.: Boberg.

A2216.7. *Formerly animals have ears like elephant's: hare bites them off.* India: Thompson-Balys.

A2217. *Appearance of animal from marking or painting.*

A2217.1. *Birds painted their present colors.* Lithuanian: Balys Index No. 3158; N. Am. Indian: *Boas RBAE XXXI 664, (Tahltan): Teit JAFL XXXII 208 No. 1 (10), (Cherokee): Alexander N. Am. 66 (robin redbreast).

A2217.2. *Chipmunk's back scratched: hence his stripes.* As he is trying to escape, bear catches him with his claws and marks him permanently. (Cf. A2413.2.) — Seneca: Curtin-Hewitt RBAE XXXII 111 No. 13, 422 No. 78, Curtin Seneca 437, 505.

A2217.3. *Marks on certain fish from fingerprints.* Tuamotu: Stimson MS (z—G 13/317, t—G 3/600).

A2217.3.1. *Marks on certain fish from St. Peter's fingerprints.* (Cf. A901, A2217.2, A2412.4). — Dh II 180 ff., III 55. — Flemish: DeMeyer FFC XXXVII 89 No. 119b; Irish: Beal XXI 305; England: Baughman.

A2217.3.2. *Marks on certain fish from devil's fingerprints.* England: *Baughman.

A2218. *Animal characteristics from burning or singeing.* (Cf. A2378.8.4, A2411.1.2.5, A2411.1.3.2, A2411.1.4.1, A2411.1.6.5, A2411.2.1.1, A2411.2.1.4, A2411.2.1.9, A2411.2.1.7, A2411.2.1.11, A2411.2.5.2, A2411.2.5.1, A2411.2.1.15, A2411.2.6.8, A2411.4.2, A2411.4.3, A2411.5.3.) — Dh III 71ff; Chinese: Graham.

A2218.1. *Raven caught in smoke-hole: hence is black.* (Cf. A2411.2.1.5.) — Dh III 72, 77ff. — N. A. Indian: *Boas RBAE XXXI 652, (Tahltan): Teit JAFL XXXII 203 No. 1 (3).

A2218.1.1. *Animal scorches self while putting out fire* in land of fire, woe and darkness. Wales: Baughman.

A2218.2. *Jackal carries sun in bag on back; burns his back black.* (Cf. A721.1, A2356.3.2.) — Hottentot: Bleek 67 No. 29.

A2218.3. *Animal who steals fire scorched: cause of his color.* (Cf. A1415.) — Dh III 93ff. — India: Thompson-Balys.

A2218.4. *Coyote burnt when hay is set afire: hence yellow patch behind his ears.* Salinan: Mason U. Cal. XIV 88, cf. 107.

A2218.5. *Robin steals fire, has breast scorched.* England: Baughman.

A2218.6. *Raven singes feet on hot stones: why its wings clap when it flies.* (Cf. A2442.2.1.) — Dh III 72. — Finnish: Aarne FFC VIII 17 No. 91.

A2218.7. *Rabbit burns self under chin when he steals an ember.* S. Am. Indian (Toba): Métraux MAFLS XL 109.

A2218.8. *Eel burned by torch: hence red eyes.* Marquesas: Handy 80.

A2219. *Other accidents to ancient animal.*

A2219.1. *Animal has color spilled on him: cause of his color.* (Cf. A2391.1, A2411.1.1.1, A2411.1.2.4, A2411.1.3.1, A2411.2.1.1, A2411.1.4.2, A2411.1.6.3, A2411.2.1.4, A2411.2.1.6, A2411.2.4.1, A2411.2.6.1, A2411.2.6.5, A2411.2.6.6, A2411.2.6.11, A2411.4.1.) — Dh III 64ff. — India: Thompson-Balys; Ila (Rhodesia): Smith and Dale 366 No. 17; S. Am. Indian (Cashinawa): Métraux BBAE CXLIII (3) 685.

A2219.2. *Cow swallows book; cause of maniplies in stomach.* Cheremis: Sebeok-Nyerges.

A2219.3. *Only one serpent had sting: fed poison to the rest.* India: Thompson-Balys.

A2532.1. Why snakes are venomous.

A2220. Animal characteristics as reward.

A2220.1. *Hedgehog's skin reward for good deed.* (Cf. A2311.4.) — Esthonian: Aarne FFC XXV 146 No. 44.

A2221. *Animal characteristics reward for pious act.* (Cf. A2231.).

A2287. Jesus causes animal characteristics. B131.5. Cock crows, "Christus natus est." B250. Religious animals. Q20. Piety rewarded. V. Religion.

A2221.1. *Animals blessed for honoring infant Jesus.* (Cf. A2231.4, A2356.2.7, A2381.1.) — Dh II 15f., 195ff.; Flemish: DeMeyer FFC XXXVII 86 No. 58c (cross on back of ass). — Finnish: Aarne FFC VIII 13 No. 67 (hog has good flesh); French: Sébillot France III 256.

V211.1. The Nativity of Christ.

A2221.2. *Animals blessed for good services at crucifixion.* (Cf. A2231.2.)

V211.2.3. The Crucifixion.

A2221.2.1. *Flies on Christ's body rewarded.* They look like nails and prevent more nails being driven. They may eat at the king's table. (Cf. A2545.1.) Estonian: Aarne FFC XXV 150 No. 68 (cf. No. 69).

B483. Helpful fly.

A2221.2.2. *Blood from cross on robin redbreast:* He helps Jesus; rewarded with red breast. (Cf. A2353.2.) — Fb "rodkjælk". — Finnish: Aarne FFC XXXIII 54 No. 92**; Livonian: Loorits FFC LXVI 90 No. 82; Flemish: DeMeyer FFC XXXVII 87 No. 92**; Lithuanian: Balys Index No. 3130, Legends Nos. 229ff.; England: Baughman.

A2221.2.3. *Blood of scourged Christ on certain spiders.* (Cf. A2411.3.2.) — Flemish: DeMeyer FFC XXXVII 89 No. 122a.

A2221.2.4. *Swallows lift Christ's crown of thorns from his brow:* why their nests are not destroyed. (Cf. A2431.3.5.) — Fb "svale" III 660b; Sebillot RTP III 156.

Q150. Immunity from disaster as reward.

A2221.2.4.1. *Swallows put on mourning at crucifixion:* have never taken it off. Spanish: Boggs FFC XC 37 No. *243.

A2221.2.4.2. *Crossbill, attempting to draw thorn from the crown of thorns, twists bill* in the attempt. England: Baughman.

A2221.3. *Markings on animals as recollections of Christ's life and sufferings.* (Cf. A2412.) — Dh II 227ff.

A2221.4. *Ant collects incense and myrrh for Christ: grows thin in middle.* (Cf. A2451.1, A2453.1.) — Livonian: Loorits FFC LXVI 93 No. 98.

A2126. Origin of flounder from Virgin Mary's half-eaten fish.

A2221.5. *Animal blessed for helping holy fugitive.* (Cf. A2231.7.1.) — Dh II 53ff. — Irish: Beal XXI 306; Livonian: Loorits FFC LXVI 93 No. 100.

B487. Helpful spider. B523.1. Spider-web over hole saves fugitive. R220. Flights.

A2221.5.1. *Ox helps patriarch who in joy kisses him on the lips:* hence no hair on ox's lips. Jewish: bin Gorion Born Judas III 118, 304, *Neuman.

A2221.6. *Animal blessed for obedience to deity.*

A2221.6.1. *Bird coloring as reward for obedience to deity.* India: Thompson-Balys.

A2411.2. Origin of color of bird.

A2221.7. *Dove returns to ark in obedience to Noah:* receives sheen of raven. Irish myth: Cross.

A1021.2. Bird scouts sent out from Ark.

A2221.8. *Squirrel's markings and immunity from falling as reward by deity.* India: Thompson-Balys.

A2412.1. Markings of mammals. A2441.1. Animal's gait or walk — mammals.

A2221.9. *Why sheep walk with bowed heads: they have remained so after having bowed to God.* India: Thompson-Balys.

A2441.12. Cause of sheep's walk.

A2221.10. *Sheep helpful to the Lord: get wool.* Irish: Beal V 271.

A2221.11. *Deity rewards animal for bringing him water:* cause of present characteristics. Maori: Clark 54.

A2222. *Animal characteristics reward for hospitality.*

A2431.4.1. Why sparrow may build nest near people's houses: reward for hospitality. Q45. Hospitality rewarded.

A2222.1. *Thrush's hospitality to peacock rewarded by being given motley coat of feathers.* (Cf. A2411.2.1.1.) — Type 235. — Livonian: Loorits FFC LXVI 90 No. 81.

A2223. *Animal characteristics reward for helpfulness.*

A2223.1. *Cat helps man build house: may occupy chimney corner.* (Cf. A2233.2, A2433.3.1.) — Dh III 203f.

A2223.2. *Bird carries deity (his daughter) home from land of skulls: given brilliant plumage.* (Cf. A2313.4, A2321.6, A2421.5.) — African (Ekoi): Talbot 276.

E485. Land of skulls.

A2223.3. *Mouse gathers rice for man: may eat a little of his rice daily.* India: Thompson-Balys.

A2435. Food of animal.

A2223.4. *Pike helps Christ cross stream: made king of fishes.* Lithuanian: Balys Legends No. 286.

B243. King of fishes.

A2223.5. *Dog guards master's life and wealth: may eat before other animals.* India: Thompson-Balys.

A2545.3. Why dog eats first.

A2223.6. *Tortoise given hard shell when it ferries rice-goddess across stream.* India: Thompson-Balys.

A2312.1. Origin of tortoise's shell.

A2223.7. *Ravens show Adam how to bury dead: are born with white feathers.* Jewish: Neuman.

A2223.8. *Chameleon saves hero's life: may change color.* Fang: Einstein 96.

A2229. *Animal characteristics as reward — miscellaneous.*

A2229.1. *Dog rescues cow's teats from fire: origin of his black muzzle.* (Cf. A2335.4.3.) — *Dh III 72ff., 500 — Finnish: Aarne FFC VIII 10 No. 48, XXXIII 53 No. 48; Estonian: Aarne FFC XXV 143 No. 27.

A2229.2. *Dog lets devil into church to steal: rewarded with dog-skin.* (Cf. A2311.1.) — Finnish: Aarne FFC VIII 10 No. 50.

A2229.3. *Owl will not betray curate: therefore may live in steeple.* (Cf. A2433.4.1.) — Flemish: DeMeyer FFC XXXVII 88 No. 98b.

A2229.4. *Fly steals fire from spider: may eat everywhere.* Spider brings fire from hell. Fly steals it from him on the way. (Cf. A2545.1.) — Livonian: Loorits FFC LXVI 93 No. 101.

A2229.5. *Cuckoo delivers other birds from their cruel king: they agree to hatch out cuckoo's young.* Lithuanian: Balys Index No. 3137; Legends Nos. 253ff.

A2431.2.1. Why cuckoo has no nest.

A2229.6. *Bird has red spot on its tail as reward for having moved woman's organ to its present position.* India: Thompson-Balys.

A1313.3. Misplaced genitalia. A2378.8. Origin of color of animal's tail.

A2230. Animal characteristics as punishment.

A2231. *Animal characteristics: punishment for impiety.* (Cf. A2221, A2311.8, A2422.2, A2302.2, A2355.1.2, A2542.1.) — Dh II 252f. (fish). — Spanish Exempla: Keller; Finnish: Aarne FFC VIII 17 No. 97, XXXIII 54 No. 97 (hazelcock).

A2287. Jesus causes animal characteristics. B250. Religious animals. C94. Tabu: rudeness to sacred person or thing. M400. Curses. Q220. Impiety punished. V. Religion.

A2231.1. *Animal characteristics: punishment for discourteous answer to God (saint).* (Cf. A2411.2.6.) — Jewish: Neuman; Maori: Clark 53.

A2231.1.1. *Discourteous answer: why cow (horse) is always eating.* When God (Peter) wants to use the cow (horse) the excuse is made that she (he) is eating. Curse: "May you always be eating!" (Cf. A2472.1, A2478.) — Dh II 93; *Fb "hest" IV 211b. — Finnish: Aarne FFC VIII 11 No. 59 (horse); ibid. 12 No. 62 (cow); Esthonian: Aarne FFC XXV 143 No. 32 (horse); Lithuanian: Balys Index No. 3094, Legends Nos. 163—175.

M411.2. Beggar's curse. Beggar is refused request. "May your bread turn to stones!"

A2231.1.2. *Discourteous answer: flounder's crooked mouth.* When God asks him where he is going, instead of answering he turns to go toward God. His mouth becomes crooked. (Cf. A2341.1.) — Dh III 24f. — Finnish: Aarne FFC VIII 21 No. 117; Livonian: Loorits FFC LXVI 91 No. 92; Flemish: DeMeyer FFC XXXVII 89 No. 117; Lithuanian: Balys Index No. 3178, Legends Nos. 273 — 281.

A2252.4. Flounder complains in race: crooked mouth.

A2231.1.3. *Discourteous answer: why crab has eyes behind.* (Cf. A2332.4.1.) — Estonian: Aarne FFC XXV 151 No. 74; Lithuanian: Balys Index No. 3178, Legends Nos. 273 — 281.

A2231.1.4. *Discourteous answer: tortoise's shell.* Zeus celebrates a wedding and invites the animals. Tortoise is late. Why? "I like my house." "May you bear your house always." (Cf. A2312.1.) — Dh IV 275f. — Wienert FFC LVI 76 (ET 424), 139 (ST 443); Halm Aesop No. 154.

A2231.2. *Animal characteristics: punishment for hostility at crucifixion.* (Cf. A2221.2.) — Dh II 202ff. — Lithuanian: Balys Legends Nos. 251f., 264.

P445.1. Why weavers are the most unhappy of men. They gave a nail for the crucifixion. Q221.2. Punishment for opposition to Christ at crucifixion.

A2231.2.1. *Crane will not weep at crucifixion: must suffer thirst* in August and break bills. Is the only bird who will not weep. (Cf. A2234.1, A2435.4.2.) — Köhler-Bolte I 3.

Z351. Only one person refuses to weep at hero's death.

A2231.2.2. *Swallows torment Christ on cross: lose voice.* (Cf. A2422.9.) — Fb "svale" III 660b.

A2231.3. *Animal characteristics: punishment for working on holy day.*

C631. Tabu: breaking the Sabbath.

A2231.3.1. *Cuckoo builds nest on Annunciation Day: has no nest.* (Cf. A2431.2.1.) — Dh II 6.

A2231.3.2. *Bees work on Sabbath: may not get honey from red clover.* (Cf. A2435.5.1.) — *Dh III 306ff. — North Carolina: Brown Collection I 634.

A2231.4. *Frog fails to honor infant Jesus: loses tail.* (Cf. A2221.1, A2378.2.3. — Dh II 17.

A2231.5. *Spider vies with Virgin Mary in spinning: cursed.* Dh II 253.

A2091.1. Arachne transformed to spider. Vies with goddess in spinning.

A2231.6. *Spider steals thread from Christ: has thread in back of body.* (Cf. A2356.2.8.) — Finnish: Aarne FFC VIII 22 No. 123; Estonian: Aarne FFC XXV 149 No. 65.

A2231.7. *Animal harmful to holy person cursed.*

A2145.5. Adder harmful to holy person transformed to blindworm. Q227. Punishment for opposition to holy person.

A2231.7.1. *Animal cursed for betraying holy fugitive.* (Cf. A2221.5.) — Dh II 51ff.; Child V 491 s.v. "partridge"; Ireland: Baughman.

A2231.7.1.1. *Beetle cursed for betraying Holy Family* on way to Egypt; beetle now has its eyes always on the ground. Ireland, Scotland: *Baughman.

A2231.7.2. *Animal cursed for refusing to carry holy fugitive across stream.* (Cf. A2371.2.1.) — Dh II 88ff. — Lithuanian: Balys Legends No. 286.

A2231.7.3. *Tortoise cursed for going under water while ferrying rice-goddess:* people will be able to kill it with iron-made spears. India: Thompson-Balys.

A2231.8. *Toad refuses to weep over its dead children:* dries up when dead. Cursed by Virgin Mary. (Cf. A2234.4, A2468.2.) — Dh II 247f.

A2231.9. *Fish in deluge deride God: are flattened with blow.* They mock God for his powerlessness over them. (Cf. A2213, A2305.1, A2354.1.) — Dh I 290.

A2231.10. *Crab beats deity's forbidden drum:* eyes lift out of body. (Cf. A2332.4.2.) — Fjort: Dennett 123.

A1731. Creation of animals as punishment for beating forbidden drum. C0. Tabu: contact with supernatural. C500. Tabu: touching. C916.2. Animals produced when forbidden drum is beaten.

A2231.11 *Beetle demands return of gold from God: must hum.* In his overweening pride he hits fence and ever afterward has hummed. (Cf. A2426.3.1.) — Dh. III 376. — Finnish: Aarne FFC VIII 22 No. 121.

A2231.12. *Buffaloes fail to come at god's leavetaking: now are killed by tigers.* India: Thompson-Balys.

A2231.13. *Loris refuse to look at sun* who comes out when they are dancing: hence never looks at sun. India: Thompson-Balys.

A2232. *Animal characteristics: punishment for immoderate request.* Dissatisfied animal finds that when his request is granted he is worse off than before. — *Dh III 176ff.

L420. Overweening ambition punished. Q338. Immoderate request punished. W128. Dissatisfaction.

A2232.1. *Camel asks for horns: punishment, short ears.* (Cf. A2325.4.) — Dh IV 265f.; *Köhler-Bolte I 579; *Crane Vitry 148f. No. 37; Jewish: Neuman; *Chauvin II 110 No. 76, 118 No. 102 (ass); Sebillot RTP II 492; Wienert FFC LVI 78 (ET 437); 109 (ST 215, 389); Halm Aesop No. 184.

J950. Presumption of the lowly. L400. Pride brought low.

A2232.2. *Bees pray for sting: punishment, first sting suicidal.* (Cf. A2346.1.) — Dh IV 266; Wienert FFC LVI 77 (ET 434), 110 (ST 216); Halm Aesop No. 287.

A2232.3. *Beetle makes immoderate request; ant moderate:* inverse awards. Creator hears wishes of animals. Beetle wants strong, noble appearance. Ant is modest. Beetle punished by being made to creep on ground. Ant is given own castle. (Cf. A2441.3.1.) Livonian: Loorits FFC LXVI 92 No. 97.

A2232.4. *Griffin disdains to go on ark; drowned:* hence extinct. Dh I 288.

A1021.1. Pairs of animals in ark. A2291. Animal characteristics obtained during deluge. B42. Griffin.

A2232.5. *Animals ask for goddess's perfume: punishment, bad odor.* (Cf. A2416.1.) — Tshi: Ellis 338.

A2232.6. *Birds who aspire to blackbird's coat punished.* (Cf. A2412.2.2.) — Ila (Rhodesia); Smith and Dale 351 No. 6.

A2232.7. *Peacock given ugly feet so as to prevent too great arrogance.* (cf. A2375.2.2.) — Dh I 196.

A2232.8. *Dog's embassy to Zeus chased forth; dogs seek ambassador:* why dogs sniff each other under leg. (Cf. A2471.1.) — *Dh IV 137ff.

J950. Presumption of the lowly. L400. Pride brought low. Q433.3. Zeus has embassy of dogs imprisoned for fouling his court.

A2232.9. *Ants ask God to give them wings: wind blows them away.* Cyprus: Hadjioannou 64.

A2232.10. *Raven attempts to imitate dove: punished with awkward gait.* Jewish: Neuman.

A2232.11. *Donkeys ask immediate reward from God: eat their own excrements.* Jewish: Neuman.

A2233. *Animal characteristics: punishment for laziness.* S. Am. Indian (Toba): Métraux MAFLS 79.

Q321. Laziness punished.

A2233.1. *Animals refuse to help dig well (make road) and are punished.* *Type 55; *Dh III 312ff., 323.

A2233.1.1. *Animals refuse to help dig well: may not drink from river or spring.* (Cf. A2435.1.1.) — Type 55; Dh III 312ff. — Estonian: Aarne FFC XXV 148 No. 54; Livonian: Loorits FFC LXVI 90 No. 83; Lithuanian: Balys Index No. 3096, Legends Nos. 176—182.

18

A2233.1.2. *Snake refuses to help make road: dies on road.* (Cf. A2441.4.1.) — Type 55. — Finnish: Aarne FFC VIII 19 No. 108.

A2233.1.3. *Shrew refuses to help make road: dies on road.* (Cf. A2468.1.) — Dh III 323f.; cf. Type 55. — Finnish: Aarne FFC VIII 15 No. 80; Lithuanian: Balys Index No. 3098, Legends Nos. 183—191.

A2233.1.4. *Sloth refuses to help make road: may not look upon sun.* India: Thompson-Balys.

A2233.2. *Dog will not help build house: must remain out of doors.* (Cf. A2223.1, A2433.3.2.) — Dh III 203f.

A2233.2.1. *Too cold for hare (dog) to build house in winter, not necessary in summer:* must go without house. Lithuanian: Balys Index No. 72*, Legends No. 214; Finnish: Aarne Index No. 72*; Russian: Andrejev No. 72**.

J2171.2.1. Does not need roof when it is fair, cannot put it on when it rains.

A2233.3. *Owl as watchman goes to sleep: does not see by day.* He is placed as watchman of wren who is imprisoned in a mousehole. (Cf. A2332.6.6.) — Type 221; *Dh IV 172ff.

A2233.4. *Grasshopper builds no house for winter; ant strikes him blind:* therefore born blind. (Cf. A2332.6.3.) — Dh III 21.

J711.1. Ant and lazy cricket (grasshopper).

A2233.4.1. *Bird neglects to build nest: goes without.* (Cf. A2431.2.) — Dh. III 202ff.

A2234. *Animal characteristics: punishment for disobedience.* India: Thompson-Balys.

C94. Tabu: rudeness to sacred person or thing. M400. Curses. Q220. Impiety punished. Q325. Disobedience punished.

A2234.1. *Raven does not return to Noah: must suffer thirst and break bill.* (Cf. A2231.2.1, A2411.2.1.5, A2435.4.3.) — Variant: he is cursed to be black or to eat carrion. *Köhler-Bolte I 3; Dh I 284; Irish myth: Cross.

A1021.2. Bird scouts sent out from ark. A2291. Animal characteristics obtained during deluge.

A2234.1.1. *Raven does not return to ark in obedience to Noah: black color is resulting punishment.* Irish myth: Cross; Jewish: Neuman.

A2221.7. Dove returns to ark in obedience to Noah: receives sheen of raven.

A2234.2. *Animals eat deity's forbidden fruit: punished.* (Cf. A2371.3.1.) — African (Ekoi): Talbot 377.

C621. Forbidden fruit.

A2234.3. *Lemur looks where forbidden: has big eyes.* (Cf. A2332.3.1.) — Fang: Nassau 235 No. 3.

C300. Looking tabu.

A2234.4. *Hare weeps for mother when forbidden: moon hits him and cleaves lip.* (Cf. A2211.2, A2231.8, A2342.1.) — Bushman: Bleek and Lloyd 59.

C762.2. Tabu: too much weeping for dead.

A2235. *Animal characteristics caused by animal's lateness at distribution of qualities.* (Cf. A2378.2.5.) — Dh III 182ff. — India: Thompson-Balys; Mpongwe: Nassau No. 11 (hog lacks horns); Gold Coast:

Barker and Sinclair 145 No. 28 (leopard cannot catch game that passes him on right side); Congo: Weeks 213 No. 9 (water snake lacks poison): Zulu: Callaway 355 (hydrax lacks tail); Ila (Rhodesia): Smith and Dale 368 No. 19 (zebra lacks horns); Marshall Islands: Davenport 222.

A2236. *Animal characteristics: punishment for planning man's downfall.* Jewish: Neuman.

A2236.1. *What creature has sweetest blood: gnat's tongue torn out.* Assembly to decide who has the sweetest blood so that it may be the food for the serpent. Gnat discovers that man has the sweetest blood. Rather than let him tell this secret, swallow tears out his tongue. Gnat can only buzz. (Cf. A2344.2, A2426.3.2.) — Dh I 281, 332ff.; Circassian: Nicolaides and Carnoy RTP I 80; Lithuanian: Balys Legends No. 192.

K961.0.1. Blood of certain animal said to be sweet.

A2236.2. *Animal characteristics: punishment for carrying devil into paradise.*

A1331. Paradise lost.

A2236.2.1. *Snake carries devil into paradise: loses feet.* (Cf. A2371.3.1.) — Dh I 207 — India: Thompson-Balys.

A2236.2.2. *Peacock has snake carry devil into paradise: cursed with ugly voice and feet.* (Cf. A2375.2.2, A2423.1.2.) — Dh I 206.

A2236.3. *Animal punished for not warning of devil's temptation in Eden.* India: *Thompson-Balys.

A2236.4. *Magpie tells man he is to die next day: no tongue and long tail.* God pulls out his tongue and makes his tail long for doing this forbidden thing. (Cf. A2344.2.6, A2378.3.1.) — Finnish: Aarne FFC VIII 16 No. 89.

A2236.5. *Animal punished for not heralding dawn.* India: *Thompson-Balys.

A2236.6. *Nit tries to bore through man's head: must remain at edge of hair.* (Cf. A2433.5.1.) — Estonian: Aarne FFC XXV 151 No. 72; Livonian: Loorits FFC LXVI 94 No. 106.

A2236.7. *Jay carries sulphur to devil in hell: must be quiet at noon.* North Carolina: Brown Collection I 633.

A2236.8. *Cat commanded to pray so as not to slay man: why cat purrs.* Lithuanian: Balys Index No. 3121, Legends Nos. 222ff.

A2237. *Animal characteristics punishment for meddling.*

Q340. Meddling punished.

A2237.1. *Animal reveals mistress's adultery: punished by master.* (Cf. A2411.2.1.5, A2422.1.1.). — Greek: Fox 280 (raven becomes black). — Zuñi: Handy JAFL XXXI 464 No. 17 (dog loses power of speech).

B131.3. Bird reveals woman's infidelity. B134.1. Dog betrays woman's infidelity. J551.1. Cocks who crow about mistress's infidelity killed. Discreet cock saves his life. J2365. Fool discloses woman's adultery: lover kills him. Q241. Adultery punished. T230. Faithlessness in marriage.

A2238. *Animal characteristics: punishment for greed.*

A2261.2. Spider transformed for greediness: now occupies dark corners. Q272. Avarice punished.

A2238.1. *Rabbit (frog) eats seed-grain from fields: nose closed during sowing season.* (Cf. A2335.2.4.) — Finnish: Aarne FFC VIII 21 No. 119; Lithuanian: Balys Legends No. 290.

A2238.2. *Ring-dove eats man's grain: man may kill him.* Similarly francolin and guinea fowl. Ila (Rhodesia): Smith and Dale 351 No. 6.

A2238.3. *Fish eat other fish: guilty must swim deep.* (Cf. A2444.1.) — Finnish: Aarne FFC VIII 19 No. 104.

A2238.4. *Diver eats nests of small birds: must not nest away from water.* (Cf. A2431.3.2.) — Finnish: Aarne FFC VIII 19 No. 104.

A2239. *Animal characteristics from miscellaneous punishments.*

A2239.1. *Hare punished for perjury: eyes deep in head.* (Cf. A2332.4.1.). — Finnish: Aarne FFC VIII 13 No. 70.

Q263. Lying (perjury) punished.

A2239.2. *Fly punished for failing to answer question:* is speechless, buzzes and associates with foul things. (Cf. A2426.3.3, A2433.5.2.) Africa (Ekoi): Talbot 384.

A2239.3. *Ass betrays deity's secret: hence his ugly bray.* India: Thompson-Balys.

A2423.1. Animal's ugly voice.

A2239.3.1. *Owl reveals deity's secret: power of speech removed.* India: Thompson-Balys.

A2239.4. *Woodpecker punished for stinginess.* North Carolina: Brown Collection I 633.

A2239.5. *Animals punished for assaulting women.* India: Thompson-Balys.

A2239.6. *Ass has cross on shoulders from being struck by Balaam.* (Cf. A2356.2.7.) — England: Baughman.

A2239.7. *Crocodile is punished for trying to attack man he is carrying: has only half tongue.* India: Thompson-Balys.

A2239.8. *Animal punished for hardheadedness* (frog toothless, mole sightless). Jewish: Neuman.

A2239.9. *Why mouse is crushed whenever she crosses a road: elephant's curse.* Africa (Sandeh): Casati I 221.

A2239.10. *Why elephant hurts himself when running through the grass: mouse's curse.* Africa (Sandeh): Casati I 221.

A2240. Animal characteristics: obtaining another's qualities. Jewish: Neuman.

A2221.7. Dove returns to Ark in obedience to Noah: receives sheen of raven.

A2241. *Animal characteristics: borrowing and not returning.* Animal borrows a member (or quality) from another and refuses to return it. (Cf. A2242, A2313.3, A2345.1, A2351.3, A2375.2.1, A2421.4, A2435.4.1.) — *Dh III 130 ff. — Lithuanian: Balys Legends No. 268ff.; India: Thompson-Balys.

K230. Other deceptions in the payment of debt. K232. Refusal to return borrowed goods. K351.2. Thief borrows cloak so as to carry food. Disappears with it.

A2241.1. *Stag's horns borrowed from dog.* (Cf. A2326.1.1.) — Dh. III 131.

A2241.2. *Owl's wings borrowed from rat* (or other animal). Dh III 131.

A2241.3. *Partridge's voice borrowed from tortoise.* Dh III 132.

A2241.4. *Cuckoo borrows food from other birds.* (Cf. A2435.4.1.) — Dh III 133.

A2241.5. *Nightingale borrows blindworm's eye.* Each has one eye. Nightingale borrow's blindworm's and will not return it. (Cf. A2332.6.1.) — *Type 234; *Dh III 136ff.; *Köhler-Bolte I 72. — Finnish: Aarne FFC XXXIII 55 No. 110** (frog in place of nightingale). — Japanese: Ikeda; English: Shakespeare Romeo and Juliet III v. 31.

E781.1. Substituted eyes. Lost eyes are replaced by those of another person or animal.

A2241.6. *Jay borrows cuckoo's skin.* (Cf. A2313.1.) — *Type 235.

A2241.7. *Squirrel borrows coney's tail.* When coney's tail is not returned, he goes in shame to live among rocks. (Cf. A2378.1.5, A2433.3.5.) — Ila (Rhodesia): Smith and Dale 357 No. 10.

A2241.8. *Boy borrows python's hands and feet:* hence python lacks them. (Cf. A2371.3.1.) — Africa (Ekoi): Talbot 374.

A2241.9. *Hornbill borrows tomtit's bill.* (Cf. A2343.1.4.) — Ila (Rhodesia): Smith and Dale 374 No. 24.

A2241.10. *Beaver borrows muskrat's tail* and never gives it back. Menomini: Skinner and Satterlee PaAM XIII 405.

A2241.11. *Monkey borrows tail from deer* and refuses to return it. India: Thompson-Balys.

A2242. *Animal characteristics: obtaining for feast and not returning.* (Cf. A2378.1.5, A2378.2.6.) — *Dh III 133ff.

A2243. *Animal characteristics: lending and refusing to receive back.* Indonesian: DeVries's list No. 117.

A2243.1. *Spider hands box to ant and refuses to take it back:* hence ants carry huge loads. Gold Coast: Barker and Sinclair 66 No. 9.

A2245. *Animal characteristics: stolen from another animal.* (Cf. A2313.3, A2375.2.2.) — Dh III 127f. — India: Thompson-Balys.

A2245.1. *Thrush steals woodcock's song.* (Cf. A2423.1.1, A2423.2.1.) — Finnish: Aarne FFC VIII 18 No. 98.

A2247. *Animal characteristics: exchange of qualities.* (Cf. A2313.2, A2326.1.2. A2326.1.4, A2326.2.1,. A2332.6.5,A2345.4, A2378.1.3, A2378.1.4, A2421.2, A2421.3, A2431.3.3, A2431.3.4, A2435.3.1, A2435.3.2.) — Dh III 123—126. — Eskimo (West Hudson Bay): Boas BAM XV 307, (Labrador): Hawks GSCan XIV 159.

A2742. Plant characteristics from exchange of qualities.

A2247.1. *Buffalo and cow exchange hides:* hence bad fitting hides. (Cf. A2311.6.) — Indonesian: *DeVries's list No. 97.

A2247.2. *Snake and turtle exhange head for fangs.* Explains snake's fangs and snake-like head of turtle. (Cf. A2320.2, A 2345.5.) — Australian: Dixon 291.

A2247.3. *Rhinoceros exchanges his red hide for hippopotamus's black.* (Cf. A2411.1.6.2., A2411.1.6.7.) — Ila (Rhodesia): Smith and Dale 372 No. 22.

A2247.4. *Dove and magpie exchange eggs* — dove's seven for magpie's two: why dove has two eggs. (Cf. A2486.3.) — *Type 240.

A2247.5. *Toad trades his tail for mole's eyes.* Spanish: Boggs: FFC XC 38 No. 287.

A2247.6. *Beaver and muskrat exchange tails.* Malecite: Speck JAFL XXX 481f.

A2250. Animal characteristics: result of contest. *Dh III 141ff. — Arawak and Carib: Alexander Latin American 274; India: Thompson-Balys; Chinese: Graham.

A2250.1. *Cock and ptarmigan in contest: winner to live in town.* (Cf. A2433.1.1, A2433.4.2, A2433.4.3.) — Finnish: Aarne FFC XXXIII 54 No. 83*; Esthonian: Aarne FFC XXV 147 No. 49.

A2250.1.1. *Man and tiger in contest: winner to live in town.* India: Thompson-Balys.

A2250.2. *Lizard wins contest with toad: why snakes and lizards change their skins.* India: Thompson-Balys.

A2251. *Animal characteristics from contest in carrying.*

A2251.1. *Ant carries load as heavy as himself.* Defeats bear, raven (or other bird). Various explanations. (Cf. A2435.3.3, A2486.1.) — *Type 280; *Dh III 144.

A2252. *Animal characteristics determined by race.* *Dh III 142ff.

A2252.1. *Race of animals to see where each shall live.* (Cf. A2433.1.1.) — *Dh III 145.

A2252.2. *Race of ox and horse: ox must labor.* Horse wins and ox must serve as draft animal. (Cf. A2515.1.) — *Dh III 144.

A2252.3. *Race of culture hero with ostrich:* ostrich loses beautiful feathers. (Cf. A2402.2.) — Dh III 145.

A2252.4. *Flounder complains in race: crooked mouth.* In race between fish he cries out in jealousy because herring is winning. He is punished with crooked mouth. (Cf. A2341.1.) — *Dh IV 192—197; *BP III 284 (Gr. No. 172).

A2231.1.2. Discourteous answer: flounder's crooked mouth.

A2253. *Animal characteristics from jumping contest.*

A2253.1. *Dog burned in jumping contest over fire: enmity between dog and hare.* Dh III 324.

A2254. *Bird characteristics from flying contests.* German: Grimm No. 171.

B242.1.2. Wren king of birds. Wins contest for kingship.

A2255. *Animal characteristics result of lawsuit.*

A2255.1. *Wool on his forehead awarded sheep in lawsuit.* He is given the privilege of keeping it when the rest of his body is shorn. (Cf. A2322.5.) — Finnish: Aarne FFC VIII 12 No. 64.

A2255.2. *Lizard loses lawsuit: must bob his head.* Lizard and ant accused of theft of king's crow. Ant pours boiling water down lizard's throat. When case is tried, lizard cannot talk but only bobs head up and down. Adjudged guilty and condemned to bob his head eternally. (Cf. A2474.1.) — Gold Coast: Barker and Sinclair 48 No. 5.

A2256. *Animal characteristics from contest in watching.*
K52. Contest in seeing sunrise first.

A2256.1. *Hare and man contest in watching for leaf to fall off tree.* First one to succeed may eat other. Hare loses. India: *Thompson-Balys.

A2257. *Animal characteristics from duel.*

A2257.1. *Why tiger does not attack wild boar until latter is old:* result of duel. India: Thompson-Balys.
K97.1. Boar to duel with tiger cakes mud on body; defeats tiger.

A2258. *Animal characteristics: as a result of quarrel.* India: Thompson-Balys.

A2260. Animal characteristics from transformation.

A2261. *Animal characteristics from transformation of animal.*
A2275.3. Animal cries reminiscent of former life as man.

A2261.1. *Shepherd transformed to bird still calls sheep:* explanation of bird cries. Usually told of hoopoe and bittern. (Cf. A1952, A1965.2, A2275.3, A2425, A2426.2.3, A2426.2.4.) — *Dh III 392—396; BP III 285 (Gr. No. 173). — Japanese: Ikeda; Chinese: Eberhard FFC CXX 123 No. 83, 127.

A2261.2. *Spider transformed for greediness: now occupies dark corners.* (Cf. A2433.5.3.) — Gold Coast: Barker and Sinclair 69 No. 10.

A2261.3. *Catfish transformed from woman still carries women's tatoo marks.* India: Thompson-Balys.
A2412.4. Markings on cod-fish.

A2261.3.1. *Catfish transformed from children still carry marks* of children's knife holder. India: Thompson-Balys.

A2261.4. *Woodpecker transformed from stingy woman: therefore stingy.* North Carolina: Brown Collection I 633.

A2261.5. *Weeping man turned into owl; still bewails sorrows.* India: Thompson-Balys.

A2261.6. *Snipe messenger for warriors because he was a messenger when a man.* Tuamotu: Stimson MS (z—G 13/10).

A2262. *Animal characteristics from transformation of implement* (or other object). (Cf. A2335.3.1, A2378.3.3, A2378.4.1.) — *Dh III 14ff.

A2262.1. *Horse originally had eyes on feet: put out and became eyelike marks.* (Cf. A2371.2.7.) — Dh III 45. — Finnish: Aarne FFC VIII 12 No. 61.

A2262.2. *Pegs driven into backs of baboons become tails.* (Cf. A2378.9.2, A2378.1.1.) — Bushman (South of Zambesi): Theal 56.

A2262.3. *Serpent steals from God's coat a stick for his back.* (Cf. A2356.1.1.) — Finnish: Aarne FFC VIII 19 No. 109.

A2270. Animal characteristics from miscellaneous causes.

A2271. *Animal characteristics learned from another animal.*

A2271.1. *Thrush teaches dove to build nest.* (Cf. A2431.3.1.) — *Type 236; Dh III 191ff. — Finnish: Aarne FFC VIII 17 No. 93; Flemish: DeMeyer FFC XXXVII 88 No. 93.

A2271.2. *Sparrow taught to sing by lark* but not sufficiently: where sparrow got voice. Lithuanian: Balys Legends No. 266.

A2272. *Animal characteristics: imitation of other animal or object.*

A2272.1. *Animal cries: imitation of sounds.* (Cf. A2425.) — *BP II 283, III 365.

A2272.1.1. *Nightingale hears boy call oxen:* learns her song. (Cf. A2426.2.1.) — Estonian: Aarne FFC XXV 147 No. 53.

A2272.1.2. *Cricket hears water hiss on hot iron:* learns his song. (Cf. A2426.3.4.) — Livonian: Loorits FFC LXVI 93 No. 99.

A2272.1.3. *Garden warbler hears smith beat iron:* learns his song. (Cf. A2426.2.2.) — Estonian: Aarne FFC XXV 148 No. 55.

A2272.2. *Lizard's tail imitated from snake's.* Finnish: Aarne FFC VIII 20 No. 110, XXXIII 55 No. 110.

A2275. *Animal habit a reminiscence of former experience.*

A2275.1. *Animal cries a lament for person lost when animal was transformed.* (Cf. A2260, A2425.) — Dh III 387. — Benga: Nassau 163 No. 21; India: *Thompson-Balys.

A2275.2. *Animal cries a lament over animal's transformation.* (Cf. A2425, A2426.2.5.) — *Dh III 376ff.

A2275.3. *Animal cries reminiscent of former life as man.* (Cf. A2261.1, A2426.2.3, A2426.2.4.) — Dh III 394ff., 398ff.; India: *Thompson-Balys.
E601. Reincarnation: former lives remembered.

A2275.4. *Animal cries recall ancient adventure.* The ancient animal cries out in difficulty. The present animal has the same cry. (Cf. A2426.1.1, A2426.4.1.) — India: Thompson-Balys; Ibo (Nigeria): Basden 139; Angola: Chatelain 217 No. 38.

A2275.4.1. *Green pigeon cheated out of its chick: is always mourning.* India: Thompson-Balys.

A2275.5. *Animal's seeking attitude from ancient loss.* The ancient animal loses something. Its descendants are forever seeking for the lost object. This explains the characteristic bearing of certain animals. (Cf. A2471.)

A2275.5.1. *Hog loses pancake in mud: still seeks it.* (Cf. A2471.2, A2477.1, Z24.1.) — *Dh III 280ff.; (Cf. Type 2025.)

A2275.5.2. *Hawk (vulture) loses grandmother: still hovers and seeks her.* (Cf. A2471.3.) — Ibo (Nigeria): Basden 274, (Cameroon): Mansfield 233.

A2275.5.3. *Bat, diver, and thornbush shipwrecked.* Bat brought money, bush put on clothes, and diver brought leather. All shipwrecked. Diver is looking for his leather. Bush looks for his clothers and holds fast to all passers-by. Bat is abroad only at night to escape creditors. (Cf. A2471.4, A2491.1.) — *Dh IV 273f; *BP I 137. (Gr. No. 18). — Wienert FFC LVI 35; Halm Aesop No. 306.

A2275.5.4. *Dolphins seek King Solomon's ring.* He loses his magic ring in the sea. They are sent by God to get it. This is why they go up and down in the sea. (Cf. A2444.2.) — Dh I 331; Jewish: Neuman.

B548.2.1. Fish recovers ring from sea. D1335.5.2. Solomon's power to hold kingdom dependent on ring: drops in water. H1132.1. Task: recovering lost ring from the sea. N211.1. Lost ring found in fish.

A2275.5.5. *Dog loses his patent right; seeks it: why dogs look at one another under the tail.* (Cf. A2471.1.) Dh IV 129. — U.S.: Baughman.

A2275.6. *Son accidentally kills father, who returns to life as cuckoo* and tells people when to sow grain. India: Thompson-Balys.

A2281. *Enmity between animals from original quarrel.* (Cf. A2494.1.1, A2494.1.3, A2494.2.3.) — Dh III 331. — Finnish: Aarne FFC VIII 11 Nos 56, 57; Esthonian: Aarne FFC XXV 143 No. 31; Livonian: Loorits FFC LXVI 88 No. 62; Flemish: DeMeyer FFC XXXVII 86 No. 56; Jewish: Neuman; Japanese: Ikeda; Korean: Zong in-Sob 36 No. 20; Benga: Nassau 99 No. 6.

A2281.1. *Cat loses dog's certificate: enmity between cats and dogs.* Dog is given a certificate of nobility. Through cat's carelessness it is lost. (Cf. A2275.5, A2494.1.2.) *Type 200. — Finnish: Aarne FFC VIII 11 No. 53; Estonian: Aarne FFC XXV 143 No. 30; Livonian: Loorits FFC LXVI 88 No. 61; Flemish: DeMeyer FFC XXXVII 85 No. 53.

A2281.1.1. *Cat garbles message from man to tiger: enmity between man and tiger.* India: *Thompson-Balys.

A1335.1. Origin of death from falsified message.

A2281.1.2. *Quarrel of dog and cat about which was higher caste.* India: Thompson-Balys.

A2281.2. *Squirrel steals dog's needle: enmity between them.* (Cf. A2494.4.1.) — Finnish: Aarne FFC VIII 11 No. 52.

A2281.3. *Why cat and dog fight: dog ate up cat's part in master's reward.* India: Thompson-Balys.

A2282. *Present habitat of animals result of ancient quarrel.* (Cf. A2433.3.3, A2433.3.4, A2433.3.21, A2433.6.1.) — Benga: Nassau 202 No. 32; Ila (Rhodesia): Smith and Dale 372, 381.

A2283. *Two animals learn songs together — one successfully, the other unsuccessfully.* (Cf. A2425.) — *Dh III 365ff.

A2284. *Origin of animal characteristics: animal persuaded into self-injury.*

K1000. Deception into self-injury.

A2284.1. *Animal persuaded to amputate limb: therefore lacks it.* (Cf. A2371.2.10, A2377.1.) — Australian: Dixon 146 (kangaroo's forepaws), 288 (emu's wings).

A2284.2. *Bustard persuaded to kill all but two children: has but two eggs.* (Cf. A2486.2.) — Australian: Dixon 289.

A2284.3. *Worm, thinking that world is coming to end, blinds self* so as not to see calamity. (Cf. A2332.6.4.) — Dh III 21.

A2284.4. *Elephant tricked into eating own testicles.* Has them inside. (Cf. A2365.1.1.) — Ila (Rhodesia): Smith and Dale 361 No. 14.

A2284.5. *Coyote persuaded to break leg: therefore has thin right leg.* (Cf. A2371.2.6.) — Dh III 46.

A2284.6. *Jackal persuades hyena to jump and break foot.* Latter has short left hind foot. (Cf. A2375.2.5.) — Hottentot: Bleek 14 No. 14.

A2286. *Animal characteristics established by deity.* Yunca (Peru): Alexander Lat. Am. Myth 229.

A2286.0.1. *God makes serpent ugly.* (Cf. A2402.1, A2494.) — Finnish: Aarne FFC VIII 19 No. 109.

A2286.1. *Creation interrupted since God must go to a fire.*

A2286.1.0.1. *Animal characteristics because creator had not enough time to finish what he began.* S. Am. Indian (Caingang): Métraux BBAE CXLIII (1) 474.

A2286.1.1. *Creation of hog incomplete since God has to go to a fire: cause of hog's round snout.* (Cf. A2335.4.2.) — Dh III 24, 493. — Finnish: Aarne FFC VIII 12 No. 65.

A2286.2. *Animal characteristics result of contest between God and devil.*

A2286.2.1. *Devil's animals devour God's.* God makes white fish, devil a pike to eat it up; God a worm, devil a frog to eat it, etc. (Cf. A1751.) — Finnish: Aarne FFC VIII 20 No. 115; Estonian: Aarne FFC XXV 149 No. 63.

A2286.2.2. *Devil gives horse four eyes; God reduces them to two.* Esthonian: Aarne FFC XXV 144 No. 33.

A2286.2.3. *Devil's cows one-horned; God makes them two-horned.* (Cf. A2326.3.1.) — Livonian: Loorits FFC LXVI 88 No 63.

A2286.2.4. *God changes color (tails) of devil's cows.* Devil makes all animals of same color (or all tailless). When God makes them of different colors (or with tails) devil no longer recognizes them. (Cf. A2378.1.) — Esthonian: Aarne FFC XXV 146 No. 47; Lithuanian: Balys Index No. 3083, Legends Nos. 134—137.

A2287. *Jesus causes animal characteristics.* (Cf. A2221, A2231.)

A2287.1. *Jesus drives evil spirits into hogs: hence short snouts.* (Cf. A2335.4.1.) — Dh II 81. — Finnish: Aarne FFC VIII 12 No. 66.

A2287.1.1. *Jesus drives evil spirits into hogs: hence "toes" on back of foreleg.* (Cf. A2371.2.2.) — Dh II 82.

A2291. *Animal characteristics obtained during deluge.* Jewish: Neuman; Achawoi: Alexander Lat. Am. 270.

A1020. Escape from deluge. A2211.7. Birds cling to sky in flood: cause of tail colors. A2232.4. Griffin disdains to go on ark; drowned: hence extinct. A2234.1. Raven does not return to Noah: must suffer thirst and break bill. A2214.3. Unicorn thrown from ark and drowned: hence they no longer exist. A2382.1. Magpie is hybrid of dove and raven; was not baptized by water of the flood in Noah's time. B754.4. Male rabbit bears young. Female rabbit escaped Noah on ark and drowned.

A2292. *Animal characteristics: change for convenience.* India: *Thompson-Balys.

A2294. *Wild animals lose their ferocity through fear of Behemoth.* Jewish: Neuman.

A2300—A2399. Causes of animal characteristics: body.

A2300. Origin of animal characteristics: body.

A2300.1. *Shape of bee's body.* Dh I 129.

A2301. *Animal's body made larger.* (See A2213.3.) — India: Thompson-Balys.

A2301.1. *Mouse's body made larger.* Tahltan: Teit JAFL XXXII 231.

A2301.2. *Spider's body made larger.* Sinkyone: Kroeber JAFL XXXII 347.

A2301.3. *Coyote's body made larger.* (See A2213.3.) — Dh III 3.

A2301.4. *Bat's body made larger.* (See A2213.3.) — Dh III 4.

A2301.5. *Flying-squirrel's body made larger.* (See A2213.3.) — Dh III 4.

A2302. *Animal's body made smaller.* (See A2213.1.) — India: Thompson-Balys.

A2302.1. *Mouse's body made smaller.* Jamaica: Beckwith MAFLS XVII 260 No. 55; Tahltan: Teit JAFL XXXII 231.

A2302.2. *Hazel-cock's body made smaller.* (See A2231, A2213.1.) Dh III 2. — Lappish: Qvigstad FFC LX 38 No. 51.

A2302.3. *Squirrel's body made smaller.* (See A2213.1.) — Dh III 2.

A2302.4. *Eagle's body made smaller.* (See A2213.1.) — Dh III 6.

A2302.5. *Wolf's body made smaller.* (See A2213.1.) — Dh III 7.

A2302.6. *Lice made smaller.* India: Thompson-Balys.

A2305. *Origin of animal's flat body.*

A2305.1. *Origin of fish's flat body.* (See A2231.9.) — Flemish: DeMeyer FFC XXXVII 89 No. 119a.

A2305.1.1. *Origin of steel-head salmon's flat body.* Tahltan: Teit JAFL XXXII 242.

A2305.1.2. *Origin of flounder's flat body.* (See A2126.) — *Dh I 248, 290, II 1ff., 269, III 35.

A2305.1.3. *Why lobster is flat.* (Cf. A2213.2.4.). — Chinese: Eberhard FFC CXX 13 No. 2.

A2305.2. *Why bedbug is flat.* Korean: Zong in-Sob 36 No. 20.

A2306. *Why animal is slippery.*

A2306.1. *Why eel is slippery.* Marshall Is.: Davenport 226.

A2310. Origin of animal characteristics: body covering.

A2311. *Origin of animal's skin.* Dh III 7ff.

A2311.1. *Origin of dog's skin.* (See A2210, A2229.2.) — Dh I 98ff., III 7.

A2311.2. *Origin of cat's skin.* (See A2210.) — Dh I 157, III 7.

A2311.3. *Origin of wolf's skin.* (See A2210.) — Dh I 151f., III 7.

A2311.4. *Origin of hedgehog's skin.* (See A2210, A2220.1.) — Dh III 7. — Lithuanian: Balys Index No. 3127, Legends No. 228.

A2311.5. *Origin of porcupine's skin.* (See A2210.) — Dh III 7ff.

A2311.6. *Origin of cow's and buffalo's hides.* (See A2247.1.) — Indonesian: De Vries's list No. 97.

A2311.7. *Why crocodile has rough skin.* (Cf. A2315.2.) — India: Thompson-Balys.

A2311.8. *Why frog has rough skin.* India: *Thompson-Balys.

A2311.9. *Why snakes and lizards change skins.* (See A2250.2.)

A2312. *Origin of animal shell.* Tahiti: Henry 339.

A2312.1. *Origin of tortoise's shell.* (See A2215.3, A2231.1.4, A2213.3, A2211.10.) — Dh III 9. — India: Thompson-Balys; Japanese: Ikeḍa; Yoruba: Ellis 273 No. 6.

A2223.6. Tortoise given hard shell when it ferries rice-goddess across stream.

A2312.1.1. *Origin of cracks in tortoise's shell.* Ila (Rhodesia): Smith and Dale 373 No. 23.

A2312.2. *Origin of snail's shell.* Jewish: Neuman; Africa (Fang): Trilles Proverbes 176.

A2312.3. *Origin of dents in crab's shell.* Tuamotu: Stimson MS (3—G 13/420).

A2313. *Origin of bird's feathers.*

A2402.2. How ostrich lost beautiful feathers.

A2313.1. *Origin of cuckoo's feathers.* (See A2241.6.) — Dh. III 140. — Finnish: Aarne FFC VIII 17 No. 94 (cf. A2411.2.6.10).

A2313.2. *Origin of magpie's feathers.* Exchanges with dove. See A2247.

A2313.3. *Origin of peacock's feathers.* (See A2241, A2245.) — Lithuanian: Balys Index No. 3142, Legends No. 256f.

A2313.4. *Origin of nkundak's feathers.* (See A2223.2.)

A2313.5. *Why young ravens have white feathers.* Jewish: Neuman.

A2315. *Origin of fish's scales.*

A2315.1. *Origin of shell-fish's black scales.* Lappish: Qvigstad FFC LX 39 No. 59.

A2315.2. *Origin of alligator's scales.* (Cf. A2311.7.) — Dh III 10. — Am. Negro: (Georgia): Harris Nights 26.

A2317. *Why certain animals are bare of covering.* Dh III 10ff.

A2317.1. *Why swine's belly is bare.* Dh III 10.

A2317.2. *Why fly is bald.* Dh III 11.

A2317.3. *Why buzzard is bald.* Dh III 11. — Ojibwa: Skinner JAFL XXXII 282.

A2317.4. *Why crow's head is bald.* Dh III 13.

A2317.5. *Why raven is bald.* Dh III 13. — Tahltan: Teit JAFL XXXII 221.

A2317.6. *Why magpie is bald.* Dh III 14.

A2317.7. *Why vulture is bald.* Dh. III 14. — Menomini: Skinner und Satterlee PaAm XIII 78; S. Am. Indian (Toba): Métraux MAFLS XL 161.

A2317.8. *Why bat is bald.* Dh I 95.

A2317.9. *Why bird's feet are bare.* Dh II 261.

A2317.10. *Why baboon has bare place on back.* (See A2213.2.3.)

A2317.11. *Why john-crow has bald head.* Jamaica: Beckwith MAFLS 259 No. 47.

A2317.12. *Why opossum has bare tail.* Am. Negro (Georgia): Harris Remus 129 No. 27; Cherokee: Alexander N. Am. 65.

A2317.12.1. *Why kangaroo-rat's tail is not bushy.* Salinan: Mason UCal XIV 83.

A2317.12.2. *Why jackal has bare tail.* India: Thompson-Balys.

J681.2. Jackal and leopard tie tails together for mutual protection. Frightened, they run apart and injure each other.

A2317.12.3. *Why rat's tail is round and without any hair.* (Cf. A2378.9.5.) — India: Thompson-Balys.

A2320. Origin of animal characteristics: head.

A2320.1. *How snake got small head.* (See A2213.1.) — Jewish: Neuman.

A2320.1.1. *Why weaver bird's head is small.* India: Thompson-Balys.

A2320.2. *How turtle got snake-like head.* (See A2247.2.)

A2320.3. *How lizard got red head.* (See A2211.8.) — Jewish: Neuman.

A2320.3.1. *Origin of mudhen's red head.* Hawaii: Beckwith Myth 230.

A2320.4. *Why crab has no head.* India: Thompson-Balys.

A2320.5. *Why bird's head is so large.* India: *Thompson-Balys.

A2320.6. *Why crocodile has marks of water pot on head.* India: Thompson-Balys.

A2320.7. *Why palm-rat has swollen head.* Africa (Congo): Weeks Jungle 455.

A2321. *Origin of bird crests.* Dh III 18f. — Tahltan: Teit JAFL XXXII 208f.

A2321.1. *Origin of goose's crest.* Dh III 18.

A2321.2. *Origin of hoopoe's crest.* Dh III 18.

A2321.3. *Origin of woodpecker's crest.* Dh III 18.

A2321.4. *Origin of crested-lark's crest.* Dh III 19.

A2321.5. *Origin of kingfisher's crest.* Dh III 19.

A2321.6. *Origin of nkundak's crest.* (See A2223.2.)

A2321.7. *Origin of buzzard's crest.* Cherokee: Alexander N. Am. 65.

A2321.8. *Origin of red lump on rail's head.* (See A2215.4.)

A2321.9. *Origin of willow-grouse's crest.* Tahltan: Teit JAFL XXXII 209.

A2321.10. *Origin of cock's red crest.* Lithuanian: Balys Index 3160; India: Thompson-Balys.

A2321.10.1. *Why the cock's comb becomes white when he is angry.* Jewish: Neuman.

A2321.11. *Origin of woodpecker's crest.* India: Thompson-Balys.

A2322. *Origin of hair and mane.* Dh III 34f.

A2322.1. *How buffalo got hair under chin.* Dh III 34.

A2322.3. *How zebra got its mane.* Ila (Rhodesia): Smith and Dale 368 No. 19

A2322.4. *How goat got his beard.* Dh I 2, 181.

A2322.4.1. *How goat got his mane.* India: Thompson-Balys.

A2322.5. *Why sheep may keep wool which grows on his forehead.* (See A2255.1.)

A2322.6. *Why the gorilla and chimpanzee have hair all over the body.* Punishment for not guarding possessions at creation. Bulu: Krug 111f.

A2325. *Origin of animals' ears.*

A2325.1. *Why rabbit has long ears.* Chuh: Kunst JAFL XXVIII 354.

A2325.2. *Why hare's ears are black.* (See A2212.1.)

A2325.3. *Why ass has long ears.* Flemish: DeMeyer FFC XXXVII 86 No. 58b.; Lithuanian: Balys Index No. 3125, Legends No. 226.

A2325.4. *Why camel has short ears.* (See A2232.1.)

A2325.5. *Why zebra has long ears.* Ila (Rhodesia): Smith and Dale 368 No. 19.

A2325.6. *Why cat has jagged ears.* Irish myth: Cross.

A2325.7. *Why camel has no ears.* (Cf. A2232.1.) — Jewish: Neuman.

A2325.8. *Why serpent has no ears.* Jewish: Neuman.

A2326. *Origin and nature of animal's horns.* Dh III 30ff. — India: Thompson-Balys.

A2326.1. *How animals got horns.* Africa (Fang): Tessman 16f.

A2326.1.1. *How stag got antlers.* From camel. See A2241.1.

A2326.1.1.1. *Why deer has antlers: as reward for not cheating.* Jewish: Neuman; India: Thompson-Balys.

A2326.1.2. *How caribou got antlers.* Exchanged his teeth for walrus's horns. (See A2247.) Eskimo (Labrador): Hawks GSCan XIV 159.

A2326.1.3. *How sheep got horns.* Lithuanian: Balys Index No. 3126; Tahltan: Teit JAFL XXXII 215.

A2326.1.4. *How ox got horns.* Exchanged for horse's teeth. (See A2247.)

A2326.1.5. *How goats got horns.* Tahltan: Teit JAFL XXXII 215.

A2326.1.6. *How horned-viper got horns.* Dh III 34.

A2326.2. *Why some animals have no horns.*

A2326.2.1. *Why cats have no horns.* See A2247; Dh III 125; Sebillot RTP II 491.

A2326.2.2. *Why dog has no horns: they were stolen by deer* (goat). India: Thompson-Balys.

A2326.2.3. *Originally cock had horns.* Chinese: Eberhard FFC CXX 13.

A2326.3. *Nature of animal's horns.*

A2326.3.1. *Why cows have two horns.* (See A2286.2.3.)

A2326.3.2. *How stag got long antlers.* Dh III 30.

A2326.3.3. *Why antelope's antlers reach backward.* Dh III 30.

A2326.3.4. *Why buffalo's horns are bent.* Dh III 30.

A2326.3.5. *Why mountain-sheep's horns are close together.* Kaska: Teit JAFL XXX 430.

A2330. Origin of animal characteristics: face.

A2330.1. *How wildcat got his mashed face.* (See A2213.2.1.)

A2330.2. *How lynx got his squint.* (See A2211.1.)

A2330.3. *Why monkey's face is black.* India: Thompson-Balys.

A2330.4. *Origin of marks on tiger's face.* India: Thompson-Balys.
A2412.1. Markings of mammals.

A2330.5. *Why flea's face is red.* Korean: Zong in-Sob 36 No. 20.

A2330.6. *Why pheasant's cheeks are red.* Korean: Zong in-Sob 32 No. 15.

A2330.7. *Why dove's head is marked as it is.* Korean: Zong in-Sob 32 No. 15.

A2330.8. *Why rail (bird) has red forehead.* New Hebrides: Codrington 361.

A2332. *Origin and nature of animals' eyes.*

A2332.1. *Origin of animals' eyes.*

A2332.1.1. *How mouse got his eyes.* Dh III 19.

A2332.1.2. *How fly got his eyes.* Dh III 19.

A2332.1.3. *How herring got his eyes.* Dh III 44.

A2332.1.4. *How fox got his eyes.* Stole from birch tree. (See A2245.) — Dh III 129.

A2332.1.5. *Where owl got his eyes.* Eskimo (Alaska): Jenness 32.

A2332.2. *Number of animal's eyes.*

A2332.2.1. *Why horse has only two eyes.* (See A2286.2.2.)

A2332.3. *Size of animals' eyes.*

A2332.3.1. *Why lemur has big eyes.* (See A2234.3.)

A2332.3.2. *Why zabi's eyes are narrow:* because he laughs so hard. India: Thompson-Balys.

A2211.2. Rabbit laughs: cause of harelip.

A2332.3.3. *Why caribou has small eyes.* Eskimo (Labrador): Hawks GSCan XIV 161.

A2332.4. *Shape and position of animal's eyes.* Lithuanian: Balys Legends No. 281.

A2332.4.1. *Why hare has deep-set eyes.* (See A2239.1.)

A2332.4.2. *Why crab lifts eye out of body or has eye behind.* (See A2231.10, A2231.1.3.)

A2332.4.3. *Why frog's eyes bulge out.* Africa (Congo): Weeks Jungle 459.

A2332.5. *Color of animal's eyes.* Dh III 60f.

A2332.5.1. *Why coyote has yellowish eyes.* Zuñi: Handy JAFL XXXI 461.

A2332.5.2. *Why cuckoo has red eyes.* Sébillot RTP III 262.

A2332.5.3. *Why water-hen has red eyes.* Plains Cree: Skinner JAFL XXIX 349.

A2332.5.4. *Why toad has red eyes.* Dh III 60. — Jewish: Neuman.

A2332.5.5. *Why turkey has red eyes.* Dh III 61.

A2332.5.6. *Why wooddove has green eyes.* Dh III 61.

A2332.5.7. *Why wild duck has red eyes.* Dances for trickster. *Dh III 61.

K826. Hoodwinked dancers. A trickster induces ducks to dance with closed eyes and kills them.

A2332.5.8. *Why herring's eyes are red.* Fb "sild".

A2332.6. *"Blindness" in animals.* Animals really or supposedly blind. Dh III 19ff.

A2332.6.1. *Why blindworm has no eyes.* (See A2241.5.)

A2332.6.2. *Why giant lizard is blind.* Chose poison instead of eyes. Dh III 21. — Jewish: Neuman.

A2332.6.3. *Why grasshopper is born blind.* (See A2233.4.)

A2332.6.4. *Why worm is blind.* (See A2284.3.) — Japanese: Ikeda.

A2332.6.5. *Why mole is blind.* — (See A2239.8, A2247, A2378.1.4.) — Spanish: Boggs FFC XC 38 No. 287; Jewish: Neuman.

A2332.6.6. *Why owl is blind by day.* (See A2233.3.) — Lithuanian: Balys Index No. 3140.

A2332.6.7. *Why elephant sees half-blindly.* India: Thompson-Balys.

A2332.6.8. *Why leech is blind.* India: Thompson-Balys.

A2332.6.9. *Why bee is blind.* India: Thompson-Balys.

A2335. *Origin and nature of animal's nasal organ* (nose, snout, proboscis, etc.).

A2335.1. *Origin of animal's nose.*

A2335.2. *Nature of animal's nose.* (See A2213.4.3.)

A2214.6. Bat falls from high perch due to extreme heat of sun's rays, breaks bones, etc. Hence peculiar feet and nose.

A2335.2.1. *Why deer has white mark on nose.* From white ashes. Dh III 79.

A2335.2.2. *Why lynx has short, blunt nose.* Kaska: Teit JAFL XXX 455.

A2335.2.3. *Why raven has nose marked as if it had been broken off.* Tahltan: Teit JAFL XXXII 225.

A2335.2.4. *Why hare's nose is closed during sowing season.* (See A2238.1.)

A2342.1. Why hare's lip is split.

A2335.2.5. *Why steer has no hair on his nose.* (See A2221.5.1.)

A2335.3. *Origin and nature of animal's proboscis.*

A2335.3.1. *Origin of anteater's proboscis.* Transformed digging-stick. (See A2262.)

A2335.3.2. *Why tapir has long nose.* S. Am. Indian (Yagua): Steward-Métraux BBAE CXLIII (3) 736.

A2335.4. *Origin and nature of animal's snout (muzzle).*

A2335.4.1. *Why hog has short snout.* (See A2287.1.) — Africa (Fang): Trilles 179.

A2335.4.2. *Why hog has round snout.* Creation of hog incomplete since God had to go to fire. (See A2286.1.1.)

A2335.4.3. *Why dog has black muzzle.* (See A2229.1.) India: Thompson-Balys.

A2335.4.4. *Why coyote has long muzzle.* (See A2213.4.1.)

A2335.4.5. *Why the wolf's muzzle is black.* Lithuanian: Balys Index No. 3087, Legends No. 147.

A2335.4.6. *Why rat has long snout.* Africa (Cameroon): Mansfield 231.

A2341. *Origin and nature of animal's mouth.* Dh III 22—27.

A2341.1. *Why flounder's mouth is crooked.* (See A2252.4, A2231.1.2.) — Irish: Beal XXI 327.

A2341.2. *Why animal's mouth is large.*

A2341.2.1. *Why opossum's mouth is large.* Choctaw: Alexander N. Am. 64.

A2341.2.2. *Why zebra's mouth is large.* Ila (Rhodesia): Smith and Dale 368 No. 19.

A2341.3. *Why animal's mouth is closed.*

A2341.3.1. *Why serpent's mouth is closed.* Jewish: Neuman.

A2342. *Origin and nature of animal's lips.*

A2342.1. *Why hare's lip is split.* (See A2234.4, A2216.3, A2211.2.) — Dh III 22f.; BP III 75 n. 1; Fb "hare" IV 201a; Types 47, 70. — Micmac: Speck JAFL XXVIII 65; Chitimacha: Swanton JAFL XXX 476.

A2003. Origin of insects: released from sack. Hare laughs. Cause of hare-lip. A2335.2.4. Why hare's nose is closed during sowing season.

A2342.2. *Why ox has no hair on his lips.* (See A2221.5.1.)

A2343. *Origin and nature of bird's beak.* Dh III 26.

A2343.1. *Origin of bird's long beak.*

A2343.1.1. *Where kingfisher got his long beak.* Dh III 27; Korean: Zong in-Sob 35 No. 19.

A2343.1.2. *Where snipe got his long beak.* Tahltan: Teit JAFL XXXII 219.

A2343.1.3. *Why loon has big beak.* Tahltan: Teit JAFL XXXII 209.

A2343.1.4. *Where hornbill got his big beak.* (See A2241.9.) — Africa (Cameroon): Mansfield 234.

A2343.2. *Why bird's beak is colored.*

A2343.2.1. *Why parrot's beak is black.* India: Thompson-Balys.

A2343.2.2. *Why toucan's beak is black.* S. Am. Indian (Chiriguano): Métraux RMLP XXXIII 178.

A2343.3. *Origin of other features of birds' beak.*

A2343.3.1. *Why starling's beak is split.* India: Thompson-Balys.

A2343.3.2. *Why woodpecker has sharp beak.* India: Thompson-Balys.

A2344. *Origin and nature of animal's tongue.* Dh III 27ff.

A2344.1. *Why animal has short tongue.*

A2344.1.1. *Why crocodile has short tongue.* Dh III 28. — Jewish: Neuman; India: Thompson-Balys.

A2344.1.1.1. *Why crocodile has half a tongue.* (Cf. A2239.7.) — India: Thompson-Balys.

A2344.1.1.2. *Why crocodile has no tongue.* India: Thompson-Balys.

A2344.1.2. *Why alligator has short tongue.* Dh III 28.

A2344.2. *Why animal has no tongue.*

Q451.3. Loss of speech as punishment. Q451.4. Tongue cut off as punishment. S163. Mutilation: cutting (tearing) out tongue.

A2344.2.1. *Why gnat has no tongue.* (See A2236.1.)

A2344.2.2. *Why eel has no tongue.* Dh III 27.

A2344.2.3. *Why swallow has no tongue.* Dh III 29.

A2344.2.4. *Why titmouse has no tongue.* Dh III 28.

A2344.2.5. *Why cormorant has no tongue.* (Cf. A2422.8.) — Dh III 28. — N. A. Indian: *Boas RBAE XXXI 678.

K825.1. Cormorant's tongue pulled out by putting louse on it.

A2344.2.6. *Why magpie has no tongue.* (See A2236.4.)

A2344.3. *Cause of color of animal's tongue.*

A2344.3.1. *Why sheep's tongue is black.* Kaska: Teit JAFL XXX 430.

A2345. *Origin and nature of animal's teeth.*

A2345.1. *Where horse got his upper teeth.* Borrowed them from buffalo. (See A2241.)

A2345.2. *Where coyote got his long teeth.* Dh III 33f.

A2345.3. *Where reindeer got his small teeth.* Dh. III 34.

A2345.4. *Where walrus got his tusks.* Traded antlers with caribou for tusks. (See A2247.)

A2345.5. *Where snake got his fangs.* (See A2247.2.) — Jewish: Neuman.

A2345.6. *How elephant got its tusks.* India: Thompson-Balys.

A2345.7. *Why animal lacks teeth.*

A2345.7.1. *Why cow has no upper teeth.* Chinese: Graham.

A2345.7.2. *Why frog has no teeth.* (Cf. A2239.8.) — Jewish: Neuman.

A2345.7.3. *Why caribou has no teeth.* Eskimo (Cumberland Sound): Boas BAM XV 168, 306, (Central Eskimo): Boas RBAE VI 587, (Alaska): Jenness 80, (West Hudson Bay): Boas BAM XV 536, 554, (Labrador): Hawks GSCan XIV 160, (Bering Strait): Nelson RBAE XVIII 449, 460.

A2345.8. *Why hen has no teeth.* Africa (Cameroon): Mansfield 233.

A2345.9. *Why gorilla and chimpanzee have large teeth* in mouth: punishment for neglecting possessions. Bulu: Krug 111f.

A2346. *Origin and nature of insect's sting.*

A2346.1. *Why bees die after they sting.* (See A2232.2.) — Breton: Sébillot Incidents s.v. "abeilles"; Lithuanian: Balys Index 3204, Legends Nos. 296—300.

A2346.2. *Why bee's sting is no longer fatal to man.* India: Thompson-Balys.

A2350. Origin of animal characteristics: trunk.

A2351. *Origin and nature of animal's neck.*

A2351.1. *Why camel's neck bends upwards.* Dh III 35.

A2351.2. *Why eagle-owl's head turns on its neck.* Type 230. — Finnish: Aarne FFC VIII 18 No. 100.

A2351.3. *Where Jahrvogel (rhytidoceros) got its necklace.* Borrowed form dove. (See A2241.) — Dh III 133.

A2351.4. *Origin of animal's long neck.*

A2351.4.1. *Origin of stork's long neck.* India: Thompson-Balys.
A2231. Animal characteristics: punishment for impiety.

A2351.4.2. *Why magpie has long neck.* India: Thompson-Balys.

A2351.4.3. *Origin of antelope's long neck.* Africa (Cameroon): Mansfield 224.

A2351.5. *Why tortoise's neck is outstretched toward the sky:* is looking for his wife, the star. India: Thompson-Balys.

A2471. Why animals continually seek something.

A2351.6. *Where horse got arched neck:* arches neck to kick tiger from rear; remains so. India: Thompson-Balys.

A2351.7. *Why munia wears his crop on the back of his neck.* India: Thompson-Balys.

A2353. *Origin and nature of animal's breast.*

A2353.1. *Why apia (bird) is flat-chested.* Told wife that he was going away to dine. Was too late for his meal. — Ibo (Nigeria): Basden 278.

A2353.2. *Why robin has red breast.* (See A2221.2.2.) — Breton: Sébillot RTP III 157.

A2353.3. *Elephant loses its breasts.* India: Thompson-Balys.

A2353.4. *Why bears do not have breasts for nursing.* Jewish: Neuman.

A2354. *Origin and nature of animal's belly.*

A2354.1. *Why flounder is flat-bellied.* (See A2231.9.)

A2355. *Origin and nature of animal's waist.*

A2355.1. *Why animal has small waist.* Dh III 36ff.

A2355.1.1. *Why spider has small waist.* Dh III 36ff.

A2355.1.2. *Why ant has small waist.* (See A2214.2.) — India: *Thompson-Balys; Korea: Zong in-Sob No. 16, 35 No. 19.

A2356. *Origin and nature of animal's back.* Dh III 42ff.

A2356.1. *Origin of animal's back.*

A2356.1.1. *Origin of snake's back.* From a stick. (See A2262.3.)

A2356.2. *Origin of shape of animal's back.*

A2356.2.1. *Why frog has hunchback.* Dh III 42ff. — Jewish: Neuman.

A2356.2.2. *Why wolf has straight back.* (See A2211.3.) —Dh III 43.

A2356.2.3. *Why cat has arched back.* Dh I 166, III 44.

A2356.2.4. *Why certain fish have bowed backs.* Dh III 44.

A2356.2.5. *Why water-hen has broad back.* Plains Cree: Skinner JAFL XXIX 349.

A2356.2.6. *Why bear has hump on back.* Ojibwa: Jones JAFL XXIX 368.

A2356.2.7. *Why ass has cross on back (shoulders).* (See A2221.1, A2239.6.) — England: Baughman.

A2356.2.8. *Why spider has thread in back of body.* (See A2231.6.)

A2356.2.9. *Why tortoise has humpy back.* (See A2213.2.2.) — Jewish: Neuman.

A2356.2.10. *Why helldiver has flat stern.* Culture hero kicked him. Menomini: Skinner and Satterlee PaAM XIII 269.

A2356.2.11. *Why alligator has rough back.* Am. Negro: (Georgia) Harris Nights 141 No. 26.

A2356.2.12. *Why cow's body has hollow on one side.* India: Thompson-Balys.

A2356.2.13. *Why camel has humped back.* India: Thompson-Balys.

A2356.3. *Origin of color of animal's back.*

A2356.3.1. *Why eagle's back is brown.* Lappish: Qvigstad FFC LX 38 No. 48.

A2356.3.2. *Why jackal has black back.* (See A2218.2.)

A2356.3.3. *Why wolverine has peculiar marks on back.* Kaska: Teit JAFL XXX 458.

A2356.3.4. *Why spider has markings on back.* Kaska: Teit JAFL XXX 241.

A2362. *Origin and nature of animal's buttocks.*

A2362.1. *Why monkey's buttocks are red.* India: *Thompson-Balys.

A2363. *Origin and nature of animal's teats.*

A2363.1. *Why cow has so few teats.* Finnish: Aarne FFC VIII 12 No. 63, (Cf. No. 48).

A2364. *Origin and nature of animal's loins.*

A2364.1. *Why wolverine has red hair on loins.* Tahltan: Teit JAFL XXXII 248.

A2365. *Origin and nature of animal's genitals.* India: Thompson-Balys.

A2365.1. *Nature of animal's testicles.*

A2365.1.1. *Why elephant has testicles inside.* Persuaded to eat them. (See A2284.4.)

A2365.2. *Nature of animal's penis.*

A2365.2.0.1. *Why goat's and cat's members are as they are.* India: Thompson-Balys.

A2365.2.1. *Why animal's penis is large (long).*

A2365.2.1.1. *Why horse's penis is long.* India: Thompson-Balys.

A2365.2.1.2. *Why elephant's penis is large.* India: Thompson-Balys.

A2365.2.1.3. *Why donkey's penis is large.* India: Thompson-Balys.

A2367. *Animal characteristics: inside of body.*

A2367.1. *Animal characteristics: bones.*

A2367.1.1. *Why sucker has small bones in body.* Tahltan: Teit JAFL XXXII 242.

A2367.2. *Animal characteristics:* internal markings.

A2367.2.1. *Why grizzly bears have three stripes on inside of stomach.* Tahltan: Teit JAFL XXXII 208.

A2367.3. *Animal characteristics: blood.*

A2367.3.1. *Origin of serpent's blood and venom.* Jewish: Neuman.
A2532.1. Why snakes are venomous.

A2370. Animal characteristics: extremities.

A2371. *Origin and nature of animal's legs.* Dh III 45.

A2371.1. *Origin of animal's legs.*

A2371.2. *Shape of animal's legs.*

A2371.2.1. *Why sheep has thin legs.* (See A2231.7.2.) — Dh II 91.

A2371.2.2. *Why hog has "toes" on back of foreleg.* Mark of devil's teeth. (See A2287.1.1.)

A2371.2.3. *Why ravens have crooked legs and walk lame.* Tahltan: Teit JAFL XXXII 226.

A2371.2.4. *Why bears have short, crooked legs.* Tahltan: Teit JAFL XXXII 217.

A2371.2.5. *Why there is meat in front of the caribou's lower legs.* Tahltan: Teit JAFL XXXII 217.

A2371.2.6. *Why coyote's right leg is thin.* (See A2284.5.)

A2371.2.7. *Why horse has eye-like marks on forelegs.* (See A2262.1.) — Lithuanian: Balys Legends No. 162.

A2371.2.8. *Why he-goat has shaggy legs.* Braved the wolf, who tore his legs. Dh III 46.

A2371.2.9. *Why diver (loon) holds legs backward.* (See A2215.6.)

A2371.2.10. *Why kangaroo has short front legs.* (See A2284.1.)

A2371.2.11. *Why hare has short pair of legs.* Dh III 23. — Finnish: Aarne FFC VIII 13 No. 73.
A2317.9. Why birds' feet are bare.

A2371.2.12. *Why daddy-long-legs has long legs.* India: Thompson-Balys.
A2221. Animal characteristics reward for pious act.

A2371.3. *Why animal lacks legs.*

A2371.3.1. *Why snake has no legs.* (See A2234.2, A2236.2.1, A2241.8.) — Dh I 116, 207, 216, 219f. — Jewish: Neuman; India: Thompson-Balys.

A2371.4. *Origin of color of animal's legs.*

A2371.4.1. *Why curlew has red legs.* Australian: Dixon 292.

A2371.4.2. *Why fox's legs are black.* Am. Negro (Georgia): Harris Friends 10.

A2375. *Origin and nature of animal's feet.* Dh III 45ff.
A2214.6. Bat falls from high perch due to extreme heat of sun's rays, breaks bones, etc. Hence peculiar feet and nose.

A2375.1. *Where animal got feet.*

A2375.2. *Nature of animal's feet.*

A2375.2.1. *Why partridge has pretty feet.* Exchanged with peacock. (Also told of jay and flamingo.) (See A2241.) — India: Thompson-Balys.

A2375.2.2. *Why peacock has ugly feet.* (See A2232.7, A2236.2.2, A2375.2.1.)

A2375.2.3. *Why dog has hairy paws.* Stole from rabbit. (See A2245.)

A2375.2.4. *Why rabbits have soft pads on feet.* Tahltan: Teit JAFL XXXII 222.

A2375.2.5. *Why hyena has short left hind foot.* Deceived into jumping by jackal. (See A2284.6.)

A2375.2.6. *Why mole has hand like man.* Dh I 156.

A1311.1. The lizard hand. Man's hand is modeled on that of the lizard.

A2375.2.7. *Why mole's "hands" are turned backward.* Sinkyone: Kroeber JAFL XXXII 349.

A2375.2.8. *Explanation of duck's feet.* Calif. Indian: Gayton and Newman 73; S. Am. Indian (Chiriguano): Métraux RMLP XXXIII 178.

A2375.2.9. *Why toad has no thumbs.* India: Thompson-Balys.

A2230. Animal characteristics as punishment.

A2375.2.10. *Why the guinea fowl has red feet.* Cheated and could not stand the ordeal of hot oil poured on his feet. Cameroon: Mansfield 226.

A2376. *Animal characteristics: claws and hoofs.*

A2376.1. *Why cow has cloven hoof.* Dh. III 47. — India: Thompson-Balys.

A2376.1.1. *Why ass does not have cloven hoof.* Jewish: Neuman.

A2376.2. *Dog's claws as grains under paws.* In the great famine, God leaves the dog grain under his paws. From this grows new seed. Estonian: Aarne FFC XXV 143 No. 29.

A2376.3. *Why porcupine has only four claws.* Tahltan: Teit JAFL XXXII 226, 246.

A2376.4. *How crab got its claws.* India: Thompson-Balys.

A2376.5. *Why crab has legs like teeth of a comb.* India: Thompson-Balys.

A2377. *Animal characteristics: wings.*

A2377.1. *Why emu has no wings.* (See A2284.1.)

A2378. *Origin and nature of animal's tail.* Dh III 47ff.

A2317.12. Why opossum has bare tail. A2317.12.1. Why kangaroo-rat's tail is not bushy.

A2378.1. *Why animals have tail* (See A2286.2.4.)

A2378.1.1. *Where baboon got tail.* (See A2262.2.)

A2378.1.2. *Where rat got tail* (See A2241.7.)

A2378.1.3. *Where lizard got tail.* From the snake. (Cf. A2247.) — Finnish: Aarne FFC VIII 20 No. 110, XXXIII 55 No. 110; Jewish: Neuman.

A2378.1.4. *Where mole got tail.* Traded eyes for it. (See A2247, A2332.6.5.) — Spanish: Boggs FFC XC 38 No. 287.

A2378.1.5. *Where squirrel got tail.* (See A2241.7, A2242.)

A2378.1.6. *Where beaver got tail.* (See A2241.10.)

A2378.1.7. *How dog got its tail.* India: Thompson-Balys.

A2378.1.8. *How monkey got its tail.* India: Thompson-Balys.

A2378.1.9. *How peacock got its tail.* India: Thompson-Balys.

A2378.2. *Why animals lack tail.*

A2378.2.1. *Why quail has no tail.* Tricks crab into pulling out tail instead of killing her. Says that gripping her neck would not hurt but that pulling tail will be fatal. Dh III 54. — Flemish: DeMeyer FFC XXXVII 87 No. 90a; Jewish: Neuman, India: Thompson-Balys.
K580. Captor persuaded into illusory punishment.

A2378.2.2. *How goats lost tails.* (See A2216.2.)

A2378.2.3. *How frogs lost tails.* (See A2231.4, A2236.3.) — Jewish: Neuman.

A2378.2.4. *How bear lost tail.* (See A2216.1.)

A2378.2.5. *Why hydrax has no tail.* (See A2235.)

A2378.2.6. *How frog lost tail.* (See A2242, lent to squirrel.) — Dh III 54.

A2378.2.7. *How toad lost tail.* Dh III 54. — Spanish: Boggs FFC XC 38 No. 287.

A2378.2.8. *Why flies lack tail.* Africa (Duala): Ebding 142ff.

A2378.3. *Why animal has long tail.*

A2378.3.1. *How magpie got long tail.* (See A2236.4.)

A2378.3.2. *How muskrat got long, thin tail.* Dh III 51.

A2378.3.3. *How wolf got long tail.* (See A2215.1; Cf. A2262.)

A2378.3.4. *Why fox has long tail.* (See A2213.4.2.)

A2378.4. *Why animal has short tail.*

A2378.4.1. *Why hare has short tail.* (See A2215.2, A2262.) — Dh III 47ff. — Japanese: Ikeda; Virginia (negro): Smiley JAFL XXXII 361; Antigua: Johnson JAFL XXXIV 67.

A2378.4.2. *Why bear has short tail.* (Cf. A2378.2.4.) — Loucheux: Barbeau JAFL XXVIII 256.

A2378.4.3. *Why marmot has short tail.* Dh III 51.

A2378.4.4. *Why tortoise has short tail.* (See A2216.4.) — Dh III 52ff. — Jewish: Neuman.

A2378.4.5. *Why jackal's tail is short.* India: Thompson-Balys.

A2378.4.6. *Why monkey has short tail.* India: Thompson-Balys.

A2378.4.7. *Why crow has short tail.* India: Thompson-Balys.

A2378.5. *Why animal has forked tail.*

A2378.5.1. *Why swallow has forked tail.* (See A2214.1.) Dh III 54. — Cf. Flemish: DeMeyer FFC XXXVII 87 No. 85; Lithuanian: Balys Index No. 3100, Legends Nos. 28, 192, 262.

A2378.5.2. *Why hawk has forked tail.* (See A2216.5.)

A2378.6. *Why animal has bushy tail.*

A2378.6.1. *Why fox has bushy tail.* Virginia (negro): Smiley JAFL XXXII 361.

A2378.7. *Why animal has flat tail.*

A2378.7.1. *Why beaver has flat tail.* (See A2247.6, A2241.10, A2378.1.6.) Dh III 51.

A2378.7.2. *Why magpie's tail is like a chisel.* Lithuanian: Balys Legends No. 262.

A2378.8. *Origin of color of animal's tail.* India: Thompson-Balys.

A2229.6. Bird has red spot in its tail as reward for having moved woman's organ to its present position.

A2378.8.1. *Why end of fox's tail is white.* (See A2215.5.)

A2378.8.1.1. *Why end of fox's tail is black.* Central American: Krickeberg Märchen der Azteken und Inkaperuaner 282.

A2378.8.2. *Why tail of West African grey parrot is red.* Ibo (Nigeria): Basden 276.

A2378.8.3. *Why tip of weasel's tail is black.* Plains Ojibwa: Skinner JAFL XXXII 290.

A2411.1.3. Why weasel is white with dark tip to tail.

A2378.8.4. *Why tip of ermine's tail is black.* (See A2218.) Dh III 74.

A2411.1.4. Color of ermine. A2412.2.1. Markings on tailfeathers of ruffed grouse.

A2378.8.5. *Why minivet has red tail.* India: Thompson-Balys.

A2378.8.6. *Why swallow has black feathers in tail and only two feathers.* India: Thompson-Balys.

A2378.8.7. *Why bird has two beautiful feathers in his tail.* India: Thompson-Balys.

A2378.9. *Nature of animal's tail — miscellaneous.*

A2378.9.1. *Why king-salmon is thick around root of tail.* Tahltan: Teit JAFL XXXII 242.

A2378.9.1.1. *Why salmon has tapering tail.* Icel.: MacCulloch Eddic 146, Boberg.

A2378.9.2. *Why baboons have crooked tails.* (See A2262.2.)

A2378.9.3. *Why hares have cotton tail.* Deity rubs cotton on hare. India: *Thompson-Balys.

A2378.9.4. *Why deer's tail tastes like liver.* India: Thompson-Balys.

A2378.9.5. *Why rat's tail looks like a folded leaf.* (Cf. A2317.12.3) — New Hebrides: Codrington 360.

A2380. Animal characteristics: other bodily features.

A2381. *Flesh of animal.*

A2381.1. *Why hog has good flesh.* (See A2221.1.) — India: Thompson-Balys.

A2382. *Why animal is a hybrid.*

A2382.1. *Magpie is a hybrid of dove and raven;* was not baptized by water of the flood in Noah's time. (Cf. A2291.) — England: Baughman.

A2542.1.1. Magpie refuses to get into ark, sits around outside, jabbering over drowned world, is unlucky.

A2385. *Excrements of animals.*

A2385.1. *Why dung of ass is triangular.* Flemish: DeMeyer FFC XXXVII 86 No. 58d.

A2385.2. *Why red dog's excrement contains animal hair.* India: Thompson-Balys.

A2385.3. *Honey as excrement of bees.* India: Thompson-Balys.

A2385.4. *Why cat hides its excreta.* India: Thompson-Balys.

A2386. *Gall-bladder of animal.*

A2211.13. Stag defeated by snail vomits his gall-bladder: hence no gall-bladder.

A2391. *Nature of bird's eggs.*

A2391.1. *Why canary's eggs are yellow.* (See A2219.1.) — Dh III 65.

A2400—A2499. Causes of animal characteristics: appearance and habits.

A2400. Animal characteristics: general appearance.

A2401. *Cause of animal's beauty.*

A2402. *Cause of animal's ugliness.*

D1337. Magic objects makes beautiful or hideous.

A2402.1. *Cause of serpent's ugliness.* (See A2286.0.1.)

A2402.2. *How ostrich lost beautiful feathers.* (See A2252.3.)

A2410. Animal characteristics: color and smell.

A2411. *Origin of color of animal.*

A2286.2.4. God changes color of devil's animals. A2330.8. Color of animal's head. A2332.5. Color of animal's eyes.

A2411.1. *Origin of color of mammals.*

A2411.1.1. *Origin of color of felidae.*

A2411.1.1.1. *Color of leopard.* (See A2219.1.) — Dh III 69.

A2411.1.1.2. *Color of jaguar.* Dh III 62.

A2411.1.2. *Origin of color of mustelidae.*

A2411.1.2.1. *Why weasel is white with dark tip to tail.* Plains Cree: Skinner JAFL XXIX 350.

A2411.1.2.1.1. *Why weasel is part black.* Chinese: Graham.

A2411.1.2.2. *Color of ermine.* Loucheux: Barbeau JAFL XXVIII 257.

A2378.8.4. Why tip of ermine's tail is black.

A2411.1.2.3. *Color of otter.* Dh III 64.

A2411.1.2.4. *Color of skunk.* (See A2219.1.) — Dh III 71.

A2411.1.2.5. *Color of mink. Singed by sun.* (See A2218). — Dh III 84.

A2411.1.3. *Color of canidae and other carnivora.*

A2411.1.3.1. *Color of fox.* (See A2219.1.) — Dh III 64, 66.

A2411.1.3.2. *Color of coyote.* (See A2218.) — Dh III 79.

A2411.1.4. *Origin of color of rodentia.*

A2411.1.4.1. *Color of squirrel.* (See A2218.) — Dh III 76f.; India: Thompson-Balys.

A2411.1.4.2. *Color of beaver.* (See A2219.1.) — Dh III 71.

A2411.1.4.3. *Color of rat.* Dh III 91. — India: Thompson-Balys.

A2411.1.4.4. *Color of hare.*

A2411.1.4.4.1. *Why hare is grey in summer.* Cheremis: Sebeok-Nyerges (A2411.1.22).

A2411.1.5. *Origin of color of primata.*

A2411.1.5.1. *Color of monkey.* India: *Thompson-Balys.

A2411.1.5.1.1. *Why ape has red back.* China: Eberhard FFC CXX 177 No. 119, 411 s.v. "Affenmutter".

A2411.1.5.2. *Color of baboon.*

A2411.1.5.2.1. *Why baboon's face and hands are black.* India: Thompson-Balys.

A2231. Animal characteristics: punishment for impiety. A2230. Origin of animal characteristics: face. A2375. Origin and nature of animal's feet.

A2411.1.6. *Origin of color of ungulata.*

A2411.1.6.1. *Color of horse.* Dh III 86.

A2411.1.6.2. *Color of hippopotamus.* (See A2247.3.)

A2411.1.6.3. *Red color of bush-buck.* From blood. (Cf. A2219.1.) — Ila (Rhodesia): Smith and Dale 366 No. 17.

A2411.1.6.4. *Color of cow.* Dh I 188—191, III 86. — India: Thompson-Balys.

B182.0.1. White cow. B182.2.0.3. Magic white cow with red ear. B731.4.1. Cows with white ears. Q153.1. Cows white-headed during reign of good king.

A2411.1.6.5. *Color of deer.* (See A2218.) — Dh III 79, 88.

A2411.1.6.6. *Color of elk.* Dh III 88.

A2411.1.6.7. *Color of rhinoceros.* (See A2247.3.)

A2411.1.7. *Origin of color of other mammals.*

A2411.1.7.1. *Origin of color of hyena* (365 colors): Jewish: Neuman.

A2411.2. *Origin of color of bird.* Lithuanian: Balys Index Nos. 3158, 3165, Legends No. 261f.; Chinese: Eberhard FFC CXX 127; Japanese: Ikeda; N. A. Indian (Canadian Dakota): Wallis JAFL XXXVI 66; (Southern Ute): Lowie JAFL XXXVII 32 No. 18, 69 No. 38, (Tahltan): Teit JAFL XXXII 208f.; S. Am. Indian (Toba): Métraux MAFLS XL 39f.

A2221.6.1. Bird coloring as reward for obedience to deity.

A2411.2.1. *Origin of color of passeriformes.*

A2411.2.1.1. *Color of thrush.* (See A2222.1, A2218). — Dh III 76.

A2411.2.1.2. *Color of water-ousel.* Lappish: Qvigstad FFC LX 38 No. 49.

A2411.2.1.3. *Color of wag-tail.* Lithuanian: Balys Legends No. 262.

A2411.2.1.4. *Color of swallow.* (See A2218, A2219.1, A2221.2.4.1.) — Dh III 64, 75, (Cf. III 58). — Japanese: Ikeda.

A2411.2.1.5. *Color of raven.* (See A2237.1, A2234.1, A2231.1, A2218.1). — Dh III 59, 63, 65, 143. — Greek: Frazer Apollodorus II 15 n. i; Finnish: Aarne FFC VIII 16 No. 90, XXXIII 54 No. 90; Jewish: Neuman; India: *Thompson-Balys; Eskimo (Labrador): Hawks GSCan XIV 160, (Alaska): Jenness 71, (East Greenland): Rasmussen I 146, (Cumberland Sound): Boas BAM XV 220, (Smith Sound): Kroeber JAFL XII 174, (Central Eskimo): Boas RBAE VI 641; N. A. Indian (Tahltan): Teit JAFL XXXII 203, (Upper Thompson): Teit JAFL XXIX 329.

A2234.1.1. Raven does not return to ark in obedience to Noah: black color is resulting punishment. D1337.6. Magic leaves turn white bird black.

A2411.2.1.6. *Color of crow.* (See A2219.1) — Dh III 59, 65f. — Lithuanian: Balys Legends No. 262; Flemish: DeMeyer FFC XXXVII 87 No. 90a; Breton: Sébillot Incidents s.v. "corbeaux". — Japanese: Ikeda; Thompson River: Teit JAFL XXIX 329; Calif. Indian: Gayton and Newman 58.

A2411.2.1.7. *Color of rook.* (See A2218) — Dh III 75.

A2411.2.1.8. *Color of jay.* Dh III 86.

A2411.2.1.9. *Color of blackbird.* (See A2218) — Dh III 71.

A2411.2.1.10. *Color of magpie.* Dh III 63.

A2411.2.1.11. *Color of sparrow.* (See A2218) — Dh III 75. — Japanese: Ikeda.

A2411.2.1.12. *Color of goldfinch.* Dh. III 185. — Flemish: DeMeyer FFC XXXVII 88 No. 94c.

A2411.2.1.13. *Color of red-bird.* Dh III 63.

A2411.2.1.14. *Color of canary.* Flemish: DeMeyer FFC XXXVII 88 No. 94b.

A2411.2.1.15. *Color of trumpet-bird* (psophia crepitans). (See A2218) — Dh III 82.

A2411.2.1.16. *Color of starling.* India: Thompson-Balys.

A2411.2.1.17. *Color of martin.* Eskimo (East Greenland): Rasmussen I 146.

A2411.2.2. *Origin of color of falconiformes.*

A2411.2.3. *Origin of color of charidriiformes.*

A2411.2.3.1. *Color of woodcock.* Lappish: Qvigstad FFC LX 38 No. 49.

A2411.2.4. *Origin of color of caraciiformes.*

A2411.2.4.1. *Color of woodpecker.* See A2219.1; Dh III 70, 89.

A2411.2.4.2. *Color of owl.* Eskimo (Cumberland Sound): Boas BAM XV 220.

A2411.2.5. *Origin of color of ciconiiformes.*

A2411.2.5.1. *Color of cormorant.* (See A2218.) — Dh III 77.

A2411.2.5.2. *Color of heron.* (See A2218.) — Dh III 82.

A2411.2.5.3. *Color of stork.* Dh III 59.

A2411.2.5.3.1. *Why stork has black back.* Lithuanian: Balys Legends Nos. 233, 236, 238f., 243ff.

A2003. Origin of insects: released from sack. D155.1. Transformation: man to stork.

A2411.2.5.4. *Color of gull.* Eskimo (Alaska): Jenness 71.

A2411.2.6. *Origin of color of other birds.*

A2411.2.6.1. *Color of loon.* (See A2219.1.) — Dh III 69—71.

A2411.2.6.2. *Color of swan.* Lappish: Qvigstad FFC LX 38 No. 49.

A2411.2.6.3. *Color of goose.* Dh III 89.

A2411.2.6.4. *Color of duck.* Eskimo (Alaska): Jenness 71.

A2411.2.6.5. *Color of turkey.* (See A2219.1.) — Dh III 70.

A2411.2.6.6. *Color of guinea-fowl.* (See A2219.1.) — Dh III 67. — Am. Negro (Georgia): Harris Nights 193 No. 33; Africa (Cameroon): Mansfield 226.

A2411.2.6.7. *Color of peacock.* India: *Thompson-Balys.

A2411.2.6.8. *Color of partridge.* (See A2218, A2219.1.) — Dh III 62, 75. — Lithuanian: Balys Legends No. 261; India: Thompson-Balys.

A2411.2.6.9. *Color of pheasant.* Dh III 62.

A2411.2.6.10. *Color of cuckoo.* Type 235; Dh III 140. — Finnish: Aarne FFC VIII 17 No. 94; Lappish: Qvigstad FFC LX 38 No. 49.

A2411.2.6.11. *Color of parrot.* (See A2219.1.) — Dh III 70. — India: Thompson-Balys; Africa (Cameroon): Mansfield 234.

A2411.3. *Origin of color of insect.* Japanese: Ikeda.

A2411.3.1. *Origin of color of bee.* Dh I 129. — India: Thompson-Balys.

A2411.3.2. *Color of spider.* (See A2221.2.3.)

A2411.4. *Origin of color of fish.*

A2411.4.1. *Color of halibut.* (See A2219.1.) — Dh III 67. — Tsimshian: Boas RBAE XXVII 58ff.

A2411.4.2. *Color of perch.* (See A2218.) — Dh III 75.

A2411.4.3. *Color of burbot.* (See A2218.) — Dh III 75.

A2411.5. *Color of reptiles and other animal forms.*

A2411.5.1. *Color of turtle.* Dh III 63.

A2411.5.2. *Color of frog.* Dh III 63, 89.

A2411.5.3. *Color of snail.* (See A2218.) — Dh III 85.

A2411.5.4. *Color of mussel.* Dh III 90.

A2411.5.5. *Why earthworm is red at one end.* India: Thompson-Balys.

A2411.5.6. *Color of chameleon.*

A2411.5.6.1. *Why chameleon can change his color.* (Cf. A2223.8.) — Africa (Fang): Einstein 96, (Togo): Einstein 10f.

A2411.5.7. *Color of shrimp.* Hawaii: Beckwith Myth 234.

A2412. *Origin of animal markings.* (See A2211.12, A2221.3, A2221.7.) — Calif. Indian: Gayton and Newman 61, 75.

A2320.3. How lizard got red head. A2356.3. Origin of color of animal's back. A2378.8. Origin of color of animal's tail.

A2412.0.1. *Creator sends two deities to tatoo all creatures: origin of animal markings.* Marshall Is.: Davenport 222.

A2412.1. *Markings of mammals.*

A2335.4.3. Why dog has black muzzle. A2344.3.1. Why sheep's tongue is black. A2356.2.7. Why ass has cross on shoulders. A2356.3.3. Why wolverine has peculiar marks on back. A2364.1. Why wolverine has red hair on loins.

A2412.1.1. *White markings on deer.* Liberian: Bundy JAFL XXXII 417.

A2335.2.1. Why deer has white mark on nose.

A2412.1.2. *Spots on leopard.* Liberian: Bundy JAFL XXXII 411f.

A2412.1.3. *Why coyote has yellow patch behind his ears.* (See A2218.4.)

A2412.1.4. *Why kangaroo-rat has white band around his body.* (See A2218.4.)

A2412.1.5. *Why elephant has white marks on its body.* India: Thompson-Balys.

A2412.1.6. *Why peccary has spots.* S. Am. Indian (Yagua): Steward-Metraux BBAE CXLIII (3) 736.

A2412.2. *Markings on birds.* (See A2211.7.)

A2253.2. Why robin has red breast. A2321.8. Origin of red lump on rail's head. A2371.4.1. Why curlew has red legs.

A2412.2.1. *Markings on tail-feathers of ruffed grouse.* Ojibwa: Jones JAFL XXIX 370.

A2412.2.2. *Markings of francolin.* (See A2232.6.)

A2412.3. *Markings on insects.* Japanese: Ikeda.

A2356.3.4. Why spider has markings on back.

A2412.3.1. *Why louse has mark on his back.* Korean: Zong in-Sob 36 No. 20.

A2412.3.2. *Origin of butterflies' marks.* Korean: Zong in-Sob 39 No. 23.

A2412.4. *Markings on fish.* (See A2217.3, A2213.2.) — Eskimo (Labrador): Hawks GSCan XIV 155.

A2315.1. Origin of shell-fish's black scales.

A2412.4.1. *Markings on sun-fish.* (See A2217.3.)

A2412.4.2. *Markings on king-salmon.* Tahltan: Teit JAFL XXXII 242 (red marks below ears).

A2412.4.2.1. *Why salmon has purple belly.* Irish myth: Cross.

B124.2. Salmon of knowledge.

A2412.4.3. *Markings on cod-fish.* From devil's fingers. — Fb "torsk" III 830a.

A2412.4.4. *Cross on crab's back.* Saintyves Saints Successeurs 245f.

A2412.4.5. *Markings on flying fish.* New Guinea: Kerr 25.

A2412.5. *Markings on other animals.*

A2412.5.1. *Markings on tortoise's back.* India: Thompson-Balys.

A2412.5.2. *Why toads have warts on their backs.* (Cf. A2356.2.) — India: Thompson-Balys.

A2412.5.2.1. *Why frog is spotty all over.* India: Thompson-Balys.

A2413. *Origin of animal's stripes.*

A2413.1. *Stripes of zebra.* Ila (Rhodesia): Smith and Dale 369 No. 19.

A2413.2. *Stripes of chipmunk.* (See A2217.2.) — Dh III 57.

A2413.3. *Stripes of squirrel.* Dh III 56. — India: Thompson-Balys; Chinese: Graham.

A2413.4. *Stripes of tiger.* Dh III 58. — India: *Thompson-Balys; Chinese: Graham.

A2413.5. *Stripes of alligator.* Dh III 58. — India: Thompson-Balys.

A2413.6. *Stripes of cony.* Dh III 58.

A2413.7. *Stripes on trout.* Eskimo (Labrador): Hawks GSCan XIV 155.

A2416. *Origin and nature of animal's smell.* *Dh III 233f.

A2416.1. *Bad smell of goat.* (See A2232.5.) — Dh III 233; Fb "gjedebuk" IV 178b. — Ibo (Nigeria): Thomas 125; Africa (Ekoi): Talbot 226, (Cameroon): Mansfield 227.

A2416.2. *Burnt smell of mink.* Dh III 234.

A2416.3. *Bad smell of skunk.* Dh III 233. — Central America: Krickeberg Märchen der Azteken und Inkaperuaner 254.

A2416.4. *Burnt smell of wolverine.* Tahltan: Teit JAFL XXXII 248.

A2416.5. *Why ram smells bad.* Sébillot RTP II 492.

A2416.6. *Why bugs smell bad.* Lappish: Qvigstad FFC LX 39 No. 62.

A2416.7. *Why herrings have bad odor.* Italian Novella: Rotunda.

A2420. Animal characteristics: voice and hearing.

A2421. *How animal got voice.* Lithuanian: Balys Index No. 3168, Legends Nos. 263—270; Japanese: Ikeda.

A2421.1. *How night-swallow got voice.* Esthonian: Aarne FFC XXV 147 No. 51.

A2421.2. *How woodcock got voice.* Traded with turkey. (See A2247). — Dh III 123.

A2421.3. *Where crow got voice.* Traded with thunder-bird. (See A2247). — Dh III 126.

A2421.4. *How partridge got voice.* Borrowed from tortoise. (See A2241). —Dh III 132.

A2421.4.1. *How quail got voice.* Lithuanian: Balys Legends No. 267.

A2421.5. *How nkundak got voice.* (See A2223.2.)

A2421.6. *Why cocks crow.* Spanish: Boggs FFC XC 35 No. *205; Jewish: Neuman; India: Thompson-Balys.

A2421.7. *Voice of peewit.* Lithuanian: Balys Legends No. 264f.

A2421.8. *Why cat purrs.* (Cf. A2236.8.)

A2422. *How animal lost voice* (or power of speech). Dh III 231ff. — India: Thompson-Balys.

A2422.1. *Why dog lost his power of speech.* Bulu: Krug.

A2422.1.1. *Why dogs do not speak.* Dh III 232. (See A2237.1.) — Benga: Nassau 163 No. 22; Zuñi: Handy JAFL XXXI 467; Tahltan: Teit JAFL XXXII 243; India: Thompson-Balys.
B134.1. Dog betrays woman's infidelity.

A2422.2. *Why sheep do not speak.* Curse of Virgin Mary. (See A2231). — Sébillot RTP II 492.

A2422.3. *Why white crow is dumb.* Hottentot: Bleek 45 No. 22.

A2422.4. *Why tortoise has no voice.* (See A2421.4.) — Africa (Ekoi): Talbot 378.

A2422.5. *Why fly has no voice.* Africa (Ekoi): Talbot 384.

A2422.6. *Why raven cannot talk.* Dh III 232.

A2422.7. *Why frogs cannot speak.* Dh III 232.

A2422.8. *Why cormorant cannot speak.* (See A2344.2.5.) — Dh III 232f.
K825.1. Cormorant's tongue pulled out by putting louse on it.

A2422.9. *Why swallows lost voice.* (See A2231.2.2.)

A2422.10. *Why cock does not speak.* India: Thompson-Balys.

A2423. *General quality of animal's voice.*

A2423.1. *Animal's ugly voice.*

A2423.1.1. *Woodcock's ugly voice.* Exchanged with thrush. (See A2245.1.)

A2423.1.2. *Peacock's ugly voice.* (See A2236.2.2.)

A2423.1.3. *Loon's ugly voice.* Lappish: Qvigstad FFC LX 38 No. 53.

A2423.1.4. *Why ass brays.* (Cf. A2239.3.)

A2423.1.5. *Why hornbill speaks through his nose.* Africa (Cameroon): Mansfield 234.

A2423.1.6. *Origin of snail's monotonous voice.* Africa: Milligan Jungle 95.

A2423.2. *Animal's pleasing voice.*

A2423.2.1. *Thrush's beautiful voice.* Exchanged with woodcock. (See A2423.1.1, A2245.1.)

A2423.2.2. *Cuckoo's sweet voice.* India: Thompson-Balys.

A2425. *Origin of animal cries.* (See A2261.1, A2272.1, A2275.1, A2275.2.) — *Millier (A.) Petits Contes du Nivernais (Nevers, 1894); Dh III 355ff.; BP II 535; Wienert FFC LVI 40; Chauvin VIII 49 No. 17; India: Thompson-Balys.

A2261.1. Shepherd transformed to bird still calls sheep: explanation of bird cries. A2272.1. Animal cries: imitation of sounds. A2275.1. Animal cries a lament for person lost when animal was transformed. A2275.2. Animal cries a lament over animal's transformation. A2283. Two animals learn songs together.

A2425.1. *How dog began to bark.* India: Thompson-Balys.

A2425.2. *Origin of birds' morning-songs* (from singing angels). Jewish: Neuman.

A2426. *Nature and meaning of animal cries.* *Dh III 355 ff. — Finnish: *Aarne FFC IX.

A2426.1. *Cries of mammals.*

A2426.1.1. *Cry of bush-cat.* (See A2275.4.) — U.S.: Baughman.

A2426.1.2. *Cry of squirrel.* Finnish: Aarne FFC IX 3 No. 3. — Tahltan: Teit JAFL XXXII 220.

A2426.1.2.1. *Squirrel's call:* asks whether viper (who ate up his children) is his friend. Bulu: Krug 106.

A2426.1.3. *Why hog grunts.* Finnish: Aarne FFC IX 4 No. 13. — Jamaica Negro: Beckwith MAFLS XVII 259 No. 51; Angola: Chatelain 215.

A2426.1.4. *The hedgehog's cry.* Lithuanian: Balys Index No. *278.

A2426.1.5. *Why dog barks after thief.* India: Thompson-Balys.

A2326.2.2. Why dog has no horns: they were stolen by deer (goat).

A2426.1.6. *Why bats cry as they fly.* New Guinea: Kerr 7.

A2426.2. *Cries of birds.*

A2426.2.1. *Nightingale's song.* (See A2272.1.1.) — Lithuanian: Balys Index No. 3151, Balys Legends No. 260; Japanese: Ikeda.

A2426.2.2. *Garden warbler's song.* (See A2272.1.3.)

A2426.2.3. *Bittern's song* (See A2261.1, A2275.3.)

A2426.2.4. *Hoopoe's song.* (See A2261.1, A2275.3.)

A2426.2.5. *Cuckoo's song.* (See A2275.2.) — Japanese: Ikeda.

A2426.2.6. *Cawing of crow.* Dh III 126, 257, 357, 369, 371, 372. — Finnish: Aarne FFC IX 7 No. 39; Tahltan: Teit JAFL XXXII 223; Australian: Dixon 292.

A2426.2.7. *Croaking of raven.* Dh III 364, 373, 392. — Finnish: Aarne FFC IX 9 No. 46. — Tahltan: Teit JAFL XXXII 223; Eskimo (Ungava): Turner RBAE XI 261.

A2426.2.8. *Why dove coos.* *Dh III 554 s.v. "Taube". — Finnish: Aarne FFC IX 12 No. 57; Angola: Chatelain 153 No. 16; Jamaica negro: Beckwith MAFLS XVII 259 No. 50; India: *Thompson-Balys.

A2426.2.9. *Why goose quacks.* Finnish: Aarne FFC IX 6 No. 31.

A2426.2.10. *Why duck quacks.* Fb "and".

A2426.2.11. *What parrot says.* Benga: Nassau 199 No. 29; India: Thompson-Balys.

A2426.2.12. *Meaning of swallow's song.* Fb "svale".

A2426.2.13. *Cackling of guinea hen.* North Carolina: Brown Collection I 634.

A2426.2.15. *Why certain species of eagle cries like a baby:* spirit of tortured baby became an eagle. India: Thompson-Balys.

A2261. Animal characteristics from transformation of animal.

A2426.2.16. *Origin of cry of brain-fever bird.* India: Thompson-Balys.

A2426.2.17. *Origin of owl's cries.* (Cf. A2427.3.) — S. Am. Indian (Matoco): Métraux MAFLS XL 48.

J1811.1. Owl's hoot misunderstood.

A2426.2.18. *Origin and meaning of cock's cry "cock-a-doodle-do".* India: Thompson-Balys; Chinese: Eberhard FFC CXX 13.

A2426.2.18.1. *Why cock crows on roof with neck stretched out.* Korean: Zong in-Sob 25 No. 11.

A2426.3. *Sounds of insects.*

A2426.3.1. *Beetle's hum.* (See A2231.11.)

A2426.3.2. *Gnat's buzz.* (See A2236.1.)

A2426.3.3. *Fly's buzz.* (See A2239.2.)

A2426.3.4. *Cricket's chirp.* (See A2272.1.2.)

A2426.3.5. *Mosquito's buzz.* Mpongwe: Nassau 62 No. 12.

A2426.3.6. *Speech of fireflies.* India: Thompson-Balys.

A2426.4. *Other animal cries.*

A2426.4.1. *Frog's croak.* (See A2275.4.) — Jewish: Neuman; Japanese: Ikeda; Angola: Chatelain 217 No. 38; Liberia: Bundy JAFL XXXII 420.

A2426.4.1.1. *Frogs formerly were ducks* stolen from Eden by Cain. God changed them to frogs; and so frogs sound like ducks in the spring. (Cf. A2162.) — U. S.: Baughman.

A2426.4.1.2. *Why frog croaks in wet weather.* Korean: Zong in-Sob 35 No. 18.

A2426.4.2. *Toad's croak.* Jamaica Negro: Beckwith MAFLS XVII 259.

A2427. *Why animal howls (cries out) at night.*

A2427.1. *Why jackal cries in the night.* India: Thompson-Balys.

A2427.2. *Why dog howls at night.*

A2427.2.1. *Why dogs howl when man is dying.* India: Thompson-Balys.

A2427.3. *Why owl hoots at night.* (Cf. A2426.2.17.) — India: Thompson-Balys.

A2428. *Animal's hearing.*

A2428.1. *How animal lost hearing.* Dh III 231.

A2430. Animal characteristics: dwelling and food.

A2431. *Birds' nests.* (Cf. A2486.)

A2431.1. *How bird learned to build nest.* *Dh III 202.

A2431.2. *Why bird has no nest.* (See A2233.4.1.)

A2431.2.1. *Why cuckoo has no nest.* (See A2231.3.1.) — Dh III 177, 195, 200; India: Thompson-Balys; Lithuanian: Balys Legends Nos. 198f., 250, 270.

A2431.2.1.1. *Crow hatches cuckoo's egg.* India: Thompson-Balys.

A2431.2.2. *Why heron has no nest.* Congo: Weeks 220 No. 15.

A2431.3. *Nature of birds' nests.*

A2431.3.1. *Dove's nest.* (See A2271.1.) — Dh III 124, 191—201.

A2431.3.2. *Diver's nest.* (See A2238.4.) — Dh III 202.

A2431.3.3. *Ring-dove's nest. Exchanged with gull.* (See A2247.) — Dh III 124.

A2431.3.4. *Gull's nest. Exchanged with ringdove.* (See A2247.) — Dh III 124.

A2431.3.5. *Swallow's nest.* (See A2221.2.4.) — Dh III 5, 200, 415ff.; Sébillot RTP III 156; Finnish: Aarne FFC VIII 16 No. 87.

A2431.3.5.1. *Why swallow does not like green trees for her nest.* Lithuanian: Balys Index No. 3145, Legends No. 272.

A2431.3.6. *Crow's nest.*

A2431.3.6.1. *Why crow cannot enter sparrow's nest.* India: Thompson-Balys.

A2431.3.6.2. *Why crow's nest is not tightly built.* India: Thompson-Balys.

A2431.3.6.3. *Why crow must build nests far from people's houses.* India: Thompson-Balys.

A2431.3.7. *Sparrow's nest.*

A2431.3.7.1. *Why sparrow may build nest near people's houses;* reward for hospitality. India: Thompson-Balys.

A2222. Animal characteristics reward for hospitality.

A2431.3.8. *Turkey's nest.*

A2431.3.8.1. *Why brush turkey nests on the ground.* New Guinea: Kerr 107.

A2432. *Dwelling of other animal than bird.*
A2491.3. Why mole burrows underground.

A2432.1. *Why ant lives in ant-hill.* Livonian: Loorits FFC LXVI 92 No. 97.

A2432.2. *Why wasp has nest.* Dh III 189.

A2432.3. *Beaver's dwelling.* Tahltan: Teit JAFL XXXII 246.

A2432.4. *Porcupine's dwelling.* Tahltan: Teit JAFL XXXII 246.

A2432.5. *Muskrat's dwelling.* Tahltan: Teit JAFL XXXII 243.

A2432.6. *Bear's den.* Kaska: Teit JAFL XXX 444.

A2432.7. *Wart-hog's burrow.* Ila (Rhodesia): Smith and Dale 364 No. 16.

A2432.8. *Bee's hive.* India: Thompson-Balys.

A2432.9. *Why fly lives on dung heap.* Africa (Cameroon): Mansfield 229.

A2432.10. *Why the elephant lives without a hut.* Wakweli: Bender 82f.

A2433. *Animal's characteristic haunt.* *Dh III 204ff.

A2433.1. *Establishment of animal haunt.* (See A2212.2.)

A2433.1.1. *Animal haunt established by contest (race).* (See A2250.1, A2252.1.)

A2433.1.2. *Animals change their type of dwelling-place.* Dh III 215ff.

A2433.1.3. *Place to live given as patent right to dog.* Dh IV 117.

A2433.2. *Various haunts of animals.*

A2433.2.1. *Animals that live in woods.* Dh III 204ff.

A2433.2.1.1. *Why small ants live in houses while driver ants must live in bush.* Africa (Congo): Weeks Jungle 260f.

A2433.2.1.2. *Why gorilla and chimpanzee live in forests:* punishment for neglecting their possessions. Bulu: Krug 111f.

A2433.2.2. *Animals that inhabit water.* Dh III 208ff.

A2433.2.3. *Animals that live alone.* Dh III 210ff.

A2433.2.3.1. *Why leopard walks alone.* He killed treacherously his saviors and all animals deserted him. Milligan Jungle 99.

A2433.2.4. *Animals that live with men.* Dh III 213ff.

A2433.2.4.1. *Why the chimpanzee lives with men.* Africa (Duala): Lederbogen Märchen 146ff.

A2433.3. *Haunts of various animals — mammals.*

A2433.3.1. *Cat's characteristic haunt.* Jewish: Neuman.

A2433.3.1.1. *Why cat keeps chimney-corner.* (See A2223.1.)

A2433.3.2. *Dog's characteristic haunt.* (See A2233.2.) — Lithuanian: Balys Legends No. 214; Jewish: Neuman; India: Thompson-Balys; Africa (Angola): Chatelain 213 No. 35 (by the fire), (Wute): Sieber 205.

A2433.3.3. *Why hare lives in bush.* (See A2282.)

A2433.3.4. *Why hyena stays in burrow.* (See A2282.)

A2433.3.5. *Why coney lives among rocks.* (See A2241.7.)

A2433.3.6. *Why hog lives in sty.* Angola: Chatelain 215 No. 36; India: Thompson-Balys.

A2433.3.7. *Why rams live at home.* Gold Coast: Barker and Sinclair 143 No. 27; India: Thompson-Balys.

A2433.3.8. *Why goat lives with men.* Gold Coast: Barker and Sinclair 153 No. 29; Benga: Nassau 100 No. 7.

A2433.3.9. *Why squirrel lives in tree.* Ila (Rhodesia): Smith and Dale 358 No. 11.

A2433.3.9.1. *Why squirrel stays hidden in jungle.* India: Thompson-Balys.

A2433.3.10. *Why muskrats live in water.* Tahltan: Teit JAFL XXXII 243.

A2433.3.11. *Why porcupine lives in high places in mountains.* Tahltan: Teit JAFL XXXII 246.

A2433.3.12. *Why beaver lives along rivers.* Tahltan: Teit JAFL XXXII 246.

A2433.3.13. *Why elk lives in woods.* Quileute: Farrand JAFL XXXII 259.

A2433.3.14. *Why wolf lives in woods.* Africa (Gold Coast): Barker and Sinclair 153 No. 29.

A2433.3.15. *Why elephant does not live in town.* Yoruba: Ellis 267 No. 3.

A2433.3.16. *Why lion stays away from settlement.* Africa (Ekoi): Talbot 382.

A2433.3.17. *Why bear lives where he does.* Australian: Dixon 298 (trees); Kaska: Teit JAFL XXX 444 (mountains).

A2433.3.18. *Why leopard lives where he does.* Gold Coast: Barker and Sinclair 143 (woods), ibid. 153 (desert). India: Thompson-Balys.

A2433.3.19. *Why monkey lives in tree.* Mpongwe: Nassau 68 No. 14.

A2433.3.19.1. *Why monkey has first fruits of harvest in every field.* India: Thompson-Balys.

A2433.3.20. *Why mole lives underground.* Spanish: Boggs FFC XC 38 No. 287.

A2433.3.21. *Why tiger lives in jungle.* India: Thompson-Balys.

A2433.4. *Haunts of birds.*

A2433.4.1. *Why owl lives where he does.* (See A2229.3, steeple.) — Africa (Ekoi): Talbot 196 (away from other birds).

A2433.4.2. *Why cock lives in town.* (See A2250.1.) — Benga: Nassau 199 No. 29.

A2433.4.3. *Why ptarmigan lives in country.* (See A2250.1.)

A2433.4.4. *Why parrot lives in tree.* Congo: Weeks 220 No. 15.

A2433.4.5. *Why kingfisher lives in the air.* Africa (Togo): Einstein 7.

A2433.4.6. *Why fowls never shut their doors at night.* Africa (Congo): Weeks Jungle 379ff.

A2433.5. *Haunts of insects.*

A2433.5.1. *Why nit lives at edge of hair.* (See A2236.6.)

A2433.5.2. *Why fly lives amid filth.* (See A2239.2.)

A2433.5.3. *Haunts of spider.* (See A2211.6, large stones, A2261.2, dusty corners.) India: Thompson-Balys.

A2433.5.3.1. *Why spider lives under stones.* Africa: Meinhof 209.

A2433.5.4. *Why beetles live in manure.* Pueblo: Parsons JAFL XXXI 245.

A2433.5.5. *Why ants are lords of the bush.* Africa (Ekoi): Talbot 400.

A2433.5.6. *Why butterflies haunt urine-impregnated places.* India: Thompson-Balys.

A2433.5.7. *Why cockroaches live in houses.* India: Thompson-Balys.

A2433.6. *Haunts of reptiles,* etc.

A2433.6.1. *Haunts of tortoise (turtle).*

A2214.5. Why tortoise is amphibious. Hurled on rock: half falls on land, half in water.

A2433.6.1.1. *Why tortoise lives in logs in stream.* (See A2282.) — Benga Nassau 139, 207 Nos. 15, 32.

A2433.6.1.2. *Why turtle lays eggs on beach.* (Cf. A2486.) — Hawaii: Beckwith Myth 22.

A2433.6.2. *Why oyster lives in salt water.* Mpongwe: Nassau 62 No. 11.

A2433.6.3. *Haunts of crab.*

A2433.6.3.1. *Why crabs live in water.* Kaffir Kidd 249 No. 11; India: Thompson-Balys.

A2433.6.3.2. *Why crabs burrow in sand.* New Guinea: Kerr 86.

A2433.6.3.3. *Why common crab lives underground.* Africa (Cameroon): Mansfield 224.

A2433.6.4. *Why iguana lives in stream.* Benga: Nassau 106 No. 8.

A2433.6.5. *Why leeches live in water.* India: Thompson-Balys.

A2433.6.6. *Habitation of frog.* India: Thompson-Balys; Africa (Togo): Einstein 7.

A2433.6.7. *Why toad lives in cold place.* India: Thompson-Balys.

A2433.6.8. *Habitat of snake.* India: Thompson-Balys.

A2433.6.9. *Why thousand-legged worm avoids sun.* Africa (Wakweli): Bender 61.

A2434. *Habitat of animal.* The country or locality in which animal is found.

A2434.1. *Why certain animals are found everywhere.* India: Thompson-Balys.

A2434.1.1. *Why birds are everywhere.* India: Thompson-Balys; Tahltan: Teit JAFL XXXII 209.

A2434.1.2. *Why bluebirds are everywhere.* Pueblo: Parsons JAFL XXXI 219.

A2434.1.3. *Why snowbirds are everywhere.* Pueblo: Parsons JAFL XXXI 218.

A2434.1.4. *Why black ants are everywhere.* Zuñi: Handy JAFL XXXI 468.

A2434.1.5. *Why jackal may go everywhere.* India: Thompson-Balys.

A2434.2. *Why certain animals are absent from countries.* *Dh III 217ff.

A2434.2.1. *Why porcupines and skunks do not live on Cape Breton Island.* Micmac: Speck JAFL XXVIII 69.

A2434.2.2. *Why foxes do not live on a certain island:* driven out by a god. Japanese: Anesaki Japanese Myth. 252.

A2434.2.3. *Why there are no snakes in Ireland.* Irish myth: Cross.

A531.2. Culture hero banishes snakes. D2176.1. Snakes banned by magic. V229.3. Saint banishes snakes.

A2434.3. *Why animals live in certain countries.* *Dh III 217ff.

A2434.3.1. *Why locusts live in certain Pueblo towns.* Pueblo: Parsons JAFL XXXI 225.

A2434.3.2. *Why there are wild turkeys in a certain Pueblo town.* Pueblo: Parsons JAFL XXXI 235.

A2434.3.3. *Why elephant lives in Nigeria.* Gold Coast: Barker and Sinclair 153 No. 29.

A2435. *Food of animal.* *Dh III 295ff., 308ff.

A2435.1. *Assignment of food to animal.* Circassian: Nicolaides and Carnoy RTP I 80.

A2435.1.1. *Why certain birds may not drink out of river.* (See A2233.1.1.)

A2435.1.2. *How tiger formerly cooked its food and why it changed.* India: Thompson-Balys.

A2435.2. *Nature of animal's food.*

A2435.2.1. *Why animals eat everything without salt.* Zuñi: Handy JAFL XXXI 461.

A2435.2.2. *Why certain animals are carnivorous.* Jewish: Neuman.

A2435.3. *Food of various animals — mammals.* India: Thompson-Balys.

A2435.3.1. *Food of dog.* (See A2247, exchanged with cat.) — Dh III 124, IV 112ff., 121ff.

A2435.3.2. *Food of cat.* (See A2247, exchanged with dog.) — Dh III 124, IV 121ff., 128 (to eat before dog).

A2435.3.3. *Food of bear.* (See A2251.1.) India: Thompson-Balys.

A2435.3.4. *Food of wolf.* Man. — Finnish: Aarne FFC XXXIII 53. No. 75*; Esthonian: Aarne FFC XXV 144 No. 37.

A2435.3.5. *Food of wolverine.* Tahltan: Teit JAFL XXXII 247 (corpses).

A2435.3.6. *Why moose eat willows.* Tahltan: Teit JAFL XXXII 231.

A2435.3.7. *Food of mouse.*

A2435.3.7.1. *Why mice eat grease and salmon.* Joshua: Frachtenberg JAFL XXVIII 231.

A2223.3. Mouse gathers rice for men: may eat a little of his rice daily.

A2435.3.8. *Why ant-bear eats insects.* Ila (Rhodesia): Smith and Dale 366 No. 16.

A2435.3.9. *Food of tiger.*

A2435.3.9.1. *Why tigers eat dogs.* India: Thompson-Balys.

A2435.3.9.2. *Why tigers eat uncooked food.* India: Thompson-Balys.

A2435.3.9.3. *Why tigers eat human flesh.* India: Thompson-Balys.

A2435.3.9.4. *Why tiger eats buffalo.* India: Thompson-Balys.

A2435.3.10. *Food of rat.*

A2435.3.10.1. *Why rat may eat rice.* Brings original rice-plant from pond. India: *Thompson-Balys.

A2223. Animal characteristics reward for helpfulness.

A2435.3.11. *Food of reindeer.* Cheremis: Sebeok-Nyerges.

A2435.3.12. *Food of hare.* Cheremis: Sebeok-Nyerges.

A2435.3.12.1. *Why hare never drinks from rivers or streams.* India: Thompson-Balys.

A2435.3.13. *Food of squirrel.* Cheremis: Sebeok-Nyerges.

A2435.3.14. *Food of pig.* Jewish: Neuman.

A2435.3.14.1. *Why pigs feed on excreta.* India: Thompson-Balys.

A2435.3.15. *Why wildcats come and eat chickens.* Chinese: Graham.

A2435.3.16. *Food of jaguar.*

A2435.3.16.1. *Why jaguars eat men.* S. Am. Indian (Toba): Métraux MAFLS XL 83.

A2435.3.17. *Food of leopard.*

A2435.3.17.1. *Why leopards eat men.* Africa (Cameroon): Rosenhuber 79.

A2435.4. *Food of birds.* Joshua: Frachtenberg JAFL XXVIII 232 (corpses). — India: Thompson-Balys; Japanese: Ikeda.

A2435.4.1. *Food of cuckoo.* (See A2241.4.) — Dh III 133.

A2435.4.2. *Why crane suffers thirst.* (See A2231.2.1.)

A2435.4.3. *Why raven suffers thirst.* (See A2234.1.)

A2435.4.4. *Food of eagle.* Tahltan: Teit JAFL XXXII 242 (fish). — Ila (Rhodesia): Smith and Dale 372 No. 21.

A2435.4.5. *Food of buzzard.* Ojibwa: Skinner JAFL XXXII 282.

A2435.4.5.1. *Carrion as food of vultures.* India: *Thompson-Balys.

A2435.4.6. *Food of hawks.* Ibo (Nigeria): Basden 140; Angola: Chatelain 111 No. 7.

A2435.4.7. *Food of crow.* Why crows peck at flesh of men. India: Thompson-Balys.

A2435.4.7.1. *Why crow eats excrement.* India: Thompson-Balys.

A2435.4.8. *Food of cock.*

A2435.4.8.1. *Why cock scratches for food.* Am. Negro: (Georgia) Harris Nights 56 No. 11.

A2435.4.9. *Food of owl.* Cheremis: Sebeok-Nyerges.

A2435.4.9.1. *Why owl eats no grain.* India: Thompson-Balys.

A2435.4.9.2. *Why owl drinks no water.* India: Thompson-Balys.

A2435.4.10. *Food of jackdaw.* Cheremis: Sebeok-Nyerges.

A2435.4.11. *Food of wren.*

A2435.4.11.1. *Why wren eats no berries.* Africa (Wakweli): Bender 69f.

A2435.5. *Food of insects.* India: Thompson-Balys.

A2435.5.1. *Why bees may not get honey from red clover.* (See A2231.3.2.)

A2435.5.1.1. *Why bees eat their own children.* India: Thompson-Balys.

A2435.5.2. *Insect fries human blood and eats it.* India: Thompson-Balys.

A2435.6. *Food of fish, reptiles,* etc.

A2435.6.1. *Food of tortoise.* Jewish: Neuman; Ila (Rhodesia): Smith and Dale 370 No. 21.

A2435.6.2. *Food of snake.* Jewish: Neuman; Africa (Ekoi): Talbot 386; India: Thompson-Balys.

A2435.6.2.1. *Snake sucks milk from woman's breast.* India: Thompson-Balys.

A2435.6.3. *Why leech feeds on human blood.* India: Thompson-Balys.

A2435.6.6. *Food of hawks.* Chinese: Graham.

A2436. *Why animals lack fire.* Sent to steal fire but are lazy and fail. African (Fang): Tessman 18.

A1415.2. Theft of fire by animals.

A2440. Animal characteristics: carriage. Dh III 219ff.

A2441. *Animal's gait or walk.*

A2441.1. *Animal's gait or walk — mammals.*

A2441.1.0.1. *Animals (and men) hop* because ground is often so dry that it cracks: they have to jump over the cracks. Canada: Baughman.

A2441.1.1. *Cause of monkey's walk.* Dh III 223, 229. — Africa (Fang): Trilles 179.

A2441.1.2. *Why baboon walks on all fours.* Hottentot: Bleek 36 No. 17.

A2441.1.3. *Cause of dog's walk.* Dh III 221.

A2441.1.4. *Cause of hyena's walk.* Dh III 223.

A2441.1.5. *Cause of wolverine's walk.* Tahltan: Teit JAFL XXXII 248.

A2441.1.6. *Cause of skunk's walk.* Ila (Rhodesia): Smith and Dale 360 No. 12.

A2441.1.7. *Cause of elephant's walk.* Dh III 226. — India: Thompson-Balys.

A2441.1.8. *Cause of ox's walk.* Dh III 227.

A2441.1.9. *Cause of leopard's walk.* Dh III 228.

A2441.1.10. *Cause of cat's walk.* Dh III 229.

A2441.1.11. *Cause of hare's hopping gait.* Cheremis: Sebeok-Nyerges; India: Thompson-Balys.

A2441.1.12. *Cause of sheep's walk.* India: Thompson-Balys.

A2221.9. Why sheep walk with bowed heads: they have remained so after bowing to God.

A2441.2. *Cause of bird's walk.*

A2441.2.1. *Why raven hops.* Jewish. Neuman.

A2441.2.2. *Graceful step of dove.* Jewish: Neuman.

A2441.3. *Cause of insect's walk.*

A2441.3.1. *Why beetle creeps on ground.* (See A2232.3.) — Dh III 227.

A2231.7.1. Animal cursed for betraying holy fugitive.

A2441.3.2. *Cause of flea's movement.* Dh III 222f.

A2441.3.3. *Cause of fly's movement.* Dh III 227.

A2441.4. *Cause of movement of reptile,* etc.

A2441.4.1. *Why snake does not go on the road.* (See A2233.1.2.)

A2441.4.2. *Cause of crab's walk.* Dh III 219ff.

A2441.4.3. *Cause of toad's hop.* Dh III 222.

A2441.4.4. *Cause of chameleon's movement.* Dh III 222. — Jewish: Neuman.

A2442. *Method and position of bird's flight.* Jewish: Neuman.

A2442.1. *High and low flight of birds.*

A2442.1.1. *Why some birds cannot fly high.* Dh III 230.

A2442.1.2. *Why parrots fly high.* Africa (Congo): Weeks 221.

A2442.2. *Flight of various birds.*

A2442.2.1. *Why raven claps wings in flying.* (See A2218.6.)

A2442.2.2. *Why cuckoo flies with difficulty,* and sings with wings spread. Sébillot RTP III 265.

A2442.2.3. *Why lapwing flies in curves.* Sébillot RTP III 160.

A2442.2.4. *Bluejay's flight.* Ila (Rhodesia): Smith and Dale 348 No. 2.

A2442.2.5. *Hawk's flight.* Africa (Ekoi): Talbot 189.

A2442.2.6. *Water-birds' flight and diving.* Dh III 224ff.

A2442.2.7. *Wild-goose's flight.* Dh III 223.

A2442.2.8. *Eagle's flight.* Jewish: Neuman.

A2442.3. *How birds began to fly.* India: Thompson-Balys.

A2444. *Animal's method of swimming.*

A2444.1. *Why some fish swim deep; others shallow.* (See A2238.3.)

A2444.2. *Why dolphins swim up and down.* (See A2275.5.4.)

A2444.3. *How salmon swims.* Dh III 222. — Irish: Beal XXI 327.

A2450. Animal's daily work.

A2451. *Animal's occupation: carrying.*

A2451.1. *Why ants carry large bundles.* (See A2221.4.)

A2452. *Animal's occupation: hunting.* *Dh III 272ff. (For animal's favorite prey, see A2494, Why certain animals are enemies.)

A2452.1. *Why dogs hunt.* Sébillot RTP II 437.

A2452.2. *Why stork must hunt for living.* Dh III 284ff.

A2452.3. *Why hawks put heads of mice, etc. on pile of stones.* Zuñi: Handy JAFL XXXI 455.

A2453. *Animal's occupation: collecting.*

A2453.1. *Why ant collects resin.* (See A2221.4.)

A2455. *Animal's occupation: stealing.* Dh III 255.

A2455.1. *Why wolf is thief.* Dh III 295.

A2455.2. *Why swallow is thief.* Flemish: DeMeyer FFC XXXVII 87 No. 84b.

A2455.3. *Why raven is thief.* Because he has none of ten commandments and carries a black stamp on his breast. — Livonian: Loorits FFC LXVI 90 No. 84.

A2455.4. *Why hen does not know how to steal.* Flemish: DeMeyer FFC XXXVII 88 No. 98a.

A2455.5. *Why wolverine is a thief.* Kaska: Teit JAFL XXX 470f.

A2456. *Animal's occupation: boring.*

A2456.1. *Why woodpecker bores in wood.* Am. Negro (North Carolina): Brown Collection I 633; Jamaica Negro: Beckwith MAFLS XVII 259 No. 53.

A2456.2. *Why wood-worm bores wood.* Tahltan: Teit JAFL XXXII 243.

A2457. *Animal's occupation: rolling.*

A2457.1. *Why tumble-bug rolls in dung.* Jamaica Negro: Beckwith MAFLS XVII 258 No. 46.

A2460. Animal characteristics: attack and defense.

A2461. *Animal's means of defense.* Dh III 234ff.

A2461.1. *Hare sleeps with open eyes as defense.* Dh III 234.

A2461.2. *Toad remains still when he hears footsteps* (defense). Dh III 235.

A2461.3. *Killer-whale uses dorsal fin as weapon.* Joshua: Frachtenberg JAFL XXVIII 236.

A2461.4. *Why deer run, stop, and run on again* (defense). Quileute: Farrand JAFL XXXII 251.

A2462. *Animal's habits when attacked.*

A2462.1. *Why squirrel barks when attacked.* Dh III 237.

A2462.2. *Why beaver splashes his tail in water and dives when attacked.* Quileute: Farrand JAFL XXXII 251.

A2462.3. *Why mouse does not defend self against cat.* Jewish: Neuman.

A2463. *Animal's means of attack.*

A2463.1. *Why leopard cannot capture animal who passes him on right side.* Gold Coast: Barker and Sinclair 146 No. 28.

A2464. *Why animal does not attack.*

A2464.1. *Why lion does not attack dog.* Jewish: Neuman.

A2465. *Means of capturing animal.*

A2465.1. *Why fish are caught in nets.* (Cf. Type 253.) — Finnish: Aarne FFC VIII 21 No. 118, XXXIII 55 No. 118.

A2466. *Animal's habits when caught.*

A2466.1. *Why opossum plays dead when caught.* Dh III 236f. — Am. Negro (Georgia): Harris Remus 11 No. 3.

A2466.2. *Why turtle beats with forelegs when caught.* Gold Coast: Barker and Sinclair 87 No. 15.

A2468. *Animal's behavior at death.*

A2468.1. *Why shrew dies on road.* (See A2233.1.3.)

A2468.2. *Why toad dries up when dead.* (See A2231.8.) — Jewish: Neuman.

A2468.3. *Why dragon dies by means of fire.* Ila (Rhodesia): Smith and Dale 379 No. 4.

B11. Dragon.

A2470. Animal's habitual bodily movements.

A2471. *Why animals continually seek something.* (See A2275.5.)

A2471.1. *Why dogs look at one another under tail.* (See A2275.5.5, A2232.8; also *Dh IV 129ff.) — Sébillot RTP ii 433; England, U.S.: Baughman.

A2471.1.1. *Why dogs sniff at one another.* Lithuanian: Balys Index No. *202; Prussian: Plenzat 10.

A2471.2. *Why hogs inspect one another:* seek pancake. (See A2275.5.1.)

A2471.3. *Why hawk (vulture) hovers over camp-fire:* seeks grandmother. (See A2275.5.2.)

A2471.4. *Why diver always looks at sea.* (See A2275.5.3.).

A2471.5. *Why lynx squints:* is looking afar at view. Ojibwa: Jones JAFL XXIX 378.

A2471.6. *Why dog is always looking.* Jamaica negro: Beckwith MAFLS XVII 259 No. 48.

A2471.6.1. *Why dog looks back at person who has beaten him.* Liberian: Bundy JAFL XXXII 421.

A2471.6.2. *Why dogs howl, looking at sky.* Joshua: Frachtenberg JAFL XXVIII 225.

A2471.7. *What hawks are looking for.* Gold Coast: Barker and Sinclair 128 No. 22.

A2471.8. *Why mason-wasp looks for fireplace.* Ila (Rhodesia): Smith and Dale 346 No. 1.

A2471.9. *Why animals always look down.* Jewish: Neuman.

A2472. *Why animals ruminate.*

A2472.1. *Why cows ruminate.* (See A2231.1.1.) — Chinese: Graham.

A2473. *Why animals lift their legs.*

A2473.1. *Why dogs lift their legs.* Dh III 261. — Sébillot RTP II 436; Japanese: Ikeda.

A2473.1.1. *Why dogs leave droppings at crossroads.* India: Thompson-Balys.

A2473.2. *Why pigs in mud lift their legs.* Jewish: Neuman.

A2474. *Why some animals continually shake head.*

A2474.1. *Why lizard bobs head up and down.* (See A2255.2, A2211.9.)

A2474.2. *Why hare shakes head.* Bushman: Bleek and Lloyd 65.

A2474.3. *Why owl shakes head.* India: Thompson-Balys.

A2475. *Why animals scent from distance.*

A2475.1. *Why deer scent people from distance.* Sinkyone: Kroeber JAFL XXXII 346.

A2476. *Why animals move mouth, nose, etc.*

A2476.1. *Why rabbit continually moves mouth.* Zanzibar: Bateman 22 No. 1.

A2477. *Why animals root in ground.*

A2477.1. *Why hog roots in ground.* (See A2236.3, A2275.5.1.) — India: Thompson-Balys.

A2236.8. Why hog roots: was doing so when he should have warned man of devil's temptation in Garden of Eden.

A2477.2. *Why hen scratches in ground.* Africa (Cameroon): Mansfield 233.

A2478. *Why certain animals are continually eating.* (See A2231.1.1.)

A2478.1. *Why zebra is continually eating.* Ila (Rhodesia): Smith and Dale 369 No. 19.

A2479. *Other habitual bodily movements of animals.*

A2479.1. *Why wagtail moves tail up and down.* Dh III 226.

A2479.2. *Why hare skips about like a leaf.* India: *Thompson-Balys.

A2479.3. *Why jackals make noise at night when seeking food.* India: Thompson-Balys.

A2479.4. *Why the hedgehog draws himself up:* shame at sight of a good man. Cheremis: Sebeok-Nyerges.

A2479.6. *Why caterpillars climb trees.* Marquesas: Handy 115.

A2479.7. *Why ants fall upon every man.* Africa (Cameroon): Mansfield 231.

A2479.8. *Why dog snaps every fly.* Fly laughed at dog's (feigned) death. Africa (Cameroon): Mansfield 227.

A2479.9. *Why flies fly around ox's eyes.* Africa (Cameroon): Mansfield 230.

A2480. Periodic habits of animals.

A2481. *Why animals hibernate.*

A2481.1. *Why bears hibernate.* Dh III 257. — Finnish: Aarne FFC XXXIII 53 No. 78**.

A2482. *Why animals migrate.* Dh III 257ff.

A2482.1. *Why swallows migrate.* Dh III 258. — Finnish: Aarne FFC VIII 16 No. 86; Flemish: DeMeyer FFC XXXVII 87 No. 86.

A2482.2. *Why caribou migrate.* Tahltan: Teit JAFL XXXII 232.

A2482.3. *Why wren does not migrate.* Flemish: DeMeyer FFC XXXVII 87 No. 86a.

A2483. *Why animals shed periodically.*

A2483.1. *Why snake sheds skin.* Flemish: DeMeyer FFC XXXVII 88 No. 110a; Jewish: Neuman; India: Thompson-Balys.

A2484. *Why animals crowd together seasonally.*

A2484.1. *Why fish come in seasonally.* New Guinea: Ker 25; Tonga: Gifford.

A2486. *Why animals lay eggs as they do.* (Cf. A2431, A2433.6.1.2.)

A2486.1. *Why raven lays eggs in March.* (See A2251.1.)

A2486.2. *Why bustard hatches but two eggs.* (See A2284.2.)

A2486.3. *Why dove lays but two eggs.* (See A2247.4.)

A2486.4. *How birds began to lay eggs.* India: Thompson-Balys.

A2489. *Animal's periodic habits — miscellaneous.*

A2489.1. *Why cock wakes man in morning.* India: Thompson-Balys; Mpongwe: Nassau 58 No. 9.

A2489.1.1. *Why cock crows to greet sunrise.* India: *Thompson-Balys.

J2272.1. Chanticleer believes that his crowing makes the sun rise.

A2490. Other habits of animals.

A2491. *Why certain animals avoid light.* Dh III 266ff.

A2491.1. *Why bat flies by night.* (See A2275.5.3.) — Dh III 267. — Lithuanian: Balys Index No. 3170; Legends No. 271; Japanese: Ikeda.

A2491.1.1. *Why bat sleeps by day.* (See A2236.3.) — India: Thompson-Balys.

A2491.2. *Why owl avoids daylight.* Dh III 270. — Ibo (Nigeria): Thomas 162; (Wakweli): Bender 39, 46.

A2491.3. *Why mole burrows underground.* Dh III 267. — Cherokee: Alexander N. Am. 64.

A2491.4. *Tiger cursed with short sight in day time:* good sight only at night. India: Thompson-Balys.

A2491.5. *Why grasshoppers and locusts hide in day.* India: Thompson-Balys.

A2492. *Why certain animals go in herds.*

A2492.1. *Why jackals do not go in herds.* Ila (Rhodesia): Smith and Dale 368 No. 18.

A2492.2. *Why birds do not live in societies.* New Guinea: Ker 77.

A2493. *Friendships between the animals.* Dh III 324ff. — Bödker Exempler 290 No. 45—46. — Indonesian: DeVries's list No. 86.

K815. Victim lured by kind words, approaches trickster and is killed.
M246. Covenant of friendship.

A2493.0.1. *Former friendship between domestic and wild animals.* India: Thompson-Balys.

A2493.1. *Friendship of prairie-dog and owl.* Dh III 352.

A2493.2. *Friendship of bat and owl.* Dh III 355.

A2493.3. *Friendship of tiger and buffalo.* India: Thompson-Balys.

A2493.4. *Friendship between man and dog.* India: Thompson-Balys; Africa (Kweli): Sieber 92f.

A2493.5. *Friendship between deer and fish.* India: Thompson-Balys.

A2493.6. *Friendship between squirrel and quail.* India: Thompson-Balys.

A2493.7. *Friendship between leopard-cat and squirrel.* India: Thompson-Balys.

A2493.7.1. *Friendship between leopard-cat and night-jar.* India: Thompson-Balys.

A2493.8. *Friendship between leopard and goat.* Africa (Congo): Weeks Jungle 433ff.

A2493.9. *Friendship of cat and mouse.* Grimm No. 2.

A2493.9.1. *Oath of friendship between cat and rat.* India: Thompson-Balys.

A2493.10. *Friendship of fox and titmouse.* Cheremis: Sebeok-Nyerges.

A2493.11. *Friendship between jackal and crocodile.* India: Thompson-Balys.

A2493.11.1. *Friendship between jackal and alligator.* India: Thompson-Balys.

A2493.11.2. *Friendship between jackal and elephant.* India: Thompson-Balys.

A2493.11.3. *Friendship between jackal and tiger.* India: Thompson-Balys.

A2493.11.3.1. *Jackal and tiger as business partners.* India: Thompson-Balys.

A2493.11.4. *Friendship between jackal and partridge.* India: Thompson-Balys.

A2493.12. *Friendship between turtle and heron.* New Hebrides: Codrington I 1.

A2493.12.1. *Friendship between turtle and wallaby.* Papua: Ker I.

A2493.13. *Friendship between hare and parrot.* India: Thompson-Balys.

A2493.14. *Friendship between monkey and elephant.* India: Thompson-Balys.

A2493.14.1. *Friendship between monkey and tiger.* India: Thompson-Balys.

A2493.14.2. *Friendship between monkey and lion.* India: Thompson-Balys.

A2493.14.3. *Friendship between monkey and stork.* India: Thompson-Balys.

A2493.14.4. *Friendship between monkey and rabbit.* India: Thompson-Balys.

A2493.14.5. *Friendship between partridge, monkey and elephant.* Buddhist myth: Malalasekera I 1008.

A2493.15. *Friendship between wolf and ass.* India: Thompson-Balys.

A2493.16. *Friendship between cock and dog.* India: Thompson-Balys.

A2493.17. *Friendship between tiger and deer (fawn).* India: Thompson-Balys.

A2493.18. *Friendship between cat and tiger.* India: Thompson-Balys.

A2493.19. *Friendship between crab and cobra.* India: Thompson-Balys.

A2493.20. *Friendship between frog and cricket.* India: Thompson-Balys.

A2493.21. *Friendship between grasshopper and dungbeetle.* India: Thompson-Balys.

A2493.22. *Friendship between goat and hog.* India: Thompson-Balys.

A2493.23. *Friendship between louse and crow.* India: Thompson-Balys.

A2493.24. *Friendship between cow and tiger, calf and cub.* India: Thompson-Balys.

A2493.25. *Friendship between snake and crow.* India: *Thompson-Balys.

A2493.26. *Friendship between parrot and maina.* India: Thompson-Balys.

A2493.27. *Friendship between bird and crab.* India: *Thompson-Balys.

A2493.28. *Friendship between mouse and butterfly.* Papua: Ker 100.

A2493.29. *Friendship between ant and pheasant.* Papua: Ker 118.

A2493.30. *Friendship between tiger and lion.* Buddhist myth: Malalasekera II 623, 823.

A2493.30.1. *Friendship between lion and jackal.* Buddhist myth: Malalasekera I 775, II 895.

A2493.30.2. *Friendship between cow and lioness.* Buddhist myth: Malalasekera II 1028.

A2493.31. *Friendship between dog and elephant.* Buddhist myth: Malalasekera I 137.

A2493.32. *Friendship between antelope, woodpecker and tortoise.* Buddhist myth: Malalasekera I 642.

A2493.33. *Friendship between pike and crawfish.* Africa (Wakweli): Bender 41.

A2493.34. *Friendship of hen and duck.* Africa (Wakweli): Bender 81f.

A2493.34.1. *Friendship between hen and sparrow.* Africa (Wakweli): Bender 51.

A2493.35. *Why we know that the parrot comforts and helps man.* Africa (Wakweli): Bender 70.

A2494. *Why certain animals are enemies.* *Dh III 324ff. — (See A2286.0.1.) — India: Thompson-Balys; Africa: Stanley 78, (Wakweli): Bender 88f.

A2004. Insects from devil's post-hole. Stopped by burning log. Why insects hate smoke. A2585. Why there is enmity between certain animals and man.

A2494.1. *The cat's enemies.*

A2494.1.1. *Enmity between cat and mouse.* (See A2281.) — Dh IV 112ff., 144ff.

A2494.1.2. *Enmity between cat and dog.* (See A2281.1.) — Dh IV 117ff., 142ff.

A2494.1.3. *Enmity between cat and hare.* (See A2281.) — Dh III 332.

A2494.1.4. *Enmity between cat and rat.* Dh III 328 (wildcat). — India: Thompson-Balys; Liberian: Bundy JAFL XXXII 419f.

A2494.1.5. *Enmity between cat and hen.* Dh III 329ff.

A2494.1.6. *Enmity between cat and tiger.* Dh III 333f. — India: *Thompson-Balys; Indonesian: DeVries's list No. 93.

A2494.1.7. *Enmity between cat and spider.* Dh III 331.

A2494.1.8. *Enmity between civet cat and chicken.* Africa (Wakweli): Bender 65ff., 71f.

A2494.2. *The leopard's enemies.* Benga: Nassau 163, 226 Nos. 20, 33; Congo: Weeks 211 No. 7.

A2494.2.1. *Enmity between leopard and antelope.* Dh III 335. — India: Thompson-Balys; Fjort: Dennett 73 No. 15.

A2494.2.2. *Enmity between leopard and lion.* Dh III 338. — Spanish Exempla: Keller.

A2494.2.3. *Enmity between leopard and goat.* (See A2281.) — Africa (Benga): Nassau 99 No. 6, (Angola): Chatelain 195 No. 24, (Vai): Ellis 240 No. 47, (Wakweli): Bender 54.

A2494.2.4. *Enmity between leopard and deer.* Liberia: Bundy JAFL XXXII 417.

A2494.2.5. *Enmity between dog and leopard.* Africa: Stanley 196, (Benga): Nassau 189 No. 25.

A2494.2.6. *Enmity between leopard and sheep.* Ibo (Nigeria): Thomas 72.

A2494.2.7. *Enmity between leopard and monkey.* India: Thompson-Balys.

A2494.3. *The hyena's enemies.*

A2494.3.1. *Enmity between hyena and ass.* Dh III 337.

A2494.3.2. *Enmity between hyena and jackal.* Dh III 338.

A2494.3.3. *Enmity between hyena and weasel.* Dh III 338.

A2494.3.4. *Enmity between hyena and cow.* Dh III 338.

A2494.3.5. *Enmity between hyena and wildcat.* Dh III 329.

A2494.4. *The dog's enemies.*

A2494.4.0.1. *Dog driven away from other animals because of his barking.* India: Thompson-Balys.

A2494.4.1. *Enmity between dog and squirrel.* (See A2281.2.)

A2494.4.2. *Enmity between dog and crocodile.* Dh III 327.

A2494.4.3. *Enmity between dog and mouse.* Dh IV 112ff.

A2494.4.4. *Enmity between dog and rabbit.* Dh III 328; Am. Negro (Georgia): Harris Nights 349 No. 61.

A2494.4.5. *Enmity between dog and fox.* Dh III 328.

A2494.4.6. *Enmity between dog and cat.* (See A2494.1.2, A2281.1.)

A2494.4.7. *Enmity between dog and lion.* Dh III 338.

A2494.4.8. *Enmity between dog and bull.* India: Thompson-Balys.

A2494.4.9. *Enmity between dog and tiger.* India: Thompson-Balys.

A2494.4.10. *Enmity between dog and cow.* India: Thompson-Balys.

A2494.4.11. *Enmity between dog and rooster.* Duala: Lederbogen Märchen V 128.

A2494.4.12. *Enmity between fowl and dog.* Africa: Weeks Cannibals 209.

A2494.4.13. *Enmity between palm rat and dog.* Africa: Weeks Jungle 382f.

A2494.5. *The jackal's enemies.*

A2494.5.1. *Enmity between jackal and wild hen.* Dh III 341.

A2494.5.2. *Enmity between jackal and kite.* Dh III 341.

A2494.5.3. *Enmity between jackal and crab.* Dh III 349; India: Thompson-Balys.

A2281. Enmity between animals from original quarrel.

A2494.5.4. *Enmity between jackal and alligator.* India: Thompson-Balys.

A2494.6. *The rabbit's enemies.*

A2494.6.1. *Enmity between lynx and rabbit.* Penobscot: Speck JAFL XXVIII 54.

A2494.6.2. *Enmity between rabbit and coyote.* Chuh: Kunst JAFL XXVIII 356.

A2494.6.3. *Enmity between fisher and rabbit.* Penobscot: Speck JAFL XXVIII 53.

A2494.7. *The lion's enemies.*

A2494.7.1. *Enmity between monkey and lion.* Vai: Ellis 231 No. 40.

A2494.7.2. *Enmity between lion and wolf.* Dh III 339. — Africa (Angola): Chatelain 201 No. 27.

A2494.7.3. *Enmity between lion and man.* Wute: Sieber 182f.

A2494.8. *The bear's enemies.* (Cf. A2494.10.3.)

A2494.8.1. *Enmity between bears and goats.* India: Thompson-Balys.

A2494.8.2. *Enmity between bear and ant.* Dh III 143.

A2494.9. *Enemies of fox.* (Cf. A2494.4.5.)

A2494.9.1. *Enmity between baboon and fox.* Dh III 332.

A2494.9.2. *Enmity between fox and chicken.* Liberian: Bundy JAFL XXXII 424.

A2494.10. *The tiger's enemies.*

A2494.10.1. *Enmity between tiger and man.* India: Thompson-Balys.

A2494.10.2. *Enmity between tiger and boar.* India: Thompson-Balys.

A2494.10.3. *Enmity between tiger and bear.* India: Thompson-Balys.

A2494.11. *The elephant's enemies.*

A2494.11.1. *Enmity between elephant and thousand-leg.* Dh III 339.

A2494.11.2. *Enmity between crocodile and elephant.* India: Thompson-Balys.

A2494.11.3. *Enmity between elephant and ant.* India: Thompson-Balys.

A2494.12. *Miscellaneous enmities of mammals.* (Cf. A2494.13.3, A2494.13.5.)

A2494.12.1. *Enmity between panther, antelope, and tortoise.* Dh III 335.

A2494.12.2. *Enmity between mongoose and snake.* Buddhist myth: Malalasekera II 2, 854.

A2494.12.3. *Enmity between ox and antelope.* Africa (Mpongwe): Nassau 58 No. 10.

A2494.12.3.1. *Enmity between cattle and snails.* China: Eberhard FFC CXX No. 79.

A2494.12.4. *Enmity between coyote and meadowlark.* Pueblo: Parsons JAFL XXXI 227.

A2494.12.5. *Enmity between raven and mink.* Dh. III 351.

A2494.12.6. *Enmity between marten and squirrel.* Dh III 339.

A2494.12.7. *Enmity between deer and terrapin.* North Carolina: Brown Coll. I 103.

A2494.12.8. *Enmity between rat and spider.* India: Thompson-Balys.

A2494.12.9. *Enmity between chimpanzee and man.* Nyang: Ittman 65ff.

A2494.12.10. *Enmity between porcupine and snail.* Wakweli: Bender 78.

A2494.13. *Enmities of birds.* (Cf. A2494.12.4, A2494.16.4.)

A2494.13.1. *Enmity between crow and owl.* Spanish Exempla: Keller; India: Thompson-Balys; Panchatantra III introduction (transl. Ryder); Buddhist myth: Malalasekera I 437; Japanese: Ikeda.

A2494.13.2. *Enmity between kite and crow.* Japanese: Ikeda; Zanzibar: Bateman 57 No. 4.

A2494.13.3. *Enmity between fowl and cockroach.* Antigua: Johnson JAFL XXXIV 66.

A2494.13.4. *Enmity between owl and mouse.* Dh III 343.

A2494.13.4.1. *Enmity between owl and fowl.* Africa: Weeks Jungle 436ff.

A2494.13.5. *Enmity between crow and prairie-dog.* Dh III 341.

A2494.13.6. *Enmity between raven and marshsnipe.* Dh III 348.

A2494.13.7. *Enmity between raven and mink.* Dh III 351.

A2494.13.8. *Enmity between woodpecker and weaver-bird.* Wakweli: Bender 50.

A2494.13.9. *Enmity between bird and rat.* India: Thompson-Balys.

A2494.13.10. *The hen's enemies.*

A2494.13.10.1. *Enmity between hen and all other animals.* Dh III 344.

A2494.13.10.2. *Enmity between hen, beetle, and duck.* Dh III 347.

A2494.13.10.3. *Enmity between hawk and hen.* Dh III 343. — Africa (Cameroon): Rosenhuber 69f.

A2494.13.10.4. *Enmity between falcon and hen.* Dh III 348.

A2494.13.10.5. *Enmity between hen and tiger.* Fang: Trilles 246.

A2494.13.10.6. *Enmity between birds of prey and chickens.* Africa (Cameroon): Meinhof 42.

A2494.13.11. *The starling's enemies.*

A2494.13.11.1. *Enmity between grasshopper and starling.* Dh III 349.

A2494.13.11.2. *Enmity between starling and locust.* India: Thompson-Balys.

A2494.13.11.3. *Enmity between parrot and starling.* India: Thompson-Balys.

A2494.13.12. *Enmity between fowl and falcon.* Buddhist myth: Malalasekera I 613.

A2494.14. *The insects' enemies.* (Cf. A2494.13.3, A2494.13.10.2, A2494.13.11.1.)

A2494.14.1. *Enmity between spider and fly.* Dh III 349. — Esthonian: Aarne FFC XXV 150 No. 67.

A2494.14.2. *Enmity between spider and wasp.* India: Thompson-Balys.

A2494.14.3. *Why stinging flies sit on eyes of cattle.* Wakweli: Bender 64.

A2494.15. *The fish's enemies.*

A2494.16. *Enemies of reptiles and other animal forms.* (Cf. A2494.11.2, A2494.12.7.)

A2494.16.1. *Enmity between frog and snake.* Dh III 349f.

A2494.16.2. *Enmity between chameleon and lizard.* Dh III 349.

A2494.16.3. *Enmity between cobra and viper.* Dh III 350.

A2494.16.4. *Enmity between bird and lizard.* Latter muddies water. India: Thompson-Balys.

A2494.16.5. *Enmity between crab and spider.* India: Thompson-Balys.

A2494.16.6. *Enmity between earthworm and rattlesnake.* S. Am. Indian (Toba): Métraux MAFLS XL 67.

A2494.16.7. *Enmity between octopus and rat.* Tonga: Gifford 206.

A2495. *Animal's treatment of its excrements (urine).*

A2495.1. *Why cat buries its excrements.* Cyprus: Hadjioannou No. 9; India: Thompson-Balys.

A2495.2. *Why ass smells his own excrements.* Jewish: Neuman.

A2495.3. *Why donkeys always urinate when others begin.* Jewish: Neuman.

A2496. *Sexual intercourse of animals.* India: Thompson-Balys.

A2496.1. *Why dogs get stuck in copulation.* (Cf. A2236.3, A2236.5.) — Jewish: Neuman; India: Thompson-Balys.

A2496.2. *Copulation of serpents.* Jewish: Neuman.

A2496.3. *Why men, fish and serpents face each other in copulation.* Jewish: Neuman.

A2497. *Monogamy among animals.*

A2497.1. *Monogamous life of dove.* Jewish: Neuman.

A2499. *Other habits of animals: miscellaneous.*

A2499.1. *Why tigers do not kill women who run away after quarreling with their husbands.* India: Thompson-Balys.

A2500—A2599. Animal characteristics—miscellaneous.

A2500. Animal characteristics—miscellaneous.

A2510. Utility of animals.

A2510.1. *Why reindeer has so many qualities.* Flemish: DeMeyer FFC XXXVII 86 No. 58e.

A2511. *Why flesh of animal is good.*

A2511.1. *Why black bears are better eating than grizzly bears.* Kaska: Teit JAFL XXX 448.

A2512. *Animal useful because of power of scenting.*

A2512.1. *Why dog can follow animal's scent.* India: Thompson-Balys.

A2513. *Why certain animals serve men.* Dh III 249ff. — Lithuanian: Balys Index No. 3108.

A2513.0.1. *Existence of animals depends upon existence of man.* Jewish: Neuman.

A2513.1. *Origin of dog's service.* Dog must serve and obey man for meager recompense. Lithuanian: Balys Index No. 3109; India: *Thompson-Balys.

A2513.1.1. *Dog looks for the most powerful master.* Stays for good in man's service, since man fears no one. Lithuanian: Balys Index No. *205.

A2513.2. *How cat was domesticated.* India: Thompson-Balys.

A2513.3. *How pig was domesticated.* India: Thompson-Balys.

A2513.4. *Why goat lives with man.* India: Thompson-Balys.

A2513.5. *Why ox serves man.* India: Thompson-Balys.

A2515. *Animal useful for bearing burdens.*

A2515.1. *Why ox is draft animal.* (See A2252.2.)

A2520. Disposition of animals.

A2521. *Why animal is sad.*

A2521.1. *Why turtle-dove is sad.* Sébillot RTP III 159.

A2522. *Why animal is disliked.*

A2522.1. *Why sparrow is disliked.* Sébillot RTP III 159.

A2522.2. *Why shrike is disliked.* Sébillot RTP III 159.

A2522.3. *Why white ants are a pest.* Africa (Gold Coast): Barker and Sinclair 67 No. 7.

A2522.4. *Why skunk is disliked.* Inca: Krickeberg Märchen der Azteken und Inkaperuaner 254.

A2522.5. *Why crow is disliked.* India: Thompson-Balys.

A2522.6. *Why wren is disliked.* Irish myth: Cross.

A2522.7. *Why fly is hated.* Africa (Fang): Tressman 79ff.

A2523. *Why animal is evil.* Jewish: Neuman.

A2523.1. *Why hog has evil spirit.* (See A2287.1.)

A2523.2. *Why snakes are proud.* India: Thompson-Balys.

A2523.2.1. *Why rattlesnake is dangerous.* S. Am. Indian (Toba): Métraux MAFLS XL 69.

A2524. *Why animal is pugnacious (brave, bold).*

A2524.1. *Why grizzly bears are pugnacious.* Kaska: Teit JAFL XXX 448.

A2524.2. *Why sandpiper (machetis pugnax) fights.* Finnish: Aarne FFC XXXIII 54 No. 104**.

A2524.3. *Why bears attack men.* India: Thompson-Balys.

A2524.4. *Why fish attack anything they find.* India: Thompson-Balys.

A2524.5. *Why lion is brave.* Jewish: Neuman.

A2524.6. *Why dog is bold.* Jewish: Neuman.

A2525. *Why animals are deceptive.*

A2525.1. *Why hare is deceptive.* Ila (Rhodesia): Smith and Dale 375 No. 1.

A2525.2. *Why crab is cunning.* India: Thompson-Balys.

A2525.3. *Why fox is sly.* Jewish: Neuman.

A2526. *Why animals are unrestrained.*

A2526.1. *Why dog lacks restraint.* Ojibwa: Jones JAFL XXIX 369.

A2527. *Why animal is vain.*

A2527.1. *Why cock is vain and selfish.* Jewish: Neuman.

A2527.2. *Why peacock is vain.* Buddhist myth: Malalasekera II 8.

A2528. *Why animal is strong.*

A2528.1. *Why leopard is strong.* Jewish: Neuman.

A2531. *Why animal is harmless.*

A2531.0.1. *Wild animals lose their ferocity.* Jewish: Neuman. (Cf. A2295.)

A2531.1. *Why water serpents are not venomous.* (Cf. A2532.1.) — India: Thompson-Balys; Pueblo: Parsons JAFL XXXI 250; Congo: Weeks 213 No. 9.

A2531.2. *Why grizzly bear is peaceable.* Calif. Indian: Gayton and Newman 95, (Joshua): Frachtenberg JAFL XXVIII 241.

A2531.3. *Why elephant is peaceable.* Congo: Weeks 214 No. 10.

A2531.3.1. *Why elephant flees when cock crows.* Africa (Dinka): Casati I 49.

A2532. *Why animals are venomous.*

A2532.1. *Why snakes are venomous.* (Cf. A2235.) — Choctaw: Alexander N. Am. 64; India: Thompson-Balys; Jewish: Neuman.

A2219.3. Only one serpent had sting.

A2532.2. *Why hairy caterpillar is venomous.* India: Thompson-Balys.

A2534. *Why animal is timorous.*

A2534.1. *Why crab is afraid in dark.* Jamaica Negro: Beckwith MAFLS XVII 259 No. 54.

A2536. *Animals of good omen.*

B147. Animal of ill omen.

A2536.1. *Why swallow brings good luck.* Flemish: DeMeyer FFC XXXVII 86 No. 84a.

A2536.2. *Why ring-dove brings good luck.* Ila (Rhodesia): Smith and Dale 353 No. 7.

A2536.3. *Why spider brings good luck.* Africa (Fang): Einstein 99. (Cf. A523.1.)

A2537. *Why animal is stupid.*

A2537.1. *Why fish is stupid.* Jewish: Neuman.

A2537.2. *Why ass is stupid.* Jewish: Neuman.

A2540. Other animal characteristics.

W154.3.1. Lion rescued from net by rat: eats rat.

A2541. *Why animal is sacred.*

A2541.1. *Why bee is sacred.* Dh I 215; Sébillot RTP III 158.

A2541.2. *Why stork is holy.* (See A2221.5.) — Dh III 286; Sébillot RTP III 128.

A2542. *Why animal is cursed.*

A2542.1. *Why magpie is cursed.* (See A2231.) — Sébillot RTP III 159.

A2542.1.1. *Magpie refuses to get into ark,* sits around outside, jabbering over drowned world, is unlucky. (Cf. A2232.4.) England: Baughman.

A2542.2. *Why spider is cursed.* (See A2231.5.)

A2545. *Animal given certain privilege.*

A2545.1. *Why flies may eat anywhere.* (See A2221.2.1, A2229.4.)

A2545.2. *Why cat eats first.* Lithuanian: Balys Legends No. 225; S. Carolina negro: Davis JAFL XXVII 244 (eats before washing).

A2545.3. *Why dog eats first.*

A2223.5. Dog guards master's life and wealth: may eat before other animals.

A2545.4. *Dog granted proper food.* Dh IV 112.

A2545.5. *Why wild pigs ravage rice-fields.* India: Thompson-Balys.

A2546. *Animal granted patent of nobility.*

A2546.1. *Dog granted patent of nobility.* Dh IV 117ff.

A2546.2. *Wolf granted patent of nobility.* Dh IV 125.

A2547. Why certain animal is king.

B240. King of animals.

A2547.1. *Why certain bird is king of birds.* India: Thompson-Balys; Ibo (Nigeria): Basden 281.

A2551. *Why game is easy to hunt.* Tahltan: Teit JAFL XXXII 218.

A2552. *Why game animals are elusive.* S. Am. Indian (Toba): Métraux MAFLS XL 59, (Cavina, Tumapasa): Métraux BBAE CXLIII (3) 448.

A2555. *Why certain animals are swift.*

A2555.1. *Why sheep is a good runner.* Tahltan: Teit JAFL XXXII 231.

A2561. *Why certain animals are sterile.*

A2561.1. *Why mule is sterile.* Sébillot RTP II 492. — Laguna and Zuñi: Parsons JAFL XXXI 259.

A2571. *How animals received their names.* *Dh III 186ff. — Marshall Islands: Davenport 222.

A2571.0.1. *Adam gives name to all animals.* Jewish: Neuman.

A2571.0.2. *Adam names male animals, Eve, female.* Jewish: Neuman.

A2571.0.3. *God gives animals their name on first Sabbath.* Jewish: Neuman.

A2571.0.4. *Names of animals explained by their characteristics.* Jewish: Neuman.

A2571.1. *How the blackbird (merulus) received its name.* Irish myth: Cross.

A2575. *Quarrels introduced among animals.* Africa (Congo): Weeks 205 No. 2.

A1599.11. Origin of quarrels.

A2576. *Why monkeys do not fall from trees.* India: Thompson-Balys.

A2577. *Why tiger cannot come down a tree head foremost.* India: Thompson-Balys.

A2578. *Why animal has long life.* Jewish: Neuman.

A2578.1. *Why daddy-long-legs has long life.* India: Thompson-Balys.

A2578.2. *Why eagle has long life.* Jewish: Neuman.

A2581. *Why tiger lacks some qualities of cats:* cat, his teacher, omitted to teach him all he knew. India: Thompson-Balys.

A2582. *Why certain animals are plentiful.*

A2582.1. *Why pigs are plentiful.* New Guinea: Ker 13.

A2584. *Why particular animals are not found in certain place.*

A2584.1. *Why certain district is free of mosquitoes.* Korean: Zong in-Sob 58, No. 32.

A2584.2. *Why ants no longer live on the back of the hare.* Korean: Zong in-Sob 33 No. 16.

A2585. *Why there is enmity between certain animals and man.* Jewish: Neuman.

A2585.1. *Origin of enmity between serpent and man.* Jewish: Neuman.

A2600—A2699. Origin of trees and plants.

A2600—A2649. VARIOUS ORIGINS OF PLANTS

A2600. Origin of plants. Dh I 170f. — **Wünsche Die Pflanzenfabel in der Weltliteratur (Leipzig 1905). — Persian: Carnoy 281; Hawaiian: Dixon 38; Maori: Clark 15.

A2601. *Origin of plants: creator sends down the insects, who plant them.* India: Thompson-Balys.

A2602. *Planting the earth.* India: Thompson-Balys.

A2610. Creation of plants by transformation.
D210. Transformation: man to vegetable form.

A2611. *Plants from body of slain person or animal.* Dh I 79. — India: *Thompson-Balys; Chinese: Eberhard FFC CXX 23, 129; S. Am. Indian (Mataco): Métraux MAFLS XL 128, (Caingang): Métraux BBAE CXLIII (1) 473.
E631. Reincarnation in plant (tree) growing from grave.

A2611.0.1. *Plants from grave of dead person or animal.* India: Thompson-Balys; Mono-Alu: Wheeler 67; S. Am. Indian (Brazil): Oberg 109, (Toba): Métraux MAFLS XL 38, (Paressi): Métraux BBAE CXLIII (3) 359f., (Cashinawa): Métraux ibid. 686.

A2611.0.2. *Plants from foetus or body of stillborn child.* India: Thompson-Balys.

A2611.0.3. *Human placenta transformed into plant.* India: Thompson-Balys.

A2611.0.4. *Parts of body of god transformed into plants.* India: Thompson-Balys; Hawaii: Beckwith Myth 188.

A2611.0.4.1. *Women transformed into flowers.* Marquesas: Handy 135.

A2611.0.5. *Parts of human or animal body transformed into plants.* India: Thompson-Balys; Chinese: Eberhard FFC CXX 130f. Nos. 85, 89; S. Am. Indian (Mataco): Métraux MAFLS XL 128.

A2611.1. *Corn from body of slain person.* (Cf. A2685.1.) — Babylonian: Spence 140; India: Thompson-Balys; N. A. Indian: *Thompson Tales 293 n. 77; S. Am. Indian (Amazon): Alexander Lat. Am. 292; Yunca (Peru): ibid. 225, (Paressi): Métraux BBAE CXLIII (3) 360, (Brazil): Oberg 108; (Caingang): Métraux BBAE CXLIII (1) 473.

A1420.1. Origin of food from body of slain food-goddess.

A2611.2. *Tobacco from grave of bad woman.* Finnish: Aarne FFC VIII 23 No. 128, XXXIII 56 No. 128; Esthonian: Aarne FFC XXV 152 No. 76; Livonian: Loorits FFC LXVI 96 No. 125; Lithuanian: Balys Index No. 3240, Legends Nos. 326—337; S. Am. Indian (Paressi): Métraux BBAE CXLIII (3) 359, (Toba): Métraux MAFLS XL 62.

A2611.2.1. *Tobacco from grave of virgin.* India: Thompson-Balys.

A2611.3. *Coconut tree from head of slain monster.* Oceanic (Samoa, Union Group, Mangaia, Tahiti): Dixon 55; (Cook Is.): Beckwith Myth 104, (Solomon Is.): ibid. 104, (Papua): Ker 92, (Tuamotu): Beckwith Myth 103.

A2611.4. *Pepper plant from body of slain person.* (Cf. A2686.3.) — Zuñi: Cushing 183.

A2611.5. *Mandrake from blood of person hanged on gallows.* (Cf. A2664.) — **Starck Der Alraun; *Taylor JAFL XXXI 561f.; Penzer III 153.; *Fb "alrunerod" IV 10a.

A2611.6. *Hair transformed into plants.* India: Thompson-Balys.

A2611.6.1. *Grass from hair of slain person.* India: *Thompson-Balys.

A2683. Origin of grass.

A2611.7. *Origin of rue: from drops of Christ's blood.* Lithuanian: Balys Index No. 3218, Legends No. 304.

A2612. *Plants from tears.*

D1454.4.3. Flowers from tears.

A2612.1. *Tears of Adam and Eve leaving paradise become trees.* (Cf. A2681.) — Dh I 223ff.

A1331. Paradise lost.

A2612.2. *Tears of Mary at Annunciation become daisies.* (Cf. A2651.) — — Dh II 7.

A2612.3. *God's tears become peas.* (Cf. A2686.2.) — Finnish: Aarne FFC VIII 23 No. 126.

A2613. *Plant from spittle.*

A2613.1. *Mushroom from spittle of deity.* (Cf. A2686.1.) — Dh II 107; Lithuanian: Balys Index No. 3230, Legends No. 325.

A2615. *Object transformed to plant.* Jewish: Neuman.

D450. Transformation: object to another object. D462. Transformation of plants to another object.

A2615.1. *Mary hides in ground nail to be used for cross: origin of thistles.* (Cf. A2688.1.) — Dh II 216.

A2615.2. *Plant from mother's milk.* India: Thompson-Balys.

A2615.3. *Canoe transformed into coconut tree.* Hawaii: Beckwith Myth 232.

A2615.4. *Seaweed becomes vegetation.* Eskimo (Labrador): Hawkes GSCan XIV 152.

A2616. *One plant transformed into another.* India: Thompson-Balys; Eskimo (Labrador): Hawks GSCan XIV 152.

A2617. *Plants from transformed person (animal).*

A2617.1. *Living boys or girls transformed into plants.* India: Thompson-Balys.

A2617.2. *Living animals transformed into plants.* India: Thompson-Balys.

A2620. Plants originate from experience of holy person.

V200. Sacred persons.

A2621. *Plants from tread of holy person.* Dh II 7. — Japanese: Anesaki 240.

A2621.1. *Flowers from under the feet of Virgin Mary.* (Cf. A2650.) — *Dh II 258; BP I 100 n. 1.

A2621.2. *Plants from tread of goddess.* Greek myth: Grote I 5 (Aphrodite).

A2622. *Peter lets key of heaven fall: origin of "Heaven Key" (primrose).* Peter hears that duplicate key to heaven has been made. In his excitement he lets his key drop to earth. It is returned by an angel. Where it dropped are the "Heaven Keys". (Cf. A2653.) — *Dh II 190.

A2623. *St. Peter's grass.* Created by the saint as medicine for snakebite. Lithuanian: Balys Legends No. 301.

A2532.1. Why snakes are venomous.

A2624. *Origin of plant from staff of holy person.*

A2624.1. *Origin of thorn tree from staff of Joseph of Arimathea.* England: Baughman.

A2625. *Plants from clothing of deity.* (Cf. A2615.) — Hawaii: Beckwith Myth 282; Tahiti: Henry 338.

A2630. Other types of plant origins.

A2631. *Origin of plant as punishment.* (Cf. A2230.)

A2631.1. *Punishment for first murder: thistles, etc.* Until murder was committed, only useful plants grew on earth; since then, thistles. (Cf. A2688.1.) — Dh I 248.

Q211. Murder punished.

A2631.1.1. *Punishment for Fall of Man: thistles, etc.* Jewish: Neuman.

A2632. *Origin of plant as reward.*

A2632.1. *Willow shelters Holy Family: becomes weeping willow.* (Cf. A2681.1.) — Flemish: DeMeyer FFC XXXVII 91 No. 132c.

A2632.2. *Origin of tree for crucifixion of Christ.* Planted by Adam's son on the grave of primeval father. Lithuanian: Balys Legends No. 66.

A2634. *Plants created by direct divine agency.* India: Thompson-Balys; S. Am. Indian (Viracocha): Steward-Métraux BBAE CXLIII (3) 550, (Toba): Métraux MAFLS XL 41.

A2650—A2699. ORIGIN OF VARIOUS PLANTS AND TREES

A2650. Origin of flowers. (See A2617.1, A2621.1.) — India: Thompson-Balys.

E631.1.1. Lily from grave. E631.1.2. Rose from grave.

A2651. *Origin of daisy.* (See A2612.2.) — Flemish: DeMeyer FFC XXXVII 92 No. 253*.

A2653. *Origin of primrose.* (Cf. A2622.) — Flemish: DeMeyer FFC XXXVII 91 No. 250.

A2654. *Origin of "Mary's bed straw"* (thymus serpyllum). Flemish: De Meyer FFC XXXVII 91 No. 251*.

A2655. *Origin of bindweed* (convolvulus sepium). Flemish: DeMeyer FFC XXXVII 91 No. 252*.

A2656. *Origin of rose.*

A2656.1. *Origin of mossrose.* Flemish: DeMeyer FFC XXXVII 92 No. 254*

A2656.2. *Origin of York and Lancaster rose.* From dust and blood of slain of War of the Roses — a variety of rose unknown before that time. England: Baughman.

A2657. *Origin of forget-me-not.* Flemish: DeMeyer FFC XXXVII 92 No. 255*.

A2658. *Origin of lady-slipper* (calceolaria hybrida). Flemish: DeMeyer XXXVII 92 No. 256*.

A2661. *Origin of snowdrop* (galanthus nivatis). Flemish: DeMeyer FFC XXXVII 92 No. 257*.

A2662. *Origin of hellebore.* Flemish: DeMeyer FFC XXXVII 92 No. 259*.

A2663. *Origin of clove.* Flemish: DeMeyer FFC XXXVII 92 No. 261*.

A2664. *Origin of mandrake.* (See A2611.5.)

A2665. *Origin of wild morning glory.* Hawaii: Beckwith Myth 282.

A2665.1. *Origin of narcissus.* Chinese: Eberhard 131 No. 87.

A2666. *Origin of rue.* (See A2611.0.4.1.)

A2680. Origin of other plant forms.

A2681. *Origin of trees.* (See A2612.1.) — Finnish: Kalevala rune 2; Icel.: MacCulloch Eddic 325—26; India: Thompson-Balys.

A2681.1. *Origin of weeping willow.* (See A2632.1.)

A2681.2. *Origin of oak.* Finnish: Kalevala rune 2.

A2681.3. *Poplars from weeping maidens transformed by god.* *Frazer Pausanias II 72.

A2681.4. *Origin of birch trees.*

A2681.4.1. *First birch trees in Ireland.* Irish myth: Cross.

A2681.5. *Origin of palms.* Jewish: Neuman; India: Thompson-Balys.

A2681.5.1. *Origin of coconut tree.* (See A2611.3.) — Oceanic (Cove Is.): Hawaii: Beckwith Myth 104, (Tahiti): ibid. 101, (New Guinea): ibid. 102, (Marshall Is.): Davenport 223, (Marquesas): Handy 30.

A2681.6. *Origin of bamboo.* India: *Thompson-Balys.

A2681.7. *Origin of sandalwood tree.* India: Thompson-Balys.

A2681.8. *Origin of dammar tree.* India: Thompson-Balys.

A2681.9. *Origin of mulberry tree.* Marquesas: Handy 123.

A2681.10. *Origin of banyan tree.* Marquesas: Handy 123.

A2681.11. *Origin of breadfruit tree.* Hawaii: Beckwith Myth 68, 971, 101.

A2681.12. *Origin of palm-wine tree.* Africa (Bushonga): Torday 236.

A2681.13. *Origin of cedar tree.* Jewish: Neuman.

A2682. *Origin of creepers.* India: Thompson-Balys; S. Am. Indian (Mataco): Métraux MAFLS XL 128.

A2683. *Origin of grass.* India: Thompson-Balys.

A2611.6. Hair transformed into plants. A2611.6.1. Grass from hair of slain person.

A2684. *Origin of cultivated plants.* (Cf. A2685, A2691.2.) — Jibaro: Karsten, cf. JAFL XXXII 446; Tonga: Gifford 17f.; Japanese: Beckwith Myth 102.

A2684.1. *Origin of flax.* Lithuanian: Balys Legends No. 112.

A2684.2. *Origin of hemp.* India: Thompson-Balys.

A2684.2.1. *Origin of sorghum.* Africa (Wute): Sieber 204.

A2684.3. *Origin of cotton plant.* S. Am. Indian (Paressi): Métraux BBAE CXLIII (3) 359.

A2685. *Origin of cereals.*

A1423.2. Acquisition of rice.

A2685.1. *Origin of corn.* (See A2611.1.) — India: Thompson-Balys.

A2685.1.1. *Origin of maize.* India: Thompson-Balys; S. A. Indian (Chiriguano): Métraux RMLP XXXIII 172, (Tembe): Métraux ibid. 140, (Kaigua, Apapocuva-Guarani): Métraux ibid. 136, (Tenetehara): Wagley-Galvão BBAE CXLIII (3) 148.

A2685.2. *Origin of straw.* Formerly whole blade became grain. Straw left for dog. Finnish: Aarne FFC VIII 10. No. 49, XXXIII 53 No. 49; Estonian: Aarne FFC XXV 143 No. 28; India: Thompson-Balys.

A2685.3. *Origin of rye.* Finnish: Aarne FFC VIII 23 No. 129; India: Thompson-Balys.

A2685.4. *Origin of barley.* Finnish: Kalevala rune 2; Jewish: Neuman.

A2685.5. *Origin of manioc.* S. Am. Indian (Paressi): Métraux BBAE CXLIII (3) 360, (Mataco): Métraux MAFLS XL 128.

A2686. *Origin of vegetables.* India: Thompson-Balys.

A2686.1. *Origin of mushroom.* (Cf. A2613.1.) — Dh II 107; India: *Thompson-Balys.

A2686.2. *Origin of peas.* (See A2612.3.) — India: Thompson-Balys.

A2686.3. *Origin of pepper plant.* (See A2611.4.) — S. Am. Indian (Brazil): Oberg 109.

F954.4. Chile plant so hot it causes dumb man to speak: thus discovered for eating.

A2686.3.1. *Origin of kava plant.* Tonga: Beckwith Myth 101, Gifford 72, 75.

A2686.4. *Origin of edible roots.* India: Thompson-Balys.

A2686.4.1. *Origin of sweet potato.* Hawaii: Beckwith Myth 242; S. Am. Indian (Brazil): Oberg 109.

A2686.4.2. *Origin of taro.* Mono-Alu: Wheeler 67; Hawaii: Beckwith Myth 98.

A2686.4.3. *Origin of yams.* Tonga: Gifford 17.

A2686.5. *Origin of turmeric.* India: Thompson-Balys.

A2686.6. *Origin of beans.* S. Am. Indian (Caingang): Métraux BBAE CXLIII (1) 473.

A2686.7. *Origin of gourds.* S. Am. Indian (Caingang): Métraux BBAE CXLIII (1) 473.

A2686.8. *Origin of cinnamon.* Jewish: Neuman.

A2687. *Origin of fruits.*

A2687.1. *Origin of blood-oranges.* Sébillot RTP III 25.

A2687.2. *Origin of melons.* S. Am. Indian (Mataco): MAFLS XL 128.

A2687.3. *Origin of berries.* Hawaii: Beckwith Myth 188, 282.

A2687.4. *Origin of pumpkin.* S. Am. Indian (Jivaro): Steward-Métraux BBAE CXLIII (3) 627.

A2687.5. *Origin of banana.* Tonga: Gifford 17.

A2688. *Origin of weeds.* India: Thompson-Balys; Tonga: Gifford 22.

A2688.1. *Origin of thistles.* (See A2615.1, A2631.1.) — Irish myth: Cross; Finnish: Aarne FFC VIII 23 No. 130; Jewish: Neuman.

A2688.1.1. *Origin of thorn-bush.* Fb "torn" III 827a; Jewish: Neuman; India: Thompson-Balys.

A2691. *Origin of narcotic plants.*

A2691.1. *Origin of coffee.* Finnish: Aarne FFC VIII 23 No. 127.

A2691.2. *Origin of tobacco.* (See A2611.2, A2611.2.1.) — Chinese: Eberhard FFC CXX 131 No. 88; India: *Thompson-Balys; Calif. Indian: Gayton and Newman 58; S. Am. Indian (Cariri): Lowie BBAE CXLIII (1) 559.

A2691.3. *Origin of ganja.* India: Thompson-Balys.

A2691.4. *Origin of opium.* India: *Thompson-Balys; Chinese: Eberhard 131 No. 88.

A2733. Poppy characteristics from series of reincarnations.

A2691.5. *Origin of betel.* India: Thompson-Balys.

A2692. *Origin of poisonous plants.* India: Thompson-Balys; S. Am. Indian (Cashinawa): Métraux BBAE CXLIII (3) 686; Africa (Tonga): Gifford 27.

A2700—A2799. Origin of plant characteristics.

A2700—A2749. VARIOUS ORIGINS OF PLANT CHARACTERISTICS

A2700. Origin of plant characteristics. Jewish: Neuman.

A2710. Plant characteristics as reward.

F1099.4.1. Blades of corn grow through hair of saint as reward for guarding corn kiln.

A2711. *Plant blessed for pious act.* (Cf. A2221.)

Q20. Piety rewarded.

A2711.1. *Plant blessed for help at Jesus' birth.* Dh II 19f.

A2711.2. *Trees blessed that made the cross.* Dh II 207.

A2711.2.1. *Elder tree is never struck by lightning* because it was used in making the cross. England: Baughman.

A2711.3. *Plant blessed for helping holy fugitive.* Dh II 58ff. — Spanish Exempla: Keller; Lithuanian: Balys Legends Nos. 197f., 202ff.; Irish: Beal XXI 306.

R220. Flights.

A2711.4. *Tree protects Jesus from rain: is green all year.* (Cf. A2765.1.) — Esthonian: Aarne FFC XXV 152 No. 80 (fig); Livonian: Loorits FFC LXVI 94 No. 113 (pine).

A2711.4.1. *Hazel gives Virgin Mary shelter.* Blessed. *BP III 477; Lithuanian: Balys Legends No. 198f., 204.

D950.1. Magic hazel tree. D1402.10.1. Rod from magic hazel tree kills snake immediately.

A2711.4.2. *Thistle serves as milk-cup for Virgin Mary: white spots on leaves.* England: Baughman.

A2711.4.3. *Plant receives name because of service to Virgin Mary.* German: Grimm No. 207.

A2711.5. *Rowan helps Thor out of river.* Icel.: MacCulloch Eddic 84.

A2711.6. *How the plum tree came to be so hardy: blessed by Ram.* India: Thompson-Balys.

A2771. Budding and bearing of plant.

A2711.7. *Fig tree stays with the angels: rewarded with sap of all other trees.* India: Thompson-Balys.

A2720. Plant characteristics as punishment.

A2688.1. Origin of thistles.

A2721. *Plant cursed for impious act.*

A2721.1. *Plant cursed for disservice to child Jesus.* (Cf. A2772.2.) — Flemish: DeMeyer FFC XXXVII 90 No. 130a (rush).

A2721.2. *Plant cursed for disservice at crucifixion.* (Cf. A2711.2.) — Lithuanian: Balys Index No. 3222, Legends No. 323.

Q221.2. Punishment for opposition to Christ at crucifixion.

A2721.2.1. *Tree cursed for serving as cross.* (Cf. A2751.3.1, A2751.3.2, A2755.2, A2762.1, A2775.) — Dh II 207ff. — Finnish: Aarne FFC VIII 23 No. 131, XXXIII 56 No. 131; Esthonian: Aarne FFC XXV 152 No. 77; Livonian: Loorits FFC LXVI 94 No. 108; North Carolina: Brown Collection I 636.

Z352. All trees except aspen refuse to make Christ's cross.

A2721.2.1.1. *Aspen cursed for serving as cross.* (Cf. A2762.1.) — England, Scotland: Baughman.*

A2721.2.1.2. *Poplar cursed for serving as cross.* (Cf. A2762.2.) — U.S.: Baughman.

A2721.2.1.3. *Cottonwood cursed for serving as cross.* U.S.: Baughman.

A2721.2.1.4. *Elder cursed for serving as cross.* (Cf. A2766.1.) — England: Baughman.

A2721.2.2. *Indentations on plants from Christ's biting them at crucifixion.* (Cf. A2751.3.1.) — Dh II 198.

A2721.3. *Plant punished for ungracious answer to holy person.*

A2721.3.1. *Man tells Jesus he is sowing stones.* "You shall get stones." Why peas do not soften in boiling. Esthonian: Aarne FFC XXV 152 No. 78; cf. Livonian: Loorits FFC LXVI 96 No. 124; Lithuanian: Balys Index No. 3016.

Q591.2. Punishment: man says salt he carries is stones; immediately becomes so.

A2721.3.2. *Farmer tells begging monk that potatoes are hard as stones:* why potatoes are hard. Japanese: Anesaki Japanese Myth 252.

A2721.4. *Plant cursed for betraying holy fugitive.* Dh II 58ff.

R220. Flights.

A2721.5. *Tree on which Judas hanged himself cursed.* Dh II 236ff.; **Taylor "The Gallows of Judas Iscariot" Washington University Studies (Humanistic series) IX (1922) 135ff.

A2721.6. *Why the mogli flower and the lime are cursed by gods.* India: Thompson-Balys.

A2721.7. *Trees fail to come at god's leavetaking, now bear bitter fruit.* India: Thompson-Balys.

A2721.8. *Barren trees as punishment of earth for disobedience at man's fall.* Jewish: Neuman.

A2722. *Plant punished for disobedience.*

A2722.1. *Plantain disobeys mother:* hence bears but one stalk. (Cf. A2771.2.) — Mpongwe: Nassau 76 No. 16.

A2723. *Plant punished for discontent.* Chinese: Eberhard FFC CXX 134 No. 91.

A2723.1. *Discontented pine-tree: cause of pine needles.* Pine tree given silk leaves, glass leaves, etc. Always discontented. Finally has needles again. (Cf. A2767.1.) — *Dh III 337. — Livonian: Loorits FFC LXVI 94 No. 114.

A2723.2. *God changes nature of plant to punish wastefulness of man:* yield of plant is decreased. German: Grimm No. 194.

A2725. *Plant punished for tardiness.*

A2725.1. *Ash-tree late at distribution of qualities* at creation: therefore buds last. (Cf. A2771.1.) — Livonian: Loorits FFC LXVI 95 No. 115.

A2726. *Plant punished for tale-telling.*

A2726.1. *Curse of tale-telling banana affects all others.* India: Thompson-Balys.

A2730. Miscellaneous reasons for plant characteristics.

A2731. *Plant characteristics from transformation.*

A2615. Object transformed to plant.

A2731.1. *Trickster's burnt flesh becomes gum on trees.* N. A. Indian: Thompson Tales 304 n. 1091.

A2731.2. *Plant characteristics from tears.* (Cf. A2755.3.1, A2755.3.2.) — Greek: Frazer Apollodorus II 82 n. 2, 86 n. 2.

A2731.2.1. *Plant characteristics from Virgin Mary's tears.* *Dh II 255ff.

A2731.2.1.1. *Plant characteristics from Virgin Mary's milk.* England: Baughman.

A2711.4.2. Thistle serves as milk-cup for Virgin Mary; white spots on leaves.

A2731.3. *Blood from wizard becomes red grain of cedar.* Bleeding head of wizard who tries to kill the sun placed on top of a tree. (Cf. A2755.1.) — Yuchi: Alexander N. Am. 64.

A2731.4. *Why agar-tree has magic properties.* A transformed magician. India: Thompson-Balys.

A2733. *Poppy characteristics from series of reincarnations.* Opium produces each of the appropriate qualities. India: Thompson-Balys.

A1371.2. Bad women combination of nine different animals. A2691.3. Origin of opium.

A2734. *Plant characteristics from object thrown by devil.*

A2734.1. *Devil throws sand at aspen: hence rough bark.* Angered because aspens will not cease quivering. (Cf. A2751.2.1.) — Finnish: Aarne FFC VIII 23 No. 132.

A2734.2. *Devil throws tar at tree: hence tar in tree-heart.* (Cf. A2755.3.) — Finnish: Aarne FFC VIII 4 No. 10. Cf. Type 153.

A2736. *Evil spirit in spite puts bark and thorns on tree.* (A2751.1, A2752.) — Persian: Carnoy 283.

A2738. *Christ puts knots in wood.* Peter, angry at carpenters wants Christ to have iron knots in wood. Christ does make hard knots but not iron. (Cf. A2755.4.) — Dh II 174ff.

A2741. *Plant characteristics from accident to original plant.*

A2741.1. *Bean laughs till it splits: cause of black stripe.* (Cf. A2793.1, F1025.1.) — Type 295. — Flemish: DeMeyer FFC XXXVII 90 No. 126a; Livonian: Loorits FFC LXVI 95 No. 121.

A2741.2. *Yams dropped by bird and split: why some are good and some bad.* (Cf. A2793.3.) — New Hebrides (Leper's Island): Dixon 144.

A2741.3. *Sky rests on top of trees: hence flat leaves.* (Cf. A2761.3.) — Polynesian: Dixon 51 n. 55.

A2741.4. *Bush loses clothes in shipwreck: hence catches passerby* looking for clothes. (Cf. A2792.1.) — See A2275.5.3.

A2741.5. *Why khijur leaves are long and narrow: split with an arrow.* India: Thompson-Balys.

A2760. Leaves of plant.

A2742. *Plant characteristics from exchange of qualities.* India: Thompson-Balys.

A2247. Animal characteristics: exchange of qualities.

A2743. *Plant characteristic because plant belongs to the devil.*

G303. Devil.

A2743.1. *Fuschia belongs to devil: hence ball and red petals.* North Carolina: Brown Coll. I 635.

A2750—A2799. ORIGIN OF VARIOUS PLANT CHARACTERISTICS

A2750. Interior and bark of plant.

A2751. *Bark of plant.*

A2751.1. *Origin of bark on plants.* (See A2736.)

A2751.2. *Texture of bark of plant.*

A2751.2.1. *Why aspen's bark is rough.* (See A2734.1.)

A2751.2.2. *Why bark of red willow is thin.* Tahltan: Teit JAFL XXXII 223.

A2751.2.3. *Why tinsa tree has no bark at bottom of trunk.* India: Thompson-Balys.

A2751.3. *Markings on bark of plant.*

A2751.3.1. *Indentions in stem of reed.* (See A2721.2.1, A2721.2.2, A2732.) — Flemish: DeMeyer FFC XXXVII 90 No. 130b.

A2751.3.2. *Crosses on certain trees.* (See A2721.2.1.)

A2751.4. *Color of bark of plant.*

A2751.4.1. *Why birch has white bark.* Livonian: Loorits FFC LXVI 94 No. 110; Flemish: DeMeyer FFC XXXVII 91 No. 132f.

A2751.4.2. *Why ebony tree is black.* India: Thompson-Balys.

A2751.4.3. *Why tamarind bark is black.* India: Thompson-Balys.

A2751.4.4. *Why bark of saja and tinsa is white.* India: Thompson-Balys.

A2751.4.5. *Why broom-corn is covered with blood-red spots.* Korean: Zong in-Sob 10 No. 3.

A2751.4.6. *Why kava plant is grey.* Tonga: Gifford 72.

A2752. *Thorns on plants.* (See A2736). — Jewish: Neuman; India: Thompson-Balys.

A2688.1. Origin of thistles.

A2752.1. *Why bombax tree has thorns.* India: Thompson-Balys.

A2755. *Internal parts of plant.*

A2755.1. *Origin of red grain of cedar.* (See A2731.3.)

A2755.2. *Origin of blood-colored sap in trees.* (See A2721.2.1.) — India: Thompson-Balys.

A2755.2.1. *Why the saja tree has no sap.* India: Thompson-Balys.

A2755.3. *Origin of tar in heart of trees.* (See A2734.2.) — Tahltan: Teit JAFL XXXII 210.

A2755.3.1. *Origin of amber in poplar trees.* (Cf. A2731.2.) — Greek: Frazer Apollodorus II 82 n. 2.

A2755.3.2. *Origin of gum in myrrh tree.* (Cf. A2731.2.) — Greek: Frazer Apollodorus II 86 n. 2.

A2755.4. *Origin of knots in wood.* (See A2738.) — Irish myth: Cross.

A2755.4.1. *Why there are knots on the saja tree.* India: Thompson-Balys.

A2756. *Why the bamboo has nodes.* India: *Thompson-Balys.

A2757. *Why certain reeds are hollow.* Buddhist myth: Malalasekera II 36.

A2760. Leaves of plant.

E631.0.2. Flower from grave bears letters. These commemorate the buried person.

A2760.1. *Why all trees have leaves.* India: Thompson-Balys.

A2761. *Shape of leaves of plant.*

A2761.1. *Why oak-leaves are indented.* Flemish: DeMeyer FFC XXXVII 91 No. 132b.

A2761.2. *Why vine-leaves are hand-shaped.* Flemish: DeMeyer FFC XXXVII 91 No. 132b.

A2761.3. *Why plant-leaves are flat.* (See A2741.3.)

A2762. *Movement of leaves.*

A2762.1. *Why aspen-leaves tremble.* — *Fb "asp" IV 18a; Lithuanian: Balys Index No. 3105, Legends Nos. 203—213.

A2721.2.1.1. Aspen cursed for serving as cross.

A2762.2. *Why poplar-leaves tremble.* Flemish: DeMeyer FFC XXXVII 90 No. 131.

A2721.2.1.2. Poplar cursed for serving as cross.

A2762.3. *Why pipal leaves tremble.* India: Thompson-Balys.

A2763. *Why certain leaves have holes in them.* India: Thompson-Balys.

A2764. *Why certain leaves are hollow.*

A2764.1. *Why taro leaves are hollow.* Hawaii: Beckwith Myth 229.

A2765. *Why leaves are evergreen.* (See A2711.4.)

A2766. *Why certain tree bleeds.*

A2766.1. *Why elder tree bleeds when cut.* (A2721.2.1.4.) — England: Baughman.

A2767. *Origin of tree's needles.*

A2767.1. *Origin of pine-needles.* (See A2723.1.)

A2768. *Why leaves hang head downward.* Maori: Clark 96.

A2769. *Leaves of plant — miscellaneous.*

A2769.1. *Why tamarind leaves are small.* India: Thompson-Balys.

A2770. Other plant characteristics.

A2771. *Budding and bearing of plant.*

A2771.1. *Why ash-tree buds last.* (See A2725.1.) — Lithuanian: Balys Index No. 3222, Legends No. 324.

A2771.2. *Why plantain bears but one stalk.* (See A2722.1.) — India: Thompson-Balys.

A2771.3. *Why sago bears fruit from the stem.* India: Thompson-Balys.

A2742. Plant characteristics from exchange of qualities.

A2771.4. *Why banana bears fruit from crown of tree.* India: Thompson-Balys.

A2771.4.1. *Why rice has ears only at top.* Chinese: Eberhard FFC CXX 130 No. 86.

A2771.5. *Trees bear first buds to commemorate reign of primitive hero.* Irish myth: Cross.

A901. Topographical features caused by experiences of primitive hero (demigod, deity).

A2771.6. *Why certain willow tree bears fruit when fruit trees bear.* Irish myth: Cross.

A2771.7. *Why sorrel grows on certain rock every winter.* Irish myth: Cross.

A2771.8. *Why tree has bitter fruit.*

A2721.7. Trees fail to come at god's leavetaking, now bear bitter fruit.

A2771.8.1. *Why olive is bitter.* Jewish: Neuman.

A2771.8.2. *Why laurel tree is bitter.* Jewish: Neuman.

A2771.9. *Why big trees have small fruit.* India: Thompson-Balys.

A2771.10. *Why willow flowers do not bear fruit.* Chinese: Graham.

A2772. *Color of plants.*

A2772.1. *Origin of rose's color.* Sébillot RTP II 549.

A2772.2. *Why end of rush is black.* (See A2721.1.)

A2772.3. *Why the heartsease (polygonum persicaria) has red stripes.* Flemish: DeMeyer FFC XXXVII 90 No. 129a.

A2772.4. *Why ebony tree has black wood and smoke-colored leaves.* India: Thompson-Balys.

A2774. *Why trees remain fixed.* India: Thompson-Balys.

A2774.1. *Why ayikha-bush is firmly rooted.* India: Thompson-Balys.

A2775. *Why certain trees are dwarfed.* (See A2721.2.1.)

A2775.0.1. *Why plants no longer reach sky.* Chinese: Eberhard FFC CXX 134 No. 90.

A2776. *Why certain plants are cursed.*

A2776.1. *Why birch is cursed.* Flemish: DeMeyer FFC XXXVII 91 No. 132d.

A2776.2. *Why weeping-willow is cursed.* Flemish: DeMeyer XXXVII 91 No. 132d.

A2777. *Why certain plants (trees) are blessed.*

A2777.1. *Why fig tree is chief priest of the trees.* India: Thompson-Balys.

B252.2. Priest of snakes.

A2777.2. *King of trees.* India: Thompson-Balys.

A2778. *Why certain tree is tall.*

A2778.1. *Why coconut tree is tall.* Hawaii: Beckwith Myth 98.

A2778.2. *Why palm is tall.* India: Thompson-Balys.

A2781. *Origin of plant names.* Jewish: Neuman.

A2782. *Origin of combustible property of wood.* Tonga: Gifford 23.

A2783. *Medicinal properties of trees.* Jewish: Neuman.

A2785. *Origin of shape of particular tree.*

A2785.1. *Origin of shape of wiliwili tree.* Hawaii: Beckwith Myth 495.

A2788. *Why certain tree is hardy.*

A2711.6. How the plum tree came to be so hardy: blessed by Ram.

A2791. *Sundry characteristics of trees.*

A2791.1. *Why trees do not talk.* All ask to be spared when man begins cutting them. Esthonian: Aarne FFC XXV 151 No. 75; Livonian: Loorits FFC LXVI 94 No. 107; Lithuanian: Balys Index No. 3215, Legends No. 302f.; India: Thompson-Balys.

A2791.2. *Why lightning spares the nut-tree.* Flemish: DeMeyer FFC XXXVII 91 No. 132e.

A2791.3. *How banyan got its milk.* India: Thompson-Balys.

A2791.4. *Why no one can find flower of wild fig.* India: Thompson-Balys.

A2791.5. *Why tamarind fruit is sour.* India: Thompson-Balys.

A2791.7. *Why some trees have no fruit.* India: Thompson-Balys.

A2791.8. *Why sap comes from top of palm.* India: Thompson-Balys.

A2791.9. *Why fruit of sago palm looks like an eye.* India: Thompson-Balys.

A2791.10. *Why sago palm gives abundant sap.* India: Thompson-Balys.

A2791.11. *Why fruit of date palm looks like breasts of old woman.* India: Thompson-Balys.

A2791.12. *Why the bija tree is often struck by lightning.* India: Thompson-Balys.

A2791.13. *Why the roots of the banyan hang down.* India: Thompson-Balys.

A2792. *Sundry characteristics of shrubs.*

A2792.1. *Why bush holds on to passer-by.* (See A2275.5.3, A2741.4.)

A2793. *Sundry characteristics of grains and vegetables.*

A2793.1. *Why bean has black stripe.* (See A2741.1.)

A2793.1.1. *Why beans bear everywhere.* Chinese: Graham.

A2793.2. *Why grain of wheat is divided.* Flemish: DeMeyer FFC XXXVII. 90 No. 126b.

A2793.2.1. *Why wheat must be planted in one year and harvested in the next.* Chinese: Graham.

A2793.3. *Why some yams are good, some bad.* (See A2741.2.)

A2793.4. *Why potatoes are hard.* (See A2721.3.2.)

A2793.5. *Why grain grows only at top of stalk* (punishment for men's sinfulness). Grimm No. 194; BP III 417ff.; Lithuanian: Balys Index No. 3220, Legends Nos. 305—313; Cheremis: Sebeok-Nyerges.

A2793.5.1. *Why corn does not yield in the middle.* Chinese: Graham.

A2793.6. *Origin of shapes of grain.* Lithuanian: Balys Index No. 3221, Legends Nos. 315—322.

A2793.7. *Why rice is so abundant.* Chinese: Graham.

A2793.8. *Why millet is red on top.* Chinese: Graham.

A2793.9. *Why buckwheat produces twice a year.* Chinese: Graham.

A2794. *Sundry characteristics of vegetables.*

A2794.1. *Why mushrooms are slimy.* India: Thompson-Balys.

A2794.2. *Why yams are small but plentiful in certain place.* New Hebrides: Codrington No. II 3.

A2795. *Sundry characteristics of flowers.*

A2795.1. *Why some flowers have no scent.* India: Thompson-Balys.

A2800—A2899. Miscellaneous explanations.

A2800—A2849. MISCELLANEOUS EXPLANATIONS: ORIGINS

A2811. *Origin of silk.* Chauvin VII 59 No. 77 n. 1.

A2812. *Origin of musk.* Chauvin VII 59 No. 77 n. 1.

A2813. *Origin of honey.* Chauvin VII 59 No. 77 n. 1.; Jewish: Neuman; India: Thompson-Balys; Icel.: Boberg.
A2012.2. First bees in Ireland.

A2814. *Origin of spices.* Chauvin VII 59 No. 77 n. 1.

A2815. *Origin of floating webs in summer.* *Dh II 254.

A2816. *Origin of smoke.* Esthonian: Aarne FFC XXV 152 No. 81.

A2817. *Origin of the will-o'-the-wisp* (jack-o'-lantern). Type 330. — Africa (Fang): Trilles 138.
F491. Will-o'-the-wisp.

A2817.1. *Smith outwits devil, is admitted to neither heaven nor hell.* The devil gives him a light to find his way back in the dark; he is known as the will-o'-the-wisp or jack-o'-lantern. England, Ireland, Scotland, U.S.: *Baughman.

A2817.2. *Will-o'-the-wisp is girl cursed by her mother for gathering plants for dyestuffs on Sunday.* Will-o'-the-wisp is seen where girl disappeared. Scotland: Baughman.

A2823. *Origin of churning stick.* India: Thompson-Balys.

A2824. *Origin of drum.* India: Thompson-Balys.

A2825. *Origin of canes:* from whip thrust into ground. India: Thompson-Balys.

A2826. *Origin of shells.* Eskimo (East Greenland): Rasmussen I 114.
D233. Troll turns to shell.

A2827. *Origin of pearls.* Jewish: Neuman.

A2828. *Origin of particular kinds of basket.* Tonga: Gifford 140.

A2831. *Origin of demons.* Jewish: Neuman.
G302. Demons. G303. Devil.

A2834. *Origin of fish drug.* S. Am. Indian: Wagley-Galvão BBAE CXLIII (3) 253.

A2847. *Origin of scum on stagnant water.* India: Thompson-Balys.

A2849. *Miscellaneous origins.*

A2849.1. *Miscellaneous Jewish origins.* Jewish: **Neuman.

A2850—A2899. MISCELLANEOUS EXPLANATIONS: CHARACTERISTICS

A2851. *The four characteristics of wine.* Devil helps Noah plant vineyard and kills various animals over it. These illustrate the four qualities of wine. Peacock: brilliant colors; ape: jokes; lion: boldness; hog: drunkenness. — *Dh I 298ff.; *Pauli (ed. Bolte) No. 244; *Köhler-Bolte I 577; Basset III 31; *Krappe Bull. Hispanique XXXIX 48; Spanish Exempla: Keller; Lithuanian: Balys Index No. 3242; Jewish: Neuman; India: Thompson-Balys.

A2853. *Why sexes differ in form and temperament.* Jewish: Neuman.

A2854. *Why men like tobacco, but spit when smoking.* Adam in paradise spat upon the tobacco plant. Lithuanian: Balys Index No. 3242, Legends No. 338f.

A2855. *Trees classified as "pleasant trees, herb trees, shrub trees."* Irish myth: Cross.

A2861. *Why men become old.* India: Thompson-Balys.

A2862. *Why spirits are invisible.* India: Thompson-Balys.

A2871. *Why soil in certain country is poor.* India: Thompson-Balys.

A2872. *Why coral is soft.* Africa (Tonga): Gifford 136.

A2875. *Why babies have soft spots in head.* Hawaii: Beckwith Myth 507.

A2877. *Why palm oil is red.* Africa (Cameroon): Mansfield.

B. ANIMALS

DETAILED SYNOPSIS

B0 —B99. Mythical animals
- B10. Mythical beasts and hybrids
- B20. Beast-men
- B30. Mythical birds
- B40. Bird-beasts
- B50. Bird-men
- B60. Mythical fish
- B70. Fish-beasts
- B80. Fish-men
- B90. Other mythical animals

B100—B199. Magic animals
- B100—B119. *Treasure animals*
  - B100. Treasure animals — general
  - B110. Treasure-producing parts of animals
- B120—B169. *Animals with magic wisdom*
  - B120. Wise animals
  - B130. Truth-telling animals
  - B140. Prophetic animals
  - B150. Oracular animals
  - B160. Wisdom-giving animals
- B170—B189. *Other magic animals*
  - B170. Magic birds, fish, reptiles, etc.
  - B180. Magic quadrupeds
  - B190. Magic animals: miscellaneous motifs

B200—B299. Animals with human traits
- B210. Speaking animals
- B220. Animal kingdom (community)
- B230. Parliament of animals
- B240. King of animals
- B250. Religious animals
- B260. Animal warfare
- B270. Animals in legal relations
- B280. Animal weddings
- B290. Other animals with human traits

B300—B599. FRIENDLY ANIMALS

B300—B349. Helpful animals — general
- B310. Acquisition of helpful animal
- B320. Reward of helpful animal
- B330. Death of helpful animal
- B340. Treatment of helpful animal — miscellaneous

B350—B399. Grateful animals
- B360. Animals grateful for rescue from peril of death
- B370. Animals grateful to captor for release
- B380. Animals grateful for relief from pain
- B390. Animals grateful for other kind acts

B400—B499. Kinds of helpful animals
B400—B449. *Helpful beasts*
B400. Helpful domestic beasts
B430. Helpful wild beasts
B450. Helpful birds
B470. Helpful fish
B480· Helpful insects
B490. Other helpful animals

B500—B599. Services of helpful animals
B500. Magic power from animal
B510. Healing by animal
B520. Animals save person's life
B530. Animals nourish men
B540. Animal rescuer or retriever
B550. Animals carry men
B560. Animals advise men
B570. Animals serve men
B580. Animals help men to wealth and greatness
B590. Miscellaneous services of helpful animals

B600—B699. Marriage of person to animal
B610. Animal paramour
B620. Animal suitor
B630. Offspring of marriage to animal
B640. Marriage to person in animal form
B650. Marriage to animal in human form

B700—B799. Fanciful traits of animals
B710. Fanciful origin of animals
B720—B749. *Fanciful physical qualities of animals*
B720. Fanciful bodily members of animals
B730. Fanciful color, smell, etc. of animals
B740. Fanciful marvelous strength of animals
B750. Fanciful habits of animals
B770. Other fanciful traits of animals

B800—B899. Miscellaneous animal motifs
B870. Giant animals

B. ANIMALS

B0—B99. Mythical animals.

B0. Mythical animals.
Lum (Peter) Fabulous Beasts (New York, 1951). — Irish myth: Cross; Jewish: Neuman.

A113. Totemistic gods, having animal associations. A131. Gods with animal features. A132. God in animal form. A417.1. Beast guardians of the four quarters of the world. A522. Animal as culture hero. A1700—2199. Creation of animal life. A2200—2599. Animal characteristics. D1840.2. Magic invulnerability of animals. F167.1. Animals in other world. F234.1. Fairy in form of an animal. F980. Extraordinary occurrences concerning animals.

B1. *Animal elders.* Mythical ancestors of the present animals.— Irish myth: Cross. — N. A. Indian: *Alexander N. Am. 292 No. 40, ibid. 69 (Cherokee), 81 (Pawnee), 156 (Navaho).

A1614.1.2. Origin of "goat-heads" from curse of Ham. A2210. Animal characteristics: change in ancient animal.

B1.1. *Angels of animals.* Each kind of animal has its angel in heaven. Jewish: Neuman.

B2. *Animal totems.* Irish myth: Cross.

A113. Totemistic gods. B630. Offspring of marriage to animal. C221.2. Tabu: eating totem animal. C841. Tabu: killing certain animals. V12.4. Animal as sacrifice.

B2.1. *Dog as totem animal.* Irish myth: Cross.

B5. *Fantastic beasts, birds, etc., in art.* Irish myth: Cross.

B7. *Animals in the heavens.*

B7.1. *Animals rule celestial spheres.* Jewish: Neuman.

B7.2. *Mythical animals surround God's throne.* Jewish: Neuman.

B7.3. *Mythical bird running before the sun* bears inscription of golden letters. Jewish: Neuman.

B10. Mythical beasts and hybrids.

B11. *Dragon.* **Smith Dragon; *Fb Drager, lindorme, slanger i folkets tro (Særtryk af Naturen og Mennesket, 1894, pp. 164—196); *Nyrop Dania II 341ff.; *Róheim Drachen und Drachenkämpfer; *Hdwb. d. Abergl. II 364 ff.; Meyer Germanische Mythologie (1891) 95ff.; **Du Bose The Dragon, Image and Demon (London, 1886); Norlind Skattsägner 44f., 77f., Solheim Register 17; Danish: Kristensen Danske Sagn II (1893) 133ff., 176ff., (1928) 119ff. — *Type 300; *BP I 547. — Icel.: MacCulloch Eddic 216; Celtic: *Henderson Celtic Dragon Myth (Edinburgh, 1911), *Cross; Lettish: Auning Ueber den lettischen Drachenmythus; Armenian: Ananikian 76ff; Jewish: Neuman; Chinese: Ferguson 101; India: Thompson-Balys; Korean: Zong in-Sob 169, No. 73.

A139.3. Dragon god. A162.2. Combat between god of light and dragon of ocean. A1072.4. Fettered monster as dragon. A1142.2. Thunder from flying dragon. A1265. Men created from sown dragon's teeth. A2001.

Insects from body of slain monster. B91.3. Horned snake. B163.1. Animal languages learned from eating dragon's heart. B498. Helpful dragon. C92.2. Tabu: killing sacred dragon. D199.2. Transformation: man to dragon. D419.1.1. Transformation: sea dragon to serpent. D429.1.1. Transformation: dragon king to gust of wind. D659.4.2. Sea dragon in serpent form to accompany hero. D812.7. Magic object received from dragon king. D1846.4. Invulnerability through bathing in dragon's blood. E263. Adulteress returns from dead as devastating dragon. E738.1. Soul in form of dragon. H1024.5. Task: sowing dragon's teeth. H1274. Quest in hell for three dragon feathers.

B11.1. *Origin of dragon.*

B11.1.1. *Dragon from cock's egg.* (Cf. B12.1.) — *Fb "drage"; Hdwb. d. Abergl. II 600—603.

B11.1.2. *Dragon from transformed horse.* White horse plunges into water and is changed into a dragon. Chinese: Werner 368.

B318. Helpful animals transformed from other animals. D410. Transformation: one animal to another.

B11.1.3. *Dragon from transformed man lying on his treasures* (Fáfnir). (Cf. B11.6.2.) — Hdwb. d. Abergl. II 367; Eisen Esthnische Mythologie 74ff.; Icel.: *Boberg.

B11.1.3.0.1. *Transformed princess as dragon.* Irish myth: Cross; German: Grimm No. 88.

B11.1.3.1. *Dragon from worm.* Irish myth: Cross.

B11.1.3.1.1. *Dragon develops from small worm placed on gold.* It grows together with the gold. DeVries Studien over Faerosche Balladen 122ff.; Hdwb. d. Abergl. II 384f.; Icel.: *Boberg.

B11.1.4. *Devil in form of dragon.* German: Grimm No. 125.

B11.2. *Form of dragon.* *Smith Dragon, passim.; Chinese: Werner 208ff.

B11.2.0.1. *She-dragon.* Irish myth: Cross.

B11.2.1. *Dragon as compound animal* (Cf. B14.) — Smith Dragon 81 (serpent or crocodile, with scales of a fish for covering, and feet and wings and sometimes also the head, of an eagle, falcon, or hawk, and the forelimbs and sometimes the head of a lion). — Chinese: Werner 208 (ears of an ox, feet of a tiger, claws of an eagle, horns of a deer, head of a camel, eyes of a devil, neck of a snake, abdomen of a cock, scales of a carp); Egyptian: Smith op. cit. 79 (lioness, falcon, human being).

B11.2.1.1. *Dragon as modified serpent.* Smith Dragon 92, 101f., 107ff. (American Indian, Japanese, East Indian). — Icel.: *Boberg; Japanese: Ikeda; Chinese: Eberhard FFC CXX 65.

B11.2.1.2. *Dragon as modified lizard.* Smith Dragon 109.

B11.2.1.3. *Dragon as modified fish.* Smith Dragon 108f.; Irish myth: Cross; Chinese: Eberhard FFC CXX 65.

B16.9. Devastating man-eating sea-monster. B21.5. Sea-serpent. B175. Magic fish. B875. Giant sea-monster.

B11.2.1.4. *Dragon as modified shell-fish.* Smith Dragon 165ff.

B11.2.1.5. *Dragon as modified toad.* Smith Dragon 109.

B11.2.1.6. *Dragon as modified elephant.* Smith Dragon 109.

B11.2.1.7. *Dragon as modified horse.* Smith Dragon 97f. Japanese: Ikeda.

B11.2.1.9. *Dragon as modified ram.* Smith Dragon 134 (Egyptian, Soudanese, West African, Hindu, Chinese, Japanese, American Indian). The evidence of this identification is merely the spiral horn.

B11.2.1.10. *Dragon as modified deer.* Smith Dragon 131.

B11.2.1.11. *Dragon as modified eagle.* Smith Dragon 92f., 108.
B11.4.1. Flying dragon.

B11.2.1.12. *Dragon as other modified animal.* Smith Dragon 108 (falcon), 165ff. (octopus, whale).

B11.2.2. *Color of dragon.* Smith Dragon 108 (blue), 137 (red). — Breton: Sébillot Incidents s.v. "dragons" (regiment of green dragons). — Icel.: Bósa saga 62 (golden).

B11.2.2.1. *Dragon with golden feathers.* Icel.: *Boberg.

B11.2.3. *Many-headed dragon.* (Cf. B15.1.2.) — Danish: Fb "hoved" 65b; Jones PMLA XXIII 569. — Greek: Fox 87 (hundred); Persian: Carnoy 265 (three); Japanese: Anesaki 228 (eight), 333 (nine).
F531.1.2.2. Many-headed giant. G361.1.3. Many-headed ogre. G304.1.3. Many-headed troll.

B11.2.3.1. *Seven-headed dragon.* *Type 300; Smith Dragon 211f. — Breton: Sébillot Incidents s.v. "bête". Missouri French: Carrière; Spanish: Boggs FFC XC 42 No. 302*A: Gaster Thespis 80f, 186. — India: Thompson-Balys; Araucanian: Alexander Lat. Am. 327.
G11.17. Seven-mouthed cannibal ogre. G215.1. Seven-headed witch.

B11.2.3.2. *Three-headed dragon.* Cheremis: Sebeok-Nyerges; Africa (Fulah): Frobenius Atlantis VI 182ff. No. 4.

B11.2.3.3. *Six-headed dragon.* Cheremis: Sebeok-Nyerges.

B11.2.3.4. *Nine-headed dragon.* Cheremis: Sebeok-Nyerges.

B11.2.3.5. *Twelve-headed dragon.* Cheremis: Sebeok-Nyerges.

B11.2.3.6. *Two-headed dragon.* England: Baughman.

B11.2.4. *Feet of dragon.*
F551. Remarkable feet.

B11.2.4.1. *Feet of dragon — number.* Irish myth: Cross; Japanese: Smith Dragon 101f.; Chinese: Werner 368.

B11.2.4.2. *Feet of dragon — nature.* Cloven hoofs: Smith Dragon 137. — Claws: Chinese: Werner 368.

B11.2.5. *Horns of dragon.* Smith Dragon 137. — Chinese: Werner 368, Eberhard FFC CXX 73, 85.

B11.2.6. *Wings of dragon.* Smith Dragon 137. — Chinese: Werner 368.

B11.2.7. *Snakes issue from dragon's shoulders.* Persian: Carnoy 320.

B11.2.8. *Tail of dragon.* Smith Dragon 137; Fb "drage" (if one throws fire over dragon's long tail, the tail falls and is full of treasure).

B11.2.8.1. *Dragon encircles city with its tail.* India: Thompson-Balys.

B11.2.9. *Heart of dragon.* Fb "hjærte" 631b.
D1015.1.2. Magic dragon heart. D1500.1.9.3. Dragon's heart-blood as remedy.

B11.2.10. *Scales of dragon.* Chinese: Werner 368.

B11.2.11. *Fire-breathing dragon.* *Type 300; Hdwb. d. Abergl. II 391; Fb. "drage", "gloende" (glowing eyes and tongue), "ild" (fire from mouth). Irish myth: Cross; Icel.: *Boberg.

B16. Devastating animals. B742. Animal breathes fire. D1337.11. Dragon's breath renders hideous. M357.1. Prophecy: fiery bolt from a dragon to kill world population.

B11.2.11.1. Dragon spews venom. Icel.: *Boberg.

F582.2. Man spews venom.

B11.2.11.2. *Breath of dragon kills man.* Scotland, England: *Baughman; Chinese: Werner 236. — N. A. Indian (Iroquois): BBAE XXX pt. 2, 720 s.v. "Teharonhiawagon".

B14.1. Chimera breathes fire. B16. Devastating animals. B742. Animal breathes fire. D1337.11. Dragon's breath renders hideous. M357.1. Prophecy: fiery bolt from a dragon to kill world population.

B11.2.12. *Dragon of enormous size.* Jewish: Bin Gorion Born Judas II 170, 349, Neuman; Irish myth: Cross; African (Fang): Einstein 47.

B870. Giant animals. F531. Giant.

B11.2.13. *Blood of dragon.* Irish myth: Cross.

D1016. Magic blood of animal.

B11.2.13.1. *Blood of dragon venomous.* Irish myth: Cross.

B776.5. Blood of animal considered venomous.

B11.2.14. *Dragon with jewel in head.* Irish myth: Cross.

B108.2. Serpent with jewel in head.

B11.3. *Habitat of dragon.*

B11.3.1. *Dragon's home in bottom of sea.* Smith Dragon 82. — Chinese: Werner 210 (only in autumn and winter); Icel.: Boberg.

F420. Water-spirits.

B11.3.1.1. *Dragon lives in lake.* Irish myth: Cross.

B11.3.1.2. *Dragon's home beneath waterfall.* (Cf. F426.) Icel.: Boberg.

B11.3.2. *Dragon's home at top of mountain.* His breath forms clouds to hide the mountain. — Smith Dragon 82. — Scotland: Baughman.

B11.3.3. *Dragon's visit to sky.* Chinese: Werner 210 (only in spring and summer). (Cf. B11.4.1.)

B11.3.4. *Dragons live beneath castle.* Mediaeval Romance: Wells Manual of Writings 39 (Nennius's Historia Britonum) 42f. (Arthour and Merlin).

B11.3.5. *Dragon lives under the ground.* By his movements a building or village will be dislodged. (Cf. A1070.) — Zingerle Zs. f. deutsche Mythologie und Sittengeschichte II 347; Hdwb. d. Abergl. II 890. — Irish myth: Cross.

F450. Underground spirits.

B11.3.6. *Dragons live in hell.* Irish myth: Cross; Icel.: MacCulloch Eddic 319, 352.

A671. Hell. Lower world of torment. B11.6.4. Dragon guards bridge to otherworld. Q568.2. Sinners in hell swallowed by dragon.

B11.3.7. *Dragon lives beneath tree.* Danish: Kristensen Danske Sagn II (1893) 179ff., (1928) 122ff. — Icel.: MacCulloch Eddic 319.

B11.3.8. *Dragon lives in isolated island.* German: Grimm No. 129.

B11.4. *Dragon's habits.*

B11.4.1. *Flying dragon* (Cf. B11.2.1.11.) — BP III 423; *Fb "drage" (flies over the mountain). — Icel.: MacCulloch Eddic 319, 345; *Boberg; Greek myth: *Frazer Apollodorus I 38 n. 2 (air-going chariot and dragons); Irish myth: Cross; India: Thompson-Balys.
B40. Bird-beasts. F796. Dragon seen in sky.

B11.4.2. *Dragon as giver of omens.* Smith Dragon 97.
D1812.5. Future learned through omens.

B11.4.3. *Sleepless dragon.* Greek Myth (Jason): *Frazer Apollodorus I 95 n. 2.

B11.4.4. *Dragon travels on sea or land.* Irish myth: Cross.

B11.4.5. *Talking dragon.* Irish myth: Cross.
B123. Wise serpent. B211. Animal uses human speech.

B11.5. *Powers of dragon.*

B11.5.1. *Dragon's power of self-transformation.* Chinese: Werner 223.

B11.5.2. *Dragon's power of magic invisibility.* Chinese: Werner 209.
D1361. Magic object renders invisible. D1980. Magic invisibility.

B11.5.3. *Dragon's miraculous vision.* Can see a fly miles away. — Africa (Gold Coast): Barker and Sinclair 97 No 18.

B11.5.4. *Dragon's miraculous speed.* Gold Coast: Barker and Sinclair 97 No. 18.

B11.5.5. *Self-returning dragon's head* (Cf. B11.2.3, B11.11.2.) — *Type 300; BP I 547; Eng.: Baughman; Greek: Fox 81 (hydra). — Onondaga: Beauchamp JAFL II 261.
D1602.12. Self-returning head. E783. Vital head. F531.1.2.6. Giant's self-returning head.

B11.6. *Deeds of dragons.*

B11.6.1. *Dragon helps hero out of gratitude.* Dickson Valentine and Orson 121 n. 64.

B11.6.1.2. *Grateful dragon saves hero and rescues him from prison.* Chinese: Eberhard 180.

B11.6.2. *Dragon guards treasure.* *Norlind Skattsägner 77f.; Gould Scandinavian Studies and Notes IX (1917) 170 No. 4; Penzer III 133; Smith Dragon 157—165; Finnish-Swedish; Wessman 76, 78 Nos. 632, 657; Icel.: Boberg; Danish: Kristensen Danske Sagn II (1893) 133ff., (1928) 119ff., III (1895) 454ff., (1931) 311ff.; Greek: *Grote I 219; U.S.: Baughman; Wienert FFC LVI 37; Phaedrus IV 21; Chinese: Werner 209.
B11.1.3. Dragon from transformed man lying on his treasures. B576.2. Animal guards treasure. D950.0.1. Magic tree guarded by serpent (dragon). H335.7. Suitor task: to kill treasure-guarding snake lying around the princess' chamber. N511.4. Treasure found in snake hole. N557. Serpent guards treasure. N570. Guardian of treasure.

B11.6.2.1. *Dragon must give up treasure when steel is thrown on him.* Fb "stål". III 647a; Finnish-Swedish: Wessman 76 No. 632.

B11.6.2.2. *Serpents play with precious green stone.* Icel.: *Boberg.

B11.6.2.3. *Dragon's pearl stolen.* Chinese: Eberhard FFC CXX 233 No. 181.

B11.6.3. *Dragon feeds on treasure.* Oberwallis: Jegerlehner 321 No. 75; Chinese: Werner 210.

B11.6.4. *Dragon guards holy land.* Irish myth: Cross.

B11.6.5. *Dragon guards hermit's food,* frightens off robbers. Spanish Exempla: Keller.

B11.6.6. *Dragon guards bridge to otherworld.* Icel.: *Boberg.

B11.3.6. Dragons in hell. F152. Bridge to otherworld. F721.2.2. Monster guards door of habitable hill.

B11.6.7. *Dragon eats an ox at every meal.* Icel.: Boberg.

B11.6.8. *Dragon flies to its nest with human being.* Icel.: *Boberg.

B31.2.2. The bird Gam flies away with human being. R13. Abduction by animal.

B11.6.8.1. *Dragon flies away with lion.* Icel.: *Boberg.

B11.11.6. Dragon fight in order to free lion.

B11.6.9. *Dragon gnaws the roots of tree.* Icel.: MacCulloch Eddic 332.

B11.6.10. *Sandalwood tree is guarded by dragon with venomous breath.* India: Thompson-Balys.

B776. Venomous animals.

B11.7. *Dragon as rain-spirit.* Smith Dragon 1, 78, 82, 90. — Chinese: Werner 208.

A287. Rain-god.

B11.7.1. *Dragon controls water-supply.* Hindu: Keith, Thompson-Balys; Japanese: Ikeda.

A1111. Impounded water. Water is kept by a monster so that mankind cannot use it. F420.4.9. Water-spirit controls water-supply.

B11.7.1.1. *Dragon causes deluge.* China: Eberhard FFC CXX 233 No. 181.

B11.7.2. *Dragon guards lake.* Penzer VII 235 N. 2; Irish myth: Cross; India: Thompson-Balys.

B11.8. *Dragon as power of good.* Smith Dragon 82, 97. — Chinese: Werner 208ff., Graham. Icel.: Boberg.

B11.9. *Dragon as power of evil.* So considered everywhere except in the East, where are also found beneficent dragons. — Smith Dragon 82. — Irish myth; Chinese: Werner 208 (introduced by the Buddhists).

B11.10. *Sacrifice of human being to dragon.* *Type 300; Penzer VII 236, 240; Dickson Valentine and Orson 226f.; Gaster Thespis 176; Hartland Legend of Perseus passim; Fb "drage", "pige". — Irish myth: Cross; Greek: Fox 34; Persian: Carnoy 320; India: *Thompson-Balys; Breton: Sébillot Incidents s.v. "exposition"; French Canadian: Barbeau JAFL XXXIX 17; Missouri French: Carrière; Africa (Zulu): Callaway 41; Japanese: Anesaki 249.

B16.6. Giant devastating serpent. R111.1.3. Rescue of princess (maiden) from dragon. S262. Periodic sacrifices to a monster.

B11.10.0.1. *Sacrifice of animals to dragon.* Irish myth: Cross.

V12.4. Animal as sacrifice.

B11.10.1. *Dragon keeps maiden tied with golden chain.* Köhler-Bolte I 128.

B11.10.2. *Dragon eats people for his rent.* Chinese: Graham.

B11.10.3. *Dragon devours children.* India: Thompson-Balys; Eng., U.S.: Baughman.

B11.11. *Fight with dragon.* *Type 300; *BP I 547; *Smith Dragon 79ff., 104; *Róheim Drachen und Drachenkämpfer; *Norlind Skattsägner 67f., *Liebrecht Zur Volkskunde 70; **von Sydow Sigurds Strid med Fåvne; *Schoepperle Tristan and Isolt I 204 nn. 1, 2; Clouston Pop. Tales and Fictions I 155ff.; *Spence 80; *E. Siecke Drachenkämpfe; Fb "Jörgen" II 67a (St. George and the Dragon). — Germanic: Hdwb. d. Abergl. II 371; Heusler Altnordische Dichtung und Prosa von Jung Sigurd (Sitzungsberichte der Berliner Akad. v. Wissenschaften, 1919, 162—195); **H. Sandkühler Der Drachenkampf des heiligen Georg in englischer Legende u. Dichtung vom 14. bis 16. Jahrhundert (Diss. München 1914); *Loomis White Magic 65, 119; Greek: *Frazer Apollodorus 27 no. 4 (Apollo and Python), I 153 n. 1 (Bellerophon and Chimera); Celtic: MacCulloch Celtic 130ff.; Irish myth: Cross; Icel.: *Boberg; Jewish: Neuman, Gaster Thespis 140 ff., 326ff.; Egyptian: Müller 127; Persian: Carnoy 266, 270, 273, 322, *325, 329f.; Hindu: Keith 33 (Indra); India: *Thompson-Balys; Armenian: Ananikian 77; Japanese: Anesaki 228; Chinese: Werner 224, 361, Eberhard FFC CXX 105, 138; Arabian: Burton I 172. — English: Wells Manual of Writings 16 (Guy of Warwick), 115 (Sir Eglamour), 117 (Torrent of Portyngale); Missouri French: Carrière; Africa (Fang): Einstein 44, 47. — Cf. *Olrik Ragnarök 57ff. (fight with giant serpent).

A531. Culture hero overcomes monsters. B524.1.1. Dogs kill attacking dragon. B875.2. Giant sea-monster overpowered by saint (hero). C422.1. Tabu: revealing dragon-fighter's identity. D1385.14. Milk of two king's children protects hero in dragon fight. D1402.14. Magic circle of saliva kills dragon. D1795. Dragon-fighter's magic sleep. F962.10.1. Mist settles over lake after fight with serpent. G357.1. Hero overcomes devastating animal. H105.1. Dragon-tongue proof. H1333.3.0.1. Quest for branches of tree guarded by dragon. H1561.6. Test of valor: fight with giant. K835. Dragon deceived into listening to tale: hero cuts off his head. K1052. Dragon attacks own image in mirror. R111.1.4. Rescue of princess (maiden) from dragon. T68.1. Princess offered as prize to rescuer.

B11.11.1. *Dragon fight: respite granted and dragon returns with renewed strength.* French Canadian: Barbeau JAFL XXXIX 21; Missouri French: Carrière.

B11.11.2. *Hero's dogs (horse) prevent dragon's heads from rejoining body.* (Cf. B11.2.3.) — *Type 300; *BP I 547.

B11.5.5. Self-returning dragon's head.

B11.11.3. *Dragon combats attack with showers of fiery spines.* Irish myth: Cross.

B11.2. Form of dragon. B11.12.3. Fiery dragon.

B11.11.4. *Dragon fight in order to free princess.* Icel.: *Boberg. (See also R111.1 and most of the references to B11.11.).

B11.11.5. *Dragon fight in order to free man.* Icel.: *Boberg.

B11.11.6. *Dragon fight in order to free lion.* Icel.: *Boberg.

B11.6.6.1. Dragon flies away with lion.

B11.11.7. *Woman as dragon-slayer.* India: Thompson-Balys.

B11.11.8. *Dragon doubles his demand after men's rebellion.* Africa (Fang): Einstein 42.

B11.12. *Other traits of dragon.*

B11.12.1. *Dragon cannot be killed with weapons.* Wesselski Mönchslatein 171 No. 136; Irish myth: Cross; Eng.: Baughman; Gaster Oldest Stories 69.

A2468.3. Why dragon dies by means of fire. K1840.2. Magic invulnerability of animals.

B11.12.1.1. *Dragon which cannot be killed with weapons is kicked in vulnerable spot.* England: Baughman.

B11.12.1.2. *Dragon dips wounded part in holy well,* is healed immediately. England: Baughman.

B11.12.2. *Dragon's shriek makes land barren.* Irish myth: Cross; Mac Culloch Celtic 130.

B741. Lion's roar causes havoc at 300 miles. B741.1. Cry of giant ox impregnates all fish. D2081. Land magically made sterile.

B11.12.3. *Fiery dragon.* Irish myth: Cross.

B11.2.11. Fire-breathing dragon. B11.11.3. Dragon combats attack with showers of fiery spines. B15.7.13. Bird with fiery beak. B15.7.14. Bird with tail of fire. B19.4. Glowing animals. D1271. Magic fire. F574. Luminous person.

B11.12.4. *Dragon is fond of milk.*

B11.12.4.1. *Dragon is fed great quantities of milk to keep him pacified.* England: *Baughman.

B11.12.5. *The dragon-king.* Chinese: Eberhard 25 No. 13,65, 87 No. 7,158, 245 No. 190.

B11.12.6. *Dragon can hear a child cry even at great distance.* India: Thompson-Balys.

B11.12.7. *Human-dragon marriage.* Chinese: Eberhard 49, 64f., 103, 135, No. 92.

B12. *Basilisk.* A mythical lizard or serpent whose hissing drives away all other serpents. — *Polívka Zs. f. Vksk. XXVII 46ff.; *Fb "basilisk"; *A Guichot y Sierra El Basilisco (Folklore Español III 9—83); *Norlind Skattsägner 46 n. 1; Hdwb. d. Abergl. s.v. "Basilisk"; Köhler-Bolte I 133. — English: Wells Manual of Writings 105 (Prose Alexander); Jewish: Neuman.

B12.1. *Basilisk hatched from cock's egg.* Usually, a seven-year-old cock. Egg must lie in manure. (Cf. B11.1.1.) — *Polívka Zs. f. Vksk. XXVIII 46ff.; *Fb. "basilisk" I 53a, IV 29a; De Vries Het Sprookje 19—97; Taylor PMLA XXXVI 35ff.; Hdwb. d. Abergl. s.v. "Basilisk".

B19.3. Horse born of egg. B710. Fanciful origin of animal.

B12.2. *Basilisk's fatal glance.* Renders powerless or kills. — *Fb "basilisk" I 53a, IV 29a, "øje" III 1167b; Penzer VIII 75 n.l.

D2061.2.1. Death-giving glance. D2071. Evil Eye.

B12.3. *Basilisk killed by seeing own image.* *Fb "basilisk" I 53a, "spejl" III 48a; Ward Catalogue of Romances III 194; Oesterley Gesta Romanorum No. 139; Hdwb. d. Abergl. I 935.

B13. *Unicorn.* (Cf. B15.7.2.) — *Type 1640; *BP I 164; **Odell Shepard The Lore of the Unicorn (London, 1929); **Robert Brown Jr. The Unicorn, a Mythological Investigation (London, 1881); Howey Horse in Magic and Myth 232f.; Hdwb. d. Abergl. s.v. "Einhorn"; Bolte Reise der Söhne Giaffers 212; Icel.: *Boberg; Jewish: Neuman; Chinese: Ferguson 98.

K771. Unicorn tricked into running horn into tree. A2214.3. Unicorn thrown from ark and drowned: hence extinct.

B14. *Other hybrid animals.*

B16.1.1. Monster cat born of a pig.

B14.1. *Chimera.* Combination of lion, dragon, and goat. Breathes fire. — *Frazer Apollodorus I 151 n. 2, 153 n. 1; Fox 39. — Egyptian: Müller 169.

B11.2.11. Fire-breathing dragon. B742. Animal breathes fire.

B14.2. *Animal with body of horse, legs of hound.* Irish myth: Cross.

B14.3. *Hybrid monster: calf-sheep.* S. A. Indian (Araucanian): Cooper BBAE CXLIII II 753.

B15. *Animals with unusual limbs or members.*

B20. Beast-man. B50. Bird-man. B80. Fish-man. B700. Fanciful traits of animals. B720. Fanciful bodily members of animal. D1010. Magic bodily members — animal. F241.1.3.1. Fairy horse, one-legged.

B15.1. *Animal unusual as to his head.*

B15.1.1. *Headless animals.* *Fb "hovedløs" IV 223a.

B15.1.1.1. *Headless dog.* North Carolina: Brown Coll. I 636.

B15.1.2. *Many-headed animal.* (Cf. B15.7.2.) — Irish myth: Cross; N. A. Indian: Thompson Tales 357 n. 287f. — Africa (Angola): Chatelain 93 No. 5.

B11.2.3. Many-headed dragon. D1846.2. Invulnerability bestowed by many-headed monster. F531.1.2.2. Many-headed giant. G304.1.3. Many-headed troll. G361.1. Many-headed ogre.

B15.1.2.1. *Two-headed animal.* U.S.: Baughman; Jewish: Neuman.

B15.1.2.1.1. *Two-headed serpent.* One head in front and one at rear. — Penzer V 135 n. 2.

B15.1.2.1.2. *Two-headed tiger.* S. A. Indian (Chiriguano): Métraux RMLP XXXIII 142—158 passim.

B15.1.2.1.3. *Jaguar with two heads.* S. A. Indian (Chiriguano): Métraux RMLP XXXIII 155.

B15.1.2.1.4. *Two-headed dog.* Greek: *Frazer Apollodorus I 211 n. 3 (Orthus).

B15.1.2.2. *Three-headed animal.*

B15.1.2.2.1. *Three-headed bird.* Irish myth: Cross.

B15.1.2.2.2. *Three-headed serpent.* Persian: Carnoy 311; Hindu: Keith 36, 154.

B15.1.2.3. *Four-headed animal.*

B15.1.2.3.1. *Four-headed monster.* Irish myth: Cross.

B15.1.2.4. *Five-headed animal.*

B642.1.1. Marriage to person in form of five-headed snake.

B15.1.2.5. *Six-headed animal.*

B15.1.2.6. *Seven-headed animal.*

B11.2.3.1. Seven-headed dragon. G11.17. Seven-mouthed cannibal ogre.

B15.1.2.6.1. *Seven-headed serpent.* Gaster Thespis 80f.; Hindu: Keith 154; Zanzibar: Bateman 134.

G215.1. Seven-headed witch.

B15.1.2.7. *Eight-headed animal.*

B15.1.2.8. *Nine-headed animal.*

B15.1.2.8.1. *Hydra: nine-headed monster.* Middle head immortal. — *Frazer Apollodorus I 187 n. 3.

F1041.5. Poison of hydra corrodes the skin.

B15.1.2.8.2. *Nine-headed serpent.* Fb. "hugormekonge".

B15.1.2.9. *Ten-headed serpent.* Hindu: Keith 154.

B15.1.2.10. *Other many-headed animals.*

B15.1.2.10.1. *Twelve-headed serpent.* Cheremis: Sebeok-Nyerges. India: Thompson-Balys.

B15.1.2.10.2. *Hundred-headed serpent* (monster). Irish myth: Cross.

B15.1.2.10.3. *Thousand-headed serpent.* Hindu: Penzer VI 61 n. 1, VI 176.

A842.1. Serpent supports the earth. Thousand-headed serpent.

B15.1.3. *Animal with head of bone.* Irish myth: Cross.

F511. Person unusual as to his head. F558. Man covered with horn.

B15.2. *Many-mouthed animal* (Cf. B15.7.2.).

B15.2.1. *Six-mouthed serpent.* Persian: Keith Ind. Myth. 36.

B15.3. *Animal unusual as to his horns.*

F511.3. Person with horns. G361.1.2.1. Monster with two horns, each having human head on it.

B15.3.0.1. *Hornless cow.* Irish myth: Cross.

B15.3.0.1.1. *Hornless bull.* Irish myth: Cross.

B15.3.0.2. *One-horned ox.* Jewish: Neuman.

B15.3.1. *Many-horned animal.*

B15.3.1.1. *Three-horned deer.* Irish: MacCulloch Celtic 129, Cross.

B15.3.1.2. *Nine-horned sheep.* Irish myth: Cross.

B15.3.1.3. *Ox with three horns.* Icel.: *Boberg.

B15.3.1.3.1. *Ox with four horns.* Icel.: *Boberg.

B15.3.2. *Animal with a gold (silver) horn.*

B15.3.2.1. *Deer with a gold and a silver horn.* *Fb "hjort" I 625 a.

B15.3.2.2. *Goat with a gold and a silver horn.* Cheremis: Sebeok-Nyerges.

B15.3.2.3. *Ox with golden horns.* French Canadian: Sister Marie Ursule.

B15.3.2.3.1. *Cow with silver horns.* Cheremis: Sebeok-Nyerges.

B15.3.3. *Deer with giant antler.* Irish myth: Cross.

B106.1.1. Stag with golden antlers. B870. Giant animals. F234.1.4. Fairy in form of stag.

B15.3.4. *Animal usually harmless has horns.*

B15.3.4.1. *Hare with horns.* India: Thompson-Balys.

B15.3.4.2. *Horned armadillo lives underground.* S. A Indian (Chaco): Belaieff BBAE CXLIII (1) 379.

B15.3.5. *Animal with horn on his head pointing to the sky.* Chinese: Graham.

B15.4. *Animals with unusual eyes.* (Cf. B15.7.2.) Irish myth: Cross.

B721. Cat's luminous eye. F541. Remarkable eyes.

B15.4.1. *Many-eyed animal.*

B15.4.1.1. *Many-eyed antelope.* Southern Ute: Lowie JAFL XXXVII 49 No. 24.

B15.4.1.2. *Four-eyed tiger.* S. A. Indian (Yuracare): Métraux RMLP XXXIII 144.

B15.4.1.3. *Four-eyed jaguar.* S. A. Indian (Yuracare): Métraux BBAE CXLIII (3) 503.

B15.4.1.4. *Eight-eyed bat.* Hawaii: Beckwith Myth 233.

B15.4.2. *Beasts with fiery eyes.*

B15.4.2.1. *Dog with fire in eyes.* (Cf. B19.4.) — Fb "ild". — Gaster Thespis 214.

E42.3.6. Ghosts as dogs with glowing tongues and eyes. E501.4.1.3. Dogs with fiery eyes in wild hunt.

B15.4.3. *Dogs with eyes like plates, tea-cups, etc.* Fb. "øje" 1165b.

B15.4.4. *Animal with human eyes (transformed man).* Icel.: *Boberg.

B15.4.5. *One-eyed pig.* Irish myth: Cross.

B15.5. *Animal unusual as to his nose (snout).*

F514. Person unusual as to his nose. F543. Remarkable nose.

B15.5.1. *Horse with fire-breathing nostrils.* (Cf. B19.1.) — Fb "ild" II 12a; Icel.: *Boberg.

B742. Animal breathes fire. E501.4.2.4. Horse in wild hunt breathes fire.

B15.5.2. *Animal with snout of iron.* Irish myth: Cross. (Cf. B15.7.13.1.)

B15.6. *Animals with unusual legs or feet.* (Cf. B19.1.)

B11.2.4. Feet of dragon. E501.4.2.6. Two-legged horse in wild hunt. F551. Remarkable feet. H609.5. Symbolical interpretation of fight between one-legged bird and twelve-legged bird. X1381. Lie: animal with long and short legs for mountain climbing.

B15.6.0.1. *One-footed animal.* Irish myth: Cross.

B15.6.1. *Three-legged quadrupeds.* Fb. "trebenet"; Zingerle Sagen aus Tirol 590; Tobler Epiphanie der Seele 20; *Hdwb. d. Abergl. II 420. Mannhardt Germanische Mythen 409; Wehrhan Freimauerei 53 (hare). — Swiss: Jegerlehner Oberwallis 324 No. 152.

E501.4.1.6. Three-legged dogs in wild hunt. E521.2. Three-legged ghost of horse. F241.1.3. Fairies ride on three-legged horses.

B15.6.2. *Empousa.* Monster with one foot of brass and another of an ass. — Greek: Fox 278.

B15.6.3. *Animals with many legs.* Ipolyi Zs. f. deutsche Mythologie II 269. — Hindu: Penzer III 259 n. 1 (sarabhas); Irish myth: Cross.

B15.6.3.1. *Six-legged quadruped.*

B15.6.3.1.1. *Six-legged horse.* Cheremis: Sebeok-Nyerges.

A135. Sleipnir: eight-legged horse of Odin.

B15.6.3.2. *Twelve-legged bird.* Irish myth: Cross.

B172. Magic bird. H619.5. Symbolical interpretation of fight between one-legged bird and twelve-legged bird.

B15.6.3.3. *Seven-legged beast.* India: Thompson-Balys.

B15.6.4. *Bull with human hands and feet.* India: Thompson-Balys.

B15.7. *Other animals with unusual limbs or members.* (Cf. B20, B142, B92.) Irish myth: Cross.

B15.7.1. *Cerberus.* The hell hound with three heads, a serpent's tail, and a writhing tangle of snakes from his body. Irish myth: Cross; Greek: Fox 88, 142.

A673. Hound of hell. Cerberus (monstrous dog) guards the bridge to the lower world.

B15.7.2. *Monster three-legged ass.* Stands in the ocean. Has three feet, six eyes, nine mouths, two ears, one horn, a white body. Two eyes are in eye position, two on top of his head, two on his hump. He renders powerless by the sharpness of his eyes. He has three mouths in his head, three in his hump, and three in the inner parts of his flanks. Each mouth is the size of a cottage. (Cf. B13, B15.1, B15.2, B15.4.) — Persian: Carnoy 270.

B871. Giant animals. G350. Animal ogres.

B15.7.3. *Bird with head of gold and wings of silver.* Irish myth: Cross.

B15.7.4. *Fox with eight-forked tail.* Japanese: Anesaki 325, Ikeda.

B15.7.5. *Ghormuhas: men's bodies, horses' heads, one leg, cannibals.* (Cf. B21.) India: Thompson-Balys.

B15.7.6. *Three-tailed turtle.* Korean: Zong-in-Sob 169 No. 73.

B15.7.7. *Leopard with nine tails.* Africa (Chaga): Gutman Globus XCI 239ff.

B15.7.7.1. *Nine-tailed fox.* Korean: Zong-in-Sob 230 No. 99, 20 No. 9, 38 No. 22; Japanese: Ikeda; Chinese: Eberhard FFC CXX 141.

B15.7.8. *Boar with nine tusks in each jaw.* Irish myth: Cross.

B16.4. Giant devastating boar. B183. Magic boar. B871.2. Giant boar.

B15.7.9. *Cow with tallow liver.* Irish myth: Cross.

B182. Magic cow. H1331.3.2. Quest for cow with liver of tallow. U35. Rich man seizes poor widow's cow.

B15.7.9.1. *Cow with two bags: one containing a one-legged bird; the other, a twelve-legged bird.* Irish myth: Cross.

B182. Magic cow (ox, bull).

B15.7.10. *Animal unusual as to skin.* Irish myth: Cross.

B15.7.10.1. *Animal with horny skin.* Irish myth: Cross.

F558. Man covered with horn.

B15.7.10.2. *Animal with hair of iron pins.* Irish myth: Cross.

B15.7.11. *Animal with one head, two bodies, six legs.* Irish myth: Cross. (Cf. B15.6.3.5, B15.7.9.1.)

B15.7.12. *Eel with fiery mane.* Irish myth: Cross.

B17.2.1.2. Hostile eel attacks hero. D1271. Magic fire.

B15.7.13. *Bird with fiery beak.* Irish myth: Cross.

B11.12.3. Fiery dragon. B33.1. Other devastating birds. D1271. Magic fire.

B15.7.13.1. *Bird with beak of iron.* Irish myth: Cross; Icel.: *Boberg.

B15.7.14. *Bird with tail of fire.* Irish myth: Cross.

B15.7.15. *Monster with 100 hands,* 100 palms on each hand, and 100 nails on each palm. Irish myth: Cross.

B15.7.16. *Eagle with twelve wings* and three heads. Jewish: Moreno Esdras (B172.6.)

B16. *Devastating animals.* India: *Thompson-Balys.

B11.2.11. Fire-breathing dragon. B11.12.2. Dragon's shriek makes land barren. B17. Hostile animals. B33. Man-eating birds. B776. Venomous animals. E263. Adulteress returns from dead as devastating dragon. F366.3. Fairies in form of devastating animals kill flocks. F981.4. Fiery bolt from heaven kills devastating animal. G346. Devastating monster. H1161. Task: killing ferocious beast. H1362. Quest for devastating animals.

B16.0.1. *Beasts that destroy vineyards and steal fruit.* Irish myth: Cross.

B16.0.2. *Tormenting beast in man's stomach.* Irish myth: Cross.

B16.0.3. *Man-eating monster (in cave).* Irish myth: Cross.

B16.1. *Devastating domestic animals.*

B16.1.1. *Monster cat devastates country.* Welsh: MacCulloch Celtic 191; Irish myth: Cross; Breton: Sébillot Incidents s.v. "chat"; India: Thompson-Balys.

B184. Magic cat. B871.10. Giant cat. H1411.2. Fear test: spending night in haunted house infested by cats. R13.2. Cat abducts person.

B16.1.1.1. *Monster cat born of a pig.* Welsh: MacCulloch Celtic 191.

B871. Giant animals.

B16.1.1.2. *Cat leaps through man like arrow of fire* and burns him to ashes. Irish myth: Cross.

B19.4. Glowing animals. B184. Magic cat. F831.2. Arrows of fire. B916. One animal jumps through body of another.

B16.1.1.3. *Cat devours flesh of man's legs.* Irish myth: Cross.

B16.1.2. *Devastating dog (hound).* Irish myth: Cross; India: Thompson-Balys.

B16.1.2.1. *Giant devastating hound.* Irish myth: Cross.

B871.13. Giant dog (hound).

B16.1.3. *Devastating horse.*

B16.1.3.1. *Man-eating mares.* *Frazer Apollodorus I 200 n. 1.

B16.1.4. Devastating swine. Irish myth: Cross.

B183. Magic boar (pig).

B16.1.4.1. *Giant devastating boar.* Irish myth: Cross; Icel.: *Boberg; Greek: Fox 82; Italian: Basile Pentamerone I No. 2; India: Thompson-Balys.

B183. Magic boar. B871. Giant animals.

B16.1.4.2. Giant devastating sow. Irish myth: Cross; Icel.: MacCulloch Celtic 187, *Fb "so" III 450a.

B16.1.5. *Man-eating cattle.* India: Thompson-Balys.

B16.1.5.1. *Monster ox (bull) killed.* Babylonian: Jensen Gilgamesch-Epos VI 94ff., cf. 120—21, 129ff.; Greek: Fox 29, 62, 84, 102; Icel.: Mac Culloch Eddic 85, *Boberg; India: Thompson-Balys.

B23. Man-bull.

B16.1.5.2. *Destructive cow possessed by demons.* Irish myth: Cross. (Cf. B17.1.3.)

B16.1.5.3. *Devastating bull.* Greek: Grote I 189.

B16.1.6. *Destructive sheep.* Irish myth: Cross.

B189.1. Magic sheep. B776.1. Venomous sheep destroy enemy. B871.3. Giant sheep.

B16.1.6.1. *Devastating supernatural lamb.* Irish myth: Cross.

B16.2. *Devastating wild animals.*

B16.2.1. *Devastating fox.* Monthly human sacrifice. — *Frazer Apollodorus I 171 n. 2.

S262. Periodic sacrifices to a monster.

B16.2.2. *Devastating tiger.* India: *Thompson-Balys; Chinese: Graham.

B16.2.2.1 *Hostile tiger killed.* Icel.: *Boberg.

B16.2.3. *Giant lion overcome by hero.* Babylonian: Jensen Gilgamesch-Epos VIII; Greek: Fox 80; Icel.: *Boberg; India: *Thompson-Balys.

H1161. Task: killing ferocious beast.

B16.2.4. *Giant devastating wolf overcome by hero.* Icel.: Boberg.

B16.2.5. *Devastating bear killed.* Icel.: Boberg.

B16.2.6. *Devastating elephant.* Icel.: *Boberg; India: Thompson-Balys; Chinese-Persian: Coyajee JPASB XXIV 188.

B16.2.7. *Destructive deer.* Irish myth: Cross.

B188. Magic deer. F234.1.4. Fairy in form of deer.

B16.2.8. *Giant man-eating mice.* Irish myth: Cross.

B16.2.9. *Devastating bison (buffalo).* German: Grimm No. 197; India: Thompson-Balys.

B16.3. *Devastating birds.* (Cf. B33.)

B16.4. *Devastating fish carries off daily victim.* India: Thompson-Balys; Greek: Grote I 189.

B16.4.1. *Leviathan casts up gorge which spreads disease.* Irish myth: Cross.

B61. Leviathan.

B16.4.1.1. *Leviathan causes cataclysm* by striking earth with tail. Irish myth: Cross.

A1145.2. Earthquakes from movements of sea-monster.

B16.4.1.1.2. *Sea-beast:* when it belches landward, it causes disease; upward it kills birds; downward, fishes and sea animals. Irish myth: Cross.

B16.5. *Devastating reptiles.*

B16.5.1. *Giant devastating serpent.* India: *Thompson-Balys; Chinese: Eberhard FFC CXX 144f. — Africa (Chaga): Stamberg Zs. f. Eingeborenen-Spr. XXIII 296ff., Gutmann Volksbuch der Wadschagga 82f. No. 41, (Ganda): Baskerville King of the Snakes 1ff., (Senegambia): Béranger-Feraud Recueil de Contes Populaires de la Senegambia II 185ff. No. 2, (tribes of Western Sudan): Tauxier Le Noir du Yatengo 496 No. 1.

B16.5.1.1. *Devastating serpent with fiery breath.* India: Thompson-Balys.

B11.6.4.1. Sandal-wood tree is guarded by dragon with venomous breath.

B16.5.1.2. *Devastating (man-eating) sea-monster (serpent).* Irish myth: Cross.

B91.5. Sea-serpent. B875. Giant sea-monster (serpent). G308.1. Fight with sea- (lake-) monster.

B16.5.1.2.1. *Serpent sucks man's breath (blood).* India: *Thompson-Balys.

B16.5.2. *Devastating crocodile.* India: Thompson-Balys; Chinese: Eberhard FFC CXX II No. 188.

B16.5.3. *Devastating shell-fish.* Chinese: Eberhard FFC CXX 119f.

B16.5.4. *Man-devouring turtle.* Chinese: Eberhard FFC CXX 145.

B16.6. *Devastating insects.*

B16.6.1. *Giant man-eating ants. Irish myth: Cross.*

B874. Giant insects.

B16.6.2. *Blood-sucking chafer.* Irish myth: Cross.

B16.6.2.1. *Fierce black chafer.* Irish myth: Cross.

B16.6.3. *Destructive locusts* (with wings of iron) eat wheat crop. Irish myth: Cross.

B16.6.4. *Devastating spider.* India: Thompson-Balys.

B16.6.5. *Devastating centipede.* Chinese: Eberhard FFC CXX 232f.

B17. *Hostile animals.* Irish myth: Cross.

B16. Devastating animals. B778 Venomous animals. G346. Devastating monster.

B17.1. *Hostile beasts.* Irish myth: Cross.

B17.1.1. *Ferocious animals loosed against attackers.* Irish myth: Cross.

B776.1. Venomous sheep destroy enemy.

B17.1.2. *Hostile dog (hound).* Irish myth: Cross.

B16.18. Devastating dog. B187. Magic dog.

B17.1.2.1. *Bloodhounds decapitate victim.* Irish myth: Cross.

B17.1.2.2. *Hostile hound killed* by reaching through hollow log in its jaws — and tearing heart out. Irish myth: Cross.

F628.1. Strong man kills animals with own hands. F981. Extraordinary death of animal.

B17.1.2.2.1. *Hero kills hostile hound (monster)* by tearing (forcing) out its entrails (heart). Irish myth: Cross.

F628.1.0.1. Strong man tears out hound's heart. F981. Extraordinary death of animal.

B17.1.2.3. *Transformed man as hostile dog.* Irish myth: Cross.
D141. Transformation: man to dog.

B17.1.3. *Hostile cattle.* Irish myth: Cross. (Cf. B15.1.5.2.)

B17.1.4. *Hostile horse.* Irish myth: Cross.
B181.7. Magic horse avenges hero's death.

B17.1.4.1. *Infuriated horses kill driver.* Irish myth: Cross.

B17.1.5. *Hostile cat.* Irish myth: Cross (B16.1.4).

B17.2. *Other hostile animals.* Irish myth: Cross.

B17.2.1. *Hostile sea-beasts.* Irish myth: Cross.
B61. Leviathan. B91.5. Sea-serpent. G308. Sea-monster.

B17.2.1.1. *Hostile sea-rat.* Irish myth: Cross.
B70. Fish-beast.

B17.2.1.2. *Hostile eel attacks hero.* Irish myth: Cross.
B15.7.12. Eel with fiery mane. R262. Magic eel pursues man over land.

B17.2.1.3. *Hostile sea-cat.* Irish myth: Cross.
B73. Sea-cat.

B17.2.2. *Hostile griffin.* Irish myth: Cross.
B42. Griffin.

B17.2.3. *Hostile raven.*

B17.2.3.1. *Raven plucks out men's eyes.* India: Thompson-Balys.

B17.2.4. *Hostile scorpion.*

B17.2.4.1. *Scorpion scoops out men's eyes.* India: Thompson-Balys.

B18. *Behemoth:* mythical gigantic animal. Jewish: Neuman.

B19. *Other mythical beasts.* Fb "solulv".
A673. Hound of hell. A878.3.1. Hart(s) eating of the earth-tree. A878.3.2. Chattering squirrel in the earth-tree.

B19.1. *Brazen-footed, fire-breathing bulls.* (Cf. B15.6, B15.5) — Frazer Apollodorus I 109 n. 4, 110 n. i.
A141.1. God makes automata and vivifies them. Hephaistos thus makes brazen giant, brazen-footed bulls, and gold and silver dogs. B182.3. Magic bull. B742. Animal breathes fire.

B19.2. *Nectar-yielding cow.* Hindu: Keith 37.
B182. Magic cow. B530. Animals nourish man. D1472. Food and drink from magic object. D1665.2. Cow whose milk tastes like honey and intoxicating wine.

B19.2.1. *The cow Audhumla.* Icel.: MacCulloch Eddic 324.
A14. Cow as creator.

B19.3. *Horse born of egg.* Mythical hero will come riding on such a horse. — Fb "Holger Danske" I 640b, "æg" III 1142b.
A580. Culture hero's expected return. B12.1. Basilisk hatched from cock's egg. B710. Fanciful origin of animal. B811.1. Helpful horses descended from heaven.

B19.3.1. *Immortal horses.* Greek: Grote I 11.

B19.3.2. *Mythical horse belonging to water-spirit.* S. A. Indian: Toba Métraux MAFLS XL 50.

B19.4. *Glowing animals.* Horses, swine, etc. which glow. (Cf. B15.4.2.) — *Wuttke Der deutsche Volksaberglaube der Gegenwart 59; *Hdwb. d. Abergl. s.v. "glühend"; *Fb "gloende". — Irish myth: Cross; Jewish: Neuman; Icel.: Boberg.

B11.12.3. Fiery dragon. B16.1.2. Cat leaps through man like arrow of fire and burns him to ashes. B172.8. Magic osprey produces lightning. B721. Cat's luminous eye. D1645. Self-luminous eyes. E501.4.1.2. Dogs with fiery tongues in wild hunt. E501.4.2.5. Horse with fiery eyes in wild hunt. E501.4.1.3. Dogs with fiery eyes in wild hunt.

B19.4.1. *Burrowing swine heat ground.* Irish myth: Cross.

B183.2. Magic swine issue from elf-mound.

B19.4.2. *Fiery serpent.* Irish myth: Cross.

B11.2.3. Fiery dragon.

B19.4.3. *Sheep with fiery collar.* Irish myth: Cross.

B189.1. Magic sheep.

B19.4.4. *Hound flame of fire by night.* Irish myth: Cross.

B187. Magic dog.

B19.5. *Horse with golden mane.* Icel.: MacCulloch Eddic 66, 153.

B19.6. *Herd which came from heaven.* India: Thompson-Balys.

B19.6.1. *Cows of the sun.* (Cf. Odyssey.) India: Thompson-Balys.

B19.7. *The goat Heidrun.* Icel.: MacCulloch Eddic 313—14.

B535.1. Goat feeds other animals from its body.

B19.8. *Mythical antelope.* Jewish: Neuman.

B19.9. *Eternal bats.* S. A. Indian (Guarani): Métraux BBAE CXLIII (3) 93.

B19.10. *Mythical tiger.* Jewish: Neuman.

B19.11. *Mythical donkey.* Jewish: Neuman.

B20. Beast-men. Combinations of bestial and human form.

B92. Beast with human head and shape of smith's bellows. F510. Monstrous persons. F526. Person with compound body. F540. Remarkable physical organs. T611.10.1. Girl suckled by wolf has nail "like wolf's nail".

B20.1. *Army of half-animals, half-men.* Jewish: Neuman.

B20.2. *Beast-men in the lower world.* Jewish: Neuman.

B21. *Centaur:* man-horse. Trunk and head of man, body of horse. — **P. V. C. Baur Centaurs in Ancient Art (Berlin, 1912); *Frazer Apollodorus I 191 n. 3, 261 n. 1; Pauli (ed. Bolte) No. 413; Howey Horse in Magic and Myth 225ff.; **Dumézil (G.) Le Probleme des Centaures (Paris, 1929); Irish myth: Cross; Jewish: Neuman; Hindu: Penzer I 202.

A132. God in animal form. B25.1.1. Dog-headed man has mane of horse (cattle). B29.8. Man with horse's mouth. B181. Magic horse.

B21.1. *Norse man-horse: "fingalkn" or "fingalp".* Icel.: Boberg.

B21.2. *Body and hands human,* head and ears those of a horse. India: Thompson-Balys.

B21.3. *Man with horse's mouth.* Irish myth: Cross.

B22. *Man-ass.* Body of man, hoofs of ass. — *Chauvin VII 82 No. 373bis, n. I; Jewish: Neuman.

B22.1. *Body of man, head of ass.* Jewish: Neuman.

B22.2. *Ass with human intelligence.* German: Grimm No. 144.

B23. *Man-bull.*

B23.1. *Minotaur.* Body of man, head of bull. Result of union of woman with bull. — Icel.: Boberg; Greek: Fox 61; Roscher Lexikon s. v. "Acheloos"; Frazer Apollodorus I 307 n. I, II 120 n. I. — Chauvin VII 87 No. 373bis n. 3. — Chinese: Ferguson 30.

B16.11. Monster ox (bull) killed. F781.1. Labyrinth. T465. Bestiality.

B23.2. *Bull with man's head.* Persian: Carnoy 333.

B23.3. *Man with (two) horns on his head.* Irish myth: Cross; Icel.: Boberg.

A131.6. Horned god.

B24. *Satyr.* Combination of man and goat. — Greek: Fox 268; Jewish: Neuman.

B29.5. Man-goat. F442. Pan. F611.1.3. Wild man son of woman and satyr who overpowers her.

B24.1. *Satyr reveals woman's infidelity.* Italian Novella: Rotunda.

B130. Truth-telling animals. U119.1. Revelations of a satyr.

B24.2. *Man with goat's head.* (Cf. A1614.1.2.) Irish myth: Cross (B29.5).

B25. *Man-dog.* Icel.: *Boberg; American Indian and Siberian: *Jochelson JE VI, 1912, 336; Eskimo (Greenland): Rasmussen I 205, III 226, 246, Holm 50, Rink 47, 111, (Central Eskimo): Boas RBAE VI 633; Hawaii: Beckwith Myth 205.

B187. Magic dog. B635.4. Son of dog. D141.0.1. Kynanthropy.

B25.1. *Man with dog's head.* *Chauvin VII 77 No. 121; H. Cordier RTP V 72ff.; Fb "hundetyrk". — Loomis White Magic 114; Irish myth: Cross; Icel.: Boberg; Jewish: Neuman; India: Thompson-Balys; Chinese: Eberhard FFC CXX 72.

B25.1.1. *Dog-headed man has mane of horse* (cattle). Irish myth: Cross.

B21. Centaur.

B25.1.2. *Dog-headed people.* Peasants persecuted by one-eyed and dog-headed savages. — Estonian: M. J. Eisen Estnische Mythologie (Leipzig 1925) pp. 202—206; Livonian: Loorits FFC LXVI 73 No. 232; Lithuanian: Balys Index No. 3911.

B25.2. *Dog with human head.* India: Thompson-Balys.

B26. *Man-tiger.* Hindu: Keith 96, Thompson-Balys.

B26.1. *Girl with tiger's legs and ears.* Indo-Chinese (Wa tribe): Scott 291.

B27. *Man-lion.* Man with lion's head. — Greek: *Grote I 7; Jewish: Neuman; Chauvin VII 87 No. 373bis n. 3.

B51. Sphinx.

B28. *Man-elephant.* Man with elephant's head. — Hindu: Keith 181.

B29. *Other combinations of beast and man.*

B29.1. *Lamia.* Face of woman, body of serpent (or body of sow, and legs of horse). — *Bolte FFC XXXIX 5 n. 1 — Icel.: Herrmann Saxo II 603; Czech: Machal Slavic 265; India: Thompson-Balys.

F582.1. Serpent damsel.

B29.2. *Echidna.* Half woman, half serpent. — Frazer Apollodorus I 131.

B29.2.1. *Serpent with human head.* Jewish: Neuman.

B29.2.2. *Man with serpent's head.* Jewish: Neuman.

B29.2.3. *Snake body-woman's head.* Aurora (New Hebrides): Codrington No. III 12.

B29.3. *Man-hog.* Irish myth: Cross; Chinese: Werner 335.

A132.7. Swine-god. B183.2. Magic swine. D136. Transformation: man to swine. F241.3.1. Fairy-swine.

B29.4. *Man-cat.* Irish myth: Cross.

B29.4.1. *Man with cat's head.* Irish myth: Cross.

A131.3. Cat-headed god.

B29.4.1.1. *Man with head and tail of cat.* Irish myth: Cross.

C7369.4. Ogre has head and tail of a cat.

B29.5. *Man-wolf.* Icel.: Boberg.

D113.1.1. Wer-wolf.

B29.6. *Man-elk.* Hrolfs saga kr. ch. 20.

B29.7. *Man-bear.* Jewish: Neuman.

B29.8. *Man-hedgehog.* Upper half of body like hedgehog. — German: Grimm 108.

B29.9. *Man-ape.* Jewish: Neuman.

B30. Mythical birds. Penzer VII 56 n.; Hawaii: Beckwith Myth 29.

A132.6.1. Bird-god. F234.1.15. Fairy in form of bird.

B30.1. *Mythical white albatross.* Hawaii: Beckwith Myth 92.

B30.2. *Mythical cock.* Icel.: MacCulloch Eddic 276, 303, 313, 331, Boberg.

B171. Magic cock.

B31.1. *Roc.* A giant bird which carries off men in its claws. — Irish myth: Cross; German: Grimm Nos. 51, 161; Penzer I 103ff., II 219; Chauvin VI 3 No. 181 n. 3; Burton I 154 n., V 122f., VI 16n, 48ff., S III 186, S VII 249. —Hawaii: Beckwith Myth 45. — N. A. Indian: Thompson Tales 318 n. 151.

B552. Man carried by bird. G351. Eagle as ogre. K186.1.1. Hero sewed up in animal hide so as to be carried to height by bird. K521.1.1. Man sewed in animal's hide carried off by birds.

B31.1.0.1. *The bird Ziz,* Hebrew counterpart of roc. Jewish: Neuman.

B31.1.1. *Roc's egg.* *Chauvin VI 93 No. 256, VII 10 No. 373B.

X1036. The great egg.

B31.1.2. *Roc drops rock on ship.* Rock is so large that it destroys ship. — *Chauvin VII 21 No. 373E n. 1; *Basset 1001 Contes I 158.

B31.2. *The Bird Gam.* Throws sand in a stream and makes a lake. Appears at turn of century. Also carries men. Leaps into the sea and sleeps. — Fb "Fugl Gam", "Gam" IV 173b. — Kristensen Danske Sagn II (1893) 131ff., (1928) 94. — Icel.: *Boberg.

F531.1.8.8. Giant in a gam's shape. G531. Eagle as ogre. N812.1. Giant ogre as helper. P272. Foster-mother.

B31.3. *Giant ravens.* They sit on mountain; when they fly, avalanche comes. — Swiss: Jegerlehner Oberwallis 323 No. 139.

B31.3.1. *Giant swimming raven.* Irish myth: Cross.

B31.4. *Giant bat.* *Chauvin VII n. 9.

B31.5. *Simorg:* giant bird. — Chauvin VII 12; Malone PMLA XLIII 404.

B31.6. *Other giant birds.* Penzer I 104, VI 123 n. — Chinese: Giles Strange Stories of a Chinese Studio (New York, 1927) 547. — Africa (Basuto): Jacottet 222 No. 33.

A284.2. Thunderbird.

B31.6.1. *Giant blackbird.* Irish myth: Cross.

B172.10. Black birds.

B31.6.2. *Giant bird pulls up oak tree* by roots. Irish myth: Cross.

F531.3.10. Giants carry trees. F621.2. Trees pulled up by giant.

B31.6.2.1. *Giant bird alighting on oak tree causes it to tremble.* Irish myth: Cross.

B32. *Phoenix.* *Hdwb. d. deutschen Aberglaubens I 180; *Gunkel Das Märchen im alten Testament 36f.; Roscher Lexikon III 3450 s. v. "Phoinix". — Fb "Phoenix". — Medieval Romance: Wells Manual of Writings 105 (Prose Alexander). — Chinese: Ferguson 98, Eberhard FFC CXX 117 No. 73; Irish myth: Cross; Jewish: Neuman.

B32.1. *Phoenix renews youth.* Fb "ørn" III 1183b; Egyptian: Müller 165f.

B32.1.1. *Phoenix renews youth when 1,000 years old.* Jewish: Neuman.

B33. *Man-eating birds.* Irish myth: Cross; Greek: Fox 84; S. A. Indian (Toba): Métraux MAFLS XL 72.

B16. Devastating animals.

B33.1. *Other devastating birds.* Irish myth: Cross.

B15.7.13. Bird with fiery beak. B.16. Devastating animals.

B33.1.1. *Devastating birds wither everything* with their breath. Irish myth: Cross.

D1500.4.2. Magic breath causes disease.

B33.1.2. *Devastating birds destroy grass.* Irish myth: Cross.

F234.1.15. Fairy in form of bird.

B33.1.3. *Black birds destroy crops.* Irish myth: Cross.

B33.1.4. *Devastating birds with poisonous spells on their wings.* Irish myth: Cross.

D1273.Magic formula (charm). D2061.1.3. Poisoning by magic.

B34. *Bird of dawn.* Golden plumage; three feet. — Chinese: Werner 186.

B35. *Camrōsh.* Giant bird which collects seeds and sees that they are properly placed. Carries off the people's enemies. — Persian: Carnoy 289; Penzer I 103.

B36. *Milk-producing bird.* Africa (Zulu): Callaway 101; India: Thompson-Balys.

B37. *Immortal bird.* (cf. B32.) Irish myth: Cross; Jewish: Neuman.

B39. Other mythical birds.

A878.3.3. Wise eagle in the earth-tree. A878.3.4. Hawk in the earth-tree.

B39.1. *Bird from paradise.* India: Thompson-Balys.

B40. **Bird-beasts.** Breton: Sébillot Incidents s.v. "ailes".

B11.4.1. Flying dragon. E501.4.1.7. Winged dogs in wild hunt.

B41. *Bird-horse.*

B41.1. *Pegasus.* Winged horse. — Greek: Fox 34, 39, 213.

B41.2. *Flying horse.* Sometimes represented as having wings, sometimes as going through the air by magic. — *Chauvin V 228 No. 130; Fb "hest" IV 211a; BP II 134; *Hdwb. d. deutschen Märchens s. v. "Arabische Motive"; Penzer II 224; Rösch FFC LXXVII 110. — Icel.: Mac Culloch Eddic 43 (Sleipnir), 185 (Hofvarpnir). — Arabian: Burton I 160, V 246 n., VI 8, VII 46, 53, S II 85; India: *Thompson-Balys; Buddhist myth: Malalasekera II 838, 1358; Indo-Chinese: Scott Indo-Chinese 314.

A171.1. God rides through air on wind-swift horse. A724.1. Charioteer of the sun. Sun drives his horse and chariot across sky. B542.2. Escape on flying horse. B552. Man carried by bird. D1532. Magic object bears person aloft. D1626.1. Artificial flying horse. D2135. Magic air journey. F460.2.2. Mountain folk ride through air on horses.

B41.2.1. *Angel horse.* Horse draws angels' chariot. — *Howey Horse in Magic and Myth 17ff.

B42. *Griffin.* Half lion, half eagle. — *Chauvin VII 13 No. 313B; *Hdwb. d. Abergl. III 1129f.; Penzer I 104, 141 n. 2; Irish myth: Cross; Icel.: *Boberg; Jewish: Neuman.

A2232.4. Griffin disdains to go on ark; drowned: hence extinct. B17.2.2. Hostile griffin. B542.2.1. Transportation to fairyland on griffin's back. N575. Griffin as guardian of treasure.

B42.1. *Hippogriff.* Horse with fore-quarters of griffin. — Howey Horse in Magic and Myth 232.

B43. *Winged bull.* Spence Myths of Bab. & Assyr. 289f.; India: Thompson-Balys; Jewish: Neuman.

B1823. Magic bull.

B43.1. *Flying buffalo.* India: *Thompson-Balys.

B44. *Bird-bear.* Icel.: Herrman Saxo II 174ff., *Boberg.

B45. *Air-going elephant.* Hindu: Tawney I 328, II 540; India: *Thompson-Balys.

B447.11.2. Hero rides on winged elephant. D411.2.1. Transformation: white rat to white-winged elephant. J2133.5.2. Numskull going to heaven holding on tail of divine elephant, loses his hold to make gesture. He and all holding on to him fall.

B46. *Vasa Mortis.* Bird with four heads, middle like a whale, feathers and feet of a griffin. — Old English: Solomon and Saturnus (Grein-Wülcker) III (2) 58—82, lines 262ff.

B47. *Winged camel.* Jewish: Neuman; India: Thompson-Balys.

B48. *Flying crustacean.* (Cf. B62, B94.) India: Thompson-Balys.

B49. *Bird-beasts — miscellaneous.*

B49.1. *Bird with crocodile head.* Jewish: Neuman;

B49.2. *Flying ape.* Chinese: Eberhard FFC CXX 235.

B49.3. *Flying fox.* Chinese: Eberhard FFC CXX 235.

B50. **Bird-men.** Irish myth: Cross.

A132.6.2. Goddess in form of bird. F234.1.15. Fairy in form of bird.

B51. *Sphinx.* Has face of woman, body and tail of lion, wings of bird. — **Laistner Rätsel der Sphinx; *Frazer Apollodorus I 349 n. 1; **J. Ilberg Die Sphinx in der griechischen Kunst und Saga (Leipzig, 1896); Köhler-Bolte I 115.

B27. Man-lion. C822. Tabu: solving sphinx's riddle. H541.1.1. Sphinx propounds riddle on pain of death. H761. Riddle of the sphinx.

B52. *Harpy.* Bird with arms and breasts of woman. — Greek: Fox 111, *Grote I 216f.; Buddhist myth: Malalasekera II 564.

B53. *Siren.* Bird with woman's head. — *Encyclopaedia Britannica s.v. "sirens"; Bolte Zs. f. Vksk. XIX 310 n. 1 (here considered as half fish, half woman); Roscher Lexikon s.v. "Seirenen"; Penzer VI 282 n. 6; *Frazer Apollodorus I 21, II 291 n. 2; *Weicker Der Seelenvogel in d. alten Literatur und Kunst. — Slavic: Machal 260; Livonian: Loorits FFC LXVI 41 No. 26. — Breton: Sébillot Incidents s.v. "sirène"; Gascon: Bladé II 342 No. 10; Jewish: Neuman.

D1275. Magic song. D1355.1.1. Love-producing song. F302.3.1. Fairy entices man into fairyland. J672.1. Ears stopped with wax to avoid enchanting song. Odysseus and the Sirens.

B53.0.1. *Siren in mermaid form.* Irish myth: Cross.

B81. Mermaid. F302.3.1. Fairy entices man into fairyland. J672.1. Ears stopped with wax to avoid enchanting song. Odysseus and the Sirens.

B53.1. *Drowning man rescued by siren.* Breton: Sébillot Incidents s. v. "noyé".

N810. Supernatural helpers.

B53.2. *Man suckled by siren.* Dickson Valentine and Orson 110 n. 26, 112.

T611. Suckling of children.

B53.3. *Gold thrown on shore by siren.* Breton: Sébillot Incidents s. v. "or".

B53.4. *Siren's song causes sleep.* Irish myth: Cross.

B55. *Man with bird's head.* Chauvin VII 77 No. 121.

B56. *Garuda-bird.* Lower part man, upper part bird. — *Penzer I 103, VII 56 n. X 159; Chauvin V 228, VII 12. — Siberian: Holmberg Siberian 345. — Indonesian: Dixon 224. — Panchatantra (trans. Ryder) 94ff.; Penzer-Tawney X 159 "Garuda".

B57. *"Finngálkn"*, bird with a man's head. Icel.: *Boberg.

B60. **Mythical fish.** India: *Thompson-Balys.

B11.2.1.3. Dragon as modified fish. B17.2.1. Hostile sea-beasts. B91.5. Sea-serpent. B175. Magic fish. B872. Giant fish. G308. Sea- (lake-) monster.

B60.1. *Parent of all fishes.* Hawaii: Beckwith Myth 24.

B61. *Leviathan.* Giant fish. — Hebrew: Job 41:1, Psalms 104:26, Isaiah 27:1; Jewish: *Neuman. — Irish myth: Cross; India: Thompson-Balys.

A876.1. The Leviathan that surrounds the globe. A1145.2. Earthquakes from movements from sea monster. B16.4.1. Leviathan casts up gorge which spreads disease. F911.4. Jonah. X1723. Lies about swallowing.

B62. *Flying fish.* Irish myth: Cross.

24

B63. *Mythical octopus.* Hawaii: Beckwith Myth 22; Marquesas: Handy 74.

B64. *Mythical eel.* Hawaii: Beckwith Myth 102f.

B65. *Mythical shark.* Hawaii: Beckwith Myth 128—132.

B68. *Horned water-monster.* S. A. Indian (Chaco): Beliaeff BBAE CXLIII (1) 379.

B70. **Fish-beasts.** *Loomis White Magic 64f.

B17.2.1. Hostile sea-rat. F420.1.2. Water-spirit in animal form. F713.3. Lake-monster turning over causes lake to overflow surrounding mountains.

B71. *Sea horse.* Horse living in sea. — *Chauvin VII 7 No. 373a n. 1; *Howey Horse in Magic and Myth 133ff.; Tobler Epiphanie der Seele 97. — Irish myth: Cross; Scotch: MacDougall and Calder 309ff.; Livonian: Loorits FFC LXVI 42 No. 31. — Chinese: Ferguson 30.

A171.0.1. God drives chariot over waves. B401.1. Helpful water-horse. B611.3.1. Sea-horse paramour. F241.1. Fairies' horses.

B72. *Sea cow.* Cow living in sea. — Irish myth: Cross. — Livonian: Loorits FFC LXVI 42 No. 32; Danish: Kristensen Danske Sagn (1893) 153ff., (1928) 105ff.; India: Thompson-Balys.

B184.2.2.2. Magic cow from water world.

B72.1. *Three sea-cows:* one red, one white, one black. Irish myth: Cross.

F421.2. Fairies' cows. Z65.1.1. Red as blood, white as snow, black as raven.

B73. *Sea-cat.* Irish myth: Cross.

B17.2.1.3. Hostile sea-cat. B184. Magic cat.

B80. **Fish-men.** Tobler Epiphanie der Seele 98.

B53. Sirens.

B80.1. *Seal-man.* Irish myth: Cross.

B80.2. *Monster half-man, half-fish.* S. A. Indian (Toba): Métraux MAFLS XL 30.

B81. *Mermaid.* Woman with tail of fish. Lives in sea. — BP III 324; *Fb "havfrue" I, 569, IV 204a; Thien Motive in König Rother 42; Tobler Epiphanie der Seele 98. — Breton: Sébillot Incidents s.v. "poisson". Icel.: *Boberg; Estonian: Hartland Science of Fairy Tales 201; Irish myth: Cross; Livonian: Loorits FFC LXVI 41 No. 26; Lappish: Qvigstad FFC LX 46 Nos. 58—63; North Carolina: Brown Collection I 636; Jewish: Neuman; India: Thompson-Balys.

B53.0.1. Siren in mermaid form. D361.1. Swan maiden. D1410.4. Possession of mermaid's belt gives power over her. D1719.7. Magic power of mermaid. D1812.5.1.9. Sight of mermaid bad omen. F423. Sea-spirits. F611.2.2. Strong hero suckled by mermaid. R137. Mermaid rescues heroine, who has been thrown overboard. S214. Child promised to mermaid.

B81.0.1. *Mermaids are like fishes in the water,* like men on land. Icel.: Boberg.

B81.0.2. *Woman from water world.* Irish myth: Cross.

F212. Fairyland under water.

B81.1. *Mermaids from Pharoah's children.* They were drowned in the Red Sea. — Livonian: Loorits FFC LXVI 41 No. 27.

E600. Reincarnation.

B81.2. *Mermaid marries man.* Fb "havfrue" IV 204a. — Krappe Archiv für das Studium der neueren Sprachen 159 (1931) 161—175; Irish myth: Cross; Livonian: Loorits FFC XLVI 40 No. 25; Lappish: Qvigstad FFC LX 45f. Nos. 55, 57.

B600. Marriage of person to animal. F300. Marriage or liaison with fairy. F302. Fairy mistress. F460.4.1. Mountain-girl marries mortal man. T111. Marriage of mortal and supernatural being.

B81.2.1. *Mermaid has son by human father.* *Fb "havfrue" I 569b, IV 204a; Icel.: *Boberg.

B81.2.2. *Mermaids tear their mortal lovers to pieces.* Irish myth: Cross.

F302.3.4. Fairies entice men and then harm them.

B81.3. *Mermaid leads people astray.* Fb "havfrue" I 569b.

B81.3.1. *Mermaid appears at midnight,* entices people into water. England: Baughman.

B81.3.2. *Mermaid appears once each year,* sings in choir, entices young man to follow her. England: Baughman.

B81.4. *Mermaid captures a maiden.* *Fb "havfrue" IV 204a.

R11.1. Princess (maiden) abducted by monster (ogre).

B81.5. *Mermaid sits on knight's bedpost.* *Fb "havfrue" I 569b.

B81.6. *Mermaid has human midwife.* *Fb "havfrue" I 569b.

F372.1. Fairies take human midwife to attend fairy woman. T584. Parturition.

B81.7. *Mermaid warns of bad weather.* *Fb "havfrue" I 569b, IV 204a. Danish: Kristensen Danske Sagn II (1893) 143ff., (1928) 101ff.

B81.7.1. *Mermaid prophesies.* Icel.: Boberg.

D1812. Magic power of prophecy. M301. Prophets. M340. Unfavorable prophesies. N456. Enigmatical smile (laugh) reveals secret knowledge.

B81.8. *Mermaid cannot pass through ice.* *Fb "havfrue" I 569b.

B81.9. *Appearance of mermaid.* Fb "havfrue" IV 204a; Irish myth: Cross.

B81.9.1. *Mermaid's hair reaches her waist.* *Fb "hår" I 771b.

G219.4. Witches' hair reaches to ground.

B81.9.1.1. *Mermaid has wooly hair.* U.S.: Baughman.

B81.9.2. *Mermaid has large breasts.* *Fb "havfrue" IV 204a; Boberg.

B81.9.3. *Mermaid half-beautiful, half-monstrous.* Irish myth: Cross.

B81.9.4. *Giant mermaid.* Irish myth: Cross. (Cf. B81.13.13.)

F531. Giant.

B81.9.5. *Skin of mermaid.*

B81.9.5.1. *Mermaid has white skin.* Scotland: Baughman.

B81.9.5.2. *Mermaid has brown skin.* England, U.S.: *Baughman.

B81.10. *Mermaid swallows man.* Irish myth: Cross; Italian Novella: Rotunda.

F585.1. Fatal enticements of phantom women. F910. Extraordinary swallowings.

B81.11. *Mermaid's singing causes sleep.* Girl tumbles from boat and drowns. — Irish myth: Cross.

B53.4. Siren's song causes sleep. D1364.24. Music causes magic sleep. D1960. Magic sleep.

B81.12. *When mermaid appears.*

B81.12.1. *Mermaid appears at midnight.* England: Baughman.

B81.12.2. *Mermaid appears once each year.* England: Baughman.

B81.13. *Miscellaneous actions of mermaid.*

B81.13.1. *Mermaid asks captain to move boat* which blocks entrance to her dwelling. England, U.S.: *Baughman.

B81.13.2. *Mermaid is washed up on beach.* Wales, England: *Baughman.

B81.13.3. *Sight of mermaid bathing* makes man immortal. England: Baughman.

B81.13.4. *Mermaid gives mortals gold* from sea bottom. England: Baughman.

B81.13.5. *Giant mermaid (man) cast ashore.* Irish myth: Cross.

B81.13.6. *Mermaid sings divinely in church* (before enticing man away). England: Baughman.

B81.13.7. *Mermaid appears as omen* of catastrophe. Ireland, England: *Baughman.

B81.13.8. *Curse by mermaid.* Ireland, England: *Baughman.

B81.13.9. *Mermaid ruins seducer* of her adopted daughter. England: Baughman.

B81.13.10. *Mermaid prevents raising of sunken church bell.* (See C401.4.) England: Baughman.

B81.13.11. *Mermaid captured.* Irish myth: Cross.

D361.1. Swan maiden.

B81.13.11.1. *Mermaid caught by fishermen.* Irish myth: Cross.

B81.13.12. *Mermaid lives for three hundred years* under lake. Irish myth: Cross.

D1857. Magic longevity.

B82. *Merman.* Fb "havmand" IV 205a; *Chauvin V 7 No. 3. — Arabian: Burton V 215, VII 254, 264, 270, IX 169 n., 179, 182ff.; Icelandic: Hálfs saga ok Hálfsrekka (ed. Andrews) 82; Buddhist myth: Malalasekera I 723; Jewish: Neuman; India: Thompson-Balys.

D131.1. Transformation: merman to horse. D1639.3. Images at church turn backs as mark of disfavor. Done when abandoned woman or merman enters.

B82.1. *Merman marries maiden.* Fb "havmand" I 571a; English ballad: *Child I 366; Danish: Grundtvig Danmarks Gamle Folkeviser No. 38. — Literary treatment: Arnold "The Forsaken Merman".

C713. Forsaken merman. F301. Fairy lover. F322.0.1. Woman carried off by water-fairy.

B82.1.1. *Merman demands princess.* *Fb "havmand" I 571a; Gaster Thespis 176.

R11.1. Princess (maiden) abducted by monster (ogre).

B82.1.2. *Harp music makes merman restore stolen bride.* *Fb "havmand" I 571a, II 725.

B82.2. *Merman demands cattle as offering.* *Fb "havmand" I 571a.

S260. Sacrifices.

B82.3. *Youth takes service with merman.* *Fb "havmand" I 571a.
F376. Mortal as servant in fairyland.

B82.4. *Merman teaches music.* *Fb "nökke" II 725a.

B82.5. *Merman attacked by putting steel in the water.* *Fb "nökke" II 725a.
F384.2. Steel powerful against fairies.

B82.6. *Merman caught by fisherman (released).* England: Baughman.

B82.7. *Merman lays hands on side of canoe.* U. S.: Baughman.

B83. *Fish with human face.* *Chauvin 8 No. 373A n. 2.

B90. Other mythical animals.

B91. *Mythical serpent.* Borgese "Giganti e Serpenti" Archivio per lo Studio delle tradizioni popolari XX 507ff., XXI 90ff., 161ff. — Hindu: Penzer I 109 n. 2, II 90 n. 2, 266, III 259 n. 1. — Indo-Chinese: Scott 301; India: Thompson-Balys.
A876. Midgard Serpent. B11. Dragon. B15.1.2.10.2. Hundred-headed serpent. B16.9. Devastating man-eating seamonster (serpent). B19.4.2. Fiery serpent. B61. Leviathan.

B91.1. *Naga.* Serpent demon. — Penzer I 203f., VI 28 n. 2; India: Thompson-Balys; Buddhist myth: Malalasekera II 1354.

B91.2. *Plumed serpent.* Hopi, Zuñi: Alexander N. Am. 188.

B91.3. *Horned snake.* Jewish: Neuman; N. A. Indian: *Thompson Tales 357 n. 287f.; (Micmac): Parsons JAFL XXXVIII 95 No. 27; (Cherokee): Alexander N. Am. 68f.; Ladino (Honduras, Nicaragua): Conzemius BBAE CVI 169.

B91.4. *Sky-traveling snake.* N. A. Indian (Zuñi): Alexander N. Am. 188.

B91.5. *Sea-serpent.* *Oudemans (A. C.) The Great Sea-Serpent (London 1892). — Norwegian: Storaker (J.T.) Naturrigerne i den norske Folketro (Oslo 1928) 249; Solheim Register 17; Irish myth: Cross; Icel.: Boberg.
B11.3.1. Dragon's home at bottom of sea. B15.7.12. Eel with fiery mane. B16.9. Devastating (man-eating) sea-monster (serpent). B875. Giant seamonster G308. Sea- (lake-) monster. X1396.1. Lie: sea-serpent.

B91.5.1. *Sea-serpent dilates and contracts.* Irish myth: Cross.
B750. Fanciful habits of animals. D631. Size changed at will.

B91.5.2. *Lake-serpent (monster).* Irish myth: Cross.

B91.5.2.1. *Lake-serpent (monster) in form of woman.* Irish myth: Cross.
B81.2.3.1. Mermaid caught by fisherman.

B91.6. *Serpent causes flood.* Irish myth: Cross.
A1011. Local deluges.

B91.7. *Serpent is immortal.* Gaster Oldest Stories 81.

B92. *Other mythical reptiles.* Hawaii: Beckwith Myth 125.

B93. *Mythical spider.* India: Thompson-Balys.

B94. *Mythical crustacean.*

B94.1. *Mythical crab.* India: Thompson-Balys.

B95. *Vegetable lamb.* Generated from ground. Umbilical cord is in the ground and the lambs will die if it is forcibly severed. They are frightened into severing it themselves and then live. Vertebrae of the neck planted to produce new ones. — *Laufer JAFL XXVIII 115ff.

B95.1. *Vegetable lamb born from melons* (as from eggs). — Laufer JAFL XXVIII 124.

B95.2. *Marine lamb.* Wool taken from sea lamb. (Really textiles from shell-fish pinna). — Laufer JAFL XXVIII 103ff.

B96. *Beast with human head and shape of smith's bellows.* Irish myth: Cross.

B98. *Mythical frog.* S. A. Indian (Warrau): Métraux RMLP XXXIII 140.

B99. *Mythical animals — miscellaneous.* Africa (Ekoi): Talbot 371, (Zanzibar): Bateman 158 No. 8, (Basuto): Jacottet 70, 200, 276, (Ibo of Nigeria): Thomas 147, (Kaffir): Theal 84, 172.

B99.1. *Mythical salamander.* Jewish: Neuman.

B99.2. *Mythical worm.* Jewish: Neuman.

B100—B199. Magic animals.

B100—B119. TREASURE ANIMALS

B100. Treasure animals.
*Clouston Tales I 123 ff.; India: Thompson-Balys; Penzer I 20 n., VIII 59 n. 3; Cox 510 n. 54.

B300. Helpful animals. B562.1. Animal shows man treasure. D468.1.1. Transformation: handkerchief with three knots to golden leopard, golden snake, and golden monkey. D876. Magic treasure animal killed: goose that laid the golden egg. D1450. Magic object furnishes treasure. D2100. Magic wealth.

B100.1. *Treasure found in slain helpful animal.* *Cox Cinderella passim. — Lithuanian: Leskien 448 No. 25; Breton: Luzel III 134; Portuguese: Pedroso 76 No. 18.

B335. Helpful animal killed by hero's enemy.

B100.2. *Magic animal supplies treasure.* *Cox 510; BP III 60, I 346 (Gr. Nos. 130, 36). — Maliseet: Thompson CColl II 413.

B101. *Animals with members of precious metal* (jewels).

B101.1. *Bird with golden head.* Irish myth: Cross; Jewish: Neuman.

B101.1.1. *Bird with wings of silver.* Irish myth: Cross.

B101.1.2. *Bird with golden feet.* Jewish: Neuman.

B101.2. *Treasure-hog.* Alternate bristles of gold and silver; at each step a side of pork falls from him. — Fb "galt".

D1025.1. Magic pigskin.

B101.2.1. *Boar with golden bristles.* Icel.: MacCulloch Eddic 109, 266.

B101.3. *Ram with golden fleece.* Cox 510 n. 54. — Icel.: *Boberg; Greek: Fox 108.

D1025. Magic skin of animal.

B101.4. *Hind with golden horns.* Greek: *Frazer Apollodorus I 190 n. 1.
B188. Magic deer. B731.7.2. Fawn with golden lustre.

B101.4.1. *Stag with golden antlers and silver feet.* Irish myth: Cross.
B15.3.3. Deer with giant antler. B731.7. Fancifully colored deer.

B101.4.2. *Stag with gold and silver on horns and neck, and a silver bell.* Göngu-Hrólfs saga 273.

B101.5. *Monster (whale) with golden teeth.* Irish myth: Cross.
B872.3.1. Whale cast ashore — three golden teeth and five ounces in each of these teeth.

B101.6. *Fish with gold and silver heads.* *Fb "fiske".
D1011. Magic animal — head.

B101.7. *Serpent with jewel in head.* (Cf B112, B176). — *BP II 464; Cosquin Les contes indiens 256ff.; Fb "ædelsten". — Penzer IV 245; Indonesian: Dixon 159 n. 20, 328 n. 20; India: *Thompson-Balys; U.S.: Baughman; Cherokee: Alexander N. Am. 68f; Africa (Cameroon): Meinhof 60.
B11.2.14. Dragon with jewel in head. B722. Magic stone in animal's head. B722.3. Luminous jewel in animal's head. D1011. Magic head of animal. H1151.1.26. Task: bringing ruby in head of devastating serpent.

B101.8. *Cow with silver horns.* Irish myth: Cross.

B101.8.1. *Big ox with gold and silver in the horns.* Icel: *Boberg.

B101.9. *Mongoose with golden hair and silver ears.* India: Thompson-Balys.

B102. *Animal of precious metal (jewels).*

B102.1. *Golden bird.* Bird with golden feathers. *Type 550. — Cox 510 n. 54; Fb "fugl", "guldfugl", "fjer" — India: Thompson-Balys; Hindu: Keith 149, Tawney II 507; Panchatantra (trans. Ryder) 333; Missouri French: Carrière.
B122.0.2. Wise golden peacock. B143.1.5. Golden cock warns against attack. H1331.1.3. Quest for golden bird.

B102.1.1. Golden hawk. Icel.: *Boberg.

B102.1.2. *Golden peacock.* India: Thompson-Balys; Buddhist myth: Malalasekera I 1052.

B102.1.3. *Golden goose.* India: Thompson-Balys; Buddhist myth: Malalasekera II 581, 1264.

B102.2. *Golden horse.* (Cf. B181.) — Cox 510 n. 54; Fb "guldhest"; Danish: Kristensen Danske Sagn III (1895) 461ff., (1931) 316ff.; Icel.: *Boberg; India: Thompson-Balys; Missouri French: Carrière.
H1151.9. Task: stealing troll's golden horse.

B102.3. *Golden deer. India:* *Thompson-Balys; Buddhist myth: Malalasekera I 1131.

B102.4. *Golden fish.* Breton: Sébillot Incidents s.v. "poisson"; India: Thompson-Balys; Irish myth: Cross.

B102.4.1. *Fish of silver.* Irish myth: Cross.

B102.5. *Golden calf.* India: *Thompson-Balys.

B102.5.1. *Silver calf.* Chinese: Eberhard FFC CXX 85.

B102.6. *Golden serpent.* German: Grimm No. 136.

B102.7. *Golden dog.* Jewish: Neuman.

B102.8. *Golden crab.* Buddhist myth: Malalasekera I 249.

B103. *Treasure-producing animals.*

B756. Gold-digging ants.

B103.0.1. *Treasure-producing turkey.* N. Am. Indian (Zuñi): Cushing Zuñi Folk-Tales 54ff.

B103.0.2. *Magic bird produces unlimited food.* Irish myth: Cross; Indonesian: Dixon 238 n. 51.

D1652.1. Inexhaustible food.

B103.0.3. *Gold-producing ram.* Penzer I 20 n.

B103.0.4. *Gold-producing serpent.* Penzer I 20 n.

B103.0.4.1. *Grateful snake gives gold piece daily.* India: Thompson-Balys.

B103.0.5. *Treasure-giving goat.* Fb "buk" IV 77a; Boberg.

B103.0.6. *Gold-producing lion.* Penzer I 20 n.

B103.0.7. *Magic jewel obtained from elephant.* India: *Thompson-Balys.

B103.0.8. *Treasure received from tiger.* India: Thompson-Balys.

B103.1. *Treasure-dropping animals.*

B103.1.1. *Gold-producing ass.* Droppings of gold. — *Type 563; **Aarne JSFO XXVII (1909) 1—96; Cox 510 n. 54; Penzer V 11 n. 1; *BP I 349ff. (Gr. No. 36). — Breton: Sébillot Incidents s.v. "âne"; French Canadian: Barbeau JAFL XXIX 10; Missouri French: Carrière; Italian: Basile Pentamerone I No. 1; Philippine: Fansler MAFLS XII 196; Japanese: Ikeda.

B103.1.2. *Cow drops gold dung.* India: *Thompson-Balys.

B103.1.2.1. *Pearl-dropping cow.* India: Thompson-Balys.

B103.1.3. *Gold-producing dog.* Droppings of gold. — Penzer V 11 n. 1; Chinese: Eberhard FFC CXX 35f.

B103.1.4. *Gold-making deer.* Chinese: Eberhard FFC CXX 35ff.

B103.1.5. *Gold-making bird.* Chinese: Eberhard FFC CXX 35f.

B103.1.6. *Magic tortoise fed with salt gives pearls.* Chinese: Eberhard FFC CXX 222.

B103.2. *Treasure-laying animals.*

B103.2.1. *Treasure-laying bird.* Bird lays money or golden eggs or an egg at every step. — Köhler-Bolte I 409; Cox 510 n. 54; Fb "höne" I 570b. — Icel.: *Boberg; Breton: Sébillot Incidents s.v. "oiseau"; India: *Thompson-Balys, Panchatantra III 14, (Ryder tr.) 359.

B192. Magic animal killed. D876. Magic treasure animal killed: goose that laid the golden egg. D1019. Magic egg.

B103.3. *Animal giving treasure as milk.*

B103.3.1. *Goat giving coins instead of milk.* India: *Thompson-Balys.

D1454.3. Treasure from excrements.

B103.4. *Animal spitting (vomiting) treasure.*

B103.4.1. *Fish with coin in mouth.* Dh II 180.

B103.4.1.1. *Silver and gold run from cod's mouth.* Type 1654*.

B103.4.2. *Serpent with jewel in his mouth.* India: *Thompson-Balys.

B103.4.2.1. *Grateful snake spits out lump of gold for his rescuer.* India: Thompson-Balys.

B103.4.2.2. *Snake vomits jewels.* India: Thompson-Balys.

D1645.1. Incandescent jewel.

B103.4.3. *Dog vomits gold and silver.* Irish myth: Cross (B109.1.1).

B187. Magic dog. D2102.1. Gold vomited.

B103.5. *Animal laying treasure in water.*

B103.5.1. *Serpent lays treasure in lake.* Swiss: Jegerlehner 305, n. 3.

B103.6. *Animal producing treasure by bite.*

B103.6.1. *Serpent's bite produces ornaments and clothes.* India: Thompson-Balys.

B103.7. *Animal producing treasure at death.*

B103.7.1 *When destructive bird is killed, barn is found full of gold.* India: Thompson-Balys.

B105. *Animal bearing precious ornaments.*

B105.1. *Hind with gold chain on neck.* *Fb "hind".

B105.2. *Deer with string of pearls around its neck.* India: Thompson-Balys.

B106. *Animal lying on treasure.* Serpent with gold under him. — Fb "lindorm" II 433b.

B107. *Animal with treasure inside it.*

B107.1. *Fish with ingot of gold inside it.* Irish myth: Cross.

B548.2.1. Fish recovers ring from sea. N211.1. Lost ring found in fish.

B108. *Animal as patron of wealth.*

B108.1. *Serpent as patron of wealth.* Japanese: Anesaki 331.

B109. *Treasure animals — miscellaneous.*

B109.1. *Magic spider catches pearls.* Chinese: Eberhard FFC CXX 222.

B109.2. *Centipede plays at night with pearl.* Chinese: Eberhard FFC CXX 232f.

B110. Treasure-producing parts of animals.

B300. Helpful animals. B720. Fanciful bodily members of animal. D1010. Magic bodily members — animal. D1450. Magic object furnishes treasure. D1469.5. Worshipped sex organ of horse provides money, etc. D2100. Magic wealth.

B112. *Treasure-producing serpent's crown.* (Cf. B108.1, B115.1, B176). — — Type 672; BP II 463f. — Icel.: *Boberg; Estonian: Aarne FFC XXV 132 no. 79; Finnish: Aarne FFC XXXIII 46 No. 79; Livonian: Loorits FFC LXVI 73 No. 233.

B765.2. Snake lays aside his crown to bathe. D1011. Magic head of animal. D1011.3.1. Magic serpent's crown. D1361.9. Serpent's crown renders invisible.

B113. *Treasure-producing parts of bird.* **Aarne MSFO XXV 176 (extensive list of parts).

B113.1. *Treasure-producing bird-heart.* (Cf. D1015.1.1.) Brings riches when eaten. — **Aarne MSFO XXV 176; *Type 567; Penzer I 19 n 2; India: Thompson-Balys.

D1561.1. Magic bird-heart (when eaten) brings man to kingship. M312.3 Eater of magic bird-heart will become rich (or king).

B113.2. *Treasure-producing bird-head.* (Cf. D1011.0.1.) — *Aarne MSFO XXV 176.

B113.3. *Treasure from bird's feathers.* German: Grimm Nos. 60, 64.

B114. *Treasure-producing part of sheep.*

B114.1. *Treasure-producing sheepskin.* India: Thompson-Balys.

B115. *Animal with horn of plenty.* *Cox Cinderella 473 n. 2. — Greek: Fox 93. — India: *Thompson-Balys. — Africa (Kaffir): Theal 169, (Basuto): Jacottet 240 No. 35.

B530. Animals nourish men. D1011.1. Magic horn of animal. D1017. Magic flesh of animal. D1470.2.3. Horn of plenty. D1472. Food and drink from magic object.

B115.1. *Ear-cornucopia.* Animal furnishes treasure or supplies from its ears. — *Cox Cinderella 475 n. 2. — *Fb "tyr" III 908a, "øre" III 1181a. — Breton: Sébillot Incidents s.v. "oreille", "boeuf", "nourriture".

B115.2. *Wing-cornucopia.* Turkey supplies treasure from its wings. — Southern Ute: Lowie JAFL XXXVII 85 No. 56.

B115.3. *Animal with tail of plenty.* India: Thompson-Balys.

B119. *Treasure-producing parts of animals — miscellaneous.*

B119.1. *Dog (whose skin) turns water to wine (mead).* Irish myth: Cross.

B119.2. *Treasure produced by goat's entrails.* German: Grimm No. 130.

B119.3. *Armadillo with silver plate over its forehead.* S. A. Indian (Toba): Métraux MAFLS XL 71.

B120—B169. ANIMALS WITH MAGIC WISDOM

B120. Wise animals. India: Thompson-Balys.

B733. Animals are spirit-sighted. D1300. Magic object gives supernatural wisdom. J130. Wisdom (knowledge) acquired from animals. K423.0.1. Stolen animal returns to owner.

B120.0.1. *Animals have second sight.* Irish myth: Cross.

D1825.1. Second sight.

B121. *Beasts with magic wisdom.*

B121.1. *Dog with magic wisdom.* — Krappe "The dog king" Scandinavian Studies XVII (1942) 148ff., Icel.: *Boberg; Jewish: Neuman; Irish: Beal. XXI 310.

B134. Truth-telling dog. B152. Dog indicates pregnant woman (adulteress). B153. Dog indicates hidden treasure. B187. Magic dog. B421. Helpful dog. B521.3.1. Dogs warn against witch. E761.7.5. Life token: dogs pulling on leash.

B121.1.1. *Infallible hunting-dog.* Greek: Fox 72; Irish myth: Cross.

B187.3.2. Dog sight of which renders game helpless. D1653. Infallible article.

B121.2. *Fox as alchemist.* Chinese: Werner 381, Krappe CFQ III (1944) 125f.

B121.3. *Cat with magic wisdom.* Jewish: Neuman.

B121.4. *Ass (mule) with magic wisdom.* Jewish: Neuman.

B121.5. *Ox with magic wisdom.* Jewish: Neuman.

B121.6. *Lion with magic wisdom.* German: Grimm No. 67.

B122. *Bird with magic wisdom.* (Cf. A1904, B130, B211.3.) — Persian: Carnoy 291; India: *Thompson-Balys.

B122.0.1. *Wise magpie.* Calif. Indian: Gayton and Newman 57.

B122.0.2. *Wise golden peacock.* India: Thompson-Balys.
B102.1. Golden bird.

B122.0.3. *Wise owl.* India: Thompson-Balys; Buddhist myth: Malalasekera I 1038.

B122.0.4. *Prophesying parrot.* India: *Thompson-Balys; Buddhist myth: Malalasekera I 1038.

B122.0.5. *Wise eagle* (in Yggdrasil). Icel.: MacCulloch Eddic 332.

B122.1. *Bird as adviser.* *BP II 534. — Irish myth: Cross; Greek Grote I 105; Icel.: Gering-Symons Edda-Kommentar II 226; Völsunga saga ch. 19—20 (19); English and Germanic: Wimberly Folklore in Ballads 44ff. — India: *Thompson-Balys; Tibet: Schiefner-Ralston Tibetan Tales 129; Japanese: Ikeda; Chinese: Eberhard FFC CXX 67; Africa: Frobenius Atlantis III 244, IV 56; Am. Negro (Georgia): Harris Remus 107 No. 22, Nights 118 No. 22; S. A. Indian (Chiriguano): Métraux RMLP XXXIII 142.

B122.1.1. *Birds tell a secret.* Chauvin II 107. — Icel.: *Boberg, Ragnars saga ch. 9 (8) p. 134, Völsunga saga ch. 19—20 (19).
B560. Animals advise men.

B122.1.2. *Bird reveals druidic secrets.* Irish myth: Cross.

B122.2. *Birds as reporters of sights and sounds.* Sit on Odin's shoulder and report what they see and hear. — Icel.: MacCulloch Eddic 65, Krappe Etudes 29ff.
A165.0.1. Ravens as attendants of god. B575. Animal as constant attendant of man. C92.1. Tabu: killing raven (Odin's bird).

B122.3. *Bird can recite sacred writings.* Persian: Carnoy 290.

B122.4. *Bird announces time for sunrise and sunset.* Chinese: Werner 186f.
J2272.1. Chanticleer believes that his crowing makes the sun rise.

B122.5. *Wise mother eagle* distinguishes between stupid and intelligent eaglets. Irish myth: Cross.

B122.6. *Bird summarizes history.* Irish myth: Cross.

B122.7. *Cock helper advises of coming enemy.* India: Thompson-Balys.
B176. Magic serpent.

B122.8. *Parrot scout sent to enemy camp to ascertain strength.* Buddhist myth: Malalasekera II 980.
K2350. Military strategy.

B123. *Wise reptile.*

B123.1. *Wise serpent.* (Cf. B161—165, B176.) — *Scott Thumb 173. — Hebrew: Genesis 3:1; Jewish: Neuman; Arabian: Burton III 145, V 305, 328, 390; India: Thompson-Balys.

B505. Magic object received from animal.

B123.1.1. *Serpent's wisdom from eating from tree of knowledge.* Jewish: Neuman.

A165. Tree of knowledge.

B124. *Wise fish.* (Cf. B175.)

B142. Prophetic fish. B211.5. Speaking fish. B243. King of fishes. B470. Helpful fish. D1318.2.1. Laughing fish reveals unjust judgment.

B124.1. *Salmon as oldest and wisest of animals.* Welsh: MacCulloch Celtic 189; Irish myth: Cross.

B124.1.1. *Salmon of knowledge.* Irish myth: Cross.

B126. *Amphibian with magic knowledge.*

B126.1. *Frog with magic knowledge.* Jewish: Neuman.

B130. Truth-telling animals.

B120. Wise animals. B150. Oracular animals. B560. Animals attend and advise men. D1316. Magic object reveals truth. H200. Tests of truth. J130. Wisdom (knowledge) acquired from animals.

B131. *Bird of truth.* A bird which reveals the truth. (Cf. B122, B141, B172.) — *Type 707; *BP II 380 (Gr. No. 96); *Köhler-Bolte I 118; *Fb "fugl". — Breton: Sébillot Incidents s.v. "oiseau"; Jewish: Neuman; Arabian: Burton Arabian Nights SV 245; India: *Thompson-Balys; Japanese: Ikeda. — Africa (Angola): Chatelain 153 No. 16, (Ibo [Nigeria]): Thomas 48, (Fjort): Dennett 92 No. 23, (Gold Coast): Barker and Sinclair 78 No. 12.

B211.9. Speaking bird. B450. Helpful bird. H1331.1.1. Quest for bird of truth. J1154.1. Parrot unable to tell husband details as to wife's infidelity. K1591. Seventy tales of a parrot prevent a wife's adultery.

B131.0.1. *Truth-telling owl.* India: Thompson-Balys.

B131.1. *Bird reveals murder.* *Type 781; *BP I 275 n. 1; Hdwb. d. deutschen Märchens s.v. "Ibycus". — English: Child II 144, 146—155; Irish: Beal XXI 336. — Africa (Ekoi): Talbot 312, (Zulu): Callaway 219, 299, (Thonga): Junod 242, (Basuto): *Jacottet 56 n. 1. — Jamaica: Beckwith MAFLS XVII 266 No. 73. — Japanese: Ikeda. — S. A. Indian (Carib): Métraux RMLP XXXIII 129, 147, (Chiriguano): ibid. 162, Métraux BBAE CXLIII (3) 484, (Yuracare): Métraux RMLP XXXIII 144.

B215.1. Bird language. N271.3. The cranes of Ibycus. Q211. Murder punished.

B131.1. *Crows reveal the killing of mare.* Corpus Poeticum Boreale I 359.

B131.2. *Bird reveals treachery.* (Cf. B133.2.) — *Type 707; *BP II 380ff. (Gr. No. 96); Köhler-Bolte I 277; India: Thompson-Balys.

K1911.3.1. Substitution of false bride revealed by animal. N270. Crime inevitably comes to light. Q261. Treachery punished.

B131.3. *Bird betrays woman's infidelity.* (Cf. B134.1.) — Campbell Seven Sages xcviii — Greek: Fox 280; English: Child II 260; India: *Thompson-Balys; Buddhist myth: Malalasekera II 731.

A2237.1. Animal reveals mistress's adultery: punished by master. B335.4. Wife demands magic parrot who has accused her. J551.1. Cocks who crow about mistress's adultery killed. Discreet cock saves his life. Q241. Adultery punished. T230. Faithlessness in marriage.

B131.4. *Bird reveals dead rider.* Calls out in human voice at seeing living woman riding behind dead man. — English: Child V 65.

E215. The dead rider (Lenore).

B131.5. *Peacock's feathers ruffled in presence of poison.* (Cf. B143.1.2.) — Penzer I 110 n. 1.

B521.1. Animal warns against poison.

B131.6. *Bird betrays hiding-place of the Virgin.* English: Child II 8. — — Lithuanian: Balys Legends No. 198f.

A2231.7.1. Animal cursed for betraying holy fugitive.

B131.7. *Birds reveal innocence of suspect.* Jewish: Neuman.

B131.8. *Bird warns to hurry.* Chinese: Graham.

B132. *Truth-speaking cow.* India: *Thompson-Balys.

B133. *Truth-speaking horse.* Type 531; BP III (Gr. No. 126).

B149.1. Prophetic horse. B181. Magic horse. B211.3. Speaking horse. B401. Helpful horse.

B133.0.1. *Truth-telling ass (mule).* Jewish: Neuman.

B133.0.1.1. *Ass alone knows where hidden wind can be found.* India: Thompson-Balys.

B133.1. *Horse warns hero of danger.* English: Child No. 43; Icel.: *Boberg; Irish myth: Cross; Lithuanian: Leskien-Brugmann 359ff.; Russian: v. Löwis of Menar Russische Märchen 13, Rambaud La Russie épique 49; Persian: Nöldeke Das iranische Volksepos 58; India: Thompson-Balys; Missouri French: Carrière.

B521.3. Animal warns against attack. D1317. Magic object warns of danger.

B133.2. *Horse reveals treachery.* (Cf. B131.2.) — Africa (Mpongwe): Nassau 68 No. 15.

N270. Crime inevitably comes to light. Q261. Treachery punished.

B133.3. *Speaking horse-head.* The helpful magic horse (B181) is killed (B330). The head is preserved and placed on the wall. It speaks and reveals the treachery practiced against the heroine. — *Type 533; **W. Ljungman Två Folkminnesundersökningar (Göteborg 1925) 41ff; *BP II 273 (Gr. No. 89) 274 n. 1. — Hindu: Keith 122.

D1311.7.1. Oracular artificial head. K1911.3.1. Substitution of false bride revealed by animal.

B133.4. *Horse refuses to carry one who speaks falsehood.* Irish myth: Cross.

B159.2. Saint's horse lies down when grain of wheat falls from load. Q263. Lying (perjury) punished.

B133.4.1. *Horses refuse to remain with owner* who has been cursed by clerics. Irish myth: Cross.

B134. *Truth-telling dog.* India: Thompson-Balys.

B121. Dog with magic wisdom. B152. Dog indicates pregnant woman (adulteress). B153. Dog's barking indicates hidden treasure. B187. Magic dog. B211.7. Speaking dog. B421. Helpful dog. B521.3.1. Dogs warn against witch. B521.3.4. Dog warns of pursuit. E421.1.3. Ghost visible to dogs alone.

B134.1. *Dog betrays woman's infidelity.* (Cf. B131.3.) India: Thompson-Balys. — Zuñi: Handy JAFL XXXI 464 No. 17.

A2237.1. Animal reveals mistress's adultery: punished by master. A2422.1.

Why dogs do not speak. H411. Magic object points out unchaste woman. J2365. Fool discloses woman's adultery. K1271. Amorous intrigue observed and exposed. Q241. Adultery punished. T481. Adultery.

B134.1.1. *Truth-telling dog tells of incest.* India: Thompson-Balys.

B134.2. *Dog betrays murder.* *Fb "hund" I 678b. — Africa (Angola): Chatelain 127 No. 12.

B134.3. *Dog as animal of warning.* *Fb "hund" I 678. — Icel.: Boberg; India: Thompson-Balys.

B134.3.1. *Dog warns of coming.* Chinese: Graham 123, p. 3.

B134.4. *Dog chooses between opposing tribes.* Irish myth: Cross.

B134.5. *Dog returns from dead to clear master of murder.* India: Thompson-Balys.

B211.7. Speaking dog. E300. Friendly return from the dead.

B135. *Truth-telling cat.* India: Thompson-Balys.

B136. *Truth-telling deer.* Jewish: Neuman.

B140. Prophetic animals. India: Thompson-Balys.

B560. Animals attend and advise men. D1311. Magic object used for divination. D1812. Magic power of prophecy. M300. Prophecies. M312.0.2. Prophecy of future greatness given by animals.

B141. *Prophetic domestic beasts.*

B141.1. *Prophetic goat.* Africa (Angola): Chatelain 53 No. 2.

B413. Helpful goat.

B141.2. *Prophetic horse.* *Howey Horse in Magic and Myth 156ff.; *Malten Jahrb. d. Kaiserl. deutschen archäologischen Inst. XXIX (1914) 179ff.; Irish myth: Cross; Greek: Iliad Book XIX line 407.

B133. Truth-speaking horse. B181. Magic horse. B211.3. Speaking horse. B250. Religious animals. B301.4.1.1. Faithful horse weeps for coming death of saint. B401. Helpful horse. B736.2. Horse sheds tears of blood. E421.1.2. Ghosts visible to horses alone.

B141.2.1. *Horse weeps for master's (saint's) approaching death.* Irish myth: Cross.

B301.4.2. Faithful horse weeps tears of blood for master. D1812.0.1. Foreknowledge of hour of death.

B141.3. *Ass's behavior predicts the weather.* Italian Novella: Rotunda.

B141.4. *Dog with magic sight.* Fb "hund" IV 227a.

B187. Magic dog.

B141.4.1. *Dog (transformed man) prophesies coming of enemy.* Irish myth: Cross.

D1812.5.0.9. Divination from howling of dog.

B141.5. *Prophetic cow.* India: Thompson-Balys.

B142. *Prophetic wild beasts.*

B142.1. *Prophetic fox.* Chinese: Werner 370.

B126. Fox as alchemist. B147.1.2.1. Fox as beast of ill-omen. B441. Helpful fox.

B142.2. *Prophetic jackal.*

B142.2.1. *Jackal gives warning.* India: Thompson-Balys.

B142.3. *Prophetic hart.* Alphabet of Tales No. 416.

B142.4. *Prophetic lion.* German: Grimm No. 67.

B143. *Prophetic bird.* (Cf. B172.) — *Types 516, 517; BP I 322f., 323 n. 1; Rösch FFC LXXVII 116; Hdwb. d. Abergl. s.v. "Angang" I 428; India: *Thompson-Balys. — Jamaica: *Beckwith MAFLS XVII 266 No. 73.

M353. Prediction of bird that girl will have dead husband.

B143.0.1. *Swan as prophetic bird.* Fb. "Svane" III 663; Handwb. d. Abergl. VII 1403. — Icel.: MacCulloch Eddic 262.

B143.0.2. *Magpie as prophetic bird.* Fb. "Skade" III 219; Handwb. d. Abergl. III 796 "Elster".

B143.0.3. *Owl as prophetic bird.* India: Thompson-Balys.

B143.0.4. *Raven as prophetic bird.* Jewish: Neuman; Icel.: Boberg.

B143.0.5. *Hen as prophetic bird.* Jewish: Neuman.

B143.0.6. *Dove as prophetic bird.* Jewish: Neuman.

B143.0.7. *Eagle as prophetic bird.* Jewish: Neuman.

B143.0.8. *Crow as prophetic bird.*

B143.0.8.1. *Crows announce coming of hero to otherworld.* Irish myth: Cross.

F0. Otherworld journeys. M394. Hero's coming prophesied.

B143.1. *Bird gives warning.* (Cf. B131.5.) — English: Child I 31ff., 37, II 206 n., 496f., III 10, IV 441, V 284; India: Thompson-Balys; Japanese: Ikeda; Jamaica: *Beckwith MAFLS XVII 266 No. 73. — Africa (Benga): Nassau 142, No. 16.

B521.3. Animal warns against attack. D1317. Magic object warns of danger. D1612. Tell-tale magic objects.

B143.1.1. *Warning crow.* India: *Thompson-Balys.

B143.1.2. *Warning peacock.* India: Thompson-Balys.

B143.1.3. *Warning parrot.* India: Thompson-Balys.

B143.1.4. *Falcon saves master from drinking poisoned water.* India: Thompson-Balys.

B143.1.5. *Golden cock warns against attack.* Icel.: *Boberg.

B102.1. Golden bird. B521.3. Animals warn against attack.

B143.1.6. *Captured goose warns tortoise:* released in gratitude. India: Thompson-Balys.

B143.2. *Bird describes doomsday.* Irish myth: Cross.

A1002. Doomsday. B122. Bird with magic wisdom.

B144. *Prophetic fish.* (Cf. B175.)

B470. Helpful fish. D1318.2.1. Laughing fish reveals unjust judgment.

B144.1. *King of fishes prophesies hero's birth.* *Type 303; BP I 528 (Gr. Nos. 60, 85). — Africa (Angola): Chatelain 66 No. 3.

B311. Congenital helpful animal.

B145. *Prophetic reptile.*

B145.1. *Prophetic tortoise.* Chinese: Ferguson 100.

B145.2. *Prophetic snake.* Greek: Iliad Book II, lines 308—319.

B145.3. *Prophetic worm.* S. A. Indian (Toba): Métraux MAFLS XL 68.

B147. *Animals furnish omens.* India: Thompson-Balys.

A2536. Animals are of good omen. B521. Animal warns of fatal danger. D1812.5.1.12. Howling of dogs as bad omen. N131. Acts performed for changing luck.

B147.1. *Beasts furnish omens.*

B147.1.1. *Beasts of good omen.*

B147.1.2. *Beasts of ill-omen.*

B147.1.2.1. *Fox as beast of ill-omen.* Chinese: Werner 370; Icel.: Boberg.

B147.1.2.2. *Cat as beast of ill-omen.* Fb "kat". — Irish myth: Cross.

B16.1. Monster cat devastates country. B871.1.6. Giant cat.

B147.1.2.3. *Mouse as beast of ill-omen.* *Fb "mus" II 631a.

B147.1.2.4. *Jackal as beast of ill-omen.* India: Thompson-Balys.

B147.2. *Birds furnish omens.* *Frazer Fasti II 203, III 378ff.; Irish myth: Cross.

B147.2.1. *Bird of good omen.*

B147.2.1.1. *Raven as bird of good omen.* Irish myth: Cross; Icel.: Boberg.

B147.2.1.2. *Eagle as omen of victory.* Icel.: *Boberg.

B147.2.2. *Bird of ill-omen.* (Cf. B172.) — *Hdwb. d. Abergl. s.v. "Angang" I 428; German: Grimm No. 105.

B147.2.2.1. *Crow as bird of ill-omen.* *Fb "krage". — Icel.: Boberg; Hindu: Tawney I 284, 465 n.; Irish myth: Cross; Spanish Exempla: Keller.

B147.2.2.2. *Gull as bird of ill-omen.* *Fb "måge".

B147.2.2.3. *Raven as bird of ill-omen.* *Krappe Etudes 31ff.; Fb "ravn" III 22a; Irish myth: Cross; Icel.: Boberg.

B291.2. Raven as devil's messenger. D1812.5.1.27. Croaking of raven as bad omen.

B147.2.2.4. *Owl as bird of ill-omen.* Hdwb. d. Abergl. II 1073 s.v. "Eule". — Alphabet of Tales Nos. 87, 88. — India: Thompson-Balys; Icel.: Boberg.

E761.7.6. Life token: bird sent each day to tell of hero's condition; when owl comes it will be to announce death.

B147.2.2.5. *Eagle as bird of ill-omen.* Irish myth: Cross; Icel.: Boberg.

A1904. The oldest bird.

B147.2.2.6. *Vulture as bird of ill-omen.* Irish myth: Cross.

B147.2.2.7. *Peacock as bird of ill-omen.* India: Thompson-Balys.

B147.3. *Other animals furnish omens.*

B147.3.0.1. *Divination by fall of house-lizard.* India: Thompson-Balys.

B147.3.1. *Other animals furnish good omens.*

B147.3.1.1. *Crickets as good omens.* Hdwb. d. Abergl. III 1167.

B147.3.1.2. *Bees (ants) leave honey on lips of infant* to show future greatness. Spanish Exempla: Keller.

M312. Prophecy of future greatness for poor youth.

B147.3.2. *Other animals furnish bad omens.*

B147.3.2.1. *Crickets as bad omens.* Hdwb. d. Abergl. III 1166.

B150. Oracular animals. *Hopf (L.) Tierorakel und Orakeltiere in alter und neuer Zeit (Stuttgart, 1888). — Krappe JAFL LV 228ff.; India: Thompson-Balys.

D1311. Magic object used for divination. H171. Animal or object indicates election of ruler. H173. Disguised man recognized by dog. M300. Prophecies. N774. Adventures from pursuing enchanted animal (hind, boar, bird).

B151. *Animal determines road to be taken.* Jewish: Neuman.

B151.1. *Beast determines road to be taken.*

B151.1.1. *Horses determine road to be taken.* They are left to pick out the road themselves and to stop at the destination. — *DeCock Studien en Essays 200ff.; Wesselski Theorie 30. — Chinese: Graham.

B401. Helpful horse. B563. Animals direct man on journey. D1313. Magic object points out road. J1179.2. The hog belongs to whichever place he goes of his own accord. N774. Adventures from pursuing enchanted animal (hind, boar, bird).

B151.1.1.0.1. *Horses travel between clerics without guidance.* Irish myth: Cross.

B250. Religious animals.

B151.1.1.0.2. *Horse stops where murder has occurred.* Finnish: Aarne FFC XXXIII 39 No. 4**.

B151.1.1.0.3. *Horse allowed to go as it pleases,* finds unknown person. Chinese: Graham.

B151.1.1.1. *Mare with foal left behind finds road home.* The foal is left so that the force of nature in the mare will discover the unknown road home. — Hdwb. d. deutschen Märchens s.v. "Ariadnefaden" n. 15.

B151.1.1.2. *Ass determines road to be taken.* Jewish: Neuman.

B151.1.1.2.1. *Ass carries usurer's body to the gallows* instead of to the church. He has been denied burial in the church. — Alphabet of Tales No. 705.

N277. Oxen bear dead usurer to gallows to be buried. They are allowed to go where they will.

B151.1.1.2.2. *Baalam's ass.* Advises master that angel is barring the way. Italian Novella: Rotunda.

B151.1.2. *Bull determines road to be taken.* Irish myth: Cross.

B151.1.2.1. *Cow determines road to be·taken.* India: Thompson-Balys.

B151.1.3. *Fox determines road to be taken.* India: Thompson-Balys.

B151.1.4. *Elephant determines road to be taken.* Buddhist myth: Malalasekera II 603.

B151.1.5. *Camel determines road to be taken.* Jewish: Neuman.

B151.1.6. *Dog indicates road to be taken.* Icel.: Boberg; Wesselski Theorie 30.

B563. Animals direct man on journey.

B151.2. *Bird determines road to be taken.*

B151.2.0.1. *Bird shows way by dropping feathers* every seven steps. — Hdwb. d. deutschen Märchens s.v. "Ariadnefaden" n. 14.

R135. Abandoned children find way back by clue (bread-crumb, grain, pebble, etc.).

B151.2.0.2. *Birds show way to otherworld.* Irish myth: Cross.

F159.1. Otherworld reached by hunting animal. N774. Adventures from pursuing enchanted animal.

B151.2.0.3. *Bird shows way by singing.* South Africa: Bourhill and Drake Fairy Tales from South Africa 237ff. No. 20.

B152. *Animal selects unknown person.*

H171.2. Bird indicates election of Pope.

B152.1. *Dog indicates pregnant woman, adulteress, etc.* (Cf. B121.1, B134, B153.) — English: Child I 270 n.

B152.2. *Fly indicates successful suitor.* Girl to marry man on whom specially marked fly lights. — India: *Thompson-Balys.

H310. Suitor tests. T54. Choosing a bride by horoscope.

B152.3. *Hawk lighting on man points out criminal.* Korean: Zong-in-Sob 123 No. 59.

B153. *Dog indicates hidden treasure.* *Norlind Skattsägner 47 n. 1. — India: Thompson-Balys; Japanese: Mitford 180.

B103.4.3. Dog vomits gold and silver. B121. Dog with magic wisdom. B134. Truth-telling dog. B187. Magic dog. B421. Helpful dog. D1314. Magic object indicates desired place. D1816. Magic discovery of desired place. N530. Discovery of treasure.

B153.1. *Dog indicates other hidden objects.* Icel.: Boberg.

B154. *Animal as soothsayer.*

B140. Prophetic animals. B191. Animal as magician. D1712. Soothsayer.

B154.1. *Ox as soothsayer.* All judgments referred to it. (Cf. B182.2.) — Persian: Carnoy 335.

B154.2. *Ant as soothsayer.* Ila of Rhodesia: Smith and Dale 396.

B154.3. *Fish-eagle as soothsayer.* Ila of Rhodesia: Smith and Dale 354.

B155. *Location determined by halting of an animal.* — Irish myth: Cross. (Cf. B153.)

B256. Animal as servant of saint. B563.4. Animals lead cleric to holy place. D1314. Magic object indicates desired place. D1816. Magic discovery of desired places. V111.3.1. Birds indicate the site where a church is to be built.

B155.1. *Building site determined by halting of animal.* Where the animal stops the building is erected. — Fb "kvie" II 338a, "kirke" IV 258a; Sébillot France IV 114, 127; Günter Christliche Legende des Abendlandes 81; Dickson Valentine and Orson 54 n. 66; *Pease Classical Philology XII (1917) 8ff.; Norden on Vergil Aeneid VI, lines 136ff.; Stemplinger Neue Jahrb. XLVII (1920) 41. — Finnish-Swedish: Wessman 70 no. 598; Finnish: Holmberg Finno-Ugric 125, 145, Aarne FFC XXXIII 46 No. 82; Estonian: Aarne FFC XXV 133 No. 82;

Danish: Kristensen Danske Sagn III (1895) 167ff., (1931) 117ff.; Irish myth: Cross; Eng., Wales: Baughman.

B563.4. Animal leads cleric to holy place. V111.3.1. Birds indicate the site where a church is to be built.

B155.1.0.1. *Building site determined by other action of animal.* Irish myth: Cross.

B155.2. *City founded on spot where cow lies down.* Greek: Frazer Apollodorus I 315 n. 1, II 38 n. 1; India: Thompson-Balys.

B155.2.1. *Village founded on spot when cock crows,* dog barks, and mithian bellows. India: Thompson-Balys.

B155.2.2. *Location of settlement at place a cow stops* and where milk flows by itself. India: Thompson-Balys.

B155.2.3. *Birds indicate the place where a town (castle) is to be built.* Krappe Revue de l' histoire des Religions CXIV (1936) 236—246.

V111.3.1. Birds indicate site where a church is to be built.

B155.2.4. *Pursued animal indicates where city is to be built.* India: Thompson-Balys.

B155.3. *Animal determines burial place of saint.* Günter Christliche Legende des Abendlandes 55; Sloet De Dieren in het Germanische Volksgeloof in Volksgebruik 153f.; Irish myth: Cross; Jewish: Neuman.

B155.4. *Neighing of horse indicates important spot.* Korean: Zong in-Sob IV No. 2.

B157. *Animal leads searchers.*

B157.1. *Whistling of bird leads searcher.* Calif. Indian: Gayton and Newman 68.

B159. *Miscellaneous oracular animals.*

B159.1. *Birds drop quill when man requires pen.* Irish myth: Cross.

B159.2. *Horse lies down when grain of wheat falls from load.* Irish myth: Cross.

B159.3. *Cleric goes with saint whom his cow follows.* Irish myth: Cross.

B159.4. *Vulture's chicks will not eat dead hero's leg,* since they know he has been treacherously murdered. India: Thompson-Balys.

B160. Wisdom-giving animals. India: Thompson-Balys.

A1591.1. Burial learned from watching raven bury its dead. D1300. Magic object gives supernatural wisdom. D1319. Magic object gives supernatural information. D1811. Magic wisdom. Q552.4. Ear of stolen animal protrudes from thief's mouth.

B161. *Wisdom from serpent.* *Cox 496 n. 32; Fb "hugormekonge" IV 225a; *Scott Thumb 173. — Irish myth: Cross. — Armenian: Ananikian 74; India: Thompson-Balys.

B123. Wise serpent. B165.1. Animal languages learned from serpent. B217.1.1. Animal languages learned from eating serpent. B491. Helpful serpent. D1032. Magic meat.

B161.1. *Power of soothsaying from serpents' licking ears.* (Cf. B165.1.1., B176.) Frazer Apollodorus II 48 n. 2.

B161.2. *Fortune learned from serpent.* Fb "orm" II 759b.

B161.3. *Wisdom from eating serpent.* (Cf. B176.) — *Scott Thumb 173; Fb "hugormekonge"; Chauvin V 255ff. No. 152. — Scotch: Campbell II 377. — Cf. Diegueño: Du Bois AA n.s. VII 628.

D1793. Magic results from eating or drinking. D1811.1. Magic wisdom from eating or drinking.

B161.4. *Power of seeing whether the dead go to heaven or hell* is gained from serpent. India: Thompson-Balys.

E750. Perils of the soul.

B162. *Wisdom from fish.* (Cf. B175.)

B124.2. Salmon of knowledge.

B162.1. *Supernatural knowledge from eating magic fish.* (Cf. B175.) — *Nutt FLR IV 1ff. — Irish myth: Cross; Icel.: *Boberg; Japanese: Ikeda.

D1811.1.1. Thumb of knowledge. M315. Prophecy: man will eat magic salmon and gain knowledge.

B163. *Wisdom from other animal.*

B163.1. *Wisdom from fox.* Jewish: Neuman.

B163.1.1. *Wisdom from eating fox's heart.* Jewish: Neuman.

B165. *Animal languages learned from animal.*

B216. Knowledge of animal languages. B217.1. Animal languages learned from eating animal.

B165.1. *Animal languages learned from serpent (not eaten).* (Cf. B176.) — *Type 670; Aarne FFC XV 28ff. — Greek: *Frazer Apollodorus I 86 n. 2; India: Thompson-Balys.

B165.1.1. *Animal languages learned by having ears licked by serpent.* (Cf. B161.1.) — *Penzer VII 3 n. 2; *BP I 133.

B165.1.2. *Animal languages from stolen serpent's crown.* (Cf. B176.) — *Type 672A; cf. BP II 464.

B165.1.3. *Cobra writes letters on prince's tongue:* "Having heard all kinds of creatures talk, you will understand them." — India: Thompson-Balys.

B165.2. *Animal languages learned from frog.* *Type 670B*; Jewish: Neuman.

B170—B189. OTHER MAGIC ANIMALS

B170. Magic birds, fish, reptiles, etc.

R262. Magic eel pursues man over land.

B171. *Magic chicken (hen, cock).* India: Thompson-Balys.

B171.1. *Demi-coq.* A cock is cut in two and is made magic. Carries robbers, foxes, and stream of water under wings. — *Type 715; *BP I 258. — Missouri French: Carrière.

D915.2. River contained under cock's wings. D1010. Magic bodily members — animal. K481. Demi-coq by means of his magic animals and magic water collects money.

B171.1.0.1. *Magic cock carries great loads in his ear* (load of grain, fox, tiger, bees, wasps, etc., also fire and water). — India: Thompson-Balys.

B171.1.1. *Demi-coq crows in king's body,* when the king eats him. — Type 715. India: *Thompson-Balys.

D1619.2. Magic object speaks from inside person's body. F915. Victim speaks from swallower's body.

B171.2. *Magic fighting cock.* India: Thompson-Balys.

B172. *Magic bird.* Irish myth: Cross; Jewish: Neuman; Hawaii: Beckwith Myth 203. (Cf. B101—B103 passim, B113, B115.2, B122, B131, B141, B143, B147.2, B151.2, B155.2.3, B157.1, B159.1, B159.4, B171.)

B297.1.1. Bird plays timpan. B594.1. Bird rejuvenates person. F262.3.2. Fairy minstrel's birds sing accompaniment H1331.1. Quest for marvelous bird.

B172.1. *Magic bird petrifies those who approach.* Chauvin VI 8 No. 273 n. 1.

B172.2. *Magic bird's song.* Brings joy and oblivion for many years. Wakes the dead. — *Pauli (ed. Bolte) No. 562; Hartland Science 188f., *Krappe Bull. Hispanique XXXIX 29. — Irish myth: Cross, Plummer clxxxvi; Welsh: MacCulloch Celtic 104.

D2011.1. Years seem moments while man listens to song of bird. E55.1. Resuscitation by song.

B172.2.1. *Magic bird's song brings sleep.* Irish myth: Cross.

D1364.24. Music causes magic sleep.

B172.2. *Magic bird's song dispels grief.* Irish myth: Cross.

B292.5. Bird sings to console man (saint). B1359.3.1. Magic music causes joy.

B172.3. *Magic bird collects seeds.* Sees that they are properly placed. Also carries off people's enemies. — Persian: Carnoy 289.

B172.4. *Bird with magic bones and feathers.* Persian: Carnoy 290.

D1013. Magic bone of animal. D1021. Magic feather.

B172.5. *Magic falcon gets water of life for hero.* Italian Novella: Rotunda.

E80. Water of life.

B172.6. *Magic birds lure hunters to certain places.* Irish myth: Cross.

D659.10. Transformation to lure hunters to certain place. F159.1. Otherworld reached by hunting animal. F241.0.1. Fairy animal hunted. N774. Adventures from pursuing enchanted animal.

B172.7. *Magic birds chained in couples.* Irish myth: Cross.

B845.2. Animals chained in couples.

B172.8. *Magic osprey (transformed man) produces lightning.* Irish myth: Cross.

D2140. Magic control of the elements.

B172.9. *Magic birds cause hosts to sleep by shaking wings.* Irish myth: Cross.

D1364. Object causes magic sleep. D1960. Magic sleep.

B172.10. *Black birds.*

A485.1. Goddess of war. B31.6.1. Giant blackbird. B147.2.2.1. Crow as bird of ill-omen. B147.2.2.3. Raven as bird of ill-omen. D1293.4. Black as magic color. D1385.12.1. Saint's bell rung against blackbirds. F401.3.7.1. Demon in form of crow. F402.1.5.1. Demons seek to carry off king's soul. G303.3.3.3.3. Devil in form of blackbird.

B172.10.1. *Innumerable birds (black birds) fly into and out of tower (steeple) of fire.* Irish myth: Cross.

B172.11. *Bird steals island.* India: Thompson-Balys.

B175. *Magic fish.* (Cf. B107.1, B124, B144.) Chinese: Eberhard FFC CXX 82; Irish myth: Cross.

B243. King of fishes. B470. Helpful fish. D1318.2.1. Laughing fish reveals unjust judgment. D1613.1. Magic fish talk so that ogre thinks hero has many brothers with him. F989.18. Stranded fish do not decay for a year.

B175.1. *Magic salmon carries hero over water.* Welsh: MacCulloch Celtic 189; Irish myth: Cross; Japanese: Ikeda.

B142.2. Salmon of knowledge. B214.1. Salmon as oldest and wisest of animals. B541.1. Escape from sea on fish's back. B551. Fish carries man across water. F911.3.2. Winged serpent as boat: passengers within. R245. Whale-boat.

B175.2. *Magic tunny (grateful); carries out hero's wish.* Later he saves him from drowning and restores his sanity. — Italian Novella: Rotunda.

B540. Animal rescuer.

B176. *Magic reptile.*

B176.1. *Magic serpent.* (Cf. B108, B112, B123, B161—165.) — Type 516; BP I 42f. (Gr. No. 6); *Liljeblad Tobiasgeschichte 184f.; Norlind Skattsägner 41ff.; Irish myth: Cross; India: Thompson-Balys.

T172.2. Bridal chamber invaded by magic dragon (serpent).

B176.1.1. *Serpent as deceiver in paradise.* Hebrew: Genesis 3:1; Jewish: Neuman; Irish myth: Cross; Spanish Exempla: Keller. — Indo-Chinese: Scott Indo-Chinese 269.

A1331. Paradise lost.

B176.1.2. *Magic snake can compress himself to minute size* and expand to giant size. India: Thompson-Balys.

B177. *Magic amphibia.*

B177.1. *Magic toad.*

V34.2. Princess sick because toad has swallowed her consecrated wafer.

B177.1.1. *Magic toad under king's bed causes sickness.* French Canadian: Barbeau JAFL XXIX. Cf. Christiansen FFC XXIV 83.

B177.2. *Magic frog.* Hdwb. d. Abergl. III 124 s.v. "Frosch"; Jewish: Neuman.

B177.3. *Magic sea-turtle sucks men to the bottom.* Irish myth: Cross.

F910. Extraordinary swallowings.

B178. *Magic crustacean.*

B178.1. *Magic crab.* Chinese: Eberhard FFC CXX 222.

B180. Magic quadrupeds.

B181. *Magic quadrupeds—felidae.*

B181.1. *Magic cat.* (Cf. B211.8, B422.) — BP 146f.; Norlind Skattsägner 47 n. 1; Irish myth: Cross. See also references to B422.

B292.6. Black cat as servant of giant. B871.1.6. Giant cat. G225.3. Cat as servant of witch. G241.1.4. Witch rides on cat. G252. Witch in form of cat has hand cut off. Recognized next morning by missing hand. H1417. Fear test: night watch with magic cats. R13.12. Cat abducts person.

B181.1.1. *Cat with remarkable powers of sight.* India: Thompson-Balys.

B181.3. *Magic tiger.* Chinese: Eberhard FFC CXX 160.

B182. *Magic quadrupeds—canidae.*

B182.1. *Magic dog.* Irish myth: Cross; India: Thompson-Balys.
D1380.16. Magic dog protects. D1566.1.6. Magic dog's breath burns dead bodies. H1331.6. Quest for marvelous dog.

B182.1.0.1. *Toy (lap) dogs.* Irish myth: Cross.
A1831.2. First lap-dog in Ireland.

B182.1.0.1.1. *Magic lap-dog.* Irish myth: Cross.

B182.1.0.2. *Magic dog transformed person.* Irish myth: Cross.
D17.1.2.3. Transformed man as hostile dog. D141. Transformation: man to dog. T257.2.3. Jealous wife transforms rival to hound.

B182.1.0.3. *Magic dog transformed supernatural being.* Irish myth: Cross.

B182.1.1. *Magic dog vomits any liquor required of him.* Irish myth: Cross.
B109.1.1. Dog vomits gold and silver.

B182.1.2. *Magic hostile bitches issue from elf-mound.* Irish myth: Cross.
B17. Hostile animals. F241.6. Fairy dogs. F360. Malevolent or destructive fairies.

B182.1.3. *Dog sight of which renders game helpless.* Irish myth: Cross.

B182.1.3.1. *Magic whelp kills hound by springing down its throat.* Irish myth: Cross.
F916.2. Whelp leaps through body of hound.

B182.1.4. *Dog that is hound by night and sheep by day.* Irish myth: Cross.

B182.1.5. *Dog that is hound by day and flame of fire by night.* Irish myth: Cross.

B182.1.6. *Magic dog fragrant.* Irish myth: Cross.

B182.1.7. *Magic bitches (in human form) enchanted by fairy music.* Irish myth: Cross.
D1275.1. Magic music. F252.3.1. Fairy as helper.

B182.1.8. *Magic brazen dog.* Jewish: Neuman.

B182.2. *Magic bear.* Lithuanian: Balys Index Nos. *163, *482; Russian: Andrejev No. *160 I, 480*C.
B447. Helpful bear. D113.2. Transformation: man to bear. E235.4. Return from dead to punish theft of part of corpse. G211.6. Witch in form of bear.

B183. *Magic quadrupeds—rodentia.*

B183.1. *Magic mouse.* India: Thompson-Balys.

B183.1.1. *Magic mouse to be flayed.* Mouse orders hero to flay him and to use skin for magic purposes. Later the skin is returned to the mouse. — Africa (Zulu): Calaway 97.
D1025.3. Magic mouse skin. D1532.1. Magic mouse-skin bears person aloft.

B183.1.2. *Magic mouse causes disease.* Irish myth: Cross.
D2064. Magic sickness.

B184. *Magic quadrupeds—ungulata.*

B184.1. *Magic horse.* — Types 314, 502, 550; BP II 274, *III 111, 113 n. 4; *Fb "føl", "hest" IV 211b; Penzer VI 72 n. 1; Meyer Germanische Mythologie (1891) 105; *Jones PMLA XXIII 569; Norlind Skattsägner 46 n. 4. — Irish myth: Cross; Lithuanian: Balys Index Nos. *530A, *530B, *531, *533A, *651; French Canadian: Barbeau JAFL XXIX 15; Breton: Sébillot Incidents s.v. "cheval"; Missouri French: Carrière; Arabian: Burton V 1ff.; India: *Thompson-Balys; Cape Verde Is.: Parsons MAFLS XV (1) 277 No. 91, 281 No. 92. Africa (Mpongwe): Nassau 68 No. 15; Buddhist myth: Malalasekera I 624.

B211.3. Speaking horse. B316. Abused and pampered horses. B401. Helpful horse. C762.3. Tabu: whipping magic horse more than once on journey. C942.2. Magic horse becomes powerless because of broken tabu. D491.1.2. Magic folding mule. D1654.2. Horse magically becomes immovable. D1734. Magic power by crawling through ear of magic horse. D1846.3. Magic horse renders rider invulnerable. H1154.8. Task: capturing magic horse. H1331.4. Quest for marvelous horse. K985. Magic horse lent by fairy in disguise brings about death of mortal.

B184.1.1. *Horse (mule) with magic speed.* *Chauvin V 259 No. 154 n. 1; *Fb "hest" I 598v. — Greek: Fox 119; Irish myth: Cross; Icel.: Boberg; India: Thompson-Balys; Chinese: Werner 294.

D2122. Journey with magic speed.

B184.1.1.1. *Horse so fast fly cannot light on him.* India: Thompson-Balys.

B184.1.1.2. *Horse as swift as a bird.* Icel.: Boberg.

B184.1.1.3. *Swiftest horse on earth.* Irish myth: Cross.

B184.1.2. *Magic horse goes underground.* Fb "øg" III 1161b.

D1533.2. Vehicle travels above and below ground. D2131. Magic underground journey.

B184.1.3. *Magic horse from water world.* *Chauvin VII 7; Icel.: Boberg Irish myth: Cross. — Armenian: Chalatiank Zs. f. Vksk. XIX 152; Japanese: Ikeda.

B72. Sea horse. B401.1. Helpful water horse. C918. Mare from water world disappear when she is scolded. F133.1. Marine counterpart of land.

B184.1.4. *Magic horse travels on sea or land.* Fb "hest" I 598b; Malten (J.) Jahrbuch des kl. deutschen arch. Inst. XXIX 189; Type 516; Rösch FFC LXXVII 108; Irish myth: Cross; Greek: Iliad Book 20 line 273.

A171.0.1. God drives chariot over waves. D1524.1. Magic object permits man to walk on water. D1533. Magic amphibian vehicle. D2125. Magic power to walk on water. F159.2. Journey to otherworld on horseback. F213.3. Sea-riding horse carries mortal to fairyland. F721.1. Underground passages. Journey made through natural subways.

B184.1.5. *Breath of magic horse blows off or sucks in those he pursues.* Welsh: MacCulloch Celtic 190; Irish myth: Cross.

D1005. Magic breath.

B184.1.6. *Flight on magic horse.* *Type 314; BP III 94ff. (Gr. No. 136). Irish myth: Cross; India: Thompson-Balys; Japanese: Ikeda; Missouri French: Carrière.

B41.2. Flying horse.

B184.1.6.1. *Flight on invisible horse.* Cox Cinderella 476 n. 6.

D1980. Magic invisibility.

B184.1.7. *Magic horse avenges hero's death.* Irish myth: Cross; Japanese: Ikeda.

B301. Faithful animal. B401. Helpful horse.

B184.1.8. *Immortal horse.* Greek: Grote I 173.

B184.1.9. *Magic horse mysteriously recognized by everyone.* Scottish: Campbell-McKay No. 1 (and n. 3).

B184.1.10. *Magic horse makes prodigious jump.* India: Thompson-Balys.

F1071. Prodigious jump.

B184.1.11. *Magic invulnerable horse.* Irish myth: Cross.

D1840.2. Magic invulnerability of animals. D1846.3. Magic horse renders rider invulnerable.

B184.1.12. *Magic horse goes through fire.* Icel.: Boberg.

B184.2. *Magic cow (ox, bull).* Krappe Balor 1; Irish myth: Cross; Icel.: Boberg; India: *Thompson-Balys.

D491.1.1. Herd of cattle put into magic cup. D1652.3. Cow with inexhaustible milk. H1331.3. Quest for marvelous cattle. K476.8. Cheating by substitution of a common cow instead of a magic one.

B184.2.0.1. *Magic white cow.* Irish myth: Cross.

B259.11.1. Brilliantly white cow comes to be milked for infant saint. B731.4.1. Cow with white ears. D1515.3. Bath in milk of white hornless cow as antidote for poison. E33.1. Cooked part of white cow is brown after resuscitation. H1331.3.1. Quest for bald white-headed cow. Q153.1. Cow is white-headed during reign of good king.

B184.2.0.1.1. *Magic white cows with red ears.* Irish myth: Cross.

D1500.1.38. Flesh of white cow with red ears is only cure for mysterious illness. F241.2.1.2. Fairies' cows have red ears.

B184.2.1. *Magic cow.*

B184.2.1.1. *Magic cow gives extraordinary milk.*

B184.2.1.1.1. *Magic cow gives red milk.* Swiss: Jegerlehner Oberwallis 305 No. 2.

B411. Helpful cow. D1018. Magic milk of animal. D1036. Magic dairy products. D1043. Milk as magic drink.

B184.2.1.1.2. *Magic cow gives impossible quantity of milk.* India: Thompson-Balys.

B184.2.1.2. *Magic soldier-producing cow.* Hindu: Keith 145f.

D1475. Magic object furnishes soldiers.

B184.2.1.3. *Cow grants all desires.* Penzer II 45 n. 2; India: Thompson-Balys (B109.4).

B184.2.2. *Magic ox.* (Cf. B154.) — Types 510, 511; cf. Wesselski Märchen before Grimm, introd. — French Canadian: Barbeau JAF XXXIX 16. — Icel.: Boberg; Jewish: *Neuman. — Africa (Kaffir): Theal 169, (Basuto): Jacottet 240 No. 35. — Cf. also the giant blue ox of Paul Bunyan (B871.1.1).

B184.2.2.1. *Magic ox from unusual sexual union of animals.* Irish myth: Cross.

B754.0.1. Unusual sexual union of animals.

B184.2.2.2. *Magic cow (ox, bull) from water world.* Irish myth: Cross.

B72. Sea cows. F133.1. Marine counterpart to land. F241.2. Fairies' Cows.

B184.2.3. *Magic bull.* Arabian: Burton VIII 120 n., 121, XVII 366f.; Jewish: Neuman.

A132.9. Bull-god. A137.7. The bull with three cranes. B19.1. Brazen-footed, fire-breathing bull. B43. Winged bull. B871.1.2. Giant bull.

B184.2.3.1. *Magic bull to be flayed.* The bull orders the hero (heroinè) to flay him and to use his skin for magic purposes. (Cf. B192, B335, B411.1.) — Cox Cinderella 365 (Swedish). — Wyandot: Thompson CColl II 412.

D1025. Magic skin of animal.

B184.2.3.2. *Magic bull can be milked.* Irish myth: Cross.

B184.2.3.3. *Indra sends down buffalo whose milk is offered to the saints.* India: Thompson-Balys.

B184.2.4. *Magic ox.* Jewish: Neuman.

B184.2.5. *Magic calf.* Jewish Neuman.

B184.3. *Magic swine.*

B16.4. Giant devastating boar. B16.4.3. Magic swine blight corn and milk. B16.4.4. Magic swine make land sterile. B192.1. Magic pig burned to prevent resuscitation. D1281.1. Magic dead pig. D1359.3.2. Happiness from eating magic pig. D1449.3. Swine summoned out of magic harp. D1500.2.5. Eating magic pig prevents disease. D1652.1.9. Inexhaustible pig. E155.5. Slain pigs revive nightly. F989.8. Swine kick trees to cause fruit to fall. H1331.2. Quest for marvelous boar (pig). K525.4. Animal jumps out of skin so that only skin is caught. Q482.2. Magic swine cause robbers to be drowned.

B184.3.0.1. *Magic swine issue from elf-mound.* Irish myth: Cross.

F234.1.3. Fairy in form of wild boar. F241.3.1. Fairy swine.

B184.3.0.2. *Magic swine disappear underground.* Irish myth: Cross.

F241.0.1. Fairy animal hunted.

B184.3.0.3. *Magic red swine.* Irish myth: Cross.

D1293.1. Red as magic color.

B184.3.0.4. *Magic swine transformed person.* Irish myth: Cross.

D136. Transformation: man to swine.

B184.3.0.5. *Herd of magic swine that cannot be counted twice* with the same result. Irish myth: Cross.

B184.3.1. *Magic boar.* Meyer Germanische Mythologie (1891) 102; Irish myth: Cross; Icel.: Boberg.

B184.3.1.1. *Magic boar drowns houndpack.* Irish myth: Cross.

B184.3.2. *Magic pig.*

B184.3.2.1. *Magic invisible pig.* Irish myth: Cross.

D1980. Magic invisibility.

B184.3.2.2. *Magic pig turns water into wine for nine days.* Irish myth: Cross.

B119.1. Dog (whose skin) turns water to wine. D477.1. Transformation: water becomes wine.

B184.3.2.3. *Skin of magic pig heals wounds.* Irish myth: Cross.

D1503.2. Magic pigskin heals wounds.

B184.4. *Magic deer.* Irish myth: Cross.

B184.5. *Magic goat.*

B184.5.1. *Magic fighting goat.* India: Thompson-Balys.

B184.6. *Magic sheep.* Irish myth: Cross.

B16.19. Destructive sheep. B19.4.3. Sheep with fiery collar. D1652.14. Sheep with inexhaustible wool.

B184.6.1. *Wethers leap from well;* payment for saint's baptism. Irish myth: Cross.

B190. Magic animals: miscellaneous motifs.

B250. Religious animals. B500. Magic power from animals. B771.1. Animal tamed by holiness of saint. D684.0.1. Transformation by magic animal. D1611.13. Magic louse answers for fugitive. D1840.2. Magic invulnerability of animals. D1841.3.1. Magic animal proof against burning. D1841.6.1. Magic animal proof against drowning. F167.1. Animals in otherworld. F241. Fairies' animals. F980. Extraordinary occurrences concerning animals. H1251. Quest to other world for samples of magic animals' food.

B191. *Animal as magician.* (Cf. B154.) — India: Thompson-Balys.

B120. Wise animals. D684.0.1. Transformation by magic animal. D1711. Magician.

B191.1. *Weasel as conjurer.* Swiss: Jegerlehner Oberwallis 321 No. 74.

B191.2. *Ox-demon as magician.* Chinese: Werner 361.

B191.3. *Tiger as magician.* India: Thompson-Balys.

D1711. Magician.

B191.4. *Rat gives magic medicine.* India: Thompson-Balys.

B191.5. *Hedgehog builds castle.* Icel.: Boberg.

B191.6. *Bird as magician.* India: Thompson-Balys.

B191.7. *Serpent as magician.* Jewish: Neuman.

B192. *Magic animal killed.* Irish myth: Cross; N. A. Indian (Seneca): Curtin-Hewitt RBAE XXXII 161 No. 27.

B17.1.2.2. Hostile hound killed by reaching through hollow log in its jaws and tearing heart out. B182.3.1. Magic bull to be flayed. B187.3.3. Magic whelp kills hound by jumping down its throat. B330. Death of helpful animal. F981. Extraordinary death of animal.

B192.0.1. *Magic birds die when owner is killed.* Irish myth: Cross.

E765.2. Life bound up with that of animal.

B192.1. *Magic pig burned to prevent resuscitation.* Irish myth: Cross.

B183. Magic boar. E0. Resuscitation. E32. Resuscitated eaten animal.

B192.2. *Rain-withholding deer killed: rain released.* India: Thompson-Balys.

A1111. Impounded water.

B192.3. *Treasure-producing bird killed to please a paramour.* India: Thompson-Balys.

B104. Treasure-producing animal.

B193. *Otter carries flaming wood in mouth.* Irish myth: Cross.

B195. *Magic animal used by hero in contest grows bigger* with every round. India: Thompson-Balys.

K0. Deceptions.

B200—B299. Animals with human traits.

B200. Animals with human traits. See in general the literature dealing with fables, with the Romance of Reynard, with the bear-fox cycle of Europe, with the rabbit fox cycle of America, etc. — Irish myth: Cross Fables: Wienert FFC LVI; Hervieux Les Fabulistes latins; Jacobs

The Fables of Aesop; Jewish: Neuman; Reynard the Fox: Graf FFC XXXVIII; Bear-fox cycle: Krohn Bär (Wolf) und Fuchs JSFO VI; Dh IV; Rabbit-fox cycle: Parsons MAFLS XV (1) notes; Beckwith MAFLS XVII notes. See also Panchatantra. — Marquesas: Handy 79; S. A. Indian (Warrau): Métraux RMLP XXXIII 146, (Chiriguano): ibid. 161, 179.

A522. Animal as culture hero. B773. Animal with human emotions. D682.3. Partial transformation: animal with human mind. F981. Extraordinary death of animal. J1706. Stupid animals. Q557. Miraculous punishment through animals.

B210. Speaking animals. India: Thompson-Balys.

D1610. Magic speaking objects.

B210.1. *Person frightened by animals successively replying to his remarks.* Example: Man riding horse and followed by dog tells horse to jump over a hole. Horse says, "I will not." Man turns to dog and says, "Isn't that strange — a horse talking!" The dog says, "Yes, isn't it." Often the man runs, meeting other animals which answer him, until he falls exhausted. — U.S.: *Baughman.

B210.2. *Talking animal or object refuses to talk on demand.* Discoverer is unable to prove his claims: is beaten. — U.S. Negro: Baughman.

B210.3. *Formerly animals and man spoke the same language.* God took the power of speech from the animals because men refused to kill speaking beasts. — India: Thompson-Balys.

B211. *Animal uses human speech.* *Chauvin VIII 126 No. 113; *BP I 331. — Irish myth: Cross; Breton: Sébillot Incidents s.v. "animaux"; French Canadian: Barbeau JAFL XXIX 13; Hindu: Tawney II 599; India: *Thompson-Balys; Chinese: Eberhard FFC CXX 40 No. 28. See also references given under B200.

B11.4.5. Talking dragon. N451. Secrets overheard from animal conversation.

B211.0.1. *Animals speak, praising God, on the night of Christ's Nativity.* Irish myth: Cross.

B251.1. Animals rejoice at Christ's birth.

B211.1. *Speaking beasts — domestic.*

B211.1.1. *Speaking sheep.* Breton: Sébillot Incidents s.v. "mouton"; Missouri-French: Carrière.

B211.1.1.1. *Speaking ram.* Irish myth: Cross; Greek: Grote I 117; Breton: Sébillot Incidents s.v. "belier".

B211.1.1.1.1. *Ram stung by hornet on Sabbath says, "Damn!"* Pious owner resolves to sell it next day. — U.S.: Baughman.

B211.1.2. *Speaking goat.* Breton: Sébillot Incidents s.v. "chèvre"; India: Thompson-Balys; Africa (Angola): Chatelain 55 No. 2.

K366.5. The speaking goat swallows gold coins in temple: voids for master.

B211.1.3. *Speaking horse.* *Types 531, 532; BP II 274f., III 18; Penzer II 57; Fb "hest" I 598b; *Loomis White Magic 61; Missouri French: Carrière; Greek: Malten Jahrb. d. Kaiserl. deutschen archäologischen Inst. XXIX (1914) 203f. — Russian: v. Löwis of Menar Russische Märchen 313 No. 53, Rambaud La Russie épique 79; Lithuanian: Leskien-Brugmann Nos. 5, 9; Modern Greek: Hahn Griechische und alban. Märchen Nos. 6, 37; Bulgarian: Strauss Bulgarische Volksdichtungen 212, 309; Turkish: Giese Türkische Märchen 37; Hungarian: Ipolyi Zs. f. deutsche Mythologie II 270; India: *Thompson-Balys.

B133. Truthspeaking horse. B149.1. Prophetic horse. B181. Magic horse. B210.1. Person frightened by animals successively replying to his remarks. B401. Helpful horse.

B211.1.3.1. *Speaking ass.* Type 534*. — Breton: Sébillot Incidents s.v. "âne"; Jewish: Neuman.

B211.1.3.2. *Speaking mule.* Africa (Kordofan): Frobenius Atlantis IV 53ff. No. 6.

B211.1.4. *Speaking hog.* Irish myth: Cross; Missouri-French: Carrière; India: Thompson-Balys; Africa (Benga): Nassau 81 No. 1.

B183. Magic boar (pig).

B211.1.4.1. *Boar sings song.* Irish myth: Cross.

B214. Animal whistles (sings, etc.).

B211.1.5. *Speaking cow.* French-Canadian: Sister Marie Ursule (B211.19); Lithuanian: Balys Index Nos. *543, 481; India: *Thompson-Balys.

B211.1.5.1. *Speaking ox.* Buddhist myth: Malalasekera I 812.

B211.1.5.2. *Speaking buffalo.* India: Thompson-Balys.

B211.1.5.3. *Speaking bullock.* India: Thompson-Balys.

B211.1.5.4. *Speaking yak.* India: Thompson-Balys.

B211.1.5.5. *Speaking calf.* Jewish: Neuman.

B211.1.6. *Speaking camel.* Loomis White Magic 61; India: Thompson-Balys.

B211.1.7. *Speaking dog.* Irish myth: Cross; Breton: Sébillot Incidents s.v. "chien"; Missouri-French: Carrière; India: Thompson-Balys; Africa: Stanley 105.

B134.5. Dog returns from dead to clear master of murder. B187. Magic dog.

B211.1.7.1. Dog sings song. Africa (Zulu): Callaway 363.

B214. Animal whistles (sings, etc.).

B211.1.8. *Speaking cat.* *Type 545; BP I 329, III 487 (Gr. No. 214). — Danish: Fb "kat" II 108b; Breton: Sébillot Incidents s.v. "chats"; Missouri-French: Carrière; India: Thompson-Balys; Japanese: Mitford 253, Ikeda; German: Grimm No. 4.

B184. Magic cat. B422. Helpful cat.

B211.2. *Speaking beast—wild.*

B211.2.1. *Speaking stag.* Irish myth: Cross; Breton: Sébillot Incidents s.v. "cerf"

B211.2.2. *Speaking lion.* *Loomis White Magic 59; German: Grimm No. 60, 67, 88; French-Canadian: Gautier, Sister Marie Ursule (B211.20); Moreno: Esdras (B211.15).

B211.2.2.1. *Speaking tiger:* French-Canadian: Sister Marie Ursule (B211.21); India: *Thompson-Balys; Chinese: Graham, Eberhard FFC CXX 41; S. A. Indian (Chiriguano): Métraux RMLP XXXIII 155, 166.

B211.2.2.2. *Speaking jaguar.* S. A. Indian (Chiriguano): Métraux RMLP XXXIII 155.

B211.2.3. *Speaking bear.* German: Grimm Nos. 60, 114, 161; French-Canadian: Sister Marie Ursule (B211.22).

B211.2.4. *Speaking wolf.* Irish myth: Cross (B211.25); German: Grimm Nos. 8, 26, 37, 60; Jewish: Neuman.

B211.2.5. *Speaking fox.* German: Grimm Nos. 8, 57, 60, 191; Jewish: Neuman.

B211.2.6. *Speaking hare (rabbit).* Irish myth: Cross; German: Grimm Nos. 8, 60, 66.

B211.2.7. *Speaking sea-beast.* Irish myth: Cross (B211.17).

B211.2.7.1. *Speaking seal.* Irish myth: Cross (B211.17.1).

B80.1. Seal-man. B631.2. Human beings descended from seals.

B211.2.8. *Speaking mouse.* India: Thompson-Balys.

B211.2.9. *Speaking rat.* India: *Thompson-Balys.

B211.2.10. *Speaking monkey.* India: *Thompson-Balys; Chinese: Eberhard FFC CXX 42.

B211.3. *Speaking bird.* Type 516; *Cox 527—9; Penzer I 48; Dickson Valentine and Orson 51 n. 60; Tobler Epiphanie der Seele 53; *Fb "fugl"; Krappe Hispanic Review I (1933) 67ff.; Irish myth: Cross; Breton: Sébillot Incidents s.v. "oiseau". — Arabian: Burton III 126n, 129ff., SV 300; Bloomfield On Talking Birds in Hindu Fiction (Festschrift für Ernst Windisch) 349ff.; India: *Thompson-Balys; Chinese: Graham; Missouri-French: Carrière; Jewish: Neuman; Africa: Bouveignes 109, (Upoto): Einstein 137, (Duala): Lederbogen V 139. — Cf. Type 720 (BP I 412).

A1904. Oldest bird. B122.2. Birds as reporters of sights and sounds. B131. Bird of truth. B172. Magic bird. B251.3. Birds in otherworld sing religious songs. B450. Helpful bird. D2006.1.3. Forgotten fiancée reawakens husband's memory by having doves converse. H1331.1.4. Quest for speaking bird.

B211.3.1. *Speaking turkey.* Zuñi: Cushing Zuñi Folk Tales 54ff.

B211.3.2. *Speaking cock.* Fb "kok" II 248b.; Missouri-French: Carrière; Jewish: Neuman.

B211.3.2.1. *Speaking chicken.* Jewish: Neuman.

B211.3.3. *Speaking goose.* India: Thompson-Balys.

B211.3.4. *Speaking parrot.* India: *Thompson-Balys.

D157. Transformation: man to parrot.

B211.3.5. *Speaking dove.* Greek: Grote I 355; India: Thompson-Balys; Jewish: Neuman; S. A. Indian (Chiriguano): Métraux RMLP XXXIII 181; Africa (Ba Ronga): Einstein 25.

B211.3.6. *Speaking raven.* Jewish: Neuman.

B211.3.7. *Speaking sparrow.* India: Thompson-Balys.

B211.3.8. *Speaking vulture.* Jewish: Neuman.

B211.3.9. *Speaking crow.* French-Canadian: Sister Marie Ursule (B211.10.1); India: Thompson-Balys.

B211.4. *Speaking insects.*

B211.4.1. *Speaking ant.* French-Canadian: Sister Marie Ursule (B211.23).

B211.4.2. *Speaking bee.* German: Grimm No. 107.

B211.5. *Speaking fish.* *Type 303. Breton: Sébillot Incidents s.v. "poisson"; Jewish: Neuman; India: Thompson-Balys; Missouri-French: Carrière; Africa (Duala): Lederbogen VI 92.

B124. Wise fish. B130. Truth-telling animal. B142 Prophetic fish. B175. Magic fish. B243. King of fishes. B470. Helpful fish. D1318.2.1. Laughing fish reveal unjust judgment.

B211.6. *Speaking reptile.*

B211.6.1. *Speaking snake (serpent).* Loomis White Magic 63; Tobler Epiphanie der Seele 55. Cf. Satan in the Gardén of Eden. — Irish myth: Cross; Jewish: Neuman; India: *Thompson-Balys; Missouri-French: Carrière (B211.14).

B211.7. *Speaking amphibia.*

B211.7.1. *Speaking frog.* Cf. Type 440; BP I 1 (Gr. No. 1); Fb "frø"; S. A. Indian (Chiriguano): Métraux RMLP XXXIII 171; India: Thompson-Balys.

B493. Helpful frog.

B211.7.2. *Speaking toad.* Breton: Sébillot Incidents s.v. "crapaud"; Missouri-French: Carrière (B211.13).

B212. *Animal understands human speech.* Irish myth: Cross.

B212.0.1. *All kinds of animals understand the language of heaven.* Irish myth: Cross; Jewish: Neuman.

A1482.1. Hebrew the language of the inhabitants of heaven.

B212.0.2. *First animals knew human language.* Jewish: Neuman.

B212.1. *Fox understands human speech.* Nouvelles Recreations No. 29.

B214. *Animal whistles (sings, etc.).* Chinese: Graham.

B214.1. *Singing animal.*

B214.1.1. *Singing cow.* Jewish: Neuman.

B214.1.2. *Singing boar.* Irish myth: Cross (B211.5.1).

B214.1.3. *Singing cat.* Jewish: Neuman.

B214.1.4. *Singing dog.* Africa (Zulu): Callaway 363.

B214.1.5. *Singing lion.* Jewish: Neuman.

B214.1.6. *Singing fox.* Jewish: Neuman.

B214.1.7. *Singing frog.* Jewish: Neuman.

B214.1.8. *Singing crab.* India: Thompson-Balys.

B214.1.8.1. *Crab sings about his captivity.* India: Thompson-Balys.

B214.1.9. *Singing mouse.* Jewish: Neuman.

B214.1.10. *Singing snake.*

B214.1.11. *Singing hippopotamus.* Africa (Nyang): Ittman 49.

B214.1.12. *Singing elephant.* Africa (Nyang): Ittman 49.

B214.2. *Whistling animals.*

B214.2.1. *Whistling toad.* Chinese: Graham.

B214.3. *Laughing animal.*

B214.3.1. *Laughing toad.* Chinese: Graham.

B214.4. *Weeping animal.*

B214.4.1. *Weeping toad.* Chinese: Graham.

B215. *Animal languages.* The various animals have languages of their own. (Cf. B251.1.2.) — *Type 517, 670, 671; *BP I 131, 322, 323 n. 1; **Aarne FFC XV; *Chauvin V 180, 296.

B215.0.1. *Animals taught one another's language.* India: Thompson-Balys.

B215.1. *Bird language.* *Types 517, 671, 781; *BP I 322; Cox 497 n. 32; *W. Seelman "Die Vogelsprachen (Vogelparlamente) der mittelalterlichen Literatur" Jahrh. d. Vereins f. niederdeutsche Sprachforschung XIV 102f; Greek: Frazer Apollodorus I 86 n. 2 (Melampus); Icel.: Völsungasaga p. 45, cf. von Sydow Fåvne; Flemish: DeMeyer FFC XXXVII 87 No. 90a; Jewish: Neuman; Hindu: Penzer *II 107, IV 145; India: *Thompson-Balys.

B215.2. *Dog language.* *Type 671. — Breton: Sébillot Incidents s.v. "chien".

B215.2.1. *Dog language understood by fox.* Nouvelles Recreations No. 29.

B215.3. *Fox language.* Nouvelles Recreations No. 29.

B215.4. *Frog language.* *Type 671.

B215.5. *Serpent language.* Irish myth: Cross.
B176. Magic serpent.

B215.5.1. *Lizard's language.* India: *Thompson-Balys.

B215.6. *Insects' language.* India: Thompson-Balys.

B215.6.1. *Ant language.* India: Thompson-Balys.

B216. *Knowledge of animal languages.* Person understands them. — *Types 517, 670, 671; *Toldo Studien zur vgl. Littgsch. VIII 18; *BP I 321; Köhler-Bolte I 145, II 340; *Grunwald Hessische Blätter f. Vksk. LXI 316; Icel.: Boberg; Irish myth: Cross; Breton: Sébillot Incidents s.v. "langage"; Hindu: Penzer I 107 n. 1, VII 3 n. 2; India: *Thompson-Balys; Jewish: Neuman; Korean: Zong in-Sob 101 No. 55; Buddhist myth: Malalasekera II 68, 153, 412; Chinese: Eberhard FFC CXX 16 No. 8; Buriat: Holmberg Siberian 427. — Africa (Benga): Nassau 227 No. 34.

B165. Animal languages learned from animal. H1214. Quest assigned because of hero's knowledge of animal languages. J816.1. King brought to sense of duty by feigned conversation of birds. M302.1. Prophesying through knowledge of animal languages. N547. Understanding of animal languages leads to discovery of treasure. N451. Secrets overheard from animal conversation. V223.5. Saint understands language of wren, fly, cat.

B217. *Animal language learned.* *Types 517, 670, 671, 672, 673, 670B*, 671*, BP I 132; **Aarne FFC XV; *Frazer "The Language of Animals" Archeological Review I (1888) 166 ff.; *Chauvin VIII 49 No. 17; Cox 496 n. 32. — Wesselski Morlini 314 No. 71; Gaster Exempla 248

No. 352; Wesselski Märchen 221 No. 35; Icel.: Boberg; Jewish: Neuman; India: *Thompson-Balys; Chinese: Graham.

B165. Animal languages learned from animal. C425. Tabu: revealing knowledge of animal languages. D1301. Magic object teaches animal language. D1301.4. Bird's head (when eaten) teaches animal language. D1815. Magic knowledge of strange tongues.

B217.1. *Animal languages learned from eating animal.* Irish myth: Cross, *MacCulloch Celtic 166.

D1793. Magic results from eating or drinking. D1811.1. Magic wisdom from eating or drinking.

B217.1.1. *Animal languages learned from eating serpent.* (Cf. B176.) — *Type 673; *BP I 131 (Gr. No. 17); *Cox 496 n. 32; *Norlind Skattsägner 37ff.; **Scott Thumb; Philostratres Life of Apollonius (Loeb ed.) 57; Chinese: Eberhard FFC CXX 17 No. 8; Icel.: Boberg.

B217.1.2. *Animal languages learned from eating dragon's heart.* Smith Evolution of the Dragon 82; *BP I 131; *von Sydow Fåvne 35ff.; **Scott Thumb.

D1301.2. Drinking blood teaches animal languages.

B217.2. *Animal languages learned from eating plant.* Breton: Sébillot Incidents s.v. "herbe"; *Cox 496 n. 32.

D965. Magic plant.

B217.3. *Animal languages learned from ghosts (spirits).* Gaster Exempla 248 No. 352. — Africa (Ekoi): Talbot 99.

E373. Ghosts bestow gifts on living.

B217.4. *Animal languages learned from carrying churchyard mould in hat.* Fb. "kirkegårdsmuld".

D1301.1. Magic turf from church-roof teaches animal languages.

B217.5. *Bird language learned by having ears magically cleansed.* Greek: Frazer Apollodorus I 363 n. 2 (Athena and Tiresius).

B217.6. *Animal languages learned by exchanging tongues with helpful dragon.* Italian Novella: Rotunda.

B217.7. *Stone deity (image of) confers upon man powers of understanding animal language.* India: Thompson-Balys.

B217.8. *Language of animals learned by Adam from Eve.* Jewish: Neuman.

B220. Animal kingdom (or community). Wienert FFC LVI 47 (classic fables). — Breton: Sébillot Incidents s.v. "ville". — India: Thompson-Balys; N. A. Indian: Thompson Tales 348 n. 253a.

A2546. Animal granted patent of nobility. B240 King of animals. F127. Journey to underground animal kingdom. F531.6.2. Haunts of giants. F700. Extraordinary places.

B221. *Animal kingdom — quadrupeds.*

Q433.3. Zeus has embassy of dogs imprisoned for fouling his court. W128.2. Unsatisfied fox. In kingdom of lions laments that he always gets the worst bits of food.

B221.1. *Kingdom of monkeys.* Chauvin VII 40 No. 153; India: Thompson-Balys.

B221.2. *Kingdom of rats.* India: Thompson-Balys; Japanese: Ikeda.

B241.2.4. King of rats.

B221.2.1. *Procurator of rats.* Serpent has the office. — Fb "lindorm" II 433a.

B221.3. *Land of lions.* Icel.: Boberg.

B221.4. *Land of elephants.* Icel.: Boberg.

B221.5. *Land of mice.* India: *Thompson-Balys.

B221.6. *Land of tigers.*

B221.6.1. *Village of wer-tigers.* India: Thompson-Balys.
D112.2 Transformation: man to tiger.

B222. *Kingdom (land) of birds.* Arabian: Burton Nights VIII 91; Japanese: Anesaki 324, Ikeda.

B222.1. *Land of pigeons.* India: Thompson-Balys.

B222.2. *Land of peacocks.* India: Thompson-Balys.

B222.3. *Land of parakeets.* India: Thompson-Balys.

B222.4. *Land of parrots.* India: Thompson-Balys.

B223. *Kingdom of fishes.* India: *Thompson-Balys; Japanese: Hartland Science 174, Ikeda. — N. A. Indian: Thompson Tales 342 n. 236.

B223.1. *Kingdom of sharks.* Hawaii: Beckwith Myth 140.

B224. *Kingdom of insects.*

B224.1. *Kingdom of ants.* Chauvin VII 40 No. 153 n. 3; Jewish: Neuman.

B225. *Kingdom of reptiles.*

B225.1. *Kingdom of serpents.* Icel.: Boberg; Chauvin V 256f. No. 152; India: Thompson-Balys; Buddhist myth: Malalasekera II 388.
B244.1. King of serpents. B549.5. Frog rescues man from kingdom of the snakes. C711. Tabu: going into bath on return from serpent kingdom. R152.6. Wife gets back her husband from land of serpents by charming him with her beautiful dance.

B225.1.1. *Snake kingdom under the sea.* — India: Thompson-Balys.
F133. Submarine otherworld.

B226. *Kingdom of amphibia.*

B226.1. *Community of toads.* German: Grimm Nos. 63, 127.

B226.2. *Community of frogs.* Jewish: Neuman.

B230. Parliament of animals. E. Voigt "Odo de Ciringtonis und seine Quellen" Zs. f. d. Alterthum XXIII (N.F. XI) 283; Africa: Stanley 222, (Fang): Trilles 176, Tessman 54, (Wute): Sieber 205, (Duala): Ebding 142, (Wakweli): Bender 62; India: Thompson-Balys.

B232. *Parliament of birds.* (Cf. B236.1, B238.) — Type 220; *BP III 278ff. — *Robinson Complete Works of Chaucer 900ff.; T. Wright The Owl and the Nightingale (Percy Society, 1834); Irish myth: Cross; Breton: Sébillot Incidents s.v. "oiseaux"; Hindu: *Penzer V 100 n. 1; India: *Thompson-Balys; — Seneca (Indians): Curtin-Hewitt RBAE XXXII 695 No. 133.
K815.8. Hawk persuades doves to elect him their king. Kills them. L147.1. Tardy bird alone succeeds at bird convocation.

B232.1. *St. Valentine's Day for bird assembly.* Sartori Sitte u. Brauch III 88; M. Höfler Das Jahr im oberbayerischen Volksleben (München 1899) 11; G. L. Gomme (ed) Mother Bunch's Closet Newly Broke Open (Leipzig 1839) II (1) 357f.; E. Schröder Korrespondenzblatt des Vereins f. niederdeutsche Sprachforschung XXXVI (1917—1918) 77;

*Seelman (cf. B215 above); Sachs "Das Regiment der anderthalbhundert Vögel" (Stuttgart Verein CV) 278ff.

B233. *Parliament of fishes.* (Cf. B236.2.) — *BP III 284 (Gr. No. 172); *Dh IV 192 ff.

B233.1. *Council of fishes decide to get rid of men (who eat fish).* India: Thompson-Balys.

J671.1. Belling the cat. — J2214.6. Men must have been calves once (for they are fond of milk). Fish so reason.

B234. *School of animals.* India: Thompson-Balys.

B235. *Secrets discussed in animal meeting.* *Type 613; *BP II 481 (Gr. Nos. 6, 55, 88, 125, 119a); **Christiansen FFC XXIV; Fb "bjørn" IV 43a; Bloomfield Am. Journ. of Philology XLI 309ff.; Bloomfield in Penzer VII viii; — Missouri-French: Carrière; India: Thompson-Balys.

B513. Remedy learned from overhearing animal meeting. B561. Animals tell hero their secrets. N451. Secrets overheard from animal conversation.

B236. *Animal parliament elects king.* *Type 221; *Dh IV 192ff.; *BP III 278, 284 (Gr. Nos. 171, 172); Wienert FFC LVI 47 (ET 59—63); Penzer V100 n. 1. — Africa (Ibo, Nigeria): Basden 280, (Angola): Chatelain 211 Nos. 32, 33.

B240. King of animals. P11. Choice of kings.

B236.0.1. *Animal king chosen as result of a contest.* Type 221; *BP III 278; Dh IV 169ff. — India: Thompson-Balys; Africa (Gold Coast): Barker and Sinclair 155 No. 30.

K11. Race won by deception. K25. Flying contest won by deception.

B236.1. *Election of king of birds.* (Cf. B232.) — *Type 221; *BP III 278 (Gr. No. 171); Penzer V 100ff.; India: Thompson-Balys; Panchatantra (tr. Ryder) 304; Bødker Exempler 293 No. 53; Japanese: Ikeda.

B242.1.2. Wren king of birds. Wins contest for kingship.

B236.2. *Election of king of fishes.* (Cf. B233, B243.) — *BP III 284 (Gr. No. 172); *Dh IV 192ff.

B237. *Drinking-bout assembly of animals.* Dh II 298ff.; Riegler Wörter und Sachen VI (1914—15) 194f.

B238. *Animal council assigns place and work to all.*

B238.1. *Bird council assigns place and work to all.* Eagle as judge. (Cf. B232). — Type 220. Cf. Chaucer "Parlement of Foules".

B238.2. *Bird council assigns coats to different birds.* India: Thompson-Balys.

B239. *Parliament of animals — miscellaneous.*

B239.1. *Election of fox as mediator to appease angry lion.* Jewish: Neuman.

B240. King of animals. Breton: Sébillot Incidents s.v. "roi", "bêtes"; Fb "konge" II 265a; Jātaka Index s.v. "king"; India: Thompson-Balys; Jewish: Neuman.

A2547. Why certain animal is king. B220 Animal kingdom. B236. Animal parliament elects king. P11. Choice of kings.

B240.1. *Bear as king of animals.* *Fb "bjørn" IV 42b.

B240.2. *Rabbit as king of animals.* Chuh (Indians of Guatemala): Kunst JAFL XXVIII 353 No. 1; India: Thompson-Balys.

B240.3. *Wild man as king of animals.* Chinese: Werner 392.

B240.4. *Lion as king of animals.* (Cf. K961, K962, K1632.) — Wienert FFC LVI 47; Benfey Panchatantra I 91, 230; Bødker Exempler 277 No. 17, 303 No. 74; Jewish: Neuman; Graf FFC XXXVII passim; India: *Thompson-Balys; Japanese: Ikeda.

B240.4.1. *Minister of lion-king a crane.* India: Thompson-Balys.

B240.5. *Tortoise as king of animals.* Africa (Mbundu): Bell JAFL XXXV 135ff. No. 15.

B240.6. *Gazelle as king of animals.* Africa (Luba): De Clerq Zs. f. Kolonialspr. IV 195f. No. 8.

B240.7. *Buffalo as king of animals.* Africa (Luba): De Clerq Zs. f. Kolonialspr. IV 198ff. No. 10.

B240.8. *Fox as king of animals.* Wienert FFC LVI 47.

B240.9. *Dog as king of animals.* Wienert FFC LVI 47.

B240.10. *Wolf as king of animals.* Wienert FFC LVI 47.

B240.11. *Camel as king of animals.* Wienert FFC LVI 47.

B240.12. *Monkey as king of animals.* Wienert FFC LVI 47.

B240.13. *Tiger as king of animals.* Cheremis: Sebeok-Nyerges; India: Thompson-Balys.

B240.14. *Elephant as king of animals.* India: Thompson-Balys; Africa (Fang): Trilles 175, (Cameroon): Mansfield passim.

B240.15. *Crocodile as king of animals.* Africa (Fang): Trilles 158.

B241. *King of beasts (quadrupeds).*

B241.1. *Various beasts as king of beasts.*

B241.2. *King of the various kinds of beasts.*

B241.2.1. *King of lions.* Breton: Sébillot Incidents s.v. "roi"; Malone PMLA XLIII 409.

B241.2.2. *King of monkeys.* Cowell Jātaka III 225 No. 407; Penzer V 127ff.; Buddhist myth: Malalasekera I 287; Chinese: Eberhard 40 No. 27, 411 s.v. "Affenkönig".

J815.1. Lion rewarded by king of apes.

B241.2.3. *King of cats.* Fb "kattekonge". — English: Jacobs More Eng. 237; Irish myth: Cross.

B184. Magic cat. B342. Cat leaves house when report is made of death of one of his companions. B871.10. Giant cat.

B241.2.4. *King of rats.* Breton: Sébillot Incidents s.v. "rats"; India: Thompson-Balys; Korean: Zong in-Sob 28 No. 12.

B221.2. Kingdom of rats.

B241.2.5. *King of mice.* English: Jacobs English 82 No. 17; India: *Thompson-Balys.

M244.1. Bargain with king of mice.

B241.2.6. *King of hares.* Penzer V 101f.; Bødker Exempler 294 No. 54.

B241.2.7. *King of dogs.* Fb "hund" IV 227b.

B241.2.8. *King of tigers.* Africa (Gold Coast): Barker and Sinclair West African Folk-Tales 105ff. No. 19.; India: *Thompson-Balys.

B241.2.8.1. *Newly-born divine twins cared for by mother-of-tigers.* S. A. Indian (Chiriguano): Métraux RMLP XXXIII 161.

B241.2.9. *King of jackals.* India: *Thompson-Balys.

J951.6. King of jackals captured because of his large banner.

B241.2.10. *King of deer.* Buddhist myth: Malalasekęra II 69.

B241.2.11. *King of elephants.* Panchatantra (tr. Ryder) 275, 308; Wienert FFC LVI 47; Buddhist myth: Malalasekera I 415, 483, 921.

B241.2.12. *King of the boars.* Irish myth: Cross; Buddhist myth: Malalasekera I 986, II 819f.

B241.2.13. *King of antelopes.* India: Thompson-Balys.

B241.2.14. *King of mongooses.* Africa (Ganda): Rowling Tales of Sir Apolo 44ff.

B241.3. *Man transformed to beast becomes leader of herd.* Irish myth: Cross.

B242. *King of birds.* *Type 221; *BP III 278 (Gr. No. 171). — Irish myth: Cross; Bødker Exempler 293, 2.; Breton: Sébillot Incidents s.v. "oiseaux"; Missouri-French: Carrière; English: Jacobs English 82 No. 17; Hindu: Tawney I 183, II 65 n.; India: *Thompson-Balys; Buddhist myth: Malalasekera I 40, 437.

C841.2. Tabu: hunting birds. Supernatural lover (king of birds) tells woman that son must not do so.

B242.1. *Various birds as king of birds.*

K815.8. Hawk persuades doves to elect him their king. Kills them.

B242.1.1. *Eagle king of birds.* BP III 279; Icel.: Boberg.

B242.1.2. *Wren king of birds.* Wins contest for kingship. (Cf. B236.1.) — *Type 221; *BP III 278 (Gr. No. 171); Irish myth: Cross; Japanese: Ikeda.

B242.1.2.1. *Wren as "druid of the birds" (drui én).* Irish myth: Cross.

P427. Druid (magus).

B242.1.3. *Hornbill king of birds.* India: Thompson-Balys.

B242.1.4. *Pelican as king of birds.* Africa (Duala): Gehr Zs. f. Kolonialspr. VII 25ff.

B242.1.5. *Shrike as king of birds.* Madagascar (Merina): Renel Contes de Madagascar II 160ff. No. 100.

B242.1.6. *Jackdaw king of birds.* Wienert FFC LVI 47.

B242.1.7. *Peacock king of birds.* Wienert FFC LVI 47.

B242.1.8. *Owl as king of birds.* India: Thompson-Balys.

B242.1.9. *Swan as king of birds.* Buddhist myth: Malalasekera II 8.

B242.1.10. *Ziz as king of birds.* Jewish: Neuman.

B242.2. *King of the various kinds of birds.*

B242.2.1. *King of crows.* Breton: Sébillot Incidents s.v. "corbeaux"; India: *Thompson-Balys.

B242.2.2. *King of doves.* India: *Thompson-Balys.

B242.2.3. *King of kites.* India: Thompson-Balys.

B242.2.4. *King of pigeons.* India: Thompson-Balys.

B242.2.5. *King of peacocks.* India: Thompson-Balys.

B242.2.6. *King of quails.* India: Thompson-Balys.

B242.2.7. *King of sparrows.* India: Thompson-Balys.

B242.2.8. *King of parrots.* Buddhist myth: Malalasekera II 572.

B242.2.9. *King of geese.* Buddhist myth: Malalasekera I 948, II 581.

B242.2.10. *King of swans.* Buddhist myth: Malalasekera I 98, 210, 242, 447.

B242.2.11. *King of vultures.* Buddhist myth: Malalasekera I 269.

B242.2.12. *King of larks.* Crane Vitry I No. 4.

B243. *King of fishes.* (Cf. B236.2.) *Type 303; *BP I 528, III 284 (Gr. No. 172); *Dh IV 192ff.; Hartland Science 174. — Breton: Sébillot Incidents s.v. "poisson"; Missouri French: Carrière; India: *Thompson-Balys. — Africa (Angola): Chatelain 65 No. 3; S. A. Indian (Toba): Métraux MAFLS XL 6, 52.

B107. Treasure-fish. B124. Wise fish. B142. Prophetic fish. B142.1. King of fishes prophesies hero's birth. B175. Magic fish. B211.11. Speaking fish. B223. Kingdom of fishes. B233. Parliament of fishes. B236.2. Election of king of fishes. B375.1. Fish returned to water: grateful. B470 Helpful fish.

B243.1. *Various fishes as king of fishes.*

B243.1.1. *Herring as king of fishes.* *BP III 284, 285 n. I (Gr. No. 172).

B243.1.2. *Eel as king of fishes.* S. A. Indian (Toba): Métraux MAFLS XL 6.

B243.1.3. *Shark as king of fishes.* Hawaii: Beckwith Myth.

B243.2. *King of various kinds of fishes.*

B243.2.1. *King of salmon.* Japanese: Hartland Science 174.

B243.2.2. *King of eels.* Fb "ål" III 1190b.

B244. *King of reptiles.*

B244.1. *King of serpents (snakes).* *Type 672; BP II 463f.; *Fb "snogekonge" III 437b, "lindorm" II 433 b, "hugormekonge" I 667. — Danish: Kristensen Danske Sagn II (1893) 213ff., (1928) 139ff. — Hindu: Keith 154; Penzer VI 29; India: *Thompson-Balys; Buddhist myth: Malalasekera I 27, 64, 230, 1149, II 529, 556; Chinese: Eberhard 17 No. 8; Zanzibar: Bateman 202 No. 10.

B225.1. Kingdom of serpents. H939.4.1. Serpent-king assigns task.

B244.1.1. *Queen of watersnakes.* India: Thompson-Balys.

B244.1.2. *Serpent king resides in lake.* Buddhist myth: Malalasekera II 981.

B244.1.3. *Gigantic hood of serpent king.* Buddhist myth: Malalasekera II 796.

B244.1.4. *Four royal families of snakes.* Buddhist myth: Malalasekera I 231.

B244.2. *Naga-king.* Buddhist myth: Malalasekera I 694.

B244.3. *King of lizards.* Buddhist myth: Malalasekera I 657.

B245. *King of amphibians.*

B245.1. *King of frogs.* Type 440, Grimm No. 1; BP I 1ff.; Panchatantra (tr. Ryder) 369; Bødker Exempler 297 No. 61; Cosquin Études 530; Breton: Sébillot Incidents s.v. "roi", "grenouille". — English: Jacobs English 237; Hindu: Keith 147; India: Thompson-Balys; Chinese: Eberhard 76 No. 43.

J643.1. Frogs demand a live king. Zeus has given them a log as king.

B245.2. *Turtle king.* India: Thompson-Balys.

B246. *King of insects.*

B246.1. *King of ants.* Fb "myre".

B246.2. *King (sultan) of flies.* Africa (Swahili): Baker FL XXXVIII 183ff., No. 1.

B246.3. *King of bees.* Chinese: Eberhard 102 No. 59.

B248. *King of dragons.* Chinese: Graham.

B250. Religious animals. Günter Christliche Legende des Abendlandes 80ff.; Irish myth: Cross; Panchatantra (tr. Ryder) 334; Jewish: Neuman.

A2221. Animal characteristics as reward for pious act. A2231. Animal characteristics: punishment for impiety. B149.1.2. Horse weeps for master's (saint's) approaching death. B151.0.1. Horses travel between clerics without guidance. B563.4. Animal leads cleric to holy place. F171.5. Animals in otherworld pass in and out of church and become human beings. Q535.2. Penance: lioness foregoes meat. Q557. Miraculous punishment through animals. V. Religion. V35.1.1. Horse kneels before stolen sacrament. V331.9. Swans (transformed children) do not suffer in harsh weather after conversion to Christianity.

B251. *Animals praise or worship.*

B251.1. *Animals rejoice at Christ's birth.* Irish myth: Cross; English: Child V 485 s.v. "joy".

B211.0.1. Animals speak praising God on night of Christ's nativity. V211.1. Nativity of Christ.

B251.1.1. *Animals worship infant Jesus.* *Dh II 12ff. — Alphabet No. 554. — Irish myth: Cross; Spanish Exempla: Keller.

B251.1.2. *Animals speak to one another at Christmas.* DeCock Volkskunde XXI 52ff.; Luzel Légendes Chretiennes de la Basse Bretagne II 333; Tille Die Geschichte der deutschen Weinacht 66f.; Wossidlo Mecklenbürgische Volksüberlieferung II (1) 59, 369; Lithuanian: Balys Index No. *748; Livonian: Loorits FFC LXVI 47 No. 237; North Carolina: Brown Collection I 637.

B251.1.2.1. *Cock crows, "Christus natus est."* English: Child I 240ff., 505f., II 501, IV 451f.

B251.1.2.2. *Cows speak to one another on Christmas.* (Cf. B215.) — Fb "ko" II 240b.

B251.1.2.3. *Cows kneel in stable at midnight of Eve of Old Christmas.* England, U.S.: *Baughman.

B251.2. *Animals honor saint (cleric).* Irish myth: Cross (B251.13).

B251.2.1. *Animals sing in honor of a saint.* Köhler-Bolte I 148; Irish myth: Cross.

B292.5. Bird sings to console man (saint). D2011.1. Years seem moments while man listens to song of bird.

B251.2.2. *Fish perform races as welcome to saint.* Irish myth: Cross.

B175. Magic fish.

B251.2.3. *Wolves lick saint's shoes.* Irish myth: Cross.

B279.1. Saint makes covenant with wolves. B442. Helpful wolf. W10.2. Saint gives calf to wolf.

B251.2.4. *Fly habitually buzzes when cleric returns from matins.* Irish myth: Cross.

B259.5. Fly, wren, fox live with cleric.

B251.2.5. *Birds beat waters with wings as welcome to saint.* Irish myth: Cross.

B172. Magic bird.

B251.2.6. *Deer lick saint's tomb daily at noon.* Irish myth: Cross.

B188. Magic deer. D1775. Magic results from licking.

B251.2.6.1. *Water-monsters lick saint's feet.* Irish myth: Cross.

B251.2.6.2. *Cow licks saint's feet.* Irish myth: Cross.

B251.2.7. *Wild animals as saint's disciples.* *Loomis White Magic 63.

B251.2.7.1. *Fish come in great numbers to the bank of a stream* in order to hear Anthony of Padua preach. *Loomis White Magic 70.

B251.2.8. *Sea-monster honors saint above all others.* Irish myth: Cross.

B251.2.9. *Birds lament saint's departure.* Irish myth: Cross.

B736. Bird sheds tears.

B251.2.10. *Cow gives twelve measures of milk for the twelve apostles of Ireland.* Irish myth: Cross.

D1652.3. Cow with inexhaustible milk.

B251.2.10.1. *Brilliantly white cow comes to be milked for infant saint.* Irish myth: Cross.

B251.2.11. *Lion lies down at feet of saint.* Saintyves Saints Successeurs 133.

B251.2.12. *Birds take part at saint's funeral.* Jewish: Neuman.

B251.3. *Animals sing songs of praise.* Jewish: Neuman (cow, cat, lion, mouse, cock, vulture, fish, frog); Irish myth: Cross.

B251.3.1. *Birds in otherworld sing religious songs.* Patch PMLA XXXIII 626 n. 89; Irish myth: Cross.

F167.1. Animals in otherworld.

B251.4. *Animals pray.* Irish myth: Cross; Jewish: Neuman.

B251.4.1. *Beast invokes saint's protection.* Irish myth: Cross.
B211.17. Speaking sea-beast. D1766.10. Magic results produced in name of saint.

B251.4.1.1. *Wild beast seeks protection of saint against hunters.* *Loomis White Magic 61f.

B251.5. *Animals fast.* Irish myth: Cross (B251.4).

B251.6. *Animals keep religious precepts.* India: Thompson-Balys.

B251.7. *Animal makes religious oath.*

B251.7.1. *Wolf swears by God.* Jewish: Neuman.

B251.8. *Animals observe sacred revelation.*

B251.8.1. *Singing of birds ceases at time of revelation.* Jewish: Neuman.

B251.9. *Animals make religious responses.* Jewish: Neuman.

B251.10. *Animals lick Christ-child.* Irish myth: Cross.
D1775. Magic results from licking. V211.1. Christ.

B252. *Animal churchmen.*
P120. Church dignitaries.

B252.1. *Animal monks.* Irish: Plummer Vitae Sanctorum Hiberniae cxli.; Irish myth: Cross.

B252.2. *Birds (in otherworld) call at canonical hours.* Irish myth: Cross.
V48. The canonical hours.

B252.3. *Priest of snakes.* India: Thompson-Balys.
A2777.1. Why fig tree is Chief Priest of the trees.

B253. *Animals perform offices of church.*

B253.1. *Snakes have mass.* Swiss: Jegerlehner Oberwallis 310 No. 34.

B253.2. *Wolves have annual (church) feast.* Irish myth: Cross.

B253.3. *Fox fasts as penance.* (Cf. B251.4.) — Irish myth: Cross.
P623. Fasting (as means of distraint). Q520. Penances.

B253.4. *Spider performs penance.* India: Thompson-Balys.

B253.5. *The deer with a cross carried between their horns.* *Loomis White Magic 61.

B253.6. *Deer with candles on the tops of their antlers.* *Loomis White Magic 61.

B255. *Miracle wrought for animal.* Irish myth: Cross; Jewish: Neuman.
V221.4.0.1. Saint cures frenzied animal. V224.4. Performing fox accidentally killed, miraculously replaced by saint.

B256. *Animal as servant of saint.* (Cf. B292.) — *Loomis White Magic 63; Irish myth: Cross; Irish: Plummer cxliiff.
B300. Helpful animal. B570. Animals serve men.

B256.0.1. *Animal deluded by saint.* Irish myth: Cross.

B256.1. *Birds nest in saint's hand (cowl).* — Saints' legend (Irish): Plummer cxlvi.; Irish myth: Cross.

B256.1.1. *Birds perch on hands and head of saint.* Irish myth: Cross.

B256.2. *St. Anthony's pigs.* Pigs dedicated to saint held sacred. — Italian Novella: Rotunda.

B256.3. *Deer makes its horns available as a bookholder to a saint.* *Loomis White Magic 61.

B256.3.1. *Deer furnish bier and bear saint's corpse to church.* Irish myth: Cross.

B256.4. *Domesticated wolves.* *Loomis White Magic 60.

B256.4.1. *Wolves guard saint's cattle like watchdogs when he is absent.* *Loomis White Magic 59.

B256.5. *Obedience of the feathered creatures to the commands of saint.* *Loomis White Magic 67f.

B256.5.1. *Birds protect saint and serve him.* *Loomis White Magic 68.

B450. Helpful birds.

B256.6. *Boar serves saint.* (Cf. B183.) — Irish myth: Cross.

B256.6.1. *Boar guards holy man's swine.* Irish myth: Cross.

B576. Animal as guard.

B256.6.2. *Boar makes music for holy man.* Irish myth: Cross.

B256.6.3. *Boar acts as physician for holy man:* licks his wounded feet. Irish myth: Cross.

B251.2.3. Wolves lick saint's shoes.

B256.7. *Tiger sweeps temple for saint.* India: Thompson-Balys.

B256.8. *Saint's prayer causes wolf to bring back child.* Saintyves: Saints Successeurs 129.

B256.9. *Stags plow for saint.* Irish myth: Cross.

B256.10. *Fly, wren, fox live with cleric.* Irish myth: Cross.

B256.11. *Wolf returns sheep stolen from saint.* Irish myth: Cross.

B442. Helpful wolf. K423.0.1. Stolen animal returns to owner.

B256.12. *Whale raises back so that voyaging clerics can land to celebrate Easter.* Irish myth: Cross.

B472. Helpful whale. V75. Easter. V462.10. Asetic cleric lives for seven years on whale's back.

B257. *Animal funeral.* *Type 2021; *BP II 146 (Gr. No. 80).

Z32. The funeral procession of the hen.

B259. *Miscellaneous religious animals.*

B189.1.1. Wethers leap from well: payment for saint's baptism.

B259.1. *Ass insists upon payment of tithes.* When stolen by thieves, the ass refuses to eat for three days because the thieves' provender has not been tithed. — Hebrew: Gaster Exempla 228 No. 235; Jewish: Neuman.

B259.2. *Sabbath-keeping cow.* Refuses to work on Sabbath. — Jewish: Bin Gorion Born Judas[2] II 92, *342; Jewish: Neuman.

B259.3. *Hog will not accept food from excommunicated men.* Alphabet No. 312

B259.4. *Bees build church of wax to contain consecrated host.* (Cf. A2012.1.) — *Kittredge Witchcraft 150, 469 n. 112; Alphabet No. 695. — *Loomis White Magic 65. — Irish myth: Cross.

V30. Sacrament. V111. Churches.

B259.4.1. *Animals refrain from spoiling consecrated food.* Irish myth: Cross.

B259.5. *Bird's wings drip blood when birds hear of Day of Judgment.* Irish myth: Cross.

B260. Animal warfare. Wienert FFC LVI 48 (ET 64—68).

B260.1. *Two groups of animals make peace treaty.* Tahltan: Teit JAFL XXXII 213 No. 1 (18); Shuswap: Teit JE II 658f.

B261. *War of birds and quadrupeds.* *Type 222; BP II 435 (Gr. No. 102); *Dh III 3ff., 226, IV 197ff. — Crane Vitry No. 153; Scala Celi No. 417. Japanese: Ikeda. — Africa: Frobenius Atlantis VIII 253, IX 115, XI 128.

K2323.1. Fox's tail drops and frightens animals. War between birds and quadrupeds.

B261.1. *Bat in war of birds and quadrupeds.* Because of ambiguous form joins first one side and then the other. Discredited. — Wienert FFC LVI *48 (ET 66, 67), *52 (ET 166), 134 (ST 398, 399); Halm Aesop Nos. 307, 391; Dh IV 197ff.; India: Thompson-Balys; Japanese: Ikeda; Africa (Benga): Nassau 163 No. 21, (Ibo, Nigeria): Basden 281, Thomas 161 (hornbill), (Mpongwe): Nassau 53 No. 8 (crocodile), (Yoruba): Ellis 252 No. 3.

K2030. Double dealers.

B261.1.1. *Tame elephant not accepted by wild brethren.* India: Thompson-Balys.

B262. *War between domestic and wild animals.* *Type 104; *BP I 425. — Japanese: Ikeda.

K2323. The cowardly duelers. War between the wild and the domestic animals.

B263. *War between other groups of animals.*

B263.1. *War between toads and frogs.* Breton: Sébillot Incidents s. v. "crapauds".

B263.2. *War between elephants and ants.* Indonesian: De Vries's list No. 132.

B263.3. *War between crows and owls.* — Spanish Exempla: Keller; Hindu: Penzer V 98—113. — Panchatantra III intr. (tr. Ryder) 291ff; Bødker Exempler 293 No. 52.

B263.4. *War between birds and reptiles.* India: Thompson-Balys.

B263.5. *War between groups of birds.* Irish myth: Cross.

B263.5.1. *War between birds and eagle.* Jewish: Neuman.

B263.6. *War of monkeys and grasshoppers.* Chinese: Graham.

B263.7. *War between serpents and storks.* Jewish: Neuman.

B263.8. *War between lion and other animals.* Jewish: Neuman.

B264. *Single combat between animals.* Wienert FFC LVI 48. — Indonesia: DeVries's list No. 116. — Icel.: *Boberg; Irish myth: Cross; Jewish: Neuman.

D1812.5.0.8. Divination from animal fight.

B264.1. *Fight between animal and houndpack.* Irish myth: Cross.

B264.2. *Fight between eagle and fish.* India: Thompson-Balys.

B264.3. *Duel of buffalo and tiger.* Buffalo arms self. — India: Thompson-Balys.

B264.4. *Fight between snake and millipede.* Chinese: Eberhard 32 No. 18.

B264.5. *Fight between ape and tortoise.* Africa (Togo): Einstein 15f.

B265. *Animals continually rend each other.* Irish myth: Cross.

B266. *Animals fight.* Irish myth: Cross.

F171.4. Fighting animals seen in otherworld.

B266.1. *Thirsty cattle fight over well.* Irish myth: Cross.

B267. *Animal allies.* (Cf. A2493.)

B267.1. *Alliance of dog and wolf.* Jewish: Neuman.

B267.2. *Alliance of sheep and dog.* Jewish: Neuman.

B267.3. *Alliance of raven and crow.* Jewish: Neuman.

B267.4. *Alliance of cock and seafowl.* Jewish: Neuman.

B268. *Animal soldiers.* India: *Thompson-Balys.

F873. Extraordinary army.

B268.1. *Army of apes.* Hindu: Keith 128; India: Thompson-Balys; Chinese: Werner 328 (monkeys).

B268.2. *Cavalry of dogs.* Chauvin VII 40 No. 153.

B268.2.1. *War-dogs.* Icel.: *Boberg.

B571.3. Animals fight together with their master. H1588. Contest of dogs.

B268.3. *War-elephants.* Icel.: *Boberg.

B268.4. *Sorcerer's army of magic animals.* Icel.: Þidriks saga II 271, *Boberg.

B421. Helpful dog.

B268.5. *Army of birds.* India: Thompson-Balys.

B268.5.1. *Army of quails.* Jewish: Neuman.

B268.6. *Army of mice.* India: *Thompson-Balys.

B268.7. *Army of snakes.* India: *Thompson-Balys; Africa (Upoto): Einstein 121.

B268.7.1. *Army of snakes and scorpions.* Jewish: Neuman.

B268.8. *Insect army.* India: Thompson-Balys.

B268.8.1. *Army of hornets.* Jewish: Neuman.

B268.8.2. *Army of locusts.* Jewish: Neuman.

B268.8.3. *Army of wasps.* Jewish: Neuman.

B268.9. *Army of tigers.* India: *Thompson-Balys.

B268.10. *Army of cows.* India: Thompson-Balys.

B268.11. *Army of cats.* India: Thompson-Balys.

B268.12. *Army of boars.* Buddhist myth: Malalasekera II 819.

B268.13. *Army of hyenas.* Africa: Stanley 261.

B270. Animals in legal relations. **Cabanès Les animaux en justice (L'indiscretions de l'histoire, 5e serie, procedures singulières, Paris, 1920), **Lossouarn Les animaux en justice aux temps jadis (Bordeaux, 1905). — Spanish Exempla: Keller; Bødker Exempler 289 No. 40, 294 No. 55.; Jewish: Neuman.

J1172.3. Ungrateful animal returned to captivity. J1852. Goods sold to animals. P510. Law courts.

B270.1. *Lawsuit between the owl and kite.* India: Thompson-Balys.

B270.2. *Lawsuit between owl and mouse.* Africa. (Wakweli): Bender 38.

B271. *Animals as plaintiffs.*

B271.1. *Parrot and sparrow argue right to inherit property left by man.* Sparrow says his interests are the same as man's; parrot says that he caused all man's wealth, since man sold his feathers. People's decision for parrot. — Africa (Fang): Nassau 237 No. 5.

B271.2. *Grain as damages for injury to cat.* Swiss: Jegerlehner Oberwallis 294 No. 10.

B271.3. *Animals ring bell and demand justice.* A king has a bell which petitioners for justice may ring and thus summon him. The bell is rung by a serpent which is being menaced by a turtle (or by an old horse who wishes to complain against a cruel master). — *Pauli (ed. Bolte) No. 648; *Wesselski Theorie 20; Italian Novella: Rotunda.

B272. *Animals as defendents in court.* **Jacoby Zs. f. Vksk. XXIII (1913) 184.

E573. Ghosts tried in court.

B272.1. *Lawsuit against animals.* *Saintyves RTP XXVII 155.

B272.2. *Animal tried for crime.* *Evans (E.P.) The criminal Prosecution and Capital Punishment of Animals (New York 1926), von Amira (K). Tierstrafen und Tierprozesse (Innsbruck, 1891); *Mittheilungen d. Instituts f. öster. Geschichtsforsch. XII (1891) 545; *H. A. Berkenhoff Tierstrafe, Tierbannung und rechtsrituelle Tiertötung im Mittelalter (Strassburg 1937, diss.); Fb "stævne".

B272.2.1. *Horse tried for crime.* *Howey Horse in Magic and Myth 215ff.

B274. *Animal as judge.* Africa: Milligan 98. (See all references to J1172.3 and J1130. Cleverness in law court.)

B275. *Animal punished.* Wesselski Nasreddin I 208 No. 11, II 186 No. 356. — *Von Amira Tierstrafen und Tierprozesse (Innsbruck, 1891); Jewish: Neuman.

B253.3. Fox fasts as penance. J1860. Animal or object absurdly punished.

B275.1. *Animal executed for crime.* *Frazer Old Testament III 415—445; *Wesselski Märchen 231; **Evans The Criminal Prosecution and Capital Punishment of Animals (New York, 1906); Grimm Rechtsaltertümer II 235; Sébillot France III 27; Wilken Verspreide Geschriften IV 181ff.; Jewish: Neuman.

Q411. Death as punishment.

B275.1.1. *Horse executed for crime.* *Howey Horse in Magic and Myth 215ff.

B275.1.2. *Fox executed for thefts.* Nouvelles Récréations No. 29.

B275.1.3. *Wolf executed for thefts.*

B275.1.3.1. *Man hangs wolf who has eaten sheep left in his charge.* Spanish Exempla: Keller.

B275.1.3.2. *Wolves and wild pigs condemned to death in lion's court* for killing and eating sheep. Spanish Exempla: Keller.

B275.2. *Excommunication of animal.* *Saintyves RTP XXVII 155.

B275.3. *Animals eating corpse of holy man die.* Irish myth: Cross.

D2089.3. Animals magically stricken dead. Q558.11. Animals which eat of saint's body stricken dead. Q558.14.1. Animals stricken dead for desecration of holy place.

B275.4. *Animal's revenge for being criticized by a bird: nest destroyed.* — India: Thompson-Balys.

B276. *Animal jury.* Africa (Baukon): Ittman 89f.

B278. *Captured animal ransoms self.* *Type 159; Chauvin VI 147 No. 304, VIII 148 No. 146 note 1. — India: *Thompson-Balys.

B366. Animal grateful for ransom from captivity.

B279. *Covenant with animals.* Irish myth: Cross.

K2023.Badgers treacherously slain in violation of pledge given by prince. P312.0.1. Saint makes blood covenant with animals.

B279.1. *Saint makes covenant with wolves.* Irish myth: Cross.

B279.2. *Attitudes of animals toward oath.* Jewish: Neuman.

M100. Vows and oaths.

B280. **Animal weddings.** RTP V 16, VIII 552, JAFL XXXV 392ff. — Japanese: Anesaki 334f.; India: Thompson-Balys.

Z28.1. Louse and flea wish to marry.

B281. *Beast wedding.*

B281.1. *Wedding of fox and hyena.* Fox refuses to marry hyena, since, according to belief, hyena yearly changes sex. — Wienert FFC LVI 62 (ET 251), 131 (ST 376, 401); Halm Aesop No 405.

B281.2. *Wedding of mouse.* (See B284.1.1.)

B281.2.1. *Wedding of mouse and weasel.* Estonian: Neus Esthnische Volkslieder 352 No. 98C; Greek: Passow Pop. Carmina Graeciae Recentioris 458 No. 623.

B281.2.2. *Wedding of mouse and cockroach.* India: Thompson-Balys.

B281.3. *Wedding of wolf.* Slavic: Wenzig Westslavischer-Märchenschatz 242ff. (goat); Wendish: Haupt-Schmaler Volkslieder der Wenden I 386 (goat); Lithuanian: Balys Index No. *91; India: Thompson-Balys.

B281.4. *Wedding of lynx.* Lettish: Ulmann Lettische Volkslieder 136 No. 431 (marten), Baton Chansons nationales latviennes I[2] (Riga 1922) No. 2685 (marten).

B281.5. *Wedding of marten.* (See B281.4.)

B281.6. *Wedding of pig.* Rhaetian: Decurtins "Eine rätoromanische Ballade" Schweizerisches Archiv f. Vksk. XX 93f. (mole).

B281.7. *Wedding of ass.* French: Arnaudin Chants pop. de la Grande-Lande I 365ff.

B281.8. *Wedding of squirrel.* French: Mélusine I (1878) 287 (ant).

B281.9. *Wedding of cat.* (See B282.4.2.)

B281.9.1. *The cat as vixen's husband.* Frightens the other wild animals invited by the vixen. (Cf. K2324.) — Lithuanian: Balys Index No. *103A.

B281.10. *Wedding of monkey.* India: Thompson-Balys.

B281.11. *Wedding of rat.*

B281.11.1. *Wedding of rat and cockroach.* India: Thompson-Balys.

B282. *Bird wedding.* *RTP V 15; *Fb "ørn" III 1183b; *Hdwb. d. Aberglaubens s.v. "Vogelhochzeit"; Mélusine I 193, 287, 553; Missouri French: Carrière.

B282.1. *Wedding of turkey and peacock.* All birds invited except eagle. This omission starts great conflict. — *Type 224; *Bolte Zs. f. Vksk. XII 169.

B282.2. *Wedding of eagle with another bird.* Wendish: Haupt-Schmaler Volkslieder der Wenden II 144 No. 194 (kite).

B282.2.1. *Wedding of eagle and kite.* Kite promises to secure ostrich as attendant. Fails and is put to shame. — Wienert FFC LVI 62 (ET 250), 100 (ST 139); Thiele Der lateinische Äsop des Romulus 96.

B282.3. *Wedding of lark and another bird.*

B282.3.1. *Wedding of lark and nightingale.* German: Wossidlo Mechlenbürgische Volksüberlieferungen II (1) 255 No. 1675; Lettish: Baton Chansons nationales latviennes (Riga 1922) No. 2696.

B282.3.2. *Wedding of lark and cuckoo.* French: Perroud RTP V 15.

B282.3.3. *Wedding of lark and sparrow.* French: Tiersot RTP I 3f.

B282.3.4. *Wedding of lark and pigeon.* French: Lembert Chants et Chansons du Languedoc I 332.

B282.3.5. Wedding of lark and spotted woodpecker. Lettish: Andrejanoff Lettische Volkslieder 45 No. 134.

B282.3.6. *Wedding of lark and finch.* French: Daymard Vieux chants recueilles en Quercy 106ff., Kuhff Les Enfantines 178, Lambert Chants et Chansons du Languedoc I 327ff.; Catalonian: Mila y Fontanals Romancerillo Catalán 398f.

B282.4. *Wedding of owl.*

B282.4.1. *Wedding of owl and another bird.* French: Arnandin Chants pop. de la Grande-Lande I 350ff. (goat-sucker); Slavic: Herder Stimmen der Völker (Slavische Lieder No. 23) (wren).

B282.4.2. *Wedding of owl and cat.* English: Mother Goose rhymes.

B282.5. *Wedding of finch with another bird.* (Cf. B285.1.) — French: Rolland Faune Populaire de la France II 180ff. (greenfinch), 182ff. (goldfinch); Canadian: Gagnon Chansons pop. du Canada 279ff.

B282.6. *Wedding of goldfinch with another bird.* French: Rolland Faune pop. de la France II 182ff. (finch), Bladé Poésies pop. de la Gascogne III 104ff. (finch); Ukranian: Chodzko Les chants historiques de l'Ukraine 12f. No. 10.

B282.7. *Wedding of bullfinch with another bird.* Russian: Ralston Songs of the Russian People 11f. (quail).

B282.8. *Wedding of titmouse with another bird.* French: Wallonia V (1897) 138f. (cuckoo); Prussian: Frischbier Zehn Masurische Volkslieder 69.

B282.9. *Wedding of wren with another bird.* Slavic: Herder Stimmen der Völker (Slawische Lieder No. 23) (owl); English: FLJ I 166 (robin), Eckenstein Comparative Studies in Nursery Rhymes (London 1906) (robin); French: Kuhff Les Enfantines 345ff., Mélusine I (1878) 193f.

B282.10. *Wedding of sparrow and another bird.* French: Tiersot RTP I 3f. (lark); Bukovina: Kaindl Zs. f. Vksk. VII (1897) 427 (jackdaw). — Waldbrühl Slawische Balalaika 302. — Japanese: FLR I 131ff.

B282.11. *Wedding of blackbird with another bird.* German: Grüner Uber die ältesten Sitten u. Gebräuche der Egerländer (ed. A. John) 82f., (starling), Vorpahl Deutsche Volkslieder zur Guitarre (Sammlung I, 1915) (bullfinch), Deutsche Volkslieder Archiv (MS. Freiburg im Breisgau and University of Chicago) Nos. A74020, A72356, A63272, A93372.

B282.12. *Wedding of thrush with another bird.* German: Hainhoferi Lautenbücher II 130ff., Norrenberg Beiträge zur Localgeschichte des Niederrheins IV 102, Frischbier-Sembrzychi Hundert ostpreussische Volkslieder 52f. No. 32.

B282.13. *Wedding of woodpecker with another bird.* Estonian: Neus Esthnische Volkslieder 351f. No. 98B.

B282.14. *Wedding of magpie with another bird.* German: Hoffman-Richter Schlesische Volkslieder 75f., Haupt-Schmaler Volkslieder der Wenden (Pt. I) 256 No. 273 (raven); Lettish: Baton Chansons nationales latviennes (Riga 1922) No. 2684 (wagtail).

B282.15. *Wedding of heathcock with another bird.* German: Blätter für pommersche Volkskunde IX (1901) 42f.; Lettish: Baton Chansons nationales latviennes (Riga 1922) No. 2691.

B282.16. *Wedding of raven with another bird.* Danish: Nyerups Udvalg II 97ff.; Grüner-Nielsen Danske Skæmteviser I 34f. No. 15 (crane); Wendish: Haupt-Schmaler Volkslieder der Wenden I 256f. No. 273 (magpie).

B282.17. *Wedding of quail with another bird.* Russian: Ralston Songs of the Russian People 11f. (bullfinch).

B282.18. *Wedding of hoopoe with another bird.* Slavic: Wenzig Westslav. Märchenschatz 241; Czech.: Walda Böhmische Granaten 132 No. 163 (jay).

B282.19. *Wedding of cuckoo with another bird.* French: Perroud RTP V 15 (lark), Wallona (V 1897) 138f. (titmouse).

B282.20. *Wedding of pigeon with another bird.* French: Lambert Chants et Chansons de Languedoc I 332 (lark), Soleville Chants pop. du Bas-Quercy 303ff. (falcon).

B282.21. *Wedding of cock and hen.* German: Blätter für pommersche Volkskunde IX (1901) 43ff.

B282.22. *Wedding of crow and titmouse.*

B282.22.1. *Crow refuses to marry titmouse, since she is 100 years old.* Type 244**.

B841. Long-lived animals.

B282.23. *The courtship of the stork and the crane.* Go a-courting one another across the marshes but never come to an understanding, as each time either one or the other changes his mind. (Cf. T91.) — Lithuanian: Balys Index No. *223; Russian Andrejev No. *244 I.

B283. *Wedding of fish.* India: Thompson-Balys.

B283.1. *Wedding of crab.* Bulgarian: Rosen Bulgarische Volksdichtungen 232 (frog); Roumanian: Schuller Romänische Volkslieder 34ff. (toad).

B283.2. *Wedding of carp.* Chinese: JAFL VIII 189f.

B284. *Wedding of amphibians.*

B284.1. *Wedding of frog.* (See B283.1.)

B284.1.1. *Wedding of frog and mouse.* ("Frog went a-courtin'"). — United States: JAFL XXVI 134f., XXV 392—399 No. 138, Cox Folksongs of the South 470ff. No. 162, Scarborough On the Trail of Negro Folk-Songs 46ff., Pub. Texas Folklore Soc. V 5—48; English: Williams Folksongs of the upper Thames 133f.; Welsh: Journ. Welsh Folksong Soc. I (IV) 178 No. 18.

B284.2. *Wedding of toad.* Bulgarian: Rosen Bulgarische Volksdichtungen 233. (See also B283.1.)

B285. *Wedding of insects.*

B285.1. *Wedding of ant.* (See B281.8.) — Revue des Langues Romanes 2e Ser. IV (1877) 27ff. (louse); Rhaetian: Decurtins "Rätoromanische Christomatie" Romanische Forschungen XXVII (1910) 182f. (grasshopper); French: Arnaudin Chants pop. de la Grande-Lande I 345ff. (finch); Italian: Nigra Canti pop. de Piemonte No. 127 (cricket), *Zs. f. Vksk. XII 167f., 169n. 2 (grasshopper).

B285.2. *Wedding of cricket.* (See B285.1.) — Lettish: Andrejanoff Lettische Volkslieder 39 No. 115.

B285.3. *Wedding of grasshopper.* (See B285.1.)

B285.4. *Wedding of fly.* Danish: Abrahamson, Nyerup, og Rahbek Udvalgte Danske Viser (II) 104f. No. 40 (horsefly); German: Hoffmann-Richter Schlesische Volkslieder 71f., Jungbauer Bibliographie d. deutschen Volksliedes in Böhmen 31 (beetle); Zs. f. Vksk. XXII 421.

B285.5. *Wedding of flea.* French: Bladé Poesies pop. de la Gascogne III 291ff., Soleville Chants pop. du Bas-Quercy 310ff.; Spanish: Marín Cantos pop. Españoles I 74ff.

B285.6. *Wedding of butterfly.* French: Kuhff Les Enfantines 174, RTP V 16f, Bujeaud Chants de l'Ouest I 38.

B285.7. *Wedding of wasp.* RTP VIII 552 (hornet).

B285.8. *Wedding of cockroach and rat.* India: Thompson-Balys.

B286. *Plant wedding.*

B286.1. *Wedding of garlic and onion.* Lettish: Andrejanoff Lettische Volkslieder 39 No. 116.

B290. Other animals with human traits.

B120. Wise animals. B300. Helpful animals. F826.1. Animals with jeweled ornaments. F989.8 Mother-love induced in animal.

B290.1. *Swine march like soldiers.* Cheremis: Sebeok-Nyerges.

B291. *Animal as messenger.* Irish myth: Cross; India: Thompson-Balys; N. A. Indian: Koch-Grünberg Indianermärchen aus N. A. No. 33. — African: de Clerq Anthropos IV 451, (Fjort) Dennett 123.

A165.1.1. Birds as messengers of the gods. A1021.2. Bird scouts sent out from ark. B570. Animals serve men. E761.7.6. Life token: bird sent each day to tell of hero's condition; when owl comes it will be to announce death. F234.2.6. Fairy as messenger from fairyland. F932.5. River acts as messenger. H483. Animals compete as messengers to call father of newborn child. Their voices are tried. J1881.2.2. Fools send money by rabbit. K131. Rabbit sold as letter-carrier.

B291.0.1. *Animal tried out as messenger.* Hen (cock) the only one successful. — Africa (Basuto): Jacottet 188. No. 27, (Kaffir): Theal 63.

B291.0.2. *Unwelcome bird (insect) proves to be messenger.* *Jochelson JE VI 373 No. 16.

B291.1. *Bird as messenger.* English: Child II 113n., 356—365 passim, III 4, 8, IV 412, 482, 484f., V 234; Welsh: MacCulloch Celtic 101; Irish myth: Cross; Warncke Lais der Marie de France[2] cxxxix.; India: Thompson-Balys; Chinese: Graham; Hawaii: Beckwith Myth 90f.; Marquesas: ibid. 91; Mono: Wheeler 9, 21; Mangaia (Cook Is.): Clark 142; Africa (Fang): Einstein 148, 154, (Cameroon): Gantenbein 68.

A165.1.1. Birds as messengers of the gods. A1021.2. Bird scouts sent out from ark.

B291.1.0.1. *Bird as letter carrier.* (Cf. K131.) — India: *Thompson-Balys.

B291.1.1. *Raven as messenger.*

B291.1.1.1. *Ravens carry message to enemies.* Irish myth: Cross.

B147.1.1.3. Raven as bird of ill-omen.

B291.1.1.2. *Raven as devil's messenger.* *Fb "ravn" III 21b.

B147.1.1. Bird of ill-omen.

B291.1.2. *Crow as messenger.* India: *Thompson-Balys; Buddhist myth: Malalasekera I 567.

B291.1.3. *Dove as messenger.* Calif. Indian: Gayton and Newman 76.

B291.1.4. *Falcon as messenger.* India: Thompson-Balys.

B291.1.5. *Goose as messenger.* India: Thompson-Balys.

B291.1.6. *Parrot as messenger.* India: *Thompson-Balys.

B291.1.7. *Heron as messenger.* Buddhist myth: Malalasekera I 630.

B291.1.8. *Vulture as messenger.* Africa (Upoto): Einstein 144; Jewish: Neuman.

B291.1.9. *Eagle as messenger.* Africa (Upoto): Einstein 144; Jewish: Neuman.

B291.1.10. *Hawk as messenger.* Africa (Pooloki): Einstein 105.

B291.1.11. *Swallow as messenger.* Chinese: Eberhard 58.

B291.1.12. *Pigeon as messenger.* Jewish: Neuman.

B291.2. *Domestic beast as messenger.*

B291.2.1. *Horse as messenger.* Irish myth: Cross; India: Thompson-Balys.
B151.0.5. Horses travel between clerics without guidance. B181. Magic horse. B401. Helpful horse.

B291.2.2. *Dog as messenger.* Icel.: ASB XVII 91; India: Thompson-Balys.

B291.3. *Wild beast as messenger.*

B291.3.1. *Fox as messenger.* Irish myth: Cross.
B253.3. Fox fasts as penance. B441. Helpful fox.

B291.3.2. *Hare (rabbit) as messenger.*

B291.3.2.1. *Hares carry taxes to court.* India: Thompson-Balys.
K131. Rabbit sold as letter-carrier.

B291.4. *Other animals as messenger.*

B291.4.1. *Bee as messenger from heaven to earth.* India: Thompson-Balys.

B291.4.2. *Snake as messenger.* India: Thompson-Balys.

B291.4.3. *Whale as messenger.* Tahiti: Beckwith Myth 360.

B292. *Animal as servant to man.* Jewish: Neuman; India: Thompson-Balys; Chinese: Werner 263; Japanese: Ikeda.

B292.0.1. *Animals with human child as slave.* India: Thompson-Balys.

B292.0.2. *Animals leave wicked and go to pious master.* Jewish: Neuman.

B292.1. *Animal as shepherd for man.*

B292.1.1. *Baboon as shepherd for man.* Africa (Hottentot): Bleek 44 No. 21.

B292.1.2. *Dog as shepherd for man.* Greek Myth: Grote I 228.

B292.2. *Animal as domestic servant.* India: Thompson-Balys; Chinese: Werner 263.
B256.4. Domesticated wolves.

B292.2.1. *Monkey as domestic servant.* India: Thompson-Balys.

B292.2.2. *Bird as domestic servant.* Hawaii: Beckwith Myth 526.

B292.2.2.1. *Bird servant to deity.* India: Thompson-Balys.

B292.2.3. *Lion as domestic servant.* Jewish: Neuman.

B292.3. *Doe furnishes man milk.* Saints' legend (Irish): Plummer cxliv; Irish myth: Cross.
B188. Magic deer.

B292.4. *Stags plow for man.* Also draw chariot, bear burdens, and allow saints to use their horns as a book rest. — Saints' legend (Irish): Plummer cxliii—cxliv; Irish myth: Cross; English: Baughman.

B188. Magic deer. B445. Helpful deer. N543.2. Treasure to be found by man who plows with cock and harrows with hen.

B292.4.1. *Wild oxen plow for man.* Irish myth: Cross.

B411.2. Helpful ox.

B292.4.1.1. *Oxen draw saint's plow around whole district in one day.* Irish myth: Cross.

B292.4.2. *Tiger plows for man.* India: *Thompson-Balys.

B292.4.3. *Dog plows for man.* Chinese: Eberhard FFC CXX 44f.

B292.5. *Bird sings to console man.* Saints' legend (Irish): Plummer cxlvi (swan); Irish myth: Cross.

B172. Magic bird. D2011.1. Years seem moments while man listens to song of bird.

B292.6. *Black cat as servant of giant.* Breton: Sébillot Incidents s.v. "chat".

B184. Magic cat. E423.1.2. Revenant as cat. F531.6.1.3. Giant son of black cat. F531.8. Attendants of the giants. G100. Giant ogre. G219.7. Black witch. G225.3. Cat as servant of witch. G241.1.4. Witch rides on cat.

B292.6.1. *Thief lives alone with 20 cats that help him keep intruders away.* Icel.: *Boberg.

B292.7. *Otters supply man with fish and burning wood daily.* Irish myth: Cross.

B548.3. Otter recovers lost book from water.

B292.8. *Dog as guardian of treasure.* *Fb "hund" I 675b (cf. B576.2).

B292.9. *Animal as farm laborer.*

B292.9.1. *Frog works in fields for benefactor.* India: Thompson-Balys.

B292.9.2. *Chicken as laborer.* India: Thompson-Balys.

B292.9.3. *Rat servants cut jungle down, till soil for master.* India: Thompson-Balys.

B292.10. *Dog made king.* Icel.: Herrmann Saxo II 579, *Boberg.

B292.11. *Tiger carries load of wood for saint.* India: *Thompson-Balys.

B292.12. *Serpent as saint's whip.* India: Thompson-Balys.

B292.13. *Ass as tollkeeper.* Jewish: Neuman.

B293. *Animals dance.* India: Thompson-Balys; Africa (Luba): De Clerq Zs. f. Kolonialsprachen IV 193.

B293.0.1. *Animals dance for king.* Jewish: Neuman.

B293.1. *Dance of cats.* Breton: Sébillot Incidents s.v. "dance".

B293.2. *Dance of frog(s).* Tobler Epiphanie der Seele 76. — Breton: Sébillot Incidents s.v. "dance".

B293.3. *Dance of tigers.* French Canadian: Sister Marie Ursule. — Korean: Zong in-Sob 149 No. 65.

B293.4. *Dance of lions.* French Canadian: Sister Marie Ursule.

B293.5. *Dance of nagas (snake men).* Buddhist myth: Malalasekera II 1354.

B294. *Animals in business relations.*

B294.1. *Fox as divider of dying man's gifts.* Fb "ræv" III 113b.
B441. Helpful fox.

B294.2. *Animal handles money.*

B294.2.1. *Monkey's money stolen.* India: Thompson-Balys.

B294.2.2. *Monkey buys liquor.* India: Thompson-Balys.

B294.3. *Dog sells rotten peas on market: punished by other animals.* India: Thompson-Balys.

B294.4. *Animals hold fairs.* India: Thompson-Balys.

B294.5. *Parrot transacts business of trader.* India: Thompson-Balys.

B294.6. *Rabbit and elephant partners on trading expedition.* Africa: Stanley 245.

B294.7. *Tortoise and dog partners as thieves.* Africa (Cameroon): Meinhof 3.

B295. *Animal drives carriage.* *Type 2021; *BP II 146 (Gr. No. 80); Fb "kok" II 248b.

B295.1. *Mouse makes boat of bread-crust.* Takes animals and birds into boat. It capsizes. — Type 135*.
Z32. The funeral procession of the hen. Animals one by one join the procession. The funeral carriage breaks down or the procession drowns.

B296. *Animals go a-journeying.* *Types 130, 210; **Aarne FFC XI Die Tiere auf der Wanderschaft; BP I 75, 135, 237; Fb "væder" III 1106b, *"tyr" III 908 ab. — Jewish: Neuman; India: Thompson-Balys; Japanese: Ikeda; Indonesian, Japanese: Dixon *203 n. 41.; Missouri French: Carrière. — Africa (Tonga): Gifford 206. — Cf. N. A. Indian: Thompson Tales 302 n. 108.
F1025. Objects go journeying together. F1025.1. Bean, straw, and coal. They go journeying. Coal burns straw in two and falls into the water. Bean laughs until he splits. J1711.1. Animals helpless in sea-voyage together. Sheep, duck, and cock in peril. The duck swims; the cock flies to the mast. K1161. Animals hidden in various parts of a house attack owner with their characteristic powers and kill him when he enters.

B296.1. *Animal journeys to Rome.* Cock, geese, or dog go to Rome to become Pope. — Fb "hund" I 678b, "gås" I 528b, "Rom", "mus" II 634b.

B297. *Musical animals.*

B297.0.1. *Bull lows musically.* Irish myth: Cross (B214).
B182. Magic cow (ox, bull).

B297.1. *Animal plays musical instrument.* Africa (tribes of Western Sudan): Tauxier Le Noir du Yatenga 457 No. 56.
D1275.1. Magic music.

B297.1.1. *Bird plays timpan.* Irish myth: Cross.
B172. Magic bird.

B297.1.2. *Toad and chameleon play drum and xylophone.* Africa (Luba): De Clerq Zs. f. Kolonialsprachen IV 193.

B297.2. *Transformed women enchanted by music.*

B297.2.1. *Women transformed to bitches enchanted by music.* Irish myth: Cross.

B187.7. Magic bitches (in human form) enchanted by fairy music.

B298. *Animal plays game.*

B298.1. *Monkey plays chess.* Nouvelles Récréations No. 88.

B299. *Other animals with human traits — miscellaneous.*

B299.1. *Animal takes revenge on man.* India: *Thompson-Balys; Chinese: Graham.

B299.1.1. *Eagle takes revenge on man.* Chinese: Graham.

B299.2. *Animals dispute.*

B299.2.1. *Owls and crows dispute over merits of night or day vision.* India: Thompson-Balys.

B299.3. *Animals discover liquor and get intoxicated.* India: Thompson-Balys.

B299.4. *Bear asks boy to stay with her cubs.* India: Thompson-Balys.

B299.5. *Sympathetic animals.* Irish myth: Cross.

B295.2. Bird sings to console man.

B299.5.1. *Animal mutilates self to express sympathy.* India: Thompson-Balys.

B299.5.2. *Animal fasts to express sympathy.* India: Thompson-Balys.

B299.5.3. *Birds weep when man cuts off his hand.* Irish myth: Cross.

B736. Bird sheds tears.

B299.6. *Animal physician.* Africa (Cameroon): Rosenhuber 69, Meinhof 33, 36.

B299.7. *Festival of animals.* Jewish: Neuman; S. A. Indian (Tenetehara): Wagley-Galvão BBAE CXLIII (3) 148.

B299.8. *Animals build bridge.*

B299.8.1. *Tigers build bridge.* S. A. Indian (Amuesha): Métraux RMLP XXXIII 150.

B299.9. *Animals cultivate crops.* S. A. Indian (Chiriguano): Métraux RMLP XXXIII 179.

B299.10. *Animal christening.* German Grimm No. 74.

B300—B599. FRIENDLY ANIMALS

B300—B349. Helpful animals — general.

B300. Helpful animal. See also entire section B300—599, especially B350. — *Krappe "Guiding animals" JAFL LV (1942) 228—246; "Warning animals" FL LIX (1948) 8—15. — *Toldo Studien zur vgl. Littgsch. VIII 38. — Irish myth: Cross. — Hindu: Penzer I 101f., V 157f., 163f., VI 291, VIII 219. — India: Thompson-Balys. — N. A. Indian: *Thompson Tales 316 n. 146. — Philippine: Fansler MAFLS XII 313.

B155. Location determined by halting of an animal. B252.1. Animal monks. B256. Animal as servant of saint. B292. Animal in service of man. F601. Extraordinary companions. N800. Helpers.

B301. *Faithful animal.* Köhler-Bolte I 534; Irish myth: Cross.

B301.1. *Faithful animal at master's grave dies of hunger.* *Type 75*; *Pauli (ed Bolte) No. 428; cf. Alphabet No. 270; Icel.: *Boberg.

B301.1.1. *Faithful dog follows master's dead body when cast into river.* Supports body. — Spanish Exempla: Keller.

B301.1.2. *Faithful dog helps open mistress' grave — dies on it.* India: Thompson-Balys.

B301.1.3. *Faithful animal doesn't allow anybody to come near to master's corpse.* Þidriks saga II 154, 386.

B301.2. *Faithful animal at master's grave avenges his murder.* English: Wells Manual of Writings 121 (Sir Triamour). — *Hibbard 286.

B591. Animal avenges murder.

B301.3. *Faithful animal plans suicide when it thinks master dead.* English: Wells Manual of Writings 66 (Ywain and Gawain); Icel.: Boberg.

B301.4. *Faithful horse follows dead master to grave.* *Fb "hest" IV 212a.

B301.4.1. *Faithful horse lays his head on slain master's breast.* Irish myth: Cross.

B181.7. Magic horse avenges hero's death.

B301.4.1.1. *Faithful horse weeps for coming death of saint.* Irish myth: Cross.

B149.1.2. Horse weeps for master's (saint's) approaching death.

B301.4.2. *Faithful horse weeps tears of blood for master.* Irish myth: Cross.

B736.2. Horse sheds tears of blood. F1041.29. Tears of blood in excessive grief.

B301.4.3. *Faithful horse joins in keen at hero's death.* Irish myth: Cross.

B301.4.3.1. *Faithful horse lays his head in lap of dead master's wife.* Irish myth: Cross.

B301.4.4. *Faithful horse allows only its master to catch and ride it.* Icel.: *Boberg.

B301.4.5. *Faithful horse lies down in order that its mutilated master can mount it.* Icel.: *Boberg.

B301.4.6. *Faithful horse refuses to go before its master mounts it,* even when already loaded with two chests with gold. — Icel.: *Boberg.

B301.4.7. *Faithful horse dies together with its master.* Icel.: *Boberg.

F1041.1. Death from broken heart.

B301.4.8. *Faithful horse fights together with its master.* Icel.: *Boberg.

B571.3. Animals fight together with their master. K2. Animals help man in contest.

B301.5. *Faithful animals resuscitate master.* Italian Novella: Rotunda.

E0. Resuscitation.

B301.6. *Faithful cattle fight at master's grave* until they cast their horns. Irish myth: Cross.

A969.2. Mounds from horns cast by cattle.

B301.6.1. *Faithful cattle shed horns in grief for death of man.* Irish myth: Cross.

B301.6.2. *Faithful cow refuses to move for grief at master's death.* Irish myth: Cross.

B301.6.3. *Faithful cows lose milk at king's death.* Irish myth: Cross.

B301.7. *Faithful lapdog dies when mistress dies.* Irish myth: Cross; India: Thompson-Balys.

F1041.1. Death from broken heart.

B301.7.1. *Faithful dog helps open mistress' grave and dies on it.* India: Thompson-Balys.

F1041.1. Death from broken heart.

B301.8. *Faithful lion follows man who saved him.* Spanish Exempla: Keller; Icel.: Boberg.

B310. Acquisition of helpful animal. *Hartland Perseus III 191ff.

D810—D859. Acquisition of magic objects. N2.4. Helpful animals lost in wager.

B311. *Congenital helpful animal.* Born at same time as master and (usually) by same magic means. — *Hartland Perseus III 191ff.; *Types 300, 303; *BP I 534ff.; Köhler-Bolte I 179. — Irish myth: Cross, MacCulloch Celtic 83, Welsh ibid. 95; India: *Thompson-Balys; Africa (Zulu): Callaway 221.

B142.1. King of fishes prophesies hero's birth. B375.1. Fish returned to water: grateful. B631.1. Animal mother of man helps him. D857. Magic object born with hero. E765.2. Life bound up with that of animal. M369.8. Prophecies about fate of five boys born at the same time. P311.4. Friends born at same moment. T589.3. Birth trees. Spring forth as hero is born, act as life tokens, etc. T589.7.1. Simultaneous birth of animals and child. Z71.5.7. King with seven wives and seven mares: the seven wives pregnant for seven years, the seven mares for seven years in foal.

B311.1. *Helpful animal foster brother.* Hero reared by animal's parents. — Africa (Akan-Ashanti): Rattray Akan-Ashanti Folk Tales 206 No. 53, (Kassonke): Monteil Contes Soudanais 126ff.

B312. *Helpful animals obtained by purchase or gift.*

B312.1. *Helpful animals a gift.* German Grimm No. 60, 126; Irish myth: Cross; Spanish: Boggs FFC XC 40 No. 300; Icel.: Boberg, þiðriks saga I 314—18; India: Thompson-Balys; Japanese: Ikeda.

B312.2. *Helpful animals obtained by exchange.* *Type 300; *Hartland Perseus III 195; De Gubernatis Zool. Myth. III 36 n. — N. A. Indian: Thompson CColl II 329ff.

D851. Magic object acquired by exchange.

B312.3. *Helpful animal(s) bequeathed to hero.* Italian Novella: Rotunda; India: Thompson-Balys; Africa (Hausa): Best Black Folk Tales 71ff., Tremearne Hausa Superstitions and Customs 374ff. No. 79; Madagascar: (Marofotsy) Renel Contes de Madagascar I 65ff. No. 9.

N411.1.1. Cat as sole inheritance.

B312.4. *Helpful animal purchased.* India: Thompson-Balys; Africa (Swahili): Steere Swahili Tales 13ff., Meinhof Afrikanische Märchen 9ff. No. 1, Bateman Zanzibar Tales 99ff. No. 7.

B312.4.1. *Helpful dogs obtained by purchase.* Cheremis: Sebeok-Nyerges.

B312.5. *Helpful, strong horse caught.* Icel.: Boberg.

B313. *Helpful animal an enchanted person.* *Types 314, 328 (FFC LXXXIII), 402, 510, 530, 531, 532, 533, 545, 550, 551.

B187.0.2. Magic dog transformed person. D659.4.3. Transformation to eagle to carry hero to safety.

B313.1. *Helpful animal reincarnation of parent.* The dead mother appears to the heroine in the form of an animal. — *Cox Cinderella 475 n. 4; BP I 187, III 60ff. — India: *Thompson-Balys, *Cosquin Contes indiens 505ff.; Japanese: Ikeda.

N810. Supernatural helpers.

B313.2. *Helpful animal reincarnation of murdered child.* German: Grimm No. 47.

B314. *Helpful animal brothers-in-law.* *Type 552; *BP III 424ff. — Missouri French: Carrière.

B505.1. Magic object received from animal brother-in-law. B640. Marriage to person in animal form.

B315. *Animal helpful after being conquered.* *Type 590; BP III 1. — Icel.: *Boberg.

B316. *Abused and pampered horses.* Hero is ordered by ogre to feed and care for certain horse and to neglect other horse. Hero disobeys and feeds neglected horse. Latter is enchanted prince and helps hero. (Cf. B181.) — *Type 314, 502; BP III 18 n. 3. — French Canadian: Barbeau JAFL XXIX 15; Missouri-French: Carrière.

D1783.4. Power over monster (wizard, king) obtained by reversing orders.

B317. *Helpful bird hatched by hero.* Hero holds eagle's egg in hand and hatches it. Young eagle becomes his helper. — German New Guinea: Dixon 141.

D1783.4. Power over monster (wizard, king) obtained by reversing order.

B318. *Helpful animals transformed from other animals.* India: Thompson-Balys.

B11.1.2. Dragon from transformed horse. D410. Transformation: one animal to another.

B319. *Helpful animal otherwise acquired.*

B319.1. *Helpful animal sent by God (or a god).* Irish myth: Cross.

B319.2. *Helpful animal acquired as reward for vigil.* Cheremis: Sebeok-Nyerges.

B320. Reward of helpful animal.

B322. *Helpful animal demands food.* Breton: Sébillot Incidents s. v. "viande", "oiseau"; Japanese: Ikeda.

B322.1. *Hero feeds own flesh to helpful animal.* The hero is carried on the back of an eagle who demands food. The hero finally feeds parts of his own flesh. — *Type 301; *BP II 300 (Gr. No. 91); Chauvin VI 3 No. 181 n. 3; Panzer Beowulf 191; Clouston Tales I 241ff.; Köhler-Bolte Zs. f. Vksk. VI 164 (to Gonzenbach No. 61). — Hindu: Penzer I 84 n. 1. 85, VI 122 n. 2, VII 126 n. 2; India: Thompson-Balys; Swiss: Jegerlehner Oberwallis 304 No. 32; French Canadian: Barbeau JAFL

XXIX 15. — Missouri French: Carrière. — Apache: Goddard PaAM XXIV 94.

B542.1.1. Eagle carries man to safety. F101.3. Return from lower world on eagle. F420.5.3.6. Water-spirit demands food from those it takes across stream. K521.1.1. Man sewed in animal's hide carried off by birds. K1861.1. Hero sewed up in animal hide so as to be carried to height by bird.

B322.2. *Helpful birds demand food.* Chinese: Graham.

B325. *Animal bribed for help.* English: Child I 57ff., II 144—154, 359, IV 389f., 416; Sicilian: Gonzenbach: I 99 No. 15.

B325.1. *Animal bribed with food.* (Sop to Cerberus.) — Types 531, 551; BP III 18ff.; *Chauvin VI 6 No. 182; Finnish-Swedish: Wessman 76 No. 632; Icel.: *Boberg. Spanish: Boggs FFC XC 61 No. 445B, Spanish Exempla: Keller; India: *Thompson-Balys; N. A. Indian: Thompson Tales 308 n. 113c. — Jamaica: Beckwith MAFLS XVII 273 No. 86.

A673. Hound of hell. B391. Animal grateful for food. G582. Giants appeased by feeding them. K671. Captive throws his hat to lions who fight over it while he escapes. K2062. Thief tries to feed watchdog and stop his mouth: dog detects plan.

B330. Death of helpful animal.

B100.1. Treasure found in slain helpful animal. B192. Magic animal killed. C221.2.1. Tabu: eating animal helper. C918. Mare from water world disappears when she is scolded and her halter used for common purposes. C935. Helpful animal disappears when tabu is broken. D843. Magic object found on grave of slain helpful animal. D876. Magic treasure animal killed: goose that laid the golden egg.

B331. *Helpful animal killed through misunderstanding.*

B331.1. *Faithful falcon killed through misunderstanding.* Tries to warn the king against drinking water poisoned by snake. — *Chauvin II 122 No. 115, V 289 No. 173. — India: *Thompson-Balys.

N340. Hasty killing or condemnation. N345. The falcon of Federigo.

B331.1.1. *Faithful horse killed through misunderstanding.* Tries to warn king against drinking water poisoned by snake. India: Thompson-Balys.

B331.2. *Llewellyn and his dog.* Dog has saved child from serpent. Father sees bloody mouth, thinks the dog has eaten the child, and kills the dog. — *Pauli (ed. Bolte) No. 257; Köhler-Bolte I 534; *BP I 425 n. I; Ward Catalogue of Romances II 170; *Penzer V 138 n. 1; *Campbell Sages lxxviii ff.; Benfey Panchatantra I 479ff.; Bødker Exempler 299 No. 64; *Chauvin II 100 No. 59, VIII 67 No. 31; Clouston Tales II 167; *Kittredge Arthur and Gorlagon 223 n. 1; *Frazer Pausanias V 421 . — Spanish Exempla: Keller; Irish myth: Cross; India: *Thompson-Balys; U.S.: Baughman.

B524.1.4.1. Dog defends master's child against animal assailant. J571.1. When in anger say the alphabet. N343. Lover kills self believing his mistress dead. (Pyramus and Thisbe).

B331.2.1. *Woman slays faithful mongoose which has saved her child.* "A Classical Indian Folk-Tale as a Reported Modern Event: The Brahman and the Mongoose" Proceedings, American Philosophical Society, LXXXIII 503—13; India: *Thompson-Balys.

B449.7.1. Helpful mongoose.

B331.2.2. *Faithful dog killed by overhasty master:* thinks mistakenly he has returned home against orders. (Cf. Llewellyn and his dog.) — *Emeneau "The Faithful Dog as Security for a Debt; A Companion to the Brahman and Mongoose Story-Type" Journal of American Oriental Society LXI 1—17; India: *Thompson-Balys.

B331.3. *Faithful parrot killed by mistake.* India: Thompson-Balys.

B332. *Too watchful dog killed.* Icel.: *Boberg.

B335. *Helpful animal killed by hero's enemy.* *Types 510, 533; *BP III 60ff.; *Cox Cinderella 477 n. 7. — India: *Thompson-Balys; Japanese: Ikeda. — N. A. Indian (Menomini): Hoffman RBAE XIV 236.

B133.4. Speaking horse-head. The helpful magic horse is killed.

B335.1. *Man attempts to kill faithful serpent at wife's instigation.* Loses everything. — *Krappe Bulletin Hispanique XXXIX 20 No. 73. — *Ward III 208; *Oesterley Gesta Romanorum No. 141; *Warnke Die Quellen des Esope der Marie de France 221.

K2213. Treacherous wife.

B335.1.1. *Treacherous wife forces husband to kill helpful dog.* India: Thompson-Balys.

B335.2. *Life of helpful animal demanded as cure for feigned sickness.* Penzer V 127 n. 1; India: *Thompson-Balys.

D866.2. Magic object destroyed because of feigned sickness. H1212. Quest assigned because of feigned illness. K961. Flesh of certain animal alleged to be only cure for disease: animal to be killed. K2091. Illness feigned in order to learn secret. S268.1. Sacrifice of child demanded as cure for feigned sickness. S322.4.1. Banishment of stepchildren demanded as cure for feigned illness. S322.7. Life of children demanded as cure for feigned illness.

B335.3. *Unsuccessful attempt by enemy to kill helpful animal.* India: Thompson-Balys.

B335.4. *Wife demands magic parrot who has accused her.* India: Thompson-Balys.

B131.3. Bird betrays women's infidelity. J551.1. Cocks who crow about mistress's adultery killed. J1154.1. Parrot unable to tell husband details as to wife's infidelity. K1510. Adulteress outwits husband.

B335.5. *Faithful animal killed in battle.* Icel.: *Boberg.

B335.6. *A small animal (hare, bitch) gives timely warnings to the hero about the trap* prepared by his enemy. Animal warning about trap killed. — Lithuanian: Balys Index Nos. *452f.

B335.7. *Helpful cow to be killed because of refusal to help stepdaughter.* Chinese: Graham.

B336. *Helpful animal killed (threatened) by ungrateful hero.* — Spanish Exempla: Keller. — Africa (Hausa): Mischlich Neue Märchen aus Afrika 164ff. No. 22, Frobenius Atlantis IX 277ff., 287ff., Nos. 74 and 75, (Swahili): Steere Swahili Tales 13ff., Meinhof Afrikanische Märchen 9ff. No. 1, Bateman Zanzibar Tales 99ff. No. 7.

W154. Ingratitude.

B338. *Weapons made from bones of helpful horse.* India: Thompson-Balys.

B339. *Death of helpful animal — miscellaneous.*

B339.1. *Truth-telling dog killed so as to hide murder.* India: Thompson-Balys.

B340. Treatment of helpful animals — miscellaneous.

B341. *Helpful animal's injunctions disobeyed.* Disaster follows. — Type 531; MacCulloch Childhood 229; Missouri French: Carrière; N. A. Indian (Menomini): Hoffman RBAE XIV 183, (Zuñi): Cushing 54.

B342. *Cat leaves house when report is made of death of one of his companions.* His master has been told to say "Robert is dead". As soon as this is said, the cat leaves. — *Boberg Sagnet om den store Pans Død, København 1934. — Irish: Beal III 66. — U.S.: Baughman; Taylor Washington University Studies X (Hum. Ser.) 60ff.

F405.7. Spirit leaves when report is made of the death of one of its kind.

B343. *Large reward given for return of helpful animal.* India: Thompson-Balys.

B350—B399. Grateful animals.

B350. Grateful animals. *Types 329, 480, 531, 554, 554*, 559: *BP I 207ff. (Gr. No. 24), 227, II 21 (Gr. Nos. 17, 62, 191), 454 n. 1, III 18ff. (Gr. No. 126), 365 (Gr. No. 191); Hartland Perseus III 193ff.; Clouston Tales I 223ff.; Penzer I 100f., V 157ff., VI 291, VIII 219, IX 156; *Chauvin II 107 No. 71; *Saintyves Perrault 32ff. — Irish myth: Cross. — Greek: **Marx Griechische Märchen von dankbaren Tieren; *Frazer Apollodorus I 86 n. 2; Arabian: Burton SV 326; India: *Thompson-Balys; Japanese: Anesaki 322; Breton: Sébillot Incidents s.v. "fourmi". — N. A. Indian: *Thompson Tales 316 n. 146a., CColl II 327f., 333, 342, 417; Indonesian: DeVries's list Nos. 56, 65ff., 135; Malay: Dixon 216; *ibid. 218 n. 23; Philippine: Fansler MAFLS XII 167. — Africa (Basuto): Jacottet 214 No. 31.

B311. Congenital helpful animal. D1658. Grateful objects. E341. The grateful dead. Q10. Deeds rewarded. W27. Gratitude.

B360. Animals grateful for rescue from peril of death. *Types 554, 554*, 560; *BP II 21f., 454; *Dh IV 147ff.; Chauvin II 109 No. 73; Hartland Perseus III 194; *Brown Iwain 16 and passim, 132 n. 3; Hüsing (G.) "Zum Etanamythos" Archiv f. Religionswiss. VI 178ff.; Alphabet No. 166; Wienert FFC LVI 70 (ET 338, 339), 127 (ST 353), Halm Aesop Nos. 92, 130; *Pauli (ed. Bolte) No. 648. — Irish myth: Cross; Icel.: Boberg (B364.5). — India: *Thompson-Balys; Japanese: Anesaki 321ff., Ikeda; Chinese: Graham, Eberhard FFC CXX 29 No. 17; Korean: Zong in-Sob 175 f. No. 76. — Africa (Gold Coast): Barker and Sinclair 163 No. 32; Missouri French: Carrière.

Q53. Reward for rescuer.

B361. *Animals grateful for rescue from pit.* *Type 160; Chauvin I 106 No. 71; Ward II 196; Bødker Exempler 304 No. 75; *Oesterley Gesta Romanorum No. 119; Wienert FFC LVI 70 (ET 346), 127 (ST 357), Phaedrus III 2; BP IV 139f; *Moe Samlede Skrifter I 192ff.; Hilka Compilatio Singularis Exemplorum 23; Wesselski Märchen 246 No. 56. — Krappe Bulletin Hispanique XXXIX 31; Spanish Exempla: Keller; *Pauli (ed. Bolte) No. 649. — Hindu: *Penzer V 157; India: *Thompson-Balys; Japanese: Ikeda; Chinese: Eberhard FFC CXX 30. — Africa: Frobenius Atlantis IX 385 Nos. 103f., (Swahili): Steere 423, (Zanzibar): Bateman 81 No. 6, (Gold Coast): Barker and Sinclair 163 No. 32.

K735. Capture in pitfall. W154.8. Grateful animals; ungrateful man.

B362. *Animal grateful for rescue from drowning.* Wienert FFC LVI 59 (ET 201), 127 (ST 356), Halm Aesop No. 296 (dove rescues ant). — India: Thompson-Balys; Chinese: Graham; Japanese: Ikeda; Korea: Ikeda.

B363. *Animal grateful for rescue from net.* *Type 75; Crane Vitry 194 No. 145. — India: Thompson-Balys. — Africa (Zanzibar): Bateman: 81 No. 6.

B545. Animal rescues from trap (net).

B363.1. *Lion is freed from net by mouse.* Mouse asks that his son marry lion's daughter. Request granted. The mouse is trampled to death by his bride. — Italian Novella: Rotunda.

B364. *Animal grateful for other rescue.*

B364.1. *Animal grateful for rescue from trap.* Philippine: Fansler MAFLS XII 336; India: Thompson-Balys. — Africa (Lamba): Doke XXXII No. 15.

B364.2. *Animal grateful for rescue from fire.* Italian Novella: Rotunda.

B364.3. *Insect having fallen on back grateful for being turned over.* Africa (Ganda): Baskerville King of the Snakes 8ff.

B364.4. *Bird grateful for being saved from attacking serpent.* Cook Islands: Beckwith Myth 269.

B364.5. *Animal grateful for rescue from mud.* India: Thompson-Balys.

B365. *Animal grateful for rescue of its young.* *Hartland Perseus III 194; Köhler-Bolte I 440, 545, 560, *561. — Japanese: Mitford 261, Ikeda; India: *Thompson-Balys; Missouri-French: Carrière.

B365.0.1. *Bird grateful for rescue of its young.* India: Thompson-Balys.

B365.1. *Animal grateful for rescue of its mate.* India: Thompson-Balys.

B365.2. *Animal grateful to hero for preventing distruction of nest.*

B365.2.1. *Ant grateful for preventing distruction of nest.* German: Grimm No. 62.

B365.3. *Animal grateful for release of relative.* Chinese: Eberhard FFC CXX 65.

B366. *Animal grateful for ransom from captivity.* BP II 451 (Gr. No. 104a), *454 n. 1.; Wienert FFC LVI 70 (ET 337), 127 (ST 354, 489); Halm Aesop No. 6. — India: *Thompson-Balys; Japanese: Ikeda.

B278. Captured animal ransoms self.

B370. Animal grateful to captor for release.

B371. *Small animal released from jaws of large one: grateful.*

B371.1. *Lion spared mouse: mouse grateful.* Later releases lion from net. (Cf. B363.) — Jacobs Aesop 203 No. 11, Halm Aesop 256, cf. Type 75. — Spanish Exempla: Keller; India: *Thompson-Balys.

Q55. Reward for sparing life when in animal form.

B371.2. *Lion spares fly: fly grateful.* Later warns lion. — India: Thompson-Balys.

B374. *Other animals grateful for release.*

B374.1. *Lion rescued from snake: thankful.* Spanish Exempla: Keller.

B375. *Release of animal by hunter (fisher).* Africa (Angola): Chatelain 159 No. 19 (deer). — German: Grimm No. 60, 191. — India: Thompson-Balys.

B375.1. *Fish returned to water: grateful.* *Fb "fisk"; Hartland Science 174. — India: Thompson-Balys; Chinese: Graham. — Two special forms of this motif are common; in both the fish is returned to the water and rewards the captor. (1). The "King of the Fishes" form: a man captures the king of fishes (B243) who as a reward for the release tells the man to feed parts of his body (when he is later captured) to his wife and parts to certain animals. As a result the hero and congenital helpful animals (B311) are born: *Type 303; BP I 528 (Gr. Nos. 60, 85); Sébillot Incidents s.v. "poisson", Gaster Exempla 251 No. 373.; Missouri French: Carrière. — For other references see B243. — (2) The "Fisher and his Wife" form. The king of the fishes in this case grants the man's wife the power of fulfilling all her wishes; *Type 555; BP I 138 (Gr. No. 19); see C773.1.2.

B175. Magic fish. B211.11. Speaking fish. B470. Helpful fish. B505. Magic object received from animal. B527.1. Fish promises to spare man in coming flood. T511.5.1. Conception from eating fish.

B375.1.1. *Grateful fish grants mad hero his wish:* to impregnate a princess. Later the fish saves the hero and his family from death at sea. — Italian Novella: Rotunda.

B375.1.2. *Fish grateful for being transferred from tank to river.* India: *Thompson-Balys.

B375.2. *Frog returned to spring: grateful.* Teaches hero animals' language (Cf. B217). — *Type 670B; India: *Thompson-Balys.

B375.3. *Bird released: grateful.* — *Chauvin II 117 No. 97; India: *Thompson-Balys; Japanese: Ikeda.

B375.3.1. *Eagle released: grateful.* Lithuanian: Balys Index No. *320.

B375.4. *Squirrel released: grateful and helpful.* India: Thompson-Balys.

B375.5. *Monkey released: grateful.* India: Thompson-Balys.

B375.6. *Rat released: grateful.* India: Thompson-Balys.

B375.7. *Leopard released: grateful.* Africa (Fang): Tessman 195f.

B375.8. *Turtle released: grateful.* Korean: Zong in-Sob 169 No. 73.

B375.9. *Serpent released: grateful.* S. A. Indian (Toba): Métraux MAFLS XL 55.

B375.10. *Jackal released: grateful.* India: Thompson-Balys.

B376. *Wasp released from vase full of honey: grateful.* Italian Novella: Rotunda.

B380. Animal grateful for relief from pain. Spanish Exempla: Keller; India: Thompson-Balys.

B380.1. *Grateful hyena leads lost hermit from wilderness as reward* for his help. Spanish Exempla: Keller.

B381. *Thorn removed from lion's paw (Androcles and the Lion).* In gratitude the lion later rewards the man. — *Type 156; *BP III 1 n. 2; Cf. Type 74*; Jacobs Aesop 205 No. 23; Wienert FFC LVI 70 (ET 345), 127 (ST 357); *Krappe Bulletin Hispanique XXXIX 29; **Brodeur (A.G.) "The Grateful Lion" PMLA XXXIX 485; Herbert Catalogue of Romances III 210; Penzer V 162 n. 1, IX 47 n. 1; Alphabet No. 451; Oesterley Gesta Romanorum No. 278. — *Loomis White Magic 58—61. — Spanish Exempla: Keller. — India: *Thompson-Balys. — Chinese: Graham. — N. A. Indian (Wyandot): Barbeau GSCan XI 106 No. 29.

B525. Animal spares man he is about to devour.

B381.1. *Wolf fetches a man to remove thorn from his children's paws.* Does not attack the man's livestock. — Lithuanian: Balys Index No. *156A.

B381.2. *Thorn removed from monkey's tail.* India: Thompson-Balys.

B382. *Animal grateful for removal of bone lodged in its throat.* India: Thompson-Balys; S. A. Indian (Cashinawa): Métraux BBAE CXLIII (3) 685.

W154.3. Crane pulls bone from wolf's throat: wolf refuses payment.

B383. *Man called by animal for help to his cubs in danger.* *Loomis White Magic 59.

B384. *Saint cures the blind young ones of a hyena* or wolf by the sign of the cross and the application of his saliva. (Cf. D1500.1.8.1.) The animal mother is grateful. — *Loomis White Magic 59 f.

B385. *Serpent relieved from sand blown in eyes: grateful.* India: Thompson-Balys.

B386. *Tigress grateful for opening of abscess.* India: Thompson-Balys.

B387. *Tiger grateful for woman assisting tigress as midwife.* Chinese: Graham, Eberhard FFC CXX 29.

B388. *Cobra grateful for cure of ulcer.* India: Thompson-Balys.

N647. Thorn accidentally removed from cobra's throat by woman's finger. Grateful cobra.

B390. Animals grateful for other kind acts.

B11.6.1. Dragon helps hero out of gratitude.

B391. *Animal grateful for food.* *Types 300, 531, 550, 554; Warnke Quellen des Esope der Marie de France 221ff.; *BP II 21f., 463; Halm Aesop No. 173; Wienert FFC LVI 70 (ET 347), 127 (ST 358); Ward III 208; Oesterley Gesta Romanorum No. 141 (Cf. B335.1.) — Lithuanian: Balys Legends No. 387. — Danish: Fb "kalv"; Missouri-French: Carrière — India: *Thompson-Balys; Japanese: Mitford 185f., 270, Anesaki 313, Ikeda; Chinese: Eberhard FFC CXX 29. — Africa (Benga): Nassau No. 33.

B325.1. Animal bribed with food. Q45. Hospitality rewarded.

B391.1. *Child feeds snake from its milk-bottle.* *Type 285; BP II 459, cf. II 463. — India: Thompson-Balys.

B765.6. Snake eats milk and bread with child.

B391.1.1. *Cobra grateful to prince for milk.* India: Thompson-Balys.

B391.1.2. *Snake grateful because man feeds her young snakes milk.* India: Thompson-Balys.

B391.1.3. *Snake grateful for pouring milk into its hole.* India: Thompson-Balys.

B391.2. *Child shares food with toad.* German: Grimm No. 105.

B391.3. *Hero kills horse to feed young ravens.* German: Grimm No. 17.

B391.4. *Animals given water to drink: grateful.* Buddhist myth: Malalasekera I 150.

B392. *Hero divides spoil for animals.* *Type 300; Fb "dele" IV 96b; *BP II 22 n. 1. — Lithuanian: Balys Index No. *554A.; Italian Novella: Rotunda. — Missouri-French: Carrière; Africa (Angola): Chatelain 70 No. 3.

B392.1. *Animals grateful for being given appropriate food.* Hero finds dog with hay and horse with meat. He changes it about. — Köhler-Bolte Zs. f. Vksk. VI 63 (to Gonzenbach No. 13.); Missouri-French: Carrière.

J512.11. Camel and jackal exchange food: camel is led by his good friend to thorny fruit and thorn sticks into his throat. U147. Animals try unsuccessfully to exchange food.

B393. *Animals grateful for shelter.* Japanese: Mitford 270.

B394. *Cow grateful for being milked.* (Cf. B411.) — Type 510A; Cox passim.

B395. *Buffaloes grateful for care of their calves.* India: Thompson-Balys.

B395.1. *Buffaloes grateful for being cleaned and combed.* India: Thompson-Balys.

B396. *Cows grateful for hero's housekeeping for them.* India: Thompson-Balys.

B400—B499. Kinds of helpful animals.

B400—B449. HELPFUL BEASTS

B400. **Helpful domestic beasts.** India: Thompson-Balys.

B401. *Helpful horse.* *Type 314, 502, 531, 532; BP III 94ff., III 18ff., II 273ff; *Fb "hest"; *Köhler-Bolte I 468. — Wienert FFC LVI *70 (ET 347), 127 (ST 358); Halm Aesop No. 173 (Cf. BP III 290ff.); Welsh: MacCulloch Celtic 94; Greek: Frazer Apollodorus I 372 n. 1. — Irish myth: Cross; Icel.: *Boberg; Spanish Exempla: Keller; Italian Novella: Rotunda. — Breton: *Sébillot Incidents s.v. "animaux"; French Canadian: *Barbeau JAFL XXIX 15; Missouri French: Carrière; Cape Verde Islands: *Parson MAFLS XV (1) 277 No. 91, 281 No. 92. — India: *Thompson-Balys. — Philippine: Fansler MAFLS XII 280, 284.

B133. Truth-speaking horse. B149.1. Prophetic horse. B151. Horse determines road to be taken. B181. Magic horse. B211.3. Speaking horse.

B401.1. *Helpful water-horse.* Irish myth: Cross.

B181.3. Magic horse from water world.

B402. *Helpful ass.* *Fb "æsel" III 1155a. — India: Thompson-Balys.

B102. Gold-producing ass.

B403. *Helpful mule.* Breton: *Sébillot Incidents s.v. "mule", "animaux".

B405. *Helpful camel.* India: Thompson-Balys. Africa (Hausa): Tremearne FL XXII 464ff. No. 50, Hausa Superstitions and Customs 380ff. No. 80.

B411. *Helpful cow.* (Cf. B354.) — *Type 510A; Cox passim. — Halm Aesop No. 173, Wienert FFC LVI *70 (ET 347), 127 (ST 358). — Irish myth: Cross. — Breton: Sébillot Incidents s.v. "animaux"; India: *Thompson-Balys; Chinese: Graham, Eberhard FFC CXX 52 No. 32.

B182. Magic cow (ox, bull). B182.1. Magic cow gives red milk. B394. Cow grateful for being milked. B535.0.1. Cow as nurse cares for children.

B411.1. *Helpful bull.* (Cf. B182.3.1.) — Cox Cinderella 365 (Swedish). — Irish myth: Cross. — Breton: Sébillot Incidents s.v. "animaux". —

India: Thompson-Balys. — N. A. Indian (Wyandot): Thompson CColl II 412; Missouri-French: Carrière.

B182. Magic cow (ox, bull).

B411.2. *Helpful ox.* French Canadian: Barbeau JAFL XXIX 15. — Irish myth: Cross. — India: Thompson-Balys. — Africa (Basuto): Jacottet 76 No. 12, 240 No. 35, (Kaffir): Theal 169.

B182.2. Magic ox. X1237.2. Lie: Paul Bunyan's ox.

B411.3. *Helpful calf.* Fb "kalv".

B411.4. *Helpful buffalo.* India: *Thompson-Balys.

B411.4.1. *Helpful bison.* India: Thompson-Balys.

B411.5. *Helpful bullock.* India: Thompson-Balys.

B411.6. *Helpful steer.* Jewish: Neuman.

B412. *Helpful sheep.* Type 510; *Cox 477 n. 7.; Missouri-French: Carrière; India: Thompson-Balys.

B189.1. Magic sheep. D1652.14. Sheep with inexhaustible wool.

B413. *Helpful goat.* Type 510; Cox 473f. n. 2. — Irish myth: Cross, Beal XXI 325; Breton: Sébillot Incidents s.v. "chevre", "animaux"; Missouri French: Carrière; Swiss: Jegerlehner Oberwallis 294 No. 9, 298 No. 13, 325 No. 4. — Jewish: Neuman; India: *Thompson-Balys. —Africa (Angola): Chatelain 53 No. 2, (Benga): Nassau 202 No. 32.

B414. *Helpful hog.* Fb "svin" III 676a. — Irish myth: Cross. — India: Thompson-Balys. — Africa (Ekoi): Talbot 144, 197.

B562.1.1. Hogs root up gold for saint.

B414.1. *Helpful boar.* India: Thompson-Balys.

B183. Magic boar. B256.6. Boar serves saint.

B421. *Helpful dog.* (Cf. B524.1.1, B268.2.1. War-dogs.) *Types 300, 400, 560; *BP II 455ff., I 331, 547; *Emeneau "The Faithful Dog as Security for a Debt," Journal of the American Oriental Society LXI 1—17; *Hartland Perseus III 191ff.; *Aarne MSFO XXV 48; *Dh IV 147ff. — Fable: Halm Aesop No. 173; *BP III 290; Wienert FFC LVI *70 (ET 347), 127 (ST 358). — Irish myth: Cross; Icel.: *Boberg. — Breton: Sébillot Incidents s.v. "chien", "mort", "nourriture"; *Fb "hund" IV 226b; Alphabet of Tales No. 271. — English: Wells Manual of Writings 121 (Sir Triamour); Scotch: Campbell I 7; French Canadian: *Barbeau JAFL XXIX 15, 20; Spanish: Boggs FFC XC 48 No. 327; Jamaican: Beckwith MAFLS XVII 270 No. 82. — Jewish: Neuman. India: *Thompson-Balys. — Japanese: Anesaki 322, Ikeda; Korean: Zong in-Sob 93 No. 51. — Africa (Zulu): Callaway 51, 142, (Basuto): Jacottet 56 No. 9, 140 No. 20, (Kaffir): Kidd 226 No. 1, Theal 126, (Benga): Nassau 140 No. 16, (Angola): Chatelain 127 No. 12; N. A. Indian (Thompson River): Teit JAFL XXIX 304 (Type 403). See references in B524.1.

A35. Creator's dog. B121. Dog with magic wisdom. B134. Truth-telling dog. B153. Dog's barking indicates hidden treasure. B187. Magic dog. B211.7. Speaking dog. B521.3.1. Dogs warn against witch. B524.1.1. Dog saves life — kills cannibal (ogre).

B422. *Helpful cat.* *Types 402, 545, 560; *BP I 325, II 30, 455, III 487; *Aarne MSFO XXV 48; *Dh IV 147ff.; *Fb "kat" II 108a. — Irish myth: Cross; Italian Novella: Rotunda; Breton: Sébillot Incidents s.v. "chat"; Missouri French: Carrière; Scotch: Campbell II 279, *284ff.;

India: *Thompson-Balys; Japanese: Mitford 253; Korean: Zong in-Sob 28 No. 12; Tonga: Gifford 201.

B184. Magic cat. B211.8. Speaking cat. K722. Giant tricked into becoming mouse. Cat eats him up.

B430. Helpful wild beasts. India: Thompson-Balys.

B431. *Helpful wild beasts — felidae.*

B431.1. *Helpful leopard.* Africa (Akan-Ashanti): Rattray Akan-Ashanti Folk Tales 206 No. 53.

B431.2. *Helpful lion.* (Cf. B549.1.) — *Type 156 (see all references for B381), *Type 590; *BP III 1 (Gr. No. 121); *Fb "löve" II 518b; Dickson Valentine and Orson 107 n. 17, 118 n. 51. — Icel.: Boberg. — Irish myth: Cross; English: Wells 66 (Ywain and Gawain), 118f. (Octavian). — *Hibbard 271 n. 3. — Spanish Exempla: Keller. — Italian Novella: Rotunda. — Saintyves Saints Successeurs 252. — French Canadian: Sister Marie Ursule; Missouri French: Carrière. — Jewish: Neuman. — India: *Thompson-Balys. — Africa (Gold Coast): Barker and Sinclair 131 No. 24, (Zanzibar): Bateman 82 No. 6.

B431.3. *Helpful tiger.* India: *Thompson-Balys; Chinese: Werner 263; Korean: Zong in-Sob 82, No. 45.

B431.4. *Helpful panther.* Fable: Phaedrus III 2; Wienert FFC LVI 70 (ET 346), 127 (ST 357).

B433. *Helpful wild beasts — mustelidae.*

B433.1. *Helpful otter.* Saints' legend (Irish): Plummer cxliv; Irish myth: Cross.

B292.7. Otters supply man with fish and burning wood daily. B548.3. Otter recovers lost book from water.

B433.2. *Helpful badger.* Jewish: Neuman; Japanese: Mitford 270ff.

B433.3. *Helpful ichneumon.* India: Thompson-Balys; Africa (Nao): Held Märchen und Sagen der afrikanischen Neger 132ff.

B433.4. *Helpful mongoose.* Chauvin II 100 No. 59; Bødker Exempler 299 No. 64; India: *Thompson-Balys.

B311.2.1. Woman slays faithful mongoose which has saved her child.

B435. *Helpful wild beasts — canidae* and other *carnivora.*

B435.1. *Helpful fox.* *Types 506, 545, 550; *BP I 331, 503, III 487, 490ff.; Hdwb. d. Abergl. III 179. — Sébillot RTP III 394; *Fb "höj" I 741, "ræv" III 113b. — Irish myth: Cross; Breton: Sébillot Incidents s.v. "animaux". — Missouri French: Carrière; Jewish: Neuman; India: Thompson-Balys. — Chinese: Werner 380f., Krappe CFQ III (1944) 126, Eberhard FFC CXX 29 No. 17. — Japanese: Mitford 261ff. — N. A. Indian: Thompson Tales 342 n. 233. — Africa (Tonga): Gifford 123.

B144. Prophetic fox. B253.3. Fox fasts as penance. B259.5. Fly, wren, fox live with cleric. B291.3.1. Fox as messenger. B294. Fox as divider of dying man's gifts. B514.1. Fox as healer. B541.2. Fox rescues man from sea. B651.1. Marriage to fox in human form.

B435.2. *Helpful jackal.* BP I 331; India: *Thompson-Balys.

B563.4.1. Jackal leads lost men out of wilderness.

B435.3. *Helpful wolf.* *Type 428; *Fb "ulv" IV 971a. — English: Wells Manual of Writings 20 (William of Palerne) (werwolf). — Breton: Sébillot Incidents s.v. "animaux". — Irish myth: Cross. — Italian

Novella: Rotunda. — Jewish: Neuman. — Missouri-French: Carrière. — See also references for B535.

B435.4. *Helpful bear.* *Fb "Bjørn" IV 42a, 43a. — Italian Novella: Rotunda; Jewish: Neuman; India: *Thompson-Balys; Missouri-French: Carrière.

B435.5. *Helpful seal.* Irish myth: Cross.

B435.6. *Helpful hyena.* Spanish Exempla: Keller.

B437. *Helpful wild beasts — rodentia.* — India: Thompson-Balys; N. A. Indian: Thompson Tales 317 n. 147. — Tehuelche (Pategonia): Alexander Lat. Am. 335.

B437.1. *Helpful rat.* *Fb "rotte" III 83b. — India: *Thompson-Balys; Chinese: Eberhard FFC CXX 180. — Korean: Zong in-Sob 28 No. 12. — Africa (Basuto): Jacottet 214 No. 31, (Benga): Nassau 208 No. 33.

K1182. Rat leaves serpent behind, though spared to rescue him.

B437.1.1. *Helpful bandicoot.* India: Thompson-Balys.

B535.0.2. Bandicoot (large rat) as nurse cares for children.

B437.2. *Helpful mouse.* *Type 75, cf. Type 560. — Jewish: Neuman; Penzer V 79 n. 2. — India: *Thompson-Balys, Bødker Exempler 290 Nos 45, 46; Italian Novella: Rotunda; Missouri-French: Carrière. — Buddhist myth: Malalasekera II 268. — Africa (Kaffir): Theal 85, Kidd 230 No. 2, (Basuto): Jacottet 190 No. 28.

J426.1. Mouse helps wild cat escape from snares. K632. Mice gnaw enemies' bow-strings and prevent pursuit.

B437.3. *Helpful squirrel.* Cheremis: Sebeok-Nyerges. — India: Thompson-Balys. — Chinese: Graham. — Africa (Fang): Trilles Bulletin de la Société Neuchâteloise de Geographie XVI 238ff. No. 23.

B563.3. Squirrel points out road. H1121. Task: picking all nuts from tall tree. (Performed by grateful squirrel.

B437.4. *Helpful rabbit (hare).* Fb "hare" IV 201a; Dh I 276ff. — Breton: Sébillot Incidents s.v. "animaux". — Japanese: Anesaki 318.

B441. *Helpful wild beasts — primata.*

B441.1. *Helpful monkey.* Penzer IX 47 n. 1; BP I 331. — Jewish: Neuman. — India: *Thompson-Balys; Indonesian: DeVries' List No. 180. — Chile: Pino Saavedra 402, 404.

B441.1.1. *Helpful ape.* Chinese: Eberhard FFC CXX 180. — Africa: Rochemonteix Quelques Contes Nubiens 48ff. No. 4, 55ff. No. 5, Basset Contes populaires d'Afrique 133ff. No. 52, (Bambara): Travélé Proverbes et Contes Bambara 200f. No. 65, (Temne): Schlender 87ff. No. 7, (Swahili): Steere 13ff.

B443. *Helpful wild beasts — ungulata.*

B443.1. *Helpful deer (stag, doe).* *Fb "hjort", "hind". — Irish myth: Cross; Saints' legend (Irish): Plummer cxlii—cxliv. — Jewish: Neuman. — India: *Thompson-Balys. — Korean: Zong in-Sob 22 No. 11. — Africa (Angola): Chatelain 159 No. 19.

B188. Magic deer. B292.4. Stags plow for man. Also draw chariot, bear burdens, and allow saints to use their horns as a book rest.

B443.2 *Helpful antelope.* Southeastern Africa: Macdonald FL III 352ff. No. 4.

B443.3. *Helpful elephant.* *Pauli (ed. Bolte) No. 649; India: *Thompson-Balys.

B443.4. *Helpful gazelle.* BP I 331.

B443.5. *Helpful wild hog (boar).* Madagascar: Sibree FLJ II 45ff., Renel Contes de Madagascar I 65ff. No. 9, 140ff. No. 25, Ferrand 102ff. No. 32.

B443.6. *Helpful hippopotamus.* Africa (Ganda): Baskerville King of the Snakes 47f.

B443.7. *Helpful wild ox.* Irish myth: Cross.

B557.2. Saint carried by wild oxen.

B449. *Helpful wild beasts — miscellaneous.*

B449.1. *Helpful hedgehog.* Dh I 276ff.; India: Thompson-Balys.

B449.2. *Helpful mole.* Canadian: Gautier (B449.13).

B449.3. *Helpful bat.* N. A. Indian: Thompson Tales 318 n. 151b.

B450. Helpful birds. *Köhler-Bolte I 185, 277; *Type 781; *Chauvin II 109 No 73, V 242 No. 142; *Basset 1001 Contes III 295; *Fb "fugl"; Wesselski Märchen 231. — Welsh: MacCulloch Celtic 101; Irish myth: Cross; English: Child Eng.-Scot. Pop. Ballads II 113 n., 356ff., 362f., 365f., III 4, 8; IV 412, 482, 485f.; V 234. — Italian Novella: Rotunda; Missouri French: Carrière. — Jewish: Neuman; India: *Thompson-Balys; Japanese: Ikeda. — Indonesian: DeVries' List No. 209. — Mono-Alu: Wheeler 20, 36, 46, 60f. — Papua: Ker 41, 45, 57, 64, 103. — New Hebrides: Codrington No. III 8. N. A. Indian (Pawnee): Alexander N. Am. 81. — Africa (Benga): Nassau 140 No. 16, (Ekoi): Talbot 233, (Angola): Chatelain 145 No. 14, (Kaffir): Theal 37, 47, 127, (Swahili): Steere 199, (Basuto): Jacottet 104 No. 15.

A34. Birds as creator's servants. A165.1.1. Birds as messengers of the gods. A1021.2. Bird scouts sent out from ark. B101. Treasure bird. B141. Prophetic bird. B172. Magic bird. B256.5.1. Birds protect saint and serve him. B523. Animal saves man from pursuer. B538.1. Bird gives shelter with wings. B541.3. Bird rescues man from sea. B552. Bird carries man.

B451. *Helpful birds — passeriformes.*

B451.1. *Helpful lark.* Madagascar (Imerina): Ferrand Contes populaires Malgaches 102ff. No. 32.

B451.2. *Helpful nightingale.* *Chauvin II 117 No. 97; India: Thompson-Balys.

B451.3. *Helpful wren.* Irish myth: Cross; India: Thompson-Balys.

A1348.1. Wren helps mankind restore prosperity to the world. B259.5. Fly, wren, fox live with cleric.

B451.4. *Helpful crow.* India: *Thompson-Balys; Chinese: Graham. — Africa (Hausa): Tremearne FL XXII 464ff. No. 50, Hausa Superstitions and Customs 380 ff. No. 80.

B451.5. *Helpful raven.* *Fb "ravn" III 23a; *Zingerle Sagen aus Tirol 588. — Irish: MacCulloch Celtic 36; Spanish Exempla: Keller; Bødker Exempler 290 Nos. 45, 46; Jewish: Neuman. — Chinese: Eberhard FFC CXX 53.

B147.1.2.1. Raven as bird of good omen. B291.1.1. Ravens carry messages to enemies.

B451.6. *Helpful magpie.* Chinese: Werner 190, Graham.

B451.7. *Helpful sparrow.* Irish myth: Cross; Japanese: Anesaki 318.

B455. *Helpful birds — falconiformes.*

B455.1. *Helpful vulture.* Greek: Grote I 105; India: *Thompson-Balys.

B455.2. *Helpful falcon.* Italian Novella: Rotunda.

B172.5. Magic falcon gets water of life for hero.

B455.3. *Helpful eagle.* See references in B322.1. — *Fb "fjer", "ørn" IV 1183b; Köhler-Bolte I 545, 560, *561; Reinhard PMLA XXXVIII 433 nn. 24, 26; Gaster Exempla 186 No. 5; Fables: Halm Aesop Nos. 92, 120, Babrius No. 144, Wienert FFC LVI 70 (ET 338, 339), 127 (ST 353). — Irish myth: Cross; Greek: Fox 118; Finnish: Kalevala rune 7; Breton: Sébillot Incidents s.v. "oiseau", "nid". — Missouri French: Carrière; Jewish: Neuman; India: Thompson-Balys. — German New Guinea: Dixon 141f.; Africa (Vai): Ellis 242 No. 49.

B522.4. Eagle carries off abandoned child. B542.1.1. Eagle carries man to safety.

B455.4. *Helpful hawk.* Scottish: Campbell-McKay No. 1; India: Thompson-Balys.

B455.5. *Helpful kite (bird).* Hindu: *Penzer IV 192 n. 1; India: *Thompson-Balys.

B457. *Helpful birds — charidriiformes.*

B457.1. *Helpful dove.* (Cf. B362.) — Fable: Halm Aesop No. 296, Wienert FFC LVI 59 (ET 201), 127 (ST 356); Breton: Sébillot Incidents s.v. "talisman". — Missouri-French: Carrière; Italian Novella: Rotunda. — Jewish: Neuman; Irish myth: Cross; India: *Thompson-Balys.

A2221.7. Dove returns to ark in obedience to Noah. E754.2.1. Souls carried to heaven by doves. V231.1. Angel in bird's shape.

B457.2. *Helpful pigeon.* Jewish: Neuman.

B461. *Helpful birds — coraciiformes.*

B461.1. *Helpful woodpecker.* Africa (Shangani): Bourhill and Drake 43ff. No. 5, (Fjort): Dennett 74ff. No. 16.

B461.2. *Helpful owl.* India: Thompson-Balys.

B463. *Helpful birds — ciconiiformes.*

B463.1. *Helpful sea-bird.* Type 554*. — Saints' legend (Irish): Plummer cxlvi; Irish myth: Cross.

B463.2. *Helpful heron.* India: *Thompson-Balys; S. A. Indian (Ceuici): Alexander Lat. Am. 304.

B463.3. *Helpful crane.* India: *Thompson-Balys; Japanese: Ikeda, Anesaki 323. — N. A. Indian: Thompson Tales 340 n. 227.

Q557.6. Saint's pet crane picks out eye of spying person. R246. Crane-bridge. Fugitives are helped across a stream by a crane who lets them cross on his leg.

B463.4. *Helpful stork.* Hartland Science 194; India: *Thompson-Balys.

B469. *Helpful birds — miscellaneous.*

B469.1. *Helpful grebe.* Madagascar (Imerina): Ferrand Contes populaires Malgaches 102ff. No. 32.

B469.2. *Helpful swan.* Irish myth: Cross; Saints' legend (Irish): Plummer cxlvi. — Hindu: Keith 108; India: *Thompson-Balys.

D361.1. Swan maiden. H411.17. Swan as chastity test.

B469.3. *Helpful goose.* *Köhler-Bolte I 347; India: Thompson-Balys.
K1816.5.1. Geese betray beauty of disguised goose-girl.

B469.3.1. *Helpful wild goose.* Cheremis: Sebeok-Nyerges (B469.5); India: Thompson-Balys.

B469.4. *Helpful duck.* Fb "and" IV 12b. — Japanese: Anesaki 321, Ikeda; India: Thompson-Balys.

B469.4.1. *Helpful wild duck.* Africa (Betsileo): Renel Contes de Madagascar I 140ff. No. 25, (Imerina): Ferrand 102ff. No. 32.

B469.5. *Helpful cock.* *Type 670; *Aarne FFC XV 49ff.; Missouri-French: Carrière; Jewish: Neuman; India: Thompson-Balys. — Africa (Fjort): Dennett 105 No. 29.

B469.5.1. *Helpful chicken.* Jewish: Neuman.

B469.6. *Helpful guinea-fowl.* Africa (Hottentot): Bleek 65 No. 28.

B469.7. *Helpful turkey.* N. A. Indian (Zuñi): Cushing 54ff.

B469.8. *Helpful cuckoo.* Lithuanian: Balys Index Nos. 454f.

B469.9. *Helpful parrot.* Clouston II 196ff.; India: *Thompson-Balys. — Africa (Ekoi): Talbot 252.
K1591. Seventy tales of a parrot prevent a wife's adultery.

B469.9.1. *Helpful paroquet.* India: Thompson-Balys.

B469.10. *Helpful pheasant.* Korean: Zong in-Sob 97 No. 53.

B470. Helpful fish. See B375.1 and references. — *Fb "ring" III 61a, "fisk" I 296. — Italian Novella: Rotunda; Missouri-French: Carrière. — Breton: Sébillot Incidents s.v. "animaux", Hartland Science 174; Arabian: Burton S V 326; Hindu: Keith 99; India: *Thompson-Balys; Indonesian: DeVries Volksverhalen uit Oost Indië I No. 72 (also in some versions of No. 35). — Polynesian (Celebes): Dixon *72 n. 56; Indonesian, Japanese, N. Pacific Coast American Indian (Micmac): Dixon *157 n. 6; Africa (Angola): Chatelain 65 No. 3.
B107. Treasure fish. B124. Wise fish. B142. Prophetic fish. B175. Magic fish. B211.11. Speaking fish. B243. King of fishes. B375.1. Fish returned to water: grateful. B548.2 Fish recovers object from sea. B551. Fish carries man.

B470.1. *Small fish as helper.* Marquesas: Handy 99.

B471. *Helpful shark.* Fb "haj". — Tahiti: Dixon 64; Tonga: Gifford 76; Mono-Alu-Fauru: Wheeler 65.

B472. *Helpful whale.* Irish myth: Cross; India: Thompson-Balys. — N. A. Indian: *Thompson Tales 327 n. 179. — Jamaica: Beckwith MAFLS XVII 256ff. Nos. 38, 39, 275 No. 86. — Maori: Dixon 83.
R245. Whale-boat. A man is carried across the water on a whale (fish). V462.10. Ascetic cleric lives seven years on whale's back.

B473. *Helpful dolphin.* *Chauvin V 4 No. 2; *Pauli (ed. Bolte) No. 868. — Jewish: Neuman; Greek: Fox 101.

B474. *Helpful salmon.* *Type 675.
B175.1. Magic salmon carries hero over water.

B475. *Helpful pike.* *Fb "gjedde".

B476. *Helpful eel.* Hawaii: Beckwith Myth 478, 511.

B477. *Helpful octopus.* Marquesas: Handy 76.

B478. *Helpful crab.* Africa (Mpongwe): Nassau 41 No. 6; India: *Thompson-Balys.

B480. Helpful insects. India: *Thompson-Balys; Jewish: Neuman; Chinese: Graham.

B481. *Helpful insects — hymenoptera.*

B481.1. *Helpful ant.* (Cf. B362.) — Fb "myre". Fable: Halm Aesop No. 296, Wienert FFC LVI 59 (ET 201), 127 (ST 356). — Breton: Sébillot Incidents s.v. "fourmi", "animaux". — Missouri-French: Carrière. — Africa (Fjort): Dennett 126. — India: *Thompson-Balys; Indonesian: Dixon 217, DeVries Volksverhalen I No. 67, II No. 170; Chinese: Graham.

H1091. Task: sorting a large amount of grains (beads, beans, peas) in one night.

B481.2. *Helpful termite.* Africa (Nao): Held 132ff.

B481.3. *Helpful bee.* *Fb "bi" IV 36b. — Finnish: Kalevala rune 15; Italian Novella: Rotunda; Jewish: Neuman; Japanese: Ikeda, Anesaki 323.

A33. Bee as God's spy. B259.4. Bees build church of wax to contain consecrated host.

B481.3.1. *Helpful bumblebee.* Africa (Ganda): Baskerville 8ff.

B481.4. *Helpful wasp.* *Type 559; Jewish: Neuman; Africa (Madagascar): Sibree FLJ I (1883) 45ff.

B481.5. *Helpful hornet.* Type 559; Jewish: Neuman; N. A. Indian (Micmac): Rand 42 No. 6.

B482. *Helpful insects — coleoptera.*

B482.1. *Helpful firefly.* Indonesian: DeVries Volksverhalen I No. 35, II No. 170.

B482.2. *Helpful dungbeetle.* Type 559; *BP II 454 n. 1.

B483. *Helpful insects — diptera.*

B483.1. *Helpful fly.* Type 772*; Dh II 214. — Africa (Ekoi): Talbot 209; India: *Thompson-Balys.

A2221.2.1. Flies on Christ's body rewarded. B251.7. Fly habitually buzzes when cleric returns from matins. B259.5. Fly, wren, fox live with cleric. H322. Suitor test: finding princess.

B483.1.0.1. *Fly warns saint against devil hidden in a cup with liquor.* *Loomis White Magic 66.

B483.2. *Helpful flea.* *Chauvin II 197 No. 29.

B484. *Helpful insects — lepidoptera.*

B484.1. *Helpful caterpillar.* French Canadian: Sister Marie Ursule (B489.2).

B485. *Helpful insects — hemiptera.*

B486. *Helpful insects — orthoptera.*

B486.1. *Helpful locusts.* Arabian: Burton S VI 9.

B486.2. *Helpful cricket.* India: *Thompson-Balys.

B489. *Helpful insects — miscellaneous.*

B489.1. *Helpful spider*[1] *Dh I 144, II 66ff. — N. A. Indian (Jicarilla Apache): Russell JAFL XI 256; *Loomis White Magic 66; Africa (Duala): Lederbogen Märchen V 141; India: Thompson-Balys.

B490. Other helpful animals.[2]

B491. *Helpful reptile.*

B491.1. *Helpful serpent.* *Types 612, 670, 672, 673; *BP I 128, 131, II 463; Dh I 276ff. (cf. A2145.2), IV 147ff. (Type 560); *Fb "hugorm" I 666; "snog" III 436b, "blad" IV 44a; *Chauvin II 106 No. 71, VII 25 No. 373F n. 5; Köhler-Bolte I 440; *Pauli (ed. Bolte) No. 648; *Ward Catalogue of Romances III 208; Oesterley Gesta Romanorum No. 141; *Warnke Quellen des Esope der Marie de France 221ff.; Dickson Valentine and Orson 53; *Penzer I 101 n. 1. — Italian Novella: Rotunda; Missouri-French: Carrière. — Greek: *Frazer Apollodorus I 86 n. 2, 312 n. 2; Jewish: Neuman; Swiss: Jegerlehner Oberwallis 305 No. 3; Estonian: Aarne FFC XXV 132 No. 78; Finnish: Aarne FFC XXXIII 46 No. 78. — Burmese: Scott Indo-Chinese Myth. 274; Indonesian: DeVries Volksverhalen I No. 67. — Sumatran: Dixon 163; India: *Thompson-Balys; Korean: Zong in-Sob 95, No. 52. — Africa (Gold Coast): Barker and Sinclair 163 No. 32, (Zanzibar): Bateman 222 No. 10, (Benga): Nassau 208 No. 33.

B108.6. Serpent's bite produces ornaments and clothes. B123. Wise serpent. B161. Wisdom from serpent. B165.1. Animal languages learned from serpent. B176. Magic serpent. B217.1.1. Animal languages learned from eating serpent. B511.1. Snake as healer. B524.3. Helpful snake protects man from attack. S222.2. Woman promises unborn daughter to snake as wife for ferrying her across stream.

B491.2. *Helpful lizard.* Breton: Sébillot Incidents s.v. "animaux". — India: Thompson-Balys; Chinese: Graham. — N. A. Indian (Jicarilla Apache): Russell JAFL XI 256.

B491.3. *Helpful crocodile.* India: Thompson-Balys. — Africa (Madagascar): Sibree FLJ I 2-2ff., Larrouy RTP IV 305, (Temne): Schlenker Temne Traditions 87ff. No. 7.

B491.4. *Helpful worm.* Chinese, Persian: Coyajee JPASB XXIV 197f.; Jewish: Neuman.

B491.4.1. *Helpful centipede.* Chinese: Graham, Eberhard FFC CXX 30. — Africa (Benga): Nassau 208 No. 33.

B491.4.2. *Helpful angleworm.* Chinese: Graham.

B491.5. *Helpful turtle (tortoise).* Hawaii: Beckwith Myth 514; Tonga: Gifford 50; Africa (Fjort): Dennett 74ff. No. 16.

B493. *Helpful amphibian.*

B493.1. *Helpful frog.* *Type 402, 440, 670B*; *BP I 1ff. (Gr. No. 1), II 30ff. (Gr. No. 63). — Jewish: Neuman; India: *Thompson-Balys: Chinese: Eberhard FFC CXX 30, 180. — Chile: Pino Saavedra 405. — Africa (Zulu): Callaway 241, (Ba Ronga): Einstein 288, (Basuto): Jacottet 202 No. 30.

B211.12. Speaking frog. B375.2. Frog returned to spring: grateful.

---

[1] In folk thought, an insect.

[2] B490—B499 has been reorganized as follows:

Old Number	New Number
B491	B491.1
B492	B491.2
B493	B493.1
B494	B493.2
B496	B491.4.1
B498	B498.1

B493.2. *Helpful toad.* Type 402; BP II 30ff. (Gr. No. 63). — Missouri-French: Carrière; Chinese: Graham.

B495. *Helpful crustacean.*

B495.1. *Helpful crab.* India: Thompson-Balys; Africa (Mpongwe): Nassau 41 No. 6.

B495.2. *Helpful lobster.* Chinese: Eberhard FFC CXX 180.

B498. *Helpful mythical animal.*

B498.1. *Helpful dragon.* (Cf. B11.) — Italian Novella: Rotunda; Swiss Jegerlehner Oberwallis 328 No. 17; Chinese: Graham.

B500—B599. Services of helpful animals.

B500. Magic power from animals. — Type 675; Fb "ønske" III 1179a. — Italian Novella: Rotunda; Jewish: Neuman; India: *Thompson-Balys; Missouri French: Carrière; N. A. Indian: *Thompson Tales 317 n. 146c; Africa (Angola): Chatelain 71 No. 3. (Cf. B100—B199 Magic animals.)

B109.1.2. Dog whose skin turns water into wine. D684. Transformation by helpful animal. D810. Magic object a gift. D1720. Acquisition of magic power. D1834. Magic strength from helping animal. D1903. Power of inducing love given by animals. F405.5. Cat, dog, and mouse ward off evil spirit. Man takes these animals along with him as protection F980. Extraordinary occurrences concerning animals.

B501. *Animal gives part of body as talisman for summoning its aid.* *Types 531, 552, 553; BP III 18ff., 424ff.; Malone PMLA XLIII 407; *Fb "fjer" I 301, "hår" I 771b. — Breton: Sébillot Incidents s.v. "talisman"; French Canadian: Barbeau JAFL XXIX 15; Missouri-French: Carrière; Italian Novella: Rotunda; India: *Thompson-Balys. — Persian: Carnoy 290, 331. — Africa (Kaffir): Theal 85, (Swahili): Steere 199; N. A. Indian (Pawnee): Dorsey MAFLS VIII 102.

D532. Transformation by putting on claw, feather, etc. of helpful animal. D1021. Magic feather. D1023. Magic hair of animal. D1421. Magic object summons helper. D2074.1. Animals magically called.

B501.1. *Buffalo give hero horns for summoning them.*

D1011.1. Magic animal horn. D1421.5.1. Magic horn summons army for rescue. D2074.1.1. Buffalo magically called.

B501.1.1. *Merry horn and angry horn for summoning buffalo.* When all is well hero is to blow on merry-horn; when in trouble on angry-horn. — India: Thompson-Balys.

B501.2. *Kite teaches rhyme by which he may be summoned for help.* India: Thompson-Balys.

D1273. Magic formula (charm). H12. Recognition by song (music).

B501.3. *Animal gives jewel for summoning him when in need of help.* India: Thompson-Balys.

B501.4. *Birds give hero feather to burn if he is in difficulty.* India: Thompson-Balys.

B505. *Magic object received from animal.* *Types 560, 561; *Aarne MSFO XXV 3—82; BP II 451ff., 537; Type 554*; *Köhler-Bolte I 440; Hartland Perseus III 199; Breton: Sébillot Incidents s.v. "talisman"; Missouri-French: Carrière. — India: *Thompson-Balys; Chinese: Eberhard FFC CXX 37 No. 24. — Africa (Zanzibar): Bateman 221 No. 10, (Basuto): Jacottet 214 No. 31. See also references in B375.1.

D810. Magic object a gift. J130. Wisdom (knowledge) acquired from animals.

B505.1. *Magic object received from animal brother-in-law.* *Type 552. — N. A. Indian (Micmac): Thompson CColl II 409ff.

B314. Helpful animal brothers-in-law.

B505.2. *Animal tells hero where to find magic object.* (Cf. B560.) — French Canadian: Sister Marie Ursule.

B505.3. *Magic song received from fish* (Cf. B470.) — Chinese: Graham.

B510. Healing by animals.

D1342. Magic object gives health. D1500. Magic object controls disease. D2161. Magic healing power. F950. Marvelous cures.

B511. *Animal as healer.*

B511.1. *Snake as healer.* *Chauvin VII 25 No. 373 F note 5; *Pauli (ed. Bolte) No. 648; Jewish: Neuman; India: Thompson-Balys.

B491.1. Helpful serpent.

B511.1.1. *Snake creeps into man's mouth and heals him.* Estonian: Aarne FFC XXV 132 No. 78; Finnish: Aarne FFC XXXIII 46 No. 78.

B511.1.2. *Snake heals mutilated maiden with magic herbs.* Italian Novella: Rotunda.

B511.1.3. *Helpful hedgehog forces snake to suck out poison from bitten raja.* India: Thompson-Balys.

B511.2. *Pig as healer.*

B183. Magic boar (pig).

B511.2.1. *Magic pig heals wound its skin touches.* Irish myth: Cross.

B183.9. Skin of magic pig heals wounds.

B511.2.2. *Magic pig heals wounds by licking.* Irish myth: Cross.

B511.3. *Faithful horse pushes sleep thorn out of its master's head,* so that he awakes. Icel.: Boberg.

D1364.2. Sleep-thorn. D1978.3. Waking from magic sleep by removal of enchanting instrument.

B511.4. *Rat cures man of wound.* S. A. Indian (Cashinawa): Métraux BBAE 143 III 685.

B511.5. *Bird heals man.* Chinese-Persian: Coyajee JPASB XXIV 185f.; Alu: Wheeler 60; Papua: Ker 103.

B511.5.1. *Vulture cures blindness.* India: Thompson-Balys.

B512. *Medicine shown by animal.* It heals another animal with a medicine (herb, water, etc.) and thus shows the man the remedy. Sometimes the medicine resuscitates the dead. (The animal is most frequently the serpent. (Cf. B491.) — *Type 160, 303, 590, 612; *BP I 128; Chauvin II 106 No. 71; Kittredge Gawain 153 n. 4; Wesselski Märchen 239f. No. 50. — *Krappe Papers and Trans. of Jubilee Cong. of Folk-Lore Soc. 277ff. — *Fb "blad" IV 44a; *Frazer Apollodorus I 312 n. 2. — Icel.: Boberg, Völsunga saga ch. 8.; Jewish: Neuman; India: *Thompson-Balys; Japanese: Ikeda. N. A. Indian: Thompson Tales 354 n. 279.

D955. Magic leaf. D965. Magic plant. D1500.1.18. Magic healing water. D1505.5. Magic water restores sight. E80. Water of life. E105. Resuscitation by herbs (leaves). E181. Means of resuscitation learned. N452. Secret remedy overheard in conversation of animals (witches). W154.8. Grateful animals; ungrateful man.

B513. *Remedy learned from overhearing animal meeting.* The hero learns how to cure his own blindness and the sickness of the king (princess).— Spanish Exempla: Keller; Missouri-French: Carrière; India: Thompson-Balys. — See references for B235.

B235. Secrets discussed in animal meeting. B561. Animals tell hero their secrets.

B514. *Animal fetches remedy for man.* Missouri-French: Carrière.

B514.1. *Grateful fox fetches fox liver as remedy.* Japanese: Mitford 261ff.

B441. Helpful fox.

B514.2. *Bee fetches balm from heaven to restore hero's speech.* Finnish: Kalevala rune 15.

B514.3. *Snake gives man antidote for poison.* Africa (Gold Coast): Barker and Sinclair 163 No. 32.

D1317.0.1. Magic object detects poison. D1383. Magic object protects from poison. D1515. Magic antidote for poison.

B515. *Resuscitation by animals.* *Types 300, 665. Italian Novella: Rotunda; Jewish: Neuman; India: *Thompson-Balys.

E0. Resuscitation.

B516. *Sight restored by animal.* India: Thompson-Balys; Eskimo (Greenland): Holm 31, Rasmussen I 312, III 203, Rink 100, (Smith Sound): Kroeber JAFL XII 169, (Cumberland Sound): Boas BAM XV 169, (Central Eskimo): Boas RBAE VI 626.

B520. Animals save person's life. See also B540. — Greek: Frazer Apollodorus I 372 n. 1 (horse). — Icel.: *Boberg; Missouri-French: Carrière; Panchatantra III 8 (tr. Ryder) 334; Buddhist myth: Malalasekera II 1260; Chinese: Eberhard FFC CXX 25, 28, 31, 84; Africa (Duala): Lederbogen 76.

D699.1. Eyes of hero's buffalo friend turn into two powerful dogs that protect his wife. K528.1. Substitute smoker. K640. Escape by help of confederate. K645. Monkey saves condemned birds through feigned dream. K644. Monkey attracts attention of mowers until young birds can fly away from the harvest field. K2351. Animals help in military victory. R243. Fugitives aided by a helpful animal.

B521. *Animal warns of fatal danger.* India: *Thompson-Balys; Jewish: Neuman; U.S.: Baughman; Africa (Duala): Lederbogen Märchen 75, (Fang): Trilles 138, (Loango): Pechuël-Loesche 109.

B140. Prophetic animals. R243. Fugitives aided by a helpful animal.

B521.1. *Animal warns against poison.* Fable: Halm Aesop No. 120, Wienert FFC LVI 70 (ET 338), 127 (ST 353), (eagle). — India: Thompson-Balys; Africa (Basuto): Jacottet 76 No. 12 (ox).

B131.5. Peacock's feathers ruffled in presence of poison. D1317.0.1. Magic object detects poison. D1383. Magic object protects from poison. D1515. Magic antidote for poison.

B521.1.1. *Horse advises hero not to wash in water* (as his false wife told him to) or his eyes will pop out. — India: Thompson-Balys.

B521.1.2. *Animal warns man against drinking.* India: Thompson-Balys.

B521.2. *Animal warns against accident.*

B521.2.1. *Eagle saves man from falling wall.* The grateful eagle swoops down and takes the man's hat, and thus gets him away from the wall that is about to fall. — Fable: Babrius No. 144, Halm Aesop No. 92, Wienert FFC 70 (ET 339), 127 (ST 353).

B521.3. *Animals warn against attack.* Icel.: Boberg; Jewish: Neuman; India: *Thompson-Balys; Africa (Zulu): Callaway 87.

B133.1. Horse warns of danger. B141.1. Bird gives warning. D1317. Magic object warns of danger.

B521.3.1. *Dogs warn against witch.* Jamaica: *Beckwith MAFLS XVII 270 No. 82; Eskimo (Greenland): Rink 452.

G250. Recognition of witches.

B521.3.2. *Cackling geese spread alarm.* *Frazer Fasti II 175 n. 5.

B576.1. Animal as guard of person or house.

B521.3.3. *Flea's bite alarms king.* Robber tells flea of plan to rob king. During the robbery the flea bites and awakens the king. — *Chauvin II 197 No. 29.

B521.3.3.1. *Prince awakened by fly on his nose* in time to save himself from enemy. India: Thompson-Balys.

B521.3.4. *Dog warns of pursuit.* Irish myth: Cross; Buddhist myth: Malalasekera II 536.

B521.3.5. *Owl warns other birds from limed net.* India: Thompson-Balys.

B521.4. *Animals warn wife of husband's danger.* Africa (Ekoi): Talbot 252.

B521.5. *Owl saves man from plunging over cliff.* Flaps wings and arrests man's attention. — Hawaii: Beckwith Myth 124.

B521.6. *Birds warn of enemy's approach.* Hawaii: Beckwith Myth 390.

B522. *Animal saves man from death sentence.* India: Thompson-Balys; Jewish: Neuman.

J1130. Cleverness in law court.

B522.1. *Serpent shows condemned man how to save prince's life.* Bites the prince and then shows the man the proper remedy (cf. B512). By thus ingratiating himself the man is freed from false accusation. — *Type 160; Chauvin II 106 No. 71. — Spanish Exempla: Keller; Clouston Tales I 230; Bødker Exempler 304 No. 75; India: *Thompson-Balys; Japanese: Ikeda. — Africa (Vai): Ellis 230 No. 39.

W154.8. Grateful animals; ungrateful man.

B522.2. *Kite steals jewels and thus saves condemned man.* Innocent man in possession of stolen jewels, is about to be apprehended. Kite carries off the jewels and saves him. — *Penzer IV 192 n. 1; India: *Thompson-Balys.

N352. Bird carries off ring which lover has taken from sleeping mistress' finger. He searches for the ring and becomes separated from her.

B522.3. *Woman slandered as adulteress is thrown into lion pit.* Lions do not harm her. — Italian Novella: Rotunda.

B443. Helpful lion. D1714. Magic power of chaste woman. F980. Extraordinary occurrences concerning animals. H413. Special powers of chaste woman. K2110. Slanders.

B522.4. *Eagle carries off condemned child.* Irish myth: Cross.

B552. Man carried by bird. R122. Miraculous rescue. R131. Exposed or abandoned child rescued.

B522.4.1. *Circling cranes carry away girl.* Eskimo (Bering Strait): Nelson RBAE XVIII 480.

B523. *Animal saves man from pursuer.* Missouri-French: Carrière.

B521.3.4. Dog warns of pursuit. D1393. Magic object helps fugitive. R246. Crane-bridge.

B523.1. *Spider-web over hole saves fugitive.* (Cf. A2221.5.) — Type 967*; *Dh II 66f. — *Wesselski Theorie 42. — Jewish: Neuman, Bin Gorion Born Judas[2] III 115ff., Grünbaum Neue Beiträge zur Semitischen Sagenkunde 195; Lappish: Qvigstad Lappiske Eventyr I No. 32, II No. 68. — India: Thompson-Balys; Japanese: Ikeda; Africa (Fang): Trilles 139.

B523.2. *Whale fights monster pursuing saint.* Irish myth: Cross.

B472. Helpful whale.

B523.3. *Great clam fights hero's pursuer.* Tahiti: Beckwith Myth 260.

B524. *Animal overcomes man's adversary.* India: *Thompson-Balys.

D2156.8.1. Saint sends tigers against murderers. H1588. Contest of dogs. Two opponents test their powers by having their dogs fight.

B524.1. *Animals overcome man's adversary by force.* English: Wells Manual of Writings 66 (Ywain and Gawain); Irish myth: Cross; Spanish: Boggs FFC XC 98 No. 327; India: *Thompson-Balys; Eskimo (Bering Strait): Nelson RBAE XVIII 493, (Cumberland Sound): Boas BAM XV 187.

B17. Hostile animals. B187.3.3. Magic whelp kills hound by jumping down its throat. B776.1. Venomous sheep destroy enemy.

B524.1.1. *Dogs kill attacking cannibal (dragon).* *Type 300; *BP I 547. — Irish myth: Cross; French Canadian: Barbeau JAFL XXIX 20. — Africa (Basuto): Jacottet 56 No. 9, (Zulu): Callaway 51, (Kaffir): Kidd 226 No. 1.

B11.11. Fight with dragon. B11.11.2. Hero's dogs (horse) prevent dragon's heads from rejoining body. B187. Magic dog. G275.2. Witch overcome by helpful dogs of hero.

B524.1.2. *Dogs rescue fleeing master from tree refuge.* *Parsons Zs. f. Ethnologie LIV 1—29, MAFLS XVII 271 No. 82. — See also most of African references in B421.

G275.2. Witch overcome by helpful dogs of hero. R251. Flight on a tree, which ogre tries to cut down.

B524.1.2.1. *Dogs break bonds and kill master's attacker.* Type 327; India: Thompson-Balys.

B524.1.3. *Cat kills attacking rat.* Japanese: Ikeda, Mitford 253ff.

B524.1.4. *Wolf defends master's child against serpent.* Malone PMLA XLIII 420; Irish myth: Cross.

B524.1.4.1. *Dog defends master's child against animal assailant.* Irish myth: Cross.

B331.2. Llewellyn and his dog.

B524.1.5. *Helpful buffaloes tramp hero's enemies to death.* India: Thompson-Balys.

B524.1.5.1. *Helpful buffaloes save hero from tiger.* India: Thompson-Balys.

B524.1.6. *Helpful bird kills snake attacking master's wife and child.* Africa (Mbundu): JAFL XXXV 136ff. No. 16.

B524.1.7. *Horse kills master's attacking enemies.* Irish myth: Cross.

B524.1.8. *Shut in with elephants, blackbird orders ants to burrow themselves into the elephants' brains.* India: Thompson-Balys.

B524.1.9. *Grateful hawk attacks hero's enemies.* Chinese: Graham.

B524.1.10. *Helpful centipede kills ogre.* Chinese: Graham.

B524.1.11. *Hero contests with demons, using fighting animals:* cock, goat, bull, horse, wild bull, peacock. — India: Thompson-Balys.

B524.1.12. *Hero saved from ravaging snake by crab companion.* India: Thompson-Balys.

B524.2. *Animals overcome man's adversary by strategy.* Type 545; BP I 325ff., III 487 (Gr. 33a, 214). — Icel.: Boberg; Indonesian: DeVries' list No. 48. — Africa (Kaffir): Kidd 230 No. 2, (Ekoi): Talbot 233, (Basuto): Jacottet 114 No. 27.

K427. Clever animal betrays thief. K722. Giant tricked into becoming mouse. Cat eats him up.

B524.2.1. *Helpful bees (hornets) sting opposing army.* Spanish Exempla: Keller; Jewish: *Neuman, Bin Gorion Born Judas[2] III 113ff.; India: *Thompson-Balys; Japanese: Anesaki 323.

K2351.2. Bees thrown into redoubt drive out enemies.

B524.2.1.1. *Saint sends swarm of bees or wasps against enemies.* *Loomis White Magic 65f.

V229.8. Invaders miraculously defeated by saints.

B524.3. *Helpful snake protects man from attack.* India: Thompson-Balys.

B524.4. *Supernatural bird prevents mother from killing babe.* Irish myth: Cross.

B172. Magic bird. S12. Cruel mother.

B524.5. *Broom, transformed into porcupine, drives away would-be ravisher.* India: Thompson-Balys.

B524.6. *Grateful hare raises animal army for hero.* India: Thompson-Balys.

B524.7. *Faithful dog kills would-be murderer of sleeping master.* India: Thompson-Balys.

B524.8. *Chicken picks out one of attacker's eyes.* Jewish: Neuman.

B525. *Animal spares man he is about to devour.* Spanish Exempla: Keller; Buddhist myth: Malalasekera I 851. — See all references to B381.

B525.1. *Tiger hides woman from all other tigers.* S. A. Indian (Chiriguano): Métraux RMLP XXXIII 155, 161, (Carib): ibid. 146.

B526. *Animal saves man from death by burning.*

D1382. Magic object protects against cold or burning. D1841.3 Burning magically evaded.

B526.1. *Helpful animals quench execution fire.* Master is to be burned at stake. — Dh I 315.

D1391.1. Miraculous rain extinguishes fire used at stake. J1180. Clever means of avoiding legal punishment.

B526.2. *Helpful mare cools boiling bath for master.* Hero is made to bathe in boiling mare's milk. His mare blows on the milk and cools it. — *Köhler-Bolte I 468.

B527. *Animal saves man from death by drowning.* Saints' legend (Irish): Plummer cxlvi (sea birds); Irish myth: Cross; Buddhist myth: Malalasekera II 747.

F1088.3.2. Fisherman dragged through sea by seal escapes.

B527.1. *Fish promises to spare man in coming flood.* (Cf. B375.1.) — Hindu: Keith 99; India: Thompson-Balys.

A1028. Rescue from deluge by fish.

B527.2. *Helpful animal stops leak in Noah's Ark.* Dh I 276ff.

A1020. Escape from deluge. A2145.2. Snake preserved in ark: to stop hole with tail.

B527.3. *Owl saves man from drowning:* flaps wings to call attention to direction of land. Hawaii: Beckwith Myth 125.

B529. *Animal saves person's life — miscellaneous.*

B529.1. *Animals (sow, bitch, mare) hide boy in their belly to protect him.* India: Thompson-Balys.

B529.2. *Dragon swallows arrow (thunderbolt) intended for hero.* Italian Novella: Rotunda.

B530. **Animals nourish men.** Provide food, shelter, or other necessities. — India: Thompson-Balys. — Zanzibar: Bateman 85 No. 6 (ape, lion, snake).

B19.2. Nectar-yielding cow. B115. Animal with horn of plenty.

B530.1. *Mythical frog as host to woman.* S. A. Indian (Warrau): Métraux RMLP XXXIII 146.

B530.2. *Elephants look after ascetic in jungle.* Buddhist myth: Malalasekera I 44.

B531. *Animals provide food for men.* *Basset 1001 Contes III 295 (birds); *Wesselski Märchen 249 No. 57; Toldo Studien zur vgl. Littgsch. VIII 21; *Fb "hind" I 612 (deer); Alphabet Nos. 361. 636. — Irish myth: Cross, Saints' legend (Irish): Plummer cxliv (otter). — Breton: Sébillot Incidents s.v. "nourriture" (bird, dog); French Canadian: *Barbeau JAFL XXIX 15 (dog); Missouri-French: Carrière; Spanish Exempla: Keller; Swiss: Jegerlehner Oberwallis 328 No 17 (dragon). — Jewish: Neuman; India: *Thompson-Balys; Buddhist myth: Malalasekera I 217, II 655, 1158; Chinese : Graham; Africa: Stanley 329, (Angola): Chatelain 129 No. 19; Eskimo (Greenland): Rasmussen I 143, III 80, 198, Rink 227, 413, 462, Holm 84, (Cumberland Sound): Boas BAM XV 222, (Central Eskimo): Boas RBAE VI 638, (Smith Sound): Kroeber JAFL XII 176. — S. A. Indian (Toba): Métraux MAFLS XL 6, (Chiriguano): Métraux RMLP XXXIII 155.

B531.1. *Infants fed by bees.* *Pease Cicero De Divinatione 391 (Bk. I 79), 597; S. A. Indian (Kaiguá): Métraux RMLP XXXIII 139.

B531.2. *Unusual milking animal.*

B531.2.1. *Does, tigresses, she-wolves milked into pond,* which becomes a pond of milk. India: Thompson-Balys.

B531.3. *Helpful animal recovers magic food-producing skin from river bottom.* India: Thompson-Balys.

B531.4. *Helpful animal drops magic food.* India: Thompson-Balys.

B531.5. *Birds save man from hunger by pitching themselves to roast in fire he has made.* India: Thompson-Balys.

B535. *Animal nurse.* Animal nourishes abandoned child. — *Frazer Fasti II 369ff., especially 369 n. 3, 375; Dickson Valentine and Orson 36, 103, 107, 112, 169; *Liebrecht Zur Volkskunde 17ff.; *Nutt FLR IV 1ff.; Penzer II 294; *Fb "ulv" III 971 a (Wolf); *BP II 317, III 60ff. — Irish myth: Cross; Greek: Fox 22 (doe), 56 (bear), 118, 155 (goat, crow, sow), 280, Frazer Apollodorus I 397, II 47 n. 2, Roscher s.v. "Achilleus"; Roman: Fox 307 (Romulus and Remus) (wolf); Persian: Carnoy 330; Breton: Sébillot Incidents s.v. "chien" (dog); Missouri-French: Carrière; McCartney Papers of Michigan Academy of Science, Arts, and Letters IV (1924) 15—42; Wesselski Theorie 19; Icel.: Þiðriks saga I 302—03 (hind), Boberg; English: Wells 118 (Octovian) (lion); Chinese: Ferguson 41. — N. A. Indian: Thompson CColl II 387 (Mt. 707), Thompson Tales 316 n. 146b; S. A. Indian (Brazil): Ehrenreich International Congress of Americanists XIV 662. — Indonesian: DeVries Volksverhalen I Nos. 22, 89; India: *Thompson-Balys; — Africa (Basuto): Jacottet 104 No. 15, 190 No. 28, (Wakweli): Bender 49f.

A511.10.2.1. Culture hero suckled by wolf. B259.11.1. Brilliantly white cow comes to be milked for infant saint. B331.2. Llewellyn and his dog. B524.1.4. Wolf defends master's child against serpent. F611.2.1. Strong hero suckled by animal. L111.2.4. Future hero found in wolf den. L111.7. Future hero (heroine) raised by animal. N215. Child borne off by tiger, which is caught by griffin, which is killed by lioness, who rears child with her whelps. R13.0.1. Children carried off by animals. R131. Exposed or abandoned child rescued. S352. Animal aids abandoned child(ren). T611. Suckling of children. T611.10.1. Girl (princess, man, saint) suckled by wolf. T670. Adoption of children.

B535.0.1. *Cow as nurse cares for children.* India: Thompson-Balys.

B535.0.1.1. *Bison as nurse for child.* India: Thompson-Balys.

B535.0.2. *Bandicoot (large rat) as nurse.* Cares for children. — India: *Thompson-Balys.

B535.0.3. *Goat as nurse for child.* Jewish: Neuman; India: Thompson-Balys.

B535.0.4. *Dog as nurse for child.* India: Thompson-Balys.

B421. Helpful dog.

B535.0.5. *Abandoned prince grows up in eagle's nest.* India: Thompson-Balys.

B535.0.6. *Frog as nurse for child.* India: Thompson-Balys; S. A. Indian (Warrau): Métraux RMLP XXXIII 146.

B535.0.7. *Bird as nurse for child.* Chinese-Persian: *Coyajee JPASB XXIV 188.

B535.0.7.1. *Stork as nurse for child.* India: Thompson-Balys.

B535.0.7.2. *Crane as nurse for child.* India: Thompson-Balys.

B535.0.8. *Tiger as nurse for child.* S. A. Indian (Chiriguano): Métraux RMLP XXXIII 161, (Amuesa): ibid. 129.

B535.0.9. *She-wolf as nurse for child.* *Loomis White Magic 60; Roman myth: Fox 307.

B535.0.10. *Sheep and oxen protect exposed child.* Chinese: Coyajee JPASB XXIV 188.

B535.0.11. *She-wolf cares for baby exposed in the forest.* *Loomis White Magic 60.

B535.0.12. *Eagle cares for baby while mother works in field.* Africa (Fang): Tessman 134.

B535.0.13. *Crab as nurse for child.* S. A. Indian (Cashinawa): Métraux BBAE 143 III 684.

B535.0.14. *Serpent as nurse for child.* Greek: Grote I 44; Buddhist myth: Malalasekera II 529.

B535.1. *Goat feeds other animals from its body.* Permits them to feed from it internally. — Africa (Benga): Nassau 202 No. 32.

B19.7. The goat Heidrun.

B535.2. *Animal nurses fight with real parent for children.* India: Thompson-Balys.

J391. Kind foster-parents chosen rather than cruel parents.

B536. *Helpful animal cares for wounded (sick) master.*

B536.1. *Helpful bird cares for blinded master.* India: Thompson-Balys.

B537. *Animals adopt mysterious housekeeper.* India: Thompson-Balys.

N831.1. Mysterious housekeeper.

B538. *Animals provide shelter.*

B538.1. *Bird gives shelter with wings.* (Cf. B450.) — Irish myth: Cross; Günter Christliche Legende des Abendlandes 125; Singer Zs. f. deutsch. Altertum XXXV 184f.; Dunlop-Wilson History of Fiction I 428; Saintyves Saints Successeurs 134; Dh I 321ff.; Hand. d. Abergl. I 187. — Jewish: Neuman; Africa (Basuto): Jacottet 104 No. 15.

B538.2. *Wolf-tail blankets.* Wolves shelter man with their tails. — N. A. Indian (Ojibwa): Jones-Michelson PAES VII (1) 77, Carson JAFL XXX 491 No. 1.

B540. Animal rescuer or retriever. Rescue person or retrieve lost object. — Japanese: Anesaki 320.

D1390. Magic object rescues person. R150. Rescuers.

B540.1. *Birds throw some of their feathers to the hero in danger* and he flies off. Lithuanian: Balys Index Nos. *3270, *404.

D532. Transformation by putting on claws, feathers, etc. of helpful animals. F1021.1. Flight on artificial wings.

B540.2. *Helpful horse rescues children.* India: Thompson-Balys.

B541. *Animal rescues man from sea.* Type 506; BP III 494ff.; Liljeblad Tobiasgeschichte 94; Missouri-French: Carrière.

F1088.3.2. Fisherman dragged through sea by seal escapes.

B541.1. *Escape from sea on fish's back.* (See also B551.) — *Pauli (ed. Bolte) No. 868; *Chauvin V 4 No. 2.

B175.1. Magic salmon carries hero over water. B551.1. Fish carries man across water. F911.3.2. Winged serpent as boat: passengers within. R245. Whale boat.

B541.1.1. *Fish swallows man to rescue him from sea.* India: Thompson-Balys.

B541.2. *Fox rescues man from sea.* Type 506; BP III 494ff.; — N. A. Indian: Thompson CColl II 405ff. (Passamaquoddy, Shuswap).

B441. Helpful fox. E341. The grateful dead.

B541.3. *Bird rescues man from sea.* (Cf. B542, B450.) — *Liljeblad Tobiasgeschichte 94. — N. A. Indian (Ojibwa): Thompson CColl II 408.

B541.4. *Dog rescues drowning man.* Type 540*.

B541.4.1. *Boat towed by dog.* Eskimo (Bering Strait): Nelson RBAE XVIII 505, (Greenland): Rink 196.

B541.5. *Fish rescues ship.* (Cf. B470.) — *Charpentier Kleine Beiträge 34 n. 1.

B542. *Animal carries man through air to safety.*

B542.1. *Bird flies with man to safety.* India: *Thompson-Balys.

B552. Man carried by bird. X1133.5. Buzzards carry man to safety.

B542.1.1. *Eagle carries man to safety.* *Type 301; BP II 300 (Gr. No. 91). See all references under B322.1. — Irish myth: Cross; Missouri-French: Carrière; Finnish: Kalevala rune 7; Japanese: Hartland Science 194, Ikeda. — Africa (Kaffir): Theal 47, 127, (Vai): Ellis 242 No. 49.

B451. Helpful eagle. B522. Animal saves man from death sentence. B522.4. Eagle carries off abandoned child. D659.4.3. Transformation to eagle to carry hero to safety. F101.3. Return from lower world on eagle. K521.1.1. Man sewed in animal's hide carried off by birds. K1861.1. Hero sewed up in animal hide so as to be carried to height by bird.

B542.1.2. *Bat rescues man from height.* Bat lets him down in a spider-web basket. — N. A. Indian: Thompson Tales 318 n. 151b, Calif. Indian: Gayton and Newman 95.

B542.1.3. *Measuring worm rescues from a height.* Calif. Indian: Gayton and Newman 76.

B542.2. *Escape on flying horse.* (Cf. B41.2.) — *Chauvin V 227f. No. 130; Missouri-French: Carrière; India: *Thompson-Balys.

B542.2.1. *Transportation to fairyland on griffin's back.* India: Thompson-Balys.

B42. Griffin.

B543. *Animal finds stolen person.* Scotch: Campbell I 1ff. (dog, hawk, otter). — India: Thompson-Balys; Africa (Basuto): Jacottet 232 No. 34.

B543.0.1. *Animal helps on quest for vanished wife.* India: Thompson-Balys.

H1385.3. Quest for vanished wife (mistress).

B543.1. *Bottlefly finds stolen woman in sky.* Calif. Indian: Gayton and Newman 79.

B543.2. *Animal finds stolen goods.* India: Thompson-Balys.

B543.3. *Stolen child rescued by animal nurse.* (Cf. B535.) — Irish myth: Cross; India: Thompson-Balys; *Krappe Balor 80ff.

R131. Exposed or abandoned child rescued.

B543.3.1. *Elephant rescues stolen girl.* India: Thompson-Balys.

B437. Helpful elephant.

B544. *Animal rescues captive.* *Fb "höj" I 741 b (fox); Missouri-French: Carrière; India: *Thompson-Balys; Chinese: Eberhard FFC CXX 17 No. 8. — Africa (Zulu): Callaway 147, 241 (dog, frog), (Cameroon): Meinhof 88, 102.

G552. Rescue from ogre by helpful animals. R100. Rescues. R121.4. Ants carry silk threads to prisoner, who makes rope and escapes.

B544.1. *Animals help imprisoned master.* India: Thompson-Balys; Chinese: Eberhard FFC CXX 180.

B545. *Animal rescues from trap (net).* *Type 75. See references to B363. — Penzer V 79 n. 2 (mouse); Japanese: Ikeda.

K1182. Rat leaves serpent behind, though spared to rescue him.

B545.1. *Deer in net freed by friendly animals,* a crow, a mouse and a tortoise. Spanish Exempla: Keller.

B545.2. *Rat (mouse) gnaws net.* India: *Thompson-Balys.

B546. *Animal searches for dead man.* Breton: Sébillot s.v. "mort" (dog).

B547. *Animal rescues man from dangerous place.*

B547.1. *Animal rescues man from well.* India: *Thompson-Balys.

B547.2. *Raven rescues man from pit.* French-Canadian: Sister Marie Ursule (B542.3).

B547.2.1. *Man falls in hole with horse;* buzzards gather; he lassoes a number of buzzards, ties them together, frightens them; all fly at once, carry him from hole. (Tall tale.) Cf. Type 1882. — U.S.: Baughman.

B547.3. *Centaur rescues man from beast-infested jungle.* Greek: Grote I 109.

B547.4. *Frog rescues man from kingdom of the snakes.* India: Thompson-Balys.

B225.1. Kingdom of serpents. B493. Helpful frog.

B548. *Animal retrieves lost object.*

A941.5.4. Spring breaks forth where animal delivers book left behind by saint. D882. Stolen magic object stolen back by helpful cat and dog. D882.1. Recovered magic objects dropped by rescuing animals into sea.

B548.1. *Animals recover lost wishing ring.* Grateful cat, dog, and snake compel mouse to steal it from thief. — *Type 560; **Aarne MSFO XXV 3—82; *BP II 455ff.; Dh IV 147ff. — Missouri-French: Carrière; India: *Thompson-Balys. — Indonesian: DeVries' list No. 186; Chinese: Eberhard FFC CXX 24ff. No. 13, 68.

D882. Stolen magic object stolen back by helpful cat and dog. D882.1. Recovered magic objects dropped by rescuing animals into sea. D1076. Magic ring.

B548.1.1. *Martens recover lost magic ring from kite.* India: Thompson-Balys.

B548.1.2. *Otters recover lost magic ring from fish.* India: Thompson-Balys.

B548.2. *Fish brings lost object from bottom of sea.*

B548.2.1. *Fish recovers ring from sea.* *Type 554; *BP II 19ff.; *Fb "gjedde" I 440a, "ring" III 61a; Wünsche (A.) Die Sage vom Ring des Polykrates in der Weltliteratur (Beilage zur Allgemeinen Zeitung, 1893, Nos. 179, 180, 185, 188); Chauvin V 17; Köhler-Bolte II 209; Clouston Tales I 398ff.; Saintyves Essais de folklore biblique 402. — Irish myth: Cross; Italian Novella: Rotunda; Greek: Fox 101; Spanish: Boggs FFC XC 69 No. 515; Jewish: Neuman; India: *Thompson-Balys. Cf. L412.1. Woman casts ring into sea.

A2275.5.4. Dolphins seek King Solomon's ring. B107. Treasure fish. B571. Animals perform tasks for man. H1132.1. Task: recovering lost ring from sea. N211.1. Lost ring found in fish. N211.1.0.1. Lost articles found in interior of fish through virtue of saint.

B548.2.2. *Fish recovers key from sea.* *Type 554; *BP II 19ff.; *Fb "haj" I 534, "fisk" I 296, "ring" III 61a. — Irish myth: Cross, Beal XXI 308; Missouri-French: Carrière.

H1132.2. Task: recovering lost key from sea.

B548.2.2.1. *Frog recovers keys from sea.* French Canadian: Sister Marie Ursule.

B548.2.2.2. *Duck recovers lost key from sea.* German: Grimm No. 62.

B548.2.3. *Fish recovers lost fish-hook from sea.* Hatt Asiatic Influences 90f.; *Dixon 157 n. 6 (Indonesian, Japanese, N. Pac. Coast Am. Indian, Micmac); Japanese: Ikeda.

B548.2.4. *Fish recovers pen from sea.* *Type 531.

H1132.4. Task: recovering pen from sea.

B548.2.5. *Fish recovers lost urn from sea.* Irish myth: Cross.

B548.3. *Otter retrieves lost magic object from bottom of lake.* India: Thompson-Balys.

B548.4. *Ducks recover lost object from water.* Madagascar (Marofotsy): Renel Contes de Madagascar I 65ff. No. 9.

B548.5. *Frog recovers Sacred Host from water.* French Canadian: Sister Marie Ursule.

B548.6. *Jewel recovered from sea by helpful parrot.* India: Thompson-Balys.

B549. *Animal rescuer — miscellaneous.*

B549.1. *Girl saved by lion from ravishment.* (Cf. B443.) — Alphabet No. 775; *Loomis White Magic 58; U.S.: Baughman.

B549.2. *Dragon makes bridge across stream for holy man.* (Cf. B11.) — Jewish: Bin Gorion Born Judas[2] II 170, 349.

B549.3. *Abandoned child rescued by dog.* Italian Novella: Rotunda.

R131. Exposed or abandoned child rescued. R150. Rescuers.

B549.4. *Animal rescues from cave.* Chinese: Eberhart FFC CXX 180.

B549.5. *Hero saved from ravaging snake by crab companion.* India: *Thompson-Balys.

B550. **Animals carry men.** — India: *Thompson-Balys.

F213.3. Sea-riding horse carries mortals to fairyland. F982. Animals carry extraordinary burden. R13. Abduction by animal. V462.10. Ascetic cleric lives seven years on whale's back.

B551. *Animal carries man across water.* India: Thompson-Balys.

B551.1. *Fish carries man across water.* See also B541.1; also all references in R246. — Günter Die Christliche Legende des Abendlandes 17, 56, 80 (dolphin). — Chinese: Werner 366. — *Dixon 72 n. 56 (Hawaii, Tahiti, Celebes).

B175.1. Magic salmon carries hero over water. B541.1. Escape from sea on fish's back. F420.5.3.6. Water-spirit demands food from those it takes across stream. F911.3.2. Winged serpent as boat: passengers within. M205.1.1. Turtle carrying man through water upsets him because of a broken promise. R245. Whale boat.

B551.1.0.1. *Fish carries man to upper world.* Spanish: Boggs FFC XC 42 No. 302* A.

B551.2. *Acquatic bird carries man across water.* India: Thompson-Balys.

B551.2.1. *Parrots carry couple across the sea.* India: Thompson-Balys.

B551.3. *Crocodile carries man across river (ocean).* India: *Thompson-Balys; Buddhist myth: Malalasekera I 365.

B551.4. *Water snake carries boy across river.* India: Thompson-Balys.

S222.2. Woman promises unborn daughter to snake as wife for ferrying her across stream.

B551.5. *Turtle (tortoise) carries person across river (ocean).* Buddhist myth: Malalasekera I 997; Tonga: Gifford 53.

B552. *Man carried by bird.* See all references in B542.1 and B542.1.1. — Chauvin V 230 No. 130, VII 12; *Reinhard PMLA XXXVIII 433 nn. 24, 26. — Greek: Frazer Apollodorus II 37 n. 4 (Ganymede); Jewish: Neuman*, Bin Gorion Born Judas[2] I 228; Breton: Sébillot Incidents s.v. "nid"; Irish myth: Cross, Saints' legend (Irish): Plummer cxlvi. — Missouri-French: Carrière. — German New Guinea: Dixon 141f.; India: *Thompson-Balys; Japanese: Ikeda; Chinese: Eberhard FFC CXX 38f.; Africa: Stanley 83, (Boloki): Weeks 202f., (Upoto): Einstein 138, (Pangwe): Tessman 370, (Fang): ibid. 160.

B31.1. Roc. B41.2. Flying horse. B45. Air-going elephant. B450. Helpful bird. B522.4. Eagle carries off condemned child. B582.2.1. Hero carried by bird to mistress' chamber. D1532. Magic object bears person aloft. E754.2.1. Souls carried to heaven by doves. F62. Bird carries person to or from upper world. F531.6.3. Eagle carries giant to its nest. F1021. Extraordinary flights through air. K1861.1. Hero sewed up in animal hide so as to be carried to height by bird.

B552.1. *Alexander carried by two birds with meat held in front of them.* Jewish: Neuman; Gaster Exempla 186 No. 5.

F1021.2.2. Flight so high that eyelids drop from cold.

B552.2. *Man carried by peacock.* India: Thompson-Balys.

B552.3. *Indra carried by cock.* India: Thompson-Balys.

B555. *Animals serve as bridge across stream.* Jewish: Neuman (snake); Persian: Carnoy 289 (ox); Burmese: Scott Indo-Chinese 274 (snake); Chinese: Werner 190 (magpie); Korean: Zong in-Sob 6 No. 2. (fish and tortoise). — India: Thompson-Balys; S. A. Indian (Ceuici): Alexander Lat. Am 304 (herons).

R246. Crane-bridge.

B556. *Sea-beast allows voyager to land upon his back.* Irish myth: Cross.

B256.12. Whale raises back so that voyaging clerics can celebrate Easter.

B557. *Unusual animal as riding-horse.* *BP II 483 (Gr. 108) (cock); Tobler Epiphanie der Seele 72f. (goat, goose, snake); *Fb "buk" IV 77a (goat); Penzer II 143. — Missouri-French: Carrière; Icel.: Boberg; English: Wells 114 (lion, unicorn, leopard); Jewish: Bin Gorion Born Judas[2] III 148; India: Thompson-Balys; Chinese: Werner 392 (tiger).

A136. Gods with unusual riding or draft animals. F535.1.1.6. Thumbling has cat as riding horse. F989.4. Man rides on back of fleeing wild boar. G241.1. Witch rides on unusual animal. J2132.4. Numskull rides on tiger's back. K1241. Trickster rides dupe horseback.

B557.1. *Man carried on goat's horns.* (Goat is transformed man.) — German: Grimm No. 163.

B557.2. *Saint carried by wild oxen.* Irish myth: Cross.

B557.3. *Man carried by deer.* Irish myth: Cross; *Loomis White Magic 61; India: *Thompson-Balys.

B557.4. *Crocodile as means of transportation for a saint.* *Loomis White Magic 64.

B557.5. *Person carried by lion.* Irish myth: Cross; India: Thompson-Balys.

B557.6. *Magic dog carries owner in his ear.* Eskimo (Mackenzie Area): Jenness 64.

B557.7. *Person carried by cat.* India: Thompson-Balys.

B557.8. *Person carried by cobra.* India: *Thompson-Balys.

B557.9. *Person carried by locust.* India: Thompson-Balys.

B557.10. *Person carried by tiger.* India: *Thompson-Balys.
G241.1.7. Witch rides on tiger.

B557.11. *Person (animal) carried by elephant.*

B557.11.1. *Hero rides on animated wax elephant.* India: Thompson-Balys.

B557.11.2. *Hero rides on winged elephant.* — India: Thompson-Balys.
B45. Air-going elephant.

B557.11.3. *Hare rides on winged elephant.* Africa (Cameroon): Meinhof 12.

B557.12. *Person carried by peacock.* — India: *Thompson-Balys.

B557.13. *Jackal rides on fox.* India: Thompson-Balys.

B557.14. *Person carried by frog.* India: Thompson-Balys.

B557.15. *Wolf carries man.* Cheremis: Sebeok-Nyerges.

B558. *Unusual draft-animal.*
A136. Gods with unusual riding or draft animals. B256. Animal as servant of saint. B292. Animal in service of man.

B558.1. *Boat drawn by swans (geese).* **Boekenoogen Ridder metter Swane 166ff. — Krappe Balor 44; *Fb "svane" III 664 — Icel.: Mac Culloch Eddic 262. — N. A. Indian: Thompson Tales 358 n. 287 n.

B558.2. *Swans harnessed to chariot.* Chauvin V 230 No. 130. — Greek: Sappho "Ode to Aphrodite" (Team of sparrows). — Hindu: Keith 108, Penzer VIII 151f.

B558.3. *Hen hitched to wagon.* *Fb "höne" I 750b.

B558.4. *Deer hitched to wagon.* Irish myth: Cross.
B188. Magic deer. B256. Animal as servant of saint. B292. Animal as servant to man. B443.1. Helpful deer.

B558.5. *Mice hitched to wagon.* Fb. "mus".

B558.6. *Wild animals yoked by saint to his plough.* *Loomis White Magic 60.

B558.7. *Winged serpents pull chariot through sky.* Greek: Grote I 112 (Medea).

B91.4. Air-traveling snake. F911.3.2. Winged serpent as boat.

B559. *Animals carry men — miscellaneous.*

B559.1. *Man carried by toad.* Chinese: Graham.

B560. Animals advise men. Type 400 and references on the whole section in this work concerned with Helpful Animals (B300—599), since advice is very frequently part of the help. — *BP I 134; India: *Thompson-Balys; Chinese: Eberhard FFC CXX 28.

B130. Truth-telling animals. B131. Bird of truth. B133. Truth-speaking horse. B133.1. Horse warns hero of danger. B140. Prophetic animals. B141.1. Bird gives warning. B521.3. Animal warns against attack. D1312. Magic object gives advice. D1814. Magic advice. J150. Other means of acquiring wisdom (knowledge).

B560.1. *Grateful dragon king gives hero advice.* Korean: Zong in-Sob 170, No. 73.

B561. *Animals tell hero their secrets.* Do so voluntarily. — *BP II 482.

B235. Secrets discussed in animal meeting. B513. Remedy learned from overhearing animal meeting.

B562. *Animals' advice leads man to wealth.* India: *Thompson-Balys.

B581. Animal brings wealth to man.

B562.1. *Animal shows man treasure.* Irish myth: Cross; Icel.: Boberg; Finnish-Swedish: Wessman 78 No. 651. — India: *Thompson-Balys; *Norlind Skattsägner 37ff., 41ff.; Chauvin II 109 No. 73, *117 No. 97. — Chinese: Graham, Werner 380; Japanese: Ikeda; Africa (Swahili): Steere 13ff.

B100—119. Treasure animals. B581. Animal brings wealth to man. B583. Animal gives treasure to man. N530. Discovery of treasure.

B562.1.0.1. *Helpful animal discovers jewel.* Africa (Swahili): Steere 13ff., Meinhof Afrikanische Märchen 9ff. No. 1, Bateman 99ff. No. 7.

B562.1.1. *Hogs root up gold (treasure) for saint.* Irish myth: Cross.

B183. Magic boar (pig). B414. Helpful hog.

B562.1.2. *Horse kicks up jewel.* Irish myth: Cross.

B562.1.3. *Birds show man treasure.* Doves saved by monk from death show him where to dig for treasure. — Spanish Exempla: Keller; Bødker Exempler 305 No. 77.

B562.2. *Animal advises about investment.* Chinese: Werner 381 (fox).

B563. *Animals direct man on journey.* Type 400; Schoepperle Tristan and Isolt I 190f.; Dickson Valentine and Orson 54 n. 67; *Günter Christliche Legende des Abendlandes 235 s.v. "Führung"; *DeCock Studien en Essays 200ff.; *Fb "Ravn" III 23a. — India: *Thompson-Balys; Africa (Benga): Nassau No. 33, (Basuto): Jacottet 140 No. 20, 202 No. 30, (Ekoi): Talbot 209.

B153.2. Dog indicates road to be taken.

B563.1. *Lion leads lost king from forest.* (Cf. B431.2.) — Dickson Valentine and Orson 123 n. 75.

B549.2. Animal leads lost man home. D1313. Magic object points out road.

B563.1.1. *Horses carry lost riders to safety.* India: Thompson-Balys.

B563.1.2. *Chimpanzee leads lost hunter home.* Africa (Duala): Lederbogen 146.

B563.2. *Birds point out road to hero.* (Cf. B151.0.3.). — E. Norden P. Vergilius Maro Æneis Buch VI p. 170; Icel.: MacCulloch Eddic 216 (ravens); Jewish: Neuman; India: Thompson-Balys.

B151.0.3.1. Birds show way to other world. B172.6. Magic birds lead hunters to certain places.

B563.3. *Squirrel points out road.* India: Thompson-Balys.

B563.4. *Animal leads cleric to holy place.* Irish myth: Cross (B549.7).

B155. Location determined by halting of an animal. B256. Animal as servant of saint.

B563.4.1. *Animal leads lost man home.* Irish myth: Cross (B549.7).

R130. Rescue of abandoned or lost persons.

B563.4.1.1. *Tiger guides lost man home; hence men do not eat tigers.* India: Thompson-Balys.

B444. Helpful tiger. C221.2.1. Tabu: eating animal helper.

B563.4.1.2. *Jackal leads lost men out of wilderness.* Spanish Exempla: Keller.

B563.5. *Wild leopards guide Jesus and the Holy Family through wilderness* in flight to Egypt. Spanish Exempla: Keller.

B563.6. *Birds as scouts.* Hawaii: Beckwith Myth 466.

B563.7. *Bird conducts navigators to landing place.* Hawaii: Beckwith Myth 92.

B565. *Parrot gives advice to queen playing chess,* and she always wins. India: Thompson-Balys.

B569. *Animals advise men — miscellaneous.*

B569.1. *Owl advises old man of projected visit by gods (in disguise).* India: Thompson-Balys.

B569.2. *Owl advises old man where to plant his crops* after listening in to council of gods concerning rainfall distribution for the year. — India: Thompson-Balys.

B569.3. *Mosquito gives hero advice as to which choice to make.* Korean: Zong in-Sob 18 No. 8.

B570. Animals serve men. India: *Thompson-Balys.

A34. Birds as creator's servants. B256. Animal as servant of saint. B292. Animal as servant of man. K2. Animals help man in contest.

B571. *Animals perform tasks for man.* *Type 554; BP I 134, II *21ff.; Köhler-Bolte I 397; *Fb "fugl" I 381a; Köhler Zs. f. Vksk. VI 71 (to Gonzenbach No. 32). — Arabian: Burton S VI 9—11. — Indonesian, Malay: Dixon 216, 217, *218 n. 23. — India: *Thompson-Balys; Chinese: Eberhard FFC CXX 28, 80 No. 46. — Carib: Alexander Lat. Am. 264; Chincha: ibid. 231; Quiché: ibid. 174; Italian Novella: Rotunda; Missouri-French: Carrière.

B292. Animal in service to man. B548.2.1. Fish recovers ring from sea. B563.8. Deer indicate cave through which king escapes. H561. Solvers of riddles. H970. Help in performing tasks. H982. Animals help man perform task. H1091.1. Task: sorting grains; performed by helpful ants. H1091.2. Task: sorting grains; performed by helpful birds. H1092.1. Helpful animal performs spinning task. H1093. Task: embroidering blanket in one day (help from animals). H1121. Task: picking all nuts from tall tree. (Performed by grateful squirrel.) H1233. Animals help hero on quest.

B571.1. *Animals help man overcome monster with external soul.* Discover where he keeps his soul. — BP I 134; Type 302. — Missouri-French: Carrière.

B571.2. *Animal who arrives late performs tasks for man.* (Cf. L147.1.) — Cosquin I 49f.; Missouri-French: Carrière.

B571.3. *Animals fight together with their master.* Icel.: *Boberg.

B268.2.1. War-dogs. B301.4.8. Faithful horse fights together with its master. K2351. Animal betrays himself to his enemies by talking.

B571.4. *Bear husks millet for man.* India: Thompson-Balys.

B572. *Animals as carpenter (builder).* Buddhist myth: Malalasekera I 188, II 819.

B572.1. *Animals build palace (house) for man.* India: Thompson-Balys; Samoa: Beckwith Myth 536 (rats).

B572.2. *Birds build canoe for master.* Maori: Clark 98.

B574. *Animals as domestic servants.* India: Thompson-Balys; Buddhist myth: Malalasekera I 798 (elephant).

B575. *Animal as constant attendant of man.* *Pauli (ed Bolte) No. 649; Type 74*; Fb ("orne" II 760, "ravn") III 23a (boar, raven); *Zingerle Sagen aus Tirol 588 (ravens). — Irish myth: Cross; Scotch: Campbell II 279—289; French Canadian: Barbeau JAFL XXIX 15; Swiss: Jegerlehner Oberwallis 298 No. 13; English: Wells 20 (William of Palerne), 118f. (Octovian); Jewish: Neuman (steer); Buddhist myth: Malalasekera II 921 (owl), Hawaii: Beckwith Myth 37 (birds); Maori: Clark 54 (birds); Africa (Angola): Chatelain 53 No. 2.

A165.0.1. Ravens as attendants of god. B122.2. Birds as reporters of sights and sounds. E501.4.4. Two ravens follow wild huntsman.

B575.1. *Wild animals kept as dogs.* Icel.: *Boberg; N. A. Indian: Thompson Tales 308 n. 113d; Eskimo (E. Greenland): Rasmussen I 318, 363, Rink 248 (fox), (Central Eskimo): Boas RBAE VI 599 (walrus).

B843. Wild animals herded. F368. Human beings as game in fairy hunt. K133. Wild animals sold as watch-dog. K1725. "St. George's Dogs" (wolves). The man says, "St. George's dogs are coming!" The ogre flees.

B575.2. *Bird rests on person's shoulders.* Type 709. — Scottish: Campbell-McKay No. 2 (and note 2).

B576. *Animal as guard.* Jewish: Neuman; India: Thompson-Balys; Tonga: Gifford 77 (shark), 84; Fiji: Beckwith Myth 131 (hawk, prawn).

D950.0.1. Magic tree guarded by serpent (dragon). F152.0.1. Bridge to other world guarded by animals.

B576.1. *Animal as guard of person or house.* Rösch FFC LXXVII 107 (Type 516); *Fb "bjørn" IV 42a, "løve" II 518; Chauvin VI 6 No. 182; *Loomis White Magic 63; Dickson Valentine and Orson 198; Irish myth: Cross; Missouri French: Carrière; English: Wells 60 (Syre Gawene and the Carle of Carelyle). — Jewish: Neuman; India: *Thompson-Balys; Buddhist myth: Malalasekera II 704 (elephant); Hawaii: Beckwith Myth 24 (bird), 129 (shark), 84, 349 (dog). — N. A.

Indian: *Thompson Tales 308 n. 113c. — Jamaica: Beckwith MAFLS XVII 273 No. 86; Africa (Hottentot): Bleek 55 No 28.

B256.6.1. Boar guards holy man's swine. B521.3. Animals warn against attack. D950.0.1. Magic tree guarded by serpent (dragon) coiled around its roots. D1380.16. Magic dog protects. F152.0.1. Bridge to otherworld guarded by animals. F771.5.1. Castle guarded by beasts. K1591. Seventy tales of a parrot prevent a wife's adultery.

B576.1.1. *Guardian animals evaded.* N. A. Indian: Thompson Tales 367 n. 113a.

B576.1.2. *Robbers frightened by grateful dog.* India: Thompson-Balys.

B576.2. *Animals guard treasure.* *Fb "höne" I 750b, "hund", I 675 b (hen, dog) — Breton: Sèbillot Incidents s.v. "animaux"; Swiss: Jegerlehner Oberwallis 294 No. 9, 325 No. 4. — *Norlind Skattsägner 53; *Winter Deutsche Schatzsagen 54, 61; Danish: Kristensen Da. Sagn III (1895) 455ff.; (1931) 311ff. — England-U.S.: *Baughman (dog, cat, sow, goat, snake, bird, crow, raven, cock, drake, swan and night-bird). India: *Thompson-Balys; Chinese: Graham (tiger).

B11.6.2. Dragon guards treasure. B292.8. Dog as guardian of treasure. N570. Guardian of treasure. N577. Serpent guards treasure.

B576.3. *Animal as herdsman.*

B576.3.1. *Fish guards cow for master.* India: Thompson-Balys.

B576.4. *Animal guards master's dead body.* Jewish: Neuman.

B576.5. *Animal as guard of shop.* Azov JPASB II 403.

B578. *Dogs track down law-breakers.* Italian Novella: Rotunda.

B579. *Animals serve man otherwise.*

B579.1. *Animal accompanies man on journey.* Irish myth: Cross; India: Thompson-Balys; Chinese: Graham.

B579.2. *Helpful cow strikes at flies, while boy eats.* Chinese: Graham.

B579.3. *Animal corrects examination paper for his rescuer.* Chinese: Graham.

B579.4. *Animals help repair leaky pot.* India: *Thompson-Balys.

B579.5. *Serpent acts as a rope to collect wood for man.* India: Thompson-Balys.

B579.6. *Faithful dog is offered as security for a debt.* India: Thompson-Balys.

B579.7. *Animal earns money for master.* Buddhist myth: Malalasekera I 166.

B580. Animal helps men to wealth and greatness. *Type 671; BP I 322; *Ward Catalogue of Romances III 208, Oesterley Gesta Romanorum No. 141, *Warnke Quellen des Esope der Marie de France 221ff. — India: *Thompson-Balys; Buddhist myth: Malalasekera I 189; Papua: Ker XLI 147.

B160. Wisdom-giving animals. B165. Animal languages learned from animal. B291. Animal as messenger. H151.2. Attention drawn by helpful animal's theft of food from wedding table: recognition follows. K1952.1. Poor boy said by helpful cat to be dispossessed prince. This is believed. K1954.1. Helpful cat borrows measure for his master's money.

B581. *Animal brings wealth to man.* *Type 545; BP I 325, *331; Fb "hjort" I 625a, "kat" IV 225b. — Breton: Hartland Science 174; Missouri-French: Carrière; Italian Novella: Rotunda; Jewish: Neuman; India: *Thompson-Balys; Japanese: Ikeda, Mitford 270 ff.

B562.1. Animal shows man treasure. K366. Theft by trickster's trained animal.

B582. *Animal helps person to success in love.*

K1917.3. Penniless wooer: helpful animal reports master wealthy and thus wins girl for him. T66.1. Grateful dead man helps hero win princess.

B582.1. *Animal wooer.* India: Thompson-Balys.

B582.1.1. *Animal wins wife for his master (Puss in Boots).* *Type 545B; BP I 325, III 487; Fb "kat"IV 255b. — Italian Novella: Rotunda; India: *Thompson-Balys; Chinese: Graham; Korean: Zong in-Sob 89 No. 48; Philippine: Fansler MAFLS XII 336.

N411.1.1. Cat as sole inheritance.

B582.1.1.1. *Goose brings master sleeping princess.* India: Thompson-Balys.

D1960.3. Sleeping beauty.

B582.1.2. *Animal wins husband for mistress.* *Type 545A; *BP I 325ff., III 487. — Indonesian: DeVries' List Nos. 180, 209 (monkey, bird).

B582.2. *Animals help hero win princess.* *Type 554, 559, cf. 552, 553; *BP I 134, II 21, 454 n. 1, III 425. — Italian Novella: Rotunda; India: *Thompson-Balys; Chinese: Eberhard FFC CXX 28.

B582.2.1. *Hero carried by bird to mistress' chamber.* *Chauvin V 242 No. 142.

B552. Man carried by bird.

B582.2.2. *Rat digs underground passage to girl's chamber for hero.* India: *Thompson-Balys.

B582.2.3. *Swan as matchmaker.* India: Thompson-Balys.

B582.2.4. *Bee as matchmaker.* Chinese: Eberhard FFC CXX 175f.

B582.2.5. *Dove helps deity draw his wife into a net.* Marquesas: Handy 115.

B583. *Animal gives treasure to man.* India: *Thompson-Balys; Africa (Yoruba): Frobenius Atlantis X 222ff., No. 14, (Swahili): Stigand Black Tales for White Children 97ff. No. 15.

B562.1. Animal shows man treasure.

B583.1. *Grateful whales disgorge gold.* India: Thompson-Balys.

B100. Treasure animals.

B584. *Animal gives man other gifts.* India: Thompson-Balys; Chinese: Eberhard FFC CXX 29.

B584.1. *Fox holds in its mouth a beautiful flower which he gives to hero.* India: Thompson-Balys.

B587. *Animal wins contest for man.*

B587.1. *Magic horse wins jumping contest for man.* India: Thompson-Balys.

B587.2. *Fly helps loathly suitor pass suitor test.* India: Thompson-Balys.

H310. Suitor tests.

B587.3. *Grateful bull draws one hundred carts for wager for master.* Buddhist myth: Malalasekera II 29.

B589. *Animal helps man to wealth and greatness — miscellaneous.*

B589.1. *Eagle regains throne for deposed king.* India: Thompson-Balys.

B590. Miscellaneous services of helpful animals.

A34. Birds as creator's servants. A165.1.1. Birds as messengers of the gods. A165.1.2. Cock as ambassador of god. A812. Earth diver. A1021.2. Bird scouts sent out from ark. A1415.2. Theft of fire by animals. A2221.2.1. Flies on Christ's body rewarded. B292. Animal in service to man.

B591. *Animal avenges murder.* Jewish: Neuman.

B301.2. Faithful animal at master's grave avenges his murder. Q211. Murder punished. Q557. Miraculous punishment through animal.

B591.0.1. *Animals refuse to devour Cain to avenge murder of Abel.* Jewish: Neuman.

B591.1. *Lion kills wolf who has killed mistress' sheep.* Africa (Gold Coast): Barker and Sinclair 131 No. 24.

B591.2. *Horse kicks to death master's murderer.* India: Thompson-Balys.

B592. *Animals bequeath characteristics to man.* Horse gives him the characteristics of youth (fiery), cow of middle age (avaricious), and the dog of old age (fractious). — Fable: Halm Aesop No. 173; BP III 290; Köhler-Bolte I 42ff.; Babrius No. 74; Wienert FFC LVI *70 (ET 347), 127 (ST 358).

A1321. Man and animals readjust span of life. Man is given a portion of animals' lives.

B593. *Animal as house-spirit.*

A411. Household gods. F480. House-spirits.

B593.1. *Snake as house-spirit.* *Fb "snog" III 436b.

B594. *Animal rejuvenates person.*

D1338. Magic object rejuvenates. D1880. Magic rejuvenation.

B594.1. *Bird rejuvenates person* (Cf. B172). — *Chauvin VI 73f. No. 239.

B596. *Animal helps saint by setting fire to neglected church.* Irish myth: Cross.

B597. *Cow gives marvelous supply of milk through virtue of saint.* Irish myth: Cross.

B109.4.3. Cow gives milk without cessation. B182. Magic cow. D1652.3. Cow with inexhaustible milk.

B598. *Animal as confederate of adulterous wife.*

K1591. Seventy tales of a parrot prevent a wife's adultery.

B598.1. *Boar as confederate of adulterous wife.* India: Thompson-Balys.

B598.2. *Deer as confederate of adulterous wife.* India: Thompson-Balys.

B599. *Other services of helpful animals.*

B599.1. *Cock and hen build pyre for benefactor.* India: Thompson-Balys.

B599.2. *Animal helps person pass test.* India: Thompson-Balys.

H162. Recognition of disguised princess by bee lighting on her.

B599.3. *Elephant draws plow to mark boundaries of empire.* Buddhist myth: Malalasekera II 528.

B600—B699. Marriage of person to animal.

B600. Marriage of person to animal. Extremely common. Only a few references are given. — *Wesselski Märchen 247 No. 57; *Chauvin V 177f. No. 101; Fb "kvinde" II 339b; India: *Thompson-Balys; Philippine: Fansler MAFLS XII 303. — N. A. Indian: Thompson Tales 273 n. 3.

B81.2. Mermaid marries man. D658.1. Transformation to animal to seduce woman. T91. Unequals in love. T110. Unusual marriage. T465. Bestiality. Intercourse of a human being and an animal. T554. Woman gives birth to animal.

B600.1. *Various animals tried out as wives.* Only one accepted. — N. A. Indian: *Thompson Tales 348 n. 254b.

B600.1.1. *Various animals tried out as wives: none accepted.* India: Thompson-Balys.

B600.2. *Animal husband provides characteristic animal food.* Eskimo (Mackenzie Area): Jenness 52, (Greenland): Thalbitzer 6.

B601. *Marriage of person to beast.* (Cf. B641, B651).

B601.1. *Marriage to bear.* (Cf. B611.1, B631, B635.1). — *Fb "björn" IV 42b.; Icel.: Boberg; India: *Thompson-Balys; Chinese: Eberhard FFC CXX 64, 178.

K1911.1.6. She-bear as false bride.

B601.1.1. *Bear steals woman and makes her his wife.* Cheremis: Sebeok-Nyerges; India: Thompson-Balys.

B601.2. *Marriage to dog.* (Cf. B611.2, B641.1.) — Irish myth: Cross; N. A. Indian: Thompson Tales 272 n. 2. — Africa (Benga): Nassau 165 No. 22; Dobu: Beckwith Myth 349.

B635.4. Son of dog ("cú", person).

B601.3. *Marriage to rat.* Spanish Exempla: Keller; Bødker Exempler 297 No. 60; India: Thompson-Balys; Africa (Duala): Lederbogen Märchen V 192, (Mpongwe): Nassau 41 No. 6.

B601.3.1. *Marriage to mouse.* Cheremis: Sebeok-Nyerges.

B601.4. *Marriage to leopard.* Africa (Benga): Nassau 85 No. 4.

B601.5. *Marriage to elephant.* Africa (Hottentot): Bleek 61 No. 27.

B601.6. *Marriage to lemur.* Africa (Ekoi): Talbot 349.

B601.7. *Marriage to monkey.* India: *Thompson-Balys; Japanese: Ikeda; Philippine: Fansler MAFLS XII 183; Chinese: Eberhard FFC CXX 411 s.v. "Affenmutter"

B601.7.1. *Person plans to marry monkey.* India: Thompson-Balys.

B601.8. *Marriage to swine.* Italian Novella: Rotunda.

D733.2. Swine bridegroom.

B601.9. *Marriage to tiger.* India: *Thompson-Balys; Chinese: Eberhard FFC CXX 62f.; S. A. Indian (Jivaró): Métraux RMLP XXXIII 142.

B601.10. *Marriage to deer.* Irish myth: Cross.

B611.5. Deer paramour.

B601.11. *Marriage to jackal.* India: *Thompson-Balys.

B601.12. *Marriage to cat.* India: Thompson-Balys.

B601.13. *Marriage to hare.* India: *Thompson-Balys.

B601.14. *Marriage to fox.* India: Thompson-Balys; Chinese: Eberhard FFC CXX 63, 214; Eskimo (East Greenland): Rasmussen I 137, 143; S. A. Indian (Chiriguano): Métraux RMLP XXXIII 174.

B601.15. *Marriage to jaguar.* S. A. Indian (Mataco, Toba): Métraux MAFLS XL 62, 64, (Jivaró): Steward-Métraux BBAE 143 III 627, (Eastern Brazil): Lowie ibid. I 434, (Yuracare): Métraux ibid. III 504.

B601.16. *Marriage to wolf.* Eskimo (Mackenzie Area): Jenness 38, (Bering Strait): Nelson BBAE XVIII 482. — Chinese: Eberhard FFC CXX 49.

B601.17. *Marriage to coati-puri.* S. A. Indian (Cashinawa): Métraux BBAE III 143, 685.

B601.18. *Marriage to seal.* Koryak: Jochelson JE VI 153; Eskimo (Greenland): Rink 127.

B602. *Marriage to bird.* (Cf. B644.) — India: *Thompson-Balys. — Marquesas: Handy 120; New Hebrides: Codrington 397; Papua: Ker 57; Mono Alu: Wheeler 20. — Eskimo (Mackenzie Area): Jenness 52, 75; (Greenland, Cape York): Rasmussen III 57, 83.

B602.1. *Marriage to eagle.* India: *Thompson-Balys; N. A. Indian: *Thompson Tales 341 n. 231.

B602.2. *Marriage to fulmar.* *N. A. Indian: Thompson Tales 272 n. 2.

B602.3. *Marriage to pigeon.* Africa (Zulu): Callaway 78.

B602.4. *Marriage to vulture.* Arawak, Carib: Alexander Lat. Am. 274.

B602.5. *Marriage to crane.* India: Thompson-Balys.

B602.6. *Marriage to goose.* Eskimo (Mackenzie Area): Jenness 47, 77.

B602.7. *Marriage to parrot.* S. A. Indian (Chiriguano): Métraux RMLP XXXIII 175.

B602.8. *Marriage to kingfisher.* Africa (Togo): Einstein 7.

B603. *Marriage to fish (whale).* (Cf. B612.) — India: *Thompson-Balys; Japanese: Ikeda. — *N. A. Indian: Thompson Tales 341 n. 231.

B603.1. *Marriage to shrimp.* Eskimo (Greenland): Rasmussen I 144.

B603.2. *Marriage to eel.* Tuamotu: Beckwith Myth 103.

B604. *Marriage to reptile.* (Cf. B613, B622.1, B642, B652.)

B604.1. *Marriage to snake.* (Cf. B613.1.) — Fb "slange" III 363a; *BP II 251. — India: *Thompson-Balys; Buddhist myth: Malalasekera II 388, 1354; Japanese: Ikeda; Chinese: Eberhard FFC CXX 49, 176. — Jamaica: *Beckwith MAFLS XVII 272; Buin: Wheeler 43; San Cristoval (Solomon Islands): Beckwith Myth 104. — Eskimo (Mackenzie Area): Jenness 75, (Greenland): Rink 186, Rasmussen I 148, (Cumberland Sound): Boas BAM XV 178f., (West Hudson Bay): Boas BAM XV 555; (Bering Strait): Nelson RBAE XVIII 516. — S. A. Indian (Toba): Métraux MAFLS XL 65.

R111.1.5. Rescue of woman from snake-husband.

B604.2. *Marriage to tortoise.* India: *Thompson-Balys; Africa (Benga): Nassau 134 No. 15.

B604.2.1. *Marriage to turtle.* India: *Thompson-Balys.

B604.3. *Marriage to crocodile.* India: Thompson-Balys.

B604.4. *Marriage to lizard.* India: Thompson-Balys; Africa (Fang): Einstein 152.

B604.5. *Marriage to frog.* India: *Thompson-Balys; Africa (Luba): DeClerq Zs. f. Kolonialsprachen IV 211, (Togo): Einstein 7.

B605. *Marriage to dragon.* Chinese: Eberhard FFC CXX 64f.

B610. Animal paramour.

C841.2. Tabu: hunting birds. Supernatural lover (king of birds) tells woman that son must not do so. T118. Girl married to (enamoured of) monster. T465. Bestiality.

B610.1. *Girl's animal lover slain by spying relatives.* BP I 69f. (Gr. No. 8a). — Jamaica: Beckwith MAFLS XVII 267 No. 78. — N. A. Indian: Thompson Tales 345 n. 244.

B611. *Beast paramour.* (Cf. B601.)

B611.1. *Bear paramour.* (Cf. B601.1., B631, B635.) India: Thompson-Balys. — N. A. Indian: Thompson Tales 345 nn. 244, 245.

T511.0.2. Eaten meat of bear lover causes unborn son to have animal characteristics.

B611.2. *Dog paramour.* (Cf. B601.2, B642.) — India: Thompson-Balys; Buddhist myth: Malalasekera II 456; Siberian and North Pacific Coast Natives: Jochelson JE VI 374.

B611.3. *Horse paramour.* Hindu: Penzer IV 16, IX 153; Japanese: Ikeda; *N. A. Indian: Thompson Tales 348 n. 254a.

B611.3.1. *Sea-horse paramour.* Irish myth: Cross.

B71. Sea-horse. B634.1. Monstrous offspring of sea-horse and woman.

B611.3.2. *Lake-horse paramour.* Irish myth: Cross.

B611.4. *Bull paramour.* Greek: Frazer Apollodorus I 305 n. (Pasiphoe), I 299 n. 2. (Europa); Am. Negro (Georgia): Harris Friends 81 No. 11.

B611.5. *Deer paramour.* Irish myth: Cross.

B611.6. *Monkey paramour.* India: Thompson-Balys.

B611.7. *Rat paramour.* India: Thompson-Balys.

B611.8. *Tapir paramour.* S. A. Indian (Toba): Métraux MAFLS XL 60.

B612. *Fish paramour.* (Cf. B603.) — *Cape Verde Islands: Parsons MAFLS XV (1) 140 n. 1. — Japanese: Ikeda. — Africa (Ekoi): Talbot 187.

B612.1. *Eel paramour.* Maori, Mangaia: Dixon 55; Samoa, Mangaia: Beckwith Myth 103; Hawaii: ibid. 136.

B612.2. *Dolphin as paramour.* Jewish: Neuman.

B613. *Reptile paramour.* (Cf. B604.)

B613.1. *Snake paramour.* (Cf. B604.1.) Armenian: Ananikian 74; India: *Thompson-Balys; Japanese: Ikeda, Anesaki 332. — N. A. Indian:

*Thompson Tales 344 n. 239. — S. A. Indian (Warrau, Carib): Alexander Lat. Am. 272; (Amazonia) ibid. 286; (Toba): Métraux MAFLS XL 65f. — Africa (Basuto): Jacottet 142 No. 20.

B613.1.1. *Snake woman as paramour.* India: Thompson-Balys.

B613.2. *Crocodile paramour.* Africa (Fang): Trilles 162, (Ekoi): Talbot 333.

B613.3. *Lizard paramour.* India: Thompson-Balys.

B614. *Bird paramour.* India: Thompson-Balys.

D641.1. Lover as bird visits mistress.

B620. **Animal suitor.** Missouri-French: Carrière.

D641.1. Lover as bird visits mistress.

B620.1. *Daughter promised to animal suitor.* *Types 425, 552; *BP II 232, III 424ff. — India: Thompson-Balys; Japanese: Ikeda. — Africa (Angola): Chatelain 65 No. 3.

H188. Princess appears before crane (who had demanded her in marriage) and is recognized by him despite loathly disguise. S215.1. Girl promises herself to animal suitor. S221.1. Bankrupt father sells his daughters in marriage to animals. S222.2 Woman promises unborn daughter to snake as wife for ferrying her across stream. S232. Daughter promised to tiger in marriage for help in carrying load. S247. Daughter unwittingly promised to dog rescuer. T68. Princess offered as prize.

B621. *Beast as suitor.*

B621.1. *Bear as suitor.* (Cf. B601.1, B611.1, B635.1.) — Fb "björn" IV 43a.

B314. Helpful animal brothers-in-law.

B621.2. *Lion as suitor.* Fable: Halm Aesop No. 249, Babrius No. 98, Wienert FFC LVI 45 (ET 32), 70 (ET 344), 107 (ST 198).

J642.1. Lion suitor allows his teeth to be pulled and his claws to be cut.

B621.3. *Tiger as suitor.* Chinese: Graham; India: Thompson-Balys; S. A. Indian: (Jivaró): Métraux RMLP XXXIII 148.

B621.4. *Rat as suitor.* Cheremis: Sebeok-Nyerges.

B621.5. *Leopard as suitor.* India: Thompson-Balys.

B621.6. *Pig as suitor.* Chinese: Eberhard FFC CXX 77.

B621.7. *Horse as suitor.* Chinese: Eberhard FFC CXX 79.

B621.8. *Wolf and wolverine fight over girl.* Eskimo (Mackenzie Area): Jenness 38.

B622. *Reptile as wooer.*

B622.1. *Serpent as wooer.* Fb "slange" III 363a.; Jewish: Neuman; India: *Thompson-Balys.

B622.2. *Crocodile as wooer.* India: Thompson-Balys.

B622.3. *Tortoise as wooer.* India: Thompson-Balys.

B623. *Bird as wooer.*

B623.1. *Crane as wooer.* India: Thompson-Balys.

B623.2. *Owl as suitor.* Cheremis: Sebeok-Nyerges; S. A. Indian (Toba): Métraux MAFLS XL 154.

B623.3. *Magpie as suitor.* Cheremis: Sebeok-Nyerges.

B623.4. *Crow as suitor.* Cheremis: Sebeok-Nyerges.

B623.5. *Cock as suitor.* Chinese: Eberhard FFC CXX 77.

B625. *Fish as wooer.*

B625.0.1. *Half-man, half-fish as wooer.* S. A. Indian (Toba): Métraux MAFLS XL 30.

B630. Offspring of marriage to animal. India: Thompson-Balys.

A1224. Descent of man from animals. B2. Animal totems. B23.1. Minotaur. Body of man, head of bull. Result of union of woman and bull. B81.2.1. Mermaid has son by human father. T554. Woman gives birth to animal.

B631. *Human offspring from marriage to animal.* *Type 301, 650; *BP II 300ff., 285ff., especially 293; *Dickson Valentine and Orson 123 n. 76; *Krappe Le Moyen Age XLI 96ff. — Irish myth: Cross; Gaster Oldest Stories 169; India: *Thompson-Balys. — Japanese: Anesaki 332; N. A. Indian (Thompson River): Teit MAFLS XI 42; Danish: Boberg.

F611.1.5. Strong man son of man and she-bear. F611.1.6. Strong man son of man and mare.

B631.0.1. *Son warns animal mother.* Irish myth: Cross.

A511.10.1. Culture hero son of deer mother.

B631.0.2. *Boy kills his animal father for reward.* Buddhist myth: Malalasekera II 1169.

B631.1. *Animal mother of man helps him.* Burmese: Scott Indo-Chinese 274.

B631.2. *Human beings descended from seals.* Irish myth: Cross.

B80.1. Seal-man. B81.2.1. Mermaid has son by human father.

B631.3. *Fish bears men-children.* Has swallowed rinsings of man's mouth. — India: Thompson-Balys.

T531. Conception from casual contact with man.

B631.4. *Lioness bears man child.* Africa (Lamba): Doke MAFLS XX 14 No. 11.

P311.3. Human sons of animal companions go together on adventure.

B631.5. *Cow bears man child.* Africa (Lamba): Doke MAFLS XX 14 No. 11.

B631.6. *Tigress bears men-children.* India: Thompson-Balys.

B631.7. *Human offspring of marriage of person and jaguar.* S. A. Indian (Toba): Métraux MAFLS XL 62, (Eastern Brazil): Lowie BBAE CXLIII I 434.

B631.8. *Human offspring of marriage of person and lion.* Buddhist myth: Malalasekera II 1170.

B631.9. *Human offspring of marriage of person and snake.* S. A. Indian (Tapirape): Wagley-Galvão BBAE 143 III 253.

B632. *Animal offspring from marriage to animal.* *Fb "kvinde" II 339b, "menneske" II 577b; *MacCulloch Childhood 263ff.; Cox 487. — Icelandic: Boberg; India: *Thompson-Balys. — Eskimo (Greenland):

Rink 413, 465, Holm 56, 82, Rasmussen I 363, III 200, (Cumberland Sound): Boas BAM XV 167, 226, (Central Eskimo): Boas RBAE VI 637, (Mackenzie Area): Jenness 80. — N. A. Indian (Seneca): Curtin Hewitt RBAE XXXII No. 9; cf. Thompson Tales 347 n. 247, 248. — Africa (Zulu): Callaway 79, 349.

T554. Woman gives birth to animal.

B633. *Human and animal offspring from marriage to animal.* *Wesselski Märchen 247 No. 57.

B634. *Monstrous offspring from animal marriage.* Irish myth: Cross; Buddhist myth: Malalasekera II 1169, 1354.

T550. Monstrous births.

B634.1. *Monstrous offspring of sea-horse and woman.* Irish myth: Cross.

B71. Sea-horse.

B635. *Human foster-child with animal qualities.*

B635.1. *The Bear's Son.* Human son of woman who marries a bear acquires bear characteristics. (Cf. B601.1.) — *Type 301; *BP II 300ff.; Cosquin I 6; MacCulloch Childhood 270; Panzer Beowulf I 246; *Wesselski Märchen 249 No. 57; *Fb "bjørn" IV 42b; *Dickson Valentine and Orson 118 nn. 49, 50, 172 n. 30.

F611.1.1. Strong man son of bear who has stolen his mother.

B635.1.1. *Eaten meat of bear-lover causes unborn son to have bear characteristics.* (Cf. B611.1.) — Hrolfs saga Kraka 53.

D1017. Magic flesh of animal. D1032. Magic meat. D1352. Magic object has prenatal influence.

B635.1.2. *Bear's foster child not used to sun and light.* Eskimo (Mackenzie Area): Jenness 53.

B635.1.3. *Bear says he is boy's father; asks food.* Eskimo (Mackenzie Area): Jenness 47.

B635.2. *Wolf boy (girl) running around with wolf and cubs recovered by parents* after six years: recognized by scar. India: Thompson-Balys.

B635.3. *Child of mortal and deer has deer's hair on temple.* Irish myth: Cross.

A511.10.1. Culture hero son of deer mother. D114.1.1. Transformation: girl to deer.

B635.3.1. *Culture hero licked by deer mother.* Irish myth: Cross.

D1775. Magic results from licking.

B635.4. *Son of dog* ("cu," person). Irish myth: Cross.

B635.4.1. *Son of three dogs* ("con," persons). Irish myth: Cross.

B25. Man-dog. T611.10. Man suckled by dog called "maccon" (son of dog).

B636. *Offspring of human and animal intercourse.* India: Thompson-Balys.

B640. Marriage to person in animal form.

B314. Helpful animal brothers-in-law. B505.1. Magic object received from animal brothers-in-law. D734. Disenchantment of animal by admission to woman's bed.

B640.1. *Marriage to beast by day and man by night.* (Cf. D621.) — *Type 425. See references for D621. — *Tegethoff Amor-Psyche 17; Missouri-French: Carrière; India: *Thompson-Balys.

C32. Tabu: offending supernatural husband. D621.1. Animal by day; man by night. T111. Marriage of mortal and supernatural being. T113. Marriage to man alive by night but dead by day. T117.5.1. Marriage to tree by day, man by night.

B641. *Marriage to person in beast form.* (Cf. B601, B651.)

B641.1. *Marriage to person in dog form.* (Cf. B635.4, D141.) — Irish myth: Cross, MacCulloch Celtic 168; India: *Thompson-Balys; Chinese: Werner 421. — Eskimo (Greenland): Rasmussen II 244; N. A. Indian: *Thompson Tales 347 n. 247; S. A. Indian (Chaco): Métraux BBAE CXLIII (1) 369.

B635.4. Son of dog ("cu", person).

B641.2. *Marriage to woman in deer form.* (Cf. D114.1.) Irish myth: Cross, MacCulloch Celtic 168; India: Thompson-Balys.

B611.5. Deer paramour.

B641.2.1. *Marriage to man in deer form.* Africa (Swazi): Bourhill and Drake Fairy Tales from South Africa 212ff. No. 18.

B641.3. *Marriage to god in bull form.* (Cf. B611.4, D133.2) — *Frazer Fasti IV 74 nn. 2, 3 (Europa).

B611.4. Bull paramour. D658.1. Transformation to animal to seduce woman. K1310. Seduction by disguise or substitution. T111.1. Marriage of a mortal and a god.

B641.4. *Marriage to person in ass form.* (Cf. D132.1.) — *Type 430.

B641.5. *Marriage to person in hedgehog form.* *Type 441; BP II 234, 482.

B641.6. *Marriage to person in horse form.* Africa (Hausa): Mischlich Neue Märchen aus Africa 186ff.

B641.7. *Marriage to person in monkey form.* India: Thompson-Balys.

B641.8. *Marriage to person in opossum form.* S. A. Indian (Tupinamba): Métraux BBAE CXLIII (3). 132.

B642. *Marriage to person in bird form.* (Cf. B602, D150.). — Type 432; India: *Thompson-Balys.

B643. *Marriage to person in insect form.*

B643.3. *Marriage to person in caterpillar form.* India: Thompson-Balys.

B644. *Marriage to person in fish form.* India: Thompson-Balys; Eskimo (Mackenzie Area): Jenness 52.

B645. *Marriage to person in amphibian form.*

B645.1. *Marriage of person to transformed toad.* Korean: Zong in-Sob 176 No. 76.

B645.1.1. *Marriage to person in toad form.* India: Thompson-Balys.

B645.1.2. *Marriage to person in frog form.* India: Thompson-Balys.

B645.2. *Marriage to person in crocodile form.* (Cf. D194.) — Africa (Kaffir): Theal 38; India: Thompson-Balys.

B646. *Marriage to person in reptile form.* (Cf. B604, B652.)

B646.1. *Marriage to person in snake form.* (Cf. D191.) Type 433. — India: *Thompson-Balys. — Africa (Zulu): Callaway 57, 321, (Kaffir): Theal 48, (Basuto): Jacottet 126 No. 18, 146 No. 20.

B646.1.1. *Marriage to person in form of five-headed snake.* Africa (Hausa): Stigand Black Tales for White Children 83ff. No. 13.

B647. *Marriage to person in animal form — miscellaneous.*

B647.1. *Marriage to person in crustacean form.*

B647.1.1. *Marriage to person in crab form.* India: *Thompson-Balys.

B648. *Man becomes deer and marries deer.* N. A. Indian: Thompson Tales 348 n. 252.

B650. **Marriage to animal in human form.** Burmese: Scott Indo-Chinese 272.

C31. Tabu: offending supernatural wife. C35. Tabu: offending animal wife. C35.1. Tabu: mentioning origin of animal wife. D300. Transformation: animal to person. K1822. Animal disguised as human being.

B650.1. *Animal transformed to man wants to marry woman.* Indonesian: DeVries' list No. 156.

B651. *Marriage to beast in human form.* (Cf. B601, B641.)

B651.1. *Marriage to fox in human form.* *N. A. Indian: Thompson Tales 342 n. 233 ("The Fox Woman"). — Chinese: Krappe CFQ III (1944) 124, 129ff., 136f., 141, Eberhard FFC CXX 49, 214. — Eskimo (Greenland): Rink 144, 427, Rasmussen I 150, III 76, (Cumberland Sound): Boas BAM XV 222—224, (Labrador): Hawkes GSCan XIV 156, (Ungava) Turner RBAE XI 264; Koryak: Jochelsen JE VI 364; S. A. Indian (Toba): Métraux MAFLS XL 144ff.

C35.1. Tabu: mentioning origin of animal wife. N831.1. Mysterious housekeeper. Men find their house mysteriously put in order. Discover that it is done by a girl (frequently an animal transformed into a girl).

B651.2. *Marriage to buffalo in human form.* N. A. Indian: *Thompson Tales 339 n. 222 ("The Piqued Buffalo Wife").

B651.3. *Marriage to lion in human form.* Africa (Angola): Chatelain 145 No. 15.

B651.4. *Marriage to dog in human form.* Icel.: MacCulloch Eddic 258; Chinese: Werner 421.

B651.5. *Marriage to deer in human form.* India: Thompson-Balys; S. A. Indian (Maropa): Métraux BBAE CXLIII (3) 448.

B651.6. *Marriage to wolf in human form.* Icel.: MacCulloch Eddic 258. — Eskimo (Mackenzie Area): Jenness 38.

B651.7. *Marriage to bear in human form.* Eskimo (Smith Sound): Kroeber JAFL XII 176, (Greenland): Holm 82, (Central Eskimo): Boas RBAE VI 638f., (Mackenzie Area): Jenness 76.

B651.8. *Marriage to seal in human form.* Helge Holmström Svanjungfrumotivet 1919, 84ff.; Icel.: MacCulloch Eddic 258.

B651.9. *Marriage to tiger in human form.* India: *Thompson-Balys.

B651.10. *Marriage to squirrel in human form.* India: Thompson-Balys.

B651.11. *Marriage to leopard in human form.* Africa (Wakweli): Bender 52.

B652. *Marriage to bird in human form.*

B652.1. *Marriage to swan-maiden.* See all references for D361.1.
D361.1. Swan maiden. T56.3. Wooing bathing nymphs by stealing their clothes.

B652.2. *Man marries crane in human form.* Japanese: Ikeda, Anesaki 324.

B652.3. *Marriage to dove-maiden.* Icel.: MacCulloch Eddic 260.

B652.4. *Marriage to woodpecker in human form.* S. A. Indian (Toba): Métraux MAFLS XL 146.

B653. *Marriage to insect in human form.*

B653.1. *Marriage to bee in human form.* Indonesian: Dixon 219.

B654. *Marriage to fish in human form.* Irish myth: Cross (B612.0.1); India: Thompson-Balys; Chinese: Eberhard FFC CXX 47f., 142; Africa (Congo): Weeks 216.

B655. *Marriage to amphibia in human form.*

B656. *Marriage to reptile in human form.* (Cf. B604, B642.)

B656.1. *Marriage to python in human form.* Africa (Kaffir): Kidd 249.

B656.2. *Marriage to serpent in human form.* Hindu: Penzer VI 73 n. 2; India: *Thompson-Balys; Indo-Chinese: Scott 276; S. A. Indian (Toba): Métraux MAFLS XL 66; Eskimo (Greenland): Rasmussen III 76, 201. — Krappe CFQ III (1944) 138ff.

B659. *Marriage to other animals in human form.*

B670. Unusual mating between animals.

B671. *Goose mates with crow.* Buddhist myth: Malalasekera II 884.

B672. *Mythical tiger has family of jaguars.* S. A. Indian (Chiriguano): Métraux RMLP XXXIII 155.

B690. Marriage of person to animal — miscellaneous.

B691. *Relatives kill animal-husband but wife throws herself into pyre.* India: Thompson-Balys.

B700—B799. Fanciful traits of animals.

B700. Fanciful traits of animals.

A2200. Animal characteristics. B15. Animal with unusual limbs or members. F980. Extraordinary occurrences concerning animals. H1186. Task: making pigs dance. T591.1.2. Milk of hornless, single-colored cow drunk by man to make wife fruitful.

B710. Fanciful origin of animals.

A1700. Creation of animals. B12.1. Basilisk hatched from cock's egg. B16.14.1. Devastating elephant from divine world. B19.3. Horse born of egg. T573.0.1. Short pregnancy in animals.

B710.1. *Fanciful origin of the jackal.* India: Thompson-Balys.

B710.2. *Clever and swift horse of fanciful origin.*

B710.2.1. *Clever and swift horse fed with worms' milk on the gold mountain Tecklen* in India. Icel.: *Boberg.

B710.2.2. *Clever and swift horse of dromedary-family.* Göngu-Hrólfs saga 239.

B712. *Barnacle goose.* Goose born from barnacles. — *Chauvin VII 18 No. 373C; Fb "and" IV 12b; Hdwb. d. Abergl. s.v. "Baumgans"; Jewish: Neuman.

B95. Vegetable lamb.

B713. *Animal born from animal carcass.* Jewish: *Neuman.

B713.1. *Bees born from carcass of ox.* Frazer Fasti of Ovid II 157.

A2001. Insects from body of slain monster.

B713.2. *Animal born from putrification.* Jewish: Neuman.

A1853.2. Mice engendered after flood from rottenness: no mice on ark.

B714. *Worm (monster) from caul born with child.* Irish myth: Cross.

T551.8. Child born with caul (containing serpent).

B715. *The cow Audhumla sprang from the dripping rime* of the creation of the universe. (Cf. A1245.4. and B19.2.1.) — Icel.: MacCulloch Eddic 324.

B716. *Animal born from human or animal bones.* Jewish: Neuman.

B717. *Animal born from earth.* Jewish: Neuman.

A401. Mother Earth.

B720. Fanciful bodily members of animals.

B15. Animals with unusual limbs or members. B15.1.2. Many-headed animal. B15.2. Many-mouthed animal. B15.3.1. Many-horned animal. B15.4. Animal with unusual eyes. B15.6. Animal with unusual legs or feet. B110. Treasure-producing parts of animal. D1010. Magic bodily members of animal.

B721. *Cat's luminous eye.* — Breton: Sébillot Incidents s.v. "œil".; Icel.: Boberg.

B15.4. Animal with unusual eyes. B19.4. Glowing animals. D1645. Self-luminous objects. F541.1. Flashing eyes.

B722. *Magic stone in animal's head.* Irish myth: Cross; India: Thompson-Balys.

B108.2. Serpent with jewel in head. D992. Magic head. D1071. Magic jewel.

B722.1. *Magic love-working stone in swallow's head.* — Fb. "svale" III 661b.

D1355. Love-producing magic object.

B722.2. *Magic stone in dog's forehead.* Fb "hund" I 678.

B722.3. *Luminous jewel in animal's head.* *Cosquin Contes indiens 254ff.; India: Thompson-Balys.

B108.2. Serpent with jewel in its head. D1645.1. Incandescent jewel.

B722.4. *Earthworm has light in its tail.* India: Thompson-Balys.

B723. *Tortoise has no liver or teeth.* India: Thompson-Balys.

B724. *Spider has no blood in body.* India: Thompson-Balys.

B725. *Female bears have no breasts to nurse their young;* suck paws. Jewish: Neuman.

B726. *Double snake — male and female.* Africa (Baluba): Einstein 182.

B730. Fanciful color, smell, etc. of animals.

B731. *Fanciful color of animal.* Irish myth: Cross.
B15.7.3. Bird with head of gold and wings of silver. F527. Person of unusual color. F985. Animals change color.

B731.0.1. *Animals of strange and varied coloring.* *Schoepperle Tristan and Isolt II 322 n. 1.

B731.1. *Green she-goat.* Breton: Sébillot Incidents s.v. "chèvre".

B731.2. *Green horse.* Howey Horse in Magic and Myth 7.

B731.2.1. *Horse with crimson mane and green legs.* Irish myth: Cross.
F233.1. Green fairy. F233.3. Red fairy. F241.1. Fairy's horses.

B731.2.2. *Artificially colored horses.* Irish myth: Cross.

B731.2.3. *Striped horse with purple mane and white feet.* Irish myth: Cross.

B731.3. *Multicolored llama.* Wool red, blue, and yellow. No need to dye it for weaving. — Chincha (Peru): Alexander Lat. Am. 230.

B731.4. *Cow with changing colors.* Changes every four hours: white, red, black. — Greek: Frazer Apollodorus I 310 n. 3.

B731.4.1. *Cow with white ears.* Irish myth: Cross.
B182.0.1. Magic white cow. C316.1. Tabu: seeing herd: redheaded and white-starred. D1515.3. Bath in milk of white hornless cows as antidote for poison. Q153.1. Cows whiteheaded during reign of good king.

B731.4.2. *Cow with red ears.* Irish myth: Cross.
D1500.1.38. Flesh of white cow with red ears as only cure for mysterious illness. F241.2.1.2. Fairy cows have red ears.

B731.5. *Silver, gold, and diamond birds.* Czech: Tille FFC XXXIV 162.

B731.6. *Hound of every color.* Irish myth: Cross.

B731.6.0.1. *Polychromatic dogs.* Irish myth: Cross.
F241.6. Fairy dogs.

B731.6.1. *Hound half white, half green.* Irish myth: Cross.

B731.6.2. *Blue dogs and cats.* Irish myth: Cross.

B731.7. *Fancifully colored deer.* Irish myth: Cross.
F234.1.4. Fairy in form of stag (deer).

B731.7.1. *Stag with stripe of every color.* Irish myth: Cross.
B106.1.1. Stag with golden antlers and silver feet.

B731.7.2. *Fawn with golden lustre.* Irish myth: Cross.
M314.1. Prophecy: son who catches certain fawn will become king.

B731.8. *Red (green) swine.* Irish myth: Cross.

B731.9. *Purple wether.* Irish myth: Cross.

B731.9.1. *Ram with green feet and horns.* Irish myth: Cross.

B731.10. *Multicolored worm (serpent).* Irish myth: Cross.

B731.11. *Blue serpent.* Irish myth: Cross.

B731.12. *Silver fish with gold fins.* Irish myth: Cross.

B731.13. *Bird with changing color.* Jewish: Neuman.

B731.14. *Hyena with three hundred sixty-five different colors.* Jewish: Neuman.

B732. *Panther's sweet smell protects him from other beasts.* Herbert Catalogue of Romances III 37ff. (Odo of Cheriton), Hervieux Fabulistes latins IV No. 60.

B733. *Animals are spirit-sighted.* Scent danger. — Swiss; Jegerlehner Oberwallis 298 No. 9 — Irish myth: Cross. Cf. B120. Wise animals.

B147. Animals furnish omens. E421.1.2. Ghost visible to horses alone.

B733.1. *Balaam's ass perceives angel.* Jewish: Neuman.

B733.2. *Dogs howling indicates death.* Argentina: Jijena Sanchez Perro Negro 115; Fb "hund" I 676 b; Hdwb. d. Abergl. IV 473.

B733.2.1. *Cock hears inaudible voice of dying man.* Jewish: Neuman.

B735. *Bird gives milk.* Africa (Basuto): Jacottet 102 No. 15, (Kaffir): Theal 33; India: *Thompson-Balys.

B736. *Animal sheds tears.*

B736.1. *Bird sheds tears.* (Cf. D1505.5.1.) — Spanish Boggs FFC XC 59 No. 425D.; Irish myth. Cross.

B259.10. Birds lament saint's departure. B303.1. Birds weep when man cuts off his hand.

B736.2. *Horse sheds tears (of blood).* Irish myth: Cross.

B149.2. Horse weeps for master's approaching death. B301.4.2. Faithful horse weeps tears of blood for master. F1041.29. Tears of blood from excessive grief.

B736.3. *Dog sheds tears.* Irish myth: Cross.

B736.4. *Fox sheds tears.* Jewish: Neuman.

B736.5. *Stag sheds tears.* German: Grimm No. 11.

B736.6. *Calf sheds tears.* Jewish: Neuman.

B737. *Fish with coat of wool.* Irish myth: Cross.

B738. *Animal's skin revolves while flesh and bones remain stationary.* Irish myth: Cross.

B739. *Fanciful color, smell etc. of animals — miscellaneous.*

B739.1. *Magic cock has elixir in his body which makes people light.* Chinese: Eberhard FFC CXX 222.

B740. Fanciful marvelous strength of animals.

B741. *Lion's roar causes havoc at 300 miles.* At 300 miles all women miscarry, at 200 teeth of all men drop out. — Gaster Exempla 187 No. 7; Jewish: Neuman.

B11.12.2. Dragon's shriek makes land barren.

B741.1. *Cry of giant ox impregnates all fish.* Persian: Carnoy 289.

B182.2. Magic ox.

B741.2. *Neighing of stallion in Assyria impregnates mares in Egypt.* — *DeVries FFC LXXIII 375.

H572. Reductio ad absurdum of riddle: stallions of Babylon.

B741.3. *Cow whose bellowing defeats army.* *Liebrecht Zur Volkskunde 71; Norse: *Boberg.

B741.4. *Bellow of bull heard over entire land.* Irish myth: Cross.

B742. *Animal breathes fire.* Gaster Oldest Stories 69.

B11.2.11. Fire-breathing dragon. B14.1. Chimera breathes fire. B15.5. Horse with fire-breathing nostrils. B19.1. Brazen-footed, fire-breathing bulls. E501.4.2.4. Horse in wild hunt breathes fire.

B742.1. *Lion breathes fire.* Breton: Sébillot Incidents s.v. "lion".

B742.2. *Birds spit fire.* English: Wells 104 (Alexander and Dindimus); Irish myth: Cross.

B742.3. *Fire-breathing horses.* Hartland Science 243.

B742.4. *Fire-breathing dogs.* Irish myth: Cross.

B743. *Blowing serpent.* Can blow through seven church walls but not through a pair of hose. — Fb "blæseorm".

B744. *Animal travels extraordinary distance.* Irish myth: Cross.

B745. *Indestructibility of leech.* India: Thompson-Balys.

B746. *Bear could formerly lift mountain.* India: Thompson-Balys.

B747. *Animal's strong teeth.*

B747.1. *Strong teeth of lion.* Jewish: Neuman.

B747.2. *Locusts with jaw teeth strong as lion's.* Jewish: Neuman.

B747.3. *Mice gnaw through metal vessels.* Jewish: Neuman.

B748. *Snake shoots rapids of mighty river.* S. A. Indian (Pilcomayo River Tribes): Belaieff BBAE CXLIII (1) 379.

B750. Fanciful habits of animals.

D631.2. Animal's size changed at will. T589.6.1. Children brought by the stork.

B751. *Animal's fanciful treatment of their young.*

B725. Female bears have no breasts to nurse their young: must suck paws.

B751.1. *Snake swallows young to protect them.* *Speck JAFL XXXVI 298; England, U.S.: Baughman; North Carolina: Brown Coll. I 637f.

B751.2. *Pelican kills young and revives them with own blood.* Herbert Catalogue of Romances III 37ff. (Odo of Cheriton), Hervieux Fabulistes latins IV No. 57.

D1889.3. Rejuvenation by song of pelican.

B751.3. *Eagle tests eaglets by having them gaze at sun.* Herbert III 38 (Odo of Cheriton), Hervieux Fabulistes latins IV No. 10; Gaster Thespis 30.

B751.4. *The lion blows first life into its cubs three days after their birth.* Zs. für deutsche Philol. XXVI 25.

B751.5. *Animal neglects its young.* Jewish: Neuman (raven, jackal, ostrich).

B751.6. *Wolf strongly attracted to his own children.* Jewish: Neuman.

B752. *Fanciful behavior of animal at death.*

B752.1. *Swan song.* Swan sings as she dies. — Fb "svane" III 663b.
N651. Pet swan saves self by singing death song.

B752.2. *Snake does not die before sunset.* — Fb "orm" II 759a; U.S.: Baughman.

B752.3. *Snake kills itself by biting part of body* (when in danger or torture). U.S.: Baughman.

B754. *Sexual habits of animals.* Jewish: *Neuman.
T. Sex.

B754.0.1. *Unusual sexual union of animals.* Irish myth: Cross.
B182.2.0.1. Magic ox from unusual sexual union of animals.

B754.1. *Animal changes sex periodically.*

B754.1.1. *Hyena changes sex yearly.* Fable: Halm Aesop 405, Wienert FFC LVI 62 (ET 251), 131 (ST 376, 401); Jewish: Neuman.

B754.1.2. *Hare changes sex periodically.* Jewish: Neuman.

B754.2. *Elephants have sexual desire only after eating mandrakes.* English: Wells 182 (The Bestiary).

B754.3. *Lions do not mate with their fellows, but prefer leopards.* (Cf. Q551.3.) — *Krappe Balor 82; Frazer Apollodorus I 401.

B754.3.1. *Female rattlesnakes mate with black snakes* rather than with male rattlesnakes. U.S.: Baughman.

B754.4. *Male rabbit bears young.* Female rabbit escaped Noah on ark and drowned. — Nouvelles Récréations No. 66.
A1021.1. Pairs of animals in ark. Seed of all beings put into ark to escape destruction. A2211. Animal characteristics: accidental action of ancient animal.

B754.5. *Cocks kept from intercourse with hens have tenderest meat.* Nouvelles Récréations No. 86.

B754.6. *Peacock pregnant without intercourse.* Male spits up semen and female eats it. This as a curse. (Cf. A2236.5.) — India: *Thompson-Balys; Jewish: Neuman (raven).

B754.6.1. *Unusual impregnation of animal.*

B754.6.1.1. *Animal impregnated through mouth (ears).* Jewish: Neuman.

B754.7. *Unusual parturition of animal.*
T540. Miraculous birth.

B754.7.1. *Crab's offspring born through its chest.* India: Thompson-Balys.

B754.7.2. *Eagle catches gazelle's young as it is born.* Jewish: Neuman.

B755. *Animal calls the dawn.* The sun rises as a result of the animal's call. — Africa (Benga): Nassau 204 No. 32, (Ekoi): Talbot 384.
J2272.1. Chanticleer believes that his crowing makes the sun rise. K494. Wolf announces dawn prematurely to collect debt.

B756. *Gold-digging ants.* *Chauvin VII 87 No. 373bis; **F. Schiern Ueber den Ursprung der Sage von den goldgrabenden Ameisen (Copenhagen-Leipzig, 1873).

B757. *Rats leave sinking ship.* Fb "rotte" III 83a.

B758. *Eagle renews youth.* Feathers fall off and regrow. — *Wensinck "Tree and Bird as Cosmological symbols in Western Asia" Verhandelingen der Koninklijke Akademie von Wetenschappen n.s. XXII no. 1 (1921) 38; Hdwb. d. Aberg. I 180 s.v. "Adler". — Herbert Catalogue of Romances III 69 (Odo of Cheriton); Gaster Oldest Stories 80.
B32.1. Phoenix renews youth. D1881. Magic self-rejuvenation.

B761. *Turtle holds with jaws till it thunders.* Ojibwa: Jones-Michelson PAES VII (2) 347 No. 44; American Negro (Georgia): Harris Friends 167 No. 23.

B762. *Monkeys attack by throwing coconuts.* *Chauvin VII 22 n. 3.

B762.1. *Animal attacks by throwing pebbles.* Irish myth: Cross.

B765. *Fanciful qualities of snakes.* (Cf. B91.3, B751.1, B752.2.) — Jewish: *Neuman.

B765.1. *Snake takes tail in mouth and rolls like wheel.* Fb "stålorm".
X1321.3.1. The hoop snake.

B765.2. *Snake lays aside his crown to bathe.* Hoffman-Krayer Zs. f. Vksk. XXV 120 n. 2.; India: Thompson-Balys.
B112. Treasure-producing serpent's crown.

B765.3. *Snake sucks poisonous dew from grass.* *Fb "hugorm".

B765.4. *Snake milks cows at night.* *Kittredge Witchcraft 484 f. nn. 23, 24. — Swiss: Jegerlehner Oberwallis 300 No. 9.

B765.4.1. *Snake attaches itself to a woman's breast* and draws away her milk while she sleeps. India: Thompson-Balys.

B765.5. *Snake crawls from sleeper's mouth.* Fb "hugorm". — Fr. v.d. Leyen Das Märchen 39ff.
B784. Animal lives in person's stomach.

B765.6. *Snake eats milk and bread with child.* Type 672c.; BP II 463; Fb "snog" III 437a.
B391.1. Child feeds snake from its milk bottle.

B765.6.1. *Snake drinks milk.* India: Thompson-Balys.

B765.7. *Jointed snake can join its segments when it is broken into pieces.* Chinese: Werner 393; U.S.: Baughman.

B765.7.1. *Snakes may be killed, but do not die.* India: Thompson-Balys.

B765.7.2. *Snake grows back together after it has been severed.* U.S.: Baughman.

B765.8. *Snake sucks poison from bite it has itself made.* **Wesselski Erlesenes 3ff.

B765.9. *Poisonous snakes in certain region have no venom.* Irish myth: Cross.

B765.10. *Snake cracks self like coach whip and chases man.* North Carolina: Brown Coll. I 637. U.S.: Baughman.

B765.11. *Snake's venom kills tree.* North Carolina: Brown Coll. I 637.
F970. Extraordinary behavior of trees and plants. X1205.1. Snake strikes object, causing it to swell.

B765.12. *Venomous snakes play with precious stones.* Icel.: Boberg.

B765.13. *Copperhead guides rattlesnake to its prey.* U.S.: Baughman.

B765.14. *Snake has hypnotic stare: person cannot move.* U.S.: *Baughman.

B765.14.1. *Serpent reduces man to a heap of ashes by its fiery gaze.* India: Thompson-Balys.

B765.15. *Snake stands up, whistles.* U.S.: Baughman.

B765.16. *Snake has stinger.* U.S.: *Baughman.

B765.17. *Bullets have no effect on giant serpent;* only stroke of lightning effective. Ladino: Conzemius BBAE CVI 169.

B765.18. *Snake avoids object.*

B765.18.1. *Snake avoids white ash.* U.S.: *Baughman.

B765.18.2. *Snakes will not cross rope made of hair.* U.S.: Baughman.

B765.18.3. *Snakes will not cross a ring made of Irish earth.* U.S.: Baughman.

B765.19. *Detached snake fang kills person or animal.* U.S.: *Baughman.

B765.20. *Snake kills man who has killed snake's mate.* U.S., West Indies: *Baughman.

B765.21. *Snake revives snakes which have been injured (the doctor snake).* U.S.: Baughman.

B765.22. *King snake: kills and eats any snake* that does not accept his authority. U.S.: Baughman.

B765.23. *Snake with legs.* U.S.: Baughman.

B765.24. *Dragon fly serves as snake's servant, feeds snake;* it is called snake-feeder. U.S.: Baughman.

B765.24.1. *Dragon fly acts as doctor to injured snakes.* U.S.: Baughman.

B765.25. *Female snake seven years pregnant.* Jewish: Neuman.

B765.26. *Palm tree grows on serpent's body.* S. A. Indian (Toba): Métraux MAFLS XL 71.

B766. *Fanciful dangers from animals.*

B766.1. *Cat mutilates corpses.* *Kittredge Witchcraft 178 n. 41; U.S.: Baughman; North Carolina: Brown Collection I 638.

E731.3. Soul in form of mouse. G262.1. Witch sucks blood.

B766.1.1. *Cat must be kept from dying person* because it will catch the person's soul issuing (from mouth) in form of mouse. (Cf. E731.3.) — England, U.S.: Baughman.

B766.2. *Cat sucks sleeping child's breath.* *Kittredge Witchcraft 178 n. 40; England: Baughman; North Carolina: Brown Collection I 638.

B766.3. *Toads suck blood.* *Kittredge Witchcraft 183 n. 88.

B766.4. *Bite of white she-mule causes certain death.* Jewish: Neuman.

B767. *Animals attracted by music.* German: Grimm Nos. 8, 114.

B767.1. *Fish follow sound of music.* Jātaka II 157.

B768. *Fancied nourishment of animals.*

B768.1. *Partridge subsists on moonbeams.* Penzer II 235 n. 3.

B768.2. *Salamander subsists on fire.* Hertz Gesammelte Abhandlungen 257 n.; Irish myth: Cross; Jewish: *Neuman.

B768.3. *Swans live on pearls.* India: Thompson-Balys.

B768.4. *Serpent subsists on dust.* Jewish: Neuman.

B770. Other fanciful traits of animals.

B771. *Wild animal miraculously tamed.*

B771.0.1. *Wild animal will not harm chaste woman.* Italian Novella: Rotunda.

B522.3. Woman slandered as adulteress is thrown into lion pit. Lions do not harm her.

B771.1. *Animal tamed by maiden's beauty.* Penzer VII 52 n. 2, VIII 111; Herbert III 234; Oesterley Gesta Romanorum No. 115; Dickson Valentine and Orson 198 n. 86. — India: Thompson-Balys.

B851. Girl removes dog from lion's claw without being harmed. H413.4. Special power of chaste woman: raising fallen elephant. L300. Triumph of the weak. T300. Chastity and celibacy.

B771.2. *Animal tamed by holiness of saint.* Saint's legend: Plummer cxlvi; Irish myth: Cross; Jewish: Neuman; Icel.: Boberg.

A2434.2.3. Why there are no snakes in Ireland. B256. Animal as servant of saint. D1713. Magic power of hermit (saint). D2156. Magic control of animals.

B771.2.1. *Hungry lions do not harm saint.* Loomis White Magic 58.

B848. Man unharmed in den of animals.

B771.2.2. *Animal tamed by saint's prayer.* Irish myth: Cross.

D1766.1. Magic results produced by prayer.

B771.2.3. *Lions made tame by Moses' rod.* Jewish: Neuman.

B771.3. *Wild animal will not attack royal person.* Dickson Valentine and Orson 198 n. 86.

B771.4. *Fish trained to answer person's call.* Africa: Stanley 54.

B771.5. *Wild animal performs for king.* Irish myth: Cross.

B772. *Shipwrecked man repulsed by animals.* As he floats to shore animals push him back into water. — Chauvin V 149 No. 73 n. 2.

B773. *Animals with human emotions.*

B200. Animals with human traits. B250. Religious animals. B300 Friendly animals. B736. Animals shed tears. F989.8. Mother-love induced in animal. M414.8. Animals cursed.

B773.1. *Animal feels agitation at sight of native land.* Irish myth: Cross.

B773.2. *Animal (lion) pines away with grief upon his friend's grave.* *Loomis White Magic 59.

B773.3. *Lion (wolf) protects the saint's body.* *Loomis White Magic 58, 60.

B775. *Stork is man while hibernating in Egypt.* Fb "stork" III 592a.

B776. *Venomous animals.*

B11.6.4.1. Sandalwood tree is guarded by dragon with venomous breath. B16. Devastating animals. B17. Hostile animals. F582.3. Venomous man. S111. Murder by poisoning.

B776.0.1. *Garlic juice dangerous to poisonous animals.* Penzer II 296.

B776.1. *Venomous sheep destroy enemy.* Irish: MacCulloch Celtic 63, Irish myth: Cross.

B16.19. Destructive sheep. B17.1.1. Ferocious animals loosed against attackers.

B776.2. *Toad considered venomous.* (Cf. B776.5.1.) — Kittredge Witchcraft 181 nn. 67—71; Jewish: Neuman.

K2116.3. Girl falsely accused of murdering her lover. Investigation reveals poisonous breath of toad as cause of death.

B776.3. *Venomous hound.* Irish myth: Cross.

A673.1. Dogs in hell. B16.18. Devastating dog (hound). B17.1.2. Hostile dog. B187. Magic dog. B871.1.7. Giant dog.

B776.3.1. *Venomous dog loosed against saint.* Irish myth: Cross.

B776.3.2. *Mud puppy considered poisonous.* U.S.: Baughman.

B776.4. *Venomous swine.*

B776.4.1. *Pig with venomous bristles.* Irish myth: Cross.

B776.4.2. *Venomous boar.* Irish myth: Cross.

B16.4. Giant devastating boar. B871.2. Giant boar.

B776.5. *Blood of animal considered venomous.* Irish myth: Cross.

B11.2.13.1. Blood of dragon venomous.

B776.5.1. *Blood of toad venomous.* Irish myth: Cross.

B776.5.2. *Blood of lion venomous.* Irish myth: Cross.

B776.5.3. *Blood of snakes venomous* (Cf. B776.7.) — Irish myth: Cross.

B776.5.4. *Blood of otter venomous.* Irish myth: Cross.

B776.5.5. *Blood of bear venomous.* Irish myth: Cross.

B776.6. *Venomous worm.* Irish myth: Cross.

B776.7. *Venomous serpent.* (Cf. B776.5.3.) — Irish myth: Cross; Norse: Herrmann Saxo II 602, MacCulloch Eddic 105, Boberg; India: Thompson-Balys.

B777. *Breath of bird withers.* Irish myth: Cross.

B781. *Animal "drinks apart" mixed liquids.* Separates the parts while drinking. — *M. Bloomfield in Penzer VII xviii — xix.

D2168.1. Poison magically separated from drink.

B782. *Sheep sleeps if anyone ties shoe to its ear.* India: Thompson-Balys.

B783. *Swine maddened by smell of oak forest.* Irish myth: Cross.

B784. *Animal lives in person's stomach.*

B784.0.1. *Frog living in person's stomach rises into throat,* croaks every spring. England: Baughman.

B784.1. *How animal gets into person's stomach (or body) (various methods).*

B784.1.1. *Person drinking from brook swallows animal eggs (frog or newt).* England, Ireland, U.S.: *Baughman.

B784.1.2. *Person swallows pebble on beach; snake grows in stomach.* U.S.: Baughman.

B784.1.3. *Person swallows snake semen or egg while eating watercress.* England: *Baughman.

B784.1.4. *Girl swallows frog spawn; an octopus grows inside her* with tentacles reaching to every part of her body. Eng.: Baughman.

B784.1.5. *Swallowed blackbeetle reproduces inside person's body.* England: Baughman.

B784.1.6. *Girl eats plums and maggots in them; maggots multiply inside her body.* England: Baughman.

B784.1.7. *Scaly lizard jumps into person's mouth.* U.S.: Baughman.

B784.1.8. *Salamander gets into veins through cracks in feet* when person goes barefoot. U.S.: Baughman.

B784.2. *Means of ridding person of animal in stomach.*

B784.2.0.1. *No remedy possible.* England: Baughman.

B784.2.1. *Patient fed salt: animal comes out for water.* The patient is fed salt or heavily salted food and allowed no water for several days. He then stands with mouth open before a supply of fresh water, often a running brook. The thirsty animal emerges to get fresh water. — Ireland, U.S.: *Baughman; Italian Novella: Rotunda (J1115.2.3).

F582. Poison damsel. F950. Marvelous cures. G274.1. Witch snared.

B784.2.1.1. *Snake (frog) in human body enticed out by milk (water).* India: Thompson-Balys.

B784.2.1.2. *Husband ties a cock near wife's feet:* snake-parasite in her stomach comes out to catch the cock and is killed by husband. — India: Thompson-Balys.

B784.2.2. *Patient sits before tempting meal without eating; animal emerges.* Ireland, England, U.S.: *Baughman.

B784.2.3. *Frog is enticed from patient's mouth by offering it a piece of cheese.* England: Baughman.

B784.2.4. *Physician removes animal from stomach of patient.* U.S.: *Baughman.

B785. *Animal wards off spirits.* Irish myth: Cross.

B524. Animal overcomes man's adversary.

B786. *Monkeys always copy men.* India: Thompson-Balys.

B787. *Birds mock ascetic's devotions.* India: Thompson-Balys.

B788. *Bats keep fireflies to light their houses.* India: Thompson-Balys.

B791. *Elephants have power of bringing rain.* Buddhist myth: Malalasekera I 41.

B792. *Why certain animals are thought of as good or bad.* Jewish: Neuman.

B800—B899. Miscellaneous animal motifs.

B800. Miscellaneous animal motifs.

B801. *Elephants in folktales.* *Penzer I 134.

B802. *Horses in tales and legends.* (Cf. B41.1, B41.2, B103, B133, B149.1, B151, B181, B811.1.) — **Howey Horse in Magic and Myth passim; *Malten Jahrb. d. Kaiserl. deutschen archäologischen Inst. XXIX (1914) 179ff.

A132.3. Horse deity. F343.9.1. Horses as fairy gifts. K2383. Tying cat to balky horse's tail to make him move. Q589.1. Horses fail when owner refuses load to saint.

B811. *Sacred animals.* Egyptian: Müller 159ff.; Icel.: Boberg.

A132. God in animal form. A155. Animals of the gods. B11.10.0.1. Sacrifice of animals to dragon. B100. Treasure animals. C65. Tabu: offending sacred animals. C92. Tabu: killing sacred being. Q228. Punishment for trying to harm sacred animal. V1.3. Animal worship. V10. Religious sacrifices. V134.3. Fish in water from certain well: water refuses to boil till fish are returned to well.

B811.1. *Sacred horse.* (Cf. B802.) — Penzer II 57 n. 1.

A132.3. Horse deity. B181. Magic horse.

B811.1.1. *Helpful horses descended from heaven.* India: Thompson-Balys.

B811.2. *Sacred armadillo.* S. A. Indian (Chiriguano): Métraux BBAE CXLIII (3). 484.

B811.3. *Sacred animal: cow.* India: *Thompson-Balys.

C2211.1.1.1. Tabu: killing and cooking sacred cow.

B811.3.1. *Sacred buffalo.* India: Thompson-Balys.

B811.3.2. *Sacred bull.* Jewish: Neuman.

B811.3.3. *Sacred cattle of sun god.* Greek myth: Grote I 313.

B811.4. *Sacred cat.* India: Thompson-Balys.

B811.5. *Sacred swan.* India: Thompson-Balys.

B811.6. *Sacred fox.* S. A. Indian (Chiriguano): Métraux BBAE CXLIII (3) 484.

B831. *Animals try in vain to repair sleigh.* They get unsatisfactory materials. — Type 158.

B841. *Long-lived animals.* — Frazer Pausanias IV 217; **Wesselski Archiv Orientalni IV 1ff.

A1881.0.1. Horse lives from time of Adam on. A1904. The oldest kind. B37. Immortal bird. B124.1. Salmon as oldest and wisest of animals. D1345. Magic object gives longevity. D1857. Magic longevity.

B841.1. *Animals debate as to which is the elder.* **Wesselski Archiv Orientalni IV 1ff.; *Baum JAFL XXX 378 ff.; India: Thompson-Balys; Korean: Zong in-Sob XXXIII No. 17; Japanese: Ikeda. — Africa (Benga): Nassau 95, 109 Nos. 5, 10, (Fang): Nassau 239 No. 7.

F571.2. Sending to the older. Old person refers inquirer to his father, who refers to his father, and so on for several generations.

B841.2. *Ages of animals (birds, fish) compared with age of human beings.* Irish myth: Cross.

B841.2.1. *Crow lives nine generations of men,* deer 36, raven 108, phoenix 972, nymphs 9720. — Frazer Pausanias IV 217.

B841.3. *Dog so old his head is skinless.* Eskimo (Greenland): Holm 80.

B841.4. *Stags live one thousand years.* Tupper and Ogle Map 4.

B842. *Faithful old dog to be killed.* *Type 101.

B842.1. *Faithful old horse to be abandoned.* German: Grimm No. 132.

B843. *Immortal animals.* Jewish: Neuman.
B37. Immortal bird. D1850. Immortality.

B843.1. *Immortal serpent.* Gaster Oldest Stories 81.

B843.2. *Immortal donkey.* Jewish: Neuman.

B845. *Wild animals herded.* *Fb "hare" IV 201a; *Type 570; Irish myth: Cross.
B575.1. Wild animals kept as dogs. D1444. Magic object catches animal. H1112. Task: herding rabbits. H1154. Task: capturing animals.

B845.1. *Wild pigs kept by demigod as if domesticated.* India: Thompson-Balys.

B845.2. *Animals chained in couples.* Irish myth: Cross.
B172.7. Magic birds chained in couples.

B846. *Monkeys construct a bridge across the ocean.* Penzer II 84 n. 1, 85 n.
B549.3. Dragon makes bridge across stream for holy man.

B847. *Lions placed in city to prevent entrance.* Penzer I 108 n. 3.

B848. *Man unharmed in den of animals* (Cf. B771.2.1.) — Type 403; Spanish Exempla: Keller; Jewish: *Neuman.

B848.1. *The musician in the wolf-trap:* meets wolf already trapped, and saves himself by playing music. (Cf. K551.3.1.) — Lithuanian: Balys Index No. *168; Estonian: Aarne in FFC XXV No. 2002.
B767. Animal attracted by music.

B848.2. *Girl removes dog from lion's claws without being harmed.* Italian Novella: Rotunda.
B771. Animal tamed by maiden's beauty.

B852. *When cow calls her calf, all cattle graze.* Irish myth: Cross.
B182. Magic cow (ox. bull).

B853. *Birds perch on ears of cows.* Irish myth: Cross.

B854. *Each of grazing herd of cows eats same amount.* Irish myth: Cross.

B855. *Man and bear in the rick of hay.* The bear, persecuted by wolves, runs onto the hay-rick where the man was hidden, and defends himself from the wolves with bunches of hay. — Lithuanian: Balys Index No. *167.

B857. *Animal avenges injury.* Chinese: Eberhard FFC CXX 18 No. 9; Africa (Fang): Tessman 117f.
N261. Train of troubles for sparrow's vengence. Q211.6. Killing an animal avenged.

B870. Giant animals. (Cf. B16.1, B16.4, B15.7.12) — Coulter Trans. Am. Philological Association LVII 32ff.
B11.2.12. Dragon of enormous size. B15.3.3. Deer with giant antler. B31. Giant bird. B81.2.4. Giant mermaid cast ashore. F234.1.0.1. Fairy in form of giant animal. F531. Giant. A person of enormous size. F989.11. Animal as mighty drinker. X1200. Lie: the great animal.

B870.1. *Animal extraordinarily heavy for size.* Irish myth: Cross.

B871. *Giant beasts.*

B871.1. *Giant domestic beasts.*

B871.1.1. *Giant cow.* Irish myth: Cross.

B871.1.1.1. *Giant ox.* Persia: Carnoy 289; Japanese: Ikeda.
A1791. Giant ox ancestor of all animals. B182.2. Magic ox. X1237. Lie: remarkable ox or steer.

B871.1.1.1.1. *Gigantic ox-rib (in otherworld).* Irish myth: Cross.
F343.16. Gigantic ox-rib as gift from fairies.

B871.1.1.2. *Giant bull.* Irish myth: Cross; *Loomis White Magic 82.

B871.1.1.3. *Giant buffalo.*
G357.1. Hero overcomes devastating animal (buffalo).

B871.1.2. *Giant boar.* Irish myth: Cross; India: Thompson-Balys.

B871.1.2.0.1. *Giant boar with hinder part as large as can be carried by nine men.* Irish myth: Cross.
B164. Giant devastating boar (pig).

B871.1.2.1. *Giant hog.* Fb "svin" III 676a.; India: Thompson-Balys; Irish myth: Cross.

B871.1.2.1.1. *Gigantic hog-rib (in otherworld).* Irish myth: Cross.
F343.16. Gigantic ox-rib as gift from fairies.

B871.1.3. *Giant sheep.* Irish myth: Cross.

B871.1.4. *Giant goat.* Africa (Benga): Nassau 202 No. 32.

B871.1.5. *Giant horse: hair from the tail is seven yards.* Nornagests þ. ch. 7 p. 67.

B871.1.6. *Giant cat.* Irish myth: Cross.
B161. Monster cat devastates country.

B871.1.7. *Giant dog (hound).* Irish myth: Cross; Eskimo (Greenland): Rasmussen III 114, Holm 24.

B871.2. *Giant wild beasts.*

B871.2.1. *Giant elephant.* Icel.: *Boberg; Buddhist myth: Malalasekera I 737, II 409; Africa (Mpongwe): Nassau 37 No. 5.

B871.2.2. *Giant tiger.* *Chauvin VII 86 n. 7.

B871.2.3. *Giant panther.* *Chauvin VII 86 n. 6.

B871.2.4. *Giant hippopotamus.* Chauvin VII 86 n. 5.

B871.2.5. *Giant lion.* Malone PMLA XLIII 402f.; Irish myth: Cross.

B871.2.6. *Giant walrus.* Irish myth: Cross.

B871.2.7. *Giant mice.* Irish myth: Cross.
B16.21. Giant man-eating mice.

B871.2.8. *Giant hare.* Icel.: Boberg.

B871.2.9. *Giant armadillo.* S. A. Indián (Toba): Métraux MAFLS XL 71.

B872. *Giant birds.*

B872.1. *Giant eagle.* India: Thompson-Balys.

B872.2. *Giant gull.* Eskimo (Greenland): Rink 455, (Cumberland Sound): Boas BAM XV 195.

B872.3. *Giant falcon.* Eskimo (Greenland): Rasmussen III 207.

B872.4. *Giant auk.* Eskimo (Greenland): Rink 430.

B873. *Giant insects.*

B16.7. Giant man-eating ants.

B873.1. *Giant louse.* *Type 621; *BP III 483 (Gr. No. 212). See also all references to F983.2.

F983.2. Louse fattened. H522.1. Test: guessing origin of certain skin.

B873.2. *Giant scorpion.* *Chauvin VII 86 No. 373bis.; Jewish: *Neuman.

B873.3. *Giant spider.* Buddhist myth: Malalasekera I 347.

B873.4. *Giant ant.* Jewish: Neuman.

B874. *Giant fish.* *Chauvin VII 8 No. 373A n. 2; *Reinhard PMLA XXXVIII 447 n. 81; Irish myth: Cross; Jewish: Neuman; Buddhist myth: Malalasekera I 40, 269f., 1014, II 29; Japanese: Ikeda. — Eskimo (Mackenzie Area): Jenness 78, (Central Eskimo): Boas RBAE VI 640, (West Hudson Bay): Boas BAM XV 539.

B11.2.1.3. Dragon as modified fish. B60. Mythical fish.

B874.1. *Giant river catfish.* Ladino: Conzemius BBAE CVI 130f.

B874.2. *Giant eel.* Irish myth: Cross.

B15.7.12. Eel with fiery mane.

B874.3. *Giant whale.* Irish myth: Cross; Marquesas: Handy 116.

B874.3.1. *Whale cast ashore* — three golden teeth and five ounces in each of these teeth. Irish myth: Cross.

B107.6. Monster (whale) with golden teeth.

B874.3.2. *Giant whale cast ashore on the night of Christ's Nativity:* "fifty men were on the upper parts of its head, and (there was) the limit of vision between each two of them. Such was the amount of ground which the animal occupied. Irish myth: Cross.

B81.2.4. Giant mermaid cast ashore.

B874.4. *Giant salmon.* Irish myth: Cross.

B874.5. *Giant shark.* Marquesas: Handy 110.

B874.6. *Giant clam.* Tahiti: Beckwith Myth 266.

B875. *Giant reptiles.*

B875.1. *Giant serpent.* *Chauvin VII 10 No. 373B n. 2; Jātaka Index s.v. "Nāga". — Icel.: MacCulloch Eddic 216f.; Norwegian: Solheim Register 17; India: *Thompson-Balys; Chinese: Werner 181; Irish myth: Cross; Missouri-French: Carrière; Jewish: Neuman; Japanese: Ikeda. — Eskimo (Greenland): Thalbitzer 5; Tonga: Gifford 178;

Ladino: Conzemius BBAE CVI 169. — S. A. Indian (Toba): Métraux MAFLS XL 57, 59, 71.

A876. Midgard serpent. B11. Dragon. B61. Leviathan. B91.5. Sea serpent. D449.7. Transformation: brain to giant serpent. G308. Sea monster. X1321.1. The great snake.

B875.2. *Giant crocodile.* *Chauvin VII 86 No. 373bis n. 8; Jewish: *Neuman; Buddhist myth: Malalasekera I 480. — Africa (Fang): Einstein 36f., Trilles 158.

B875.3. *Giant turtle.* *Chauvin VII 16 No. 373C n. 2.

B875.4. *Giant tortoise.* Jewish: Neuman; Africa (Zulu): Callaway 339.

B876. *Giant amphibia and other animal forms.*

B876.1. *Giant frog.* Jewish: *Neuman.

B876.2. *Giant crustacean.*

B876.2.1. *Giant crab.* Buddhist myth: Malalasekera I 249, 472; Chauvin VIII 83 No. 373bis n. 1.

B877. *Giant mythical animals.*

B877.1. *Giant sea monster.* Irish myth: Cross.

B16.9. Devastating (man-eating) sea-monster (serpent). B61. Leviathan. B91.5. Sea-serpent. G308. Sea-monster.

B877.1.1. *Giant water monster attacks man.* Irish myth: Cross.

B877.1.2. *Giant sea monster overpowered by saint.* Irish myth: Cross.

B11.11. Fight with dragon.

B877.2. *Gigantic animal ("reem").* Jewish: *Neuman.

B877.3. *Djun, gigantic and ferocious river animal.* Africa (Fang): Trilles 186.

B878. *Giant flock of animals (birds.)*

B878.1. *Giant flock of birds.*

B878.1.1. *Flock of birds so numerous* that it shakes trees upon which it perches. Irish myth: Cross.

C. TABU

DETAILED SYNOPSIS

C0 —C99. Tabu connected with supernatural beings
- C0. Tabu: contact with supernatural
- C10. Tabu: profanely calling up spirit (devil, etc.)
- C20. Tabu: calling on ogre or destructive animal
- C30. Tabu: offending supernatural relative
- C40. Tabu: offending spirits of water, mountain, etc.
- C50. Tabu: offending the gods
- C70. Tabu: offending other sacred beings
- C90. Other tabus in connection with sacred beings

C100—C199. Sex tabu
- C100. Sex tabu
- C110. Tabu: sexual intercourse
- C120. Tabu: kissing
- C130. Tabu connected with puberty
- C140. Tabu connected with menses
- C150. Tabu connected with childbirth
- C160. Tabu connected with marriage
- C170. Tabu connected with husband's or wife's relatives
- C180. Tabu confined to one sex
- C190. Sex tabu — miscellaneous

C200—C299. Eating and drinking tabu
- C200—C249. *Eating tabus*
  - C200. Tabu: eating (general)
  - C210. Tabu: eating in certain place
  - C220. Tabu: eating certain things
  - C230. Tabu: eating at certain time
  - C240. Tabu: eating food of certain person
- C250—C279. *Drinking tabus*
  - C250. Tabu: drinking
  - C260. Tabu: drinking at certain place
  - C270. Tabu: drinking certain things
  - C280. Miscellaneous eating and drinking tabus

C300—C399. Looking tabu
- C300. Looking tabu
- C310. Tabu: looking at certain person or thing
- C320. Tabu: looking into certain receptacle
- C330. Tabu: looking in certain direction

C400—C499. Speaking tabu
- C400. Speaking tabu
- C410. Tabu: asking questions
- C420. Tabu: uttering secrets
- C430. Name tabu
- C440. Origin tabu
- C450. Tabu: boasting

C. TABU

For the whole subject of tabu both in tales and in practice see: Frazer Taboo and the Perils of the Soul, Vol. III of The Golden Bough (London, 1914). In the following treatment no attempt has been made to cover tabu in practice. Attention has been directed to it mainly as a motif in tales. See also: Penzer Ocean of Story X Index s.v. "Taboo"; Fb "tabu" IV 354a; Singer Taboo in Hebrew Scriptures (Chicago-London 1928).

A1587. Origin of tabus. M400. Curses. N120. Determination of luck or fate. Q200. Deeds punished. W126. Disobedience.

C0—C99. Tabu connected with supernatural beings.

C0. Tabu: contact with supernatural. **Frazer Golden Bough, III (Taboo and the Perils of the Soul), London 1914.

A2231. Animal characteristics: punishment for impiety. C13.1. Prince invites angel to wedding. Taken to other world. C501. Tabu: contact with things belonging to a king. F348. Tabus connected with fairy gifts.

C10. Tabu: profanely calling up spirit (devil, etc.). — *Halliday in Penzer VIII xiv; BP II 63 n. 1. — N. A. Indian: Thompson Tales 338 n. 217a; India: Thompson-Balys.

C432. Tabu: uttering name of supernatural creature. E380.1. Summoning souls punished: in hour of man's death they overwhelm him. F301.1.1. Girl summons fairy lover by breaking tabu.

C10.1. *Druidism forbidden.* Irish myth: Cross.

E380.1. Summoning souls punished: in hour of man's death they overwhelm him. P427. Druid. V350. Conflict between religions.

C11. *The Old Man and Death.* Weary old man wishes for death. When Death appears at the summons he asks for help with the load. — Halm Aesop No. 90; Wienert FFC LVI 81 (ET 468, 469), 109 (ST 212, cf. ST 109, 115, 141, 342); *Jacobs Aesop 216 No. 69; *BP III 294; Italian Novella: Rotunda; U.S.: Baughman; India: *Thompson-Balys.

K2065. Appearance of Death exposes hypocrisy.

C12. *Devil invoked: appears unexpectedly.*

D2141.0.2. Storm from calling up spirits to help find buried treasure. M219.1. Bargain with the devil for an heir.

C12.1. *Devil called on for help.* When the devil appears man excuses himself. — Krappe Bulletin Hispanique XXXIX 23; Estonian: Aarne FFC XXV 123 No. 47; Finnish: Aarne FFC XXXIII 41 No. 47; Lappish: Qvigstad FFC LX 42 No. 25; Spanish Exempla: Keller.

C12.1.1. *Man wishing to be conjurer fears helper he has called.* Eskimo (Greenland): Rink 452.

C12.2. *Oath: "May the devil take me if ...."* Devil does. — Type 821A; *Pauli (ed. Bolte) No. 807. — Norwegian: Christiansen Norske Eventyr 105; Irish: Beal XXI 316; North Carolina: Brown Collection I 641.

M215. With his whole heart: devil carries off judge.

C12.3. *Oath: "May the devil whet my scythe."* Devil leaves only the handle. — Finnish: Aarne FFC XXXIII 41 No. 45**.

C12.4. *Man commends wife to devil.* Devil takes the charge seriously and guards woman's chastity during husband's absence. — *Type 1352; *Wesseiski Märchen 193.

K1500. Deception connected with adultery. T230. Faithlessness in marriage.

C12.4.1. *Mother wishes lazy daughter may marry devil.* Devil appears and marries her. — Spanish: Boggs FFC XC 51 No. 340.

D1761. Magic results produced by wishing. S211. Child sold (promised) to devil (ogre).

C12.5. *Devil's name used in curse.* Appears. Alphabet No. 246. — Esthonian: Aarne FFC XXV 120 No. 32; Finnish: Aarne FFC XXXIII 40 No. 32.

C12.5.1. *Noah's curse admits devil to ark.* Devil persuades Noah's wife to stay out of ark till Noah shall call devil in. Noah at last loses patience and calls out, "The devil! Come in!" The devil comes in and turns himself into a mouse. — Dh. I 258ff.

G303.23. The devil and the ark. K485. The devil gets into the ark. K2213.4.2. Noah's secret betrayed by his wife.

C12.5.2. *Man curses and devil fulfills his wish: takes the stone away.* Lithuanian: Balys Legends Nos. 497ff.

C12.5.3. *Girl fond of dancing uses devil's name.* (See Q386.1.) Canada, England: Baughman.*

C12.5.4. *Lost parson says he would rather have devil for guide than clerk who is with him.* Devil appears, causes death of both. England, U.S.: Baughman.*

C12.5.5. *Man calls on devil to descend chimney when angry at wife.* The devil comes, makes pudding black. U.S.: Baughman.

C12.5.6. *Man swears he will chastise devil for poaching.* The devil appears; the man runs; the devil takes man's wife. England: Baughman.

C12.5.7. *Wife curses wicked husband: "May devil take you!"* Devil does. (See M432.) U.S.: Baughman.

C12.5.8. *Man vows he will cross water "in spite of devil."* Devil takes him. Origin of place name: En Spuyten Duyvil. U.S.: Baughman.

C13. *The offended skull (statue)* (Festin de Pierre). A skull (statue) is invited to dinner. Attends the dinner and takes his host off to the other world. — *Type 470; **D.E. MacKay The Double Invitation in the Legend of Don Juan; *BP III 483 n. 1; *Wesselski Märchen 241 No. 51; Armeto La Leyenda de Don Juan (Madrid, 1908); *DeCock Studien en Essays 108—152, 308ff.; *Lancaster PMLA XXXVIII 471 n. 1; G. de Bevotte La Legende de Don Juan (Paris, 1906) (bibliography pp. 517—521); Manning PMLA XXXVIII 479; *Waxman JAFL XXI 184; *Pauli (ed. Bolte) no. 561; *Fb "menneskehoved" II 579b; Hartland Science 167; Sébillot France IV 132; Klapper Erzählungen des Mittelalters 157 No. 164; Gering Islenzk Aeventyri I 97 No. 34.

C954. Person carried off to other world for breaking tabu. E238. Dinner with the dead. Dea man is invited to dinner. Takes his host off to other world. E235.5 Return from dead to punish kicking of skull.

C13.1. *Prince invites angel to wedding.* Taken to other world. — *Child V 290a.

C14. *"Adversity" summoned:* king says he has heard people speak of adversity but has never seen it; genius of adversity appears. India: Thompson-Balys.

C15. *Wish for supernatural husband (wife) realized.* (Cf. C26.) — English: Child I 6ff. No. 2.

F301.1.1.1. Girl summons fairy lover by wishing for him. N201. Wish for exalted husband realized.

C15.1. *Wish for star-husband realized.* **Thompson The Star-Husband Tale (Studia Septentrionalia IV [1953] 93ff.); N. A. Indian: *Thompson Tales 330 n. 193.

A762.1. Star-husband. F15. Visit to star-world. T111.2. Woman from sky-world marries mortal man.

C15.1.1. *Wish for star wife realized.* S. Am. Indian (Toba): Métraux MAFLS XL 40, 43, (Sherente): Lowie BBAE CXLIII (1) 516.

T111.2. Woman from sky-world marries mortal man.

C15.2. *Wish for tree as husband realized.* Tree comes to life. — Yuracare: Alexander Lat. Am. 314.

C16. *Tabu: offending spirits of the dead.* Eskimo (Labrador): Hawks GSCan XIV 153.

C20. Tabu: calling on ogre or destructive animal.

C21. *"Ah me!": ogre's name uttered.* He appears. Köhler-Bolte I 557; Köhler Zs. f. Vksk. VI 68; *Cosquin Études Folkloriques 532ff.

C25. *"Bear's food."* To urge on his horses a man threatens them with the bear, calling them "bear's food." The bear hears and comes for them. — *Type 154; **Krohn Mann und Fuchs 11.

C25.1. *Child threatened with ogre.* Latter takes child off. — Swiss: Jegerlehner Oberwallis 321 No. 72, 323 No. 131; Japanese: Ikeda.

J2066.5. Wolf waits in vain for the nurse to throw away the child. She has threatened to throw the child to the wolf. S211. Child sold (promised) to devil (ogre).

C26. *Wish for animal husband realized.* Girl says she will marry a certain animal. Latter appears and carries her off. (Cf. C15.) — *Type 552. — Norwegian: Christiansen Norske Eventyr 80.— N. A. Indian: Thompson Tales 341 n. 231.

N201. Wish for exalted husband realized.

C30. Tabu: offending supernatural relative.

C31. *Tabu: offending supernatural wife.* Upon slight offence the wife leaves for her old home. — *Hoffman-Krayer Zs. f. Vksk. XXV 120 n. 4; Irish myth: Cross; English: Child I 21, 485a, II 496b, 509a, IV 440b; India: *Thompson-Balys; Japanese: Ikeda; N. A. Indian: *Thompson Tales 340 n. 223a; Eskimo (Cumberland Sound): Boas VAM XV 180; Maori: Dixon 58, 72.

C435.1. Tabu: uttering name of supernatural wife. C932. Loss of wife for breaking tabu. C942. Loss of strength from broken tabu. C952. Immediate return to other world for broken tabu. F302.3.3.1. Fairy avenges herself on inconstant lover. F302.6. Fairy mistress leaves man when he breaks tabu. P210. Husband and wife. T111. Marriage of mortal and supernatural being.

C31.1. *Tabu: looking at supernatural wife.* India: *Thompson-Balys; Chinese: Graham.

C300. Looking tabu.

C31.1.1. *Tabu: looking at supernatural wife too soon.* *BP III 114 (Gr. No. 137). — Middle English romance: Wells 145 (Parthenope of Blois).

C31.1.2. *Tabu: looking at supernatural wife on certain occasion.* (Melusine). The husband must not see the wife when she is transformed to an animal. — *Krappe Bulletin Hispanique XXXV (1933) 121; *Köhler-Bolte III 265nn. 1, 2; **Köhler Der Ursprung der Melusinensage (1895); Desaivre Le Mythe de la Mère Lusine (Extrait des Memoires de la Société de Statistique, Sciences, Lettres, et Arts de Deux-Sèvres [Saint-Maixent 1883]); Keightley Fairy Mythology 480; Baring-Gould Curious Myths 470; Hartland Science 201; Holmström Studier över Svanjungfrumotivet 100; M. Nowack Die Melusinensage (Diss. 1886); *Fränkel Zs. f. Vksk. IV 387; Jegerlehner Oberwallis 307 No. 24.

B81.2. Mermaid marries man. D361.1. Swan maiden. F302.2. Man marries fairy and takes her to his home. G245.1. Witch transforms self into snake when she bathes.

C31.1.3. *Tabu: looking at supernatural wife naked.* African: Werner 191.

C312.1.1. Tabu: man looking at nude goddess. C942.3. Weakness from seeing woman naked.

C31.1.4. *Tabu: husband looking at supernatural wife in childbirth.* (Cf. C151.) — Japanese: Anesaki 266.

C31.1.5. *Tabu: opening gourd in which star-wife is kept.* When curious girls do so, she flies up to sky. S. Am. Indian (Camacoco): Métraux MAFLS XL 48.

C31.2. *Tabu: mentioning origin of supernatural wife.* (Cf. C33.1, C35.1.) — Swiss: Jegerlehner Oberwallis 296 No. 21; Fjort: Dennett 44 No. 6; Indonesian: DeVries Volksverhalen I No. 35 n.

C440. Origin tabu. C952. Immediate return to other world because of broken tabu.

C31.3. *Tabu: disobeying supernatural wife.* Congo: Weeks 206f. No. 3; Fjort: Dennett 41 No. 5. — India: Thompson-Balys; Indonesian: De Vries Volksverhalen I No. 35 n.

C31.4. *Tabu: blaming supernatural wife.* *Chauvin VI 182 No. 343. — Greek: Fox 122 (Thetis). — Indonesian: DeVries Volksverhalen I No. 35 n.

C31.4.1. *Tabu: questioning supernatural wife.* Hindu: Penzer VII 21 n. 3, II 252f.; India: Thompson-Balys; Indonesian: DeVries Volksverhalen I No. 35 n.

C31.4.2. *Tabu: scolding supernatural wife.* English: Child V 495 s.v. "scolding". — Swiss: Jegerlehner Oberwallis 296 No. 21; England: Baughman. — Melanesian: Codrington The Melanesians 172.

C31.5. *Tabu: boasting of supernatural wife.* *BP II 327; Köhler-Bolte I 308ff. — Irish myth: Cross; English: Wells 132 (Sir Launfal). — Fjort: Dennett 42 No. 6.

C453. Tabu: boasting of love-conquest. M55. Judgment: pardon given if hero produces the lady about whom he has boasted.

C31.6. *Tabu: calling on supernatural wife.* *Type 400; BP II 318ff. (Gr. No. 92); *Fb "ønske" III 1179a. — English: Wells 132 (Sir Launfal.)

D2074.2.3.1. Mistress summoned by wish.

C31.7. *Tabu: lousing supernatural wife.* Indonesian: DeVries Volksverhalen I No. 35 n.

C31.8. *Tabu: striking supernatural wife.* Irish myth: Cross; Wales: Baughman; Kassai (Congo): Frobenius Atlantis XII 106.

C31.9. *Tabu: revealing secrets of supernatural wife.* (Cf. C420). *Schofield PMLA XV 165; Irish myth: Cross.

C31.10. *Tabu: giving garment back to supernatural (divine) wife.* India: Thompson-Balys.

D361.1. Swan Maiden. F302.4.2. Fairy comes into man's power when he steals her wings. K1335. Seduction (or wooing) by stealing clothes of bathing girl.

C31.11. *Tabu: reproaching supernatural wife about her sisters.* England: Baughman.*

C31.12. *Unfaithful husband loses magic wife.* Chinese: Graham.

C32. *Tabu: offending supernatural husband.* (Cf. C36.) — *Type 425; BP II 245ff. (Gr. No. 88). — India: *Thompson-Balys; S. Am. Indian (Toba): Métraux MAFLS XL 91.

B640.1. Marriage to beast by day and man by night. C121. Tabu: kissing supernatural husband. C421. Tabu: revealing secret of supernatural husband. T111. Marriage of mortal and supernatural being. T200. Married life.

C32.1. *Tabu: looking at supernatural husband.* *Type 425a; *BP II 234, 245ff., 266ff.; *Tegethoff Studien zum Märchentypus von Amor und Psyche 32; *Lang Cupid and Psyche (1886); *Fb "lys" II 483a. — India: Thompson-Balys.

C421. Tabu: revealing secret of supernatural husband. C757.1. Tabu: destroying animal skin of enchanted person too soon. C761.2. Tabu: staying too long at home. C310. Tabu: looking at certain person or thing. C313.1.1. Tabu: goddess seeing mortal husband naked. C916.1. Trespass betrayed by dripping candle.

C32.1.1. *Tabu: wife seeing transformed husband.* Chinese: Graham.

D512.2. Transformation because wife shrieks when she sees supernatural husband in original serpent form.

C32.1.2. *Tabu: showing surprise when supernatural husband resumes his true shape.* India: Thompson-Balys.

C413. Tabu: expressing surprise in lower world of dead.

C32.2. *Tabu: questioning supernatural husband.* *Boekenoogen Ridder metter Swane 166ff; India: Thompson-Balys.

C32.2.1. *Tabu: asking name of supernatural husband.* (Cf C430.) India: *Thompson-Balys.

C32.2.2. *Tabu: asking where supernatural husband comes from.* (Cf. C421.) — India: *Thompson-Balys.

C32.2.3. *Tabu: asking for caste of supernatural husband.* India: Thompson-Balys.

C32.3. *Tabu: not to touch too soon supernatural husband on visit.* India: Thompson-Balys.

C33. *Offending supernatural child.* India: Thompson-Balys.

C33.1. *Tabu: mentioning origin of supernatural child.* (Cf. C31.2, C35.1.) — India: Thompson-Balys; Africa (Ekoi): Talbot 133 — 136; (Gold Coast): Barker and Sinclair 77ff. No. 12, (Basuto): Jacottet 110; (Ibo of Nigeria): Thomas 76, 80.

C440. Origin tabu. T540. Miraculous birth. T646. Illegitimate child taunted by playmates.

C35. *Tabu: offending animal wife.* N. A. Indian: *Thompson Tales 339 n. 223; Eskimo (Greenland): Rink 145, (Central Eskimo): Boas RBAE VI 616.

B650. Marriage to animal in human form.

C35.1. *Tabu: mentioning origin of animal wife.* (Cf. C31.2, C33.1.) — N. A. Indian: Thompson Tales 339—342 nn. 222, 223, 233, cf. 234. — Africa (Congo): Weeks 215 No. 11; (Basuto): Jacottet 108 No. 16, (Fjort): Dennett 43 No. 6, (Cameroon): Rosenhuber 44, (Duala): Lederbogen 143. — Indonesian: Dixon 219.

B651.1. Marriage to fox in human form. B655.1. Marriage to bee in human form. C440. Origin tabu.

C36. *Tabu: offending animal husband.* (Cf. C32). — Eskimo (Mackenzie Area): Jenness 38.

C36.1. *Tabu: burning animal husband.* India: Thompson-Balys.

C841.3. Tabu: burning caterpillars.

C36.2. *Tabu: spying on animal husband.* Eskimo (Greenland): Rasmussen I 145.

C37. *Tabu: offending other animal relatives.* Eskimo (Mackenzie Area): Jenness 47, 49, (Greenland): Rink 144, (Labrador): Hawkes GSCan XIV 156.

C40. Tabu: offending spirits of water, mountain, etc.

J755.1. The forgotten wind. Man allowed to manage the weather forgets to ask help of the wind. All goes wrong and he must give up management.

C41. *Tabu: offending water-spirit.* Frazer Golden Bough III 94. — North Carolina: Brown Collection I 641; Africa (Kaffir): Theal 56.

C918. Mare from water world disappears when she is scolded and her halter used for common purposes. E511.1.3. Flying Dutchman sails because he defied the storm. F420. Waterspirits. G424. Bridal party will not pass over bridge for fear of water-demon. D1432.1. Water gradually envelops girl filling pitcher.

C41.1. *Tabu: rescuing drowning man.* Breton: Sébillot Incidents s.v. "noyé."

C41.2. *Tabu: letting ball fall into water.* *Type 440; BP I 1 (Gr. No. 1.)

G423. Ball falling into water puts person into ogre's (witch's, water-spirit's) power.

C41.3. *Tabu: crossing water when spirits are offended.*

S264.1. Man thrown overboard to placate storm. T211.1.1. Woman drowns herself as sacrifice to water-gods to keep husband's boat from capsizing.

C41.3.1. *Tabu: skating over water when spirits are offended.* N. A. Indian: *Thompson Tales 277 n. 23.

C41.4. *Tabu: poisoning fish causes storm.* India: Thompson-Balys.

C42. *Tabu: offending mountain-spirit.* Finnish: Aarne FFC XXXIII 42 No. 53**.

F460. Mountain-spirits.

C43. *Tabu: offending wood-spirit.* (Cf. C51.2.2, C64). — Swiss: Jegerlehner Oberwallis 295 No. 12; India: Thompson-Balys.

F441. Wood-spirit.

C43.1. *Tabu: offending spirit of banyan tree.* India: Thompson-Balys.

C43.2. *Tabu: cutting certain trees lest tree-spirits be offended.* India: Thompson-Balys.

C43.3. *Felled tree restored for failure to make proper offerings to tree-spirit.* Tuamotu: Beckwith Myth 267.

D1602.2. Felled tree raises itself again.

C44. *Tabu: offending guardian spirits.* Icel.: MacCulloch Eddic 321; Herrmann Saxo Gr. II 586.

C45. *Tabu: offending devil.* A smith or priest continually insults the devil's statue or picture (cf. C13). The devil brings the offender into dangerous situation (suspicion of theft or murder), and saves him miraculously when he promises never again to abuse the devil's likeness. Lithuanian: Balys Index No. 3325f.; Legends Nos. 631—637, 789; Cheremis: Sebeok-Nyerges.

C46. *Tabu: offending fairy.*

F360. Malevolent or destructive fairies.

C46.1. *Tabu: breaking promise to fairy: death on twelfth day.* India: Thompson-Balys.

C50. **Tabu: offending the gods.** Irish myth: Cross; India: *Thompson-Balys.

A1346.1. Man must work as punishment for theft of fire. C311.1. Tabu: seeing supernatural creatures. Q457.1. Flaying alive as punishment for contesting with a god. V1. Objects of worship.

C50.1. *Tabu: offending goddess of fortune.* India: Thompson-Balys. N111. Fortuna.

C51. *Tabu: touching possessions of god.* India: Thompson-Balys. C916.2. Animals produced when forbidden drum is beaten.

C51.1. *Tabu: profaning shrine.* Irish myth: Cross, Beal XXI 336; Greek: Grote I 279; India: Thompson-Balys.

B596. Animal helps saint by setting fire to neglected church. C93. Tabu: trespassing sacred precincts. Q222. Punishment for desecration of holy places, images, etc. Q551.3. Punishment: transformation of lovers into lion and lioness for desecrating temple. Q558.18. Saints bring about miraculous death because of desecration of sanctuaries. R325. Church (altar) as refuge. V110. Religious buildings. V113. Shrines.

C51.1.1. *Tabu: using altar for secular purposes.* Irish: Plummer clxxxiv; Irish myth: Cross.

C51.1.2. *Tabu: stealing from altar.* (Cf. C51.2.) — Fable: Phaedrus IV 11; Wienert FFC LVI 80 (ET 465), 138 (ST 433).

C51.1.2.1. *Tabu: stealing from sacred booty.* Jewish: *Neuman.

C51.1.3. *Tabu: breathing on sacred fire.* British: *MacCulloch Celtic 11 (references given to parallels from Parsis, Brahmans, Japanese, and Germans). — Irish myth: Cross.

C51.1.4. *Tabu: misuse of money in alms box.* Swiss: Jegerlehner Oberwallis 319 No. 23.

C51.1.5. *Tabu: dancing in churchyard.* Fb "kirkegaard" II 129.

C752.1.5. Tabu: casting in graveyard after sunset. Q552.2.3. Girl sinks into earth for dancing in church.

C51.1.6. *Tabu: discontinuing use of a church.* Crane Liber de Miraculis 90 No. 20.

C943. Loss of sight for breaking tabu. Q221. Personal offences against gods punished. V111. Churches.

C51.1.7. *Tabu: peeping at sacred font.* (Cf. C300.) — Finnish-Swedish: Wessman 19 No. 187.

C51.1.8. *Tabu: allowing a drop to fall upon altar.* Irish myth: Cross.

C51.1.9. *Tabu: unworthy men to enter or see sanctuary.* (Cf. C300.) *Loomis White Magic 97.

C51.1.10. *Tabu: to enter sacred places closed to the female sex.* (Cf. C51.1.2.) *Loomis White Magic 97.

C181. Tabu confined to women.

C51.1.11. *Visits of goddess cease when her sacred spring is disturbed.* Tahiti: Henry 85.

C51.1.12. *Tabu: striking tree which belongs to deity.* Hawaii: Beckwith Myth 111.

C51.1.13. *Tabu: treating scornfully statue and dress of goddess.* Greek Myth: Grote I 84.

C51.1.14. *Tabu: leaving corpse at shrine.* Jewish: Neuman.

C51.1.15. *Tabu: wearing shoes at shrine.* Jewish: Neuman.

C51.2. *Tabu: stealing from god or saint.* (Cf. C51.1.2.) — Greek: Grote I 145; Tuamotu: Stimson MS (3—G 3/1386); S. Am. Indian (Chiriguano): Métraux RMLP XXXIII 173.

D1713. Magic power of hermit (saint). V224.3. Animal stolen from saint miraculously replaced.

C51.2.1. *Tabu: wearing unauthorized sacred robe (jewel).* Crane Liber de Miraculis 82 No. 1; Ward Catalogue of Romances II 603 No. 6, 604 No. 7; Irish saints' legend: Plummer xliv; Irish myth: Cross.

C51.2.2. *Tabu: cutting sacred trees or groves.* (Cf. C43.) — Irish saints' legend: Plummer cliii; Irish myth: Cross.

V1.1.1. Sacred tree. V114. Sacred groves.

C51.2.2.1. *Tabu: taking fruit and fish dedicated to goddess.* (Cf. C221, C225, C241.) — India: Thompson-Balys.

C51.2.3. *Tabu: stealing wife of god.* Africa (Ekoi): Talbot 129.

C51.2.4. *Tabu: stealing from holy statue.* Spanish: Boggs FFC XC 91 No. 769C.

C51.2.5. *Tabu: violating refuge with saint.* Irish myth: Cross.

C51.3. *Tabu: revealing name of god.* Jewish: Neuman; Egyptian: Müller 109; Chinese: Werner 294.

C431. Tabu: uttering name of god (or gods). C921. Immediate death for breaking tabu.

C51.3.1. *Tabu: desecration of God's name.* Jewish: *Neuman.

C51.4. *Tabu: revealing secrets of god.* Greek: Frazer Apollodorus I 363 n. 1, Grote I 145. — Swiss: Jegerlehner Oberwallis 298 No. 6 (investigating secret source of magic wine cask).

C420. Tabu: uttering secrets.

C51.4.1. *Tabu: betraying privacy of god.* Emperor visited by God conceals his wife so that she may hear. God ceases his visits. — Type 775*.

C51.4.2. *Tabu: spying on secret help of angels.* *Toldo Studien zur vgl. Littgsch. IV 52ff.; Irish myth: Cross.

C51.4.3. *Tabu: spying on secret help of fairies.* Irish myth: Cross.

C311.1.2. Tabu: looking at fairies. F361.3.1. Fairies leave work unfinished when overseen.

C51.5. *Tabu: imitating god.* Greek: Fox 106 (Salmoneus imitates Zeus's thunder), Grote I 103f.*, 128; German: Grimm No. 147; India: Thompson-Balys.

C51.6. *Tabu: falsely claiming the powers of a god.* Greek: *Frazer Apollodorus I 80 n. 3; Jewish: Neuman.

C51.7. *Tabu: touching stone image of deity with unwashed hands.* India: Thompson-Balys.

C51.8. *Tabu: giving away idol.* India: Thompson-Balys.

C51.9. *Tabu: pointing boat toward island of the gods.* Hawaii: Beckwith Myth 67.

C52. *Tabu: being in presence of god.* Greek: Fox 46 (Semele in presence of Zeus.)

C312.1.1. Tabu: man looking at nude goddess. C921. Immediate death for breaking tabu.

C52.1. *Direct communication with god fatal to all except special devotees.* India: Thompson-Balys.

C52.2. *Tabu: coming suddenly on supernatural creatures.* Tupper and Ogle Walter Map 95.

C53. *Tabu: refusing credit to god.* Type 830. — Africa (Ekoi): Talbot 177.

C53.1. *People taught by God to work: claim they learned by own efforts.* Lithuanian: Balys Index No. 3057. (Cf. A1403.)

C53.2. *Tabu: arrogance toward deity.* Jewish: Neuman.

Q330. Overweening punished.

C54. *Tabu: rivaling the gods.* Greek: *Frazer Apollodorus I 20 n. 1 (Thamyris), I 31 (Side), Fox 220 (Marsyas), Grote I 103f., 146, 238, Gaster Thespis 261f., 289; India: Thompson-Balys.

C770. Tabu: overweening pride.

C55. *Tabu: losing consecrated wafer.* Types 613, 671; BP I 322 n. 1.

C940.1. Princess's secret sickness from breaking tabu. D2064.1. Magic sickness because girl has thrown away her consecrated wafer. H1292.4.1. Question (propounded on quest): How can the princess be cured? — Answer: She must recover consecrated wafer which rat has stolen from her first communion. V34.2. Princess sick because toad has swallowed her consecrated wafer.

C55.1. *Tabu: stepping on sacred bread.* Finnish-Swedish: Wessman 19 No. 188.

C55.2. *Tabu: shooting at consecrated wafer.* Man's ghost wanders. Type 756C. — Lithuanian: Balys Index No. 3320; Legends Nos. 615—623; Livonian: Loorits in FFC LCVI 59 No. 138.

C55.3. *Bee-master puts consecrated host into beehive.* Has success with his bees. (Cf. B259.4.) — When he dies, his spirit haunts the place. Lithuanian: Balys Legends Nos. 624—627.

D1031.1.1. Consecrated bread as magic object. Q222.1. Punishment for desecration of holy things (wafers). V 35. The stolen sacrament.

C56. *Tabu: unseemly acts while carrying divine image.*

C56.1. *Tabu: defecating while carrying image of a god.* India: Thompson-Balys.

C56.2. *Tabu: stopping enroute while carrying image of a god.* India: Thompson-Balys.

C57. *Tabu: neglect of service to deity.*

C57.1. *Tabu: neglect of sacrifice to deity.* Greek: Grote I 104, 108.
Q223.3. Neglect to sacrifice punished.

C57.1.1. *Tabu: fraudulent sacrifice.* India: *Thompson-Balys; Jewish: Neuman.
D1766.2. Magic results produced by sacrifices. K171.3.1. Deceptive sacrifice of nuts and dates.

C57.1.2. *No man with a wound to be sacrificed to goddess.* India: Thompson-Balys.

C57.1.3. *Tabu: eating from offerings made to gods.* India: Thompson-Balys.

C57.2. *Punishment for having refused to take part in Bacchic rites.* Greek myth: Grote I 84.

C58. *Tabu: profaning sacred day.* Irish myth: Cross; Finnish-Swedish: Wessman 18 Nos. 163, 166; Hebrew: Exodus 20: 8—11, Neuman; Pauli (ed. Bolte) No. 390. — Swiss: Jegerlehner Oberwallis 308 Nos. 37, 38; 324 No. 147; 328 No. 11; India: Thompson-Balys.
A2231.3. Animal characteristics: punishment for working on holy day. C631. Tabu: breaking the sabbath. C886. Tabu: failing to observe certain festival. E501.3.6. Wild huntsman wanders for hunting on Sunday. V71. Sabbath.

C58.1. *Tabu: diminishing number of sacred days.* Finnish-Swedish: Wessman 19 No. 180.

C61. *Tabu: disbelief in religious teachings.*

C61.1. *Tabu: disbelief in* God. Jewish: Neuman.

C61.2. *Tabu: disbelief in immortality.* Jewish: Neuman.

C61.3. *Tabu: disbelief in scriptures.* Jewish: Neuman.

C61.4. *Tabu: disbelief in particular supernatural power.* Eskimo (Greenland): Rink 471.

C62. *Tabu: idolatry.* Jewish: Neuman.
V120. Images.

C63. *Tabu: attacking deity (sacred person).* Greek: Fox 9; Eskimo (Greenland): Rasmussen I 115; Fiji: Beckwith Myth 138; S. Am. Indian (Witoto): Métraux MAFLS XL 36.

C64. *Tabu: failing to heed message of god.* India: Thompson-Balys; Africa (Fjort): Dennett 105 No. 29.

C65. *Tabu: changing ritual.* India: *Thompson-Balys.

C66. *Tabu: murmuring against deity.* Jewish: Neuman.

C67. *Tabu: neglect of sacred fires.* Hawaii: Beckwith Myth 111.

C68. *Tabu: neglecting to fulfill vow made to god.* Greek: Grote I 202.
M100. Vows and oaths.

C70. Tabu: offending other sacred beings.

C71. *Tabu: disobeying the king.* Man dies as result of failure to obey. — Alphabet No. 241.

C75. *Tabu: offending heavenly bodies.*

C75.1. *Tabu: offending the moon.* Eskimo (Greenland): Rink 442, Rasmussen II 25, (Smith Sound): Kroeber JAFL XII 180.

C90. Other tabus in connection with sacred beings.

C91. *Tabu: stealing from spirits.* (Cf. C51.2.) — Irish saints' legend: Plummer cliii (cf. C43, C51.2). — Finnish: Aarne FFC XXXIII 42 No. 53** (cf. C42).

C51.2. Tabu: stealing from god or saint. Q212. Theft punished.

C91.1. *Tabu: stealing garment from a rock.* The rock pursues. (The offended rolling stone.) — N. A. Indian: Thompson Tales 300 n. 96.

D1431. Rock pursues person. J1873.2. Cloak given to a stone to keep it warm. R261. Pursuit by rolling object.

C91.2. *Tabu: stealing fruits from sacred tree.* (Cf. C262.3.) — India: *Thompson-Balys.

C92. *Tabu: killing sacred beings.* Swiss: Jegerlehner Oberwallis 320. No. 41.

B811. Sacred animals.

C92.1. *Tabu: killing sacred animals.* Eskimo (Greenland): Rink 442, Rasmussen II 25, (Smith Sound): Kroeber JAFL XII 180.

C92.1.0.1. *Tabu: killing animals for sacrifice.* (Cf. C57.1.) — Buddhist myth: Malalasekera I 461, II 577.

V10. Religious sacrifices.

C92.1.1. *Tabu: killing raven* (Odin's bird). Fb "ravn" III 22a. — Krappe "Arturus cosmocrator" Speculum (1945) 405ff.

A165.0.1. Ravens as attendants of god. B122.2. Birds as reporters of sights and sounds. Sit on Odin's shoulder.

C92.1.2. *Tabu: killing sacred calf.* India: Thompson-Balys.

N361.1. Brahmin unwittingly kills calf.

C92.1.3. *Tabu: killing shrew-mouse, sacred to the gods.* India: Thompson-Balys.

C92.1.4. *Tabu: killing stork.* Fb "stork" III 592 ab.

C841.1. Tabu: killing stork. N250.1. Bad luck follows man who shoots stork.

C92.1.5. *Tabu: killing scald-crow (goddess of war).* Irish myth: Cross.

A132.6.2. Goddess in form of bird. A485.1. Goddess of war. B147.1.1.1. Crow as bird of ill omen.

C92.1.6. *Tabu: killing other sacred bird.* Eskimo (Greenland): Rasmussen I 160; Tuamotu: Stimson MS (t-G 2/44).

C92.2. *Tabu: killing sacred dragon.* (Cf. B11.) — Greek: Frazer Apollodorus I 334 n. 1.

C93. *Tabu: trespassing sacred precinct.* Alphabet No. 52. — Irish: Plummer clxxxiv; Irish myth: Cross. — Swiss: Jegerlehner Oberwallis

295, No. 12. — Eskimo (Central Eskimo): Boas RBAE VI 600; Africa (Ekoi): Talbot 59 (ghost town).

C51.1. Tabu: profaning shrine. C116. Tabu: sexual intercourse in sacred precinct. C752.1.5. Tabu: casting in graveyard after sunset. H1292.4. Question (propounded on quest): How can the prince be cured? — Answer: He must remove stone which he has spit out in the church. Q222. Punishment for desecration of holy places. V100. Religious edifices. V110. Religious buildings. V114. Sacred forests. V134. Sacred wells.

C93.1. *Tabu: sleeping in saint's bed.* Irish: Plummer clxxxiv; Irish myth: Cross.

C93.2. *Tabu: profaning hallowed clothes and vessels.* Alphabet No. 696.

C93.3. *Tabu: digging in churchyard.* Irish myth: Cross.

C523. Tabu: digging.

C93.4. *Tabu: crossing bridge sacred to the gods.* India: Thompson-Balys.

C93.5. *Tabu: slaughtering buffalo in temple.* India: Thompson-Balys.

C93.5.1. *Tabu: use of palanquin within temple.* India: Thompson-Balys.

C93.6. *Tabu: cutting down tree wherein resides deity.* India: Thompson-Balys.

C93.7. *Tabu: erecting fort on holy ground.* India: Thompson-Balys.

C93.8. *Tabu: landing on floating island of the gods without invitation.* Hawaii: Beckwith Myth 68.

C94. *Tabu: rudeness to sacred person or thing.*

Q220. Impiety punished.

C94.1. *Tabu: uncivil answer to holy (or supernatural) being.* Gaster Exempla 229 No. 239; Estonian: Aarne FFC XXV 125 No. 54; Finnish: Aarne FFC XXXIII 43. — India: Thompson-Balys.

A2231.1. Animal characteristics: punishment for discourteous answer to God (saint). A2721.3. Plant punished for ungracious answer to holy person. C31.4.2. Scolding supernatural wife. F481.1. Cobold avenges uncivil answer (or treatment).

C94.1.1. *The cursed dancers.* Dancers rude to holy man (Jesus) cursed and must keep dancing till Judgment Day. — *Bolte Zs. f. Vksk. XIX 309 n. 1; *Pauli (ed. Bolte) No. 388; Ward Catalogue II 660 No. 30; *Herbert ibid, III 283, 312; Alphabet No. 215; Swiss: Jegerlehner Oberwallis 296f. Nos. 3, 28; Finnish-Swedish: Wessman 18 No. 168.

D2061.1.2. Persons magically caused to dance selves to death. D2174. Magic dancing. E493. Dance of the dead. M400. Curses. Q220. Impiety punished. Q500. Tedious punishments.

C94.1.2. *Tabu: failure to give alms to Brahmans.* India: Thompson-Balys.

C94.1.3. *Tabu: discourtesy toward priest (rabbi, etc.).* Jewish: Neuman.

C94.2. *Tabu: false and profane swearing of oath.* *Pauli (ed. Bolte) No. 448. — Jewish: Neuman.

M101.3. Death as punishment for broken oath.

C94.3. *Tabu: mocking animal.* India: Thompson-Balys.

C94.3.1. *Tabu: rudeness to sacred animal.* India: *Thompson-Balys.

C94.3.1.1. *Tabu: offending sacred cow.* India: Thompson-Balys.

C94.4. *Tabu: calling profanely on God.* Daughter of Emperor says to Rabbi: "Your God is a builder; so let him build a tent here." She becomes leprous and must be placed in a tent. (Cf. C51.3.1.) — Gaster Exempla 187 No. 10; Jewish: Neuman.

C94.4.1. *Tabu: calling profanely on the members of God.* Spanish Exempla: Keller.

C94.5. *Tabu: masking as ghost in graveyard.* Finnish: Aarne FFC XXXIII 39 No. 15**; Lithuanian: Balys Index No. 3441, Legends Nos. 854—858.

C94.6. *Tabu: throwing away holy image.* Finnish-Swedish: Wessman 19 No. 184.

C94.7. *Tabu: ringing of church bell by nun.* Irish myth: Cross.

C180. Tabu confined to one sex.

C94.8. *Tabu: refusing homage to saint's bell.* Irish myth: Cross.

C94.9. *Tabu: disturbing austerities of an ascetic.* India: Thompson-Balys.

C95. *Tabu: giving security for one excommunicated.* Irish myth: Cross.

V84. Excommunication.

C96. *Tabu: using miracle for trifling purpose.* India: Thompson-Balys.

C96.1. *Tabu: resurrecting cat for trifling purpose.* India: Thompson-Balys.

C99. *Other tabus in connection with sacred beings — miscellaneous.*

C99.1. *Tabu: facing the sun (sun-god) while urinating.* (Cf. T521.) — India: Thompson-Balys.

C99.1.1. *Tabu: urinating on fire* (fire-god). — India: Thompson-Balys.

C99.2. *Tabu: weaving leather shoes on pilgrimage.* China: Eberhard 188 No. 129.

C100—C199. Sex tabu.

C100. Sex tabu. Hebrew: Leviticus ch. 18.

Q240. Sexual sins punished. T300. Chastity and celibacy.

C101. *Sex tabu broken: child born without bones.* Icelandic: Ragnarssaga Loðbrokar 128; India: Thompson-Balys.

A1152. Boneless man turned over to produce seasons. F529.7. Person with gristle instead of bones. T462. Lesbian love. T550. Monstrous births.

C110. Tabu: sexual intercourse. *Frazer Golden Bough XII 225f. s.v. "continence", 214 s.v. "chastity"; Irish myth: Cross; Icelandic: Boberg.

C142. Tabu: sexual intercourse during menses. C566. Tabu: sex activity for warriors. E411.2. Adulterous person cannot rest in grave. F304.2. Fairy queen's beauty temporarily destroyed by intercourse with mortal. H1472. Test: sleeping by princess three nights without looking at her or disturbing her. M130. Vows concerning sex. N553.1. Tabu: incontinence while treasure is being raised. Q243. Incontinence punished — miscellaneous. Q535.3. Refraining from sexual intercourse as penance. T400. Illicit sexual relations.

C110.1. *Tabu: sexual relationship with girls of nobility while having sore on body.* Mono: Wheeler 30.

C111. *Tabu: loss of chastity.* Hero loses power with loss of chastity. — — Wesselski Mönchslatein 185 No. 144; Jewish: Neuman; Gaster Thespis 327f.; Róheim Animism, Magic, and the Divine King 1ff.; Jastrow Religion of Babylonia and Assyria 475ff. — Cf. Stories of knights of the Round Table, e.g. Galahad. — *Crane Vitry 237 No. 247; Herbert Catalogue of Romances III 20; Irish myth: Cross. — N. A. Indian: *Thompson Tales 335 n. 209a.

D1837. Magic weakness. T300. Chastity and celibacy.

C112. *Tabu: sexual intercourse with unearthly beings.* (Cf. C122.) — English: Child V 500 s.v. "unearthly". — Icel.: MacCulloch Eddic 321—22; Herrmann Saxo II 588, Boberg; S. Am. Indian (Lengua): Métraux BBAE CXLIII (1) 369.

F300. Marriage or liaison with fairy. T11. Marriage of mortal and supernatural being. T118. Girl married to a monster. T539.3. Conception from intercourse with demon.

C113. *Tabu: sodomy.* Hebrew: Leviticus 20: 15f.; Jewish: Neuman.

B600. Marriage of person to animal. T460. Sexual perversion.

C114. *Tabu: incest.* **Rank Inzestmotiv. — Hebrew: Leviticus 20: 11ff.; Jewish: Neuman; India: *Thompson-Balys.

A1018. Flood as punishment for incest. T410. Incest. Q242. Incest punished.

C114.1. *Tabu: son seeing mother perform sex act.* India: Thompson-Balys.

C312. Tabu: man looking at woman.

C114.2. *Sex tabu: man—niece.* Chinese: Eberhard FFC CXX 90 No. 50.

C115. *Tabu: adultery.* Hebrew: Leviticus 20: 10; Exodux 20:14.

Q241. Adultery punished.

C116. *Tabu: sexual intercourse in sacred precinct.* (Cf. Q551.3.) — *Krappe Balor 82ff.; Jewish: Neuman; Icelandic: Boberg.

C93. Tabu: trespassing sacred precinct.

C117. *Nuptial tabu.* Man and wife forbidden intercourse for definite time. — *Schoepperle Tristan and Isolt II 298; Crawley Mystic Rose (1902) 343ff.; *DeVries Zs. f. deutsche Philologie LIII 276ff.; Penzer II 248, VIII 25 n. 1. — Irish myth: Cross; Norse: Elton Saxo Grammaticus xxxi, 319, Corpus Poeticum Boreale II 347, Ragnarssage Loðbrókar 128; Greek: Frazer Apollodorus I 169 n. 2; India: Thompson-Balys; N. A. Indian: *Thompson Tales 335 n. 209; Calif. Indian: Gayton and Newman 99; Eskimo (Greenland): Holm 47, Rasmussen III 134.

C751.2. Tabu: sleeping with certain wife on Midsummer's Eve. T151. Year's respite for unwelcome marriage. T165. Girl may remain virgin for three days after marriage. T350. Chaste sleeping together.

C117.1. *Tabu: intercourse with resuscitated wife for particular number of days.* Marquesas: Handy 113.

C118. *Tabu: violating woman.* Irish myth: Cross.

C885.2. Tabu: listening to groans of woman being violated. T471. Rape.

C118.1. *Tabu: violating insane woman.* Irish myth: Cross.

C119. *Miscellaneous tabus concerning sexual intercourse.*

C119.1. *Tabu: sexual intercourse at certain time.* Jewish: Neuman.

C119.1.1. *Tabu: sexual intercourse during illness.* Irish myth: Cross.

C119.1.2. *Tabu: sexual intercourse on Sabbath.* Jewish: Neuman.
C631. Tabu: violating Sabbath.

C119.1.3. *Tabu: intercourse at hunting season.* Samoyed: Holmberg Finno-Ugric 84.

C119.1.4. *Tabu: sexual intercourse during religious festival* (18 days). India: Thompson-Balys.

C119.1.5. *Tabu: intercourse before worship.* India: Thompson-Balys.

C119.1.6. *Tabu: intercourse at night.* India: Thompson-Balys.

C119.2. *Tabu: failure to sleep with guest unaccompanied by husband.* Irish myth: Cross.
T281. Sex hospitality.

C120. **Tabu: kissing.** Usually causes disenchantment or magic forgetfulness. (Cf. D735, D2003.) — *Type 313C, 410. — Grimm Nos. 113, 186, 193; Italian Novella: Rotunda.
D735. Disenchantment by kiss. D1794. Magic results from kissing. D2003. Forgotten fiancée.

C121. *Tabu: kissing supernatural husband.* (Cf. C32.) *Type 425; BP II 234, 236 n. 1, 271; Sébillot France I 244, III 291; Dickson Valentine and Orson 55.

C122. *Tabu: kissing fairies.* This puts one in their power. (Cf. C112.) — English: Child I 322 and n., 325; Wimberly Folklore in Ballads 282ff.
F302.3.4.1. Fairy's kiss fatal.

C130. **Tabu connected with puberty.** Irish myth: Cross.

C131. *Tabu: girl going forth at puberty.* Kaffir: Theal 17, cf. 67. — N. A. Indian: Curtin Myths of the Modocs 68.

C132. *Tabu: male presence in girl's puberty-hut.* Zulu: Callaway 74, 85.

C140. **Tabu connected with menses.** Jewish: *Neuman; Hawaii: Beckwith Myth 530f; India: Thompson-Balys.

C141. *Tabu: going forth during menses.* Frazer Golden Bough III 145ff., X 76ff.; Hebrew: Leviticus 15: 19ff.; India: Thompson-Balys.

C141.1. *Tabu: menstrous woman not to go near any cultivated field* or crops will be ruined. India: *Thompson-Balys.

C141.2. *Tabu: not to enter cowshed during menses.* India: Thompson-Balys.

C141.3. *Tabu: not to enter water during menses.* S. Am. Indian (Toba): Métraux MAFLS XL 29.

C142. *Tabu: sexual intercourse during menses.* Hebrew: Leviticus 20: 18; Jewish: Neuman; India: *Thompson-Balys.
C110. Tabu: sexual intercourse.

C143. *Tabu: eating from hands of menstruating women.* India: Thompson-Balys.
C240. Tabu: eating food of certain person.

C144. *Ground defiled by menstrual blood.* Jewish: Neuman; India: Thompson-Balys.

C145. *Tabu: not to touch certain things during menses.* Jewish: Neuman; India: Thompson-Balys.

C500. Tabu: touching.

C146. *Women must wear certain things during menstruation.*

C146.1. *Menstruating women must wear amulet of leaves* when approaching certain valley. Hawaii: Beckwith Myth 212..

C150. Tabu connected with childbirth.

C531.1. Unbilical cord not to be cut with iron.

C151. *Tabu: man not to be present at childbirth.* (Cf. C31.1.4.) — English: Child I 179, 181—3, 245f., 502a; II 98, 106f., 414, 418, 422, 499; IV 250a, 464; V236; Dickson Valentine and Orson 169 n. 20; *Boje 125.

T580. Childbirth.

C152. *Tabus during pregnancy.* *Frazer Golden Bough I 141 n., III 147; *Fb "glød", "grav", "gryn", "hul", "hvid" I 700b, "hår" I 771a, "ild" II 11b, "karklud", "kaste" II 103a, "kniv" II 221. — India: Thompson-Balys.

T570. Pregnancy.

C152.1. *Tabu: violence to woman during pregnancy.* Irish myth: Cross.

C152.2. *Tabu: refusing unreasonable demand of pregnant woman.* Irish myth: Cross; India: Thompson- Balys.

C871. Tabu: refusing a request. T571. Unreasonable demands of pregnant woman.

C152.3. *Eating tabus for pregnant woman.*

C200. Tabu: eating — general.

C152.3.1. *Pregnant woman not to eat food baked overnight.* India: Thompson-Balys.

C152.3.2. *Certain foods tabu one (two) months before childbirth.* S. Am. Indian (Brazil): Oberg 110.

C153. *Tabu: contact with woman at childbirth.* Frazer Golden Bough III 147ff., X 20.

C153.1. *Tabu: carrying corpse of woman who died in childbirth.* Jewish: *Neuman.

C154. *Tabus following childbirth.*

C154.1. *Food tabus following childbirth.* Eskimo (Greenland): Rasmussen II 295, (Cumberland Sound): Boas BAM XV 312.

C160. Tabu connected with marriage.

C566.4. Tabu: women marrying until hero has chosen their husbands. C751.2. Tabu: sleeping with certain wife on Midsummer's Eve. T131. Marriage restrictions.

C161. *Tabus for girl going to her husband.* Kaffir: Theal 49.

C162. *Tabu: marriage with certain person.*

C567. Tabu: eloping with king's daughter.

C162.1. *Tabu: marrying queen of certain race.* Irish myth: Cross.

C162.1.1. *Tabu: fairy girl marrying mortal.* India: Thompson-Balys; Korean: Zong in-Sob 30 No. 13.

F303. Fairy weds prince.

C162.2. *Tabu: marrying unmanly person.* Irish myth: Cross.

C162.3. *Tabu: marrying outside of group (or caste).* Jewish: *Neuman.

C163. *Tabu: neglecting sexual relations in marriage.* Irish myth: Cross.

C164. *Tabu: forcing wife.* Irish myth: Cross.

C165. *Tabu: marriage with person whose blood one has drunk.* Irish myth: Cross.

P312. Blood brotherhood. T61.1. Betrothal by lovers drinking each other's blood. T410. Incest.

C167. *Tabu: playing at marriage ceremony.*

C167.1. *Boy who plays marriage-game finds he has actually been married to a spirit* (invisible during ceremony). India: Thompson-Balys.

C168. *Tabu: disregarding dream warning against marriage.*

C168.1. *Woman marries in spite of warning dream.* Bears blind child who soon dies. India: Thompson-Balys.

D1812.3.3. Divination through interpretation of dreams. T311.0.1. Woman's aversion to marriage motivated through a dream.

C169. *Tabu connected with marriage — miscellaneous.*

C169.1. *Tabu: not to lay down basket carrying bride on wedding journey.* India: Thompson-Balys.

C169.2. *Tabu: giving younger daughter in marriage before elder.* Jewish: Neuman.

C170. Tabu connected with husband's or wife's relatives.

C435.1. Tabu: uttering name of other close relations. P282.3. Stepmother in love with stepson.

C171. *Mother-in-law tabu.* Mother-in-law and son-in-law must not have anything to do with each other. — *Frazer Golden Bough XII 378 s.v. "mother-in-law"; *Andree Ethnographische Parallelen (1878) 159. — Jewish: Neuman; Africa (Zulu): Calaway 164, (Upoto): Einstein 129.

C172. *Sister-in-law tabu:* older brother must avoid younger brother's wife. Jewish: Neuman; India: Thompson-Balys.

C173. *Daughter-in-law tabu.* Jewish: Neuman.

C180. Tabu confined to one sex.

C550. Class tabu.

C181. *Tabu confined to women.* Irish myth: Cross.

C229.2. Tabu: women not to eat genitals of animals. C313.1. Tabu: woman looking at nude man. C566.3. Tabu: women leaving hero's land without his knowing it. C619.4. Tabu: women to be on certain island. D1982.1. Magic door invisible to women.

C181.1. *Tabu: woman not to touch husband's drum (magic object).* Africa (Basuto): Jacottet 176 No. 25, (Ekoi): Talbot 18.

C500. Tabu: touching.

C181.2. *Tabu: women not to participate in hunting activities.* Lappish: Holmberg Finno-Ugric 84.

C229.2. Tabu: women not to eat genitals of animals.

C181.3. *Tabu: women not to touch man's weapons.* (Cf. C835.2.) — *Krappe Études de Mythologie 115ff., Jewish: Neuman; Icelandic: Boberg.

C181.4. *Tabu: women not to climb on roof.* India: Thompson-Balys.

C181.5. *Tabu: Baiga women not to tie cloth between legs.* India: Thompson-Balys.

C181.6. *Tabu: Bondo women not to wear clothes.* India: Thompson-Balys.

C181.7. *Grave (of man) upon which no women can look* without foolish laugh or "sine crepitu ventris eius." Irish myth: Cross.

C181.8. *Tabu: women not to eat pork.* India: Thompson-Balys.

C181.9. *Tabu: Saora women not to wear gold earrings.* India: Thompson-Balys.

C181.10. *Tabu: women riding in canoe.* Marquesas: Handy 134.

C181.11. *Mare not to be yoked to cart drawing corpse.* McKay, Beal III 141.

C181.12. *Tabu: woman sacrificing in temple.* Jewish: Neuman.

C182. *Tabu confined to men.*

C312. Tabu: man looking at woman. C565. Tabus of bearded men. C686.1. Tabu: to refuse help to a woman. C867. Tabu: abusing women or children. J21.22. "Do not tell a secret to a woman." N134.1. Unlucky to have man in house while cloth is being dyed.

C182.1. *Tabu: men fishing at certain place.* India: Thompson-Balys.

C182.2. *Tabu: man entering woman's quarters in her absence.* Tonga: Gifford 53.

C190. Sex tabu — miscellaneous.

C31.5. Tabu: boasting of supernatural wife. C435. Tabu: uttering spouse's name. C453. Tabu: boasting love-conquest.

C191. *Tabu: mortal lusting after goddess.* Greek: Frazer Apollodorus I 28 n. 2; India: Thompson-Balys.

A180. Gods in relation to mortals.

C192. *Tabu: refusing to elope with woman who desires it.* Irish myth: Cross.

C567. Tabu: eloping with king's daughter. T55. Girl as wooer.

C193. *Tabu: consorting with a woman.* Irish myth: Cross; Jewish: Neuman.

C111. Tabu: loss of chastity.

C193.1. *Tabu: woman being in one's dwelling.* Irish myth: Cross.

C194. *Tabu: trysting with woman at certain place.* Irish myth: Cross.

C610. The one forbidden place.

C194.1. *Tabu: embracing at village gate.* India: Thompson-Balys.

C195. *Tabu: taking the advice of a woman.* Irish myth: Cross.

J21.22. "Do not tell a secret to a woman." T453. Getting advice from a woman in bed.

C196. *Tabu: asking for king's daughter in marriage.* India: *Thompson-Balys.

C567. Tabu: eloping with king's daughter. P40. Princesses.

C200—C299. Eating and drinking tabu.

C200—C249. EATING TABUS

C200. Tabu: eating (general). **Schurtz (H). Die Speiseverbote, ein Problem der Volkskunde (Hamburg, 1893); *Frazer Golden Bough III 116ff.; *Type 400. — Irish myth: Cross; India: *Thompson-Balys; Indonesian: DeVries' list No. 205; Borneo: Dixon 181; Lepers' Island: Ibid. 127. — Zuñi: Parsons JAFL XXIX 393.

D550. Transformation by eating or drinking. D1365.3. Food causes magic forgetfulness. D1766.8. Magic results from fasting. D1766.8.1. Fasting a part of magic ritual. P623. Fasting as a means of distraint. V462.2. Ascetic fasting.

C205. *Tabu: eating one's fill.* Africa (Wakweli): Bender 43.

C210. Tabu: eating in certain place. India: Thompson-Balys.

C211. *Tabu: eating in other world.* *Cosquin Études Folkloriques 192; *Fb "mad" II 524b; Golther Germanische Mythologie 477; Hdwb. d. Abergl. II 1053; Güntert Kalypso 154ff.; Boberg Bjergfolkenes Bagning (DF XLVI) 56ff. — Norse: Herrmann Saxo II 586ff., Mac Culloch Eddic 321; *Greek: Frazer Apollodorus I 39 n. 4, Gaster Thespis 191, Oldest Stories 232; India: Thompson-Balys; N. A. Indian: *Thompson Tales 338 n. 217c.; Melanesian: Codrington 277; Hawaii: Beckwith Myth 148.

C262. Tabu: drinking in other world. C710. Tabus connected with otherworld journeys.

C211.1. *Tabu: eating in fairyland.* *Fb "spise" III 495a; Feilberg Bjærgtagen 15f., 19, 28, 56—64, 100; Hartland Science 38—43, 144. — English-Scottish: Child I 322—5, 327, II 505, IV 455, 458, Wimberly Folklore in Ballads, 159, 275ff.; Irish myth: Cross, MacCulloch Celtic 90* n. 19; Wales: Baughman.

C242. Tabu: eating food of witch (demon). C661. Girl from elfland must eat earthly food in order to remain. C712.1. Tabu: staying too long in fairyland. F210. Fairyland. F378. Tabus connected with trip to fairyland. F384.1.2. Salt sprinkled on fairy food renders it harmless.

C211.2. *Tabu: eating in lower world.* *Penzer VI 133. — English-Scottish: Child I 322—9 passim. — Maori: Dixon 77; Jewish: Bin Gorion Born Judas I (2d. ed.) 228, VI 64.

C225.1. Tabu: eating pomegranate seed.

C211.2.1. *Tabu: eating in land of ghosts.* *Hartland Science 45. — Africa (Ekoi): Talbot 210, 240; Maori: Clark 8.

C211.2.2. *Tabu: eating in hell (hades).* *Fb "mad" II 524.

C211.3. *Tabu: sky dwellers eating on earth.* Africa (Cameroon): Rosenhuber 38.

C211.3.1. *Tabu: goddess eating on earth.* Ila: Smith and Dale 347.

C211.3.2. *Tabu: fairies eating mortal food.* Irish myth: Cross.

F243.0.1. Christianized fairy woman refuses to eat fairy food.

C215. *Married man not to eat in country of his parents.* Fjort: Dennett 43 No. 6.

C219. *Tabu: eating from certain place — miscellaneous.*

C219.1. *Tabu: eating from ground.* Youth will eat only when on ox. Zulu: Callaway 221.

C219.2. *Tabu: eating from fine pots.* Basuto: Jacottet 142 No. 20.

C219.3. *Tabu: eating off new mats.* Kaffir: Theal 86.

C219.4. *Tabu: eating from cooking hearth.* Irish myth: Cross.

C220. **Tabu: eating certain things.** India: Thompson-Balys.

A1517. Origin of eating tabus. C152.3. Pregnant woman not to eat food baked overnight. C569.2. Touching food of another caste.

C220.1. *Tabu: eating food produced by a spell.* Marquesas: Handy 114.

C221. *Tabu: eating meat.* Hdwb. d. Abergl. IX Nachträge 811; Eskimo (Greenland): Holm 93, Rasmussen II 233, (Mackenzie Area): Jenness 76, (West Hudson Bay): Boas BAM 327. — Malory Morte Darthur XV 2; Ekoi: Talbot 409.

C235. Tabu: eating flesh on Maundy Thursday.

C221.1. *Tabu: eating flesh of certain animal.* Irish myth: Cross; Hebrew: Leviticus, ch. 11; India: Thompson-Balys; Buddhist myth: Malalasekera II 636.

C221.1.1. *Tabu: eating flesh of certain beast.*

C221.1.1.1. *Tabu: eating cow.*

C221.1.1.1.1. *Tabu: eating ox.* India: Thompson-Balys; Africa (Basuto): Jacottet 72 No. 11.

C221.1.1.1.2. *Tabu: eating calf.* *Fb "kalvekjød" II 81.

C221.1.1.1.3. *Tabu: killing and cooking sacred cow.* India: Thompson-Balys.

V811.3. Sacred cow.

C221.1.1.2. *Tabu: eating horsemeat.* Irish myth: Cross.

C756.4. Tabu: entering chariot less than three weeks after having eaten horseflesh. Q499.6. Penance for three years and a half for eating horseflesh.

C221.1.1.3. *Eating seal meat.* Eskimo (Cumberland Sound): Boas BAM XV200.

C221.1.1.4. *Tabu: eating dog.* Jewish: Neuman; India: Thompson-Balys.

C221.1.1.5. *Tabu: eating pork.* Leviticus ch. 2; Isa. 65: 4; 66: 3ff.; (Egypt, Mohammedan, Crete). — Jewish: Neuman; Africa (Fang): Tessman 195.

C221.1.1.6. *Tabu: eating weasel.* Jewish: Neuman.

C221.1.1.7. *Tabu: eating mouse.* Jewish: Neuman.

C221.1.2. *Tabu: eating bird.* Marquesas: Handy 64, 131.

C221.1.2.1. *Tabu: eating cassawary.* Papua: Ker 90.

C221.1.2.2. *Tabu: eating pigeon.* Marquesas: Handy 67.

C221.1.2.3. *Eating dove.* (Cf. C549.) Jewish: Neuman.

C221.1.2.4. *Tabu: eating eagle.* Africa (Pangwe): Tessman 370, (Fang): Tessman 162.

C221.1.3. *Tabu: eating fish.* New Guinea: Ker 52; China: Eberhard FFC CXX 85f.

C221.1.3.1. *Tabu: eating certain fish.* Jewish: *Neuman.

C221.1.3.2. *Tabu: eating eel.* Rarotonga: Beckwith Myth 262.

C221.1.3.3. *Tabu: eating crabs.* Mono-Alu: Wheeler 44.

C221.1.3.4. *Tabu: eating shark.* Tonga: Gifford 80.

C221.2. *Eating totem animal* (or animal namesake). Frazer Golden Bough VIII 25ff. — Irish myth: Cross, MacCulloch Celtic 156; India: Thompson-Balys. — Hupa: Goddard UCal I 154; Iroquois: Smith RBAE II 85; Eskimo (Mackenzie Area): Jenness 52; African: *Werner African 276ff.; Tshi: Ellis Tshi-Speaking Peoples 211. — Australian: Parker 40ff.; Bougainville: Wheeler 58.

C848. Tabu: sleeping on bed made of totem-tree. B2. Animal totems. C92. Tabu: killing sacred being. C841.7. Tabu: killing totem animal. C847. Tabu: giving away gifts received from animal.

C221.2.1. *Tabu: eating animal helper.* India: Thompson-Balys; Chinese: Eberhard 217 No. 167; Wyandot: Barbeau GSCan XI 103—131, Nos. 28—38.

B330. Death of helpful animal. B549.6. Tiger guides lost man home: hence men do not eat tigers.

C221.3. *Tabu: eating certain parts of animals.* *Encyc. Religion and Ethics I 492b.

C221.3.1. *Tabu: eating animal's genitals.* (Cf. C229.2.) — Africa (Ekoi): Talbot 409.

C221.3.2. *Tabu: breaking bones of eaten animal.* Saintyves Contes de Perrault 39. Cf. also E32.

C221.3.3. *Tabu: eating bird's eggs at certain time of year.* Easter Island: Métraux Ethnology 312.

C221.3.4. *Tabu: eating blubber.* Eskimo (Greenland): Rasmussen III 244.

C221.3.4.1. *Tabu: eating fat of animals.* (Cf. C229.) — Jewish: *Neuman.

C221.3.5. *Tabu: eating heart of animal* (to commemorate relative whose heart was removed by king.) — Chinese: Graham.

C221.3.6. *Tabu: eating sinew of thigh vein.* Jewish: *Neuman.

C221.4. *Tabu: eating animal taken under certain circumstances.*

C221.4.1. *Tabu: wife eating first animal caught in trap.* Ekoi: Talbot 114.

C221.4.2. *Tabu: eating fish caught with fish-hook made without proper incantations.* Maori: Clark 154.

C221.4.3. *Tabu: eating animals recklessly killed.* Hawaii: Beckwith Myth 138.

C221.5. *Tabu: eating live animals or live parts of them.* Jewish: *Neuman.

C224. *Tabu: eating certain vegetable.*

C224.1. *Tabu: eating beans.* *Frazer Pausanias IV 240.

C224.2. *Tabu: eating forbidden herbs.* India: Thompson-Balys.

C224.3. *Tabu: eating breadfruit.* Mono: Wheeler 33.

C224.4. *Tabu: horses' eating foreign provender.* Greek: *Grote II 130.

C225. *Tabu: eating certain fruit.* Benga: Nassau 140 No. 16; India: Thompson-Balys; S. Am. Indian (Tupenamba): Métraux RMLP XXXIII 172; Jewish: Neuman.

A1331.1. Paradise lost because of forbidden fruit. C621. Forbidden tree.

C225.1. *Tabu: eating pomegranate seed.* Greek: Fox 229.

C211.2. Tabu: eating in lower world.

C226. *Tabu: eating certain plant.*

C226.0.1. *Why slayers of tigers must not eat certain plants.* India: Thompson-Balys.

C227. *Tabu: eating human flesh.*

C227.1. *Why cannibalism is out of vogue.* New Guinea: Ker 13.

G0. Cannibalism.

C229. *Tabu: eating certain thing — miscellaneous.*

C229.1. *Tabu: eating thick milk.* Kaffir: Theal 49.

C229.2. *Tabu: women not to eat genitals (heart, liver, etc.) of animals.* (Cf. C221.3.1.) — Nippigen Revue Anthropologique XIV 399. — Ekoi: Talbot 409.

C181. Tabu confined to women. C933. Luck in hunting lost for breaking tabu.

C229.3. *Tabu: eating griddle cakes* (in Garden of Eden). — India: Thompson-Balys.

C229.4. *Tabu: eating firstlings* (animals, fruit, etc.) — Jewish: Neuman.

C229.5. *Eating meat with milk.* (Cf. C271). — Jewish: *Neuman.

C229.6. *Tabu: eating salt.* Africa (Togo): Einstein 8f.; Jewish: Neuman.

C230. **Tabu: eating at certain time.** Irish: Beal XXI 314; Jewish: *Neuman.

C755. Tabu: doing thing during certain time.

C230.1. *Tabu: feasting for a week.* Irish myth: Cross.

C231. *Tabu: eating before certain time.* Irish myth: Cross.

M151. Vow not to eat before hearing of adventure.

C231.1. *Tabu: girl eating before being called by father.* India: Thompson-Balys; Zulu: Callaway 192.

C231.2. *Tabu: eating before task is finished.* Zuñi: Boas JAFL XXXV 76 No. 4.

C231.3. *Tabu: eating before offering woman food.* Irish myth: Cross.

C231.3.1. *Tabu: eating of magic catch before mother does.* Eskimo (Greenland): Rasmussen II 233.

C231.4. *Tabu: eating before house of host has been righted.* Irish myth: Cross.

C231.5. *Eight handfuls of food only to be eaten during ceremony.* India: Thompson-Balys.

C231.6. *Tabu: eating before three years have passed.* Jewish: Neuman.

C232. *Tabu: eating on journey.* Benga: Nassau 129 No. 14; India: Thompson-Balys.

C232.1. *Tabu: bride eating on journey to husband.* Kaffir: Theal 51.

C234. *Tabu: eating while on visit home.* *Type 400.

C235. *Tabu: eating flesh on Maundy Thursday.* Irish myth: Cross.
C221. Tabu: eating meat.

C236. *Tabu: eating after a guest.* Irish myth: Cross.

C237. *Tabu: feasting by night at beginning of harvest.* Irish myth: Cross.

C240. Tabu: eating food of certain person.
C143. Tabu: eating from the hands of menstruating woman.

C241. *Tabu: eating food of gods.* Babylonian: Spence 119f.; India: Thompson-Balys. — Africa (Ekoi): Talbot 183.
A153. Food of the gods. C211.1. Tabu: eating in fairy-land.

C241.1. *Tabu: tasting milk of "cow of plenty", dedicated to the gods.* India: Thompson-Balys.

C241.2. *Tabu: eating chief's food.* Samoa: Beckwith Myth 512.

C243. *Tabu: eating food of transformed husband.* Ila (Rhodesia): Smith and Dale 403.

D243.1. *Tabu: eating food of supernatural lover.* India: Thompson-Balys.

C245. *Tabu: eating food birds have pecked at.* *Fb "fugl" I 380b.

C246. *Tabu: eating with person of certain caste.* India: Thompson-Balys.
C569.2. Tabu: touching food of another caste.

C246.1. *Tabu: Jews eating with heathen.* Jewish: *Neuman.

C246.2. *Tabu: eating special food of noble girl.* Mono: Wheeler XIII 56.

C247. *Tabu: eating food laid on the grave.* Cheremis: Sebeok-Nyerges.

C248. *Tabu: eating food kept for animals.* India: Thompson-Balys.

C250—C279. DRINKING TABUS

C250. Tabu: drinking. Type 400; Penzer VI 135. — Finnish: Kalevala rune 16. — N. A. Indian: Thompson Tales 338 n. 217b.; Eskimo (Greenland): Rasmussen II 226.
D550. Transformation by eating or drinking. D1365.2. Drink causes magic forgetfulness.

C260. Tabu: drinking at certain place.

C261. *Tabu: drinking from certain fountain.* Hartland Science 225; Irish myth: Cross; Eskimo (Greenland): Rink 417, 465; Africa (Loango): Pechuël-Loesche 109.
C623. Forbidden well. V134. Sacred (holy) wells.

C262. *Tabu: drinking in other world.* *Fb "drikke" I 204. — Wales: Baughman; Icel.: Herrmann Saxo II 586ff., MacCulloch Eddic 321f., Boberg.
C211. Tabu: eating in other world. C712.1. Tabu: staying too long in fairyland.

C263. *Tabu: drinking from certain river between two darknesses.* Irish myth: Cross.

C755. Tabu: doing thing during certain time.

C270. **Tabu: drinking certain things.** Breton: Sébillot Incidents s. v. "boisson"; Irish myth: Cross.

V383.2. Hindu drinks water by mistake from Mohammedan's vessel: his fortune turns to evil.

C271. *Tabu: drinking milk.* India: Thompson-Balys.

C272. *Tabu: drinking wine.* (Cf. C251.) — Jewish: Neuman, Moreno: Esdras.

C272.1. *Tabu: drinking wine touched by hand of heathen.* Jewish: Neuman.

C272.2. *Tabu: drinking wine at certain time.* (Cf. C755.) — Jewish: *Neuman.

C272.3. *Tabu: drinking palm-drink:* only prince allowed to break it. Africa (Fang): Einstein 45, Trilles 163.

C273. *Tabu: drinking water.*

C273.1. *Tabu: drinking water during certain time.* Jewish: Neuman.

C755. Doing thing during certain time.

C273.2. *Tabu: drinking water from certain bottle.* Chinese: Eberhard 214 No. 113.

C280 **Miscellaneous eating and drinking tabus.**

C281. *Tabu: drinking without presence of dead heads.* Irish myth: Cross.

S139.2.2.1.1. Heads (tongues) of slain enemies as trophies.

C282. *Tabu: refusing a feast.* Irish myth: Cross.

C744. Tabu: accepting an invitation. P320. Hospitality. P634. Feasts. Q1. Hospitality rewarded, opposite punished.

C282.1. *Tabu: leaving a feast before it is ended.* Irish myth: Cross.

C874. Tabu: breaking up revelry before its end.

C283. *Tabu: eating without giving thanks.* Irish myth: Cross.

C284. *Tabu: eating alone.* Irish myth: Cross.

C285. *Tabu: eating in company.* Irish myth: Cross.

C286. *Tabu: partaking of certain feast.* Irish myth: Cross.

C287. *Tabu: consuming feast without discovering a new wonder.* Irish myth: Cross.

C564.1. Tabu: chief being in ale-house when there is no storytelling. M151. Vow not to eat before hearing of adventure. W213. Man will not allow food served to stranger until a man of them wrestles with him.

C288. *Tabu: refusing to eat food demanded and supplied.* Irish myth: Cross.

J1512.1. Milk from the hornless cow.

C300—C399. Looking tabu.

C300. **Looking tabu.** *Fb "se" III 172b. — Breton: Sébillot Incidents s. v. "vue"; Greek: Fox 67 (Pandrosus), Odyssey VII line 20. — Irish myth: Cross; India: *Thompson-Balys; Chinese: Graham; Javanese: Dixon 209; N. A. Indian: *Thompson Tales 338 n. 217; Eskimo (Greenland): Rink 385; S. Am. Indian (Cherentes, Amazonian): Alexander Lat. Am. 308, (Mataco): Métraux MAFLS XL 35.

D2121.2. Magic journey with closed eyes. Person must not open eyes while on the journey. E251.1.1. Vampire's power overcome by endurance and prayer. Hero continues to pray without looking or speaking while vampire punishes him.

C310. Tabu: looking at certain person or thing.

D513.1. Man looks at copulating snakes: transformed to woman.

C311. *Tabu: seeing the supernatural.* *Fb "se" III 173a; Irish myth: Cross.

C31.1. Tabu: looking at supernatural wife. C32.1. Tabu: looking at supernatural husband. C51.4.2. Tabu: spying on secret help of angels.

C311.1. *Tabu: seeing supernatural creatures.* S. Am. Indian (Toba): Métraux MAFLS XL 50.

C311.1.1. *Tabu: looking at ghosts.* Fb "sygdom" III 699a. — India: Thompson-Balys.

E561.1. Sight of dead woman spinning drives people insane.

C311.1.1.1. *Tabu: looking through the upturned sleeve of a fur coat.* One sees ghosts. Lithuanian: Balys Ghosts.

C311.1.2. *Tabu: looking at fairies.* Fb "sygdom" III 699a. — Irish myth: Cross; England, Wales: Baughman.

C51.4.3. Tabu: spying on secret help of fairies. F200. Fairies (elves). F348.5. Mortal not to recognize fairy who gives him gift. F361.3. Fairies take revenge on person who spies on them.

C311.1.3. *Tabu: looking at mountain-folk.* Fb "sygdom" III 699a.

F460. Mountain-spirits.

C311.1.4. *Tabu: looking at werewolf.* Fb "stum". — Irish myth: Cross.

D113.1.1. Werwolf.

C311.1.5. *Tabu: observing supernatural helper.* Chinese: Eberhard 217 No. 167.

N810. Supernatural helpers.

C311.1.6. *Tabu: seeing witch in her true form.* German: Grimm No. 43.

G100. Witches.

C311.1.7. *Tabu: looking at slain game before it dies.* Eskimo (Central Eskimo): Boas RBAE VI 620.

C311.1.8. *Tabu: looking at deity.* Jewish: Neuman.

C311.1.8.1. *Gods flee at approach of dawn.* (Cf. E452.) Tonga: Gifford 140.

C311.2. *Tabu: looking at holy objects.* Jewish: Neuman.

C312. *Tabu: man looking at woman.* Irish myth: Cross.

C114.1. Tabu: son seeing mother perform sex act. F1041.32. Death from shame.

C312.1. *Tabu: man looking at nude woman.* Irish myth: Cross; Icelandic: Boberg; Gaster Thespis 328, Oldest Stories 142.

A1383.3. Shame for nakedness appears to first woman. C942.3. Weakness from seeing woman naked. F1041.32.1. Girl dies of shame at being seen naked. K774. Capture by sight of woman's breasts. T55.6. Person exhibits figure.

C312.1.1. *Tabu: man looking at nude goddess.* Greek: *Frazer Apollodorus I 363 n. 1 (Tiresias), Fox 46, 185 (Acteon), Grote I 238; Jewish: Neuman; India: Thompson-Balys.

C31.1.3. Tabu: looking at supernatural wife naked. C52. Tabu: being in presence of god. C943. Loss of sight for breaking tabu. Q221. Personal offences against gods punished. Q415.1.1. Punishment: transformation to deer which is devoured by dogs.

C312.1.2. *Tabu: looking at nude woman riding through town.* (Godiva.) — Hartland "Peeping Tom and Lady Godiva" FL I 207; Liebrecht Zur Volkskunde 105; English: Baughman.

M235. Godiva.

C312.2. *Tabu: looking at woman (miscellaneous).*

C312.2.1. *Tabu: looking at princess on public appearance.* *Chauvin V 61 No. 19; India: Thompson-Balys.

P40. Princesses.

C312.2.2. *Tabu: looking at old woman helper as she eats.* Gold Coast: Barker and Sinclair 90 No. 16.

C312.2.3. *Tabu: looking at supernatural woman who is dismembered.* Cheremis: Sebeok-Nyerges.

C312.2.4. *Tabu: looking at women performing Bacchic rites.* Greek: Grote I 239.

C312.3. *Tabu: on looking at daughter for twelve years.* India: *Thompson-Balys.

C313. *Tabu: woman looking at man.*

C313.0.1. *Tabu: princess never to see male person.* All men must hide when she goes forth. India: Thompson-Balys.

C313.1. *Tabu: woman seeing nude man.* Greek: Odyssey VI line 128 (Odysseus).

F647.4. Marvelous sensitiveness: women blush. F1041.32.2. Woman dies of shame at seeing naked man (husband).

C313.1.1. *Tabu: goddess seeing mortal husband naked.* Hindu: Keith 95.

C315. *Tabu: looking at certain object.*

C51.1. Tabu: profaning shrine. C93. Tabu: trespassing on sacred precinct.

C315.1. *Tabu: looking at certain boat.* Breton: Sébillot Incidents s.v. "bateau". — Eskimo (Greenland): Rink 375, Rasmussen I 239.

C315.2. *Tabu: looking at heavenly body.*

C315.2.1. *Looking at moon when shooting game.* Bushman: Bleek and Lloyd 67.

C315.2.2. *Tabu: looking at sun.* Eskimo (Smith Sound): Kroeber JAFL XII 180, (Greenland): Rink 441, Rasmussen III 51, Holm 72.

C315.2.2.1. *Tabu: looking at sun before prince becomes fourteen years old.* India: Thompson-Balys.

C756. Tabu: doing thing before certain time. M300. Prophecies.

C315.2.3. *Tabu: looking at rainbow.* Jewish: Neuman; S. Am. Indian (Toba): Métraux MAFLS XL 39.

C315.3. *Tabu: looking at water.* India: *Thompson-Balys.

C315.4. *Tabu: looking at certain well.* Irish myth: Cross.

C261. Tabu: drinking from certain fountain. F933.7. Well floods when gazed upon until mass said over it.

C315.5. *Tabu: looking on certain island.* Maori: Beckwith Myth 349.

C316. *Tabu: looking at certain animal.*

C316.1. *Tabu: seeing herd red-headed and white-starred.* Irish myth: Cross.

B731.4.1. Cow with white ears. B731.4.2. Cow with red ears.

C316.2. *Tabu: looking at caribou.* Eskimo (Cumberland Sound): Boas BAM XV 241.

C319. *Tabu: looking at certain person or thing — miscellaneous.*

C319.1. *Tabu: king forbidden to look at his son.* India: Thompson-Balys.

C319.2. *Tabu: seeing dead man not killed by weapons.* Irish myth: Cross.

Q227.4. Punishment for looking at saint's corpse.

C320. Tabu: looking into certain receptacle.

C321. *Tabu: looking into box (Pandora).* Köhler notes to Gonzenbach Sicilianische Märchen No. 15. — Greek: Hesiod Works and Days lines 81—104. — England: Baughman; Lithuanian: Balys Index No. *320; India: *Thompson-Balys; N. A. Indian: Thompson Tales 276 n. 19.

C915.1. Troubles escape when forbidden casket is opened. C915.1.1. Music-box continues playing when it is touched contrary to tabu. C922. Death by smothering for breaking tabu. N113. Casket with Good Luck in it given to men by Zeus.

C321.1. *Tabu: opening too much of magic box at a time.* A priest gives a prince a sealed packet which he is to open in time of distress. He must open only one portion at a time. — Chinese: Werner 230.

C321.2. *Tabu: opening gift box prematurely.* India: *Thompson-Balys.

C757. Tabu: doing thing too soon.

C322. *Tabu: looking into bag.* India: Thompson-Balys; Takelau (Samoa): Beckwith Myth 25.

A2003. Origin of insects: released from sack. Looking tabu broken.

C322.1. *Bag of winds.* Wind is confined in a bag. Man breaks prohibition against looking into bag and releases winds. — Greek: Fox 137, 266, Frazer Apollodorus II 285 n. 2; Estonian: FFC XXV 140 No. 9; Livonian: Loorits FFC LXVI 81 No. 13. — N. A. Indian: Thompson Tales 292 n. 72. — Oceanian: Dixon 55 (Samoan, coconut filled with winds; Chatham Islands, basket); Australian: ibid. 296f. (bag of waters.) — Cf. H. C. Andersen "Paradisets Have."

A1174.1. Night (darkness) in package. Released.

C322.2. *Tabu: opening bag too soon.* Welsh: Hartland Science 38.

C323. *Tabu: looking into flask.* Man given magic flask on condition that he never look into it. — Hartland Science 142; Fb "tønde" III 934b.

D1472.1.17. Magic bottle supplies drink.

C324. *Tabu: looking into jug.* Woman does so and finds mouse in it. — — Type 1416; *BP III 543 n. 1; *Fb "Adam" IV 3b; *Crane Vitry 139 No. 13; Krappe Bull. Hispanique XXXIX 44; Jewish: Neuman.

H1554.1. Test of curiosity: mouse in jug.

C324.1. *Tabu: looking into magic calabash.* African: (Yoruba): Frobenius Atlantis X 232f. No. 16.

D1470.1.4. Magic wishing-calabash.

C325. *Tabu: looking into the pots in hell.* Type 475; Köhler-Bolte I 69.

E755.2.1. Souls of drowned in heated kettles in hell. Q561.2. Kettle heating in hell for certain person.

C326. *Tabu: looking under certain bell too soon.* Chinese: Werner 421.

C327. *Tabu: looking into basket.* Congo: Weeks 206f. No. 3; Marquesas: Handy 120, 122.

C328. *Tabu: opening corpse-wrapping.* India: Thompson-Balys.

C330. Tabu: looking in certain direction.

A2234.3. Lemur looks where forbidden: has big eyes.

C331. *Tabu: looking back.* *Fb "se" III 173b; *Chauvin VII 98 No. 375; Hartland Science 236, 243; Samter Geburt, Hochzeit, Tod 147ff. — *Pease Cicero De Divinatione 182 (Bk I 49); Eitrem Hermes und die Toten (1909) 40f.; McCartney Papers of Michigan Academy of Science, Arts, and Letters XVI (1931) 147f. — Greek: Fox 147, Usener Kleine Schriften IV 455; Jewish: Neuman; Hindu: Caland Die altindischen Todten- und Bestattungsgebraüche 23, 73ff.; India: *Thompson-Balys; Fr. Canadian: Barbeau JAFL XXIX 11; Lithuanian: Balys Legends Nos. 503f.; Chinese: Eberhard FFC CXX 87 No. 7; Eskimo: Holm 19, Rink 164, 169, 299, (Cumberland Sound): Boas BAM XV 225; Tonga: Gifford 22; Hawaii: Beckwith Myth 499; Tuamotu: Stimson MS (z—G 3/1241); S. Am. Indian (Yuracare): Métraux BBAE CXLIII (3) 502; Africa (Fang): Trilles 156, 269, (Luba): DeClerq Zs. f. KS IV 197.

C312.1.1. Tabu: man looking at nude goddess. C875. Tabu: carrying child back into house. C943.1. Man receives fork in eye for breaking tabu. C953. Person must remain in other world because of broken tabu. C961.1. Transformation to pillar of salt because of breaking tabu. C961.2. Transformation to stone for breaking tabu. F81.1. Orpheus. Journey to land of dead to bring back person from the dead.

C331.1. *Tabu: looking back over left shoulder.* Irish myth: Cross.

C331.2. *Travelers to other world must not look back.* (See all references to F81.1., Orpheus.) — Eskimo (Greenland): Rink 169, 299, Rasmussen III 124, (Mackenzie Area): Jenness 51.

C331.3. *Tabu: looking back during flight.* Chinese: Eberhard FFC CXX 84.

C332. *Tabu: looking around.* Africa (Ekoi): Talbot 252.

C333. *Tabu: looking up.* Finnish: Kalevala rune 7.

C334. *Tabu: looking over cemetery walls, lest one see ghosts.* India: Thompson-Balys.

E400. Ghosts and revenants — miscellaneous.

C335. *Tabu: looking down upon earth from sky world.* S. Am. Indian (Toba): Métraux MAFLS XL 42.

C336. *Tabu: woman in other world forbidden to look behind curtains.* Kodiak: Golder JAFL XVI 30.

C337. *Tabu: looking up chimney.* Roberts Type 480, p. 175.

C400—C499. Speaking tabu.

C400. **Speaking tabu.** *Fb "stum"; *Type 451, 705, 710; Frazer Golden Bough XII 461 s.v. "silence", Wuttke Volksaberglaube 161, 323; Wimberly Folklore in Ballads 281; Rantasalo FFC XXXII 69ff.; F. L. Grundtvig Dania VI 184ff. — Irish myth: Cross; Icel.: Herrmann Saxo II 586ff., MacCulloch Eddic 321f., Boberg; Spanish Exempla: Keller; India: *Thompson-Balys. — N. A. Indian (Zuñi): Parsons JAFL XXIX 393; (Navaho): Alexander N. Am. 174, (Seneca): Curtin-Hewitt RBAE XXXII 90 No. 4.

D1741.3. Silence under punishment breaks power of enchantment. E251.1.1. Vampire's power overcome by endurance and prayer. Hero continues to pray without looking or speaking while vampire punishes him. E545.0.2. The dead are silent. H1199.3. Task: shouting from forbidden place. Q451.3. Loss of speech as punishment.

C401. *Tabu: speaking during certain time.* *Frazer Golden Bough XII 461 s.v. "silence". — Spanish Exempla: Keller; German: Grimm Nos. 9, 49, 137.

C755. Tabu: doing thing during certain time. D758. Disenchantment by maintaining silence. D2020. Magic dumbness. Q451.3. Loss of speech as punishment. Q535.1. Penance: not to speak.

C401.1. *Tabu: speaking during vigil.* *Types 307, 400; *BP II 330, 335, III 534; Wesselski Mönchslatein 101 No. 86; Hartland Science 246.

H1451. Test: speechless vigil in church.

C401.2. *Tabu: speaking during seven days of danger.* As result of prophecy of seven days of danger, an injunction of silence is imposed during this period. — Chauvin VIII 34 No. 1 n. 1; Spanish Exempla: Keller.

C401.3. *Tabu: speaking while searching for treasure.* *Fb "stiltiende" III 569a, "skat" III 236b; *Norlind Skattsägner 57ff. — Swiss Jegerlehner Oberwallis 298 No. 3; German: Grimm Deutsche Mythologie II 810ff., v.d. Leyen Sagenbuch IV 238ff.; Norwegian: Skar Gamalt or Sætesdal III 135ff.; Swedish-Finnish: Finlands Svenska Folkdiktning VII (1) 857 (register); Lappish: Qvigstad Lappiske Eventyr II No. 134; Egyptian: Legrain Louqsor sans les Pharaons 97. — England, U.S.: Baughman; North Carolina: Brown Collection I 693f. — Indonesian: Hambruch Malaiische Märchen 192.

N553.2. Unlucky encounter causes treasure-seekers to talk and thus lose treasure.

C401.3.1. *Tabu: speaking about lost money which is to be regained by witchcraft.* The loser cannot refrain from speaking of his loss; the money cannot be recovered. Eng.: Baughman.

C401.4. *Tabu: speaking while raising sunken church bell.* See all references to V115.1.3.1. — England, U.S.: Baughman*.

V115.1.3.1. Church bell cannot be raised because silence is broken.

C401.5. *Tabu: speaking while gathering fernseed* to make wishes come true, at midnight on Christmas Eve when fernseed ripens and falls immediately. Scotland: Baughman.

C401.6. *Tabu: speaking while taking a bath.* Jewish: Neuman.

C402. *Tabu: speaking before certain time.* Irish myth: Cross.

C756. Tabu: doing thing before certain time.

C402.1. *Tabu: king speaking before his druids speak.* Irish myth: Cross.

C560. Tabu: things not to be done by certain class. C563. Tabus of kings.

C402.2. *Tabu: people speaking before king speaks.* Irish myth: Cross.

C405. *Silence preserved in fairyland.* Irish myth: Cross.

E545.0.2. The dead are silent.

C410. Tabu: asking questions. *Chauvin V 251, 296, VIII 47 No. 15 n. 1. — India: Thompson-Balys.

C651. The one compulsory question.

C411. *Tabu: asking about marvels which one sees.* (Cf. C423.2, C491.) — *Chauvin V 251 No. 148. — African: Werner African 187.

C651. Hero must ask meaning of strange sights he sees (Percival). J21.6. "Do not ask questions about extraordinary things": counsel proved wise by experience. Those that ask question killed.

C411.1. *Tabu: asking for reason of an unusual action.* Spanish Exempla: Keller; Persian: Bricteux Contes Persans 97 No. 4; Indonesian: De Vries Volksverhalen I No. 35 n.

C413. *Tabu: expressing surprise in lower world of dead.* India: Thompson-Balys; African: Werner African 187.

C32.1.2. Tabu: showing surprise when supernatural husband resumes his true shape. C710. Tabus connected with otherworld journeys. F81. Descent to lower world of dead (Hell, Hades).

C415. *Tabu: asking prophet for signs.* Jewish: Neuman.

C420. Tabu: uttering secrets. Fb "sten" III 553b. — Irish myth: Cross; Jewish: Neuman; India: *Thompson-Balys; S. Am. Indian (Toba): Métraux MAFLS XL 59.

C31.9. Tabu: revealing secrets of supernatural wife. C820. Tabu: finding certain secret. F511.2.2. Person with ass's (horse's) ears. H13. Recognition by overheard conversation with animals or objects. Person not daring to reveal self directly thus attracts attention. J21.22. "Do not tell a secret to a woman". K975. Secret of strength treacherously discovered. K976. Daughter pulls out father's magic lifecontaining hair. N440. Valuable secrets learned. Q62. Reward for ability to keep secrets. Q340. Meddling punished. T252.3. Wife threatens husband with death if he will not tell secrets.

C420.1. *Man (woman) persuaded to reveal fatal secret.* India: *Thompson-Balys.

C420.2. *Tabu: not to speak about a certain happening.* India: *Thompson-Balys.

H1558. Tests of friendship.

C420.3. *Tabu: uttering secret overheard.* India: Thompson-Balys.

C421. *Tabu: revealing secret of supernatural husband.* *Type 425A; *Tegethoff Amor und Psyche 33; India: *Thompson-Balys.

C31.9. Tabu: revealing secrets of supernatural wife. C32. Tabu: offending supernatural husband. C32.1. Tabu: looking at supernatural husband. C757.1. Tabu: destroying animal skin of enchanted person too soon. C761.2. Tabu: staying at home too long.

C422. *Tabu: revealing identity of certain person.* Irish myth: Cross.

C51.3. Tabu: revealing name of god. C432. Tabu: uttering name of supernatural creature.

C422.1. *Tabu: revealing dragon-fighter's identity.* Dragon-fighter forbids princess whom he has rescued to tell who he is. — *Type 300.

B11.11. Fight with dragon. K1933. Impostor forces oath of secrecy.

C423. *Tabu: revealing the marvelous.*

C423.1. *Tabu: disclosing source of magic power.* Penzer V 3 n. 1; German: Grimm No. 85; India: Thompson-Balys; Jewish: Neuman; Buddhist myth: Malalasekera I 714; Africa (Fang): Trilles 111, 269.

C423.2. *Tabu: speaking of extraordinary sight.* (Cf. C411, C491.) — *Fb "tale" III 765b; Jewish: Neuman.

C423.3. *Tabu: revealing experiences in other world.* Hartland Science 201. — India: Thompson-Balys; Africa (Ekoi): Talbot 240.

C31. Tabu: offending supernatural wife. F0. Journey to the other world. F370. Visit to fairyland.

C423.4. *Tabu: uttering secrets heard from spirits.* Type 516; Rösch FFC LXXVII 119. — India: *Thompson-Balys; Jewish: Neuman.

C423.5. *Tabu: revealing sacred mysteries.* Jewish: *Neuman; Hawaii: Beckwith Myth 144; India: Thompson-Balys.

C423.6. *Tabu: telling children about lake monster.* Eskimo (Kodiak): Golder JAFL XXII 21.

C424. *Tabu: speaking of good luck.* Breton: Sébillot Incidents s.v. "aventure".

N131. Acts performed for changing luck.

C425. *Tabu: revealing knowledge of animal languages.* *Type 670; **Aarne FFC XV; BP I 132; India: *Thompson-Balys; Jewish: Neuman.

B217. Animal languages learned. M295.1. Tiger lets man go on condition he does not tell what he has overheard. N456. Laugh reveals secret knowledge. T252.3. Wife threatens husband with death if he will not tell secrets.

C426. *Tabu: revealing secret song.* African: Werner African 209.

C427. *Tabu: revealing help of grateful animal.* India: Thompson-Balys.

C428. *Tabu: revealing time of Messiah's advent.* Jewish: Neuman.

C429. *Tabu: uttering secrets. — miscellaneous.* India: Thompson-Balys.

C429.1. *Tabu: mentioning secret water spring.* Africa (Lamami): Bouveignes 27.

C430. **Name tabu:** prohibition against uttering the name of a person or thing. — *Types 400, 500; *BP I 495; *Clodd Tom-Tit-Tot, The Magic of Names; Hdwb. d. Abergl. IX Nachträge 809; *Nyrop Navnets Magt; *Chauvin VI 106 No. 270; *Fb "navn" II 675b, 676a; Frazer Golden Bough XII 383 s.v. "names". — Irish: Cross, MacCulloch Celtic 70; Welsh: ibid. 100; English-Scottish: Child V 489 s.v. "naming"; Swiss: Jegerlehner Oberwallis 310 No. 29; French Canadian: Barbeau JAFL XXIX 17. — Jamaica Negro: Beckwith MAFLS XVII *263 No. 66, *277 No. 89. — Africa (Bushman): Bleek and Lloyd 101, (Vai): Ellis 257 No. 52, (A'Kikuyu): Barrett 42.

C31. Tabu: offending supernatural wife. C32.2.1. Tabu: asking name of supernatural husband. H323 Suitor test: learning girl's name.

C431. *Tabu: uttering name of god (or gods).* *Frazer Golden Bough XII 383 s.v. "names"; *Chauvin VI 66 No. 233; Hebrew: Exodus 20:7, Gaster Exempla 233f. No. 288; Jewish: *Neuman.

A138. God's ineffable name. C31. Tabu: offending supernatural wife. C51.3. Tabu: revealing name of god. Q221. Personal offences against gods punished.

C432. *Tabu: uttering name of supernatural creature.* Irish myth: Cross; Icelandic: Boberg.

C10. Tabu: profanely calling up spirit (devil, etc.) — C21. "Ah me!": ogre's name uttered. He appears.

C432.1. *Guessing name of supernatural creature gives power over him.* (Tom-Tit-Tot). — *Type 500; BP I 495; *Clodd Tom-Tit-Tot; Köhler-Bolte I 109; *Fb "gjætte" I 452; Henne-am Rhyn² No. 618. — Icelandic: Árnason Legends of Iceland (Powell tr.) I 49, *Boberg.

E443.3. Ghosts exorcised by name. F381.1. Fairy leaves when he is named. H521. Test: guessing unknown propounder's name. N475. Secret name overheard by eavesdropper.

C433. *Tabu: uttering name of malevolent creature (Eumenides).* To avoid the evil results of naming these creatures other names are substituted. The Furies are spoken of as Eumenides; rats and mice as "the large" and "the small". — *Fb "rotte" III 83a, "mus" II 630b; Güntert Von der Sprache der Götter und Geister (Halle, 1921) 16; ibid. Kalypso 91; Irish myth: Cross; Esthonian: Loorits Grundzüge I 239—248; Greek: Fox 276. — African: Werner African 83.

C433.1. *Person obnoxious for his sins spoken of as "the other".* Jewish: Neuman. — Krappe "L'autre" The French Review XVII (1944) 145ff.

C433.2. *Dangerous animals not to be named.* Eskimo (Greenland): Rasmussen I 134, III 70.

C435. *Tabu: uttering relative's name.*

C435.1. *Tabu: uttering spouse's name.* *MacCulloch Childhood 337; Frazer Golden Bough III 333—339 passim. — Irish myth: Cross; India: Thompson-Balys.

C190. Sex tabu: miscellaneous. D511.1. Man calls wife "my swallow"; she becomes swallow.

C435.1.1. *Tabu: uttering name of supernatural wife.* Irish myth: Cross.

C31. Tabu: offending supernatural wife.

C435.1.1.1. *Woman (fairy) causes twofold death of mortal husband who utters her name.* Irish myth: Cross.

F901.2. Extraordinary twofold death.

C435.2. *Tabu: uttering name of other close relations.* India: Thompson-Balys.

C435.2.1. *Tabu: uttering name of sister-in-law.* India: Thompson-Balys.

C436. *Tabu: disclosing own identity.* A supernatural person must not tell who he is. Irish myth: Cross.

N731.2. Father-son combat.

C437. *Tabu: giving child a name lest it die early.* Eskimo (Greenland): Rasmussen II 298.

C600. Care of children.

C440. **Origin tabu.** Prohibition against mention of origin of person or thing.

C31.2. Tabu: mentioning origin of supernatural wife. C33.1. Tabu: mentioning origin of supernatural child. C35.1. Tabu: mentioning origin of animal wife. C963. Person returns to original form when tabu is broken.

C441. *Tabu: mentioning original form of transformed person.* See references in C31.2, C33.1, and C35.1. — MacCulloch Childhood 261; Tupper and Ogle Walter Map 221; N. A. Indian: *Thompson Tales 342 n. 234; India: Thompson-Balys.

B600. Marriage of person to animal.

C441.1. *Family dares not discuss tigers, fearing that son in form of tiger will return.* Chinese.: Graham.

C442. *Tabu: mentioning land of person's birth.* Tiersot RTP VI 730; Irish myth: Cross; Jewish: Neuman; India: Thompson-Balys.

C450. **Tabu: boasting.** Irish: Beal XXI 328; Jewish: Neuman; India: Thompson-Balys; N. A. Indian (Seneca): Curtin-Hewitt RBAE XXXII 161 No. 27, Curtin 19. — Germanic: Hdwb. d. Abergl. s.v. "Berufen". — African: Stanley 110, (Loango): Pechuël-Loesche 109.

H1215. Quest assigned because of hero's boast. L400. Pride brought low. Q330. Overweening punished. Q433.12. Punishment: abridgement of freedom till extravagant boast is confirmed. T295. Husband's indiscreet boast brings about his death.

C451. *Tabu: boasting of wealth.* *Fb "rose" (2) III 81a.

C452. *Tabu: boasting of children* (Niobe). — Greek: Fox 44, 175; Germanic: Hdwb. d. Abergl. s.v. "Berufen".

C961.2. Transformation to stone for breaking tabu.

C453. *Tabu: boasting of love-conquest.* Greek: Fox 199 (Anchises and Aphrodite).

C31.5. Tabu: boasting of supernatural wife.

C454. *Tabu: boasting that one has no need of gods' help.* Types 830, 836. — Greek: Fox 135 (Ajax the less).

C455. *Tabu: boasting of fearlessness.* Swiss: Jegerlehner Oberwallis 319 No. 22.

C460. **Laughing tabu.** Type 451; BP I 71. — India: *Thompson-Balys; Chinese: Graham.

H1194. Task: making person laugh. V462.7. Ascetic cleric never smiles.

C461. *Tabu: bearded man laughing when shaken.* Irish myth: Cross.

C462. *Tabu: laughing at sight of ghosts.* Lithuanian: Balys Ghosts.

C480. **Tabu: other vocal expressions.**

C480.1. *Whistling tabu.* *Fb I 326 "fløjte".

C480.1.1. *Tabu: whistling in mine.* U.S.: Baughman (C896.1).

C481. *Tabu: singing.*

C481.1. *Tabu: birds not to sing around home of goddess.* Hawaii: Beckwith Myth 186.

C482. *Tabu: weeping.*

C482.1. *Tabu: people weeping in land of gods.* Hawaii: Beckwith Myth 69.

C710. Tabus connected with other-world journeys.

C483. *Tabu: whistling.*

C483.1. *Tabu: whistling in other world.* Tuamotu: Stimson MS (z-G 3/1301).

C484. *Tabu: coughing.*

C484.1. *Tabu: coughing in other world.* Tuamotu: Stimson MS (z-G 3/1301).

C490. **Other speaking tabus.**

C490.1. *Substitutes for tabu expressions.*

C490.1.1. *"Save it for the beggar"* (substitute for "save it for tomorrow". You may be dead by tomorrow.) — India: Thompson-Balys.

C491. *Tabu: expressing astonishment at marvel.* (Cf. C411, C423.2.) — *Köhler-Bolte I 220. — Irish: Beal XXI 314; Jamaica: Beckwith MAFLS XVII 254 No. 31.

D512.1. Transformation when one expresses astonishment at smith drawing water in an egg-shell.

C491.1. *Tabu: screaming at terrible sight.* Hartland Science 243.

C492. *Tabu: speaking to strangers.* Seneca: Curtin-Hewitt RBAE XXXII 166 No. 29.

C745. Tabu: entertaining strangers.

C493. *Tabu: thanking* (under certain circumstances). Fb "takke" III 763a; Hdwb. d. Abergl. II 171; Icel.: *Boberg.

C493.1. *Tabu: wishing good luck.* One must not wish a hunter good luck or a sailor good voyage. — Fb "ønske" III 1178b.

N131. Acts performed for changing luck.

C494. *Tabu: cursing.* Jewish: Neuman.

M400. Curses.

C495. *Tabu: using any except one certain phrase.* India: Thompson-Balys.

J1156. Judge fails to ask proper question.

C495.1. *All questions to be answered, "I don't know".* A youth is so advised by his horse. *Type 532.

C495.2. *"We three" — "For gold" — "That is right".* These expressions are the sole conversation of three men.

C495.2.1. *"We three" — "For gold" — "That is right" devil's bargain.* Three brothers have agreed to say only these things. They incriminate themselves. — *Type 360; BP II 561; India: Thompson-Balys.

J2511.2. Numskulls make silence wager. Arrested as thieves.

C495.2.2. *"We three" — "For gold" — "That is right": phrases of foreign language.* Three travelers know each one phrase of a foreign language. They incriminate themselves. *Type 1697; BP II 561; Nouvelles Récréations No. 20; India: Thompson-Balys.

M175. Pledge to say but a single phrase. In carrying out this agreement the men innocently confess a crime.

C495.2.2.1. *"Yes" — "No" — "Very well".* — India: Thompson-Balys.

C495.3. *All questions to be answered "Thanks".* Youth is so advised by old woman helper. Type 593.

C496. *Tabu: using obscene language.* Jewish: Neuman.

C497. *Tabu: speaking to the dead.* India: Thompson-Balys.

E400. Ghosts and revenants. — miscellaneous.

C498. *Speaking tabu: the one forbidden expression.*

C600. Unique prohibition. A person is forbidden to do one particular thing; everything else he is free to do.

C498.1. *Speaking tabu: the one forbidden expression — "Sorrow is not eternal".* — India: Thompson-Balys.

C499. *Additional speaking tabus.*

C499.1. *Tabu: announcing death directly.* Jewish: Neuman.

C499.2. *Tabu: complimenting.* Africa (Pangwe): Tessman 367.

C500—C549. Tabu: touching.

C500. Tabu: touching. Breton: Sébillot Incidents s.v. "toucher". — Missouri French: Carrière; India: Thompson-Balys.

A1731. Creation of animals as punishment for beating forbidden drum. C32.4. Tabu: not to touch supernatural husband on visit too soon. C145. Tabu: not to touch cooking pots during menses. C181.1. Tabu: women not to touch husband's magic drum. C855.2. Tabu: allowing spear-head to touch stone. C916.2. Animals produced when forbidden drum is beaten. D565. Transformation by touching. M172. Vow never to touch money.

C501. *Tabu: contact with things belonging to a king.* *Frazer Golden Bough[3] III passim. — Hawaii: Beckwith Myth 95, 98.

P14.7. None permitted to enter hall of king unless he possesses an art.

C510. Tabu: touching tree (plant). Breton: Sébillot Incidents s.v. "arbres". — Jewish: Neuman; Chatham Islands: Beckwith Myth 19, Notes 10, 11, 12.

D950. Magic tree. V1.1.1. Sacred tree.

C511. *Tabu: touching leaves (of tree).* Breton: Sébillot Incidents s.v. "feuilles".

D955. Magic leaves.

C512. *Tabu: plucking ear of grain.* Gold Coast: Barker and Sinclair 181 No. 36.

C513. *Tabu: breaking twig.* BP III 62f.; Hdwb. d. Märchens s.v. "Baum".

C513.1. *Tabu: cutting branches of tree.* Jewish: Neuman.

C514. *Tabu: burning saja wood* (terminalia tomentosa). — India: Thompson-Balys.

C515. *Tabu: touching (plucking) flowers.* Type 451; Hartland Science 200. — English-Scottish: Child I 360 n.; Hawaii: Beckwith Myth 17.

D515. Transformation by plucking flowers in enchanted garden. F301.1.1.2. Girl summons fairy lover by plucking flowers. T532.1. Conception from plucking flower.

C516. *Tabu: lying under tree.* Girl who does so carried off by fairies. (Cf. C520.) — English-Scottish: Child V 499 s.v. "trees" — Irish myth: Cross.

F301.1.1.3. Girl summons fairy lover by lying under tree. F320. Fairies carry people away to fairyland.

C517. *Tabu: pulling nuts.* English-Scottish: Child I 360 n.

F301.1.1.4. Girl summons fairy lover by pulling nuts.

C518. *Tabu: cutting down tree.* Jewish: Neuman; Maori: Clark 95; Tuamotu: Stimson MS (z—G 3/1174).

C518.1. *Cutting elder tree fatal to man.* (See C920.) — England: Baughman.

C518.2. *Cutting white thorn tree fatal to man who cuts it.* (Cf. C920.) Ireland: Baughman; Danish: Kristensen Danske Sagn I No. 311, Fb "hvidtjørn" I 703 a.

C519. *Tabu: touching tree (plant) — miscellaneous.*

C519.1. *Tabu: harming tree in any way before burning it.* India: Thompson-Balys.

C520. **Tabu: touching ground.** (Cf. C516.) Hartland Science 197. — Irish myth: Cross; Tahiti: Beckwith Myth 246; Africa (Zulu): Callaway 303.

C521. *Tabu: dismounting from horse.* Hartland Science 199; Irish myth: Cross.

F378.1. Tabu: touching ground on return from fairyland.

C521.1. *Tabu: dismounting from magic sack.* French Canadian: Sister Marie Ursule.

C522. *Tabu: plowing in certain place.* Fb "plove" II 849b, "höj" I 741b. — Africa (Kaffir): Theal 30 No. 1, 41 No. 2, (Basuto): Jacottet 100 No. 15, (Zulu): Callaway 99, (Yoruba): Ellis 253 No. 4.

C523. *Tabu: digging.* (Cf. C522.) — N. A. Indian: Thompson Tales 332 n. 197.

C93.3. Tabu: digging in churchyard. F56.1. Sky window from digging or uprooting plant (tree) in upper world.

C523.1. *Tabu: digging up certain stones.* India: Thompson-Balys.

C523.2. *Tabu: digging in fairy ring.* England: Baughman.

F261.1. Fairy rings on grass.

C524. *Tabu: disembarking from boat on return from other world.* Irish myth: Cross.

F378.1. Tabu: touching ground on return from fairyland.

C525. *Tabu: picking up card fallen to ground.* Breton: Sébillot Incidents s.v. "cartes".

C526. *Tabu: touching sacred mountain.* Jewish: Neuman.

C530. **Tabu: touching (miscellaneous).**

C531. *Tabu: touching with iron.* *MacCulloch Childhood 339; Hartland Science 163f.; Fb "jærn" II 61a. — Irish myth: Cross; Jewish: Neuman; India: Thompson-Balys; Eskimo (Greenland): Holm 93.

E415.1.1. Ghost unlaid until iron he hid in life is found. F384.3. Iron powerful against fairies. F408.1. Demon occupies lance (sword). Z312.2. Giant ogre can be killed only with iron club he carries.

C531.1. *Umbilical cord not to be cut with iron.* India: Thompson-Balys.

C150. Tabu connected with childbirth.

C532. *Tabu: touching water.* Irish myth: Cross.

D877.1. Magic wishing-ring loses power by touching water.

C533. *Tabu: touching box.* Eskimo (Cumberland Sound): Boas BAM XV 203.

C533.1. *Tabu: touching magic box.* (Cf. D1174.) Africa (Ekoi): Talbot 18, 178, (Vai): Ellis 187 No. 3, (Basuto): Jacottet 220 No. 33.

C535. *Tabu: stepping on bread* (or otherwise misusing it). *Fb "brød" IV 74a.

C55.1. Tabu: stepping on sacred bread. C851.1. Tabu: wiping children with bread.

C536. *Tabu: not to clean houses with cow-dung.* India: Thompson-Balys.

C537. *Tabu: touching certain animals.*

C537.1. *Tabu: touching camel after he has retired from work.* Cyprus: Hadjioannou Kypriakoi Mythoi (Leukosia, 1948) No. 22.

C537.2. *Tabu: touching hairless dog.* Hawaii: Beckwith Myth 343.

C537.3. *Tabu: touching horse or moving dead cat or dog.* India: Thompson-Balys.

C541. *Tabu: contact with the dead.* Jewish: *Neuman; Eskimo (Greenland): Rink 341, 452, Rasmussen III 104.

C319.2. Tabu:seeing dead man not killed by weapons.

C541.1. *Tabu: dead body not to be on ship.* English-Scottish: Child I 245 n.

C541.2. *Head of slain man must not be moved.* Fb "hoved" I 655a.

C541.3. *Tabu: touching bones of murdered person.* India: Thompson-Balys.

C541.4. *Tabu: lying on ancestors' bones.* Lithuanian: Balys Index No. 3541.

C541.5. *Tabu: taking down corpse of hanged man.* India: Thompson-Balys.

C541.6. *Tabu: embalming.* Jewish: Neuman.

C542. *Tabu: touching treasures of other world.* *Krappe Balor 125 n. 17. — Icel.: Herrmann Saxo II 589; MacCulloch Eddic 321, *Boberg.

C710. Tabus connected with otherworld journeys. F0. Otherworld journeys. F378. Tabus connected with trip to fairyland.

C542.1. *Tabu: contact with things on journey to hell.* Irish myth: Cross; India: Thompson-Balys.

E391. Dead returns to life and tells of journey to land of dead. E721.7. Soul leaves body to visit hell. F81. Descent to lower world of dead (Hell, Hades). V522. Sinner reformed after visit to heaven and hell.

C542.2. *Tabu: touching fire in other world.* S. Am. Indian (Toba): Métraux MAFLS XL 45.

C543. *Tabu: picking up comb from ground.* It belongs to fairy (witch) who will avenge insult. Scottish: Campbell-McKay No. 22 note. — Cheremis: Sebeok-Nyerges.

C544. *Tabu: crushing eggs.*

C544.1. *Tabu: crushing lizard's eggs.* Hawaii: Beckwith Myth 127.

C545. *Tabu: touching certain clothes.*

C545.1. *Tabu: touching old clothes.* (Abandoned clothes should be thrown away.) — Tahiti: Henry 143.

C545.2. *Tabu: touching clothes of certain person.* Eskimo (Mackenzie Area): Jenness 58.

C545.3. *Tabu: touching dress.* French Canadian: Sister Marie Ursule.

C546. *Tabu: striking certain rock.* Samoa: Beckwith Myth 19, notes 10—12.

C549. *Tabu: touching (miscellaneous).*

C549.1. *Tabu: tiger and lion after having killed a man not to touch certain animals:* cow, buffalo, pig, deer, wild goat. India: Thompson-Balys.

C549.1.1. *Tabu: touching a horse or moving a dead cat or dog.* India: Thompson-Balys.

C549.2. *Tabu: touching soldiers of enchanted (sleeping) army and their horses.* Lithuanian: Balys Historical.
E502. The sleeping army.

C550—C599. Class tabu.

C550. Class tabu. Missouri French: Carrière.

C551. *Untouchables.* Certain castes whose touch is considered a pollution. India: Thompson-Balys.

C551.1. *Tabu: touching food of another caste.* India: Thompson-Balys.
C220. Tabu: eating certain things.

C560. Tabu: things not to be done by certain class. Irish Myth: Cross.
P. Society.

C561. *Tabus of slaves.*

C561.1. *Tabu: slave going near fetish.* African (Ekoi): Talbot 27; Maori: Clark 128; Jewish: Neuman.
P170. Slaves.

C563. *Tabus of kings.* Irish myth: Cross; Jewish: *Neuman.
C402.1. Tabu: king speaking before his druids speak. C735.2.3. Tabu: king sleeping during sunrise at capital. P10. Kings. P19.4. Kings' powers. P29.1. No king to rule who is not husband of certain queen. T131.7. King may not marry girl who has been wife of another.

C563.1. *Tabu: king traveling alone.* Irish myth: Cross.

C563.2. *Tabu: king having physical blemish.* Irish myth: Cross; India: Thompson-Balys; Jewish: *Neuman.
A128.4. God with one hand. C57.1. No men with wounds to be sacrificed to goddess. P16.2. King must resign if maimed.

C563.3. *Tabu: king allowing rapine during his reign.* Irish myth: Cross.
A1101.1.1. Reign of peace and justice under certain king. Q552.3. Failure of crops during reign of wicked king.

C563.4. *Tabu: king settling quarrel among thralls.* Irish myth: Cross.

C563.5. *Tabu: appearing before king without having been summoned.* Jewish: Neuman.

C563.6. *Tabu: killing king, even at his own request.* Jewish: Neuman.

C564. *Tabus of chiefs.* Irish myth: Cross.

C564.1. *Tabu: chief being in ale-house when there is no story-telling.* Irish myth: Cross.
C287. Tabu: consuming feast without discovering a new wonder. P14.14. King requires all who come before him to tell a story.

C564.2. *Tabu: chief's troop not having a herald.* Irish myth: Cross.

C564.3. *Tabu: chief to be in large company without wolf-hounds.* Irish myth: Cross.

C564.4. *Cloth from certain bark tabu to all except chiefs.* Hawaii: Beckwith Myth 144.

C564.5. *Tabu: altar smoke from sacrifice touching young chief.* Hawaii: Beckwith Myth: 346.

C564.6. *Tabu: teaching genealogy of chiefs to commoners.* Hawaii: Beckwith Myth 309.

C564.7. *Tabu: touching head of chief.* Hawaii, Marquesas, Lau Islands: Beckwith Myth 468.

C564.8. *Tabu: chieftainess preparing food.* Maori: Clark 2.

C564.9. *Tabu: chief going outdoors in spite of provocations.* Hawaii Beckwith Myth 118.

C565. *Tabus of bearded men.* Irish myth: Cross.

C735.1.1. Tabu: bearded man sleeping at sunrise. C835.1. Tabu: bearded man refusing combat. C871.0.1. Tabu: bearded man refusing request. C891.2. Tabu: bearded man going dirty to bed. P642. Only the brave to wear beards.

C565.1. *Tabu: labor by bearded man.* Irish myth: Cross.

C565.2. *Tabu: bearded man being lazy.* Irish myth: Cross.

C566. *Tabus of heroes.* Irish myth: Cross; Jewish: Neuman.

Z200. Heroes.

C566.1. *Tabu: fish hero snaring a being in the bays of his land.* Irish myth: Cross.

C566.2. *Tabu: birds feeding on hero's land without leaving him something.* Irish myth: Cross.

C566.3. *Tabu: women leaving hero's land without his knowing it.* Irish myth: Cross.

C180. Tabu confined to one sex.

C566.4. *Tabu: women marrying until hero has chosen their husbands.* Irish myth: Cross.

C160. Tabu connected with marriage.

C566.5. *Tabu: warriors being in hero's land without receiving challenge from him.* Irish myth: Cross.

C566.6. *Tabu: sex activity for warriors.* (Cf. C110.) Jewish: Neuman.

C567. *Tabus of princesses.*

P40. Princesses.

C567.1. *Tabu: eloping with king's daughter.* Irish myth: Cross.

C100. Sex tabu. C192. Tabu: refusing to elope with woman who desires it. T131. Marriage restrictions.

C567.2. *Tabu: princess stepping in water.* Madagascar (Tsimihety): Renel I 144ff. No. 26.

C568. *Tabus of poets.* Irish myth: Cross.

C568.1. *Tabu: poets to be ignorant of national literature.* Irish myth: Cross.

P427.7.2. Extensive repertory of poets.

C572. *Tabus of a thief.* Irish myth: Cross.

C573. *Tabus of priests.* Jewish: *Neuman; Maori: Clark 132, 149.

C575. *Tabus of bastards.* Jewish: Neuman.

C576. *Tabus of strangers.* Jewish: Neuman.

C600—C699. Unique prohibitions and compulsions.

C600—C649. THE ONE FORBIDDEN THING

C600. Unique prohibition. A person is forbidden to do one particular thing; everything else he is free to do. — Celtic: *Schoepperle Tristan and Isolt. II 307. — Irish myth: Cross; Jewish: Neuman.

A1331. Paradise lost because of one sin. C498. Speaking tabu: the one forbidden expression. C868. Tabu: fighting certain person. Z300. Unique exceptions.

C601. *Unique prohibition announced by mysterious voice.* India: Thompson-Balys.

C610. The one forbidden place. Breton: Sébillot Incidents s.v. "interdits". — Irish myth: Cross; India: *Thompson-Balys; Jewish: *Neuman; Calif. Indian: Gayton and Newman 86; Africa (Luba): DeClerq Zs. f. KS. IV 219; Hawaii: Beckwith Myth 70, 186; Marquesas: Handy 36; New Hebrides: Codrington 385; Tuamotu: Stimson MS (z—G 13/317).

C194. Tabu: trysting with woman at certain place. C751.7.1. Tabu: being in certain place at sunrise. C755.4. Tabu: going to certain place in March. C853. Tabu: holding meeting at certain place. C854.1. Tabu: going to certain place in speckled garment on speckled steed. C866. Tabu: going to (leaving) certain place without combat. C891.1. Tabu: riding dirty on black-heeled horse across certain plain. H1199.3. Task: shouting from forbidden place.

C611. *Forbidden chamber.* Person allowed to enter all chambers of house except one. — Types 311, 312, 313, 314, 480, 502, 516, 710; *BP I 21; *Cox Cinderella 484; Roberts* (Type 480) 174. — *MacCulloch Childhood 306; *Chauvin V 302 No. 117; **Hartland FLJ III 193; Fb "kammer" II 83, "menneske" II 577b; Penzer II 223 n. 1, 252f., VII 21 n. 3, VIII 57 n. 1; Rösch FFC LXXVII 98; Clouston Tales I 198ff.; Köhler-Bolte I 129, 312. — Irish myth: Cross; Welsh: MacCulloch Celtic 101; Breton: Sébillot Incidents s.v. "chambre"; French Canadian: Barbeau JAFL XXIX 23; Missouri French: Carrière; Swiss: Jegerlehner Oberwallis 304 No. 30; Jewish: Neuman; India: *Thompson-Balys; Spanish Exempla: Keller. — Seneca: Curtin-Hewitt RBAE XXXII 135 No. 21; Tonga: Gifford 189.

C911. Golden finger as sign of opening forbidden chamber. C912. Hair turns to gold as punishment in forbidden chamber. C913. Bloody key as sign of disobedience.

C611.1. *Forbidden door.* All doors may be entered except one. *Kirby FLJ V 112; *Chauvin V 203 No. 117; India: Thompson-Balys; Jamaica: *Beckwith MAFLS XVII 275 No. 86; Seneca: Curtin-Hewitt RBAE XXXII 75 No. 1.

C611.1.1. *Prince not to be given eighth key until after he has ruled for five years.* India: Thompson-Balys.

C611.2. *Forbidden stables.* Person allowed to enter everywhere but into three stables. Cheremis: Sebeok-Nyerges.

C611.3. *Forbidden ladder.* India: Thompson-Balys.

C612. *Forbidden forest.* (Cf. C614.1.0.2.) — Icelandic: Boberg; India: Thompson-Balys; Hawaii: Beckwith Myth 142; African (Pahouini): Largeau 195, (Bondei): Woodward FL XXXVI 367ff. No. 12.

C614. *Forbidden road.* All roads may be taken except one. India: *Thompson-Balys; African (Zulu): Callaway 96, (Kaffir): Theal 86.

Z211. Dreadnaughts. Brothers deliberately seek dangers they have been warned against.

C614.1. *Forbidden direction of travel.* Person free to go in any other. Irish myth: Cross; Jewish: Neuman; India: *Thompson-Balys.

C614.1.0.1. *Tabu: going in a certain direction while tending cattle.* India: Thompson-Balys.

C614.1.0.2. *Tabu: hunting in certain part of forest.* (Cf. C612.) — India: *Thompson-Balys.

C614.1.0.3. *Forbidden direction: not to step outside a certain line.* India: Thompson-Balys.

C614.1.1. *Forbidden direction: north.* India: *Thompson-Balys.

C614.1.2. *Forbidden direction: south.* India: *Thompson-Balys.

C614.1.3. *Forbidden direction: west.* India: *Thompson-Balys.

C614.1.4. *Forbidden direction: east.*

C614.1.5. *Tabu: going in direction either of sunset or sunrise.* India: Thompson-Balys.

C614.2. *Tabu: going through a wicket gate.* Irish myth: Cross.

C615. *Forbidden body of water.* Mono-Alu: Wheeler 69.

C615.1. *Forbidden lake (pool).*

C615.2. *Hero not to swim in certain lake.* Irish myth: Cross.
G308.4. Lake made dangerous by haunting serpent.

C615.3. *Lake forbidden at certain time.* Irish myth: Cross.
C751. Doing thing at certain time.

C615.4. *Tabu: not to rest near a lake.* India: Thompson-Balys.

C615.5. *Certain pool to be approached only when properly attired.* Hawaii: Beckwith Myth 288.

C616. *Tabu: feasting visitor at certain place.* Irish myth: Cross.
P320. Hospitality.

C617. *Forbidden country.* Irish myth: Cross; Jewish: Neuman.
Q431.Punishment: banishment (exile).

C617.1. *Forbidden (perilous) ford.* Irish myth: Cross.
H1561.2.3. Combats at fords.

C619. *The one forbidden place — miscellaneous.*

C619.1. *Forbidden hostel.* Irish myth: Cross.

C619.2. *Tabu: going into wild boar's haunt.* Irish myth: Cross; India: Thompson-Balys.
C841.4. Tabu: hunting a pig.

C619.3. *Forbidden horse fair.* Irish myth: Cross.

C619.4. *Tabu: women to be on certain island.* Irish myth: Cross.
C181. Tabus confined to women.

C620. Tabu: partaking of the one forbidden object. India: Thompson-Balys.

C621. *Forbidden tree.* Fruit of all trees may be eaten, except one. *Frazer Testament I 45ff.; *Dh I 208ff. — Irish myth: Cross; India:

Thompson-Balys; Spanish Exempla: Keller; Jewish: *Neuman; Siberian: Holmberg Siberian 381ff.; Burmese, Indo-Chinese: Scott Indo-Chinese 265, 289. — N. A. Indian (Biloxi): Dorsey and Swanton RBAE XLVII 32; (Quiché): Alexander Lat. Am. 171; S. Am. Indian (Yuracare): ibid. 315.

A878. Earth-tree. Forbidden branches. A1331.1. Paradise lost because of forbidden fruit (drink). A2234.2. Animals eat deity's forbidden fruit: punished. C225. Tabu: eating certain fruit. C937. God's favor lost for breaking tabu. D1346.4. Tree of immortality. D1346.6. Fruit of immortality.

C621.1. *Tree of knowledge forbidden.* Dh I 212ff. — Jewish: *Neuman.

J165. Tree of knowledge.

C621.2. *Tabu: touching fruit.*

C621.2.1. *Tabu: touching apple.* Hdwb. d. Märchens s.v. *"Apfel" n. 31. — Spanish: Boggs FFC XC 41 No. 301.

C621.2.2. *Tabu: touching banana.* Hawaii: Beckwith Myth 146.

C622. *Forbidden drinking horn.* One may drink from anything else. Irish myth: Cross.

H411.4. Magic drinking horn (cup) as chastity test.

C623. *Forbidden well.* (One may not go there unless accompanied by cup-bearers.) Irish myth: Cross.

A920.1.8.1. Lake from violating tabu. C315.4. Tabu: looking at certain well. D926. Magic well.

C623.1. *Well upon which no one can look without losing his eyes.* Irish myth: Cross.

D1403.2. Magic well maims.

C624. *Forbidden barrel.* Jewish: Neuman.

C625. *Tabu: opening bottle.* Chinese: Eberhard FFC CXX 214, No. 163.

C630. Tabu: the one forbidden time. India: Thompson-Balys.

C750. Time tabus.

C631. *Tabu: breaking the sabbath.* Hebrew: Exodus 20; 8—12. — Jewish: *Neuman; Irish myth: Cross; Finnish-Swedish: Wessman 17f. Nos. 157—170.

A1751.1.1. Man in moon burns brush as punishment for doing so on Sunday. C58. Tabu: profaning sacred day. C886. Tabu: failing to observe certain festival. Q223.6. Failure to observe holiness of Sabbath punished. Q552.14. Fortress built on Sunday destroyed by tempest. V71. Sabbath.

C631.1. *Tabu: journeying on sabbath.* Jewish: *Neuman; Irish myth: Cross; India: Thompson-Balys.

C631.2. *Tabu: spinning on holy days.* Fb "spinde" III 491b — Icel.: MacCulloch Eddic 177.

C832. Tabu: spinning.

C631.3. *Tabu: washing hair on sabbath.* Irish myth: Cross; Jewis: Neuman.

C631.4. *Tabu: lighting or extinguishing lights on sabbath.* Jewish: Neuman.

C631.5. *Tabu: writing on sabbath.* Jewish: Neuman.

C631.6. *Tabu: playing music on sabbath.* Jewish: Neuman.

C632. *Tabu: going abroad on Hallowe'en.* Irish myth: Cross.

C634. *Tabu: fasting on holidays.* Jewish: *Neuman.

C635. *Tabu: giving ring at certain time.* India: Thompson-Balys.

C636. *Tabu: hunting on shortest day in the year.* Eskimo (Greenland): Rasmussen II 341.

C640. Unique prohibition — miscellaneous.

C641. *Tabu: making war against certain tribe.* Irish myth: Cross.
C856. Tabus concerning war.

C641.1. *Tabu: making war against certain tribe on Tuesday.* Irish myth: Cross.
C751. Tabu: doing thing at certain time.

C642. *Tabu: making peace with certain tribe.* Irish myth: Cross.

C643. *Tabu: turning left side of chariot toward certain place.* Irish myth: Cross.
D1791. Magic power of circumambulation.

C644. *The one forbidden thing: returning to home country after marrying fairy.* India: Thompson-Balys.
F378. Tabus connected with trip to fairyland.

C650—C699. THE ONE COMPULSORY THING

C650. The one compulsory thing. Unless one does this one thing, misfortune comes. (Sometimes one is under magic compulsion.) — **Reinhard the Survival of Geis in Mediaeval Romance. — Irish myth: Cross, MacCulloch Celtic 177ff., passim, *Schoepperle Tristan and Isolt II 307; Beal XXI 312.
M202.0.1. Bargain or promise to be fulfilled at all hazards.

C650.1. *Customs connected with unique compulsion.* Irish myth: Cross.
P600. Customs.

C651. *The one compulsory question.* Percival must ask the meaning of the strange sights he sees; else the Fisher King will not be healed. — Voretzsch Altfranz Lit. 325 (Chretien de Troyes Conte del Graal).
C735.2.9. Tabu: to rest sitting or lying until answer to a certain question is learned. F91.1. Slamming door on exit from mountain otherworld. It (almost) injures the hero because he has failed to bring back the talisman which opened the mountain. F152.2. Slamming bridge to other world. Slams as hero leaves and (almost) injures him. He has failed to do the one compulsory thing. H508. Test: finding answer to certain question. H1388. Quest: answer to certain question. J21.6. "Do not ask questions about extraordinary things." Q85. Reward for asking proper questions.

C652. *Compulsion: taking back talisman which opened treasure mountain.* Hero takes treasure and forgets the talisman. — *Krappe Balor 109ff.

C655. *Only one certain gift must be accepted.*

C655.1. *Only peacock on the steeple of the king's golden temple can be accepted as dowry.* India: Thompson-Balys.

C661. *Girl from elfland must eat earthly food in order to remain.* *Fb "spise" III 495b.
C211. Tabu: eating in other world. C710. Tabus connected with otherworld journeys. F210. Fairyland. F243.0.1. Christianized fairy woman refuses to eat fairy food.

C662. *One must eat "death vegetable" whenever one sees it.* Otherwise god will be angry. India: Thompson-Balys.

C663. *Compulsion to bathe in certain waters daily.* Irish myth: Cross.

C664. *Injunction: to marry first woman met.* Irish myth: Cross.
C100. Sex tabu. T62. Princess to marry first man who asks for her.

C664.0.1. *Injunction: to cohabit with first woman met after battle.* Irish myth: Cross.

C665. *Injunction: protect certain stone from molestation.* Irish myth: Cross.
D931. Magic rock (stone).

C666. *Compulsion to go to certain place at certain time* (or once each year). Irish myth: Cross; Jewish: Neuman.

C671. *The one compulsory song.* Beer cannot be brewed until an old man sings the song of the origin of beer. — Finnish: Kalevala rune 20.
D2084.1. Beer magically kept from brewing.

C672. *Compulsion to tell stories.*

C672.1. *Curse laid upon man by stories he fails to tell:* they creep out of his belly when he is asleep and talk. India: Thompson-Balys.

C675. *Compulsion to give food to everyone met on journey.* African (Jaunde): Nekes 251.

C680. Other compulsions.

C681. *Compulsion to answer cry.* Hero is magically compelled to do so. Irish myth: Cross.
C566. Tabus of heroes. C885. Tabu: hearing or listening. D2034. Crying induced by magic as trick to force child's mother.

C681.1. *Compulsion to regard hunting cry and follow hounds.* Irish myth: Cross.

C682. *Compulsion to invite singer to feast.* Until that is done, the beer will not stop foaming. (Cf. C671.) — Finnish: Kalevala rune 20.

C683. *Injunction: sleep where night overtakes you.* Otherwise misfortune will come. — Cape Verde Islands: Parsons MAFLS XV (1) 213 No. 73.

C684. *Compulsion to perform certain task yearly.*
C750. Time tabus.

C684.1. *Compulsion to catch blackbird alive yearly.* Irish myth: Cross.

C684.2. *Compulsion to kill one of certain hogs yearly.* Irish myth: Cross.

C684.3. *Compulsion to leap yearly over stone one's size held in palm of hand.* Irish myth: Cross.
H1020. Tasks contrary to laws of nature.

C684.4. *Compulsion to hold festival at certain intervals.* Irish myth: Cross.

C685. *Injunction: to give sample of food to dog before eating.* Misfortune follows failure to do so. — Spanish: Boggs FFC XC 63 No. 453.

C686. *Injunction: to forsake woman who arouses love.* Irish myth: Cross.
C100. Sex tabu. T55. Girl as wooer. T331. Man unsuccessfully tempted by woman.

C686.1. *Tabu: to refuse help to a woman.* Irish myth: Cross.

C687. *Injunction: to perform certain act daily.*
C750. Time tabus.

C687.1. *Injunction: to visit saint daily.* Irish myth: Cross.

C700—C899. Miscellaneous tabus.

C700. **Miscellaneous tabus.**

C710. **Tabus connected with other-world journeys.** Babylonian: Gilgamesch-Epos XII p. 64ff. — Icelandic: Boberg; Eskimo (Greenland): Rink 371, 440, Rasmussen III 170; Marquesas: Beckwith Myth 149.
C211. Tabu: eating in other world. C405. Silence preserved in fairyland. C413. Tabu: expressing surprise in lower world of dead. C423.3. Tabu: revealing experiences in other world. C542. Tabu: touching treasures of otherworld. C482.1. Tabu: weeping in land of gods. C542.1. Tabu: contact with things on journey to hell. C644. The one forbidden thing: returning to home country after marrying fairy. F378. Tabus connected with trip to fairyland.

C711. *Tabu: going into bath on return from serpent kingdom.* (Cf. C721.) — Chauvin V 257 No. 152.
B225.1. Kingdom of serpents. F127. Journey to underground animal kingdom.

C712. *Tabu: staying too long in other world.*
C211. Tabu: eating in other world. C262. Tabu: drinking in other world. C735.2.1. Tabu: sleeping in other world. C761. Tabu: doing thing too long.

C712.1. *Tabu: staying too long in fairyland.* (Cf. C713.3.) — *R. M. Meyer Zs. f. Vksk. XXI 1ff.
C211.1. Tabu: eating in fairyland. C242. Tabu: eating food of witch (demon). F210. Fairyland. F370. Visit to fairyland. F377. Supernatural lapse of time in fairyland. F378.1. Tabu: touching ground on return from fairyland.

C713. *Forsaken merman.* Tabu: association of fairy's (merman's, etc.) human wife (husband) with human relatives.
B82.1. Merman marries maiden. T294. Wife of supernatural being longs for old home and visits relatives.

C713.1. *Tabu: merman's wife not to stay till church benediction.* English: Child I 366.
D2006.2. Sight of old home reawakens memory and brings about return from other world. F382. Exorcising fairies. Fairies disappear when some name of ceremony of the Christian Church is used. G304.2.4.1. Trolls cannot endure churchbells. V50. Prayer.

C713.2. *Tabu: wife of supernatural husband seeing old home.* Usually a part of the "Star-Husband" tale of the North American Indians: Thompson Tales 332 n. 197.

C713.3. *Tabu: wife of merman staying too long at home* (on visit). (Cf. C712.1.) — Norwegian: Child I 364.
C761.2. Tabu: staying too long at home.

C713.3.1. *Tabu: beast-husband staying too long at home: becomes sick.* India: Thompson-Balys.

C713.4. *Golden apple thrown to remind merman's wife not to forget to return to him.* Child I 364f.

F813.1.1. Golden apple.

C714. *Tabus concerning requests made in otherworld.*

C714.1. *Only one present to be asked for at home of spirit son-in-law.* India: Thompson-Balys.

T111.1. Marriage of a mortal and a god.

C715. *Tabu: speaking in otherworld.* (Cf. C400.)

F370. Visit to fairyland.

C715.1. *Tabu: speaking in fairyland.* India: Thompson-Balys.

C715.2. *Tabu: making noise on way to other world.* Eskimo (Mackenzie Area): Jenness 154.

C716. *Tabu: removing hats while in otherworld.* India: Thompson-Balys.

C720. Tabu: attending toilet needs.

M120. Vows concerning personal appearance.

C721. *Tabu: bathing.* (Cf. C711.) — Jewish: Neuman; India: Thompson-Balys.

C858. Tabu: swimming with certain birds. C891. Tabu: uncleanliness.

C721.1. *Tabu: bathing during certain time.* *Types 361, 475; BP II 423, 427 (Gr. Nos. 100, 101). — Irish myth: Cross.

C755. Tabu: doing thing during certain time.

C721.2. *Tabu: bathing in certain place.* Irish myth: Cross.

C721.2.1. *Tabu: bathing in clear stream.* Africa (Ekoi): Talbot 281.

C721.3. *Tabu: bathing without straining stream afterwards.* Irish myth: Cross.

C722. *Tabu: cutting hair.* Jewish: *Neuman.

P632.5. Long hair prized by Irish heroes. P672.2. Cutting of a man's hair as an insult.

C722.0.1. *Tabu: shaving.* Jewish: Neuman.

C722.1. *Tabu: cutting hair during certain time.* *Fb "hår" I 771b.

C755. Tabu: doing thing during certain time.

C723. *Tabu: combing hair.*

C723.1. *Tabu: combing hair during certain time.* *Types 361, 475; BP II 423, 427 (Gr. Nos. 100, 101).

C725. *Tabu: attending call of nature at certain time.* Africa (Benga): Nassau 132 No. 14.

C725.1. *Tabu: use of water after attending call of nature.* India: Thompson-Balys.

C726. *Tabu: trimming fingernails.* Jewish: Neuman; German: Grimm Nos. 100, 101.

C726.1. *Tabu: throwing away nail trimmings.* Jewish: Neuman; Tahiti: Henry 143.

G303.25.5. Devil's chair in hell made from thrown-away nail parings.

C730. Tabu: resting. India: Thompson-Balys.

C731. *Tabu: resting on journey.* India: Thompson-Balys; Eskimo (Mackenzie Area): Jenness 51.

C735. *Tabu: sleeping.* Calif. Indian: Gayton and Newman 100.

C735.1. *Tabu: sleeping during certain time.* *Type 400; BP II 318 ff.; Irish myth: Cross. — N. A. Indian (Zuñi): Parsons JAFL XXIX 393; (Ojibwa): Jones-Michelson PAES VII (2) 231 No. 20, (Bella Coola): Boas JE I 58. — Africa (Congo): Weeks 217 No. 12.

C755. Tabu: doing thing during certain time. F564.1. Person of diabolical origin never sleeps.

C735.1.0.1. *Tabu: sleeping in certain position during certain time.* Irish myth: Cross.

C735.1.1. *Tabu: bearded man sleeping at sunrise.* Irish myth: Cross.

C565. Tabus for bearded men.

C735.1.2. *Tabu: sleeping before task is finished.* Tuamotu: Stimson MS (z-G 3/1174).

H1247. Sleep forbidden until quest is accomplished.

C735.2. *Tabu: sleeping in certain place.* Irish myth: Cross.

C735.2.1. *Tabu: sleeping in other world.* Africa (Ekoi): Talbot 281, (Congo): Weeks 217 No. 22.

C712. Tabu: staying too long in other world.

C735.2.1.1. *Tabu: sleeping before lapse of seven days in cloudland.* Africa (Congo): Weeks 217.

C735.2.2. *Tabu: sleeping in empty hut.* Africa (Kaffir): Theal 86.

C735.2.3. *Tabu: king (hero) sleeping after sunrise at capital.* Irish myth: Cross.

C563. Tabus of kings. C750. Time tabus.

C735.2.4. *Tabu: sleeping in house lighted after sunset.* Irish myth: Cross.

C752.1. Tabu: doing thing after sunset.

C735.2.5. *Tabu: sleeping in cemetery.* Lithuanian: Balys Ghosts.

C735.2.6. *Tabu: sleeping on the path of ghosts.* Lithuanian: Balys Ghosts.

C735.2.7. *Tabu: sleeping on feather bed.* Canadian: Gautier.

C735.2.8. *Tabu: sleeping two nights in the same place until certain result is attained.* Irish myth: Cross.

C735.2.9. *Tabu: to rest sitting or lying until answer to certain question is learned.* Irish myth: Cross.

C757. Tabu: doing a thing too soon.

C735.2.10. *Tabu: sleeping at one's own home.* Jewish: Neuman.

C740. Tabu: doing deed of mercy or courtesy.

B316. Abused and pampered horses. C493. Tabu: thanking. C493.1. Tabu: wishing good luck.

C741. *Tabu: relieving souls in hell.* Boy who tends kettles in hell not allowed to raise covers to relieve poor souls. — Köhler-Bolte I 138, *320.

E755.2.1. Souls of drowned in heated kettles in hell. Q561.2. Kettle heating in hell for certain person.

C742. *Tabu: striking monster twice.* Though monster begs that hero strike him again, hero refuses. Monster would otherwise revive. — *Chauvin VII 69 No. 348 n. 2; *Wesselski Theorie 143 and n.; *Köhler-Bolte I 469ff.; *Krappe Révue d'Ethnographie et des Traditions Populaires (1925) 432ff.; **Wesselski Erlesenes 18ff.; *BP IV 395.

C762. Tabu: doing thing too often. E11.1. Second blow resuscitates. First kills.

C742.1. *Man must be killed with first blow: others will not harm him.* Irish myth: Cross.

Z310. Unique vulnerability.

C743. *Tabu: putting house in order for one man.* Irish myth: Cross.

P320. Hospitality.

C744. *Tabu: accepting an invitation.* Irish myth: Cross.

C282. Tabu: refusing a feast.

C745. *Tabu: entertaining strangers.* Jewish: Neuman.

C745.1. *Tabu: heeding pleas of old woman for food and warmth.* (Old woman is transformed demon.) — India: Thompson-Balys.

C746. *Tabu: watching a game without helping the losing player.* Irish myth: Cross.

C747. *Tabu: not to allow any other creature on raft.* India: Thompson-Balys.

C750. Time tabus. India: Thompson-Balys.

C630. Tabu: the one forbidden time. C684. Compulsion to perform task yearly. C687. Injunction to perform certain act daily.

C751. *Tabu: doing thing at certain time.* Irish myth: Cross.

C615.1. Lake forbidden at certain time. C641.1. Tabu: making war against certain tribe on Tuesday C725. Tabu: attending call of nature at certain time. C856.1. Tabu: leaving track of army at certain place, time. N128. Unlucky days.

C751.1. *Tabu: lighting fire at certain time.* *Chauvin VII 116 No. 385; Irish myth: Cross; Jewish: *Neuman.

C751.1.1. *Tabu: lighting fire before king lights one.* (Cf. C756.) — Irish myth: Cross.

C751.2. *Tabu: sleeping with certain wife on Midsummer's Eve.* Irish myth: Cross.

C100. Sex tabu. C160. Tabu connected with marriage.

C751.3. *Tabu: convening certain hunt at certain time.* Irish myth: Cross.

C751.4. *Tabu: going on water Monday after May Day.* Irish myth: Cross.

C751.5. *Tabu: making treaty at certain time.* Irish myth: Cross.

C751.6. *Tabu: leaving capital every ninth night.* Irish myth: Cross.

C751.7. *Tabu: doing thing at sunrise.* Irish myth: Cross.

C751.7.1. *Tabu: being in certain place at sunrise.* Irish myth: Cross.

C610. The one forbidden place. C735.2.3. Tabu: king (hero) sleeping after sunrise at capital.

C751.8. *Tabu: carrying food at night.* Hawaii: Beckwith Myth 144.

C752. *Tabu: doing thing after certain time.* Irish myth: Cross.

C752.1. *Tabu: doing thing after sunset (nightfall).* Irish myth: Cross.

C237. Tabu: feasting by night at beginning of harvest. C263. Tabu: drinking from certain river between two darknesses. C735.2.4. Tabu: sleeping in house lighted after sunset. C885.1. Tabu: listening to fluttering of birds after sunset.

C752.1.1. *Tabu: bringing arms to capital after sunset.* Irish myth: Cross.

C752.1.2. *Tabu: crossing certain plain after sunset.* Irish myth: Cross.

C752.1.3. *Tabu: single person entering one's house after sunset.* Irish myth: Cross.

C752.1.4. *Tabu: allowing person to come to feast after sunset.* Irish myth: Cross.

C752.1.5. *Tabu: casting in graveyard after sunset.* Irish myth: Cross.

C93. Tabu: trespassing sacred precinct.

C752.1.6. *Tabu: using magic power after nightfall.* Tuamotu: Stimson MS (z-G 13/116).

C752.2. *Tabu: doing certain thing after sunrise.*

C752.2.1. *Tabu: supernatural creatures being abroad after sunrise.* Hawaii: Beckwith Myth 333.

E452. Ghost laid at cock-crow. E501.11.1.2. Wild hunt abroad until cock-crow. F383.4. Fairy must leave at cock-crow. F451.3.2. Dwarfs turn to stone at sunrise. G273.3. Witch powerless at cock-crow. G636. Ogres powerless after cock-crow.

C752.2.2. *Conjurer must leave before sunrise.* Eskimo (Greenland): Rasmussen III 173.

C755. *Tabu: doing thing during certain time.* Irish myth: Cross.

C237. Tabu: feasting by night at beginning of harvest. C263. Tabu: drinking from certain river between two darknesses. C273. Tabu: drinking water at certain time. C401. Tabu: speaking during certain time. C631. Tabu: breaking sabbath. C721.1. Tabu: bathing during certain time. C722.1. Tabu: cutting hair during certain time. C723.1. Tabu: combing hair during certain time. C735.1. Tabu: sleeping during certain time.

C755.1. *Tabu: leaving house within certain time.* N. A. Indian (Seneca): Curtin-Hewitt RBAE XXXII 463 No. 99; Samoa: Henry 346.

C755.2. *Telling tales except at certain time of year (or day).* DeVries Het Sprookje 49. — Dakota: Wallis JAFL XXXVI 56f.

C755.3. *Tabu: coming to Ireland in time of peace.* Irish myth: Cross.

C755.4. *Tabu: going to certain place in March.* Irish myth: Cross.

C610. The one forbidden place.

C755.5. *Tabu: sitting on certain sepulchral mounds in autumn.* Irish myth: Cross.

C755.6. *Tabu: hunting in certain season.* Eskimo (Greenland): Rasmussen I 97, III 187.

C755.6.1. *Tabu: hunting in hottest season.* India: Thompson-Balys.

C755.7. *Tabu: landing on certain island during forbidden period.* Hawaii: Beckwith Myth 508, 511.

C755.8. *Tabu: going out at night by oneself.* Jewish: Neuman.

C756. *Tabu: doing thing before certain time.*

C300. Looking tabu. C402. Tabu: speaking before certain time. C842. Tabu: exposure to sunlight. C951. Girl carried off because of broken tabu. T381. Imprisoned virgin to prevent knowledge of men (marriage, impregnation).

C756.0.1. *Tabu: ringing bell before certain time.* Chinese: Eberhard FFC CXX 242 No. 188.

C756.1. *Tabu: going home before dog precedes.* Fb "hund" I 678b.

C756.2. *Tabu: letting sun shine on girl before she is thirty years old.* Fb "sol" III 458a.

C842. Tabu: exposure to sunlight. C951. Girl carried off because of broken tabu. T381. Imprisoned virgin to prevent knowledge of men (marriage, impregnation). T521. Conception from sunlight.

C756.3. *Tabu: going home before adventure is completed.* South African: Bourhill and Drake Fairy Tales from South Africa 237ff. No. 20.

C756.4. *Tabu: entering chariot less than three weeks after having eaten horseflesh.* Irish myth: Cross.

Q499.6. Penance for three years and a half for eating horseflesh.

C757. *Tabu: doing thing too soon.* India: Thompson-Balys.

C735.2.8. Tabu: sleeping two nights in the same place until certain result is attained. C735.2.9. Tabu: to rest sitting or lying until answer to certain question is learned. C761.4.1. Tabu: staying two nights in one place until certain event is brought to pass. D806.1. Magic object effective when struck on ground once only. Second blow renders useless.

C757.1. *Tabu: destroying animal skin of enchanted person too soon.* *Type 425; Tegethoff Amor und Psyche 32ff. — Missouri French: Carrière; India: *Thompson-Balys.

C32. Tabu: offending supernatural husband. C32.1. Tabu: looking at supernatural husband. C321.2. Tabu: opening box prematurely. C421. Tabu: revealing secret of supernatural husband. C761.2. Tabu: staying too long at home. D721.3. Disenchantment by destroying skin.

C757.2. *Tabu: telling adventure in otherworld too soon.* India: *Thompson-Balys; Calif. Indian: Gayton and Newman 99.

C423.3. Tabu: revealing experiences in other world.

C758. *Tabu: doing thing too hastily.*

C758.1. *Monster born because of hasty (inconsiderate) wish of parents.* **Tegethoff 24; *Types 425, 430, 433B, 441; BP II 235ff, *483, III 534; Wesselski Mönchslatein 15 No. 11; India: Thompson-Balys.

S223. Childless couple promise child to the devil if they may only have one. T548.1. Child born in answer to prayer. T553. Thumbling born as result of hasty wish of parents. They wish for a child, no matter how small he may be.

C761. *Tabu: doing thing too long.*

C761.1. *Tabu: remaining on journey too long.* English: Wells 66 (Ywain and Gawain). — Chinese: Graham.

C761.2. *Tabu: staying too long at home.* *Type 425; Tegethoff Amor und Psyche 34ff.

C32. Tabu: offending supernatural husband. C712. Tabu: staying too long in other world. C713.3. Tabu: wife of merman staying too long at home (on visit).

C761.3. *Tabu: staying too long at ball.* Must leave before certain hour. — *Type 510AB; *Cox Cinderella passim; Missouri French: Carrière.

R221. Heroine's three-fold flight from ball.

C761.4. *Tabu: staying too long in certain place.* Irish myth: Cross.

C712. Tabu: staying too long in otherworld.

C761.4.1. *Tabu: staying two nights in one place until certain event is brought to pass.* Irish myth: Cross.

C735.2.9. Tabu: to rest sitting or lying until answer to certain question is learned. M151.5. Vow not to eat or sleep until certain event is brought to pass.

C761.4.2. *Tabu: staying too long in meadow of otherworld.* India: Thompson-Balys.

F162. Landscape of otherworld.

C761.4.3. *Tabu: angel to remain on earth more than one week.* Jewish: Neuman.

C762. *Tabu: doing thing too often.*

C742. Tabu: striking monster twice.

C762.1. *Tabu: using magic power too often.* N. A. Indian: Thompson Tales 299 n. 93; Eskimo (Greenland): Rink 461.

D877. Magic object loses power by overuse. D1700—D2199. Magic powers. J2071. Three foolish wishes. Three wishes will be granted: used up foolishly. J2423. The eye-juggler. J2424. The sharpened leg.

C762.2. *Tabu: too much weeping for dead.* Persian: Carnoy 345. Eskimo (Greenland): Holm 73, 80, Rasmussen III 166, 180.

A2234.4. Hare weeps for mother when forbidden: punished. D516. Transformation through excessive grief. E324. Dead child's friendly return to parents, frequently to stop weeping. E361. Return from the dead to stop weeping.

C762.3. *Tabu: whipping magic horse more than once on journey.* India: Thompson-Balys.

B181. Magic horse.

C762.4. *Tabu: taking more than one fruit from certain tree.* India: Thompson-Balys.

D877. Magic object loses power to overuse.

C762.5. *"Take, but only twice."* Man to take money from cursed chest only twice. Lithuanian: Balys Index No. 36, 130.

C766. *Eating after one is satisfied.* Eskimo (Greenland): Rink 182.

C766.1. *Tabu: killing more cattle than one can eat.* Icelandic: Boberg.

C770. **Tabu: overweening pride.** Jewish: *Neuman.

C54. Tabu: rivaling the gods. C450. Boasting. L400. Pride brought low. L420. Overweening ambition punished. Q331. Pride punished. W116. Vanity.

C770.1. *Overweening pride in good fortune forbidden.* Man proud that he and his clan have never known unhappiness or want swallowed up by earth. Spanish Exempla: Keller.

C771. *Tabu: building too large a structure.*

C771.1. *Tabu: building too high a tower.* (Tower of Babel.) Hebrew: Genesis II 3ff.; Frazer Testament I 362ff.; Jewish: *Neuman; Hartland Science 221. — Esthonian: Loorits Grundzüge I 453 f.; India: Thompson-Balys; Indo-Chinese: Scott Indo-Chinese 266f. — Maya: Alexander Lat. Am. 132; Aztec: ibid. 96. — African (Kaffir): Kidd 237 No. 6; (Ashanti): Werner African Myth 124.

A1333. Confusion of tongues. C931. Building falls because of breaking of tabu. C966. Change of language for breaking tabu. F50. Access to upper world. F772.1. Tower of Babel: remarkably tall tower designed to reach sky.

C771.1.1. *Wicked man constructs tower neither too large nor too high.* (Santa Barbara.) Der Heiligen Leben u. Leiden (Leipzig, 1921) 101ff.

C771.2. *Tabu: piling up mountains to reach heaven.* Greek: Fox 144; *Frazer Ovid II 136.

C773. *Tabu: aspiring to too much power.* *Jamaica: Beckwith MAFLS XVII 259 No. 54.

C773.1. *Tabu: making unreasonable requests.* Given power of fulfilling all wishes, person oversteps moderation and is punished. *Type 555; *BP I 138; Grimm No. 19; *DeCock Volkssage 22ff.; *Wesselski Märchen 235; Irish myth: Cross; Lithuanian: Balys Index No. *555B; India: Thompson-Balys.

C871. Tabu: refusing a request. J1512. Impossible demand rebuked. J2071. Three foolish wishes. J2500. Foolish extreme. L210. Modest choice best. Q338. Immoderate request punished.

C773.1.1. *Tabu: asking for too great magic multiplication of coins.* *Starck Der Alraun; Taylor JAFL XXXI 561f. — India: Thompson-Balys.

D2100.2. Coin multiplies itself.

C776. *Tabu: counting possessions.* *Fb "tælle" III 923a. — Irish: Beal XXI 337; Jewish: Neuman.

C897. Tabus concerning counting.

C780. Tabu: buying, selling, etc.

C781. *Tabu: buying.* *Hdwb. d. Abergl. IX Nachträge 810.

C781.1. *Tabu: buying gallows flesh or living flesh.* — *BP I 514.

C782. *Tabu: selling.* *Hdwb. d. Abergl. IX Nachträge 810.

C782.1. *Tabu: selling used clothing.* — Fb "klæder" II 200a.

C782.2. *Tabu: selling to witch.* North Carolina: Brown Collection I 843.

G200. Witches.

C783. *Tabu: giving away.*

C783.1. *Tabu: giving certain money away.* — Breton: Sébillot Incidents s. v. "argent".

C783.2. *Tabu: giving away rings.* French Canadian: Sister Marie Ursule.

C784. *Tabu: lending.* Africa (Ekoi): Talbot 27.

C784.1. *Tabu: lending to witch.* North Carolina: Brown Collection I 644, 652.

G200. Witches.

C785. *Tabu: trying to save provision for another day.* India: Thompson-Balys.

C810. Tabu: heeding persuasive person or thing.

C742. Tabu: striking monster twice. Though monster begs that hero strike him again, hero refuses. Monster would otherwise revive. C745. Tabu: heeding pleas of old woman for food and warmth.

C811. *Tabu: heeding persuasive voices.* Tsimshian: Boas RBAE XXXI 188.

C811.1. *Tabu: heeding persuasive voice of magic drum.* Not to pick up drum that says "take me". — Roberts Type 480, p. 204; Benga: Nassau No. 11.

L215. Unpromising magic object chosen. Hero refuses to take one that cries out "Take me!"

C811.2. *Tabu: heeding magic yam that says not to take it up.* Gold Coast: Barker and Sinclair 90 No. 16.

C811.3. *Tabu: answering call when asleep.* Lithuanian: Balys Ghosts.

C812. *Tabu: pursuing certain animal.* Zulu: Callaway 117.

C815. *Tabu: listening to mother's counsel.* Fb "moder" II 600b.

C815.1. *Tabu: listening to princess's counsel.* Canadian: Gautier.

C820. Tabu: finding certain secret.

C420. Tabu: uttering secrets.

C821. *Tabu: finding age of monster.* Type 500; *BP I 497.

C822. *Tabu: solving sphinx's riddle: sphinx perishes.* Greek: Fox 49 (Oedipus).

B51. Sphinx. Has face of woman, body and tail of lion, wings of bird. G681. Ogre gives riddle on pain of death. H541.1. Sphinx propounds riddle on pain of death. H761. Riddle of the Sphinx.

C824. *Tabu: finding name of ghost.* BP I 496; Grimm No. 55.

E400. Ghosts and revenants.

C825. *Tabu: studying occult books.* Jewish: Neuman.

C830—C899. UNCLASSIFIED TABUS

C830.[1] **Unclassified tabus.**

C832. *Tabu: spinning.* Saintyves Contes de Perrault 79ff. — Lithuanian: Balys Index No. 3695, Legends No. 378f.

C631.2. Tabu: spinning on holy days.

C833. *Tabus for journeys.*

D2121.6. Magic journey during which one must not think of good or evil.

---

[1] The section C830—C899 has been revised. The following changes have been made:

First edition

Old number	New number
C831	C563
C833	C833.1
C834	C833.2
C835	C835.1
C845	C833.3

Cross, Motif-Index of Early Irish Literature

Old number	New number
C853	C853.1
C855	C835.2
C856	C845
C861	C833.4
C862	C833.5
C866	C835.3
C867	C867.1
C867.0.1	C867.1.1
C877	C867.2
C888	C833.6
C893	C833.7

C833.1. *Tabu: crossing river except at source.* Africa (Angola): Chatelain 69 No. 3.

C833.2. *Tabu: turning aside for anyone.* Irish myth: Cross.
H1400. Fear test. H1561. Tests of valor.

C833.3. *Tabu: turning back after beginning a journey.* *Fb "gå" I 525a, "vende" IV 1035b; African: Werner African 172.

C833.4. *Tabu: driving horses over ashen yoke.* Irish myth: Cross.

C833.5. *Tabu: going with dry feet over certain river.* Irish myth: Cross.

C833.6. *Tabu: traveling beyond spot where feat of skill was performed before duplicating it.* Irish myth: Cross.
C856.3. Tabu: army to advance until certain conditions are fulfilled.

C833.7. *Tabu: proceeding after mishap to chariot.* Irish myth: Cross.

C833.8. *Tabu: going to certain place in speckled garment on speckled steed.* Irish myth: Cross.

C833.9. *Men sent on mission prohibited from fishing and quarreling.* Africa (Bushongo): Torday Notes 247.

C835. *Tabus concerning fighting.*

C835.1. *Tabu: refusing combat to anyone.* Irish myth: Cross.

C835.1.1. *Tabu: bearded man refusing combat.* Irish myth: Cross.
C565. Tabus for bearded men.

C835.2. *Tabus concerning weapons.* Irish myth: Cross.
C181.3. Tabu: woman not to touch man's weapons. D1080. Magic weapons.

C835.2.1. *Tabu: failing to make gift to magic lance.* The lance kills offender. Irish myth: Cross.
C921. Immediate death for breaking tabu. D1086. Magic lance. D1402.8.3. Magic spear kills man. D1645.8.3. Magic flaming lance.

C835.2.2. *Tabu: allowing spear-head to touch stone.* Irish myth: Cross.
C500. Tabu: touching.

C835.2.3. *Tabu: putting spear-head between teeth.* Irish myth: Cross.

C835.2.4. *Tabu: slaying woman with spear.* Irish myth: Cross.

C835.2.5. *Tabu: reddening weapons without satiety.* Irish myth: Cross.

C835.2.6. *Tabu: giving arms in pledge.* Irish myth: Cross.

C835.3. *Tabu: going to (leaving) certain place without combat.* Irish myth: Cross.

C835.4. *Tabu: fighting certain person.* Irish myth: Cross.
C600. Unique prohibition.

C835.4.1. *Tabu: fighting with a hag.* Irish myth: Cross.
F234.2.1. Fairy in form of hag.

C836. *Tabu: disobedience.* All lodgers must obey host implicitly. — English Wells 60 (Syre Gowene and the Carle of Carlyle).

C837. *Tabu: loosing bridle in selling man transformed to horse.* Disenchantment follows. — Type 325; BP II 60ff, *67 (Gr. No. 68). — India: *Thompson-Balys.

D535. Transformation to horse (ass, etc.) by putting on bridle. D612. Protean sale. D722. Disenchantment by taking off bridle. D1209.1. Magic bridle.

C841. *Tabu: killing certain animals.* Irish myth: Cross; India: Thompson-Balys.

B2. Animal totems. C221.1. Tabu: eating flesh of certain animal.

C841.0.1. *Clerics' voyage unsuccessful because they sailed in boats of skin.* Irish myth: Cross.

F111.2.1. Island of Tir Tairngire (Land of Promise) cannot be reached in boat made of "dead soft skins of animals."

C841.0.2. *Tabu: wounding animal;* must be killed outright. Irish myth: Cross.

C841.0.3. *Tabu: killing animal which takes refuge with one.* India: Thompson-Balys.

C841.1. *Tabu: killing stork.* Bird was once maiden. (Cf. A1715, A1966.) — Dh III 286. — Fb "stork" III 592.

C92.5. Tabu: killing stork as sacred being. N250.1. Bad luck follows man who shoots stork.

C841.2. *Tabu: hunting birds.* Supernatural lover (king of birds) tells woman that son must not do so. — Irish myth: Cross.

C841.3. *Tabu: burning caterpillars.* India: Thompson-Balys.

C32.3. Tabu: burning animal husband.

C841.4. *Tabu: hunting a pig.* Irish myth: Cross.

C619.2. Tabu: going into wild boar's haunt. M397. Prophecy: hunters will encounter certain wild boar.

C841.5. *Tabu: killing a swan.* Irish myth: Cross.

D161. Transformation: man to swan.

C841.6. *Tabu: killing golden duck.* Cheremis: Sebeok-Nyerges.

C841.7. *Tabu: killing totem animal.* Irish myth: Cross.

B2. Animal totems. C221.2. Tabu: eating totem animal. E765.2. Life bound up with that of animal.

C841.8. *Tabu: killing deer.* India: *Thompson-Balys.

C841.8.1. *Tabu: killing antelope.* Africa (Fang): Tessman 190f.

C841.9. *Tabu: killing certain fish.* India: Thompson-Balys.

C841.10. *Tabu: killing albatross.*

C841.10.1. *Killing albatross causes misfortune to follow killer.* England: Baughman.

C841.11. *Tabu: killing a cat.* India: Thompson-Balys.

C842. *Tabu: exposure to sunlight.* Köhler-Bolte Zs. f. Vksk. VI 72 (to Gonzenbach No. 34); Grimm No. 88; Gaster Oldest Stories 169. — African (Basuto): Jacottet 184, 186 No. 27, (Kaffir): Theal 56, (Ibo, Nigeria): Basden 276, (Pangwe): Tessman 367.

C756.2. Tabu: letting sun shine on girl before she is thirty years old. T521. Conception from sunlight.

C842.1. *Tabu: working iron under direct rays of sun.* India: Thompson-Balys.

C843. *Tabu: pointing.* Fb "pege" II 800.

C843.1. *Tabu: pointing at rainbow.* *Fb "regnbue" III 31b.

C844. *Tabu: playing flute.* *Fb "flöjte" I 326.

C845. *Tabus concerning war.* Irish myth: Cross.

C641. Tabu: making war against certain tribe. C642. Tabu: making peace with a certain tribe. C878.2.1. Tabu: going to battle without being clothed in silk. P550. Military affairs.

C845.1. *Tabu: bringing head of slain enemy within village walls.* India: *Thompson-Balys.

C846. *Tabu: removing landmarks.* Alphabet Nos 46, 47. — Norwegian: *Solheim Register 17; Danish: Kristensen Da. Sagn V nos. 1409ff.

C847. *Tabu: giving away gifts received from animal.*

C847.1. *Tabu: giving away gifts received from fish.* India: Thompson-Balys.

C848. *Tabu: sleeping on bed made of totem-tree.* India: Thompson-Balys.

C221.2. Eating totem animal (or animal namesake). C510. Tabu: touching tree (plant).

C851. *Tabu: wastefulness.*

C851.1. *Tabu: using food for unworthy purpose.*

F931.2. Punishment for washing child with fish.

C851.1.1. *Tabu: wiping children with bread.* *Smyser Harvard Studies and Notes in Phil. and Lit. XV (1933) 62 n. 5.

C535. Tabu: stepping on bread. F944. City sinks into sea.

C851.1.2. *Tabu: using grain to clean child.* German: Grimm No. 194.

C851.2. *Tabu: throwing "living fire" into river.* India: Thompson-Balys.

C853. *Tabus concerning entry into assembly.* Irish myth: Cross.

P632. Customs concerning recognition of rank.

C853.1. *Tabu: holding meeting at certain place.* Irish myth: Cross.

C610. The one forbidden place.

C853.2. *Tabu: going to assembly of women at certain place.* Irish myth: Cross.

C854. *Tabu: doing thing in certain manner.* (Cf. C643, D1791.) Irish myth: Cross, Köhler-Bolte II 651ff.

C854.1. *Tabu: going to certain place in speckled garment on speckled steed.* Irish myth: Cross.

C854.2. *Tabu: making withershins circuit.* (Cf. D1791.2.) Irish myth: *Cross.

C857. *Tabu: inciting horse at certain place.* Irish myth: Cross.

C858. *Tabu: swimming with certain birds.* Irish myth: Cross.

C721. Tabu: bathing.

C863. *Tabu: following three red men to certain place.* Irish myth: Cross.

F233.3. Red fairy. F527. Person of unusual color.

C865. *Tabu: running a race.* Irish myth: Cross.

C865.1. *Tabu: racing pigeons.* Jewish: Neuman.

C867. *Tabu: unusual cruelty.*

C867.1. *Tabu: abusing women or children.* Irish myth: Cross.

C180. Tabu confined to one sex. S400. Cruel persecutions. T600. Care of children. W11.5.12. Hero in battle refuses to slay women.

C867.1.0.1. *Tabu: bearded men abusing women and children.* Irish myth: Cross.

C565. Tabus of bearded men.

C868. *Tabu: leaving land entirely unoccupied.* Tuamotu: Stimson MS (t-G 3/711).

C871. *Tabu: refusing a request.* Irish myth: Cross.

C152.2. Tabu: refusing unreasonable demand of pregnant woman. M158. Vow never to refuse food to any man. M202.0.1 Bargain: a promise to be fulfilled at all hazards. M223. Blind promise. P319.7. "Friendship without refusal." W11.15. Generous person refuses no man anything.

C871.0.1. *Tabu: bearded man refusing request.* Irish myth: Cross.

C565. Tabus for bearded men.

C872. *Tabu: turning away from (refusing requests of) poets.* Irish myth: Cross.

P427.7. Poet (fili, ollamh, scelaige, anchaid).

C874. *Tabu: breaking up revelry before its end.* Irish myth: Cross.

C282.1. Tabu: leaving a feast before it is ended.

C875. *Tabu: carrying child on one's back into house.* Irish myth: Cross.

C876. *Tabu: leaping a camping place.* Irish myth: Cross.

C878. *Tabu concerning clothing.* Irish myth: Cross; Jewish: *Neuman.

C878.1. *Tabu: wearing satin.* Irish myth: Cross.

C878.2. *Tabu: wearing silk.* Irish myth: Cross.

C878.2.1. *Tabu: going to battle without being clothed in silk.* Irish myth: Cross.

C856. Tabus concerning war. P550. Military affairs.

C881. *Tabu: grumbling.*

Q312. Fault-finding punished.

C881.1. *Tabu: grumbling at narrowness of certain boat.* Irish myth: Cross.

C882. *Tabu: watching game without aiding loser.* Irish myth: Cross.

C300. Looking tabu.

C883. *Tabu: crossing graveyard without alighting.* Irish myth: Cross.

C884. *Tabu: concerning riding horses.*

C884.1. *Tabu: halting or unloading horse.* Irish myth: Cross.

C884.2. *Tabu: allowing horse to lose his bridle, stray or stale.* Irish myth: Cross.

A920.1.6. Lake from urine of horse.

C885. *Tabu: hearing or listening.*

C681. Compulsion to answer cry.

C885.1. *Tabu: listening to fluttering of birds after sunset.* Irish myth: Cross.

C752.1. Tabu: doing thing after sunset.

C885.2. *Tabu: listening to groans of women being violated.* Irish myth: Cross.

C118. Tabu: violating woman.

C885.3. *Tabu: listening to certain lute.* Irish myth: Cross.

C886. *Tabu: plowing with ass and ox together.* Jewish: Neuman.

C887. *Tabu: being in same house with fire, weapon, dog.* Irish myth: Cross.

C888. *Tabu: using leaven for cooking.* Jewish: *Neuman.

C891. *Tabu: uncleanliness.* Irish myth: Cross.

C720. Tabu: attending toilet needs.

C891.1. *Tabu: riding dirty on black-heeled horse across certain plain.* Irish myth: Cross.

C610. The one forbidden place.

C891.2. *Tabu: bearded man going dirty to bed.* Irish myth: Cross.

C565. Tabus for bearded men.

C891.3. *Tabu: urinating on fire.* India: Thompson-Balys.

C892. *Tabu: stranger to play with someone without asking permission.* Irish myth: Cross.

C893. *Tabu: making use of blood.* Jewish: *Neuman.

C895. *Tabu: using stone fish-hooks.* Easter Island: Métraux Ethnology 363.

C897. *Tabus concerning counting.* *Fb "tælle" IV 923b.

C897.1. *Tabu: counting the stars.* England: Baughman; Fb "stjærne" III 577b.

C897.2. *Tabu: taking census.* Jewish: *Neuman.

C897.3. *Tabu: calculating time of Messiah's advent.* Jewish: Neuman.

C898. *Tabus concerned with mourning.* Jewish: *Neuman.

C899. *Additional unclassified tabus.*

C899.1. *Tabu: hiding iron.* India: Thompson-Balys.

C900—C999. Punishment for breaking tabu.

C900. **Punishment for breaking tabu.** India: *Thompson-Balys.

F361. Fairy's revenge. Q200. Deeds punished. Q400. Kinds of punishment.

C901. *Tabu imposed.* Irish myth: Cross.

Q431. Imposition of tabu as punishment.

C901.1. *Tabu imposed by certain person.* Irish myth: Cross.

C901.1.1. *Tabu imposed on son by father before death.* India: Thompson-Balys.

C901.1.2. *Tabu imposed by druid.* Irish myth: Cross.

D1711.4. Druid as magician. G583. Demons coerced by geasa of druids. P427. Druid.

C901.1.3. *Tabu imposed by lover.* Irish myth: Cross.

F301. Fairy lover.

C901.1.3.1. *Tabu imposed by forthputting woman.* Irish myth: Cross.
T55. Girl as wooer.

C901.1.4. *Tabu imposed by host.* Irish myth: Cross.
P320. Hospitality.

C901.1.5. *Tabu imposed by fairy.* Irish myth: Cross.
C841.2. Tabu: killing birds. F361. Fairy's revenge.

C901.1.6. *Tabu imposed by saint.* Irish myth: Cross.
D1713. Magic power of hermit (saint).

C901.2. *Tabu imposed at birth.* Irish myth: Cross.
T583. Accompaniments of childbirth.

C901.3. *Tabu imposed by magic.* Irish myth: Cross.
D2060. Death or bodily injury by magic. D2070. Bewitching.

C901.4. *Punishment for breaking tabu: assigner of punishment suffers his own penalty.*
T258.1. The curious wife: wait and see.

C901.4.1. *King breaks his own tabu and meets with the punishment he has set for violation of it.* (His nose is cut off). India: Thompson-Balys.

C905. *Supernatural being punishes breach of tabu.*

C905.1. *Dwarf punishes for breach of tabu.* Eskimo (Greenland): Rasmussen I 322.

C905.2. *Moon punishes for breach of tabu.* Eskimo (Greenland): Rasmussen I 90—95.

C910. **Permanent sign of disobedience for breaking tabu.** French Canadian: Barbeau JAFL XXIX 11.
A2231.3. Animal characteristics: punishment for working on holy day. A2234. Animal characteristics punishment for disobedience.

C911. *Golden finger as sign of opening forbidden chamber.* (Cf. C611.) — *Type 710; BP I 21 (Grimm Nos 3, 136). — Missouri French: Carrière.
D475.1. Transformation: objects to gold. D2100. Magic wealth.

C912. *Hair turns to gold as punishment in forbidden chamber.* (Cf. C611.) — *Types 314, 480; Fb "hår" I 771b; German: Grimm No. 136; Roberts Type 480 p. 174.
D475.1.10. Transformation: hair to gold. D1454.1. Hair furnishes treasure. D2100. Magic wealth.

C913. *Bloody key as sign of disobedience.* (Cf. C611, C813.) — *Types 311, 312: BP I 404ff.
D474.1. Transformation: key becomes bloody. D1176. Magic key. D1654.3. Indelible blood.

C913.1. *Bloody egg as sign of disobedience.* German: Grimm No. 46.

C915. *Contents of forbidden receptacle are released.*

C915.1. *Troubles escape when forbidden casket is opened.* See references to C321 (Tabu: looking into box).

C915.1.1. *Music-box continues playing when it is touched contrary to tabu.* — Köhler's notes to Gonzenbach Sicilianische Märchen No. 15.
A1174.1. Night (darkness) in package released. A2003. Origin of insects: released from sack. Looking tabu broken. C322.1. Bag of winds. Wind is confined in a bag. Man breaks prohibition against looking into bag and releases winds.

C915.2. *Animals escape when forbidden baskets opened.* Origin of animals. India: Thompson-Balys.

A1731. Creation of animals as punishment for beating forbidden drum.

C915.2.1. *Animals escape when forbidden calabash is opened.* African (Yoruba): Frobenius Atlantis X 232f. No. 16.

C916. *Continuous action started by breaking tabu.*

D94.1.1. The cursed dancers. Dancers rude to holy man cursed and must keep dancing till Judgment Day. D1793. Magic results from eating or drinking. D2172. Continuing magic acts.

C916.1. *Trespass betrayed by dripping candle.* (Cf. C31.1, C32.1.) — *Type 425; *Tegethoff 39; *BP III 114.

C916.2. *Animals produced when forbidden drum is beaten.* Gold Coast: Barker and Sinclair 90, No. 16.

A1731. Creation of animals as punishment for beating forbidden drum. A2231.10. Crab beats deity's forbidden drum: eyes lift out of body.

C916.3. *Magic porridge-pot keeps cooking.* Against command, mother of owner bids pot to cook. It fills house with porridge and will not stop until ordered by mistress. — *Type 565; BP II 438ff.; *Aarne JSFO XXVII 67, 80; *Christensen Molboerne 177.

A1115.2. Why the sea is salt. Magic salt mill is stolen by sea-captain, who takes it aboard and orders it to grind. It will stop only for its master; ship sinks and keeps grinding salt. D1171.1. Magic pot. D1601.10.1. Self-cooking pot. D1651.3. Magic cooking-pot obeys only master.

C916.4. *Spinning wheel continues spinning because woman has worked at forbidden time.* Finnish-Swedish: Wessman 18 No. 166.

C917. *Object magically appears when tabu is broken.*

C917.1. *Tabued pot broken: town appears.* Africa (Vai): Ellis 187, No. 3.

C918. *Mare from water world disappears when she is scolded* and her halter used for common purposes. Irish myth: Cross.

C41. Tabu: offending water spirits. F989.13. Animal dives into lake and disappears.

C918.1. *Marvelous cow offended disappears.* Irish myth: Cross.

D1652.3. Cow with inexhaustible milk.

C920. Death for breaking tabu. Type 311; BP I 398ff (Grimm No. 46). — — Irish myth: Cross; Icelandic: Boberg; India: Thompson-Balys; Hawaii: Beckwith Myth 68, 118, 134, 138, 371, 508; Marquesas: Handy 60, 67, 138; Tuamotu: Stimson MS (t-G 3/912, z-G 13/127, 317, z-G 3/1174); Eskimo (Greenland): Rink 341, Rasmussen II 341, (Mackenzie Area): Jenness 51, 58, (Central Eskimo): Boas RBAE VI 600; Calif. Indian: Gayton and Newman 101; S. Am. Indian (Toba): Métraux MAFLS XL 47; African (Angola): Chatelain 219 No. 39, (Ekoi): Talbot 178, (Kaffir): Kidd 237 No. 6, (Wakweli): Bender 43.

C822. Tabu: solving sphinx's riddle: sphinx perishes. F361.12. Fairies take vengeance for destruction of fairy mound. M101.3. Death as punishment for broken oath. M370. Vain attempts to escape fulfillment of prophecy. N101.2. Inexorable fate: death for violating tabus. Q411. Death as punishment.

C920.1. *Death of children for breaking tabu.* India: Thompson-Balys; Jewish: Neuman.

C920.2. *Death of wife for breaking tabu.* India: Thompson-Balys; Jewish: *Neuman.

C921. *Immediate death for breaking tabu.* (Cf. C52, C51.3, C453, C533.) — Irish myth: Cross; Greek: Fox 46 (Semele), 199 (Anchises). — Jewish;

*Neuman; India: *Thompson-Balys; Chinese: Werner 294; Eskimo (Greenland): Rink 375; African (Ekoi): Talbot, 18, 99, (A'Kikuyu): Barrett 41, (Yoruba): Parkinson 104, (Pangwe): Tessman 370f., (Fang): Tessman.

C855.1. Tabu: failing to make gift to magic lance. The lance kills.

C922. *Death by smothering for breaking tabu.* Man given secret box conveying the power of making women love him. He disobeys warning and opens it. The women smother him to death. (Cf. C321.) — N. A. Indian: *Thompson Tales 376 n. 19a.

D1355. Love-producing magic object. D1904. Love-compelling man sickens of bargain. F112.1. Man on Island of Fair Women overcome by loving women.

C922.1. *Death by choking for breaking tabu.* Hawaii: Beckwith Myth 146.

K951. Murder by choking.

C923. *Death by drowning for breaking tabu.* Irish myth: Cross; Greek: Fox 135 (Ajax the less), Grote I 284; Jewish: Neuman; Hawaii: Beckwith Myth 118; Samoa: ibid. 25, 512; Tuamotu: Stimson MS (t-G 2/44, z-G 13/441); Marquesas: Handy 134; Eskimo (Greenland): Rasmussen I 115, III 124.

A920.1.8.1. Lake from violating tabu. A1018. Flood as punishment. F933.6.1. Desecrated well overflows. Q552. Prodigy as punishment.

C924. *Death by thirst for breaking tabu.* (Cf. C949.4.) — African (Bushman): Bleek and Lloyd 67.

C925. *Death from rattlesnake bite because of breaking tabu.* Calif. Indian: Gayton and Newman 100.

C926. *Man (woman) vanishes on breaking of tabu.* Calif Indian: Gayton and Newman 100; Eskimo (Greenland): Rasmussen III 147.

C927. *Burning as punishment for breaking tabu.* Irish myth: Cross; Jewish: Neuman; Hawaii: Beckwith Myth 264; S. Am. Indian (Chamacoco): Métraux MAFLS XL 48; Eskimo (Greenland): Rink 441, Rasmussen III 51, Holm 72.

Q414. Punishment: burning alive.

C927.1. *Person turned to dust.* India: Thompson-Balys.

C927.2. *Falling to ashes as punishment for breaking tabu.* Irish myth: Cross; India: Thompson-Balys.

D2061.1.1. Person magically reduced to ashes. F378.1. Tabu: touching ground on return from fairyland.

C927.3. *Burning and drowning as punishment for breaking tabu.*

C435.1.1. Woman causes twofold death of mortal husband who utters her name. F901.2. Extraordinary twofold death: burning, drowning. K955. Murder by burning. M341.2.4.2. Prophecy: threefold death: wounding, burning, drowning. Q562.2. Souls in hell alternatively drown and burn.

C928. *Death from insanity as punishment for breaking tabu.* Irish myth: Cross.

C949.1. Insanity for breaking tabu.

C929. *Death for breaking tabu — miscellaneous.*

C929.1. *"Shame and disgrace" threatened for refusing love of forthputting woman.* Irish myth: Cross.

M438. Curse: humiliation. T55. Girl as wooer.

C929.2. *Death from specific disease for breaking tabu.*

C929.2.1. *Death from paralysis for breaking tabu.* African (Luba): De Clerq Zs. f. KS. IV 219.

C929.3. *Beheading for breaking tabu.* Cyprus: Hadjioannou Kypriako, Mythoi (Leukosia, 1948) No. 22; Jewish: Neuman.

C929.4. *Death by stoning for breaking tabu.* Jewish: *Neuman.

C929.5. *Death by being swallowed for breaking tabu.* Rarotonga: Beckwith Myth 262.

C929.6. *Man sacrificed to the gods for breaking tabu.* Hawaii: Beckwith Myth 511.

C930. **Loss of fortune for breaking tabu.** Irish myth: Cross; India: *Thompson-Balys; Eskimo (Greenland): Rasmussen I 322, (Cumberland Sound): Boas BAM XV 234; African (Loango): Pechuël-Loesche 109.

C841.0.1. Clerics' voyage unsuccessful because they sailed in boats of skin. N558. Raised treasure turns into charcoal (shavings). Q585. Fitting destruction (disappearance) of property as punishment.

C930.1. *Dishonor to children because of breaking tabu.* Jewish: *Neuman.

C931. *Building falls because of breaking of tabu.* (Cf. C771.1.) — Hartland Science 221; Gaster Exempla 229 No. 239; Jewish: *Neuman; English: Wells 42 (Arthour and Merlin); Swedish: Wessman 71 No. 605; India: Thompson-Balys. — Eskimo (Greenland): Rasmussen III 245, (West Hudson Bay); Boas BAM XV 234.

Q552.14. Fortress built on Sunday destroyed by tempest. S261. Foundation sacrifice.

C932. *Loss of wife (husband) for breaking tabu.* Aarne-Thompson Types 400, 425; Cheremis: Sebeok-Nyerges; India: Thompson-Balys; Maori: Beckwith Myth: 249; African (Loango): Bechuël-Loesche 109.

C31. Tabu: offending supernatural wife. H1385.3. Quest for vanished wife (mistress). H1385.4. Quest for vanished husband.

C933. *Luck in hunting (fishing) lost for breaking tabu.*

C933.1. *Luck in hunting lost for breaking tabu.* (Cf. C229.2.) — Africa (Ekoi): Talbot 409; Marquesas: Handy 64.

C933.2. *Luck in fishing lost for breaking tabu.* Tonga: Gifford 601; Easter Island: Métraux Ethnology 363; Tuamotu: Stimson MS (t-G 3/600).

C934. *Food supply fails because of broken tabu.* Eskimo (Greenland): Rink 452, (West Hudson Bay): Boas BAM XV 200; Hawaii: Beckwith Myth 111; Samoa: ibid. 450.

C934.1. *Loss of crops because of broken tabu.* Cheremis: Sebeok-Nyerges.

C934.2. *Land made sterile because of broken tabu.* Jewish: Neuman.

D2081. Land made magically sterile.

C934.3. *Elves set country afire because of broken tabu.* Irish myth: Cross.

F369.1. Fairies set fire to buildings.

C935. *Helpful animal disappears when tabu is broken.* *Fb "spise" III 495e; Hartland Science 142; Irish: Beal XXI 329, 337; Eskimo (Greenland): Rasmussen III 245.

C918. Mare from water world disappears when she is scolded and her halter used for common purposes.

C936. *War lost because of breaking tabu.* Greek: *Grote II 130.

C937. *God's favor lost for breaking tabu.* (Cf. C621.) — Jewish: Neuman; India: *Thompson-Balys; Tahiti: Henry 85; New Hebrides: Codrington 387; African (Ekoi): Talbot 129.

A1331. Paradise lost because of one sin.

C937.1. *Immortality lost because of breach of tabu.* African (Congo): Weeks 217.

A1335. Origin of death.

C938. *Rulers of inferior character after tabu is broken.* Irish myth: Cross.

P10. Kings. Q552.3. Failure of crops during reign of wicked king.

C939. *Loss of fortune for breaking tabu — miscellaneous.*

C939.1. *Punishment for breaking tabu: water withdrawn from lake.* India: *Thompson-Balys.

C939.2. *Punishment for broken tabu: good money turns to counterfeit.* India: Thompson-Balys.

C939.3. *Felled trees (cut weeds) return to their places because of broken tabu.* Maori: Clark 95; Tonga: Gifford 22.

D1602.2. Felled tree raises itself again.

C939.4. *Golden Age ends as result of broken tabu.* (Cf. A1101.1.) S. Am. Indian (Lengua): Métraux BBAE CXLIII (1) 369.

C940. **Sickness or weakness for breaking tabu.** Fb "sygdom" III 699a. — Irish myth: Cross; India: *Thompson-Balys; Eskimo (Greenland): Rink 375; S. Am. Indian (Chiriguano): Métraux RMLP XXXIII 173.

C31. Tabu: offending supernatural wife. C311. Tabu: seeing the supernatural. D1336. Magic object gives weakness. D1837. Magic weakness. D2064. Magic sickness.

C940.1. *Princess's secret sickness from breaking tabu.* (Cf. C55.) — *Type 613; BP I 322 n. 1 (Grimm No. 33).

D2064.1. Magic sickness because girl has thrown away her consecrated wafer. H1292.4.1. Question (propounded on quest): How can the princess be cured? — Answer: She must recover consecrated wafer which rat has stolen from her first communion. V34.2. Princess sick because toad has swallowed her consecrated wafer.

C940.2. *Daughters' sickness because of father's breaking tabu.* India: Thompson-Balys.

C941. *Particular disease caused by breaking tabu.*

F362. Fairies cause disease.

C941.1. *Leprosy from breaking tabu.* Gaster Exempla 187 No. 10. — Irish myth: Cross; India: Thompson-Balys; Jewish: Neuman.

C941.2. *Swelling of limbs from breaking tabu.* India: Thompson-Balys.

C941.3. *Sores on body from breaking tabu.* India: Thompson-Balys.

C941.3.1. *Sore mouth as punishment for breaking tabu.* Hawaii: Beckwith Myth 133; Eskimo (Greenland): Rasmussen II 233.

C941.4. *Plague for breaking tabu.* See references for Q552.10.

Q552.10. Plague as punishment.

C941.5. *Paralysis as punishment for broken tabu.* African (Luba): De Clerq Zs. f. KS. IV 220.

C942. *Loss of strength from broken tabu.* Irish myth: Cross; Danish: Fb "klæder" II 200a.

D1336. Magic object gives weakness. D1410. Magic object renders helpless. D1837. Magic weakness. D2064. Magic sickness. T583.1. Couvade. Z357. Unique exceptions from curse.

C942.1. *Loss of magic strength by smoking.* India: Thompson-Balys.

C942.2. *Magic horse becomes powerless because of broken tabu.* India: Thompson-Balys.

B181. Magic horse.

C942.3. *Weakness from seeing woman (fairy) naked.* Irish myth: Cross.

C312.1. Tabu: man looking at nude woman. F362.3. Fairies cause weakness. F397. Fairy woman exhibits her figure to warriors.

C942.4. *Woman's breasts dry up because of broken tabu.* India: Thompson-Balys.

C943. *Loss of sight for breaking tabu.* (Cf. C51.2.) — See C312.1.1, C312.1.2 for references. — *Fb "öje" III 1166b; Irish myth: Cross; Jewish: Neuman; India: Thompson-Balys; Tahiti: Henry 143; Eskimo (Cumberland Sound): Boas BAM XV 241.

C311.1.2. Tabu: looking at fairies. C312.1.2. Tabu: looking at nude woman riding through town. D1331.2. Magic object blinds. D2062.2. Blinding by magic. F362.1. Fairies cause blindness. Q451.7. Blinding as punishment.

C943.1. *Man receives fork in eye for breaking tabu.* (Cf. C331.) — Swiss: Jegerlehner Oberwallis 295 No. 13.

C943.2. *Loss of one eye for breaking tabu.* S. Am. Indian (Toba): Métraux MAFLS XL 39.

C943.3. *Sore eyes from breaking tabu.* Eskimo (Cumberland Sound): Boas BAM XV 241.

C944. *Dumbness as punishment for breaking tabu.* (Cf. C311.1.4.) — Type 710; Fb "stum"; Jewish: Neuman.

D2021.1. Dumbness as curse. Q451.3. Loss of speech as punishment.

C945. *Magic forgetfulness for breaking tabu.* *Fb "spise" III 495a; German: Grimm Nos. 113, 127, 186, 193; Italian Novella: Rotunda; India: Thompson-Balys.

D1365. Object causes magic forgetfulness. D2000. Magic forgetfulness.

C946. *Limbs affected by breaking tabu.*

C946.1. *Limb broken for stepping on grave.* (Cf. C520.) — India: Thompson-Balys.

C946.2. *Arm shortened for breaking tabu.* Pauli (ed. Bolte) No. 488.

C946.3. *Magic growth of members for breaking tabu.* Eskimo (Greenland): Rasmussen I 83.

C947. *Magic power lost by breaking tabu.* India: Thompson-Balys; Jewish: Neuman.

D1741. Magic powers lost.

C948. *Mutilation as punishment for breaking tabu.* Irish myth: Cross; Jewish: Neuman.

D2062. Maiming by magic. S160. Mutilations.

C948.1. *Mouth expanded because of broken tabu.* Irish myth: Cross.

C948.2. *Nose to be cut off as punishment for breaking tabu.* India: Thompson-Balys.

C948.3. *Tongue of woman who breaks tabu protrudes* and entwines itself around a post in the home. India: Thompson-Balys.

C948.4. *Man's liver snatched away because of broken tabu.* Hawaii: Beckwith Myth 118; African (Pangwe): Tessman 370, (Fang): Tessman 161.

Q501.4. Punishment of Prometheus.

C948.5. *Man's lungs cut out because of broken tabu.* Eskimo (Greenland): Rasmussen I 89.

C948.6. *Hand cut off for broken tabu.* Jewish: Neuman.

C948.7. *Face chilled because of broken tabu.* Jewish: Neuman.

C948.8. *Head shattered for breaking tabu.* India: Thompson-Balys.

C949. *Sickness or weakness for breaking tabu — miscellaneous.* Irish myth: Cross.

C949.1. *Insanity for breaking tabu.* Irish myth: Cross; India: Thompson-Balys; Icel.: Boberg.

C928. Death from insanity as punishment for breaking tabu.

C949.2. *Baldness from breaking tabu.* Irish myth: Cross; Tahiti: Henry 143.

C949.3. *Sterility from breaking tabu.* Jewish: Neuman.

C949.4. *Bleeding from breaking tabu.* Eskimo (Greenland): Rasmussen II 164.

C949.5. *Continued thirst from breaking tabu.* (Cf. C924.) — Buddhist myth: Malalasekera II 636.

C950. Person carried to other world for breaking tabu.

A751.1.1. Man in moon burns brush as punishment for doing so on Sunday.

C952. *Immediate return to other world because of broken tabu.* (Cf. C31, C31.4, C327.) — Type 710 (Gr. No. 3); Greek: Fox 229 (Persephone), 122 (Thetis); India: Thompson-Balys; Japanese: Ikeda; Africa (Congo): Weeks 206 No. 3; (Fjort): Dennett 41 No 5.

C31. Tabu: offending supernatural wife. C932. Loss of wife for breaking tabu.

C953. *Person must remain in other world because of broken tabu.* Greek myth: Grote 137; Swiss: Jegerlehner Oberwallis 295 No. 13; Jewish: Neuman; Marquesas: Handy 120, 122; Eskimo (Greenland): Rink 371.

F81.1. Orpheus. Journey to land of dead, to bring back person from the dead.

C954. *Person carried off to other world for breaking tabu.* Type 470; Fb "sol" III 458a; India: Thompson-Balys.

F325.1. Fairies kidnap boy when he breaks tabu by going outside mansion under earth before twelve years.

C955. *Banishment from heaven for breaking tabu.* German: Grimm No. 3; Jewish: Neuman.

C960. Transformation for breaking tabu. India: *Thompson-Balys; Jewish: Neuman.

D510. Transformation by breaking tabu. D660. Transformation as punishment. F348.0.1. Fairy gift disappears or is turned to something worthless when tabu is broken.

C961. *Transformation to object for breaking tabu.*

C961.1. *Transformation to pillar of salt for breaking tabu.* (Cf. C331.) — — *Fb "se" III 173b, "sten" III 553b; Spanish Exempla: Keller; Hebrew: Genesis 19: 26; Jewish: Neuman.

F531.6.12.3. Slain giant turns to salt stone.

C961.2. *Transformation to stone for breaking tabu.* (Cf. C331, C452.) — *Type 516; *Rösch FFC LXXVII 119, 132ff.; *Chauvin VII 98 No. 375; *Fb "se" III 173b, "sten" III 553b. — *Loomis White Magic 80; Greek: Fox 175 (Niobe); India: *Thompson-Balys; Maori: Beckwith Myth 349; S. Am. Indian (Aymara): Tschopik BBAE CXLIII (1) 570.

C331. Tabu: looking back. D231. Transformation: man to stone. F531.6.12.2. Sunlight turns giant or troll to stone. G304.2.5. Troll bursts when sun shines on him. Or he may become stone.

C961.3. *Transformation to wood for breaking tabu.* German: Grimm No. 43; Calif. Indian: Gayton and Newman 100.

C961.3.1. *Transformation to wooden image for breaking tabu.* Marquesas: Handy 113.

C961.3.2. *Transformation to tree for breaking tabu.* Chinese: Eberhard FFC CXX 84.

C961.4. *Transformation to mountain ridge for breaking tabu.* Hawaii: Beckwith Myth 189.

C961.5. *Transformation to anthill for breaking tabu.* India: Thompson-Balys.

C962. *Transformation to animal for breaking tabu.* Greek: Frazer Apollodorus I 334 n. 1; Jewish: Neuman; S. A. Indian (Mataco): Métraux MAFLS XL 35, (Tupinamba): Métraux RMLP XXXIII 172; Africa (Fjort): Dennett 105, No. 29.

C962.1. *Transformation to mouse for breaking tabu.* Eskimo (Mackenzie Area): Jenness 154.

C962.2. *Transformation to bird for breaking tabu.* Greek: Grote I 128.

C963. *Person returns to original form when tabu is broken.* A person originally transformed from an animal or an object returns to that form when the origin is mentioned. (Cf. C31.2, C33.1, C35.1, C440, C441.)

C963.1. *Person returns to original animal form when tabu is broken.* Africa (Congo): Weeks 215 No. 11 (fish), (Ila, Rhodesia): Smith and Dale 403 No. 3 (fish).

C963.2. *Person returns to original egg form when tabu is broken.* Africa (Basuto): Jacottet 108 No. 16.

T111.3. Marriage of man with woman who has come from an egg.

C963.3. *Person returns to original vegetable form when tabu is broken.* Africa (Gold Coast): Barker and Sinclair 78 No. 12, (Ekoi): Talbot 133, 134, 135, (Ibo, Nigeria): Thomas 80, (Fjort): Dennett 44 No. 6.

D1962.6.1. Magic sleep when hero breaks fruit open too soon.

C963.4. *Giants return to life if tabu is broken.* French Canadian: Sister Marie Ursule.

C966. *Change of language for breaking tabu.* Frazer Golden Bough XII 341 s.v. "Language". — Jewish: Neuman.

A1333. Confusion of tongues. C771.1. Tabu: building too high a tower. — Tower of Babel.

C967. *Valuable object turns to worthless, for breaking tabu.* India: Thompson-Balys.

N558. Raised treasure turns into charcoal (shavings). If one takes it along it will turn into gold.

C968. *Disenchantment for breaking tabu.* German: Grimm No. 57.

D789.4. Disenchantment by breaking tabu.

C980. Miscellaneous punishments for breaking tabu.

C100.1. Sex tabu broken: child born without bones.

C982. *Person beaten by whips for breaking tabu.* Roberts Type 480, p. 216; Jewish: Neuman; African (Benga): Nassau 113 No. 11.

C983. *Person must remain on mountain because of broken tabu.* French Canadian: Sister Marie Ursule.

C984. *Disaster because of broken tabu.*

C984.1. *Great wind because of broken tabu.* (Cf. C58.) — Swiss: Jegerlehner Oberwallis 308 Nos. 37, 38.

D906. Magic wind. D2141. Storm produced by magic. D2142. Wind produced by magic. D2143.1 Rain produced by magic.

C984.2. *Storm because of broken tabu.* Jewish: Neuman.

C984.3. *Flood because of broken tabu.* Chatham Island: Beckwith Myth 19, notes 10—12; Marquesas: Handy 114; S. Am. Indian (Toba): Métraux MAFLS XL 29.

A920.1.8.1. Lake from violating tabu. A1018. Flood as punishment for incest.

C984.4. *Tidal wave for breaking tabu.* Lau Islands: Beckwith Myth 19.

C984.4.1. *Sea rolls in over the land from all sides and a sea serpent comes because of broken tabu.* India: Thompson-Balys.

C984.5. *Disastrous lightning for breaking tabu.* Chinese: Eberhard FFC CXX 188 No. 129.

C984.6. *General conflagration for breaking tabu.* S. Am. Indian (Witoto): Métraux MAFLS XL 36.

A1030. World fire.

C984.7. *Village sinks in earth for violation of tabu.* S. Am. Indian (Toba): Métraux MAFLS XL 30.

F941.2.2. Church and congregation sink to bottom of sea.

C984.8. *Island split apart for broken tabu.* Tahiti: Beckwith Myth 468.

C985. *Physical changes in person because of broken tabu.*

C985.1. *Skin changes color because of broken tabu.* (Cf. C94.3.) — Africa (Kaffir): Theal 67.

C985.2. *Teeth blackened as punishment for breaking tabu.* Irish myth: Cross.

C985.3. *Foul breath from breaking tabu.* Irish myth: Cross.

C986. *Abduction by animal for breaking tabu.* India: Thompson-Balys; Japanese: Ikeda.

C25.1. Child threatened with ogre: latter takes child off. R13. Abduction by animal.

C986.1. *Pursuit by animal for breaking tabu.* Eskimo (Greenland): Rink 182.

C987. *Curse as punishment for breaking tabu.* Irish myth: Cross; Jewish: Neuman.

C940. Sickness or weakness for breaking tabu. D1837. Magic weakness. M343. Parricide prophecy. M400. Curses. Q556. Punishment. Z357. Unique exceptions from curse.

C991. *Quest imposed for breaking tabu.* Irish myth: Cross.

H1200. Quest.

C992. *Snake bite for broken tabu.* India: Thompson-Balys.

C993. *Unborn child affected by mother's broken tabu.* Rarotonga: Beckwith Myth 262; S. Am. Indian (Chiriguano): Métraux RMLP XXXIII 160.

T550. Monstrous births.

C994. *Punishment by adhesion for breaking tabu.* Eskimo (Greenland): Rink 465.

D2171. Magic adhesion.

C995. *Sleeplessness from breaking tabu.* Eskimo (Greenland): Rasmussen III 170.

D2063.2. Magic restlessness in bed.

C996. *Person falls because of broken tabu.* Marquesas: Handy 36; Tonga: Gifford 53; Hawaii: Beckwith Myth 127.

C998. *Trees wither because of broken tabu.* Jewish: Neuman.

www.ingramcontent.com/pod-product-compliance
Lightning Source LLC
LaVergne TN
LVHW040202080826
844660LV00001B/76
* 9 7 8 0 2 5 3 3 3 8 8 1 5 *